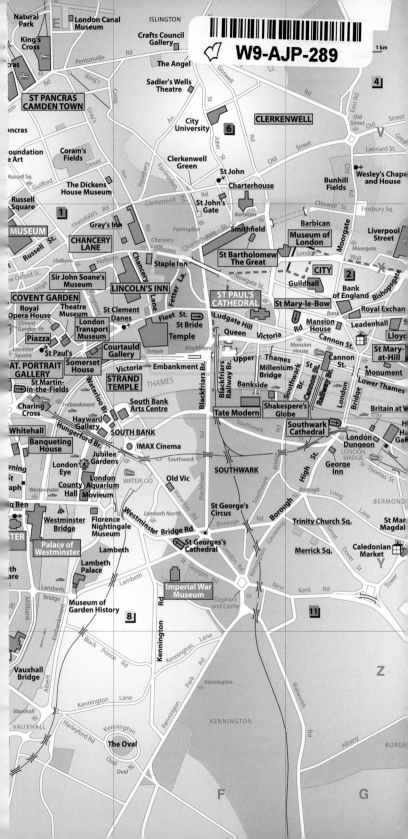

THEGREENGUIDE
London

©Philip Coblentz/Brand X Pictures

General Manager   Cynthia Clayton Ochterbeck

THE GREEN GUIDE **LONDON**

Editor   Alison Coupe
Principal Writers   Anna Meville-James, Glenn Harper
Production Manager   Natasha G. George
Cartography   John Dear
Photo Editor   Yoshimi Kanazawa
Proofreader   Jenni Rainford
Interior Design   Chris Bell
Layout   Natasha G. George, John Higginbottom
Cover Design   Chris Bell, Christelle Le Déan
Cover Layout   Michelin Apa Publications Ltd.

Contact Us   The Green Guide
                                       Michelin Maps and Guides
                                       One Parkway South
                                       Greenville, SC 29615
                                       USA
                                       www.michelintravel.com
                                       michelin.guides@us.michelin.com

                                       Michelin Maps and Guides
                                       Hannay House
                                       39 Clarendon Road
                                       Watford, Herts WD17 1JA
                                       UK
                                       ✆01923 205240
                                       www.ViaMichelin.com
                                       travelpubsales@uk.michelin.com

Special Sales   For information regarding bulk sales,
                                       customized editions and premium sales,
                                       please contact our Customer Service
                                       Departments:
                                       USA   1-800-432-6277
                                       UK   01923 205240
                                       Canada 1-800-361-8236

Note to the reader Addresses, phone numbers, opening hours and prices published in this guide are accurate at the time of press. We welcome corrections and suggestions that may assist us in preparing the next edition. While every effort is made to ensure that all information printed in this guide is correct and up-to-date, Michelin Apa Publications Ltd. accepts no liability for any direct, indirect or consequential losses howsoever caused so far as such can be excluded by law.

HOW TO USE THIS GUIDE

PLANNING YOUR TRIP

The blue-tabbed PLANNING YOUR TRIP section at the front of the guide gives you **ideas for your trip** and **practical information** to help you organise it. You'll find tours, practical information, a host of outdoor activities, a calendar of events, information on shopping, sightseeing, kids' activities and more.

INTRODUCTION

The orange-tabbed INTRODUCTION section explores London's **History**, spanning Roman Londinium to Henry VIII and to the modern day. The **Art and Culture** section covers architecture, art, literature and music, while the **London Today** delves into modern London.

DISCOVERING

The green-tabbed DISCOVERING section features Principal Sights by region, featuring the most interesting local **Sights** and **Walking Tours**. Admission prices shown are normally for a single adult.

ADDRESSES

We've selected the best hotels, restaurants, cafés, shops, nightlife and entertainment to fit all budgets. See the Legend on the cover flap for an explanation of the price categories. See Welcome to the City for a comprehensive list of hotels and restaurants.

Sidebars

Throughout the guide you will find blue, peach and green-colored text boxes with lively anecdotes, detailed history and background information.

😊 A Bit of Advice 😊

Green advice boxes found in this guide contain practical tips and handy information relevant to the sight in the Discovering section.

STAR RATINGS★★★

Michelin has given star ratings for more than 100 years. If you're pressed for time, we recommend you visit the ★★★, or ★★ sights first:

★★★	**Highly recommended**
★★	**Recommended**
★	**Interesting**

MAPS

- Principal Sights map.
- Suburbs map.
- Local town maps.
- Local area maps.

All maps in this guide are oriented north, unless otherwise indicated by a directional arrow. The term "Local Map" refers to a map within the chapter or Tourism Region. A complete list of the maps found in the guide appears at the back of this book.

PLANNING YOUR TRIP

©Philip Coblentz/Brand X Pictures

INTRODUCTION TO LONDON

DISCOVERING LONDON

CONTENTS

YOUR STAY IN LONDON

Welcome to London

One of the world's preeminent metropolitan areas, London itself is divided into 32 boroughs, each with its own character. It is renowned for its multicultural outlook, with over 300 languages along with a variety of accents spoken amongst its population. As the UK's capital and host to four UNESCO World Heritage Sites, London's sites, sounds and attractions will seduce even the most world-weary traveller.

CITY OF WESTMINSTER

(pp90–167)

Centred around Westminster Abbey, the coronation venue of kings and queens for almost a millenia, Westminster is at the same time a myriad of dynamic activity, where the grandeur of Buckingham Palace is jus a short walk from the cosmopolitan nightlife of the West End. Bargains can be sought along the hustle and bustle of Oxford Street; exotic meals can be enjoyed in Chinatown; or visitors can while away the afternoon to delight in the opulence and luxury to be found along Mayfair or simply to sit at a street café and relax while watching the street entertainers and musicians on the piazza of Covent Garden.

Horse Guards Parade ©Eur/World Pictures/Photoshot

CITY OF LONDON *(pp168–205)*

From its beginnings as the nucleus of Roman Londinium, the City has overcome disasters such as the Great Fire of 1666 and the Blitz of World War II to become one of the world's leading financial centres. A hive of bankers and traders (though the stereotype of bowler hats no

Liberty, Soho Liberty PLC

longer holds sway!) swell the Square Mile's streets during the day, amidst modern skyscrapers such as Lord Foster's Gherkin intertwined with Sir Christopher Wren's architectural legacy of 17C churches, exemplified by the iconic dome of St. Paul's Cathedral.

THE EAST END *(p206–219)*

The East End is the epitome of London's proud heritage and sense of community, where visitors can enjoy the traditional curry houses of Brick Lane; the history in the Tower of London; and the bohemian art galleries of Hoxton and Shoreditch. Regeneration projects such as the Olympic Park exemplify the vigour and vim of the area, which will be the at the centre of the world's attention when the Olympic Games come to London in 2012.

CAMDEN & ISLINGTON

(p220–231)

Home to some of London's most desirable residences and avenues, Camden and Islington personify the village feel of London's suburbs, while at the

same time encompassing a rumpus of restaurants, theatres and shopping precincts, all a short distance to the north of the City. Amongst the abundance of sights to be seen, the fashions of Camden Lock Market, the Tudor elegance of Charterhouse and the picturesque squares of Bloomsbury will entice visitors time and time again.

KENSINGTON & CHELSEA
(pp232–255)

Situated between Fulham to the west and Westminster to the east, Kensington and Chelsea are renowned for the exclusive addresses of Sloane Square and South Kensington. This is reflected in the serenity of its green parks, most notably that of Hyde Park and Holland Park; and the chic boutiques of Knightsbridge, the King's Road and Notting Hill. Cultural attractions such as the Royal Albert Hall, the Chelsea Flower Show and the Notting Hill Carnival personify the distinction of these twin royal boroughs.

SOUTHWARK, LAMBETH, WANDSWORTH *(p256–275)*

Across the river from Westminster and the eponymous City, these three boroughs are steeped in a rich literary history from Shakespeare to Dickens. This cultural influence is embodied today in the South Bank Centre, a hub of theatres and galleries, as well as architectural landmarks such as the Oxo Tower and Battersea Power Station which gracefully embellish this stretch of the River Thames.

MAJOR CENTRAL LONDON MUSEUMS *(p276–321)*

London is blessed with having cultural institutions which showcase the finest in human achievement. The British

Totem poles in the Great Court, British Museum

Y. Kanazawa/Michelin

Museum hosts a fascinating collection from every world civilisation set around the resplendent Great Court. Amongst others, visitors can delight in museums which showcase every important art movement from the Renaissance to Surrealism; decorative arts including Ming vases to the Rococo; and the extent of human endeavor which has helped shape our past and present.

SUBURBS *(p322–383)*

In order to enjoy some of London's most attractive locales, or just to escape the hurly-burly of the centre, a day trip to the suburbs should be on every visitor's itinerary. To the west lie a plethora of beautiful suburbs such as Chiswick and Richmond, not to mention the royal palaces of Hampton Court and Windsor Castle. To the south exists Wimbledon, famed for its annual tennis tournament. To the north is Hampstead, with its affluent village; and to the east, lie the pleasant vistas of Greenwich and the Docklands.

Waterlily House, Royal Botanic Gardens, Kew

D. Chapuis/Michelin

St Pancras International Station
©Monica Wells/Pictures Colour Library

When and Where to Go

WHEN TO GO
SEASONS

In **winter** most sights are open, some with reduced opening times. The **busiest periods** are from Easter to September and when other European countries enjoy a public holiday. Young people often come for the weekend to enjoy the shopping, pubs, music venues and club scene.
Spring and **autumn** are the best seasons for visiting parks and gardens when the flowers are in bloom or the leaves are turning colour.
The **summer** season is marked by traditional events: the Chelsea Flower Show, the Oxford and Cambridge Boat Race along the Thames, a tradition started in 1829, Trooping the Colour (see Calendar of Events), the pomp and circumstance of The Proms and outdoor concerts and theatre at many stately homes. Alongside these, more eclectic celebrations such as Notting Hill Carnival provide colour in the capital.
Autumn and **winter** are the best times for visiting museums or for shopping, as places are less crowded, except in the weeks before October half-term and the Christmas holidays. During the **Christmas** holidays, baubles flash in the windows of Liberty, Hamley's Toy Shop, and Harvey Nichols; Oxford and Regent Streets light up with Christmas lights and decorations. In addition to the usual school holidays in the spring and summer and at Christmas, there are mid-term breaks in Feb, May and Oct.

IDEAS FOR YOUR VISIT

A LONDON UNDERGROUND MAP is located on **page 431** *of this guide to help you plan your visit.*

WALKING TOURS
WALKWAYS

Discover dramatic sights by following these signed walks with viewpoints throughout the city:

Silver Jubilee Walkway
10mi/16km in the heart of London
Marked by special pavement markers and including two spurs to the Barbican and Bloomsbury and ten **viewpoints** with indicators identifying the neighbouring buildings: **Leicester Square** – Parliament Square – Lambeth Palace – Jubilee Gardens – National Theatre – Tate Modern – Southwark Cathedral – Hays Galleria – Tower Hill – Mansion House and the Royal Exchange. Maps can be bought from the London Tourist Board Information Centres.

Millennium Mile
A pleasant riverside walk along part of the Silver Jubilee Walkway starting from Westminster Bridge and continuing past the London Eye, Tate Modern and The Globe, London's latest landmarks, to London Bridge; the second part of the walk along the green path from Butler's Wharf takes in London Bridge, City and goes inland to Waterloo.

London Wall Walk
Less than 2mi/1.2km long
Marked by 21 panels, it follows the line of the City wall between the Tower of London and the Museum of London.

The Thames Towpath
180mi/228km
A National Trail marked by acorn signs, running from the Thames Barrier to the Cotswolds; free leaflets from the **Countryside Commission**, PO Box 124, Walgrave, Northampton NN6 9TL. *www.londonforfree.net* offers information for nine self-guided walks around different areas of the city.

GUIDED WALKS

For information on **guided walking tours**, consult the companies mentioned below or Visit London, www.visitlondon.com, which also lists a number of smaller companies. For information on new developments ℘020 7222 1234; www.tfl.gov.uk/tfl/gettingaround/walkfinder.

Big Bus Tours offer a choice of five guided walking tours which come free with the cost of your bus ticket (℘020 7233 9533; www.bigbustours.com).

Guides include trained actors, historians, professional Blue Badge holders, botanists, and authors.

Themes include: The City of London, Fleet Street, Legal London, Bloomsbury, Covent Garden Pubs, London theatres, Soho, the West End, Mayfair, Belgravia, Chelsea, Westminster, East End, Jewish East End, Docklands, Thames Pubs, Greenwich, Regent's Canal, Little Venice, Hampstead pubs, Royal London, Literary London, Shakespeare's London, many tours of Dickens' London, Sherlock Holmes' London, Beatles' London, the Swinging 60s, London Ghost Tours, London Film Locations, and more.

See **www.londonwalks.com** for more information.

A number of **museums** and exhibitions, including the City of London Museum, the Museum of Docklands, the London Canal Museum, the Theatre Museum and Shakespeare's Globe, also offer themed walks in their specialist subjects; for details see the main listings for each attraction in the *Discovering London* section (see Index also).

Discovery Walks

One of the city's most experienced and compelling guides offers a wide variety of walks with all the usuals joined by village walks of areas such as Hampstead, Highgate, Chelsea and many others, including a Harry Potter themed walk. ℘020 8530 8443. www.discovery-walks.com.

Original London Walks

Long-established company offering a huge range of walks including night walks. P O Box 1708, London NW6 4LW ℘020 7624 3978; 020 7624 WALK (9255) (recorded information). www.walks.com.

Mystery Walks

Evening Jack the Ripper and Haunted London tours. ℘020 8526 7755 or 07957 388 280. www.tourguides.org.uk.

City of London Walks

Exciting walks in the financial district. ℘020 7794 3869. www.cityoflondonwalks.co.uk.
Transport for London, www.tfl.gov.uk, lists routes for 19 free self-guided walks.

WEEKEND BREAKS
DAY 1

Highlights that should not be missed on a short visit are the romantic outlines of the **Houses of Parliament** and Big Ben in Westminster. From Westminster Bridge admire the view of the Thames and the spectacular **London Eye** on the south bank (from the Eye itself you can see the whole of London laid out at your feet).

Westminster Abbey with its glorious monuments and historical associations is a must. Walk up Whitehall with its imposing buildings to **Trafalgar Square** with the lions guarding the towering Nelson's Column, a bustling piazza where visitors have their photos taken surrounded by fat pigeons. Drop in at the **National Gallery** on the north side of the square. By now you'll need to sit down, so wander across to **Covent Garden** with its colourful markets and street entertainment as well as window shopping and an early pre-theatre supper. The **West End theatre district** is on your doorstep with everything from films to grand opera await you in the evening.

DAY 2

The **Tower of London** with its treasures exerts a great fascination. Aim to start as early as possible to avoid the crowds attracted by the Crown Jewels. The guided tour with the attendants attired in their finery highlights its long history. On a sunny day, walk under **Tower Bridge** and saunter around St Katharine Docks (picturesque marina with bars and restaurants) before crossing to the south side of the River Thames (via the Tower Bridge Experience) to explore the Bermondsey riverside (Design Museum, Bramah Museum of Tea and Coffee) and **Bankside**, which has a range of interesting attractions (HMS *Belfast*, London Dungeon, Hay's Galleria, Southwark Cathedral, Golden Hinde, Shakespeare's Globe, Tate Modern). This is London's new trendy area with a real buzz in the air, some excellent restaurants to sample and fine pubs for refreshment.

SHORT BREAKS
OPTION 1

Begin at the imposing **St Paul's Cathedral**, which is an architectural marvel, before exploring the **City** (best visited during the week when there is much activity in the financial district). From here, you can walk over the Millennium Bridge to the Tate Modern and Bankside. Alternatively, visit the **Monument**, which marks the start of the Great Fire of London, the Bank of England Museum, which explains the financial might of this City institution, wander through **Leadenhall Market** at lunchtime or have a break in the many historic pubs frequented by city workers before continuing to marvel at the modernistic Lloyd's Building. The **Guildhall** is at the heart of the administration of the city; the **Museum of London** presents fascinating aspects of the capital through the centuries. It is well worth visiting the **City Churches** with their

attractive architectural features and treasures that reflect the spirit of an age. An excellent way to round off the day is to attend a concert or theatre performance at the prestigious Barbican Centre.

OPTION 2

Located in **Bloomsbury**, once the heart of the literary set, is the prestigious **British Museum**, where treasures from around the world are exhibited. Spend the afternoon and evening in bustling Soho. Leicester Square and Piccadilly are places to visit for pubs and restaurants as well as cinemas and theatres.

OPTION 3

A visit to the charming **Wallace Collection** may be followed by a shopping spree in bustling Oxford Street, exclusive Bond Street or elegant Regent Street, which cater to all tastes.

LONGER BREAKS
OPTION 1

A day may easily be spent in the museums around **South Kensington.** Visitors interested in advances in science and technology will be fascinated by the exciting exhibits of the **Science Museum**, while those passionate about the wonders of the natural world will find much of interest in the **Natural History Museum**. Or prepare to be captivated by the wonderful treasures of the **Victoria and Albert Museum**. Nearby, the elaborate **Albert Memorial** marks the boundary of **Hyde Park** – just across the road is the **Albert Hall**, one of the city's greatest concert halls. Check the programme, particularly if the Proms are on (Jul–Sept).

Allow time to browse around the designer shops and stores in **Knights-bridge** and Sloane Street or the boutiques in South Kensington and the **King's Road**, Chelsea. The area abounds in smart pubs and eateries.

OPTION 2

To enjoy different perspectives of London take a round-trip down river from Westminster to **Greenwich**, famous for the National Maritime Museum, Queen's House, Old Observatory and Cutty Sark, combined with a return through thriving **Docklands** (Canary Wharf) with its landmark buildings and new amenities by Docklands Light Railway to Tower Gateway and the West End. Blackheath and Ranger's House are also of interest.

OPTION 3

Beyond the confines of Inner London there is **Kew**, with its world-famous gardens, which are a delight in all seasons. The splendid ceremonial rooms of **Hampton Court** are complemented by the beautiful landscaped gardens. Consider returning down river by boat (◐see OUTDOOR FUN) to admire the upper reaches of the Thames. The more intimate **Ham House, Syon Park** and **Osterley Park** in the vicinity of the gardens are also well worth a visit.

OPTION 4

Spend part of the day in **Regent's Park**, perhaps including a visit to the zoo or a break from sightseeing in the delightful rose garden. You can also visit Lord's Cricket Museum nearby. For a different aspect of London make for Camden Town with its edgy and colourful markets, pubs and eateries or Little Venice by canal boat to take in the picturesque canal scenery.

THEMED TOURS

Most museums and art galleries organise guided tours and lectures. For information, see the individual museum or gallery.
Official 'Blue Badge' guides permitted to operate in London may be contacted through the tourist information offices; they may be hired for the day or for a series of visits.

ART

London is well endowed with art venues. Besides the renowned National Gallery, National Portrait Gallery, Tate Modern and Tate Britain, which present European Art, there are several smaller galleries, which hold many treasures, such as the Courtauld Institute Galleries (one of several excellent collections in Somerset House), the Wallace Collection, the Royal Academy, the Dulwich Picture Gallery and the controversial, cutting-edge Saatchi Gallery in the Duke of York's HQ, Chelsea. Maritime art is on view at the National Maritime Museum in Greenwich.

Splendid works of art belonging to the Royal Collections are on display in royal palaces: Buckingham Palace, the Queen's Gallery, Kensington Palace, Hampton Court and Windsor.

Noble mansions such as Apsley House, Kenwood House, Ham House, Syon Park and Osterley Park also boast superb holdings of fine art.

Well-presented temporary exhibitions devoted to major artists and schools are held at the Royal Academy in Piccadilly and the Hayward Gallery on the South Bank. The ICA in the Mall, the Whitechapel Art Gallery in the East End, the White Cube Gallery in Hoxton, and many other small specialist galleries present contemporary art. Check the press for fine exhibitions put on by art dealers in Mayfair, St James's and Knightsbridge.

SCIENCE

Besides the **Science Museum**, do not miss the Royal Observatory in Greenwich and the Planetarium. The Kew Bridge Steam Museum charts industrial advances.

BIRD'S-EYE VIEWS

The biggest overview of the capital is from the **London Eye**. The viewing areas on the top floors of **Tate Modern** afford wonderful perspectives of the City of London with the majestic dome of St Paul's

Cathedral in the foregound; there is a fine view up and down the Thames spanned by the elegant Millennium Bridge. The outlook from the dome of **St Paul's Cathedral** is spectacular. The view from the elevated walkway of **Tower Bridge** embraces the graceful Tower of London and Canary Wharf on the horizon. **Wellington Arch** at Hyde Park Corner, a busy hub, is the latest viewpoint dominating Buckingham Palace, Hyde Park and Knightsbridge. To enjoy an unusual view of the rooftops of neighbouring buildings, of Nelson's Column and of the vista down Whitehall, go to the top floor of the **National Portrait Gallery**. Visitors to **Kenwood House** to the north should not miss the viewpoint in the grounds, which pinpoints the distant landmarks of the capital.

GARDENS

Gardens are a national passion and what better way of enjoying the great outdoors than to visit **Kew Gardens**, which make a glorious show in all seasons (lilac, bluebells, azaleas, magnolias, cherry blossom in spring; rhododendrons and roses in summer; heathers in autumn-winter). The heady fragrances of the **Queen Mary's Rose Garden** in Regent's Park and of the rose garden in **Syon Park** are among the delights of summer in London. The fine gardens of **Buckingham Palace**, which were previously enjoyed only by privileged guests at royal garden parties, are now accessible as part of a visit when the palace is open to the public in summer. The Edwardian sunken garden and the Flower Walk are the glories of **Kensington Gardens**.

The intricate Knot Garden, the Privy Garden and the Great Vine are special features of **Hampton Court** gardens. In spring the rhododendrons of **The Isabella Plantation** in Richmond Park gladden the eye.

Aromatic herb gardens are to be found at the **Museum of Garden History** in Lambeth and at the **Chelsea Physic Garden**. In addition to the more formal gardens, do not miss out on the city's green lungs – **Hyde Park**, **Holland Park**, **St James's Park**, **Green Park** and **Regent's Park**.

Further afield are the **Valley Gardens** with shrubs and trees and the landscaped **Savill Gardens**, both in Windsor Great Park (Egham, Windsor, 25mi/40km west of London).

ROYAL LONDON

From the earliest times the sovereigns have built their palaces in and around London. **The Tower of London**, built after the Conquest, is one of the earliest royal residences and the glittering Crown Jewels are one of its major attractions. All that remains of 11C Westminster Palace is the majestic **Westminster Hall**.

There are Tudor remnants of Whitehall Palace near Whitehall where Henry VIII held court. Also on the site is the harmonious **Banqueting House** with its wonderful interior décor and the elegant **Queen's House** in Greenwich encapsulate the sophistication of the Stuarts.

St James's Palace is a splendid example of Tudor architecture. It is the London residence of members of the royal family. **Clarence House** nearby, formerly the home of Queen Elizabeth, was also the home of the late Queen Mother (1900–2002) after the death of George VI in 1952. It is now the residence of the Prince of Wales and the Duchess of Cornwall.

The red-brick **Kensington Palace** built in Jacobean style is associated with the reign of William III and Mary II; this is where several members of the present royal family have apartments.

The royal standard flies when the sovereign is in residence at **Buckingham Palace**. The palace is open to the public in season and the fascination of wandering through the State Rooms is irresistible. Do not miss the **Changing of the Guard**, or the elaborate pageantry of state, such as **Trooping the Colour** or the Opening of Parliament.

It is well worth making an excursion to **Hampton Court** in its riverside setting, or to the majestic **Windsor Castle** and the town of Windsor (25mi/40km west of London).

STATELY HOMES

Several mansions in the vicinity of London retain the rural prospect enjoyed by their original owners. As they were built when the Thames was the main highway, many have a riverside setting. **Chiswick House**, which was intended for entertaining, epitomises 18C refinement. **Syon Park**, an imposing mansion with royal associations, reflects the tastes of discerning patrons of the arts. **Osterley Park** is an elegant stately home with splendid furnishings in the Adam style (18C). The handsome 17C **Ham House** in the Jacobean style and the charming 18C Palladian **Marble Hill House** in Twickenham boast many treasures. **Kenwood House**, which was built as a country retreat in the 18C, stands in splendid grounds on Highgate Hill; it has been the setting for several award-winning films.

MILITARY LONDON

London boasts outstanding collections of arms and armour to satisfy the most demanding amateurs. The **Royal Armouries Collection** in the Tower of London is exceptionally fine. Find out about all aspects of warfare at the **Imperial War Museum**. The story of the British Army over five centuries is traced at the **National Army Museum** in Chelsea. Excellent displays are presented at the **Wallace Collection**, **Hampton Court** and the **Victoria and Albert Museum**. The **Guards Museum** near Buckingham Palace shows the history of the great Household regiments. The grounds of the **Honourable Artillery Company HQ** in Clerkenwell were in use for military purposes as far back as the 16C. Be prepared for loud bangs at **Firepower, The Royal Artillery Museum** at the Royal Arsenal in Woolwich.

LITERARY LONDON

A plethora of writers and dramatists have plied their trade in London and are household names in the history of the English language.

The most illustrious is William Shakespeare, whose fame is associated with The Globe and other theatres on **Bankside**, an area also haunted by his contemporaries, Ben Jonson and Christopher Marlowe. Geoffrey Chaucer is linked with **Westminster Abbey**; his pilgrims started from the inns of **Southwark** and made their way to Canterbury. The poet John Milton is recorded as living in the City in the 17C. The great diarist Samuel Pepys chronicled life in the city in the late 17C, from the Plague to the Great Fire. The great 18C scholar Dr Johnson compiled his Dictionary and drafted his essays while he lived off **Fleet Street**.

Several novels by Charles Dickens are set in Victorian London, where he spent a difficult childhood. He lived in **Bloomsbury** with his family. The Bloomsbury Group, whose famous members included Virginia Woolf, EM Forster, Dora Carrington, Lytton Strachey and many others flourished around the leafy squares. Other celebrated figures are the poet Rupert Brooke, the novelist DH Lawrence and the philosopher Bertrand Russell. Thomas Carlyle, Hilaire Belloc, Oscar Wilde and AA Milne resided in **Chelsea**, as did Mark Twain, Henry James and TS Eliot. Elizabeth Barrett and Robert Browning are associated with **Marylebone**, which also lays claim to Sir Arthur Conan Doyle. Lord Byron won fame while living in **St James's**. Thomas Hardy and George Bernard Shaw were famous residents of the Adelphi, **Strand**. Karl Marx haunted the British Reading Room while researching and writing *Das Kapital* and is buried in Highgate Cemetery. Gilbert and Sullivan founded the D'Oyly Carte Company at the Savoy Theatre. The leafy groves of **Hampstead** nurtured the poet John

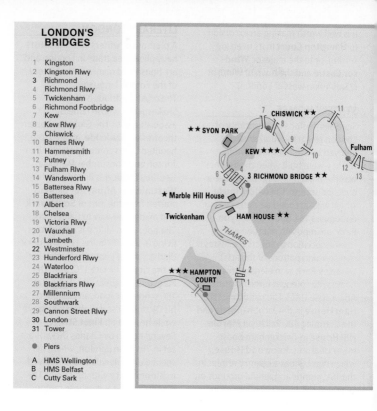

LONDON'S BRIDGES

1 Kingston
2 Kingston Rlwy
3 Richmond
4 Richmond Rlwy
5 Twickenham
6 Richmond Footbridge
7 Kew
8 Kew Rlwy
9 Chiswick
10 Barnes Rlwy
11 Hammersmith
12 Putney
13 Fulham Rlwy
14 Wandsworth
15 Battersea Rlwy
16 Battersea
17 Albert
18 Chelsea
19 Victoria Rlwy
20 Wauxhall
21 Lambeth
22 Westminster
23 Hunderford Rlwy
24 Waterloo
25 Blackfriars
26 Blackfriars Rlwy
27 Millennium
28 Southwark
29 Cannon Street Rlwy
30 London
31 Tower

● Piers

A HMS Wellington
B HMS Belfast
C Cutty Sark

Keats, Agatha Christie and the writer Ian Fleming.

CRUISES

For information about Thames Cruises, contact www.visitlondon.com.
The London Eye runs boat tours, while the Tate to Tate boat connects the Tate Britain and Modern galleries.

City Cruises

Year-round between Westminster, Waterloo (London Eye), Tower and Greenwich piers: daily 9.40am–6pm with later sailings in summer; £8.40 one way, £11 round trip Westminster–Greenwich; other legs cheaper. **River Red Rover ticket** day hop-on-hop-off ticket; adult £11.50, family £28. A **Rail River Rover ticket** additionally covers use of the Docklands Light Railway;

adult £13.50, family £33. Also offer lunch, tea, dinner, disco and cabaret cruises, plus Christmas and NY buffet and dance cruises. Cherry Gardens Pier, London SE16 4TU. ℘020 7740 0400. www.citycruises.com.

Circular Cruises

Round trip of London's famous landmarks; stops at Westminster, London Eye, St Katharine's, Bankside, and London Bridge City piers. The Old Pumphouse, Paul's Walk. ℘020 7936 2033. www.crownriver.com.

London Duck Tours

A 75min adventure on an amphibious vehicle; road tour of Westminster then a river trip. Daily 10am–sunset. Adult £19, family £57.50. ℘020 7928 3132. www.londonducktours.co.uk.

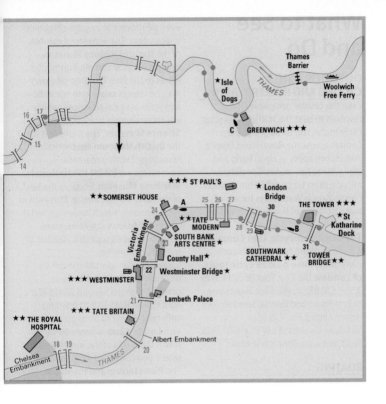

Westminster Passenger Service Association (WPSA)
Scheduled service from Westminster to Kew, Richmond and Hampton Court, daily from April–October. Adult Westminster-Hampton Court £13.50 single, £19.50 return; other legs cheaper. Journey time 3hr. Westminster Pier, Victoria Embankment, London SW1A 2JH ☎ 020 7930 2062/4721. www.wpsa.co.uk.

Lunch and Evening Cruises
- **Bateaux London**
  ☎ 020 7695 1800.
  www.bateauxlondon.com.
- **Woods River Cruises**
  ☎ 020 7481 2711.
  www.woodsrivercruises.co.uk.

BY CANAL BOAT

Services operate on Regent's Canal between Little Venice and Camden Lock, via London Zoo; dinner cruises, too.

London Waterbus Company
From Little Venice and Camden Lock. £6.50 single (50min), £9.40 round trip (110min). ☎ 020 7482 2550. www. londonwaterbus.com.

Jason's Trip
1.5hr round trip on former working boats with live commentary. Departs from Little Venice, opposite 60 Blomfield Road, London W9 2PE. ☎ 020 7286 3428. www.jasons.co.uk.

What to See and Do

OUTDOOR FUN
CYCLING AND ROLLERBLADING

Even the courier companies have resolved to beat the traffic on bicycles. Cycle routes run throughout the Capital, across the Royal Parks (speed restrictions apply in Hyde Park) and along many bus routes. Special permission must be sought from London Canals/British Waterways for use of some portions of the canal towpaths.

The London Bicycle Tour Company
As well as hiring bicycles, this company offers three **guided cycle tours of London**: the East Tour (9mi/14.5km; 3.5hr; £18.95); Royal West Tour (same as East Tour); and Central London Tour (6mi/9.6km; 2.5hr; £15.95).
56 Upper Ground SE1 9PP. ℘020 7928 6838. www.londonbicycle.com.

BOATING

For details on boating, canoeing, cycling and angling activities on the canals (and the permits) contact:
♦ **British Waterways London**
1 Sheldon Square, London W2 6TT. ℘0845 671 5530/020 7985 7200. www.waterscape.com.

Cycle permits are free via the website; angling permits cost £20 per year (℘0844 800 5386 for rod licences); short-term mooring permits are issued at locks.

Self-Drive Boat Hire
♦ **Lee Valley Boat Centre**
Old Nazeing Rd. Broxbourne, Herts EN10 6LX. ℘01992 462085. www.leevalleyboats.co.uk.

ACTIVITIES FOR CHILDREN

Children's playgrounds in most parks are very popular and there are plenty of activities for children of all ages in London. Museums and galleries have special programmes, from treasure hunts to storytelling and even sleepovers to engage children's imagination. The wonderful exhibits of the **Natural History Museum** bring ecological and environmental issues to the fore. Children take part in experiments relating to scientific and technological advances, which are entertainingly presented at the **Science Museum**. The mummies at the **British Museum** are particular favourites. Exciting maritime adventures are told at the **National Maritime Museum**. Possibly the best of the lot is the **Horniman Museum** in south London, which has a wonderful array of children's activities, many based around its superb collection of musical instruments.

Experience the spartan conditions on board the **Golden Hinde** in contrast with the Second World War light cruiser **HMS** *Belfast* bristling with twelve 6in (30.5cm) guns.

Visit **London Zoo**, where you can watch the antics of the inmates and where you can adopt an animal.

The **Planetarium** and the **Royal Observatory** at Greenwich have exciting presentations of the heavens. The grisly exhibits of the **London Dungeon** and the Chamber of Horrors at **Madame Tussaud's** will bring a thrill to some and scare others senseless, while **Pollock's Toy Museum and Shop** and the **Bethnal Green Museum of Childhood** strike a nostalgic note. The delightful shows at the **Polka Theatre for Children** in Wimbledon and at the **Little Angel Theatre** in Islington will enchant the young ones; older children can take up **brass rubbing** at Westminster Abbey, in the crypt of St Martin in the Fields and at All Hallows by the Tower. As well as all the other theatres and cinemas, there are **IMAX** screens in Waterloo and at the Science Museum. Visit London run a special website for children: www.visitlondon.com/people/family; *Time Out* magazine (www.timeout.com) carries special children's supplements during half-term and the school holidays.

SIGHTSEEING
BUS TOURS

Some tours are non-stop; some allow passengers to hop on and off and continue on a later bus with the original ticket; some include entry and guided tours of sights. Ticket prices vary (from £18). Sightseeing tours on open-topped double-decker buses *(weather permitting)* are an excellent introduction to London for those who are not familiar with the capital.

The Original London Tour

Hop-on-hop-off service, recorded commentary in 8 languages, 90 stops. Every 15–20min from 9am–6/7pm (seasonal variations). Adult ticket £22 (£20 online), child £12 (£10 online), family (2 adults and 3 children) £80 (£65 online). Starting points at Baker Street Underground, by Speaker's Corner at Marble Arch, Victoria Station, Piccadilly Underground station in Haymarket and Embankment Underground. ✆020 8877 1722. www.theoriginaltour.com.

The Big Bus Experience

Hop-on hop-off service, choice of live commentary or recorded (in 8 languages). Every 10–20min from 8.30am–6pm (4.30pm Oct–Mar). £24 (adult), £10 (child). The ticket includes three guided walking tours (Royal London, Ghosts and the Beatles), a river cruise and restaurant bonus card. Tickets available online, when boarding a tour or in advance from The Big Bus Information Centre at 48 Buckingham Palace Road. Main departure points are Baker St, Green Park, Marble Arch and Victoria. ✆020 7233 9533. www.bigbustours.com.

Evan Evans Tours

Guided bus tours of London including guided tours of major sites and excurions to Windsor, Oxford, Stratford-upon-Avon, Stonehenge and Bath. ✆020 7950 1777. **www.evanevans tours.co.uk**.

Visitors Sightseeing Tours

Half-day and full-day tours of London, themed events and tours outside London. ✆020 7636 7175. www.visitorsightseeing.co.uk.

Golden Tours

Guided and hop-on/hop-off bus tours, river cruises, evening and walking tours, themed events and out-of-town excursions. ✆0844 880 6981. www.goldentours.co.uk.

TAXI TOURS

Black cab drivers in London must pass 'The Knowledge' – a 34month training course with countless exams – in order to drive in London. Besides themed tours of central London there are also visits to "London's Villages": Hampstead, Richmond, etc. Door-to-door pickup and a 2hr Sights of London tour costs £100 (£105 Sat, Sun and Bank Holidays) per taxi (8am–6pm); London by Night costs £110 (£115 Sat, Sun and Bank Holidays) per taxi (6pm–midnight). Half-day tours to Hampton Court and Windsor are £245.

Black Taxi Tours of London

7 Durweston Mews, London W1U 6DF. ✆020 7935 9363. www.blacktaxitours.co.uk.

DISCOUNTS

Compared with the rest of the UK and other European cities, London is expensive, owing in particular to high living costs and transport. Visitors wishing to keep costs down will find information on **budget accommodation** (☺) in the section *Your Stay in the City* (☾ *see pp382–415)*, which includes Bed-and-Breakfastestablishments and guest houses as well as hotels.

Calendar of Events

Listed below are some of the popular annual events. For specific dates and full details, consult the Tourist Information Centres www.visitlondon.com.

JANUARY
New Year's Day Parade
Boat Show at Earls Court Exhibition Centre *(starts first Thursday)*
Chinese New Year in Soho *(Jan/Feb)*

FEBRUARY
Start of RBS 6 Nations Championship (Rugby Union) at Twickenham
Clowns' Church Service at Holy Trinity, Dalston *(First Sunday)*
Destinations Travel Show at Earls Court Exhibition Centre
Great Spitalfields Pancake Race *(Shrove Tuesday)*

MARCH
Chelsea Antiques Fair, Old Town Hall, Chelsea
Head of the River Race from Mortlake to Putney *(420 crews leaving at 10 second intervals)*
Oxford and Cambridge Boat Race from Putney to Mortlake
Ideal Home Exhibition at Earls Court Exhibition Centre
St Patrick's Day Parade and party, Hyde Park to Trafalgar Square

EASTER
Service and distribution of Hot Cross buns at St Bartholomew-the-Great *(Good Friday)*
Carnival Parade in Battersea Park *(Easter Sunday)*
London Harness Horse Parade in Battersea Park *(Easter Monday)*

APRIL
RHS Spring Flower Show at Westminster
London Marathon from Docklands to Westminster

The Boat Race

The annual Oxford and Cambridge Boat Race, brainchild of Charles Merivale, a Cambridge student, and Oxford student Charles Wordsworth (William Wordsworth's nephew), was first held at Henley-on-Thames in 1829. The clash transferred to the tideway between Putney and Mortlake in 1845, and today draws some 250 000 spectators to line the banks and pubs along the course. Competition is fierce: crews train for seven months for this one epic race of 4mi 374yd/6.78km. To date, Cambridge has won 79 times, Oxford 75, with one disqualification and six sinkings. Famous Boat Race oarsmen include actor Hugh Laurie and Olympic gold medalist, Matthew Pinsent.

MAY
Royal Windsor Horse Show held in Home Park, Windsor
Chelsea Flower Show at the Royal Hospital, Chelsea
F A Cup Final, Wembley Stadium
Chelsea Pensioners' Oak Apple Day Parade at the Royal Hospital, Chelsea
Covent Garden May Fayre and Puppet Festival – Punch and Judy
Open-air theatre seasons start at Shakespeare's Globe and Regent's Park Open-Air Theatre *(to September)*

JUNE
Beating Retreat at Horse Guards Parade, Whitehall
Trooping the Colour at Horse Guards Parade (Queen's Birthday)
Hampton Court Music Festival at Hampton Court Palace
Spitalfields Annual Music Festival Regent's Park **Open-Air Theatre Season**
AEGON Grass Court Championships at Queen's Club
Royal Ascot Racing Week

British Polo Open Championships at Cowdray Park

Royal Academy Summer Exhibition at Burlington House, Piccadilly

Wimbledn Championships at the All England Club, Wimbledon (*2 weeks*)

Cricket Test Matches at Lord's and The Oval

Kite Festival on Blackheath (*last Sunday*)

JULY

Hampton Court Palace **Flower Show**

The Proms – Sir Henry Wood's Promenade Concerts at the Royal Albert Hall (*8 weeks*)

The City Festival is celebrated in the City Churches and Halls

Swan Upping on the River Thames

Doggett's Coat and Badge Race rowed by 6 new freemen of the Watermen and Lightermen's Company from London Bridge to Chelsea Bridge

Opera and ballet at the Holland Park Outdoor Theatre

AUGUST

Great British Beer Festival – Olympia Exhibition Hall

RHS Summer **Flower Show** in Westminster

London Mela – Asian arts and culture festival

Notting Hill Carnival in Ladbroke Grove (*Bank Holiday Weekend*)

SEPTEMBER

Friends Provident Trophy Final at Lord's Cricket Ground

Costermongers' Harvest Festival and Church Parade, Guildhall to Cheapside

Great River Race, the Thames – 150 crafts from dragon boats to Hawaiian war canoes.

Mayor's Thames Festival – free festival with carnival and fireworks on the south bank of the Thames.

Open House weekend – buildings normally closed to the public open their doors for one weekend a year.

OCTOBER

Goldsmith's Show, **Goldsmiths Hall** (*First week*)

Chelsea Crafts Fair at Chelsea Town Hall (*two consecutive one-week shows*)

Opening of the Michaelmas Law Term: Procession of Judges in full robes to Westminster Abbey

NOVEMBER

London to Brighton Veteran Car Run departing from Hyde Park Corner (*First Sunday*)

London Film Festival organised by the BFI (*three weeks*)

Lord Mayor's Show held in the City (*Saturday nearest to 9 November*)

Remembrance Sunday Cenotaph, Whitehall (*11am service; Sunday nearest to 11 November*)

State Opening of Parliament by the Queen at Westminster

Regent Street Christmas lights are switched on

Open-air ice-rinks at Hampton Court, Somerset House, Greenwich and elsewhere (*to January*)

DECEMBER

Lighting of the **Norwegian Christmas Tree** in Trafalgar Square

Carol Services throughout the capital's churches

Notting Hill Carnival

©Jeff Gynane/Bigstockphoto.com

Know Before You Go

USEFUL WEBSITES

London offers all kinds of entertainment and the following websites will put you in the mood and help you devise your programme:

www.visitlondon.com
The **tourist office** runs a comprehensive website with full details of events and sightseeing.

www.thisislondon.co.uk
The most popular London newspaper, the *Evening Standard*, has the latest news on the capital and good entertainment listings. This is its online version.

www.timeout.com
The weekly magazine, *Time Out*, has comprehensive entertainment listings.

www.londontown.com
Comprehensive information on sightseeing, entertainment, services, shopping and many other topics is available on this website.

www.freelondonlistings.co.uk
London has a range of attractions and entertainment with **free or nearly free access**.

www.bbc.co.uk/londonlive
The online version of the **BBC**'s radio programme dedicated to London news and happenings.

Other websites worth a look include:
www.whatsonwhen.com
www.officiallondontheatre.co.uk

TOURIST OFFICES
INTERNATIONAL

The **British Tourist Authority (BTA)** provides assistance in planning a trip to London and an excellent range of brochures and maps. The addresses and telephone numbers of local tourist information centres are given in the relevant chapters.

Australia
www.visitbritain.com.au
Level 2, 15 Blue Street
North Sydney, NSW 2060
✆ 1300 858 589 (freephone)

Canada
www.visitbritain.ca
5915 Airport Road, Suite 120
Mississauga, Toronto
Ontario, L4V 1T1
✆ 1888 VISIT UK (845 4885)

France
www.visitbritain.fr
Office de Tourisme de la
Grande Bretagne,
BP 154 - 08
75262 Paris CEDEX 08
✆ 01 58 36 50 50, 0825 83 82 81

New Zealand
www.visitbritain.co.nz
17th floor, NZI House
151 Queen Street, Auckland 1
✆ Freephone 0800 700 741

South Africa
www.visitbritain.co.za
Lancaster Gate, Hyde Park Lane,
Sandton 2196
letters: PO Box 41896,
Craighall 2024, Johannesburg
✆ (11) 325 0343

United States
www.visitbritain.us
Chicago: 625 North Michigan Avenue, Suite 1001, Chicago Illinois 60611. ✆ 800 462 2748 (toll free). Fax: 312 787 9641
New York: 551 Fifth Avenue, Suite 701, New York NY 10176
✆ 1 800 462 2748 (toll free)

LOCAL

The main information centres operated by the **London Tourist Board** are located as follows (*others are listed in the coloured Orient Panels in the Discovering London section*):

Britain Visitor Centre
1 Regent Street, SW1Y 4NS
☎ 020 7808 3815 *(information line)*
☎ 0870 240 4326 *(London information pack)*

London Tourist Board
2 More Riverside, London SE1 2RR
Written enquiries only or visit
www.visitlondon.com

INTERNATIONAL VISITORS
EMBASSIES AND CONSULATES

Australian High Commission:
Australia House, Strand, WC2B 4LA
☎ 020 7379 4334
www.australia.org.uk

Canadian High Commission:
38 Grosvenor St, W1K 4AA.
☎ 020 7258 6600
www.canada.org.uk

Republic of Ireland:
Embassy of Ireland, 17 Grosvenor
Place, SW1X 7HR
☎ 020 7235 2171
www.gov.ie

New Zealand High Commission:
80 Haymarket SW1Y 4TQ
☎ 020 7930 8422
www.nzembassy.com

South African High Commission:
South Africa House, Trafalgar
Square, WC2N 5DP
☎ 020 7451 7299
www.southafricahouse.com

United States Embassy:
24 Grosvenor Square, W1A 2LQ
☎ 020 7499 9000
www.usembassy.org.uk

ENTRY REQUIREMENTS
Passports
EU nationals only need valid ID,
such as a photocard driving licence, to
enter the UK, although it is advisable
to carry a **passport**. Non-EU nationals
must have a passport and may need
a visa.

Loss or theft should be reported to the
appropriate embassy or consulate and
to the local police. It is always sensible
to photocopy the relevant pages of
your passport and keep the photocopy
separate from the passport itself.

Visas
A **visa** to visit the United Kingdom
is not required by nationals
of the member states of the
European Economic Area (EEA), the
Commonwealth (including Australia,
Canada, New Zealand, and South
Africa) and the USA. Nationals of
other countries should check with the
British Embassy and apply for a visa if
necessary in good time.
Entry visas are required by Australian,
New Zealand, Canadian and US
nationals for a stay exceeding three
months. All visitors from areas outside
the EEA must apply for a visa before
travelling if they are planning to stay
for more than six months.
For up-to-date official information on
visas, visit www.ukvisas.gov.uk.
US citizens should view *Tips for
Traveling Abroad* online (travel.state.
gov/travel/tips/brochures/brochures_
1225.html) for general information
on visa requirements, customs
regulations, medical care, etc.
American nationals may apply to the
**National Passport Information
Center** ☎ 1 877 487 2778;
http://travel.state.gov/passport/
about/npic/npic_898.html (download
passport application from website).

CUSTOMS REGULATIONS
Tax-free allowances for various commodities are governed by EU legislation except in the Channel Islands and
the Isle of Man, which have different
regulations. Details of these allowances and restrictions are available at
most ports of entry to Great Britain.
The UK Customs Office produces a
leaflet on customs regulations and the
full range of "duty free" allowances;
in the United Kingdom a sales tax of
17.5%. is added to most retail goods.
Non-EU nationals may reclaim this tax

when leaving the country; paperwork should be completed by the retailer at the time of purchase.

Prohibited Items

It is against the law to bring into the United Kingdom any drugs, firearms and ammunition, obscene material featuring children, counterfeit merchandise, unlicensed livestock (birds or animals), anything related to endangered species (furs, ivory, horn, leather) and certain plants (potatoes, bulbs, seeds, trees). It is also an offence to import duty-paid goods (to a maximum value of £145) from the EU other than for personal use.

HM Revenue & Customs (HMRC)

www.hmrc.co.uk.

For US visitors, a booklet called *Know Before You Go* is published by the **US Customs Service**; its offices are listed in the phone book in the Federal Government section under the US Department of the Treasury or can be obtained from http://travel.state.gov/travel/tips/tips_1232.html#planning.

Domestic Animals

Domestic animals (dogs, cats) with vaccination documents are allowed into the country. However, animal import legislation is complex and animals may require a period of quarantine. It is strongly suggested that you take advice several months in advance of travelling if you wish to bring your animals with you. **DEFRA Animal Health**: ✆08459 335 577. www.defra.gov.uk.

HEALTH

Medical care in the UK is free to British residents, excepting charges for prescriptions, dentistry, hearing and sight tests.

Visitors to Britain are entitled to treatment at the Accident and Emergency Departments (A&E) of National Health Service hospitals. For an overnight or longer stay in hospital, payment may well be required.

Visitors from EU countries should apply to their own National Social Security Offices for the **European Health Insurance Card (EHIC)**, which entitles them to medical treatment. If you are not entitled to free reciprocal medical care, it is crucial to take out comprehensive travel insurance including medical cover prior to departure as treatment in the UK may be extremely expensive.

Pharmacists may be able to assist with minor complaints. For a free 24hr phone or online consultation with a nurse or doctor, contact **NHS Direct** (✆0845 4647; www.nhsdirect.nhs.uk). To contact a doctor for **first aid**, **emergency medical advice** and **chemist's night service:** Medicentre (www.medicentre.co.uk).

Ask for a photocopy of any prescription. This may be important for any follow-up treatment back home. American Express offers a service, "Global Assist", for any medical, legal or personal emergency – call collect from anywhere: ✆715 343 7977.

In case of an emergency, dial the free nationwide emergency number (999) and ask for Fire, Police or Ambulance.

ACCESSIBILITY

The sights described in this guide, which are easily accessible to people of reduced mobility are indicated in the admission times and charges by the ♿ symbol. The range of possible facilities is great and readers are advised to telephone the attraction in advance to check what is available.

The **red-cover Michelin Guide Great Britain and Ireland** indicates hotels with facilities suitable for those with disabilities. Booklets for the disabled are published by organisations such as VisitBritain, National Trust and the Department of Transport. Many ticket offices, banks and other venues are fitted with hearing loops.

The **Royal Association for Disability and Rehabilitation (RADAR)** publishes a guide to hotels and holiday centres, transport, accommodation for children and activity holidays.

RADAR
12 City Forum, 250 City Road, London
EC1V 8AF. ☏020 7250 3222, minicom
020 7250 4119. www.radar.org.uk.

Artsline
Artsline provides up-to-date disability access information on cinema, theatre and gallery access. The website
allows you to search by venue.
C/o Pine Court, Wood Lodge Gardens,
Bromley BR1 2WA. ☏020 7388 2227,
minicom 020 7388 2227.
www.artsline.org.uk.

TRANSPORT
Transport for London (☏020 7222
1234. www.tfl.gov.uk) publishes
information on wheelchair-accessible
bus routes and underground stations.
There are no passes or discounts on
London public transport for visitors
with physical disabilities.

Getting There

BY PLANE
Various national and other independent airlines operate services to the five
airports that serve London – Heathrow, Gatwick, Luton, Stansted and
London City. Information, brochures
and timetables are available from the
airlines and from travel agents.
Details of how to get to the airport
may be found on the **London Tourist
Board** website (www.visitlondon.
com); for Heathrow, Gatwick and
Stansted, look at the **British Airports
Authority:** www.baa.com.

LONDON HEATHROW
Heathrow handles most major air-
line scheduled flights. It is situated
20mi/32km west of London off the
A4/M4 and is equipped with short- and
long-term car parks.
♦ **Airport Information**
☏08700 000 123
www.heathrowairport.com

To and From the Airport
By Rail – **Tube/Underground** services
to Central London are provided by
the **Bakerloo, Circle, District, Piccadilly** and **Hammersmith & City
lines** (☏see UNDERGROUND MAP,
p431). For the reverse journey, take any
of the above-listed lines to London
Paddington (c. 12min) and take the
Heathrow Connect (www.heathrow-
connect.com) or **Heathrow Express**

☺ Heathrow Express ☺

With a journey time of 15–20min,
the Heathrow Express train
provides a frequent, fast rail link
between London Paddington
Station and Heathrow Central
(Terminals 1, 2 and 3). To reach
Terminals 4 and 5, take the regular
free shuttle train service.
www.heathrowexpress.com.

(☏see box) from London Paddington
National Rail Station for c. 25–30min.
At night the N9 bus shuttles between
Heathrow (Terminals 1,2,3 5) and
Trafalgar Square every 320min.
London Transport Information
☏020 7222 1234. www.tfl.gov.uk.
By Coach/Bus – National Express
operates a coach service to and from
Heathrow Airport Central Bus Station
and London Victoria Coach Station
(to: every 10–30min, 5.25am–9.40pm;
40–45min; from: 7.15am–11.30pm;
every 30min, c. 40–80min). Around £5
(single), around £9 (return). ☏0871
781 8181. www.national express.com.
Approximate journey time 60/75min.
By Taxi – Taxis are subject to road
traffic conditions (40min on a good
day to Marble Arch, but it is best
to allow at least an hour) at an
approximate cost of £70–£90.
There are taxi desks and taxi ranks at
all terminals. Services may be booked
in advance on ☏020 7908 0271
(Computer Cabs).

LONDON GATWICK

30 miles to the south down the M25/ M23 (short- and long-term car parks at the airport). Two, 'North' and 'South,' terminals handle flights to destinations worldwide, including scheduled, charter and low-cost flights.

♦ **Airport Information**
   ℘0870 000 2468.
   www.gatwickairport.com.

To and From the Airport

By Rail – The rail link **Gatwick Express** shuttles to and from Victoria Station (30min; 35min at night and on Sun). Departures every 15min from 5am and hourly after midnight. Cost £16.90 (single), £28.80 (return). ℘0845 850 1530. www.gatwick express.com. Frequent (and cheaper) services are also offered to the City, including connections to London Bridge (**Thameslink**; www.firstcapitalconnect.co.uk) and Olympia. **Southern Trains** also runs (cheaper) stopping services between Victoria and Gatwick (℘0870 000 2468; www. southernrailway.com). **Gatwick Railway Station** has more than 900 services daily to all parts of the UK. ℘08457 48 49 50 (enquiries). www. gatwickairport.com.

By Coach/Bus – National Express runs a coach service from London Victoria Coach Station to Gatwick Airport on the hour from 7am–11.30pm; av. journey time 1hr5min–1hr35min. **Airbus A5 and National Express Speedlink** buses operate daily 4.40am–10.15pm from Gatwick North and South Terminals to Victoria Station (1hr30min) via Streatham High Road and Clapham Rd, Stockwell; and 3.30am–10pm from London Victoria Coach Station to Gatwick North and South Terminals (**A5** ℘0870 575 7747; **Speedlink** ℘0870 574 7777). From £8 return; concessions and discounts available. National Express also run a coach service between Gatwick and Heathrow Airports.

By Taxi – Taxi services are provided by the airport's official concessionaire, Checker Cars in North and South Terminals. There is a quoted fare system and the cost of the journey is made known to customers in advance. Taxis can be pre-booked, and all fares can be paid in advance by cash or credit card or at the end of the journey by cash only: **Checker Cars** ℘01293 569 790/ 0800 747 737. www.checkercars. com. Taxis are subject to traffic conditions. Allow 65–90min journey at an approximate cost of £80.

STANSTED AIRPORT

Located in Bishop's Stortford, Essex, about 34mi/54km northeast of London. ℘08700 000 303. www.stanstedairport.com.
This is the home of most of the low-cost carriers, but is also heavily used by charter services in summer.

To and From the Airport

By Rail – Stansted Express runs from Liverpool Street Station to Stansted Airport (dep. every 15–30min; journey time 50min; £18 single, £26.80 return). ℘0845 7000 0201. www.stanstedexpress.com

By Coach/Bus – Flightline coaches run hourly between Stansted and Victoria daily. ℘08717 818181. www.nationalexpress.co.uk. **Airbus A6** connects Stansted and Victoria. 0870 5747 777.

By Taxi – Taxi services are provided by **Airport Carz**: ℘01293 579224. www.airportcarz.com.

CITY AIRPORT – LONDON

City Airport lies 6mi/9.6km east of central London. The nearest rail station is Silverton and the airport generally services European business centre destinations.

♦ **Airport Information**
   ℘020 7646 0088.
   www.londoncityairport.com.

To and From the Airport

By Rail – London City Airport DLR rail station is connected to the airport with departures to London every 15min (7min to Canning Town or Woolwich Arsenal, 22min to Bank).

By Coach/Bus – Bus no. 473 runs between the airport, Stratford, Silvertown, North Woolwich and Prince Regent DLR station; **bus 474** runs between the airport, Canning Town, North Woolwich and East Beckton via Silverton.

LUTON AIRPORT

Located in Luton, Bedfordshire, 32mi/51km north of London.

- ◆ **Airport Information**
  ☎01582 405 100.
  www.london-luton.co.uk.

To and From the Airport

By Rail – First Capital Connect trains or **Midland Mainline** run from St Pancras (35min) to Luton Parkway, where there is a free airport shuttle bus (5–10min).

By Coach/Bus – National Express coaches to London Victoria (Service 422), Gatwick Airport (Service 707 and 203), and Heathrow Airport (Service 787). ☎08717 818181 (National Express/Flightline services) www.nationalexpress.co.uk.

Green Line bus 757 from Victoria Coach Station: www.greenline.co.uk. **easyBus** runs a cheap express minibus service between Luton and Baker Street (Bay 4 outside the main terminal, route 757). www.easybus.co.uk.

Parking

There are short and long-term car parks at all airports with free shuttle buses to the terminals at regular intervals.

BY SHIP

There are numerous cross-Channel (passenger and car ferries, hovercraft) and other ferry or shipping services from the Continent, the Channel Islands and Ireland. For details apply to travel agencies or to the ferry companies.

- ◆ **Brittany Ferries**
  Hants ☎0871 244 0744 (from within the UK).
  Plymouth ☎08709 000 429
  www.brittany-ferries.com

- ◆ **Norfolkline**
  ☎0844 847 5042
  www.norfolkline.com

- ◆ **Irish Ferries**
  Dublin ☎00 353 818 300 400
  Liverpool ☎08705 17 17 17
  www.irishferries.com

- ◆ **P & O Ferries**
  ☎08716 645645
  www.poferries.com

BY TRAIN/RAIL

London has 13 mainline terminals connected by the Underground and in some cases by inter-station buses. Tickets and information are available from the terminals. Tickets can be expensive, but long-distance tickets are considerably cheaper if you travel off-peak and book in advance. Many outlying areas of Greater London and much of south London are served by overground commuter trains. Travel from stations within the six zones is included on the daily and weekly travelcards and Oyster cards (☞see GETTING AROUND). Try to avoid all mainline stations during rush hours (8am–10am, 5–6.30pm).
Note for Travellers with Disabilities: It is important for disabled travellers to check procedures and facilities and arrange assistance at stations before undertaking their journey; smaller British stations are not particularly wheelchair-friendly. ☎020 7918 3015; www.railcard.co.uk.

Rail Information and Bookings

Information on fares and timetables, on special deals for unlimited travel or group travel in Europe, on rail services

The London Pass

The **London Pass** offers options with or without transport along with entry to 54 London attractions and fast track entry. Buy it from London Transport Information Centres, tourist information centres and major train and bus stations. It may be more economical to buy the version without transport, starting at £38 for one day and going up to £77 for six days per adult. **www.londonpass.com**.

and on other concessionary tickets, including combined train and bus tickets, is available from **National Rail Enquiries** ℘08457 48 49 50. www.nationalrail.co.uk.
To book train tickets and get timetable information, visit www.thetrainline. com. **For European services**, including Eurostar, and railcards, contact **Rail Europe**: ℘0845 605 0525. www.raileurope.co.uk.

MAIN LONDON STATIONS

Charing Cross – Services to south-east England.
London Bridge – Services to south, central and south-east England.
Cannon Street – Services to south-east England.
Blackfriars – Services to south-central and south-east England.
Fenchurch Street – Local commuter services to south Essex (including Basildon and Southend).

Euston – Local commuter services to the north of London including Watford, Hemel Hempstead, Northampton. intercity services to the west Midlands; north Wales; northwest England; Scotland via the west coast; Northern Ireland; Republic of Ireland.

King's Cross – Intercity services from this station to east and north-east England; Scotland via the east coast.

Local commuter services to the north of London including St Albans, Hitchin, Bedford, Stevenage and Cambridge.

Liverpool Street – Local and intercity services to: Essex, East Anglia; **Stansted Express**.

Marylebone – Services to Birmingham, including Stratford-upon-Avon.

Paddington – intercity services to the west of England and south Wales. Local commuter services to the west of London including Maidenhead, Reading and the Thames Valley. **Heathrow Express** (15–20min service every 15min to Heathrow Airport, *see GETTING THERE*).

St Pancras – Eurostar services to the Continent; Midland Mainline intercity services to the Midlands including Luton, Bedford, Leicester and Sheffield and regular First Capital Connect services to Brighton.

Victoria – Services to Gatwick Airport and central southern England; including the **Gatwick Express**.
The **Orient Express** also operates out of Victoria, ℘0845 077 2222, Brochure Line (24 hour) ℘0870 161 5060. www.orient-express.com
Waterloo – Services to southwestern England and Windsor.

EUROSTAR

Eurostar runs regular services from London (St. Pancras International Station) to Calais, Brussels, Lille, Paris (Gare du Nord), from where there are excellent connections with services across France, and Disneyland Resort Paris. Prices are comparable with the airlines and the service is far quicker with a 45min check-in and travelling time, city centre to city centre, of under 3 hours. ℘08705 186 186 (bookings); 020 7928 0660 (lost property); 01233 617 575 (from outside the UK). www.eurostar.com.

Eurotunnel Customer Service
P O Box 2000, Folkestone, Kent CT18
8XY ✆08705 353 535/08000 969 992
(free 24hr information service).
www.eurotunnel.co.uk.
Eurotunnel runs shuttle services for
vehicles through the Channel Tunnel
from Folkestone, Kent, to Calais,
France.

BY COACH/BUS

Express coach services covering all parts
of the British Isles are operated by National Express in association with other
bus operators.
Special season ticket rates, such as the
Familysaver and Tourist Trail passes
are available.
Details about ultra-cheap international coach services to Great Britain
from all parts of Europe, plus coach-
based travel passes, are available
from Eurolines.
Most coaches depart from Victoria
Coach Station (Gate 10) in Buckingham
Palace Road (5min walk from Victoria
Railway Station) or from Marble Arch.

♦ **National Express**
4 Vicarage Road, Edgbaston,
Birmingham B15 3ES

✆08705 808 080.
www.nationalexpress.com

♦ **Eurolines**
✆08705 143 219
www.eurolines.com

♦ **City Link Oxford**
✆01865 785 400
www.oxfordbus.co.uk

♦ **Greenline Coaches**
✆0844 801 7261
www.greenline.co.uk

BY CAR

See also *DRIVING IN THE UK* in
GETTING AROUND.
The Michelin companion maps and
plans for this guide are listed at the
back of the guide.
Most visitors travelling to London by
car enter the country through the
Channel ports (Dover, Folkestone,
Newhaven, Portsmouth, Bourne-
mouth, Weymouth and Plymouth),
through the Welsh ports (Port Talbot,
Pembroke Dock, Fishguard, Holyhead)
or by the east coast ports (Harwich,
Hull, Newcastle upon Tyne).

Getting Around

BY PUBLIC TRANSPORT

London is a sprawling city, but it has
a comprehensive transport network,
which makes it easy to get around.
However, the system is overloaded
and can be overcrowded at times.
Serious efforts are underway to
improve public transport with many
new buses and long-term plans
for additional underground lines
and Crossrail, a fast east–west rail
line through the centre of London,
hopefully ready for the 2012 Olympic
Games. The Docklands Light Railway is
a quick and comfortable way to travel
to the east of the city and City Airport,
connecting with the underground at
Bank and Canary Wharf.

☺ Transport for London ☺

Windsor House, 42–50 Victoria
Street, London SW1H 0TL. ✆020
7222 1234 (24hr); deaf callers
✆020 7918 3015. www.tfl.gov.uk.
Oyster Cards (see p33).

Rush Hours

Unless you have no option, avoid
travelling during the morning
and evening rush hours (Mon–Fri
8am–10am, 5pm–6.30pm) when busy
Londoners travel to and from work.

BUSES

With over 17 000 vehicles on the road
and another 2–3,000 planned over the
next few years, the famed red London
buses provide an economical and efficient way of exploring the capital and

admiring garden layouts and details of buildings above street level.

Bus maps are available from underground ticket offices, tourist information points and Transport for London. Bus routes are displayed in bus shelters as well as inside the buses themselves; note that most bus stop signs will bear the name of the stop, but if in doubt ask a passenger or the conductor. Where there are a number of routes at key points, the different bus stops have a letter (A, B, C, etc.) – check that you are at the correct stop and travelling in the right direction at the map on the bus stop sign. Reduced services on some routes operate through the night – most of them converging on Trafalgar Square. White signs with the red logo indicate bus stops at which all listed buses must stop; red signs with the white logo are request stops at which passengers must wave to the bus to indicate that it should stop to pick up passengers. Night buses (prefixed with "N" or on a blue tile located on the bus stop) stop only if requested.

Central London Bus Routes

For timetable information and bus routes in central London, visit **www.tfl.gov.uk/gettingaround/ 9440.aspx and http://journey planner.tfl.gov.uk**.

In 2005, the last of the classic Routemaster buses (tfl.gov.uk/buses/ ini-heritage-buses.asp) were taken out of service, but they continue to run on two heritage routes (every 15min 9.30am–5.30pm).

Bus Tickets

Buses are cheaper than trains or the underground, but they are also slower. Tickets cost £2 for a single journey of any length (you must pay again if you change buses during your journey);

£3.50 for a one-day London-wide bus pass (after 9.30am); £6 for a saver carnet of six tickets; £11 all zones for a 7-day pass. The price is much cheaper with a pre-pay **Oyster** card (*see box opposite*).

Children under the age of 16 years travel free; 16–17 year olds receive a 30% discount. Above the age of 11, they must have a child Oyster photocard, obtained with age ID from Oyster sellers and underground ticket offices.

In central London, you must buy a ticket before you board. There are ticket machines at every bus stop within the pre-pay area.

RAILWAY

Docklands Light Railway (DLR)

The Docklands Light Railway consists of four lines in East London: Tower Gateway to Beckton; Bank to Woolwich; Bank to Lewisham; Stratford to Lewisham.

Services are reduced at weekends. An extension link to the new Eurostar terminal at Stratford International and the Olympic Village will open mid-2010. DLR trains are fully wheelchair-accessible.

The London Overground

This system of trains is designed to provide an "orbital" network around the Capital. The East London part is still under construction, but should be completed in time for the 2012 Olympics.

THE LONDON UNDERGROUND/TUBE

The London Underground network is divided into six zones with Zone 1 covering central London.

Single or return tickets can be purchased only at underground stations. They must be retained after passing through the electronic barrier as they are required to pass through a second barrier at the end of the journey. Inspectors may also do spot checks so do not destroy or deface them. Single zone ticket extensions

Ticket Prices

Ticket price information printed in this guide is for guidance only.

must be purchased before you travel. For the most efficient and least expensive travel, purchase an Oyster Card (♿see opposite)

To calculate an estimated journey time, count three minutes between stations. Trains run from Central London Mon–Fri 5.30am–12.30am, Sun 7.30am–11.30pm.

Each line has a name and a different colour. ♿The UNDERGROUND MAP is located on page 431.

TICKETS/PASSES

Ticket Purchase

Zoned Tube tickets are sold singly at Tube stations. All children under the age of 5 years travel free on the Underground, only two per accompanying adult on the buses may travel free of charge. Passengers must have a valid ticket for their complete journey or they may be liable to pay on-the-spot penalties of up to £50 on bus, Tube, London Overground, Tramlink and DLR services.

A carnet of 10 Tube tickets within Zone 1 costs £11.50 adult; £5 child.

Travelcards

Whether or not you get an Oyster card, do use the multi-journey zoned passes, which are capped to allow you to hop on and hop off transport throughout the day without worrying about the cost. There are two versions, those that allow you to travel day and night (up to 4.30am the following day) and cheaper off-peak versions (after 9.30am Mon–Fri, all day Sat, Sun and public holidays). Price is relative to the number of zones you wish to travel in. Penalty charges apply for travelling outside your ticket's zone.

♦ A **One Day** card is £7.20 (peak) and £5.60 (off-peak) per adult for Zones 1 and 2, which cover most tourist sights. Children aged 11–15 can purchase One Day cards for £1, a good alternative to the Student Cards as only presentation of ID is required.

☺ Oyster Cards ☺

The cheapest way to travel in London is with an Oyster Card, available from underground ticket offices, designated newsagents, online or at ticket desks. This is a blue plastic 'smart' card (£3): load it up with as much money as you choose and reload as and when you need to (check the amount remaining as you swipe it at the turnstiles). You simply hold it against a reader terminal on the bus or as you enter the Tube. It acts as a single journey ticket until it reaches the cost of a day's bus pass or travelcard (depending on which form of transport you are using) when it automatically converts itself to a day pass for the rest of the day. The cards are usable on the underground, buses, trams, DLR and London Overground services. Fares are considerably cheaper with an Oyster (particularly for single journeys) than standard tickets.

©Transport for London

♦ A **Three Day** Card is £18.40 for Zones 1 and 2 (no off-peak version).

A **Photocard** is required by adults and children using a Weekly Travelcard. It is also required by 14- and 15-year-old children as a qualifier for the under-16 child fare and by youths applying for the 16–17 and Student Cards. Applications for photocards must be made several weeks in advance. Visit www.tfl.gov.uk for details.

Travel Discounts

Rail travel in the UK is not cheap, but there are various passes to help make it a little lighter on your pocket.

For students and those aged between 16 and 25, the following railcards are available:

The International Student Identity Card – ISIC (www.isiccard.com)

International Youth Travel Card – IYTC (www.istc.org)

Young Persons Railcard (www.16-25railcard.co.uk)

For all visitors to Europe, including the UK, **www.railrocket.com** gives information about travelling by rail in Europe and the various discounts available, such as BritRail, Eurail and Point-to-Point tickets.

Keep an eye on **www.tfl.gov.uk**, as there are frequently excellent **discount** deals for sightseeing, from 2-for-1 on the London Eye to 30% off tickets for West End musicals if you present a valid ticket or Oyster card.

BY TAXI

The traditional London black cab is available at railway terminals, Heathrow airport, taxi ranks and cruising the streets. An orange roof-light is displayed when the taxi is free to be hailed. There are plenty around although you may find it difficult to hail one during rush hour, at about 10.30am–11pm when the theatres and pubs turn out and if it is raining. There is a marshalled cab rank on Cranbourn Street, next to Leicester Square underground station on Friday and Saturday evenings from 10pm–3am, matching up customers with cabbies going off duty who are headed in the right direction. There are also ranks at all mainline stations (Charing Cross is the most convenient for the West End).

Minicabs

Outside the centre, there are also many local licensed minicab companies which are booked by phone (look in the local phone directory or on the Transport for London website: www.tfl.gov.uk) and offer flat-fee journeys. They are usually cheaper than black cabs but do not have meters, so be sure to ask the price when booking.

Never use the unlicensed, illegal minicabs which cruise the city centre at night and have no meter. At best you are uninsured, at worst in danger, especially lone females.

Fares

All black cabs are metered. The minimum fare is £2.20. Fares rise between 8–10pm on Mon–Fri and at weekends, and again from 10pm–6am and on public holidays. All fares are set by Transport for London, so any negotiating over the fare in central London is pointless. There is also a surcharge for luggage. Journeys beyond the limits of the Metropolitan Police District (MPD – an area broadly corresponding to but slightly less extensive than Greater London) are subject to negotiation. Taxis are not obliged to go outside the MPD nor more than 6mi/9.6km from the pick-up point within the MPD.

Few cabs accept credit cards. Those that do will have a CC sign; let them know when you get in that you will be using a card and expect a £2 handling fee. Gratuities are discretionary but up to 10% is usual. www.tfl.gov.uk/pco or www.london-taxi.co.uk.

BY BICYCLE

The London cycle network is well established in some parts of the city, although cyclists may be deterred by the dense city centre traffic. A safety helmet and face mask are essential equipment; cyclists should refrain from riding on the pavement.

Bikes may be taken on certain train lines at certain times: enquiries ✆020 7222 1234. A folding bicycle may be taken on all forms of transport without restriction (at the driver's discretion on buses; and only in a container on the DLR). *London Cycle Guides* are available free from:

- **The London Cycling Campaign** (2 Newhams Row, London SE1 3UZ; ℘020 7234 9310; www.lcc. org.uk) and **Transport for London** (www.tfl.org.uk).

- **London Bicycle Tour Company** 56 Upper Ground SE1 9PP. ℘020 7928 6838. www.londonbicycle.com.

Rental £19 first day, £9 subsequent days, £48 first week and £10 second week. 2.5hr central London bike tour daily, 10.30am (£15.95).

BY BOAT

A novel way of getting about London is by river, with many of the boats offering excellent guided sightseeing tours of the river, either upstream to Kew and Hampton Court or down the river to Greenwich.

To encourage Londoners to make more use of the river, piers have been built and regular commuter services have been introduced with hop-on-hop-off fares and valid all-day tickets; travelcard holders (including Oyster card holders with a travelcard loaded) are entitled to a 33% discount off some river service fares.

Transport for London offers downloads of timetables and fares (www.tfl.gov.uk/gettingaround/1131.aspx).

Some companies operate only weekdays and in summer, others all week and year round:

Thames Executive Charters ℘01342 820 600 **www.thamesexecutivecharters.com** Putney–Wandsworth–Chelsea Harbour–Cadogan Pier–Embankment–Blackfriars. Mon–Fri only (except bank holidays), £3.75–£7.50 (single).

Travelling by boat

Ph. Gajic/MICHELIN

Thames Clippers ℘020 7001 2222 **www.thamesclippers.com** Waterloo–Embankment–Blackfriars–Bankside–London Bridge–Tower–Canary Wharf–Greenland–Masthouse Terrace–Greenwich–QU II PIER. Mon–Fri only (except bank holidays), £5 (adult single), £2.50 (child single), £12 adult, £6 child *River Roamer* ticket.

Crown River Cruises ℘020 7936 2033 **www.crownriver.com** Westminster–St Katharine Dock Hop-on Hop-off service daily, £6 (single).

BY CAR

If you are arriving by car, it is advisable to find a place to stay on the outskirts and travel to the city centre by public transport to enjoy your visit, as London traffic is so dense and parking is very expensive – up to £30 a day in the centre. Traffic in and around towns is heavy during the rush-hour (morning and evening) as well as on major roads at the weekend, particularly in summer and more so on bank holiday weekends. Never leave anything of value in an unattended vehicle at any time.

CONGESTION CHARGE

An £8 daily charge is levied on any vehicle (except motorcycles) entering the central zone and much of Kensington and Chelsea Mon–Fri 7am–6.30pm, except public holidays. Payment must be made in advance or

before midnight on the day of travel –
£2 surcharge between 10pm and
midnight – by post, by text (SMS), at
self-service machines, on the internet,
by telephone, at retail outlets or at
certain car parks. There is a £120
penalty for non-payment, reduced to
£60 for payment within 14 days; the
penalty increases to £180 if not paid
within 28 days. ℘0845 900 1234.
www.cclondon.com.

ROAD REGULATIONS

The **minimum driving age** is 17 years
old. Traffic drives **on the left** and
overtakes on the right. Go clockwise
round roundabouts. Headlights must
be used at night and in poor visibility.
Important **traffic signs** are shown at
the end of the **Michelin Guide Great
Britain & Ireland**, and in general
correspond to international norms.

Speed Limits

MAXIMUM SPEED LIMITS	
70mph/112kph	Motorways or dual carriageways
60mph/96kph	Single carriageways
30mph/48kph	In towns and cities

Seat Belts

In Britain the compulsory wearing
of **seat belts** includes rear seat
passengers when rear belts are fitted
and all children under 14.
Infants and small children are required
to be seated in specifically designed
car seats.

Bus Lanes

Blue road signs indicate the hours
between which certain lanes are
reserved for buses and taxis. Most
bear a sign permitting use by cyclists.

Pedestrian Crossings

Give way to pedestrians on zebra
crossings and when traffic lights flash
amber or are red.

Road Signs

Road signs have different coloured
backgrounds as follows:

PARKING

Off-street parking is indicated by blue
signs with white lettering (Parking or
P); payment is made on leaving or in
advance for a certain period. In some
boroughs, such as Westminster, a Pay
by Phone option is available (call to set
up an account: ℘020 7005 0055). To
find a convenient car park, visit www.
ncp.co.uk or www.274parking.com.
There are also parking meters, disc
systems and paying parking zones; in
the last case tickets must be obtained
from ticket machines (small change
necessary) and displayed inside
the windscreen. Parking meters are
usually time-restricted and heavily
policed.

Residential parking: Parking within
London is very limited, and quite a few
places are restricted to local residents,
who pay handsomely for the privilege.
Watch for the signs. Different
boroughs operate varying restrictions
and since enforcement has been
granted to independent operators,
ticketing, clamping and removal
is common. In Covent Garden, for
example, parking on a yellow line is
permitted in some areas after 6.30pm
and after 8.30pm in others.

PENALTIES

Drinking and Driving: There are
severe penalties for driving after
drinking more than the legal limit
of alcohol. The legal limit is 80mg of
alcohol per 100ml of blood – how
much you can drink depends on your
body weight, metabolism and other
factors, but assume that anything
more than two small glasses of wine
or one pint of beer will put you close
to or over the limit. The police can
breathalyse you on the spot. Penalties
may vary from points on your licence
to losing your licence, fines of up to
£5 000 and even custodial sentences
for causing injury or death while
driving under the influence of alcohol

PARKING RESTRICTIONS

Double red line	No stopping at any time
Double yellow line	No parking at any time
Dotted yellow line	No parking for set periods as indicated on panel
White zigzag lines at a zebra crossing	No stopping or parking at any time

or drugs. For more information, see www.drinkdrivinglaw.co.uk.
Speeding: Roadside cameras (indicated) record vehicles exceeding the speed limit; fines and points on your licence follow.
Parking: Illegal parking is liable to fines and also in certain cases to the vehicle being clamped or towed away. To release your car costs £45 plus a fine of £40–80 (50% discount if you pay within 14 days). To get your car back if it has been towed will cost up to £150 plus fine. If your car has been clamped you will be given a notice of the payment centre to contact. If your car has been towed away, contact the nearest police station or call the **Trace service** hotline on ☏020 7747 4747.

PETROL/GASOLINE

In many service stations dual-pumps are the rule with **unleaded** pumps being identified by green pump handles or a green stripe. **Diesel** is available at all service stations. Most service stations are self-service.

MOTORING ORGANISATIONS

The major UK motoring organisations are the Automobile Association (AA) and the Royal Automobile Club (RAC).

- **Automobile Association**
  ☏09003 401 100 (travel information) 0800 262 050 (disability helpline)
  www.theaa.co.uk

- **Royal Automobile Club**
  ☏08705 722 722 (customer services) **www.rac.co.uk**

RENTAL CARS

There are car rental agencies at airport terminals, railway stations and in all large towns throughout Great Britain. European cars usually have manual transmissions, but automatic cars are available on demand; the driver sits on the right. An internationally recognised driving licence is required for non-EU nationals. Most companies will not rent to those aged under 25 (21 in some cases).

Rental Car Agencies
- **Avis** www.avis.com
- **Budget** www.budget.co.uk
- **Europcar** www.europcar.co.uk
- **Hertz** www.hertz.com
- **National Car Rental** www.nationalcar.co.uk

DRIVING IN THE UK

EU nationals require a valid **national driving licence**; non-EU nationals require an **international driving permit** (IDP). A permit is available from local branches of the **American Automobile Association** (1 000 AAA Drive, Heathrow, FL 32746-5063; ☏407/444-8033; www.aaa.com) or from the **National Automobile Club** (Touring Department, 1151 E Hillsdale Blvd, Foster City, CA 94404; ☏+11-800-622-7070; www.thenac.com). You also require the vehicle's **registration papers** (log-book) and a **nationality plate**.
Insurance cover is compulsory; the **International Insurance Certificate** (Green Card), though no longer a legal requirement, is the most effective proof of insurance cover and is internationally recognised by the police and other authorities.
Certain UK motoring organisations run accident insurance and breakdown service schemes for members: **Europ Assistance**, the **AA** and the **RAC** are examples; check details before travelling. The **American Automobile Association** publishes a free brochure entitled *Offices to Serve You Abroad* for its members.

Basic Information

BUSINESS HOURS

Admission times and charges are liable to change; the information printed in this guide is for guidance only.

ADMISSION TIMES
CHURCHES

Some small churches are locked when not in use for services. The cathedrals charge an entrance fee for sightseers; other churches are free but would appreciate a donation.

SHOPS

The big stores and larger shops are open Mondays to Saturdays from 9am–5.30pm or 6pm, Sundays from 10am–4pm or 11am–5pm. Some are open late (8pm) one day a week – Wednesdays in Knightsbridge, Thursdays in Oxford Street and down Regent Street. Some supermarkets are open round the clock, and certain local corner shops stay open until 10pm or later in residential areas such as Bayswater and Earl's Court.

TICKET OFFICES

These usually close 30min before closing time; only exceptions are mentioned. Some places issue timed tickets owing to limited space and facilities.

ADMISSION CHARGES

The charge given is for an individual adult. Major state-owned museums in London are all free. Most places offer reductions for families, children, students, senior citizens (old-age pensioners) and the unemployed; it may be necessary to provide proof of identity and status. Large parties should apply in advance, as many places offer special rates for group bookings and some have special days for group visits.

DATES

Dates given in this guide are inclusive. The term "weekend" means Saturday and Sunday (Sat–Sun). The term "holidays" means bank and public holidays, when shops, museums and other monuments may be closed or may vary their times of admission. The terms "school holidays" and "half-term" refer to the breaks between terms at Christmas, Easter and during the summer months and to the short mid-term breaks (one week), which are usually in February and October.

ELECTRICITY

The electric current is 230 volts AC (tolerances +10% and - 6%) (50 HZ); 3-pin flat wall sockets are standard. An adaptor or multiple point plug is required for non-British appliances.

EMERGENCIES

999 For all emergency services (no charge nationwide); ask for Fire, Police, Ambulance, Coastguard, Mountain Rescue or Cave Rescue.

LOST PROPERTY

Do not despair, precious possessions are sometimes handed in. For pro-perty lost in the street, enquire at the local police station. For property left on an underground train, London Bus or licensed taxi cabs, enquire in per-son at the **Transport for London Lost Property Office**, 200 Baker Street, NW1 5RZ (Mon–Fri 8.30am–4pm and bank holidays); enquiry forms also available from any TFL bus garage or station. ℘0845 330 9882 (recorded). Lost property forms also available on www.tfl.gov.uk. For property left on mainline trains, enquire at station.

MAIL/POST
Opening Hours

Post offices are generally open Mon–Fri 9.30am–5.30pm and Sat mornings, 9.30am–12.30pm. Late collections are made from William IV Street (between and throughout the night, and on Sun) at the principal sorting offices

Where to find Event Listings for London

Time Out – published weekly (Thursdays) – contains detailed, up-to-date information on venues and reviews for the theatre, cinemas, exhibitions, concerts, nightlife, restaurants, guided walks, cycle hire, etc.

Useful websites include:
freelondonlistings.co.uk; www.thisislondon.co.uk; www.officiallondontheatre. co.uk; www.londontheatre.co.uk; www.visitlondon.com/events

at Paddington, Nine Elms, Mount Pleasant, and St Paul's.

Stamps are available from many newsagents and tobacconists. *Poste Restante* items are held for 14 days; proof of identity is required. Airmail delivery usually takes 3 to 4 days in Europe and 4 to 7 globally.

MONEY

The decimal system (100 pence = £1) is used throughout Great Britain; Scotland has different notes including £1 and £100 notes, which are valid in England; Isle of Man and the Channel Islands have different notes and coins, which are not valid elsewhere.

The common currency – in descending order of value – is £50, £20, £10 and £5 (notes); £2, £1, 50p, 20p, 10p, 5p (silver coins) and 2p and 1p (copper coins).

Some High Street shops and department stores in central London will also accept euros.

BANKS

Opening Hours

Banks are generally open from Mon–Fri 9/9.30am–4.30/5pm; many are open 9.30am–12.30/3.30pm on Sat; all banks are closed on Sundays and bank holidays (*see Public Holidays*).

Most banks have 24hr cash dispensers (ATMs) that accept international credit cards or some debit cards, such as Maestro. *Check with your card issuer.* Exchange facilities outside banking hours are available at airports, bureaux de change, travel agencies and hotels.

Traveller's Cheques

Some form of identification is necessary when cashing traveller's cheques or Eurocheques in banks. Commission charges vary; hotels usually charge more than banks.

CREDIT CARDS

The main credit cards (EuroCard, MasterCard, Visa, Barclaycard) are widely accepted in shops, hotels, restaurants and petrol stations. Cash machines (ATMS), which accept international credit cards, are commonplace, particularly near banks but also in some small shops (transaction fee).

In case of loss or theft, the loss should be reported to the police who will issue a crime number for use by the insurance or credit card company. Always carry your credit card company's lost or stolen contact details and phone them immediately in case or loss or suspected theft.

NEWSPAPERS

Britain has an excellent selection of daily newspapers from the more serious 'broadsheets' – *The Times, Daily Telegraph, The Independent, The Guardian* and *Financial Times* – to mid-market papers such as the *Daily Mail* and the *Express* to tabloids such as the *Sun*. All have Sunday equivalents.

PUBLIC HOLIDAYS

The following days are statutory or discretionary holidays, when banks, museums and shops may be closed or may vary their times of admission: It is advisable to check boat, bus and railway timetables for changes. Most tourist sights are open on these days.

PUBLIC HOLIDAYS	
1 January	New Year's Day
Good Friday	Friday before Easter Day
Easter Monday	Monday after Easter Day
First Monday in May	May Day
Last Monday in May	Spring Bank Holiday
Last Monday in August	Bank Holiday
25 December	Christmas Day
26 December	Boxing Day

Whitsun (also a bank holiday) falls seven weeks after Easter.

SMOKING
Smoking inside public places, including bars, clubs, restaurants and pubs was banned throughout England on 1 July 2007. Customers wishing to smoke must step outside.

TELEPHONES
There are excellent **mobile/cell phone** networks using the European-standard GSM networks. US and Canadian visitors will need a tri-band phone.

PHONE CARDS
It is also possible to buy very cheap **pay-as-you-go SIM cards**. If you are wishing to make and receive a lot of overseas calls, call ✆020 7107 9700 or visit www.sim4travel.com to find international SIM cards with cheap rates. Newsagents often list prices of calls to various countries
Prepaid **British Telecom** phonecards, of varying value, are available from post offices and many newsagents; they can be used in booths with phonecard facilities for national and international calls. Most public telephones accept credit cards.

100 Operator
118 500 Directory Enquiries within the UK

999 Emergency number (free nationwide); ask for Fire, Police, Ambulance, Coastguard, Mountain Rescue or Cave Rescue.

INTERNATIONAL CALLS
To make an international call dial 00 followed by the country code, followed by the area code (without the intitial 0) followed by the subscriber's number. The codes for direct dialling to other countries are printed at the front of telephone directories and in codebooks.
Many newsagents sell **pre-pay phone cards** that offer cheap international call rates (from 2p a minute to the US); ask the shop assistant or scan the posters to find the best for your destination.

INTERNATIONAL DIALLING CODES (00 + CODE)	
Australia	✆ 61
Canada	✆ 1
Republic of Ireland	✆ 353
New Zealand	✆ 64
United Kingdom	✆ 44
United States	✆ 1
International Operator	✆ 155
International Directory	✆ 118

TIME ZONE
In winter, **standard time** throughout the British Isles is Greenwich Mean Time (GMT). In summer, clocks are advanced by an hour to give British **Summer Time** (BST). The actual dates are announced annually, but always occur at the last weekend in March and October.

CONVERSION TABLES

Weights and Measures

EU	US	UK	
1 kilogram (kg)	**2.2 pounds (lb)**	**2.2 pounds**	*To convert*
6.35 kilograms	14 pounds	1 stone (st)	*kilograms*
0.45 kilograms	16 ounces (oz)	16 ounces	*to pounds,*
1 metric ton (tn)	**1.1 tons**	**1.1 tons**	*multiply by 2.2*
1 litre (l)	**2.11 pints (pt)**	**1.76 pints**	*To convert litres*
3.79 litres	1 gallon (gal)	0.83 gallon	*to gallons, multiply*
4.55 litres	1.20 gallon	1 gallon	*by 0.26 (US)*
			or 0.22 (UK)
1 hectare (ha)	**2.47 acres**	**2.47 acres**	*To convert*
1 sq. kilometre	**0.38 sq. miles**	**0.38 sq. miles**	*hectares to*
(km²)	**(sq.mi.)**		*acres, multiply*
			by 2.4
1 centimetre (cm)	**0.39 inches (in)**	**0.39 inches**	*To convert metres*
1 metre (m)	**3.28 feet (ft) or 39.37 inches**		*to feet, multiply*
	or 1.09 yards (yd)		*by 3.28; for*
			kilometres to miles,
1 kilometre (km)	**0.62 miles (mi)**	**0.62 miles**	*multiply by 0.6*

Clothing

Women	EU	US	UK
	35	4	2½
	36	5	3½
	37	6	4½
Shoes	38	7	5½
	39	8	6½
	40	9	7½
	41	10	8½
	36	6	8
	38	8	10
Dresses	40	10	12
& suits	42	12	14
	44	14	16
	46	16	18
	36	06	30
	38	08	32
Blouses &	40	10	34
sweaters	42	12	36
	44	14	38
	46	16	40

Men	EU	US	UK
	40	7½	7
	41	8½	8
	42	9½	9
Shoes	43	10½	10
	44	11½	11
	45	12½	12
	46	13½	13
	46	36	36
	48	38	38
Suits	50	40	40
	52	42	42
	54	44	44
	56	46	48
	37	14½	14½
	38	15	15
Shirts	39	15½	15½
	40	15¾	15¾
	41	16	16
	42	16½	16½

Sizes often vary depending on the designer. These equivalents are given for guidance only.

Speed

KPH	10	30	50	70	80	90	100	110	120	130
MPH	6	19	31	43	50	56	62	68	75	81

Temperature

Celsius (°C)	0°	5°	10°	15°	20°	25°	30°	40°	60°	80°	100°
Fahrenheit (°F)	32°	41°	50°	59°	68°	77°	86°	104°	140°	176°	212°

To convert Celsius into Fahrenheit, multiply °C by 9, divide by 5, and add 32.
To convert Fahrenheit into Celsius, subtract 32 from °F, multiply by 5, and divide by 9.
NB: Conversion factors on this page are approximate.

Tower Bridge
©Philip Coblentz/Brand X Pictures

London Today

THE RIVER THAMES

The banks of the Thames ring with gaiety as the river is once again an integral part of London life. Crowds drawn to the major riverside attractions marking the beginning of the third millennium admire the splendid views of the London skyline and enjoy the pleasure of ambling along the embankment as the tide ebbs and flows. New piers and pedestrian bridges and landscaped areas add to the vitality of the riverside.

Take a river boat to beat the traffic or to make a leisurely excursion, or visit countless venues ranging from trendy pubs and restaurants and fashionable designer shops to celebrated museums and world-class theatres and concert halls. At night enjoy an entertaining evening aboard cruisers offering supper, music and dancing and gaze at the illuminated landmarks along the waterway. Some of the ships moored along the river banks are entertainment venues while others are museums of great historical interest.

From the King's Reach bend (at Waterloo Bridge) the view embraces two traditional monuments: to the east is the imposing dome of St Paul's Cathedral and to the west the multi-turreted Houses of Parliament. Across the water, adding a note of fantasy to the south bank rises the London Eye, a giant Ferris wheel, which affords a unique panorama of London extending to the far horizon.

EVENTS AND CELEBRATIONS

Events on the Thames feature prominently in the social calendar. Tradition is kept alive with **Doggett's Coat and Badge Race**, a long-established rowing contest from London Bridge to Chelsea, the **Swan Upping** ceremony at Teddington Lock (running since the 12C), when the beaks of the swans are marked by the guilds which own them (those owned by the Crown are left unmarked); both events are held in July.

Sporting challenges such as the **Oxford and Cambridge Boat Race** (Easter) attract the crowds. Regattas are held up and down the river during the summer; the highlight of the season is the **Henley Regatta** (40mi/64km upstream).

The **Greenwich and Docklands Festival** features events on or by the Thames; the exotic **Dragon Boat Races** are a Chinese tradition introduced in London in recent years. For special celebrations, spectacular fireworks displays on the river light up the night sky.

Thames Barrier

K. Brett/MICHELIN

A CHANGING SCENE

The Thames, a major river in England (215mi/346km long), meanders gently through typically English countryside of low hills, woods, meadows, country houses, pretty villages and small towns. Marinas provide moorings for private craft and locks add to the fun of a leisurely outing on the river with majestic swans and other waterfowl gliding by.

By the time the river reaches London it is a broad tidal waterway bustling with activity; barges used to ply their trade along here, and today various craft offer daytime excursions downstream to the Tower, Greenwich and the Thames Barrier or upstream to Kew and Hampton Court or evening cruises with entertainment. At low tide the muddy banks are also frequented by archaeologists and treasure-seekers in search of precious artefacts, lost or discarded objects, old ship timbers and other salvage items. The **Thames Barrier**, an impressive engineering feat, was built to contain the high tides surging upstream at the equinox, which can cause severe flooding in low-lying areas of London, especially as the land mass is tilting slowly to the south east. The marshlands of the estuary are a haven for wintering birds, waterfowl and endangered species.

Old and new now coexist as modern developments rise side by side with the old docks and warehouses. The cowls of the Thames Barrier dominate the scene at Woolwich and imaginative conversions of wharves (Butler's, Chelsea) and power stations (Bankside, Battersea, Lots Road) have turned these relics of the industrial era into the latest landmarks. Picturesque houseboats, formerly the homes of watermen and river pilots, provide desirable accommodation for the bohemian set.

MAIN THOROUGHFARE OF LONDON

Throughout the centuries the kings and nobles of England built palaces along the river from Greenwich to Hampton. Many of these grand buildings have been destroyed, but Ham House, Hampton Court and Syon Park still survive.

Until the late 17C the Thames was the capital's main highway; the royal household, the City Corporation and the city livery companies had their own barges; ordinary citizens hired the services of the watermen who plied for hire at the many landing stages, called Stairs; cargo ships and men o'war added to the congestion. Old engravings show craft of every size, which once thronged the Thames.

The first regular steamer services began in 1816 and by mid-century were carrying several million people. On weekdays the boats were crowded with workers going into the docks and boatyards, the arsenal and south bank factories; fares were a penny from one pier to the next. At other times they carried families and friends for an evening trip or for an excursion, often to the estuary and seaside towns of Herne Bay, Margate and Ramsgate.

POOL OF LONDON

London's history of importance is intertwined with its long use as a port. From the 16C to the mid-20C, the commercial prosperity of the city derived from the wharves and docks in the Pool of London stretching from London Bridge to Tower Bridge and the shipbuilding yards downstream. The yards at Deptford, founded by Henry VIII in 1513, grew rapidly and are associated with many historical events (⟲see GREENWICH).

Merchantmen unable to sail under London Bridge or to approach the wharves across the mudflats, moored in midstream and depended on a vast fleet of lighters (3 500) for loading and unloading. This system provided many opportunities for pilfering by river pirates, night plunderers, scuffle hunters and mudlarks.

This river activity is a thing of the past: wharves and warehouses have gradually been rebuilt and transformed into business and shopping centres (⟲see BANKSIDE – SOUTHWARK, Hay's Galleria) and World War II light cruiser HMS *Belfast*, moored along the South bank of the river, is an annexe of the Imperial War Museum (&see BANKSIDE – SOUTHWARK, HMS Belfast).

COMMERCIAL DOCKS

The first enclosed commercial dock, designed to cut down the opportunities for theft, was built early in the 19C. By the end of the century, there were four systems of enclosed docks extending beyond Tower Bridge over 3 000 acres/1 214ha with 36mi/58km of quays and 665 acres/270ha of dock basins: London Docks (1864), Surrey Commercial Docks (1864), East and West India Docks (1838), Royal Docks (1855–80). During World War II the docks suffered severe damage from bombing.

By the 1960s closure threatened as a result of the transfer of cargo handling being transferred to specialised riverside wharves and the dock at Tilbury.

During the 1990s, some of the surviving docks have provided good facilities for various water sporting activities, including rowing at the London Regatta Centre. The City Airport, Excel Exhibition Centre and the Millennium Dome (now the 02 Arena) are all built on former docks.

WATER SUPPLY

In the Middle Ages water supplies came from the Thames, its tributaries and from wells (Clerkenwell, Sadler's Wells, Muswell Hill). After 1285, conduits of leather or hollow tree trunks were provided by the City fathers to bring water from the Tyburn, Westbourne and Lee to lead cisterns in the City where it was collected by householders and by water carriers, who later formed a guild. During the next 300 years these provisions were augmented by private enterprise. The first pump driven by horses was set up in Upper Thames Street in 1594.

The Industrial Revolution brought steam pumping, gradually introduced from 1750 with cast-iron pipes: wooden mains could not sustain the higher pumping pressures. The widespread introduction of the water closet after 1820 resulted in sewage being discharged into the streams and rivers, polluting the water supply and bringing epidemics of typhoid and cholera (1832 and 1848). Filtration (1829), the requirement to draw water from the non-tidal river above Teddington (1856) and chlorination (1916) made London's water safe to drink.

Today, supply is maintained by reservoirs situated on the periphery of London at Datchet (8 300 million gal/37 700million l), Staines, Chingford and Walthamstow. In 1974 the Thames Water Authority was constituted to take over from the Metropolitan Water Board (1903). It levied its own rate and was responsible for the management of the Thames throughout its length and for London's water supply, sewage disposal and pollution control. The National Rivers Authority (Thames Region) was responsible for flood defence and pollution control from 1989/90 to 1996, when it was replaced by the Environment Agency. Throughout the 1980s and 1990s initiatives to clean up the pollution of the tideway were successful and meant that fish began to descend the stream and re-enter the estuary. Since 2006, some 125 species, including sole, cod, bass and even the odd seahorse have been documented in the Thames in a two-year study by the Environment Agency and London's Zoological Society. Licences for eel fishing are in demand and salmon, in particular, have returned in quantity after an absence of more than 150 years; they were once so cheap and plentiful that apprentices complained of having to eat them every day.

RIVER CROSSINGS

London grew around a fishing village at Southwark, and the only crossing was by a wooden bridge built by the Romans (&see THE CITY, London Bridge). After the Norman Conquest (1066) Richmond Bridge was the first to span the river (1139) upstream; this was followed by Putney Bridge (1729) and Westminster Bridge (1750). Tower Bridge (19C) with its high-level walkway and hydraulic lifts is a major landmark. Albert Bridge,

Thames Tributaries

Most now flow in underground pipes; some have been dammed to form lakes. There is little except streets name to recall the course of these lost waterways. Among the northern tributaries are (east–west): the Lee (or Lea); Walbrook (short) from north side of the City; the Fleet (two branches) from Hampstead and Highgate; Tyburn via Marylebone to Westminster (traced by Marylebone Lane); Westbourne via Paddington and Kensington to enter at Pimlico; Stamford Brook, which enters at Hammersmith; River Brent, which enters at Kew. Among the southern tributaries are (east–west): the Ravensbourne, which enters at Deptford Creek; Effra River, which enters in Brixton; Falcon Brook, which enters in Battersea; River Wandle, which enters at Wandsworth.

festooned by lights at night, was at the cutting edge of 19C progress with its cantilever suspension structure. The tallest liners can pass under Dartford's Queen Elizabeth II Bridge (1991), the largest suspension bridge in Europe.

The building of the Rotherhithe Tunnel (Rotherhithe–Wapping), the first underwater tunnel by Marc Brunel (1824–43), and the foot tunnel (1902, Greenwich–Isle of Dogs) by his son, Isambard Kingdom Brunel, with its two distinctive cupolas, introduced innovative engineering techniques that were later refined for the construction of the Channel Tunnel. The original Hungerford Bridge was built by Brunel; two modernistic structures for pedestrians are elegant new features. The advanced design of the pedestrian Millennium Bridge, a steel suspension bridge, evolved from the collaboration of the architect Sir Norman Foster, the engineers Ove Arup and the sculptor Anthony Caro. Initially nicknamed "the wobbly bridge" after swaying with high volumes of pedestrians crossing was reported, the futuristic structure underwent modification and is now an architectural landmark, linking Tate Modern and St Paul's Cathedral on the north bank of the Thames.

A RECURRING THEME

The Thames has inspired many artists: the celebrated views by Canaletto are of great historical interest; Monet and Turner were enthralled by the play of light on the water; the great bend of the Thames framed by idyllic scenery at Richmond was captured with great artistry by Reynolds and Turner; Whistler's paintings of Battersea Bridge (entitled *Nocturne*) are evocative works.

The following literary works and their writers found inspiration in the Thames; the plays of Shakespeare and Ben Jonson, the musings of John Evelyn, Samuel Pepys, Samuel Johnson and James Boswell, the poetry of Edmund Spenser, William Blake and TS Eliot, and the novels of Charles Dickens, Jerome K Jerome, Joseph Conrad and Virginia Woolf.

GOVERNMENT
THE REALM

Great Britain comprises England, Wales, Scotland, the Channel Islands and the Isle of Man.

The **United Kingdom**, which is ruled from London's Palace of Westminster, comprises England, Wales, Scotland and Northern Ireland, but does not include the Channel Islands or Isle of Man, which have their own parliaments and are attached directly to the Crown. Major recent constitutional reforms include devolution of some powers to a Scottish Parliament and to a Welsh Assembly.

MONARCHY

The United Kingdom is a constitutional Monarchy, a form of government in which supreme power is vested in the **Sovereign** (king or queen): in law the Sovereign is the head of the **executive** (government elected by a majority, headed by a prime minister and implemented by civil servants), an integral part of the **legislature** (the Houses of Commons and Lords responsible for deciding upon matters of law), head of the **judiciary** (Criminal and Crown Courts of law), commander-in-chief of the armed forces, temporal head of the Church of England and symbolic Head of the Commonwealth. In practice the role is strictly a formal one. During the reign of Queen Victoria (1837–1901), the monarch's right in relation to ministers was defined as "the right to be consulted, to encourage and to warn." The monarchy also acts as a last line of defence against coup as the monarch has the right to force the removal of a Prime Minister and call a new election in extreme circumstances.

PARLIAMENT

The United Kingdom has no written constitution as such, but several important statutes underpin the institution and conventions of government: **Magna Carta** (1215) sealed the king's promise to refrain from imposing feudal tax save by the consent of the Common Council of the Realm and instituted a fundamental human right: "To no man will we deny or delay right or justice"; the **Petition of Right Act** (1628) confirmed that no tax should be levied by the king without the consent of Parliament and that no person be detained without lawful cause; the **Bill of Rights** (1689) ensured ultimate supremacy of Parliament; the **Act of Settlement** (1701) established the independence of the law courts and regulated the succession to the Crown of England; the **Race Relations Act** (1968) aimed to prohibit prejudice on account of race, colour or ethnic origin; the **Representation of the People Act** (1969) gave the vote to all persons over the age of 18 listed on the electoral register save acting members of the House of Lords and those incapacitated through insanity or imprisonment.

The supreme legislature is Parliament, consisting of two bodies: the **House of Commons** and the **House of Lords** within the Palace of Westminster (🕮 see CITY OF WESTMINSTER). Regular Parliament meetings were assured after the Bloodless or Glorious Revolution (1688), when Parliament repealed James II's rule by "divine right" and appointed William III and Mary II; both houses were dominated by "landed gentry" until the 19C (MPs were paid a salary from 1911).

HOUSE OF COMMONS

Since the 17C two major parties have been predominant in Parliament (Her Majesty's Government and Her Majesty's Opposition) with Tories and Whigs, Conservatives and Liberals, Conservatives and Labour vying for power; representatives of other parties contribute to debates and may be lobbied for support by party whips to carry motions when opinion is equally divided.

Since 1992 the United Kingdom has been divided into 651 constituencies calculated to hold approximately 65 000 voters. A Member of Parliament (MP) is elected by a majority vote secured at a General Election to appoint a new government or at a by-election if the seat falls vacant in the interim. Government term is for a maximum of five years.

The House is presided over by the Speaker, appointed at the beginning of each session. MPs sit on parallel benches: members of the government cabinet sit in the first row opposite the members of the shadow cabinet (frontbenchers) while members of their respective

Horses and carriages carrying the Queen leave Buckingham Palace for the State Opening of Parliament

©Gary Lee/UPPA/Photoshot

parties sit behind (backbenchers). Their combined function is to decide upon legislation: each act is subjected to two Readings, a Committee and a Report Stage and a Third Reading before going to "the Other House" and obtaining Royal Assent.

HOUSE OF LORDS

A major reform of the House of Lords is under way. The House of Lords Act 1999 removed the rights of most hereditary peers to sit and vote in the House. An amendment enabled 92 hereditary peers, **Lords Temporal**, to remain in the House until a Royal Commission reports on the role, functions and composition of the second chamber.

Life Peers include the Lords of Appeal (Law Lords) and distinguished persons honoured for service to the Land (since 1958); the **Lords Spiritual** are the archbishops and bishops of the Church of England.

This body of the legislature debates issues officially without the bias of party politics. It also acts as the highest court of appeal in the land, although only the Law Lords are involved in such proceedings. The main body of the legal establishment, the Royal Courts of Justice and Chambers reside between Westminster and the City, where the Strand gives way to Fleet Street.

LOCAL GOVERNMENT

Since the early Middle Ages the City has been administered by the Corporation of the City of London. After the Dissolution of the monasteries (1539) Westminster and Southwark, the other urban districts, were given into the care of newly appointed **parish vestries**, which differed in character and probity.

Their powers overlapped and were insufficient to control, even where they thought it necessary, the speculators who erected tall houses with inadequate sanitation, which thus polluted the water supplies, and let off each room to one or often several families. Conditions were not, of course, uniformly bad – the "good life" was led with considerable elegance in St James's and Whitehall, in Mayfair, Marylebone, Knightsbridge, Kensington and westwards beyond.

By the 19C reform began, spurred on by traffic congestion and the dangers of poor sanitation. In 1855 the Government established a central body, the **Metropolitan Board of Works**, with special responsibility for main sewerage.

Slum clearance began as new roads were built to ease traffic congestion. Through its chief engineer, **Joseph Bazalgette**, the board reconstructed the drainage system for central London and built the embankments.

In 1888 the County of London was created with the **London County Council** (LCC) as the county authority with responsibility for an area equivalent to the present 12 inner London boroughs (Outer London has 19 boroughs).

In 1965, in the newly defined area of Greater London, the LCC was superseded by a regional authority, the **Greater London Council** (GLC). Greater London comprised the former County of London and former local authority areas surrounding London, in all a total of 610sq mi/1 579km, with a population of about 6.7 million.

Following the 1983 general election the structure of local government was reformed by Margaret Thatcher, and the GLC and other metropolitan councils were abolished (1986). The GLC's functions were devolved largely to the borough councils.

For more than a decade London was without a voice. A referendum in 1998 proved in favour of an elected mayor for London and elections were held in 2000. Since then, London has had an elected Mayor (currently Boris Johnson) whose chief functions are transport, policing, fire and emergency planning, economic development, planning, culture, environment and health. His work is assisted and carefully monitored by a 25-strong elected Greater London Assembly.

Greater London is made up of 32 boroughs, which currently have responsibility for education (excluding the universities), personal welfare services, housing, public health, environmental planning and traffic management.

Discussions are ongoing about whether the Mayor will also take increasing responsibility for policing, housing and education in the city, moving much of the power in the city away from the boroughs into a more centralised control.

LOCAL TAXATION

In 1601 a statute was passed requiring householders to pay rates to provide a dole for vagrants and the destitute, since the traditional almoners, the monastic foundations, had been suppressed by Henry VIII in 1539. For centuries the major part of the levy was employed for the relief of the poor; in 1813 out of £8.5 million raised nationally, £7 million went in relief and only £1.5 million on all other local necessities. Today, the Council Tax that supports local government is levied per property, whether owned or rented and is based on price bands. The Greater London Authority is financed by government grant and council tax.

URBAN IMPROVEMENTS

The so-called Improvement Acts of 1762 began the transformation of every street in the capital. Paving became the responsibility of the parish vestries, who replaced the deep central drains (kennels) with shallow underground sewers and lateral gutters. They provided scavengers and sweepers to clear the streets of night soil and garbage, which were still thrown out of doors.

By the 17C streets were wider and, in all but the worst areas, cleaner; the squares were cleared of accumulated refuse and were enclosed and planted.

The same 1762 Acts also instituted house numbering and street lighting. Change had begun in 1738 with the installation by the vestries of 15 000 oil-fed lamps with cotton wicks that burned from sunset to sunrise in such main thoroughfares as Oxford Street. In 1807, 13 gas lamp-posts were set up in Pall Mall. Seventy years later (1878) electricity was available and the first major street lighting project was

inaugurated with the illumination of the Embankment.

One of the greatest and least visible improvements to the city came after three bouts of cholera killed over 30,000 people and the "Great Stink" of 1858, when Joseph Bazalgette proposed, designed and built the London sewer system, a design copied across the world.

The corollary to the 1762 Improvement Acts came with the passage of the Clean Air Acts (1956, 1962) controlling the burning of coal in furnaces and open grates, so banishing the notorious London pea-soup fogs. Air quality in the capital has had a further boost with the introduction of the London Low Emission Zone in 2008, to deter lorries, coaches, large vans and other high-emission vehicles from driving in key areas. A daily charge (or penalty charge for non-payers) is levied for those vehicles wishing to drive in the zone that do not meet the LEZ emissions standard.

EDUCATION

A century ago in the capital there were only the schools of ancient foundation such as Westminster (1371) and St Paul's (1510), charity schools, Sunday schools and a few groups run by the Ragged Schools' Union, founded in 1844, attended by an estimated 12.5% of the child population.

The Education Acts of 1870 and 1876 provided schools and laid upon parents the duty of seeing that their children "received elementary education in reading, writing and arithmetic" (the The Three Rs). Responsibility later devolved on the LCC (1903) and subsequently (1965) on the Inner London Education Authority (ILEA) for Inner London. When ILEA was disbanded in 1986 education in inner London became the responsibility of the individual boroughs as it is in outer London. Under later legislation some schools opted out of local authority control. In 2005, discussions began on the possibility of transferring control of education in Greater London to the Mayor's office and Greater

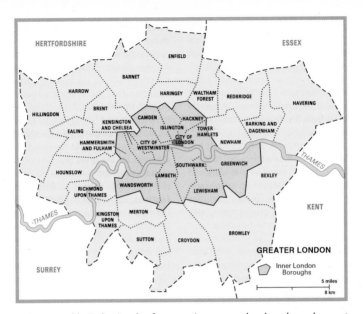

HERTFORDSHIRE
ESSEX
ENFIELD
BARNET
HARROW
HARINGEY
WALTHAM FOREST
REDBRIDGE
HAVERING
HILLINGDON
BRENT
CAMDEN
HACKNEY
KENSINGTON AND CHELSEA
ISLINGTON
BARKING AND DAGENHAM
EALING
TOWER HAMLETS
CITY OF LONDON
HAMMERSMITH AND FULHAM
CITY OF WESTMINSTER
NEWHAM
HOUNSLOW
SOUTHWARK
GREENWICH
LAMBETH
BEXLEY
RICHMOND UPON THAMES
WANDSWORTH
LEWISHAM
THAMES
KINGSTON UPON THAMES
MERTON
KENT
SUTTON
CROYDON
BROMLEY
THAMES
SURREY

GREATER LONDON
Inner London Boroughs
5 miles
8 km

London Assembly. Today, London faces challenges in its state school system: the problems of struggling schools in less affluent inner city areas are exacerbated by high property prices that mean teachers can't afford to live near to their work. Recruitment drives to attract and train more teachers and the Mayoral Key Worker Living Scheme, aiming to provide affordable housing, are under way in 2009 to offset these problems.

LIVING IN LONDON
GREEN LONDON

London is a very green city endowed with millions of trees, mostly cypresses, sycamores, ash, plane and cherry. The Royal Parks include St James's, Green Park, Hyde Park and Kensington Gardens at the very heart of Inner London, while Regent's Park, Holland Park, Greenwich Park, Richmond Park and Bushy Park extend beyond.

Many residential areas in the inner city are built around garden squares, most either lined by houses, completely hidden from the road, or locked behind high railings and only accessible to local householders with a key. Some, in areas taken over by business, are now open to all and are popular summer picnic sites among local workers, desperate for an hour of sunshine with their sandwiches. In addition many residential streets are tree-lined, while the English – gardeners to the core – insist in many cases on having lowrise houses with small back gardens and some residential areas in the outer suburbs still have allotments, areas set aside to rent out for growing vegetables.

There are some 3 500 acres/1 416ha of "common land". These are preserved today in local "commons" such as Streatham Common and Tooting Bec in south London.

Most parks are tended by the borough councils and some have sports facilities: football and cricket pitches, bowling greens, golf courses, tennis courts, bandstands, children's summer zoos and playgrounds.

In 1977 the first ecological park was created out of inner city wasteland, turning it into a renewed natural refuge where urban wildlife could thrive, bringing nature to the city-dweller for serious study or simple enjoyment; similar in purpose are the city farms.

In the 1930s a Green Belt (840sq mi/2 179sq km) was designated to run through the home counties encircling London at a radius of 20–30mi/32–48km.

51

Although in some sections the belt has disappeared completely, it has had some success in defining the limits of London and halting the metropolitan sprawl. However, with an estimated 70 000 new homes now needed in southeast England, the Green Belt is under greater threat from the developers than at any time since it was first created.

Environmental focus in London has increased over the past decade. The Recycle for London initiative was launched in 2003 by the Mayor to encourage recycling, and many London Boroughs now run their own programmes, with recycling banks, green box collections and other schemes. The Low Emissions Zone (*see Urban Improvements*) aims at improving air quality by taxing high-emission vehicles. Conversely, plans for a controversial third runway at Heathrow Airport have led some to argue that these benefits may be outweighed by a potential increase in carbon emissions. The debate continues...

The City

There is little room within the square mile for parks but since 1878 superb tracts of land "for the recreation and enjoyment of the public" have been acquired: Epping Forest (6 000 acres/2 400ha), Highgate Wood (70 acres/28ha), Queen's Park in Kilburn (30 acres/12ha), West Ham Park (77 acres) among others. The Corporation has also converted Bunhill Fields into a garden; it maintains a bowling green at Finsbury Circus, and has created gardens and courts in churchyards (Postman's Park by St Botolph's) and in the shells of blitzed or deconsecrated churches: 142 patches of green with over 2 000 trees.

SOCIAL LIFE

The green open spaces scattered across the city greatly contribute to London's social life: each of the many villages that were joined together and progressively formed the city has its own park, green or common and sometimes garden square which becomes the centre of social life as soon as the sun comes out. Sport, music, summer fairs, picnics, jumble sales... bring local residents from all walks of life together in a collective celebration of nature.

Another aspect of London that enriches its social life is its cosmopolitan character: it has always attracted people from countries around the globe who have integrated into its social fabric, and today it has the largest number of immigrants of any city in the world. This accounts for the great diversity of the capital's social and cultural events. Some of these events, such as the **Brick Lane Festival** (Bengali) or the **Notting Hill Carnival** (Jamaican), reach far beyond the communities that initiated them and have become part of the very traditional and very British London Season.

The **Season** goes back to the 16C and 17C, when London began to influence taste and fashion in the rest of the country. It originally coincided with the sitting of Parliament, starting soon after Christmas and finishing around mid-summer. It concerned the upper social classes and included social and charity events, opera and theatre performances as well as ballroom dances during which aristocratic families hoped to find suitable and advantageous matches for their sons and daughters of marrying age.

Today, the Season has considerably changed: it extends from April to August, is accessible to a wide public and main events are now mostly sponsored by major companies. An early event is the **Chelsea Flower Show** in May; the cultural scene boasts **Glyndebourne** (a quintessential south-east England event), the **Proms** (a series of concerts given at the Albert Hall) and the **Royal Academy Summer Exhibition**. In June, **Trooping the Colour** celebrates the Queen's Birthday; sporting events include the Boat Race between Putney and Mortlake (rowing), the **Lord's Test Match** (cricket), the **Wimbledon Tennis Championship** and the **Henley Royal Regatta**.

There were times during the long history of the city when being a Londoner took on a deeper meaning, when people of various origins and walks of life found a common ground in the face of adversity and responded with courage and determination: such was the case during the Blitz of 1940–41, when 30 000 civilians were killed, or during the wave of IRA bombings in the 1970s–80s and again during the terrorist bombings in July 2005.

Throughout the year, the social life of London rolls continuously; the **Theatreland** of the **West End** dazzles with the latest shows and musicals, the ENO and Royal Opera House host world-class ballet and opera performances, and music and performance of all varieties fill The South Bank, Royal Albert Hall, 02 Arena and Wembley Stadium. Smaller venues, such as the Shepherd's Bush Empire, 02 Brixton Academy and The Forum in Kentish Town provide alternative live music and gigs, stamd-up comedy shows and sporting events, such as Snooker.

Dining out is also a major part of the London social scene, from Michelin-starred restaurants to the buzz of small eateries and lively bars in places such as Soho. With the introduction of the indoor smoking ban in 2006, the streets are even more lively on warm evenings and weekends now, with many establishments putting tables outside to sit at – both for smokers and those who embrace café culture, despite the sometimes chilly temperatures.

LONDON TOMORROW

Even in uncertain global economic times, London continues to move forward with determination. As a world capital, the pace of life quickens relentlessly, entrepreneurial spirit prevails and people are working harder than ever: Britain has the longest working hours in Europe. Yet this is offset by the capital's natural dynamism, which stimulates regeneration programmes and projects, from new shopping centres, such as the vast Westfield Centre, to Heathrow Airport's new Terminal 5, and revamped entertainment venues such as the **02 Arena**, **Wembley Stadium** and the **Royal Festival Hall**. And, of course, all eyes are on preparations

for the 2012 Olympic Games, a vast and creative challenge for the capital: the site chosen for the Olympic village and the stadia, located 3mi/5km east of the City, covers an area larger than **Hyde Park**.

The Crossrail project to build two major new rail connections in the city was initially aimed to help provide access to the Olympic sites and alleviate some of the pressure on London's transport system. When finished, the two east-west tunnels will connect Paddington to Liverpool Street Station and Hackney to Chelsea. However, whether the building work will be finished in time to serve the games is currently under some speculation.

COSMOPOLITAN LONDON

London has attracted people from the four corners of the earth who have integrated into the London social fabric. The city has more than 35 ethnic groups with a population of over 100 000, leading to one of the most vibrant and cosmopolitan communities in the world.

African and Caribbean

The Afro-Caribbean communities that originally settled in Brixton and Notting Hill have since spread out all over the city, especially in northwest and south London. The Notting Hill Carnival is an international event. The lively markets in Brixton, Shepherd's Bush, north end of Portobello Road and Tooting are packed with exotic produce. The Africa Centre in King Street, Covent Garden, provides a concert venue for music and entertainment, and a craft shop. The arts of Africa are on display at the **British Museum** and at Forest Hill's **Horniman Museum**.

Jewish

London's Jewish community was well established at the time of the Norman conquest (1066) and, after many difficulties throughout the ages, has become an economic force through hard work and perseverance. The principal Jewish communities now reside in northwest London: Golders Green, Hendon, Stanmore, Barnet, Redbridge, and around.

The Jewish Museum (see ST PANCRAS) gives an introduction to the history and culture of London's Jewish community. The museum has recently undergone extensive renovation, but walking tours, temporary exhibitions, events and activities are still being held in partnership with different organisations. See www.jewishmuseum.org.uk.

Indian, Pakistani and Bangladeshi

Principal communities are located in the East End of London (Shoreditch and Whitechapel), Tooting, Shepherd's Bush, Southall and Ealing. Foodstuffs, fashion and crafts are available in London. The area around Brick Lane in the East End, and Southall are notable for their restaurants. The **Neasden Temple** (Sri Swaminarayan Mandir, off the North Circular), the first traditional Mandir temple in Europe, opened in 1995.

There are displays of the most exquisite jewellery and artefacts at the **Victoria and Albert Museum** and an exhibition on Hinduism – daily life, sacred places and devotional practices in Southern India at the **Horniman Museum**.

Far Eastern

Chinese, Thai, Malaysian, Vietnamese and Filipino communities thrive in London. At the heart of the capital is **Chinatown**★, an asian enclave that offers all kinds of services (legal advice, traditional medicine, supermarkets) and hosts the annual celebration of Chinese New Year. Limehouse in the East End is the area where the Chinese first settled.

Japanese expatriates, who live mostly in the affluent suburbs to the west and northwest, run their own schools and shops (Oriental City, 399 Edgware Road, NW9). Japanese designer stores (Muji) are famous for simple forms, practical raw materials and plain colours.

The Percival David Foundation (see BLOOMSBURY) is dedicated to the appreciation and study of Chinese culture.

Important collections of Far Eastern art are on view at the **British Museum** and the **Victoria and Albert Museum** (see MAJOR CENTRAL LONDON MUSEUMS). The Peace Pagoda in Battersea Park and Wimbledon's Thai temple are distinctive landmarks.

Mediterranean

Soho and parts of north London have been the preserve of Italian, Greek and Cypriot immigrants for decades. Spaniards and Portuguese have congregated around the top end of Portobello Road, while Greek shopkeepers have been attracted to the vicinity of **Aghia Sophia** on Moscow Road, W2.

Middle Eastern

The Edgware Road and the Bayswater area, Shepherd's Market, Kensington High Street and Westbourne Grove are frequented by the Turkish, Lebanese, Syrian, and Iranian communities. The golden dome of the **Islamic Cultural Centre** and **London Central Mosque** (146 Park Road, NW8) dominates the skyline in Regent's Park and there are mosques in Whitechapel and other areas of the city. The Ismaili Centre in South Kensington promotes Islamic culture. Rich collections of Islamic art are exhibited at the **British Museum** and the **Victoria and Albert Museum** (see MAJOR CENTRAL LONDON MUSEUMS).

History

TIME LINE
The strategic importance of the site of London as a bridgehead and trading port was recognised by the Romans almost two millenia ago.

CELTS AND VIKINGS
When the Romans invaded Britain, a Celtic fishing village had already existed since the 5C BC on the north bank of the Thames. The Romans built on the twin hills above the river crossing and Londinium grew into a major town defended by walls, with a permanent stone bridge over the Thames. The decline of the Roman Empire left the city open to Saxon and Viking invasions.

AD

43 –	Roman Londinium founded.
60 –	Revolt against the Romans by Queen Boudicca.
2C –	Roman wall constructed.
5C –	Londinium evacuated by the Romans.
8C-10C –	Viking raids and Barbarian invasions.

SAXONS AND NORMANS
Trade continued throughout the Dark Ages, despite the siege and fire of Germanic and Danish invasions. In the 8C London was recognised as the "mart of many nations by land and sea". Under Alfred for a brief period the kingdom was united and London was constituted a major city but an attempt to establish the metropolitan see in London was unsuccessful. Slowly the **City** developed into an ordered and rich community. In the 11C, when King Canute exacted tribute, the citizens contributed £10 500, an eighth of the total paid by the whole of England. The last Saxon king, **Edward the Confessor**, on being elected King by the people of the City of London, went upstream to **Westminster**; here he rebuilt the abbey and constructed a royal palace; since then the monarch and parliament have been separate from the business community in the City.

Remains of an original Roman wall in City of London
©Chris Harvey/Bigstockphoto.com

Two months after the Battle of Hastings (1066), the citizens of London submitted to **William the Conqueror**, Duke of Normandy, who was crowned as William I and soon built the Tower of London, Baynard's Castle and Mountfichet Castle on the river east and west of the City, less to defend it against future invaders than to deter the citizens from reconsidering their submission.

1016 –	Edmund Ironside elected King by the assembly *(gemut)* of London; died the same year; succeeded by **Canute**.
1042-66 –	Reign of **Edward the Confessor**.
1065 –	Westminster Abbey founded.
1066 –	Norman invasion. Coronation of William I. First royal charter granted to the City, whereby government, laws and dues devolved directly upon the citizens themselves.
1066-87 –	Reign of William I (**William the Conqueror**).
1067-97 –	Construction of the Tower of London.
1087-1100 –	Reign of William II (Rufus).
1087 –	Construction of Westminster Hall.
1100-35 –	Reign of Henry I; Royal Charter granted to the City.
1135-54 –	Reign of Stephen.
1136 –	St Paul's Cathedral and many wooden houses destroyed by fire.

Simplified diagram of the succession to the Throne

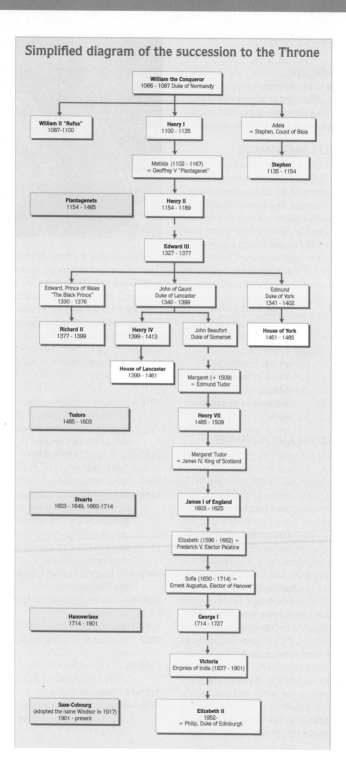

MEDIEVAL LONDON

The Roman wall, which had fallen into decay was rebuilt in the Middle Ages largely on the original foundations with an extension to the west; ruined sections are visible at London Wall and by the Tower.

In 1215, under King John, Londoners were empowered to elect annually their own mayor (elsewhere a royal appointee) who had only to submit himself formally at Westminster for royal approval; this was the origin of the Lord Mayor's Show (&see The CITY – Mansion House).

By the 13C the **City of London** had become a rich port and the capital of the kingdom. The wealthy City merchants loaned or gave money to Edward III and Henry V for wars on the Continent and, apart from the risings of Wat Tyler and Jack Cade, kept clear of strife, even during the Wars of the Roses. Indeed, the City never encroached on Westminster; with a few notable exceptions, citizens held no office under the Crown or Parliament. Many of the merchants, insurance brokers and bankers were related to landed families; younger sons, such as Richard Whittington (d. 1423), and the Hanseatics, who had arrived by 1157, were sent to seek their fortune in the City: they traded in everything and anything, particularly wool and cloth, building great timber-framed and gabled mansions and buying country estates in the West End and the outskirts of London.

Many **monasteries and magnificent churches** were erected in the City of London by the religious orders. The Dominicans, who arrived in England in 1221 constructed Blackfriars in 1276; the Franciscans (1224) began Greyfriars Church in Newgate in 1306; the Carmelites (1241) had a house off Fleet Street; the Austin friars (1253) settled near Moorgate; St John's Priory, the London Charterhouse and Rahere's priory with St Bartholomew's medical school were established on the north side of the City. At the **Dissolution of the Monasteries** (1539) Henry VIII seized their riches, destroyed the buildings and nominated himself as refounder of the hospitals – St Bartholomew's and Bedlam; this did not spoil his relations with the City, which became the home of the royal wardrobe. Under Edward VI St Paul's Cathedral, one of the great Gothic cathedrals of Europe, was stripped of its holy statues and remaining riches.

1154-89 – Reign of Henry II.

1157 – Arrival of Hanseatic merchants in the City of London.

1189-99 – Reign of Richard I (Richard the Lionheart).

1192 – Election of Henry Fitzailwin as first Mayor of the City.

1199-1216 – Reign of John (Lackland).

1209 – Construction of the first stone bridge (London Bridge) replacing the Roman bridge.

1215 – *Magna Carta* signed by King John at Runnymede, under pressure from his rebellious barons.

1216-72 – Reign of Henry III.

1224 – Law courts established at Westminster.

1290 – Jews banished from the City of London.

1272-1377 – Reigns of Edward I (1272–1307), Edward II (1307–27) and Edward III (1327–77).

1349 – Black Death: population of London reduced by half to 30 000.

1337-1453 – The Hundred Years' War between England and France began during the reign of Edward III and ended during the reign of Henry VI.

1377-99 – Reign of Richard II.

1381 – The Peasants' Revolt led by Wat Tyler.

1399-1461 – Reigns of Henry IV (1399–1413), Henry V (1413–22).

1450 – Rebellion of the men of Kent headed by Jack Cade; they occupied London for three days.

1453 – Wars of the Roses between Lancaster and York; Henry VI imprisoned in the Tower of London.

1461-83 – Reign of Edward IV.

1476 – First English printing press set up at Westminster by William Caxton.

1483 – Edward IV's sons assassinated (The Little Princes in the Tower).

1483-85 – Reigns of Edward V (1483) and Richard III (1483–85).

1485 – The battle of Bosworth marked the end of the Wars of the Roses and the beginning of the reign of Henry VII, the first Tudor King.

ELIZABETHAN LONDON

The reign of Elizabeth I dominated the second half of the 16C and marked the capital's golden age: demographic, urban and economic expansion, as well as cultural revival, particularly in literature.

Queen Elizabeth I, in whose reign the population doubled, passed the first of many Acts prohibiting the erection of any new houses within 3mi/5km of the City Gates. The reason for the royal alarm was twofold; it was feared that the newcomers, poor country people, might easily be led into rebellion and that water supplies, sewerage and burial grounds were inadequate. These and later decrees were, however, largely ignored or circumvented.

Queen Elizabeth (c. 1575) by unknown artist, National Portrait Gallery

©Imagestate/Tips Images

The Queen tried vainly to curb the growth of suburbs outside the walls. James I, however, subsidised the New River scheme which brought fresh water to the street standards.

In the age of exploration the City raised loans and fitted out and financed merchant venturers. The Elizabethan navigators were knighted by the Queen but the funds for the voyages of Drake, Frobisher, Hawkins and Raleigh were raised by the City. The aim of the adventurers was to make their fortune, of the City to establish trading posts. The result was a worldwide empire.

In 1600, under a charter of incorporation, Queen Elizabeth I granted a monopoly of trade between England and India to a new undertaking, the **East India Company**.

1509-1547 – Reign of Henry VIII.

1530 – Construction of St James's Palace.

1536 – Beheading of Anne Boleyn, second wife of Henry VIII.

1536-39 – **Reformation**: Papal authority rejected by the English Church; suppression of the monasteries.

1547-58 – Reigns of Edward VI (1547–53) and Mary I (1553–58).

1555 – Restoration of Catholicism during the reign of Mary I (Bloody Mary). Execution at Smithfield of 300 Protestants. Founding of the Muscovy Company.

1558 – Population 100 000.

1558-1603 – Reign of Elizabeth I (Good Queen Bess, the Virgin Queen).

1567 – First Exchange established in the City.

1581 – Founding of the Turkey (later Levant) Company.

1599 – Inauguration of the original Globe Theatre in Southwark.

1600 – Charter of incorporation granted to the **East India Company**.

Great Fire of London - Ludgate in the foreground and old Saint Paul's is in the distance

Mary Evans Picture Library 2008/Photoshot

THE CIVIL WAR AND THE RESTORATION

Conflict between the King and parliament led to civil war. The City merchants sided with Oliver Cromwell and his supporters against Charles I, who was always forcing loans, applying restrictions to trade and requiring gifts, ship money and tonnage.

The Jews, who had been banished in the late 13C, returned in strength during the **Commonwealth** (1649–60), a republic established by Cromwell after the execution of the King.

During the second half of the 17C, London was devastated first by the **Great Plague**, which killed almost one-fifth of the population, and, a year later, by the worst fire in the history of the capital.

The **Great Fire** (1666), which burned for four days, destroyed four-fifths of the buildings within the City walls. The Act for Rebuilding the City of London of 1667 stipulated that all future structures, houses included, should be of brick, thus reducing the risk of fire.

Christopher Wren was the main architect in charge of rebuilding the City. His great achievement was undoubtedly **St Paul's Cathedral**, but he also rebuilt many of the City's churches with money granted under acts of parliament, which increased the dues on coal entering the Port of London.

1605 – The **Gunpowder Plot** (*see CITY OF WESTMINSTER*).

1616 – Queen's House at Greenwich, the first Classical building in England, was designed by Inigo Jones.

1635 – Completion of the Covent Garden district.

1642 – The beginning of the **Civil War:** Charles I opposed by Parliament; Royalists confront Roundheads at Turnham Green.

1649 – **Execution of Charles I** on Tuesday 30 January 1649 outside the Banqueting Hall in Whitehall.

1649-60 – **Commonwealth**.

1653 – Cromwell named Lord Protector of the Commonwealth.

1660 – **Restoration**.

1660-85 – Reign of Charles II (the Merry Monarch, the Black Boy).

1660 – Royal warrants permitting theatre performances in Covent Garden.

1661 – Design of Bloomsbury Square, the first London square.

1665 – **Great Plague**: records give the total mortality as 75 000 out of a population of 460 000, rapidly spreading through London from St Giles-in-the-Fields and causing the most deaths in the poorest, most over-crowded districts on the

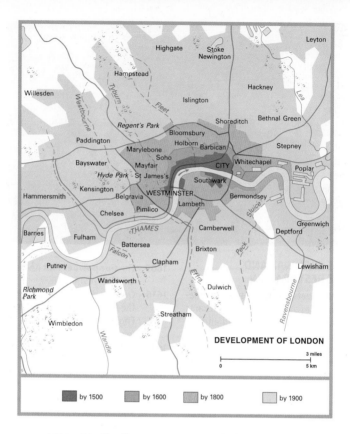

DEVELOPMENT OF LONDON

by 1500 · by 1600 · by 1800 · by 1900

3 miles
0   5 km

outskirts of the City (Stepney, Shoreditch, Clerkenwell, Cripplegate and Westminster). In June 1665 the king and the Court left London, only to return the following February; Parliament met briefly in Oxford. A vivid account of these events is given by Daniel Defoe in his *Journal of the Plague Year* (1722).

1666 – Publication of the first London newspaper.

1666 – **The Great Fire of London** (2–5 September) destroyed four-fifths of the City: St Paul's Cathedral, 87 parish churches, most of the civic buildings and over 13 000 houses.

1666-1723 – Reconstruction of St Paul's Cathedral and the City churches by Sir Christopher Wren.

1670 – The founding of the **Hudson Bay Company**, with a monopoly that lasted until 1859 in the fur trade with the North American Indians, led to British rule in Canada.

1682 – The Royal Hospital in Chelsea is founded for veteran soldiers.

1685 – Arrival of Huguenot refugees from France following the Revocation of the Edict of Nantes.

1688 – **Glorious Revolution:** flight into exile of James II; crown offered to William of Orange.

1689-1702 – Reigns of William III and Mary II until her death in 1694 and then of William alone.

1694 – Founding of the Bank of England.

1700 – Population 670 000.

1702 – Publication of the *Daily Courant* newspaper.

GEORGIAN LONDON

As the London merchants established trading posts abroad, great changes were simultaneously evolving at home as a result of the Industrial Revolution. By the mid-18C people hitherto employed in agriculture were moving into London to work in the new factories and settling east of the City in dockland, which came to be known as the **East End**. By contrast, fashionable society migrated westwards resulting in the development of the **West End** with its life of elegance and leisure.

Improved methods of transport were developed. All roads and railways, both literally and metaphorically, converged on London. Easier travel led to the development of the **London Season**, as men coming to London on business brought their wives and particularly their grown-up daughters in search of husbands.

In the 18C, during the **Age of Enlightenment**, the city began to develop from a community of merchants, bankers and craftsmen into a forum for men of letters and the arts.

1714-1830 – Reigns of George I (1714–27), George II (1727–60), George III (1760–1820) and George IV (1820–30).
1750 – Construction of Westminster Bridge.
1753 – British Museum established.
1756-63 – Seven Years' War.
1775-83 – American War of Independence.
1780 – Gordon Riots against Roman Catholics.
1801 – First census: population 1 100 000.
1811-20 – Reign of the future George IV as Prince Regent.
1812 – Regent Street created by **John Nash**.
1824 – Opening of the National Gallery.
1828 – Founding of University College.
1831 – Founding of King's College.

1836 – **University of London** incorporated by charter as an examining body.

VICTORIAN LONDON

In the 19C as more bridges were built and traffic increased, new wide streets were created to relieve congestion: King William Street as a direct route from the Bank of England to the new London Bridge; Queen Victoria Street, the first street to be lit by electricity.

One of the problems brought on by overpopulation was the Great Stink which caused engineer Joseph Bazalgette to design London's sewer system, with over 1 000 miles of tunnels and drains.

Public transport was developed through the introduction of omnibuses and the first underground railway.

Several prestigious museums were built and London hosted the first World Fair.

1837-1901 – Reign of Queen Victoria.
1835-60 – Reconstruction of the Palace of Westminster (Houses of Parliament).
1851 – First World Fair in Hyde Park. Population 2.7 million.
1852 – Founding of the Victoria and Albert Museum.
1856-1909 – Building of the South Kensington museums.

Statue of Queen Victoria

A. Taverner/MICHELIN

1860 – Horse-drawn trams introduced.
1863 – First underground railway excavated.
1888 – Jack the Ripper stalks the East End, murdering five prostitutes.
1894 – Opening of Tower Bridge.
1897 – First omnibuses (buses) introduced.

20TH CENTURY TO TODAY

The first half of the 20C was marked by a spectacular increase in the population of London, which reached almost nine million on the eve of World War II. At the same time a large proportion of Londoners settled in the **suburbs**. The 1930s saw economic depression and social unrest with an unprecedented rate of unemployment.

In 1940–41, at the beginning of World War II, German air raids concentrated on London left the City and the East End in ruins for over a decade. In the 1950s the importance of the **Port of London** faded: her smog-inducing industries were relocated and the demands for warehousing and docking dwindled. Instead efforts were concentrated on the service industries: company administration, banking, commerce, insurance.

Post-war London offered a contrast of moods: the late fifties, marred by race riots, were followed by the carefree **Swinging Sixties**, which in turn gave way to the aggressive **punk rock culture** of the seventies against a background of IRA bombings.

In the past decades, the **City** has changed beyond recognition as a result of the "Big Bang" reforms of the 1980s (computerised share dealing, monitoring of transactions and investment business by government-appointed regulators, removal of restrictions on foreign ownership); the rise and fall of Lloyd's of London; Black Monday (the collapse of the London Stock Exchange in 1987) and other financial crises; the collapse of venerable banking institutions; foreign takeovers; Bank of England independence; and the growth of

CITY OF LONDON

City of London coat of arms

Gwen Cannon/MICHELIN

the European Union. In view of these developments there is a determination to reassert the City's pre-eminence by forging new alliances in Europe. London remains, for now, one of the greatest financial and business centres in the world.

The City is governed by the **Corporation of London**, which acts through the Court of Common Council. The latter, numbering 25 Aldermen and 159 Councilmen, who represent the different wards, is presided over by the Lord Mayor and meets in Guildhall. It has its own police force. Territorial boundaries are marked by the winged dragon of St George and street signs bear the City coat of arms.

At the dawn of the 21C **London is still evolving**. The double centre remains the **City of London** for business and **Westminster** for politics.

To the outward eye the villages may have coalesced into a great urban sprawl but they are claimed with local pride by their residents. During World War II, the City and the East End suffered greatly from bombing but, as in previous periods, new amenities in tune with the age have risen from the ruins. The docks, which stimulated the growth of the city have mostly been replaced by modern industries driven by the latest technology and by the financial sector expanding east from the City and massive areas of dormitory accommodation in converted riverfront warehouses.

The East End will also be the area to benefit most from London's successful bid to host the **2012 Olympic Games**,

City Livery Companies and Ancient City Guild Halls

There are in existence 100 guilds of which 12 make up the so-called Greater Companies: Mercers, Grocers, Drapers, Fishmongers, Goldsmiths, Skinners, Merchant Taylors, Haberdashers, Salters, Ironmongers, Vintners, Clothworkers. Most are successors of medieval religious fraternities, craft or social guilds, some of which adopted uniforms and were thus styled livery companies. The number of their halls has been reduced to 25 by the Great Fire, local fires, changes of fortune and incendiary bombs – the Master Mariners have adopted a floating hall, the frigate HMS *Wellington*, which is moored in the Thames off the Victoria Embankment below the Strand.

New guilds are created by the modern professions. The Worshipful Company of Information Technologists, whose ranks number 100, held its first meeting in 1992 in Guildhall. The requirements for a new livery company are a minimum of 100 freemen, £100 000 in charitable funds and a record of charitable and educational good works.

Although in 1523 Henry VIII "commanded to have all money and plate belonging to any Hall or Crypt", many halls have collections or pieces dating back to the 15C which they either managed to hide from the king or repurchased. Notable collections reside at the Mansion House; Clothworkers' Hall *(Mincing Lane)*; Founders' Hall; Fishmongers' Hall; Tallow Chandlers' Hall *(Dowgate Hill)*; Skinners' Hall *(Dowgate Hill)*; Innholders' Hall *(College Street)* – salts and spoons; Vintners' Hall *(Upper Thames Street)*; Mercers' Hall *(Ironmonger Lane)*; Haberdashers' Hall *(Staining Lane)*; Ironmongers' Hall *(Aldersgate Street)*; Barber-Surgeons' Hall *(Monkwell Square)*.

with the games and a Channel Tunnel rail link based at Stratford. Development is booming, although Londoners struggle under a mountain of debt thanks to some of the world's highest property prices, increasingly high transport and living costs.

It is, of course, the inhabitants of London who make "London town": Londoners born and bred, adopted Londoners from the provinces, refugees from political persecution abroad (14C–17C Flemish and French Huguenots, political theorists such as Marx and Engels, post-war ex-monarchs, 20C Chileans and Ugandan Asians) or economic immigrants attracted by a higher standard of living (from the Commonwealth), men and women who achieve international recognition as artists and actors, writers and statesmen, high-flying business men and women, and the nameless millions who ply their daily trade with wit and humour.

1901-10 – Reign of Edward VII.
1901 – Population 6.6 million.

1909 – Establishment of the **Port of London Authority** to manage the docks.
1910-36 – Reign of George V.
1914-18 – Zeppelin raids on London.
1918 – After years of campaigning by the Suffragette movement, led by the Pankhurst family, women over 30 get the vote for the first time.
1919 – American-born Nancy Astor becomes Britain's first woman MP.
1933 – Establishment of London Transport to coordinate public transport: underground, bus and railway.
1936 – Accession and abdication of Edward VIII.
1936-52 – Reign of George VI.
1938 – Establishment of the **Green Belt** to protect land from development.
1939 – Population 8.61 million.
1940-41 – **London Blitz** (aerial bombardment of London) began in 1940 after the British retreat from Dunkerque

(Dunkirk) and the Battle of Britain. The first heavy raids on London by the German Air Force (Luftwaffe) began on 7 September; for 57 consecutive nights hundreds of bombers flew over London dropping heavy explosive or incendiary bombs. Only adverse weather conditions brought respite.

1951 – The **Festival of Britain**, an echo of the Great Exhibition of 1851, was promoted as a "tonic to the nation" to bring colour, light and fun to the postwar scene.

1952 – Elizabeth II is crowned Queen.

1958 – First women peers introduced to the House of Lords. Gatwick Airport opened.

1966 – Founding of the City University.

1971 – 15 February: introduction of decimal coinage.

1975 – Population 7 million.

1976 – National Theatre opens.

1979 – Margaret Thatcher elected the first woman Prime Minister.

1981 – **London Docklands Development Corporation** (LDDC) set up to regenerate the redundant London Docks. First London Marathon run. Violent confrontations in London betweeen Punks and National Front. Marriage of Prince Charles to Lady Diana Spencer at St Paul's Cathedral.

1982 – Barbican Centre opened in the City of London; Thames Barrier raised.

1986 – Deregulation of trading on the Stock Exchange. Abolition of the Greater London Council.

1988 – Jets begin landing at City Airport.

1995 – Opening of the Channel Tunnel, linking Britain with continental Europe for the first time.

1995 – National Lottery launched.

1996 – After 700 years the Stone of Scone returns to Scotland.

1997 – Inauguration of the British Library, St Pancras. Opening of the Globe Theatre.
1–6 September: London mourns Diana, Princess of Wales.

1999-2000 – London gains new landmarks to mark the third Millennium: Dome (Greenwich), Jubilee Line extension, Millennium Bridge and Tate Modern (Bankside), London Eye (South Bank).

2000 –   Ken Livingstone becomes the first elected Mayor of London, with an elected Greater London Assembly.

2005 – London wins the bid for the 2012 Olympic Games leading to massive redevelopment of east London.
7 July: 7/7 Bombings.
Prince Charles marries Camilla, Duchess of Cornwall.
Population 7 600 000.

2006 – Queen celebrates her 80th birthday.
Population 7.56 million

2007 - Tony Blair stands down as Prime Minister. Gordon Brown is appointed in his place through an internal Labour party election, before the general election is held. International Eurostar rail services move to St Pancras.

2008 – Conservative MP Boris Johnson defeats Labour MP Ken Livingstone in the Mayoral election.

2009 – Iconic music venue, The Astoria, closes after 33 years.

Art and Culture

ARCHITECTURE

As London reinvents itself to suit the demands of the time, the architecture of the capital reflects its dynamic character. Tradition is an inherent part of the modern environment and a walk around London reveals an abundance of cultural landmarks. The extension of the city to the east and commissions for major buildings have provided architects with an opportunity to show a renewed sense of flair and innovation as old buildings are put to new uses and new architectural concepts are brought into play.

St Bartholomew-the-Great

Pictures Colour Library

ROMAN INFLUENCE

None of the city gates has survived but their existence is recalled in the names of the modern streets or neighbouring churches: Ludgate, Newgate, Aldersgate, Cripplegate, Moorgate, Bishopsgate, Aldgate. The wall built by the Romans c. AD 200. was partially rebuilt between the 12C and the 17C. Demolition began in the 18C and by the 19C most of the wall had disappeared. The line of the old wall can be traced by excavated outcrops, usually consisting of an upper area of medieval construction resting on a Roman base (Barbican, St Alphage Church, All Hallows Church, Sir John Cass College and the Tower of London). The street known as London Wall more or less follows the line of the Roman Wall between Aldersgate and Bishopsgate; Houndsditch marks the course of the old ditch outside the wall.

The **London Wall Walk** *(just under 2mi/3km; about 2hr)* between the Museum of London and the Tower of London is well mapped out with 21 descriptive panels.

MATERIALS

Timber was, for a long time, the cheapest material. Stone, quarried in Kent or imported from Normandy was brought upriver to the Tower of London; **Portland stone** was first brought to London for St Paul's Cathedral (17C);

Yorkshire stone for the Houses of Parliament (1835–60). **Bricks** were made locally in Kensington and Islington. In the City, roofs were for the most part thatched until the 15C or 16C and were not uniformly tiled or slated until after the Great Fire (1666).

THE NORMAN CONQUEST

Edward the Confessor grew up in exile in Normandy before assuming the throne of England (1042–66), it was therefore natural for him to model his designs for Westminster Abbey on the Abbey at Jumièges as a symbol of the Church Militant.

The best examples of Norman architecture are to be found at St Bartholomew-the-Great, St John's Chapel in the Tower of London and the extant parts of Westminster Abbey rebuilt by Edward the Confessor before the arrival of William the Conqueror.

The boldness of design and sheer scale of the Norman style are reflected in the White Tower and in Westminster Hall – the largest to be built north of the Alps (240ft/73m long).

THE TUDOR AND JACOBEAN ERAS

The greatest examples in the public domain are St James's Palace and Hampton Court, which have the typical multi-storey gateway. At Hampton Court

St James's Palace

©Stephen Finn/Bigstockphoto.com

The result is an English interpretation of French Gothic: Westminster was consolidated with flying buttresses (cloister side of the nave). The elevation consisted of a high arcade, narrow triforium and tall clerestory with rose windows. However, what is distinctively English is the window tracery, so delicate and fluid as no longer to be considered stone masonry as such; the use of polished stone column shafts; the overall richness of applied decoration and the use of iron tie-rods as an alternative to flying buttresses.

Decorated Gothic emerged in the late 13C and may be distinguished by the richness and wealth of design in geometrical and later curvilinear tracery; from the 1290s, lierne vaulting became widespread. In essence, a spirit of experimentation and variety of approach pervaded this transitional phase.

Perpendicular, which overlapped with the previous style for 50 years, inspired architects, on occasion, to abandon the quadrangular in favour of the polygonal, thereby giving greater visual play to the windows and the illusion of a more coherent space. In some cases this led to the use of timber rather than stone for roofing.

are preserved decorative chimney-stacks, internal courtyards and the great hall with its hammerbeam roof. The first such roof and the most impressive (spanning 70ft/21m) is that in the hall of the Palace of Westminster, while other examples survive in the Middle Temple Hall (Elizabethan), Charterhouse and Eltham Palace (c. 1479); decorative pendants used at Hampton Court also survive at Crosby Hall in Chelsea. Tudor brickwork with diaper patterning is visible at Charterhouse and Fulham Palace.

THE GOTHIC STYLE

Gothic arrived in England from the continent in the 12C with the expansion of the Benedictine and, in the north, of the Cistercian Orders. It remained the predominant style for 400 years, evolving in three main phases.

Early English emerged as a distinctive style at Salisbury and was confirmed at Westminster (1220) where the fabric of the building was essentially conceived as a framework for traceried windows. In the 13C, Henry III assumed the role of pre-eminent patron of architecture in the country – an example continued until the reign of Henry VIII. When the king decided to remodel Westminster church to his taste, he selected the best craftsmen from home and abroad.

During the 15C and 16C, after the Hundred Years' War and the Wars of the Roses, the Crown returned to being the leading patron leaving us three Royal chapels in south-east England, including Henry VII's Chapel in Westminster Abbey (1503–19). Otherwise, this Perpendicular phase was the great age for secular building and for parish churches. Alas many of the London churches were damaged by the Reformation and/or destroyed in the City by the Great Fire (1666).

The rebuilding that followed, to designs by **Sir Christopher Wren** (1632–1723), marked the end of the evolution of Gothic architecture and the dawn of a different Continental influence.

EARLY CLASSICISM OR PALLADIANISM

The turning point in the evolution of English architecture comes in the mid 16C when the Duke of Northumberland sent a certain John Shute to Italy "to confer with the doings of the skilful masters in architecture". His findings, however, only superficially influenced decorative designs applied to Elizabethan country houses.

At the turn of the century, **Inigo Jones** (1573–1652) emerged as the first British architect with a definable personality moulded by the Renaissance Humanist ideal, by his affinity with Palladio's work on Italian architecture*/Quattro Libri dell'Architettura* published in Venice in 1570, and by his visits to Venice (1601 and 1605), Padua and Rome (1613). Important projects to survive undertaken for the Crown by Jones include the Banqueting House completed in 1622 (see WHITEHALL) and the Queen's House (see GREENWICH).

Queen's House, Greenwich
©Bill Bertram 2006, CC-BY-2.5/Creative Commons

CLASSICAL BAROQUE AND THE CLASSICAL REVIVAL (17C18C)

In the wake of Jones comes **Sir Christopher Wren** who is perhaps a contender for the top ten of greatest Englishmen. Wren left England only once for Paris in 1665 where he met Bernini, the famous Baroque sculptor, architect and designer from Rome. On his return to London, Wren drew up a series of designs for the rebuilding of the Old St Paul's inspired by Lemercier's dome at the Church of

the Sorbonne. In the run up to the millennium a redesign of the area around St Paul's was based in part on Wren's plans, opening up a view of the cathedral from the river.

The City Churches

Although only a few of the parish churches were drawn in detail by Wren, most were planned by the Royal Surveyor, and later supplied with steeples. The most complete surviving Wren churches include St Bride's, St Mary le Bow, St Stephen Walbrook, St Vedast, St Clement Danes and St James's.

St Paul's Cathedral

What is remarkable is that Wren lived long enough to see the completion of his masterpiece (1675–1710) which has provided later generations of architects with architectural inspiration and solutions to design problems.

Wren also worked on Hampton Court Palace (south and east wings), the Chelsea Hospital and the Greenwich Hospital, where he was certainly assisted by Hawksmoor and Sir John Vanbrugh (1664–1726) – both use Classical elements with boldness and imagination to dramatic effect.

The Clerk of Works who followed Wren, **Nicholas Hawksmoor** (1661–1736) developed his own form of English Mannerism (St Mary Woolnoth in the City; St Alfege in Greenwich; St Anne's, Limehouse; St George-in-the-East, Stepney; St George, Bloomsbury; west towers of Westminster Abbey).

NEOCLASSICISM

The rise of a new aristocracy, together with the Duke of Marlborough's great military victories, provided new opportunities for patronage and travel to the Continent. During the first decades of the 18C, **Colen Campbell** (d. 1729) published *Vitruvius Britannicus*, a compilation of British buildings in the Antique manner – a veritable manifesto for Palladianism; the other two mainstays of the movement were **Lord Burlington** (1694–1753) and **William Kent** (1685–1748), who together went on to forge a powerful partnership that provided architectural designs, interior decoration and layouts for extensive gardens-cum-parks in the manner of Palladio's Brenta villas (Chiswick Villa).

The man who bridges the gap between Wren and the new surge of Palladianism is **James Gibbs** (1682–1754), the architect of St Martin-in-the-Fields. Gibbs was a great follower of Wren – his St Mary-le-Strand is a stylistic and physical neighbour of Wren's St Clement Danes up the Strand.

GEORGIAN ELEGANCE

The next generation of eclectic designers is dominated by two rivals: **Sir William Chambers RA** (1723–96) an upholder of tradition, and the more innovative **Robert Adam** (1728–92).

Chambers, who had travelled to the Far East, was asked to remodel Kew Gardens and embellish them with exotic temples and a pagoda. He gained particular favour with George III which allowed him to exercise his taste and judgement in such important commissions as Somerset House (*see STRAND*).

Adam also travelled extensively, to France, Italy and Dalmatia to explore the Classical style and to draw inspiration direct from the example of Antique domestic architecture. In interior decoration he borrowed extensively from descriptions of Pompeii and Herculaneum and from artefacts excavated from Palmyra and Greece, most especially from Greek vase painting – he developed a light touch and delicacy that, having found favour at Osterley Park and Syon House, was quickly assimilated into 18C aesthetic movements. Few Adam town houses survive intact: Home House at 20 Portman Square, the south and east sides of Fitzroy Square, single houses in St James's Square *(no 20)*, Chandos Street and behind the Adelphi.

English Neoclassicism evolved into an informal reinterpretation of the Antique and affected all the decorative and applied arts. Multi-disciplined designers like Adam and Chambers were content to accommodate other revivalist styles in the form of follies, bowers and bandstands. **Gothic** was limited to private houses (Strawberry Hill); **chinoiserie** to garden pagodas (Kew); **Rococo** to follies or pleasure gardens (Vauxhall); the **Picturesque** contrived to imitate untamed Nature, as depicted in painting – dead trees were planted and "ruins" were artificially assembled in gardens.

THE REGENCY PERIOD (1811–30)

The main thread of the Regency style came from pre-Revolution France, copied from picture books and interpreted by Continental craftsmen. The key figure of this phase is probably **Henry Holland** (1745–1806) who designed Brooks's Club in St James's. The period up to the death of George IV is also dominated by three men: **Sir John Soane** (1753–1837) whose principal legacy was the Bank of England, now largely destroyed; **John Nash**, favourite architect of George IV, who was responsible for laying out Regent Street, the terraces of elegant residences for Members of Parliament surrounding Regent's Park (1810–11), for designing the grand Carlton House Terrace, Buckingham Palace (although much changed), the Brighton Pavilion and various country houses. **Thomas Cubitt**, quality builder and property developer, worked from George Basevi's designs to create Belgrave Square and other large sections of Belgravia (1825), Pelham Crescent (1820–30); other squares, crescents and streets stretch from Putney and Clapham to Islington, Kensington to the Isle of Dogs.

THE VICTORIAN AGE (19C)

A population explosion provoked a huge demand for urban housing that in turn necessitated a change in building practices. Materials began to be industrially manufactured (by the 1840s whole buildings were being pre-fabricated and concrete was being tested in the 1860s) and transported cheaply by rail.

The main phases may be identified as **Early Victorian**, characterised by

Ambulatory: continuation of the aisles around the east end sanctuary.

Apsidal or radiating chapel: apsed chapel radiating from the ambulatory or sanctuary.

Barrel vaulting: most basic form of tunnel vaulting, continuous rounded or pointed profile.

Blind arcading: decorative frieze of small, interlacing, arches and intervening pilaster strips; typical of Romanesque architecture in Lombardy and West Country Transitional.

Buttress: a structural member placed along the exterior wall to reinforce and counter side thrust of a vault

Capital: head or crowning feature of a column. In Classical architecture there are four orders: Doric, Ionic (with volutes), Corinthian (leaf decoration) and Composite (Ionic and Corinthian). Other forms include a Cushion capital (Romanesque cut from a cube) and a Crocket capital (decorated with stylised Gothic leaves terminating in volutes).

Caryatid: female figure used as a column (atlantes are male caryatids).

Clerestory: upper section of the elevation containing large windows.

Flamboyant: latest phase (15C) of French Gothic architecture; name taken from the undulating (flame-like) lines of the window tracery.

Flying buttress: buttress of masonry decorated with pinnacles.

Fresco: mural paintings executed on wet plaster.

Gable: triangular part of an end wall carrying a sloping roof or steeply pitched ornamental pediment of Gothic architecture.

Gargoyle: waterspout projecting from the parapet, often ornamented with a grotesque figure, animal or human.

Groined vault: produced by the intersection of two perpendicular tunnel vaults of identical shape.

Lady Chapel: chapel radiating or extending from the sanctuary dedicated to the Virgin Mary.

Lierne: a tertiary rib that neither springs

from the main springers nor passes through the central boss.

Lintel, transom: horizontal beam or stone bridging an opening of a door, window.

Pediment: low-pitched gable over a portico, usually triangular, in Classical architecture.

Pier: solid masonry structural support as distinct from a column.

Pilaster: engaged (attached) rectangular column.

Pinnacle: small turret-like decorative feature crowning spires, buttresses.

Quadripartite vaulting: one bay subdivided into four quarters or cells.

Rib vault: framework of diagonal arched ribs carrying the cells.

Rood screen: carved screen separating the chancel from the nave, sometimes surmounted by a gallery.

Semicircular arch: round-headed arch.

Tracery: intersecting stone ribwork in the upper part of a window.

Transept: transverse section of a cross-shaped church bisecting the nave.

Triforium: arcaded wall passage running the length of the nave above the arcade and below the clerestory.

Triptych: three panels hinged together, chiefly used as an altarpiece.

Capitals of Carlton House Terrace
©Anthony Baggett/Dreamstime.com

St Pancras Station

© Douglas Freer/iStockphoto.com

earnest historicism and the use of plainish materials, **High Victorian** (1850s–1870s) which reacted against archaeological correctness with bright colour, contrasting materials and strong sculptural effects, and **Late Victorian** which reverted to smooth contours and soft textures, intricate decoration and delicate colour.

A key figure who straddles all three phases was **Sir George Gilbert Scott** (1811–78). He applied his confident Gothic style as easily to religious buildings (St Mary Abbotts, Kensington) as to secular developments: St Pancras Station and Hotel, Albert Memorial, Broad Sanctuary west of Westminster Abbey. His grandson **Sir Giles Gilbert Scott** (1880–1960) proved himself to be a far more sensitive and inspired product of the Late Victorian age, bequeathing such individual landmarks of the post-industrial age as Battersea Power Station (1932–4), Waterloo Bridge (1939–45) and Bankside Power Station.

London's singlemost famous building, the Houses of Parliament, with its signature clocktower housing Big Ben, was added to the medieval Westminster Hall by **Sir Charles Barry** between 1840–1888.

At the same time, functional cast-iron building became an art in itself (Lewis Cubitt's King's Cross Station 1852, Brunel's Paddington Station 1850).

Red-brick developments were instituted by the London County Council who drew inspiration from **Philip Webb** for Bethnal Green and Millbank. Another successful exponent of this practical, unfussy style was **Richard Norman Shaw** (1831–1912) who designed Lowther Lodge in Kensington (1873, now the Geographical Society), Swan House in Chelsea (1876) and four houses in Cadogan Square (60a, 62, 68 and 72). The interior decoration and furnishings were left to the firm of the socialist **William Morris** (1834–96) and as such soon became identified with the **Arts and Crafts Movement**.

Against the tide of mass production, came a revival of craftsmanship in architectural sculpture, stained glass, practical hand-made furniture, block-printed fabrics and wallpapers. While **Alfred Waterhouse** (1830–1905) designed the Natural History Museum combining naturalistic observation with fantastic imaginary beasts applied to some great Germanic Romanesque fabric, De Morgan tiles and Morris screens spurned the development of art nouveau.

A surge in **church building** was provoked by demand to serve the new suburbs. Perpendicular spires spiked the sky as a new interest in Gothic architecture culminated in the new designs for the Palace of Westminster. As in the 18C, fads and fashions proliferated prompting a revivalist taste for neo-Norman, neo-Early Christian and, in the mid century, for neo-Italian Romanesque.

20C AND EARLY 21C

Not until the 1920s was the neo-Gothic tradition broken when **Edward Maufe** provoked a change of direction by building truly modern **churches**: St Columba's in Pont Street, St John's in Peckham.

The International Style formulated by the Belgian **Henry van der Velde** (1863–1957) and the German **Peter Behrens** (1868–1940) – both painters turned designer and architect – were followed by **Walter Gropius** (1883–1969). They advocated quality in building and practical functionality – factories and power stations should not be dressed to look like schools or cathedrals. Meanwhile, steel-frame construction (Ritz Hotel 1904) and the use of concrete led to ever shorter building time-frames.

Distinctive modern **housing** is rare: 64–66 Old Church Street in Chelsea (c. 1934) by the International Modernist **Mendelsohn** and Chernayeff, the Sun House in Hampstead (1935) by **Maxwell Fry**, Highpoint One and Two in Highgate (1936–38) by the reclusive **Berthold Lubetkin** and Tecton, **Goldfinger's** custom-built 2 Willow Road and Cheltenham Estate (Kensal Rise). Lillington Gardens, Pimlico (1960s) and Aberdeen Park in Islington (1980s) by Darbourne and Darke show that council housing need not be unattractive.

Today, important contemporary developments abound on the South Bank, in the City, Docklands, around Heathrow, Gatwick and Stansted airports, while imaginative conversions proliferate along the Thames and within London's mainline railway stations and disused markets (Billingsgate, Spitalfields) and power stations (Bankside, Lots Road). Notable landmarks on London's skyline include Centre Point, the South Bank Complex, Barbican, Telecom Tower, **Richard Rogers**'s Lloyd's Building, Tower 42, Chelsea Harbour, Vauxhall Cross, and 1 Canada Square – known simply as Canary Wharf. The Millennium Dome in Greenwich and the new offices of the Mayor of London in Bermondsey (City Hall) add a futuristic note to the riverside. The distinctive Swiss Re building designed by **Sir Norman Foster** (2002) and known to locals as "the Gherkin" continues the trend for eco-friendly buildings. Other architects are applying their skills to the 2012 Olympic Games project and to the redevelopment of the **Lower Lee Valley** around Stratford.

MUSIC AND THEATRE

It is acknowledged that the best way to capture the spirit of a place is to take part in its cultural activities. London has a proud reputation as an eclectic capital for the performing arts and Londoners have open minds and show a refreshing willingness to share new experiences. The profusion of venues and the range and quality of the offerings attest to the vibrancy of the musical and theatrical scene. The diversity of this multicultural city is a further asset to which artists from all over the world also make a contribution.

A MUSICAL MOSAIC

London is one of the concert, opera and pop capitals of the world. Tradition and modernity are often juxtaposed

City Hall and Tower Bridge

©Martinjwilliams/Dreamstime.com

to reflect diverse cultural influences at play; nowadays pop musicians and classical orchestras collaborate with great success. This significant development is a consequence of the fusion of genres, as audiences show a willingness to experiment with new musical forms. It is not unusual to mark events of national interest in a musical idiom fusing the popular and traditional styles. Opera performances are held in more accessible venues such as the arena at the Royal Albert Hall and the piazza in Covent Garden. Happy crowds enjoy the Last Night of The Proms in **Hyde Park** and the open-air concerts at Holland Park, Hampton Court and Kenwood. Popstars are equally at home at the Royal Albert Hall, The 02 Arena, Wembley Arena and the London Arena in Docklands; the Royal Festival Hall and the Barbican host jazz, folk and world music along with a superb array of classical concerts.

THE SWINGING CAPITAL

London's dizzying musical atmosphere is characterised by four prestigious orchestras, two celebrated opera companies, a multitude of pop groups, and a wide range of musical entertainment from buskers on the pavement to lunchtime church concerts and from polished orchestral performances to professionally staged rock shows and techno raves. Jazz music has achieved high status. The creative energy of the music scene which fosters inventive new styles shows no signs of abating.

A FORMIDABLE TRADITION

The light airs of Tudor England (e.g. *Greensleeves*, attributed to Henry VIII) developed into rounds, canons and finally a golden age (1588–1630) of madrigals. Much instrumental dance music was written with variations to display the performer's virtuosity; **John Dowland** excelled at solo songs accompanied by lute and viol. At the same time **Thomas Tallis** and **William Byrd** were composing religious music for the organ and voice in masses and anthems, set to the Latin and English liturgy; only in Elizabeth's reign did a distinctive Anglican style emerge.

In the latter half of the 17C composers extended their range with *Te Deums* and songs and incidental music for the theatre. **Henry Purcell** (1659–96), who dominated his own and subsequent generations, produced the first full-length opera *(Dido and Aeneas)* in 1689. Italian opera then became popular and was firmly established with *Rinaldo* (1711) by **Handel**, who had arrived in England that year. Handel resided at 25 Brooke Street, Mayfair until his death in 1759 and he produced operas based on mythological subjects, which were satirised by John Gay in *The Beggar's Opera* (1728), occasional pieces such as the *Fireworks* and *Water Music* and a great succession of oratorios about religious heroes: *Esther, Messiah.*

Mozart composed his first symphony in 1764 while residing at 180 Ebury Street; his name is perpetuated in Mozart Terrace in Pimlico. **Haydn** stayed in London in the 1790s when he was the greatest musical figure in Europe. **Mendelssohn** came to London early in the 19C and began work on the *Scottish Symphony* and incidental music to *A Midsummer Night's Dream*, which he completed some 20 years later.

THE MODERN AGE

At the end of the 19C, English music began to become widely popular. The Savoy operas – libretto by **WS Gilbert** and music by **Sir Arthur Sullivan** (1875–99) appealed to a wide audience. As radio became widespread in the 1930s, the BBC began to broadcast the **Promenade Concerts**, which had been inaugurated in 1895 by the conductor, Henry Wood, in the Queen's Hall and later held in the Albert Hall. The programmes, organised by the BBC, include orchestral works and opera by classical and modern composers, performed by national and visiting musicians and conductors. The promenaders make a spirited contribution to the Last Night, when traditional pieces are played (including Elgar's *Pomp and Circumstance*).

The opening of the 20C also saw the appearance of a host of new British composers: **Edward Elgar** (*Enigma Variations* 1899, *Dream of Gerontius* 1900), Delius, **Vaughan Williams** (nine symphonies) and **Gustav Holst** (*The Planets* 1914-16). They were joined in the 1920s by Bax, Bliss and William Walton (*Belshazzar's Feast* 1931).

After the war they were reinforced by **Michael Tippett** (*A Child of Our Time* 1941, *The Midsummer Marriage* 1955) and **Benjamin Britten** who produced a magnificent series of works – *Peter Grimes* 1945, *Albert Herring*, *Let's Make an Opera*, *Billy Budd*, *Midsummer Night's Dream*, *The War Requiem* and the operetta *Paul Bunyan*.

The second half of the 20C saw the establishment of permanent centres of opera at Covent Garden and the London Coliseum, the construction of concert halls on the South Bank and at the Barbican, the restoration of the Wigmore Hall and the birth of numerous provincial (summer) festivals.

THE BRITISH MUSICAL

From the late 1960s musicals achieved huge popularity, dominated by the talented and prolific **Andrew Lloyd-Webber**, who initially collaborated with Tim Rice (*Jesus Christ Superstar* and *Evita*) and the producer Cameron Mackintosh *(Cats)*. The shows, where the story is partly told in song, set the trend for spectacular staging, strong but simple melody and large casts. Other thrilling shows such as *Oklahoma, My Fair Lady, Les Misérables* and *Phantom of the Opera* have enjoyed long runs in the West End. Recent revivals have included *Mary Poppins, Saturday Night Fever* and *Guys and Dolls*.

The successful shows are staged in cities worldwide and have won a huge following. *The Lion King*, with music by **Elton John**, combines animation, music and song in a novel way, and there is a new trend towards reusing great pop music as the background for a plot with smash hits such as *Mamma Mia* (Abba) and *We Will Rock You* (Queen).

CODA

The rich legacy of the music hall tradition and the fantastic success of contemporary musicals are evidence of the happy fusion of two genres. Jazz music, which took over from the big dance bands, has a solid following and jazz clubs are flourishing with a high calibre of performers such as the saxophonist Courtney Pine.

Since the Swinging Sixties, the **Britpop** music scene has never been so dynamic with a proliferation of new styles, the thundering rhythmic output of famous rock and dance venues and nightclubs, the chart-topping popstars and bands and the independent groups performing in pubs and clubs.

Prestigious orchestras and celebrated artists make regular appearances at famous concert halls, opera houses, cathedrals and churches throughout London. Besides the classical repertoire, there is a drive to introduce music by modern composers to a wide public.

THE LONDON STAGE

The success of the London stage has been built on a unique tradition which spans more than five centuries. Talented playwrights and actors have helped to establish the reputation of British theatre worldwide but the capital is also receptive to foreign influences and new talent is applauded by enthusiastic and knowledgeable audiences.

Today high standards and international reputations are maintained by the Royal Shakespeare Company and the Royal National Theatre. Experimental theatre starts in the provinces and on London's fringe circuit before moving to the West End. During the summer, open-air venues in Holland Park, Regent's Park and the Globe Theatre are an unusually historical and informal way to enjoy performances, while several stately homes and parks, including Hampton Court and Kew are now hosting short seasons of open-air Shakespeare. Behind all of this, the suburbs support many smaller theatres, shared by touring productions and enthusiastic local amateur groups.

A RICH THEATRICAL HISTORY

During the Middle Ages plays were performed outside the city boundaries as the City of London authorities were steadfast in refusing to allow theatrical performances within their jurisdiction. The courts of Henry VIII and Elizabeth I at Nonsuch Palace and Hampton Court attracted contemporary dramatists and entertainers for private functions.

The first regular "public" performances were held in Clerkenwell and Shoreditch, where **James Burbage** founded the first English playhouse and then moved south of the river to Southwark.

The legal fraternity also provided facilities for the performance of plays, masques and revels; in the late 16C *The Comedy of Errors* was staged in Gray's Inn and *Twelfth Night* was played beneath the hammerbeam roof of the Middle Temple Hall.

The true theatrical tradition, however, is descended from the popular genre whose most famous exponents include **William Shakespeare** (1564–1616), **Christopher Marlowe** (1564–93), Ben Jonson (1572/3–1637), Wycherley, Congreve, Sheridan, **Oscar Wilde**, Tom Stoppard and **Harold Pinter**.

FROM RESTORATION COMEDY TO MUSIC HALL

The social climate of the Restoration is reflected in the witty comedy of manners of William **Congreve** (*The Way of the World* and *Love for Love*). The Theatres Royal of Drury Lane, Haymarket and Covent Garden opened under royal patronage in that period. The most famous performer was Nell Gwynne, a royal favourite. The 18C was an era of great acting talent such as David Garrick, the Kembles, Sarah Siddons and Dorothea Jordan. *The School for Scandal* by **Sheridan** was a triumph. In the 19C the stage was dominated by Henry Irving, Ellen Terry and the great Shakespearean actor Edmund Kean.

In the Victorian era, the growth of the urban population brought about new forms of entertainment: melodrama reflecting the popular taste for sentimentality and music hall combining

Globe Theatre

©John Tramper/Shakespeare's Globe

song and ribald comedy. The popularity of the latter genre – the star was the glamorous singer Marie Lloyd – led to grander theatres, known as Palaces of Variety, such as the London Palladium. The Hackney Empire, Collins Music Hall in Islington and Wilton's Music Hall in Wapping are rare survivals. Variety gave way to French-style revue combining songs and sketches. Its undisputed masters were Ivor Novello and **Noel Coward**, who epitomised the glamour and sophistication of the period.

A WAVE OF INNOVATION

Farce and "kitchen sink drama" were both new vogues introduced by the English Stage Company at the Royal Court Theatre which opened in 1870. Coined as the "bad boy of West End theatre," this famous institution was the launch pad for **GB Shaw** (1904–09), **John Osborne** (*Look Back in Anger* 1956) and Arnold Wesker among others who dealt with current social and political issues. The innovative style of **Harold Pinter**, his sparse use of language and challenging political themes were in tune with the mood of the time. In 2005, Pinter won the Nobel Prize for Literature.

The National Theatre Company was established to stage original works which might not be produced in the West End owing to commercial pressures. The Old Vic under Lilian Baylis had set the scene. Famous performers include many of the greatest: Sir Laurence Olivier, Sir John Gielgud, Sir Ralph Richardson, Sir Paul

Scofield, Dame Peggy Ashcroft, Dame Maggie Smith and Dame Judi Dench have won acclaim internationally. The playwrights David Hare, Alan Ayckbourn, David Storey, Edward Bond, Michael Frayn and Tom Stoppard have achieved pre-eminence on TV and in film as well as on the stage.

THE FRINGE

Alternative theatre dealing with experimental or controversial themes is performed in pubs, converted churches and small venues such as the Royal Court (Sloane Square), the King's Head (Islington), the Bush (Shepherd's Bush), the Gate (Notting Hill) and the Battersea Arts Centre. The Donmar and the Almeida are reputed for staging intelligent and provocative plays and for attracting famous names. The fringe is the proving ground of many leading writers, directors and actors.

Stand-up comedy comes into its own at The Comedy Store, Jongleurs and a host of other venues. There is an atmosphere of fun, and the shows are usually of a good quality with young hopefuls trying their luck and established comics running through new routines.

LITERATURE
A CAPTIVATING CITY

Not all have felt with William Dunbar "London thou art the flower of cities all" nor even with Dr Johnson that "there is in London all that life can afford," but at some point in their careers many writers lived in London and English literature from detective stories to diaries, from novels to biographies and histories, is permeated with scenes of London. Despite their numbers there has been no regular forum for writers down the years: groups have shifted from the pubs near Blackfriars Theatre to those on Bankside and down the Borough High Street close to the Globe; to Highgate, to Chelsea and, for a charmed circle centred on **Virginia Woolf**, to Bloomsbury; at the turn of the century a group around **Oscar Wilde**, which included Aubrey Beardsley and Max Beerbohm, and artists of the day met at the Café Royal. Since many writers have begun or earned a living as journalists, the first regular haunts were the coffee houses around Fleet Street; Addison and Steel frequented the George and Vulture and subsequently Button's at both of which they wrote copy for the *Tatler* and *Spectator*; **Dr Johnson** called at many coffee houses and taverns but nearest his own house was The Cheshire Cheese where, tradition has it, many of the great conversations took place.

VERSE

Geoffrey Chaucer (1340–1400) was a courtier and diplomat; he drew on the rich tradition of contemporary French, Latin and Italian literature to recount his *Canterbury Tales* about pilgrims journeying between Southwark and Canterbury. The Elizabethan Age is encapsulated in **Sir Edmund Spenser**'s *Faerie Queene*, a long poem populated with personifications of Justice, Temperance, Holiness, Chastity, etc. The two great masters of theatre **Christopher Marlowe** (1564–93) and **William Shakespeare** (1564–1616) used free verse enriched with powerful imagery and varied syntax.

It was not until **John Milton** (1608–74) emerged that the poetic genre heralded the Age of the Enlightenment. Intellectually provocative, Milton carefully expressed his Puritan anti-Royalist politics in prose and his views on the Fall of Man in verse *(Paradise Lost, Comus, Lycidas)*. The first Poet Laureate, **John Dryden** (1631–1700) recorded contemporary events in his poetry, criticism, drama and translations: his clear, precise verse heralds the rational climate of the period of **Alexander Pope**, **Jonathan Swift** *(Gulliver's Travels)* and **Samuel Johnson** (compiler of the first Dictionary 1755).

Such **Romantic** poets as Blake, Burns, Wordsworth and Coleridge are great and distinctive figures but, like the Brontës, Hardy and Eliot, wrote largely outside the London scene, turning instead to spirituality, Scottish patriotism, and Nature for inspiration. The quintessence of the movement exists in the tragically

Oscar Wilde

©Antique Research Center/Tips Images

short life and inspired output of **John Keats** (1795–1821) who came to London to study medicine. **William Wordsworth** mused on Westminster Bridge but lived in the Lake District; **Lord Byron** enjoyed high society.

For the Victorians, Imagination must reign over Reason – the Poet Laureate (1850–92) **Tennyson** *(Morte d'Arthur)* specialised in mellifluous poetry, **Browning** in more exclamatory verse, and **Arnold** in descriptions of the moral dilemmas of life deprived of religious faith. Pre-Raphaelite poets such as **DG Rossetti**, his sister Christina, William Morris and **Swinburne** drew their subject matter from the timeless myths and legends, and from ancient ballads. The **Aesthetes** of the 1890s, including **Oscar Wilde** (1854–1900), **Beerbohm** and **Beardsley**, were greatly impressed by the philosophical writings of Henri Bergson (1859–1941) and affected by Huysmans' Symbolist novel *A Rebours (Against the Grain* alluded to in Wilde's *Picture of Dorian Gray*). The counter-reaction this provoked was a move towards realism led by **WB Yeats** (1865–1939) and **Rudyard Kipling** whose verse was full of colloquial language, natural rhythm and vitality. The Georgian poets including **TS Eliot** (*Waste Land*, *Old Possum's Book of Practical Cats, Murder in the Cathedral*), **DH Lawrence** and Walter de la Mare defined the transition to Modernism: their work is haunted by the devastating effect of war – poignantly

captured by the War Poets (Sassoon, Owen and Brooke).

The 1930s era of depression is recorded by **WH Auden**, **Cecil Day Lewis**, **Louis MacNeice** and **Stephen Spender**: contemporaries at Oxford, their verse is direct in appeal, colloquial in language and anti-establishment in politics. **Dylan Thomas** (1914–53), on the other hand, explores childhood and innocence and **Ted Hughes** (1930–98) describes the inherent violence of Nature. **Carol Ann Duffy** is the current – and first female – Poet Laureate (Britain's "official" poet).

THE LIGHTER TOUCH

Truly English in quality is the light, humorous and entertaining light verse. Many of the major writers dabbled in it, but it is the likes of **Edward Lear** (1812–88 – *Book of Nonsense*) and **Lewis Carroll** (1832–98 – *Alice in Wonderland*) that have been the most enduring masters of nonsense and limerick. **Hilaire Belloc** (1870–1953 – *Cautionary Tales*) and AA Milne (1882–1956 – *Winnie the Pooh*) contributed their verse to *Punch* magazine – a venue that in the pictorial arts had already long perfected the parallel genre of caricature and cartoon. Perhaps the most typically English of the comic writers were **Sir John Betjeman** (1906–1984) and **PG Wodehouse** (1881–1975).

THE NOVEL

"The object of a novel should be to instruct in morals while it amuses" observed **Anthony Trollope**. The first of a line of great novelists is **Daniel Defoe** (c. 1661–1731), who managed, in *Robinson Crusoe* and *Moll Flanders*, to describe ordinary middle-class characters in credible plots. Following Defoe comes **Samuel Richardson** (1689–1761), originator of the epistolary novel with *Pamela* and *Clarissa*, which explore human thought and emotion, and the popular playwright before he became a novelist, **Henry Fielding** (1701–54) whose *Tom Jones* is the story (moralistic in tone) of a man of unknown birth who goes to London to seek his fortune. At the turn of the century

Oliver Goldsmith, Fanny Burney and Sir Horace Walpole found fame with single works prompting an interest in the Picturesque as well as mystery and terror – a tradition which was to inspire Mary Shelley's *Frankenstein* (1818).

The Romantic movement is dominated by the prolific **Sir Walter Scott** (1771–1832), a specialist of the historical novel where characters seem powerless pawns before external political predicaments *(Waverley, Rob Roy, Ivanhoe)*. By contrast, **Jane Austen** (1775–1817) drew her six novels from personal experience – notably in matters of love and marriage; she writes with wry humour and sensitivity which give her novels an enduring popularity.

The Victorian chapter is dominated by **Charles Dickens** (1812–70), who animates his great catalogue of novels, set in and around London, with colourful characterisation, inventive plots, humour and pathos (*Pickwick Papers, Oliver Twist, Nicholas Nickleby, A Christmas Carol, David Copperfield, Bleak House, Little Dorrit* and *Great Expectations*). Published as serials, his stories quickly found a large audience and stirred contemporary Humanists to reform social conditions for children, the poor and the deprived. **William Thackeray** (1811–63) sets his *Vanity Fair* in Regency England, reproaching hypocrisy and double standards.

Writing at the turn of the century, **HG Wells** (1866–1946) drew on his studies at London University to create scientific romances that lead the way for the science fiction of John Wyndham (1903–69). Travel and free thought are the principal themes of a new phase in literature: **EM Forster** (1879–1970) explored the frailty of human nature; **Virginia Woolf** (1882–1941) saw herself as an artist retaliating against the narrow-mindedness of Victorian London; she is certainly one of the most discerning and psychological novelists. **Evelyn Waugh** (1903–66) depicts social circumstances with wit, black comedy and farce that develop to realism in the face of the threat of war – a realism that pervades the work of **George Orwell**

(1903–50) and his haunting images in *1984* of a spiritless, futuristic age.

The 20C was marked by various versatile personalities living and working in London, who travelled abroad into their novels: **Graham Greene**, **Kingsley Amis**, **Muriel Spark**, **Doris Lessing**, **Iris Murdoch**, **Anthony Burgess**. *The Waterstone's Guide to London Writing* is a comprehensive survey of books set in the city. The end of the 20C saw the emergence of novelists belonging to various ethnic minorities, in particular Indian-born **Salman Rushdie** whose controversial Satanic Verses divided Islamic opinion and led to a *fatwa* death sentence being pronounced against him.

PAINTING
THE TUDOR ERA

The Renaissance master **Hans Holbein the Younger** (1497/8–1543) first came to London in 1526 with an introduction from the Humanist scholar **Erasmus**. His great draughtsmanship, penetrating eye and delicate colour suggest the artist's concern for capturing an accurate resemblance of physique and personality – formal portraits show the master keen to emphasise the exquisite detail of a jewel, brooch, brocade, silken velvet, fur or other such mark denoting status (*The Ambassadors* 1533, National Gallery). Holbein joined the court of Henry VIII and was subsequently sent abroad to paint the king's prospective brides *(Duchess of Milan*, National Gallery).

Hans Eworth who came from Antwerp in 1549, fused his own style (*Sir John Luttrell*, Courtauld Institute Galleries) with that of Holbein, in order to be promoted to court painter by Mary I and influence the likes of British-born **Nicholas Hilliard** (c. 1547–1619) who rose to become the most eminent Elizabethan portraitist in about 1570. Having been apprenticed to a goldsmith, Hilliard's jewel-like precise style was eminently suited to miniature painting (works in the Wallace Collection, V&A and Tate Britain). His greatest disciple and later rival was **Isaac Oliver** (d. 1617).

THE STUARTS

Thomas Howard, Earl of Arundel, Charles I and George Villiers, Duke of Buckingham emerge as three great patrons of the age. Religious troubles continued to provoke restlessness on the Continent, and artists were obliged to seek patrons where they could. **Van Somer** settled in London in 1616 and quickly found favour at the court (*Queen Anne of Denmark*, 1617, Royal Collection). **Daniel Mytens** came to England c 1618 from The Hague bringing a new sense of confidence both in his bold style of painting and the stances given to his subjects; he was appointed Painter to Charles I in 1625. He, together with London-born **Cornelius Johnson** (1593–1661), a master of technique, was superseded in popularity by **Sir Anthony van Dyck** (1599–1641) whose full-length official portraits project an air of gracious ease and elegance. Van Dyck's Baroque compositions are a symphony of colour and texture – shimmering silk set against a matt complexion, heavily draped curtains contrasting with solid objects that represent a distinctive attribute pertinent to the sitter. His portraits of the English royal family set a benchmark for future generations perpetuated through Dobson, Lely, Reynolds, Gainsborough, Romney, and Lawrence. (*Charles I in Three Positions* Royal Collection, *Charles I on Horseback*, National Gallery).

"The most excellent painter England hath yet bred," **William Dobson** (1610–46), was born in London and grew up to become a staunch Cavalier (Royalist). His natural style, influenced by Italian art, is less refined than Van Dyck's whom he succeeded as court painter (*Endymion Porter* Tate Britain).

Sir Peter Lely (1618–1680) was born in Germany of Dutch parentage. His early works (1640s) in England are narrative religious pieces. At the Restoration he became Principal Painter to Charles II (1661) and produced stylised portraits celebrating the image of languorous Beauty (*Windsor Beauties* at Hampton Court) or the masculine Admiralty (*Flagmen* at Greenwich): one honouring virtue, the other victory in the Second Dutch War. His "history" pictures meanwhile satisfied a less prudish market depicting the same modish voluptuous ladies (*Sleeping Nymphs* at Dulwich) in more sensual poses.

The reign of James II saw the appointment of a new Principal Painter, **Sir Godfrey Kneller** (1646/9–1723). Official portraits in the style of Lely are dignified if not beautiful in the Classical sense; well executed, they conform to a taste for formality and noble bearing (42 portraits known as the Kit-Cat series showing the head and one hand, ⓒ *see MAJOR CENTRAL LONDON MUSEUMS – National Portrait Gallery*).

Decorative Schemes

Peter Paul Rubens (1577–1640) evolved his highly energetic Baroque style from studying works by Titian, Raphael, Velázquez and epitomised the best of contemporary Continental art. In 1635, he completed the ceiling of the Banqueting House in Whitehall, a complex allegorical painting commissioned by Charles I. The impact on the English court of this bold political celebration of Charles's kingship should not be underestimated, nor should his influence on subsequent court painters be dismissed.

Lesser decorative schemes for stairways and ceilings were undertaken by foreign artists, paid by the square foot: **Antonio Verrio**, a Neapolitan, is registered in the service of the Crown from 1676 until 1688 at Windsor, St James's Palace and Whitehall. **Louis Laguerre** was trained in the Classical French tradition before coming to England at the behest of the Duke of Montagu, who was building Montagu House in Bloomsbury. **Pellegrini**, a follower of Ricci, was invited to England by the Earl of Manchester; he later became a founding member of the Royal Academy. The Venetian **Sebastiano Ricci** was responsible for the dome painting at Chelsea Hospital and a pair of large mythological paintings that hang in Burlington House. The great skill of these craftsmen, their ability to suggest luminosity and movement on a grand scale have secured their reputation as well as that of **Sir James Thornhill** (1675/6–1734), the British Baroque master of decorative painting who followed their example when engaged on such important commissions as the Painted Hall at Greenwich, the Prince's Apartments at Hampton Court and the dome of St Paul's Cathedral. Taste veered away from this French art in the manner of Lebrun only when the Neoclassical designer **William Kent** clinched the commission to decorate Kensington Palace.

Landscape

William van de Velde was an official war artist employed by the Dutch navy to document battles against the British fleet. Works at the National Maritime Museum Collection, Greenwich confirm his ability to record precise detail – a quality that endeared him to the British authorities who persuaded him to work for them; It is, however, his son William who left the more lasting impression on the evolution of British marine painting; he painted tranquil riverside views as well as warships at sea. Other Dutch painters recorded such social events as hunting scenes and the construction of major buildings; this generated a taste in sporting pictures, still-life paintings with game and flowers, topographical landscapes: genres that were to flourish throughout the 18C.

18C

The Age of Enlightenment promoted connoisseurship in the Italian art of the Renaissance and Classical art from Antiquity either from travel to the continent to study the styles at first hand or from drawings, engravings and folios; another, less intellectual but no less accomplished influence, came from Versailles in the form of a highly decorative French Baroque. Taste was a matter for stimulating debate much as were the politics of the day; preference for a particular style, therefore, varied from patron to patron.

In 1757 Edmund Burke published his treatise *A Philosophical Enquiry into the Origin of Our Ideas of the Sublime and Beautiful*. The Sublime was defined as an artistic effect that could provoke the greatest emotional feeling. The influence and impact of this work was considerable, both in Burke's own life time and on subsequent generations.

William Hogarth (1697–1764). Apprenticed as an engraver, Hogarth became popular through his "conversation" pieces like *The Beggar's Opera*. In his treatise *The Analysis of Beauty* (1753) he upholds the importance of a national style at a time when foreign artists were achieving greater success; he propounded theories on naturalism, observing that figures conform to standard expressions, gestures and stances appropriate to age; he advocated the use of the serpentine line as a basis of artistic harmony and beauty in composition (inscribed on his palette in his self-portrait in Tate Britain).

Perhaps Hogarth's greatest follower was **Thomas Rowlandson** (1756–1827), a fine caricaturist and supreme draughtsman; he produced pictures drawn from low-life and populist subjects. His talent is Rococo in its freshness, although the humour and wit are undoubtedly English.

George Lambert (1700–65) is widely regarded as "the father of British oil landscape", although his pictures were often executed in collaboration with a figure painter (Hogarth) or a marine painter (Scott).

Richard Wilson (c. 1713–82) was given a classical education by his father. When he arrived in London in the 1740s he came as a portrait painter, although early landscapes survive from 1746. In 1750 he is recorded working in and around Rome, forging a new style in the tradition of Claude and Vernet: i idyllic landscapes composed of clumped trees, buildings, paths and rivers, and populated with figures (usually drawn from Classical literature or mythology). On his return to England, the Roman Campania gently gave way to views of his own green and pleasant land.

Sir Joshua Reynolds (1723–92), a key figure in the development of British painting, was the son of an educated Devon family, a respected figure associated with the circles of Dr Johnson, David Garrick, Goldsmith and Burke. He drew inspiration from Van Dyck and the Old Master paintings known in England by engravings (Rembrandt self-portrait) or from posing his sitters according to Classical statues from Antiquity (Apollo Belvedere). The years 1752–54 he spent in Rome and studied High Renaissance Art. Returning to London via Venice, he resolved to merge the taste for the Italian "Grand Style" with the demand for "face-painting" at home. In 1768 he was rewarded with the Presidentship of the new Royal Academy and during his tenure outlined the way a British School of History might be forged. His history portraits endorsed his theories (*Three Ladies Adorning a Term of Hymen – The Montgomery Sisters* in Tate Britain) and provoked a shift in fashion towards simple Neoclassical "nightdresses" rather than billowing gowns of damask.

At his death the position of Painter to the King was taken by **Sir Thomas Lawrence** (1769–1830). Lawrence was commissioned by the Prince Regent, later George IV, to paint portraits of all the leading men who had opposed Napoleon; a large collection of sovereigns and statesmen are now hung in Windsor Castle.

> ## Antonio Canaletto (1697–1768)
>
> During the 1740s, the War of the Austrian Succession prevented British noblemen from undertaking the Grand Tour: Italian artists who had hitherto relied on their patronage decided therefore to come to England (1746–56). Canaletto transposed the sparkle and lucidity of the Venetian landscape to reaches of the Thames (pictures in the Sir John Soane Museum, and the collections of the Bank of England, Courtauld Institute Galleries, National Gallery).

Thomas Gainsborough (1727–88) developed his own very natural style while painting landscapes and "fancy pictures" for his personal pleasure. After residing several years in Suffolk, in Ipswich and in Bath (1759) he settled in London (1774) in the wake of Fashionable Society. In Bath, his portraits became more assured, full-length, life-size and set in arcadian gardens. His landscapes meanwhile echo the Dutch style of Hobbema and Ruisdael. The rich palette used for his wooded country scenes, meanwhile, is evidently drawn from Rubens: these small pictures seem to exude naturalism although the composition is carefully contrived. Gainsborough's textured rendering of foliage heralds Constable, while his skilled technique in capturing haze and flickering light foreshadows Turner.

George Stubbs (1724–1806) began as a portrait painter while studying anatomy in York. He visited Rome in 1754 in order to prove that the study of art was secondary to the observation of Nature; there he witnessed a horse being devoured by a lion, a scene that was to provide inspiration for later works. On his return to England, he applied himself to the study of the skeleton and musculature of the horse by minute observation, dissection and from Renaissance drawings with

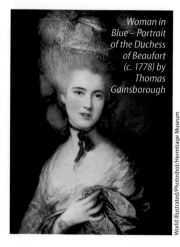

Woman in Blue – Portrait of the Duchess of Beaufort (c. 1778) by Thomas Gainsborough

World Illustrated/Photoshot/Hermitage Museum

a view to publishing his *Anatomy of a Horse* in 1766. Stubbs painted in oils, but preferred to use enamels because of their assured durability, even if the medium demanded an exacting and meticulous technique.

19C

Landscape

John Constable (1776–1834) developed his personal style and technique from observation and experimentation; his landscapes suggest topographical accuracy *(Salisbury Cathedral, Hampstead Heath)* when in fact realism has been compromised for the sake of art: trees, perspective or other such elements are contrived to better the overall composition, which in turn is unified by *chiaroscuro* (patches of light and shade). Constable refused to depend upon formal patronage and therefore was able to explore a new relationship between man and the landscape, contradicting the 18C view of Nature as a force to appease and tame rather than accept and admire for its own sake. He considered how to convey the atmosphere of a pastoral landscape *(The Haywain,* National Gallery) by comparison with the fear and dread of a storm at sea; it is interesting to note how, from 1828, after the death of his wife Maria, Constable seemed to betray a fascination for sombre skies and disturbed seas . He conveyed in landscape as much drama as any grand gesture or emotion in "high art".

He arrived at his theories by sketching from nature – in oil, a medium which took time to dry and therefore intensified his awareness of fleeting effects of light, ephemeral phenomena like rainbows and transient cloud patterns and formations. As his work met with little success, he resolved to compete in terms of size and embarked upon a series of "six-footers" *(Flatford Mill* in Tate Britain) for which he was forced to make scale sketches. In 1816 he settled permanently in London, spending the summer months in Hampstead and capturing scenes of kite flying high on the Heath. In 1824 he was awarded gold medals

for two pictures exhibited at the Paris Salon *(The Haywain,* National Gallery; *View on the Stour),* which provoked great interest from the members of the Barbizon School of outdoor painters and artists associated with the Romantic Movement, notably Delacroix.

Watercolour is a medium that found particular favour with English artists looking to capture changing qualities of light or the distance through rolling green fields to a far horizon and blue sky; for travellers on the Grand Tour it provided an efficient way of recording atmospheric details to complement topographical pencil drawings or thumb nail sketches (hence **John Ruskin**'s near-obsessional realism).

Unlike Continental predecessors, the English artists used opaque white paper which, if left blank, provided bright highlights. The leading watercolourists include Paul Sandby (1725–1809), JR Cozens (1752–97), JMW Turner (&see *below)* and **Thomas Girtin** (1775–1802).

Drawings and Illustration

Henry Fuseli (1741–1825) explored the realms of the imagination, dreams and nightmares, full of drama and extravagant movement, stylised form in vivid if horrifying detail *(Lady Macbeth Seizing the Daggers);* in 1787 he met the visionary poet **William Blake** (1757–1827), whose spirit contradicts the Age of Reason and heralds the advent of Romanticism. A large collection of Blake's works on paper is to be found at Tate Britain.

Joseph Mallord William Turner (1775–1851) showed precocious talent at painting topographical watercolours: by 1790 his work was hanging at the RA; six years later his *Fishermen at Sea* demonstrated his ability to handle oil and to show man in a natural world that was full of light, moving water and changing sky. Subsequent paintings confirmed his preoccupation with the same themes: *Snowstorm, Shipwreck 1805; Snowstorm, Hannibal and his Army crossing the Alps.* Meanwhile he continued to produce atmospheric studies of landscape (*London from Greenwich*, 1809).

He went to France and Switzerland and made several trips to Italy (1819–40) cataloguing his impressions as he went. In his sketchbooks Turner managed to suggest reflected sunlight, its blinding brilliance, its translucence and somehow its transience *(Norham Castle, Sunrise)*. In 1842 his Romantic predisposition to experience "atmosphere" at first hand was pushed to extremes: the drama captured in *Steamboat off a Harbour's Mouth* resulted from the artist insisting on being strapped to the mast of a ship pitching at sea in squally weather.

Turner also studied the work of Claude, the first artist really to attempt to paint the sun at dusk setting over rippling water (*see MAJOR CENTRAL LONDON MUSEUMS – National Gallery*).

Pre-Raphaelite Brotherhood

The initials PRB began to suffix Rossetti's signature in 1849 following discussions between the coterie of RA School artists **WH Hunt** (1827–1910), **DG Rossetti** (1828–82) and his brother William, **JE Millais** (1829–96), Collinson, the sculptor Woolner and Stephens. The Pre-Raphaelites considered the 15C Renaissance paintings by Raphael to be already too sophisticated and therefore sought to develop a style that might have predated Raphael: elaborate symbolism charged with poetic allusion, strong colour heightened by natural light and meticulous detail. Their success came with Ruskin's defence of their art before harsh criticism from Charles Dickens (especially directed at Millais' *The Carpenter's Shop*, Tate Britain). During the early 1850s, the group was dissolved.

Associated in style but independent of the Brotherhood is Sir **Edward Burne-Jones** (1833–98), a fine technician with an excellent sense of style and visual appeal honed by travels in Italy with Ruskin for whom he executed a number of studies of Tintoretto (1862); the influences of Mantegna and Botticelli are also apparent in his flat and linear designs for tapestries and stained-glass windows. In a similar vein is the **Aesthetic Movement** (*see MAJOR CENTRAL LONDON MUSEUMS – Tate Britain*) immortalised by **Oscar Wilde** in his *Portrait of Dorian Gray*, and represented by Frederic, Lord Leighton (1830–96), Albert Moore (1841–1893) and Whistler.

Foreign Artists

The American **JA McNeill Whistler** (1834–1903) trained as a Navy cartographer, hence his etching skills, before going to Paris to study painting. In 1859 he moved to London and earned notoriety for falling out with a patron over the so-called Peacock Room décor (now in the Freer Gallery of Art, Washington, DC: www.asia.si.edu), and later with Ruskin who accused the painter of "flinging a pot of paint in the public's face" when he exhibited *Nocturne in Black and Gold* (now in Detroit). Having been influenced by Courbet, Fantin-Latour, Degas and Manet during his life in Paris, Whistler introduced new perspectives to Victorian England, notably in the form of Japanese art.

Born of American expatriate parents in Italy, **JS Sargent** (1856–1925) settled in London to paint his vivid portraits and capture the elegance of Edwardian High Society with all its brilliance.

French Impressionism came to England in the form of a large exhibition put on in London in 1883: the Impressionists used pure pigments to capture the effects of bright sunlight on coloured forms; vibrancy was achieved by contrasting complementary shades; texture and movement were suggested by bold brushstrokes. Simple family scenes, informal portraiture and landscape provided them with engaging subject matter. The portrayal of circus performers and cabaret entertainers for what they are was explored by Degas, Seurat and Toulouse-Lautrec, in turn they provided subjects for Walter Sickert and Aubrey Beardsley. As for Monet, he immortalised on canvas some of London's landmarks.

In 1886 the New English Art Club was founded to provide a platform for artists ostracised by the Royal Academy: **Philip Wilson Steer** (1860–1942) and **Walter Sickert** (1860–1942) went on to set up an alternative exhibition entitled **London Impressionists**, at the Goupil Gallery.

20C

In 1910, the critic and painter **Roger Fry** organised a major show of modern French art: "Manet and the Post-Impressionists" comprised 21 works by **Cézanne**, 37 by **Gauguin**, 20 by Van Gogh and others by **Manet**, **Matisse** and **Picasso**. In 1912 he organised the "Second Post-Impressionist Exhibition", dedicated to Cubist art and large compositions by Matisse.

Augustus John's reputation as a leader in modern British art hinged on The Smiling Woman, a portrait of his mistress exhibited in 1909; a famous series of contemporary luminaries followed.

Sickert conformed with the philosophy of Impressionism which he assimilated while living in Paris. In 1910 he produced a series of works depicting the Old Bedford Music Hall, its performers, stage and audience with sympathy (Ennui, La Hollandaise); in 1911 he founded the **Camden Town Group** which attracted Robert Bevan, Spencer Gore, Harold Gilman, Charles Ginner. Bold colour, strong outlines and broad brushstrokes were dedicated to depicting the urban landscape.

The **Bloomsbury Group** collected together writers and artists: the biographer Lytton Strachey, the economist Maynard Keynes, the novelist Virginia Woolf, her publisher husband Leonard Woolf, Clive Bell, Henry Tonks, Marc Gertler and the members of the **Omega Workshop**. Vanessa Bell, Roger Fry and Duncan Grant all used bright colour to delineate bold form in the manner of Matisse; by 1914 they were experimenting with abstraction.

The **Vorticists**, led by Wyndham Lewis responded to Cubism and the dynamics of Futurism in painting and sculpture. Jessica Desmorr, Epstein, Gaudier-Brzeska were later joined in spirit by David Bomberg. Strong axes, parallel lines, harsh angles, stepped geometric forms, lurid colours proliferate, mesmerising the eye.

Pure Abstraction, which inspired **Nicholson**, Moore, Hepworth and Nash, explored form in relation to landscape. In 1936 the **International Surrealist Exhibition** was held in London, a high point in London's avant-garde artistic circles.

Among **post-war artists** are Graham Sutherland, painter of religious themes, landscapes and portraits as well as scenes of urban devastation; Sir Stanley Spencer whose visionary Biblical scenes are set in familiar surroundings and who explored eroticism as a means of exorcising the violence of war. Peter Blake, David Hockney and Bridget Riley were the exuberant exponents of **Pop Art** while the disturbing portraits and figures of **Francis Bacon** and **Lucian Freud** evoke a darker outlook.

Tate Modern, Whitechapel Gallery, Saatchi Gallery put on shows by artists such as Gilbert and George, Paula Rego, Beryl Cooke, Julian Opie, Damien Hirst, Tracy Emin, Rachel Whiteread among others, exploring new idioms – collages, installations, conceptual and performance art which challenge preconceptions and at times provoke strong reactions.

The success of the **Young British Artists** group is measured by the popularity of the White Cube Gallery, Jerwood Space, Lux Gallery, the Wapping Project and the South London Gallery, as well as alternative and artist-run spaces exhibiting contemporary art, their exhibitions and the controversial annual Turner Prize attracting much media interest which in turn is successful in drawing a young public.

Stuckism was founded in 1999 by Charles Thomson and Billy Childish in reaction to contemporary Postmodernism and in favour of a return to some form of figurative painting. Since then it has developed into an international art movement.

DECORATIVE ARTS
FURNITURE

Antique English furniture has long enjoyed favour. Distinctive types have evolved to suit changes in lifestyle and tastes in dress. Influences have been exerted by waves of craftsmen seeking refuge from Holland or France, and by the arrival of foreign pieces from Japan, China, India or other far corners of the Empire. The most complete display is to be found in the **Victoria and Albert Museum**, while most of the large houses provide period contexts in which original fixtures, fittings and furnishings may be appreciated (Ham, Osterley, Kenwood, Fenton).

The height of English furniture-making came in the **18C** when oak was replaced by imported mahogany and later by tropical satinwood, before a return was made to native walnut. These new woods were embellished with carving and enrichments of brass in the form of inlays and gilded mounts, hardwood veneers and marquetry.

A handful of names dominates English furniture of the period. **Thomas Chippendale** (1718–79), imported uncompleted furniture from France which his workshops then finished off (1769). His reputation as the pre-eminent cabinetmaker of his day was secured by his publication of *The Gentleman and Cabinet Maker's Director* (1754). Perhaps the most original Chippendale designs

Chippendale

MICHELIN

were made for the great Neoclassical houses designed or remodelled by Robert Adam and his contemporaries, by the second Thomas Chippendale (1749–1822) who went on to produce an anglicised version of Louis XVI and archetypal Regency furniture. **John Linnell** (1729–96) began as a carver but soon expanded his workshops in Berkeley Square to include cabinet-making and upholstery. His reputation was secured by his association with William Kent, Robert Adam and Henry Holland (mirrors and chairs). The partnership of **William Vile** (1700–67) and **John Cobb** (1751–1778) produced the most outstanding pieces, certainly better crafted than Chippendale if less original.

George Hepplewhite (d. 1786) achieved widespread recognition two years after his death when *The Cabinet Maker and Upholsterer's Guide* was published. This codified 300 designs for Neoclassical interiors, epitomising Adam's principles of uniting elegance with utility. It became the standard handbook for country gentlemen commissioning furniture from artisans. Hepplewhite pieces are considered as country furniture, simple, rational, extremely elegant and stylish: bow-fronted and serpentine chests of drawers, oval, heart-shaped and shield-back chairs with straight or tapered legs; Prince of Wales' feathers and wheat-ear central splats.

Post-Hepplewhite but pre-Regency comes **Thomas Sheraton** (1751–1806) whose rectilinear designs dominate the

Hepplewhite

MICHELIN

1790s, a perfect foil to Adam's intricate yet restrained interior stuccowork. His designs are recorded in *The Cabinet-Maker and Upholsterer's Drawing-Book* (1791–94). He particularly exploits the grain and textures of wood with contrasting inlays, relief panels and highly polished surfaces. Inspiration is drawn from Louis XVI furniture, notably for such subjects as small, rather feminine work tables, beautiful sideboards, secretaires and full-height bookcases.

The Goliath of Victorian taste is undoubtedly **William Morris** (1834–96) whose firm of Art Decorators at Merton Abbey supplied the full gamut of furnishings: furniture – mostly designed by Philip Webb, textiles, wallpapers, carpets, curtains, tapestries often in collaboration with Burne-Jones, tiles, candlesticks and brassware. Many designs were collated by Morris himself who drew his inspiration from historic patterns found in churches, paintings or book illumination and natural forms. Some Arts and Crafts work, which was based on craftsmanship and pre-industrial techniques, is on show at the William Morris Gallery.

In the following generation, Sir Ambrose Heal (1872–1959) designed simple solid oak furniture, sometimes inlaid with pewter and ebony, in collaboration with Charles Voysey. He supplied middle-class homes with inexpensive alternatives to flimsy reproduction or expensive Arts and Crafts furniture – a niche-market now supplied by Conran and Habitat.

CERAMICS

Tin-glazed Earthenware

The **Lambeth Potteries**, founded c 1601, are famous for their dark blue earthenware with a raised white ornamentation known as **Lambeth delft**.

The leading factory in the early 17C was the **Southwark Potteries**, founded by a Dutchman Christian Wilhelm in 1618. In 1628 he secured a 14-year monopoly for producing blue and white pieces fashioned in imitation of Chinese Ming.

Porcelain

The **Bow Factory** (identified by a variety of marks – incised, impressed or painted in underglazed blue and/or red), together with that at Chelsea were the first porcelain factories in England. It was founded by an Irish painter, Thomas Frye, with a glass merchant, Edward Heylyn, in the East End (Stratford Langthorne). In 1744 it registered a patent for wares crafted from a white clay (unaker) imported from America. In 1748 Frye also patented the use of bone ash to make **bone-china**, softer than hard-paste and cheaper to manufacture. Early pieces include plain white figures; later on, receptacles were decorated with sprigs of flowers and foliage or painted in underglazed blue or enamelled with colour (Kakiemon quail pattern) or transfers.

The earliest pieces identified with the **Chelsea Factory** (incised with a triangle) are dated 1745, most modelled on shapes then current for silver plate. The name "soft-paste" derives from the texture and translucence of the material, similar to white glass. After the first manager Charles Gouyon departed, the concern was headed by Nicholas Sprimont, a silversmith of Flemish Huguenot origin (raised anchor period 1749–52 followed by the red anchor period 1752–58 and the gold anchor period 1758–69). From 1750–70 the factory enjoyed great commercial prosperity, owing to the high technical quality of the product and the adoption of new colours, including a red tint known as claret: influence shifts from Meissen prototypes – attractive, animated figures, Sir Hans Sloane's botanical specimen plants – to a taste for French Sèvres. Despite the flavour of Continental Rococo, the highly varied Chelsea wares (vegetable tureens, fruit containers, vases, chandeliers, figurines, busts, flasks, etc.) are somehow very English, their style of painted decoration being highly naturalistic.

METALWORK

Gold and Silver

English gold and silversmiths were already known for their work in the Middle Ages, and by 1180 they had formed a guild in London. In the Elizabethan period the pieces produced showed a bold and elegant line which gave way to greater austerity in the reign of James I. The 17C was an extravagant period for London silver which was particularly influenced by Dutch Baroque. Under Charles II the French style predominated as highly skilled Huguenots (Protestant Calvinists) were expelled from France following the Revocation of the Edict of Nantes (18 October 1685).

Under Queen Anne, in the early 18C, Dutch silver design ceded to more sophisticatedly ornate designs – cut card work, strap design, cast ornaments with scrolls, escutcheons, boss beading, repoussé and chasing. The rocaille style of Paul de Lamerie (1688–1741) was followed by more sober designs produced by William Kent (1684–1748) and others working within the delicate Adam style.

Important collections of silver plate (functional receptacles made of metal: tableware, church vessels, commemorative pieces, etc.) are on view at the Tower of London, the Victoria and Albert Museum, Apsley House, the Courtauld Institute Galleries, Bank of England, the National Maritime Museum in Greenwich and the various military museums. Significant private collections, to which public access is restricted, survive at the Mansion

Bench, Victoria Embankment

House and in the halls of the City guild and livery companies.

Iron

London offers many fine examples of decorative gates, railings, balconies and balustrades ranging from the work of masters such as **Jean Tijou** (active 1689–1712) at Hampton Court to the modern design of the Queen Elizabeth Gates in **Hyde Park**.

Many City churches contain elaborate wrought-iron **sword rests** that date from the Elizabethan period (16C) when it was customary to provide a pew for the Lord Mayor of London in his own parish church furnished with a sword rest where he could deposit the Sword of State during the service.

In the 19C, design and iron casting complemented each other in the production of **street furniture**: the Egyptian-inspired bench ends along the Victoria Embankment by Cleopatra's Needle; the cannon ball and barrel bollards marking the Clink in Southwark; the beautiful dolphin lamp standards of 1870 which line the Albert Embankment; the pair of George III lamp-posts in Marlborough Road in St James's. The gold-crowned bracket lanterns at St James's Palace, made of wrought rather than cast metal, are of earlier date.

Many of the city's iron railings were melted down for munitions during World

Dolphin lamppost

War II; the discussion still continues about whether to replace them.

The first **pillar boxes** in London, 15 years after the introduction of the penny post in 1840, were erected in Fleet Street, the Strand, Pall Mall, Piccadilly, Grosvenor Place and Rutland Gate; they were rectangular with a solid round ball crowning the pyramidal roof. Subsequent hexagonal, circular, fluted, conical designs followed, flat-roofed, crowned or plain, most emblazoned with the royal cipher. A few hexagonal boxes (1866–79) survive, as do some from the 1880s "anonymous" series which the Post Office forgot to mark with its name. Pillar boxes were promoted by the writer Anthony Trollope, who was a Post Office official, and were first painted red in 1874.

Brass

From the Middle Ages until the 17C **brass tomb plates** were very popular, and a variety are still to be found in several London churches. The design was engraved with a triangular-headed graving tool and the groove was sometimes filled with enamel, or black or coloured wax. A study of these brasses shows how fashions in dress changed over the centuries: warriors clothed in chain mail from head to foot were followed by knights in armour wearing a helmet. The appearance of wives of such nobles range from the veiled simplicity of the 14C, via the rich dress and complicated headdress of the 15C, the plainer style of the Tudor period, to the ribbons and embroidery of Elizabeth's reign. In the 16C the brasses of the great churchmen were removed. In their place were rich merchants, with short hair, clean-shaven in the 15C and bearded in the Elizabethan period. **Brass-rubbing** is organised at All Hallows-by-the-Tower, St Martin-in-the-Fields and Westminster Abbey.

The long-standing tradition and patronage of fine craftsmanship and design in London is maintained today by the **Chelsea Craft Fair** and the **Goldsmith's show** at the Guildhall where international buyers come to explore ideas that will launch new trends worldwide.

SCULPTURE

The quick pace of change in popular culture has a powerful impact on all forms of art. Sculpture is no longer restricted to traditional materials and a young generation of artists has the freedom to experiment with new forms which elicit a mixed public response. As more public spaces are created in the city, monumental sculpture becomes an interesting feature of the cityscape.

In sculpture the evolution from Gothic tomb effigies to modern abstract form begins with **William Torel**, citizen and goldsmith of London, who modelled Henry III and Eleanor of Castile (1291–92), and the visiting (1511–20) early Renaissance Florentine **Torrigiano**, who cast the gilt bronze figures of Henry VII (in the Victoria & Albert), his queen, Elizabeth, and mother, Margaret, Duchess of Richmond. After the Reformation, contact with Italy was suspended, dominant influences were therefore imported from France and Flanders.

Actual portraiture appears in the 17C in the works of, among others, Nicholas Stone (John Donne), the French Huguenot **Le Sueur** (bronzes of Charles I and James I) and **Grinling Gibbons** (statues of Charles II and James II). Gibbons is better known and celebrated as a woodcarver of genius and great delicacy, who often signed his work with a peapod.

In the 18C, as a Classical style began to appeal to graduates of the Grand Tour, the Flemings, Michael Rysbrack and Peter Scheemakers, the Frenchman François **Roubiliac,** the Englishmen John Bacon, **John Flaxman** and Nollekens executed hundreds of figures until the genre became stylised and empty in the 19C. Many examples of their work are to be found in the nave and north transept of Westminster Abbey.

Vigour began to return in the 20C in portraiture and religious sculptures with works by **Jacob Epstein**, in human, near abstract and abstract themes by

Henry Moore Sculptures in London

West Wind 1928/9 (St James's Park Underground) was Moore's first open-air sculpture and first public commission; it reflects Moore's empathy for Mexican sculpture. In *Three Standing Figures* 1947/8 (west end of the lake in Battersea Park) Moore explores spatial unity of the 3D group. *Time-Life Screen* 1952/3 (New Bond St, inset on the second floor of the former Time-Life Building). The 11ft/3.3m bronze *Upright Motives* 1, 2 and 7 1955/6 (Battersea Park) show Moore working on a grand scale specifically for the outdoors. *Two Piece Reclining Figure No 1* 1959 (Chelsea School of Art). *Knife Edge Two Piece* 1962/5 (Abingdon Gardens). *Locking Piece* 1963/4 (Millbank) was inspired by two pebbles. *Two Piece Reclining Figure No 5* 1963/4 (Kenwood House). *Circular Altar* 1972 (St Stephen Walbrook, City). *Large Spindle Piece* 1974 (Spring Gardens). *The Arch* 1979/80 (Kensington Gardens). *Mother and Child: Hood* 1983 (St Paul's Cathedral).

Henry Moore, and pure abstract by **Barbara Hepworth**. In the 1930s after Dada and Surrealism had swept through Paris touching all forms of artistic consciousness, a number of painters, sculptors and architects emigrated, while others settled in Hampstead which hosted a new move towards pure abstraction: Roland Penrose, Lee Miller, Henry Moore, Barbara Hepworth, Ben Nicholson.

In addition to a large collection of mainly military dignitaries whose statues guard the streets of London, some fine contemporary sculpture adorns the open spaces created by modern town planning: the *Horses of Helios*, the Sun God, with the three Graces above, by Rudi Weller (corner of the Haymarket and Piccadilly Circus); *Boy with a Dolphin* in bronze by David Wynne (north end of Albert Bridge in Chelsea and outside the Tower Hotel in Wapping); *Fulcrum* by Richard Serra (Broadgate); a *Dancer* (Bow Street opposite the Royal Opera House); *Horse* by Shirley Pace (The Circle, Bermondsey); *The Navigators* by David Kemp (Hays Galleria, Southwark). Modern works temporarily displayed next to traditional statues in Trafalgar Square: *Ecce Homo* by Mark Wallinger, *Regardless of History* by Bill Woodrow and Plinth *(Untitled)* by Rachel Whiteread, have aroused much public interest. The sleek lines of the Millennium Bridge, built with the collaboration of the architect Sir Norman Foster, the sculptor

Sir Anthony Caro and the engineering firm Ove Arup, break new ground as an engineering masterpiece and an artistic achievement.

CINEMA

1926 – The Lodger: A Story Of The London Fog tells the story of the unsolved Whitechapel Murders of 1888; directed by Alfred Hitchcock.

1929 – Blackmail, directed by Alfred Hitchcock is considered as the first British talkie (non-so;emt film). **High Treason** creates a futurist vision of London in the 1940s; directed by M Elvey.

1941 – Dr Jekyll And Mr Hyde is evocatively set by Hollywood in London; directed by Victor Fleming.

1942 – Mrs Miniver, with Walter Pidgeon and Greer Garson, filmed in America, portrays London during the war; directed by William Wyler.

1945 – Brief Encounter, directed by David Lean, filmed at the Denham Studios.

1946 – Great Expectations was carefully filmed in London after the war under the directorship of David Lean.

1948 – Oliver Twist with stage sets recreated by David Lean from Gustave Doré's illustrations to *London* (1870).

1949 – Passport to Pimlico, is a British comedy filmed, in fact, in Lambeth; directed by H Cornelius.

1953 – Genevieve is the name of a 1906 Darracq car that takes part in the famous London to Brighton veteran car run – made by Ealing Studios; directed by H Cornelius.

1955 – The Lady Killers, set in Barnsbury, captures the Copenhagen Tunnels outside King's Cross on celluloid. **Witness for the Prosecution**, another Hitchcock, was set among the legal fraternity in and around the Royal Courts of Justice.

1964 – My Fair Lady, made by the Warner Studios in California, recreates an evocative if sentimental interpretation of the London class divisions, with Audrey Hepburn and Rex Harrison, costumes by Cecil Beaton after Bernard Shaw's *Pygmalion*; directed by George Cukor.

1966 – Blow-Up, set in the 1960s, a photographer on a fashion shoot accidentally witnesses a murder with David Hemmings, Vanessa Redgrave and Sarah Miles – the quintessential London movie; directed by Antonioni (featuring Maryon Park, Woolwich).

1966 – Alfie tracks Jack-the-lad, south-London-born Michael Caine and the easy life; directed by Lewis Gilbert.

1971 – A Clockwork Orange, Stanley Kubrick's banned cult film is about the terrors of anarchy, sequences filmed at Thamesmead.

1979 – The Long Good Friday charts the decline of the Docklands; directed by John Mackenzie.

1980 – The Elephant Man is a provocative story set in Victorian England, directed by David Lynch, starring John Hurt, Anthony Hopkins, Anne Bancroft and John Gielgud.

1985 – My Beautiful Launderette explores racial tensions in south London; directed by Stephen Frears.

1988 – A Fish called Wanda starring John Cleese, Kevin Kline, Jamie Lee Curtis in and around London Town and Docklands; directed by Charles Crichton.

1992 – Chaplin recreates the life of Charlie Chaplin in south London in the 1880s, directed by Richard Attenborough.

1994 – Madness of King George, Nigel Hawthorne in Alan Bennett's play about the mad monarch. Supported by Helen Mirren; directed by Nicholas Hytner.

1995 – Richard III, with a cast led by Ian McKellen exploits several London landmarks (Battersea and Bankside Power Stations, St Pancras).

1999 – Notting Hill, a romantic comedy with Julia Roberts and Hugh Grant set around Portobello Road; directed by Roger Mitchell.

2005 – The Libertine, Johnny Depp's portrait of the debauched 2nd Earl of Rochester in Restoration London.

2005 – Mrs Henderson Presents, Judi Dench and Bob Hoskins star in this portrait of the Windmill Theatre in WWII.

2007 – Cassandra's Dream, Woody Allen's story of two working class brothers (Colin Farrell and Ewan McGregor) who commit murder to preserve their selfish lifestyles.

2008 – RocknRolla, director Guy Ritchie's stylistic slice of London's criminal underworld.

2009 – London River, moving story set in the wake of the 2005 London terrorist attacks. Starring Brenda Blethyn.

CITY OF WESTMINSTER

Modern Central London is largely short for the City of Westminster, the borough that is home to the Monarchy, the Government and many key tourist attractions. A pop-up book of iconic sights, a single bus ride or walk can take in the elegance of Trafalgar Square, the energetic air and colour of Covent Garden and Soho, the grandeur of Buckingham Palace or the tranquillity and beauty of the city's green lungs, such as Hyde Park and St James's Park.

Highlights

1 Explore the Queen's official residence **Buckingham Palace** (p93)

2 Take a walk in the elegant surrounds of **Regent's Park** (p118)

3 Enjoy the fine art collection at the **Courtauld Institute Galleries** (p145)

4 Take a tour of the **Palace of Westminster** (p156)

5 Feel the weight of history at **Westminster Abbey** (p164).

Geography – The City of Westminster lies to the west of the City of London, and north of the River Thames. Covering 8.3sq mi/21.5sq km, it makes up much of London's central area and encompasses many of the most famous sights, including Buckingham Palace, The Houses of Parliament, Trafalgar Square, the West End and royal parks, including Hyde Park. All within Zone 1 and with Tube stations dotted everywhere, the area is easy to get around quickly and inexpensively by pubic transport. However, many sights are closer to each other than they may look on the Underground map, often no more than a five- or ten-minute walk.

The main sights are well signposted and walking really is often the best option – especially at rush hours! Alternatively, hop on a London bus for a great view – the classic Routemaster red bus still runs here along the No 9 and No 15 heritage routes.

History – One of London's two ancient cores, Westminster grew up around an 8C Benedictine abbey and royal palace built nearby after the Norman Conquest of 1066. The site was used as the principal royal residence until a fire in the 16C. Later, the remaining buildings became the location of the developing parliament. Today's Palace of Westminster remains the seat of government, including the Houses of Commons and Lords, while nearby Whitehall is home to most of the government ministries. The City of Westminster, which includes Westminster, covers a wider geographical area, and has been a London borough since 1965.

Today – The density of top London attractions in the West End and borough of Westminster itself draws a constant flow of tourists and Londoners "into town" to work or play. This is where picture-postcard London meets vibrant culture, world-class arts, grand architecture and cosmopolitan nightlife, particularly around Theatreland and the bars and restaurants of Soho.

Buckingham Palace★★

The ceremonial heart of London is a focal point for Londoners and visitors alike. State occasions are marked with the pomp and circumstance associated with the sovereign. The palace is a congregation point when national events arouse strong emotions.

A BIT OF HISTORY

Mulberry Garden to Royal Palace – In 1703 a piece of land, partly planted by **James I** as a mulberry garden, was granted by Queen Anne to the Duke of Buckingham, who built a town residence on it of brick. In 1762 **George III** purchased the property for his bride, Charlotte, and named it Queen's House.

In 1825 **John Nash** was commissioned by **George IV** to turn the house into a palace. He extended it, added a cladding of Bath stone, a grand entrance portico and a range of rooms overlooking the garden. The work was completed by Edward Blore in 1837. Three weeks after her accession **Victoria** took up residence and at last the royal standard flew on the **Marble Arch** which Nash had designed. Ten years later a new east range enclosed the courtyard; it contains the famous **balcony**, where members of the Royal Family greet the crowds in the Mall on

▷ **Location:** Map: *Inside front cover (DEY).* ⊖*Green Park; St James's Park; Victoria.* East of the palace is Westminster, with Trafalgar Sq to the northeast and St James's and Piccadilly to the north. Constitution Hill leads to Hyde Park Corner.

⊛ **Don't Miss:** The Royal Mews; the Palace Gardens; St James's Park.

◷ **Timing:** Visit the Palace and the Mews and/or the Guards' Museum in the morning then stroll through St James's Park at lunchtime when the park comes to life with Londoners working nearby.

👫 **Kids:** The Changing of the Guard; the Guards' Museum.

state occasions. In 1851, Marble Arch was moved to north-east Hyde Park. **Henry VIII** acquired **St James's Park** in 1532 for hunting purposes. **James I** established a menagerie of animals and exotic birds here. **Charles II** aligned aviaries along what came to be called Birdcage Walk and opened the park to the public. In the 19C Nash replaced the wall by iron railings and landscaped the park itself.

View of Buckingham Palace from the lake in St James's Park

A. Taverner/MICHELIN

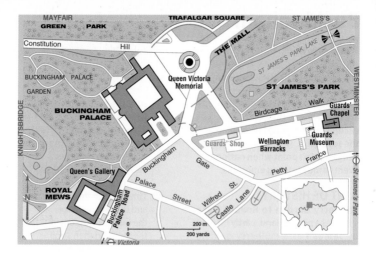

BUCKINGHAM PALACE★★

&♿⏰*Open late Jul–late Sept daily 9.45am–6pm (3.45pm last admission). 🎫Timed ticket £16.50; combined ticket with Queen's Gallery and Royal Mews £29.50. 🚶Guided tours (2–2.5hr). Brochure (6 languages). 📞020 7766 7300. www.royalcollection.org.uk.*

The interior presents the suite of Edwardian-style state rooms, decorated with treasures from the Royal Collection: Sèvres porcelain, 18C French clocks and furniture, royal portraits and chandeliers. From the Ambassadors' Entrance pass into the courtyard, dominated by the entrance portico; the pediment bears carvings of Britannia in her chariot. The Entrance Hall leads to the **Grand Staircase**, lit by a domed skylight. 18C Gobelins tapestries and magnificent chandeliers adorn the **Guard Room** leading to the **Green Drawing Room**, which has an extravagant coved white-and-gold plaster ceiling. Red and gold predominate in the **Throne Room**; note the frieze depicting the Wars of the Roses. The two chairs were used at the Coronation (1953) by the Queen and the Duke of Edinburgh.

In the **Picture Gallery** hang masterpieces from the Royal Collection: by Van Dyck (*Charles I*), Rembrandt, Vermeer (*A Lady at the Virginals*), Rubens and other artists.

On the west front are the state rooms: the **Dining Room** is adorned with royal portraits (*George IV* with his hand resting on the Commanders' Table commissioned by Napoleon in 1806 and presented to George IV by Louis XVIII in 1817). In the **Blue Drawing Room** stands the **Commanders' Table**,

---

Changing of the Guard★★★

👥 The ceremony takes place in the forecourt when the sovereign is in residence and the Royal Standard flies over the palace. The guard is mounted by the five regiments of Foot of the Guards Division. Their uniform of dark blue trousers, scarlet tunic and great bearskin is distinguished by badges, buttons and insignia: the Grenadiers (f 1656) by a white plume and buttons evenly spaced; the Coldstreams (f 1650) by a scarlet plume and buttons in pairs; the Scots (f 1642) by no plume and buttons in threes; the Irish (f 1900) by a blue plume and buttons in fours; the Welsh (f 1915) by a green-and-white plume and buttons in fives.

⏰*On fair days daily at 11.30am from May to July, and on alternate dates throughout the rest of the year.*

decorated with the head of Alexander the Great surrounded by 12 commanders of Antiquity, in Sèvres porcelain with gilt-bronze mounts. The gilded ceiling of the **Music Room** features the rose of England, the thistle of Scotland and the shamrock of Ireland with a border of fleur-de-lys.

The ornate **White Drawing Room** has Corinthian pilasters, a piano in a gilt case painted with figures and a roll-top desk by Riesener. Don't miss two graceful sculptures by Canova, *Mars and Venus* and *A Fountain Nymph* (by the Ministers' Stairs and Marble Hall).

From the garden, where garden parties are held in summer, there is a superb view of the west front of the palace.

Colourful pageantry of the foot guards
Ph. Gajic/MICHELIN

Royal Mews★★

🕑*Open Mar–Jul and Oct daily 11am–4pm (3.15pm last admission), Aug–Sept, daily 10am–5pm (4.15pm last admission).* 🕑*Closed 3, 9, 16 Jun, during state visits.* 🎫*£7.50. Combined ticket with Buckingham Palace, state rooms, Royal Mews and Queen's Gallery £29.50.* 📞*020 7766 7302. www.royalcollection.org.uk.*

The mews were built by Nash in the 1820s. The blocks around the tree-shaded courtyard house stables, harness rooms and coach houses displaying, among other royal carriages, the gold State Coach (1762), which has been used at every coronation since 1820.

Queen's Gallery★★

🕑*Open Aug–Sept daily 9.30am–5.30pm (4.30pm last admission).* 🎫*Timed ticket £8.50, combined ticket with Buckingham Palace, state rooms and the Royal Mews*

Prized Birds

St James's Park pelicans have a long-standing history: the first one, from Astrakhan, was a gift to Charles II given by a Russian ambassador – it promptly flew off and was shot over Norfolk. Peter from Karachi stayed 54 years before emigrating, no one knows where.

£29.50. 📞*020 7766 7301. www.royalcollection.org.uk.*

The gallery holds constant temporary exhibitions of treasures drawn from the Royal collections (Holbein watercolours, Canaletto paintings, furniture, sculpture, ceramics, silver and gold).

Wellington Barracks

On the south side of the parade ground stand the Wellington Barracks, built in 1833. In them, the 👥**Guards' Museum** (♿*Birdcage Walk, SW1;* 🎫*£3;* 📞*020 7414 3428; www.armymuseums.org.uk)* is

---

When We Were Very Young – A A Milne

"'They're changing the guard at Buckingham Palace –
Christopher Robin went down with Alice.
A face looked out but it wasn't the King's.
'He's much too busy a-signing things'
Says Alice'"

devoted to the Guards Regiments and charts its history from its Civil War origins to today.

Guards' Chapel – ⏱*Open as museum (except some ceremonial days).* The chapel, destroyed by a flying bomb in June 1944 (apart from the apse lined with mosaics), was rebuilt in 1963.

ADDITIONAL SIGHTS
St James's Park★★

London's oldest park is known for its flower borders and pelicans and wildfowl on the lake. Stroll by the lake or relax on the grass and enjoy band music. From the bridge there is a fine view of Buckingham Palace.

The Mall★★

In 1910 the 17C Mall was transformed into a processional way by **Sir Aston Webb**, who designed the **Queen Victoria Memorial**.

At the far end, the thoroughfare stretches through Admiralty Arch to Trafalgar Square, while the processional route leads right to **Horse Guards**.

The north side is flanked by **Green Park** and **Carlton Terrace**. A memorial statue to the Queen Mother, who died in 2002, aged 101, was unveiled here in February 2009.

Covent Garden★★

Lively crowds enjoy the animation of the central piazza until a late hour, with street entertainers and quality craft and antique markets. The refurbishment of the opera house and its facilities have given a new cachet to Covent Garden, which recalls its heyday in the 19C. Old warehouses have carefully been adapted to accommodate enticing small shops and boutiques selling off-the-peg designer clothing, while long-established businesses continue to thrive. Street cafés cater to the browsers by day and smart restaurants feed the throngs of theatregoers by night.

> ▷ **Location:** *Map: Inside front cover (EX).* ⊖*Covent Garden; Leicester Sq; Charing Cross.* Covent Garden is the area delineated by Strand, Kingsway, Charing Cross Rd and New Oxford St.
>
> ⊜ **Don't Miss:** The Floral Hall, now the sleek foyer of the Royal Opera House.
>
> ⏱ **Timing:** Spend the afternoon at the London Transport Museum or window-shopping around Neal Street, then enjoy the lively atmosphere of the Piazza in the evening.
>
> ▲▲ **Kids:** The London Transport Museum.

A BIT OF HISTORY

In the Middle Ages, Covent Garden was a 40 acre/16ha walled property belonging to the Benedictines of Westminster. Following the dissolution of the monastery at Westminster and the confiscation of the garden, several royal warrants contributed to shape the area into its present form.

When the theatres, hitherto principally in Southwark, reopened after the Restoration (1660), **Charles II** granted two royal warrants for them. The first resulted in the **Theatre Royal, Drury Lane** (1663), the second in the **Theatre Royal**, **Covent Garden** (1732). The theatrical tradition of Covent Garden was so well established that, when the monopoly of the two royal theatres was broken by the Theatre Regulation Act in 1843, some 40 new theatres mushroomed within as many years; in 1987 the Theatre Museum opened in the old Covent Garden Flower Market, but has since relocated in 2007 to galleries in the Victoria and Albert Museum.

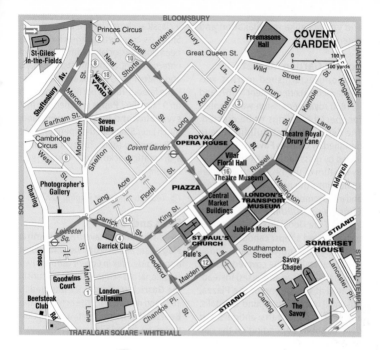

WALKING TOUR
Start from the Piazza.

The Piazza★★

The 1631 licence gave **Inigo Jones** the opportunity to design London's first square, which he modelled after those he had seen in Italy, lining the grand space on two sides with terraces of three-storey brick houses rising tall above a stone colonnade; behind the covered walkway nestled shops and coffee houses. The garden wall of the Earl's new town house ran on the south side. Bedford House was demolished in 1700 and the area was developed. Today the piazza is a meeting place for Londoners

Juggler in the Piazza, Covent Garden

©Imagestate/Tips Images

and visitors alike for relaxation and entertainment.

Covent Garden Market

The long-established market was regularised by Letters Patent in 1670 and in 1830 royal permission was granted for special buildings to be erected. The **Central Market Buildings** were designed by **Charles Fowler** (1832) and linked by glass canopies in 1872.

By the turn of the 19C/20C, the market spilled into the neighbouring streets and in November 1974 it moved to **Nine Elms** (*see SUBURBS – BATTERSEA*), leaving Eliza Doolittle's flower market to franchised shops, canopied cafés, vaulted pubs and wine bars. Today you'll find stalls in the covered Jubilee Hall Market (*see Addresses*) instead. Located at the far end of the Piazza, this small market has around 120 stalls, and sells arts and crafts, antiques and general goods depending on the day of the week (○*open Mon 5am–6pm (antiques), Tue–Fri 9.30am–6pm (general), Sat–Sun 9am–6pm (crafts); ℘020 7836 2139; www.jubileemarket.com*).

St Paul's Church★

Entrance from Bedford Street.

The Earl was unwilling to afford anything "much better than a barn" so Jones, declaring he should have "the handsomest barn in England," designed a classical church with a pitched roof. Since its completion, the church has been closely associated with the world of entertainment: actors, artists, musicians and craftsmen. Overlooking the square is the famous Tuscan portico from which on 9 May 1662 **Pepys** watched the first ever **Punch and Judy** show in England; much later **Shaw** set the opening scene of *Pygmalion* there. Today it provides a dramatic backdrop to a variety of buskers.

▷ *Leave by the alley leading to King St.*

Pubs and Clubs

The district's oldest tavern is the **Lamb & Flag** (*see Addresses*) *tucked away down a small side alley in Covent Garden*. Two traditional old-school clubs still flourish: the **Garrick** (*15 Garrick St*), founded in 1831 and named after the actor and the **Beefsteak** (*9 Irving Street*), a dining club that dates from 1876.

▷ *Walk back to Bedford St and turn left into Maiden Lane.*

At nos 34–35 is **Rule's**, London's oldest restaurant and oyster bar, established in 1798. *See YOUR STAY IN THE CITY.*

▷ *Continue north-east past the Jubilee Market. For London Transport Museum, see Additional Sights.*

Coffee Houses

The fashion for coffee houses was introduced to London during the Commonwealth (1652). Originally they served as meeting places in the City for the exchange of business intelligence. By 1715 there were over 500 not only in the City but also in Covent Garden and the Strand, St James's, Mayfair and Westminster. Customers of like interests would gather regularly, even daily, in the same houses or call at several houses at different times to pick up messages and even letters or to read the news sheets, which at first circulated from one house to another, and the later newspapers (*Daily Courant*, 1702) which were available to customers for the price of a single cup of hot chocolate or coffee. At the end of the 18C the City coffee houses reverted to being pubs, and the West End houses disappeared, except **Boodle's** and **White's**, which became clubs.

Of the 17C and 18C coffee houses for which Covent Garden was as famous as the City, none remain: Will's, frequented by "all the wits in town" (according to Pepys) used to stand at no 1 Bow Street, **Button's** in Russell Street, the **Bedford**, and the **Piazza**.

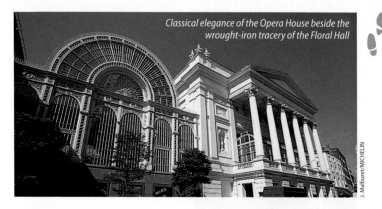

Classical elegance of the Opera House beside the wrought-iron tracery of the Floral Hall

J. Malburet/MICHELIN

▶ *Proceed along Russell St before turning left onto Bow St.*

Theatre Royal, Drury Lane

The present Georgian theatre is one of London's largest (2 283 seats) with symmetrical staircases rising beneath the domed entrance to a circular balcony. The first theatre, opened in 1663 was frequently patronised by Charles II, who met Nell Gwynne there in 1665. The second theatre, designed by **Wren**, knew a golden age under **Garrick** (from 1747 to 1776); it was replaced in 1794 by a third building, opening with **Sheridan**'s new play *The School for Scandal*. The present house, to designs by **Wyatt**, was erected in 1812. Kean, **Irving**, Ellen Terry played there; **Ivor Novello**'s dancing operettas were also staged there.

Bow Street

In the mid-18C, when **Henry Fielding**, novelist, dramatist and magistrate and his half-brother, John, the **Blind Beak**, moved into a house opposite the Opera House, they began their crusade for penal and police reform, which included the organisation in 1753 of the **Bow Street Runners**, mainly intended to fight prostitution.
The present building on the site of their house dates from 1881; in 1992 the police moved to new premises at Charing Cross.

Royal Opera House★

Charles II's patent was secured by **John Rich**, who opened his Theatre Royal, Covent Garden in 1732. In 1847, the theatre was remodelled and renamed **Royal Italian Opera**. The present house, inaugurated in 1858, became the Royal Opera House in 1892. A hundred years later, major renovation work was needed and the house was largely reconstructed between 1996 and 2000. Extensions to the west (in the 1858 style) house new dressing rooms and rehearsal facilities. The opera house now boasts an exquisitely restored auditorium with air conditioning and modern facilities for staging big productions. The iron-and-glass **Floral Hall** is used to great theatrical effect as the main foyer with escalators rising to the mezzanine galleries, which accommodate bars and restaurant, with panoramic **views** of the piazza from the loggias. **The Royal Ballet** performs here regularly, and it is also the city's premier venue for opera and visiting dance companies.

▶ *At the top of Bow St make a detour to the right before continuing along Endell St; left into Shorts Gardens.*

The Masons occupy the greater part of Great Queen Street, which includes 18C houses (nos 27–29) and the **Freemasons Hall** (1927–33).
The picturesque **Neal's Yard**★, complete with period hoists, dovecote, trees in tubs and window-boxes has attracted eco-friendly shops.

Type B Bus, London Transport Museum

London Transport Museum

Seven Dials

A 40ft/12m Doric column, adorned with a sundial on each face, was erected at the centre of seven radiating streets in the early 1690s. It was pulled down by a mob in 1773 on a rumour that treasure was buried underneath it. A replica of the pillar has been erected on the original site.

▶ *Walk down Mercer St, then Shaftesbury Ave to Princes Circus and left into St Giles High St.*

St Giles-in-the-Fields, which is of ancient foundation, was rebuilt in 1734 by Flitcroft after the styles of Wren and James Gibbs; the steeple rising directly from the façade echoes St Martin-in-the-Fields (◐*open Mon–Fri 9am–4pm and for services; ℘020 7240 2532; www.stgilesonline.org*).

ADDITIONAL SIGHTS
♟♟ London Transport Museum★

39 Wellington St, WC2E 7BB. ⊖*Covent Garden.* ♿◐*Open Sat–Thu 10am–6pm (5.15pm last admission). Fri 11am–9pm (8.15pm last admission).* ⊕*£10.* ℘*020 7565 7299 (24hr information). 020 7379 6344. www.ltmuseum.co.uk.*

The London Transport Museum, housed in part of the flower market, shows the development of one of the world's earliest and largest transport networks from trams and trolleybuses to driverless LRT (Light Rapid Transit) used by the Docklands Light Railway. Real vehicles include the Shillibeer Horse Omnibus (1829–34), Type B Bus (1910–27), Metropolitan Railway Class A Locomotive (1866), and London's beloved Routemaster bus, finally taken out of general service in December 2005.
◐The **Routemaster** still runs along two heritage routes: the no 9 from the Royal Albert Hall to Aldwych and the no 15, which passes Tower Bridge, Oxford Street and Trafalgar Square. These operate as normal, hop-on-and-ride bus services.

The museum boasts displays about cycling, walking, taxis and the River Thames and, for the first time, shows paper items such as maps, posters and engineering drawings in improved environmental conditions. Themes include transport during both World Wars, plans for the 21C and London in the context of other world cities. Interactive activities are throughout the museum.

ADDRESSES

※ LIGHT BITE

⊖ **Wagamama** – *1 Tavistock St, WC2E 7PG.* ⊖*Covent Garden.* ℘*020 7836 3330. www.wagamama.com.* Finding quick and inexpensive food around the Piazza can be difficult. Step down into this minimalist basement for healthy Asian-style dishes. The reasonable prices make this popular with Londoners and

tourists, but you may have to queue, and this is not a place for lingering, but a good choice for families.

⊖ **World Food Café** – *14 Neal's Yard, WC2H 9DP.* ⊖*Covent Garden.* ℘*020 7379 0298 . Closed Sun.* Overlooking the quaint and eco-friendly Neal's Yard, this 1st floor vegetarian restaurant is known for its hearty recipes from exotic lands around the globe, particularly Asia and Africa. Shared pine tables around a central kitchen counter. If you are pressed for time, pick up a healthy snack at one of the ground floor outlets.

The Opera Terrace at Chez Gerard – 45 East Terrace, Covent Garden Piazza, WC2E 8RF. ⊖Covent Garden. ☏020 7379 0666. www.chezgerard.com. After finding the entrance on the east corner of the Central Market, you'll be rewarded with a tranquil vantage point from which to survey the buskers and general activity of Covent Garden below. A good selection of light meals is provided, with unhurried service.

Tuttons Brasserie – 11/12 Russell St, WC2B 5HZ. ⊖Covent Garden. ☏0844 371 2550. www.tuttons.com. On the corner of the Piazza, this popular restaurant has an outdoor terrace in summer. Good, classic Modern European menu and elegant ambience.

Paul – 29 Bedford St, WC2D 1QG. ⊖Covent Garden. ☏020 7836 3304. www.paul-uk.com. Crusty bread, wonderful patisseries and great lunch-time snacks like quiche, charcuterie and soup are on offer in this delightful, old-fashioned-looking, wooden-floored – and very French – bakery group's main shop.

PUB

The Lamb & Flag – 33 Rose St, WC2E 9EB. ⊖Covent Garden. ☏0871 917 0007. Closed 1 Jan. This pub, nestling in a tiny alley, is the oldest and perhaps the most pleasant in the area. It opened in 1623 as the Cooper's Arms and became known unofficially as the Bucket of Blood from 1679, after an incident involving John Dryden, who was attacked outside while on his way home to Long Acre. Good selection of beers. Our favourite pub around Covent Garden, it is best enjoyed during off-peak hours.

SHOPPING

Birkenstock – 70 Neal St, WC2H 9PR. ⊖Covent Garden. ☏020 7240 2783. www.birkenstock.co.uk. Small but very popular shop selling over 100 different styles, colours and textures of comfortable good quality footwear developed by Birkenstock, a family of German origin, who designed the first

flexible arch support that mirrors the shape of the foot.

Jones – 13 Floral St, WC2E 9DH. ⊖Covent Garden. ☏020 7240 8312. In this spacious boutique in Floral Street, Jones offers an unrivalled choice of men's fashion featuring labels by the most feted stylists of the moment, including such luminaries as Martin Margiela, Vries van Noten and Rogan.

Jubilee Hall Market – 1 Tavistock Court, The Piazza, WC2E 8BD. ⊖Covent Garden. Stallholders sell a wide range of antiques (Mon), general goods (Tue–Fri) and handmade crafts (Sat–Sun).

Koh Samui – 65–67 Monmouth St, WC2H 9DG. ⊖Leicester Square. ☏020 7240 4280. www.kohsamui.co.uk. Closed 1 Jan. A great boutique devoted to designer favourites such as Chloe and Marc by Marc Jacobs, but also with a top selection of cutting-edge young English and European designers. Wide selection.

Monmouth Coffee House – 27 Monmouth St, WC2H 9UP. ⊖Covent Garden. ☏020 7379 3516. www.monmouthcoffee.co.uk. Closed Sun. A small shop operated by true coffee connoisseurs who will give you excellent advice on your perfect cup of java. The range of coffee changes regularly, and you can sample them on the spot.

Neal's Yard Dairy – 17 Shorts Gardens, WC2H 9AT. ⊖Covent Garden. ☏020 7240 5700. www.nealsyarddairy.co.uk. Closed Sun. This popular cheese merchant sells fabulous dairy products from the British Isles only. The house classics include Montgomery's Cheddar, Colston Bassett Stilton and Cashel Blue (a creamy Irish cheese).

Neal's Yard Remedies – 15 Neal's Yard, WC2H 9DP. ⊖Covent Garden. ☏020 7379 7222. www.nealsyardremedies.com. Established in 1981 by Romy Fraser and identifiable by its dark blue packaging, this popular brand of beauty care products and cosmetics prides itself on using only natural ingredients. Here you will find aniseed toothpaste, rosemary shampoo and all you need to make your own beauty products. There's a herbalist and homeopath; nine therapy rooms.

Paul Smith – *40–44 Floral St, WC2E 9DG. ⊖Covent Garden. ℘020 7379 7133. www.paulsmith.co.uk.* Fashion for men, women and children, designed by the man who revolutionised the British fashion world. Fans should also drop into Smith's unusual Notting Hill boutique *(122 Kensington Park Rd)* set up in a former house and designed as an exhibition hall.

Penhaligon's – *41 Wellington St, WC2E 7BN. ⊖Covent Garden. ℘020 7836 2150. www.penhaligons.com.* Perfume supplier to the aristocracy since 1870, Penhaligon counts the Royal Family among its clients. Favourite scents are "Hammam Bouquet", still made according to the original 1872 composition, or "Blenheim Bouquet", one of Churchill's favourite scents.

Crabtree & Evelyn – *Covent Garden Market, The Piazza WC2E 9RA. ⊖Covent Garden. ℘020 7836 3110. www.crabtree-evelyn.co.uk.* Classic English toiletries that evoke the feel of a genteel yesteryear, but have a modern effectiveness.

🎭 ENTERTAINMENT

Opera and Ballet Nights in the Piazza – In summer, live opera and ballet productions are broadcast from the Royal Opera House and Royal Ballet onto giant screens to enthusiastic crowds. It is a great opportunity to enjoy world-class singers and dancers in major productions in a congenial al fresco atmosphere. Enquire at the box office and check in the press and online for dates. Tickets are free but cannot be booked in advance, so be sure to get there early.

Marylebone★

The appeal of Marylebone is in the contrast between the intense activity along Oxford Street and the calm atmosphere of the dignified squares lined with attractive buildings. Famous department stores, elegant outlets along Wigmore Street and tiny shops in quaint alleyways make for a shopper's paradise. However, Marylebone has a complex identity. There are splendid 18C mansions built for high society; one now houses a famous museum (The Wallace Collection) and another is used as an exclusive club (Stratford House). Harley Street is famous as a centre of medical expertise, and cultural interest is provided by Broadcasting House, the home of the BBC, and Wigmore Hall.

A BIT OF HISTORY

The only remaining traces of St Marylebone village are Marylebone High Street and Marylebone Lane, which followed the winding course of the Tyburn River.

▷ **Location:** *Map Inside front cover (CDVX).* ⊖*Baker St; Regent's Park; Bond Street.* The main thoroughfares are Oxford Street, Wigmore Street, Portland Place and Regent Street, Baker Street and Marylebone Road.

🔎 **Don't Miss:** The Wallace Collection (see MAJOR CENTRAL LONDON MUSEUMS), the department stores on Oxford St.

🕐 **Timing:** mid-morning and mid-afternoon are the best times to shop on Oxford Street, when it is less crowded.

The land was confiscated by **Henry VIII**, who built a hunting lodge.
On old maps **Oxford Street★** appears variously as Tyburn Road, Uxbridge Road and Oxford Road. A turnpike just before the junction with Park Lane marked the western limit of what soon became London's prime shopping street.

Cavendish Square was developed early in the 18C. By the end of the century St Marylebone village and the surrounding waste land was covered by the most complete grid layout of streets in any area of London. In 1756 Marylebone Road was created to link the City directly to Paddington and west London.

⚲ WALKING TOURS
1 NORTH OF OXFORD ST★

▷ *Start from Baker St station. The Sherlock Holmes Museum (see Additional Sights) is just north of the station. Walk along Marylebone Rd past Madame Tussaud's (see Additional Sights).*

Marylebone Road is a six-lane highway, bordered by several buildings of interest. On the north side is the **Royal Academy of Music** accommodated in an attractive building (1911) in red brick and stone, with a large, elaborately decorated pediment.
Across the road is the early 19C **St Marylebone Church** by Thomas Hardwick, a large balustraded building with a three-stage tower ending in gilded caryatids upholding the cupola. The pedimented Corinthian portico was added by Nash. **Elizabeth Barrett** and **Robert Browning** were secretly married in the church in 1846. A sculptured panel commemorates **Charles Dickens**, who lived in a house on the site (*leaflet in 6 languages; ℘ 020 7563 1380; www.stmarylebone.org*).

▷ *Walk up Marylebone High St, then turn right into George St and left into Spanish Pl.*

Manchester Square
The elegant square surrounded with late Georgian houses, developed to the south of Manchester House from 1776. The house served as residence to the Spanish ambassador and then to his French counterparts (Talleyrand and Guizot, among others). In 1872 the house was bought by **Richard Wallace, Marquess of Hertford**, who

renamed it **Hertford House** and entirely remodelled it to display the **Wallace Collection**★★★ (*see MAJOR CENTRAL LONDON MUSEUMS*).

▷ *Return to George St and cross Baker St and Gloucester Place.*

On your right are two early 19C squares, **Montagu Square**, notable for its houses with shallow ground-floor bow windows – at no 39 lived the novelist Anthony **Trollope** (1873–80) – and **Bryanston Square**, graced with long stucco terraces.

▷ *Take Greater Cumberland Pl, turn left into Upper Berkeley St.*

Note, at the northwest corner of **Portman Square**★, two of the finest houses (nos 20–21) that ever graced the square. No 20 (1772–77) is by **Robert Adam**.

▷ *Right on Baker St, left on Wigmore St as far as Wimpole St (rebuilt in 20C).*

Wigmore Hall
36 Wigmore St. ℘ 020 7935 2141. www.wigmore-hall.org.uk.
The concert hall, famed for its intimate atmosphere conducive to chamber music and solo recitals, borrows its name from the street.

▷ *Turn right into Henrietta Pl.*

St Peter's
Vere Street. Open Mon–Fri 9am–5pm. Guide book. ℘ 020 7399 9555. www.licc.org.uk
This attractive small dark brick building (1721–24), designed by the architect **James Gibbs**, may have been an experimental model for St Martin-in-the-Fields (*see TRAFALGAR SQUARE*). The unexpectedly spacious interior includes galleries supported on giant Corinthian columns with massive entablatures. The quite lovely stained-glass windows were designed by Edward Coley Burne-Jones and made by William Morris & Co at their Queen's Square premises.

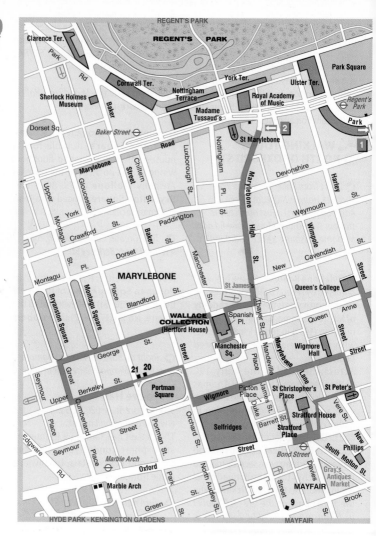

Take Marylebone Lane to Oxford St, and walk west towards Selfridges.

Stratford Place is a quiet cul-de-sac closed at its north end by **Stratford House** (now the **Oriental Club**), an imposing mansion designed in 1773 in the Palladian style.

Further on is **St Christopher's Place**, a narrow pedestrian passage restored to its Victorian appearance and well known for its outdoor cafés and its small specialist shops.

It's a great place for lunch if shopping on Oxford Street.

[2] SOUTH OF PORTLAND PLACE

Start from Regent's Park station, walking south along Portland Place.

Portland Place

In the 18C the street was a fashionable promenade; the north end was closed by gates; both sides were lined by houses designed by Robert and **James Adam**; its width was dictated by the façade of Foley House at the south end (Replaced in 1864 by the Langham Hotel). Only one **(no 46)** of the Adam

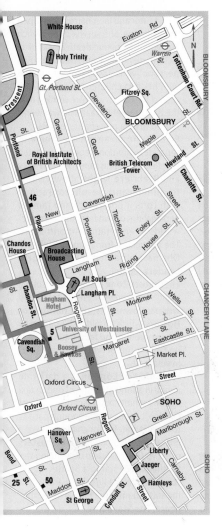

a circular portico of tall Ionic pillars, surmounted by a ring of columns supporting a fluted spire, was designed to look the same from whatever angle it was approached.

▷ *Take Portland Pl opposite.*

At the north end of **Chandos St**, facing south, stands the perfectly proportioned **Chandos House** (1771), designed by **Robert Adam**. It is built of Portland stone and the only embellishments are a narrow frieze above the second floor, the square porch and the 18C iron railings.

▷ *Turn left into Queen Anne St and into Harley St south.*

Harley Street is an architectural mixture, dating from the original Georgian to the present. The Tuscan pillared stucco portico (nos 43–49) is the entrance to **Queen's College**, the oldest English school for girls.

Before it was monopolised by the medical profession, Harley Street was home to many eminent figures, notably **Wellington** *(11)*, **Florence Nightingale** *(47)* and **Turner** *(64)*.

Cavendish Square

On the north side of the square (1717) stands a pair of stone-faced Palladian houses of the 1770s *(opposite John Lewis)*: these are now linked by a bridge designed by Louis Osman (1914–96) against which stands a moving composition of the *Madonna and Child* by **Jacob Epstein** (1950). There are late 18C and 19C houses, much altered, along the east side; no 5 was the home of Nelson in 1787. Where John Lewis, the department store, now stands used to be the house where Lord Byron was born (1788).

▷ *Turn left into Margaret St and down Regent St.*

houses has survived. The tall stone corner building (**no 66**) was erected in 1934 to celebrate the centenary of the **Royal Institute of British Architects** (RIBA). Note the distinctive curved front of **Broadcasting House,** home to BBC Radio (1931).

All Souls Church

 🕐 *Open Mon–Fri 9.30am–6pm (8pm occasionally); Sun 8am–8.30pm.* 📞 *020 7580 3522. www.allsouls.org.* The church was designed by **John Nash** as a pivot between Portland Place and Regent Street. Its unique feature,

Star-gazing at the domed Planetarium and Madame Tussaud's Waxworks

J. Malburet/MICHELIN

Oxford Street★

Oxford Street, stretching west to Marble Arch and **Hyde Park**★★★ beyond, is the main shopping centre of London with major shops including Selfridges (opened in 1908), John Lewis, House of Fraser, Debenhams and Marks and Spencer; just round the corner in Regent Street is Hamleys, the world's finest toy shop. Eastwards this major thoroughfare becomes New Oxford Street and stretches to Bloomsbury.

ADDITIONAL SIGHTS
Madame Tussaud's★

Baker Steet. Advance booking recommended, especially in high season. &O*Open Mon–Fri 9.30am–5.30pm, Sat–Sun 9am–6pm.* O*Closed 25 Dec.* &*£25–£40. Brochure (5 languages).* &*0870 400 3000. www.madame-tussauds.com.*

Marie Grosholtz (1761–1850) acquired her modelling skills from Philippe Curtius, a doctor and talented modeller who mixed with the French aristocracy. For nine years she was employed at Versailles as

an Art tutor and later narrowly escaped the guillotine. She survived the French Revolution by taking death masks of its victims, many of whom she had known personally. In 1802, she emigrated with her two children to England and toured the country before settling in at the Baker Street Bazaar. The waxworks moved to their present site in 1884.

Figures are arranged by theme in separate exhibitions regularly updated to reflect changing times. **A-List Party** and **Premiere Night** allow visitors to mingle and be photographed with contemporary rich and famous personalities drawn from the "showbiz" worlds of entertainment and sport. The politicians, from Gandhi to Barack Obama are gathered in the **World Leaders** section.

The **Culture Zone** presents some of the world's best known scientists, artists and writers. Downstairs, the **Chamber of Horrors**, which should be by-passed by the very young and faint-hearted, lines up famous murderers and serial killers in your path.

The **Spirit of London** is a dark ride *(5min)* in a simulated black London taxi cab on a whirlwind tour of the history of London, but at a gentle enough pace as to make it suitable for children.

Interactive exhibition **Music Megastars** offers you the chance to be a singing star for the day, or star in a Beatles album cover. Finish on a light note and watch the auditorium's spectacular new experience, **The Stardome**.

Sherlock Holmes Museum

O*Open daily 9.30am–6pm.* &*£6. Brochure (7 languages).* &*020 7935 8866. www.sherlock-holmes.co.uk.*

The interior of the narrow town house, built in 1815 has been arranged as described in the novels by Sir Arthur **Conan Doyle**: note in particular the familiar pipes and deerstalker hat, the magnifying glass, telescope and field-glasses, the chemical apparatus and back numbers of *The Times,* as well as photographs and paintings of the period.

Elementary My Dear Watson!

Baker Street, the wide thoroughfare, was 100 years old when **Conan Doyle** invented **221B** as the address of his famous detective **Sherlock Holmes**; 85 was then the highest number as the street was in two sections. Hansom cabs, gas lamps and fog have gone, but 221B now exists since the street was renumbered in 1930.

ADDRESSES

☼ LIGHT BITE

De Gustibus – *53 Blandford St, W1H 3AF.* ⊖*Bond Street.* ℘*020 7486 6608. www.degustibus.co.uk. Closed Sat–Sun.* Awarded by the British Baking Industry for two consecutive years, this renowned shop boasts an extensive range of freshly baked breads with Mediterranean-influenced fillings, which change daily, and other enticing snack food. Eat in the brightly decorated café, on the pavement terrace or take away.

Carluccio's – *3–5 Barrett St, St Christopher Pl, W1U 1AY.* ⊖*Bond Street.* ℘*020 7935 5927. www.carluccios.com.* Lovers of Mediterranean savours will adore this popular modern Italian deli and restaurant in a bustling square just behind Oxford Street. Full menu with good selection of classic antipasti and pastas and other traditional dishes.

The Sea Shell – *49–51 Lisson Grove, NW1 6UH.* ⊖*Marylebone.* ℘*020 7224 9000. www.seashellrestaurant.co.uk. Closed Sun.* Venture beyond the marble-tiled take-away section and take a seat in this popular fish and chip restaurant. Traditional and more adventurous seafood dishes.

The Landmark London – *222 Marylebone Rd, NW1 6JQ.* ⊖*Bond Street.* ℘*020 7631 8000. www.landmarklondon.co.uk.* At this traditional British hotel, you can take tea beneath the glass roof in the very impressive winter garden. On Sundays, brunch is served to the beat of a live jazz orchestra.

⃝ PUB

Golden Eagle – *59 Marylebone Lane, W1U 2NW.* ⊖*Marylebone.* ℘*020 7935 3228.* An old-timer traditional pub serving excellent beer.

Mayfair★

Mayfair is synonymous with elegance and luxury; Bond Street runs through the middle, agleam with handsome shop-windows full of rare and exquisite goods. There are luxurious hotels along Park Lane, which overlook the green expanse of Hyde Park. Although there are modern office buildings and the Georgian mansions are now mostly offices and embassies, the area retains its prestige with numerous art galleries, auction houses, casinos, boutiques and restaurants frequented by glamorous society people.

A BIT OF HISTORY

The name Mayfair is derived from the fair which was held annually in May until 1706. In 1735 the architect Edward Shepherd took a 999-year lease on a site just north of Piccadilly and opened a food market. Around the square and dependent streets he erected small houses, so creating Shepherd Market.

> ▷ **Location:** *Map: Inside front cover (DXY).* ⊖*Bond Street; Green Park.* Mayfair is edged by Oxford Street to the north, Regent Street to the east, Piccadilly to the south and Park Lane to the west; and bordered by two vast parks: Green Park and Hyde Park.
>
> ⊛ **Don't Miss:** Shepherd Market, the affluent atmosphere of Bond St, the secluded character of Hanover Square by contrast with bustling Oxford Street.
>
> ⊙ **Timing:** Allow half a day to stroll through Mayfair, taking in the impression of sheer luxury that pervades the area.

Large squares were the centrepiece of vast estates; elegant streets lined with Georgian mansions and houses found favour with fashionable society. Artisans' mews houses and stables have now been converted into desirable homes.

🐾 WALKING TOUR
▷ *Start in Park Lane.*

Once a winding road on the edge of **Hyde Park**, **Park Lane** is now an eight-lane highway. At the north end a few houses with graceful balconies have survived; elsewhere the town residences of local estate owners have been replaced by hotels: the **Grosvenor House** (1930), the **Dorchester** (1930), the **London Hilton** (1960s), the **InterContinental**.

▷ *Walk down Curzon St.*

Curzon Street, part residential and part commercial, is lined with 18C houses at the Park Lane end. **Disraeli** died in 1881 at no **19**. **Crewe House** (no **15**), standing back behind gates and lawns is the only surviving example of an 18C gentleman's London mansion. Built in 1730 by **Edward Shepherd** it was subsequently extended to its present seven bays with large bow-fronted wings at either end.

Shepherd Market★
A maze of alleyways and paved courts linked by archways forms the market, which contains Victorian and Edwardian pubs and houses with small shop fronts serving as pavement cafés and antique shops. It retains a village atmosphere.

▷ *Return to Curzon St and follow Chesterfield St to Charles St.*

Charles Street contains several gracious 18C houses, some remodelled in the 19C, such as no **37**; there is a small 19C–20C pub in a cobbled yard at the end.

Berkeley Square
The square, lined with 200-year-old plane trees, was laid out in 1737. On its west side a few 18C houses with ironwork balconies, lamp holders at the steps and torch snuffers survive: the façade of no **52** is in Charles Street; stone-faced and pedimented nos **46** and

KNIGHTSBRIDGE - BELGRAVIA

45 have balustraded balconies on their first floors.

▷ *Turn left into Hill St and right into Farm St.*

The **Church of the Immaculate Conception**, the 1844–49 church of the Jesuit community, has a fine high altar by **Pugin** (🕐 *open daily 7am–6.30pm;* 📞 *020 7493 7811*).

▷ *Follow South St then South Audley St on the right to Mount St.*

South Audley Street
The **Grosvenor Chapel** (1739) has a distinctive Tuscan portico, square quoined tower and octagonal turret.

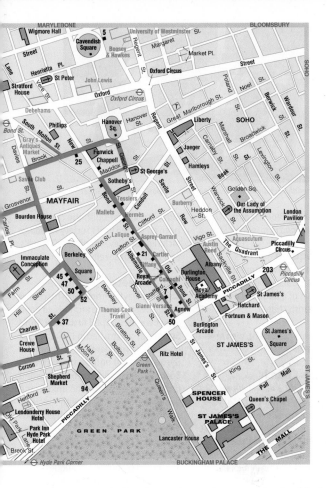

The garden became the burial ground of St George's Hanover Square (♿ see entry). 🕐 Open Mon–Fri 9.30am–1pm. 📞 020 7499 1684. www.grosvenorchapel. org.uk.

Purdeys, the gun and riflemakers at no **57**, established in 1881, bears the royal coat of arms above the door.

A leisurely air pervades **Mount Street** lined by tall, gabled terracotta brick houses of 1888 and 1893. At street level, window after window displays antique furniture, Lalique glass, porcelain, pictures and Oriental screens.

Grosvenor Square

The square (1725), one of London's largest, was redesigned in the 20C. The originally circular garden is now square with a memorial to **Franklin Roosevelt** and a monument to the RAF American squadrons. The first American resident (at no 9) was **John Adams**, the first Minister to Britain and later President. Today the neo-Georgian buildings to north, east and south are almost all US State Department offices, while the entire west side, since 1961, has been an embassy, designed by **Eero Saarinen**.

▶ Follow Grosvenor St and turn left.

Davies Street runs north from Berkeley Square to Oxford Street. At no 2 stands **Bourdon House**, built in 1723–25 as a manor-house amid fields and orchards.

Friendly exchange between Churchill and Roosevelt in Bond Street

▶ *Turn right into Brook St past Gray's Antique Market and across Bond St.*

Hanover Square

A bronze statue of **William Pitt** graces the spacious square, which was laid out c. 1715 as part of a large estate, which included a parish church.

▶ *Walk down St George St, then take Maddox St to the right.*

St George's Church

Open Mon–Fri 8.30am–3.30pm. Handel Festival (Apr–May). 020 7629 0874. www.stgeorgeshanoversquare.org. The church (1721–24) is a distinctive landmark with its portico projecting across the pavement flanked by two cast-iron game dogs. The interior is white and the reredos is from the workshop of Grinling Gibbons, framing a painting of the Last Supper by William Kent (1724).

Since it was first built, the church has been renowned for its Society Weddings including Shelley's, Benjamin Disraeli's, and Teddy Roosevelt's.

Bond Street★

Bisecting Mayfair from north to south is Bond Street. The area around Old Bond Street was developed first. **New Bond Street** was constructed in 1720 and soon boasted such residents as (Lord) Nelson, Byron, Boswell and Beau Brummell. Bond Street soon became renowned for retailing elegance, the unique and the luxurious. It is lined with specialist shops offering handmade leather goods (Hermes, Louis Vuitton, Loewe, Gucci), stationery (Smythsons), perfume and toiletries (Fenwick), antique furniture and fine art (Bond Street Antique Centre, Wildenstein, Partridge, Fine Art Society, Mallett), not forgetting haute couture (Betty Barclay, Cerruti, Louis Féraud, Guy

---

Handel in Mayfair

George Frederick Handel (1685–1759) came to England in 1711 in the wake of George IV (*see INTRODUCTION – Music and Theatre*); his Italian operas were received with great acclaim. Over a period of 18 years he wrote nearly 30 such operas and, as popularity for this genre waned, he turned to composing oratorios with as much success, setting works by Milton and Congreve – adapted by Pope and Dryden. Handel lived at **25 Brook Street** for 36 years. It was here that he composed *Messiah*. He was a practising Christian and a regular attendee at St George's. The **Handel House Museum** comprises his home and the adjoining house (no 23), once bizarrely a bolt-hole of Jimi Hendrix, with restored Georgian interiors, displays of fine and decorative arts, and biographical displays about Handel. Live concerts on Thursday evenings (*open Tue–Sat 10am–6pm (8pm Thu); Sun and bank holiday Mon noon–6pm; £5; audiotour; 020 7495 168; www.handelhouse.org).*

Laroche, Lanvin, Ballantyne, Max Mara, Valentino, Céline, Yves St Laurent).

At no 35 is **Sotheby's**, which began in 1744 as a book auctioneer and is now the biggest art auctioneer globally – the first big sale on 9 February 1798 was of Marie Antoinette's pictures. Nearby are art and antique dealers. Beyond the bronze group of Churchill and Roosevelt extends **Old Bond Street**★, lined with well-established institutions specialising in fine porcelain, jewellery and watches

(**Cartier**, **Tiffany**, **Boucheron**, **Asprey & Garrard**), Antiques and fine art (Agnew, Marlborough Fine Art, Colnaghi).

▶ *Take Royal Arcade.*

Several gracious 18C houses still survive in **Albemarle Street,** for instance no 21, which is now occupied by the **Royal Institution** (f 1799) and the **Michael Faraday Laboratory and Museum** (*℘020 7409 2992; www.rigb.org*).

ADDRESSES

✗ LIGHT BITE

Browns Hotel – *33–34 Albermarle St, W1S 4BP.* ⊖*Green Park.* ℘*020 7493 6020.* Now that Browns hotel has been refurbished, it is very elegant indeed, though still with a delightful traditional feel. Enjoy the wonderful setting and excellent afternoon tea.

The Lanesborough – *Hyde Park Corner, SW1X 7TA.* ⊖*Hyde Park Corner.* ℘*020 7259 5599. www.lanesborough. com.* Taking afternoon tea in The Conservatory by the plants and fountain is a must for all lovers of tradition.

Truc Vert – *42 North Audley St, W1K 6ZR.* ⊖*Marble Arch.* ℘*020 7491 9988. www. trucvert.co.uk.* Very classy restaurant/deli in the heart of Mayfair with a casual air and décor. Good food and particularly welcoming at breakfast for coffee and croissants or more hearty fare.

▯⏉ PUBS

The Guinea – *30 Bruton Place, W1J 6NR.* ⊖*Bond Street, Green Park.* ℘*020 7409 1728. www.theguinea.co.uk. Closed Sat– Sun.* A small and very welcoming pub with an old-fashioned charm, often used as a waiting room for the Guinea Grill restaurant in the back room.

Ye Grapes – *16 Shepherd Market, W1Y 7HU.* ⊖*Green Park, Hyde Park Corner.* ℘*020 7493 4216.* Located in the mews of Shepherd Market at the centre of Mayfair, this is a friendly pub that draws a mixed crowd. The weekends are always lively, and it is not uncommon to have to take your pint into street with you. In summer it is very busy during the week.

The Punchbowl – *41 Farm St, W1J 5RP.* ⊖*Green Park, Hyde Park Corner.* ℘*020 7493 6841.* These days The Punchbowl is most famous for being the pub bought by popstar Madonna and her ex-husband Guy Ritchie (still the owner), but this traditional pub has been slaking the thirst of the well-to-do since the 18C. The décor is dark wood panelling and the ambience upmarket. Good beer and pub food, including sausages and mash and shepherd's pie.

☺ NIGHTLIFE

Windows – *The London Hilton on Park Lane, 22 Park Lane, W1K 1BE.* ⊖*Hyde Park Corner.* ℘*020 7493 8000. www.hilton.co. uk.* One of the few London bars located high in the sky, this one is on the 28th floor of the Hilton Hotel. The décor is relatively cool but it's most worth a visit for the panoramic view over Hyde Park in the day and the lights of Knights- bridge at night.

⏊ SHOPPING

Alexander McQueen – *4–5 Old Bond St, W1S 4PD.* ⊖*Green Park.* ℘*020 7355 0088. www.alexandermcqueen.co.uk.* Originally nicknamed the "enfant terrible" of the fashion world, this stunning British designer is now a global luxury name. But dresses still astound with their brilliant tailoring and use of fabric. The place to go for a really arresting, individual look.

Bond Street – *W1.* The boutiques of international fashion designers (Cartier, Céline, Chanel, Donna Karan, Gucci, Hermès, Joseph, Louis Vuitton, Miu Miu, Polo Ralph Lauren, Prada, Ungaro, Yves Saint-Laurent) are concentrated in this major fashion street, whose parallel is Sloane Street off Knightsbridge.

Burberry – *21–23 New Bond St, W1S 2RE.* ⊖*Bond Street, Oxford Circus.* ℘*020 7968 0000. www.burberry.com.* In 1997, the somewhat stodgy English brand asked the former president of Saks in New York to give a boost to business. Rose Marie Bravo appointed talented young designers to the job of rejuvenating the brand's image.

Gieves & Hawkes – *1 Savile Row, W1S 3JR.* ⊖*Piccadilly Circus.* ℘*020 7434 2001. www.gievesandhawkes.com.* On London's premier street for gentlemen's tailoring, Gieves & Hawkes is the most famous outfitter of them all. Under the leadership of a former designer for Calvin Klein, the brand has expanded its range and now offers the British classic essentials for a man's wardrobe.

HMV – *150 Oxford St, W1D 1DJ.* ⊖*Oxford Circus.* ℘*0845 602 7800. www.hmv.co.uk.* Large music store. Impressive DVD and game console section upstairs.

Mulberry – *41–42 New Bond St, W1S 2RY.* ⊖*Bond Street.* ℘*020 7491 3900. www. mulberry.com. Closed Sun.* Established

30 years ago, this trendy establishment offers contemporary English chic. Founder Roger Saul began making leather belts on his kitchen table; now handbags and belts are the height of fashion, along with a great range of clothes and household items.

Vivienne Westwood – *44 Conduit St, W1S 2LY.* ⊖*Piccadilly Circus.* ℘*020 7924 4747. www.viviennewestwood.com. Closed Sun.* The lady known as "Queen Viv," who brought respectability to punk, still shows off her tremendous talent and extravagance, including an exquisite eye for tailoring.

South Molton Street – *W1.* An attractive pedestrian precinct lined with pavement cafés, restaurants and small fashion boutiques.

Cork Street – *W1.* The galleries offer the best in modern art.

Savile Row – *W1.* The home of tailoring businesses since the 19C, the street is lined with small custom bespoke tailors that can make you the perfect sharp suit or made-to-measure shirt, with impeccable customer service to match.

Piccadilly★

This busy thoroughfare lined with stately buildings, elegant shops and hotels is the dividing line between fashionable Mayfair and dignified St James's. To the east, Piccadilly Circus, famous for the statue of Eros and its illuminated hoardings, is a major hub and a meeting place for visitors. At the west end is the quiet elegance of Apsley House set against the luxuriant greenery of Hyde Park.

A BIT OF HISTORY

The name Piccadilly is derived from Pickadill Hall, an imposing family mansion built by a Somerset tailor who had made a fortune manufacturing frilled lace borders known as "pickadills" beloved by fashionable Elizabethans who attached them to their ruffs and cuffs.

▶ **Location:** *Map: Inside front cover (DEXY) and area map under MAYFAIR.* ⊖*Piccadilly Circus; Green Park; Hyde Park Corner.* Several thoroughfares converge on Piccadilly Circus, which is a short distance west of Leicester Square and within easy access of Soho. On the other side of Green Park are Buckingham Palace and the Mall.

⏱ **Timing:** Allow 2hr for a stroll along Piccadilly, lined with exclusive shops. Add another 1.5hr to visit one of the sights.

👥 **Kids:** The attractions inside the Trocadero in Piccadilly Circus.

WALKING TOUR
Piccadilly Circus★

The circus still draws the crowds, chiefly as the heart of nighttime London between the West End theatres, the clubs and restaurants of Soho. It was created by **John Nash** as part of his new Regent Street plan. The statue of **Eros**, officially the Angel of Christian Charity, crowns a memorial fountain erected in 1892 to the philanthropist, **Lord Shaftesbury**.

The south side of the circus is occupied by the **Criterion**, a Victorian building containing a hotel and restaurant. The 19C mosaic ceiling is still visible in the Criterion Brasserie; the **Criterion Theatre** was one of the first theatres to be lit by electricity. On the southeast corner *(at the top end of Haymarket)* stands a four horse fountain by Rudy Weller: high above, three divers reach for the sky.

The north side is taken up by the **London Pavilion**, redeveloped in the 1980s to contain shops and restaurants.

Trocadero

Open Sun–Thu 10am–midnight Fri–Sat 10am–1am. Closed 25 Dec. Charges for individual attractions. www.londontrocadero.com

A place of gentle entertainment throughout the Victorian and Edwardian eras when waltzing to Strauss was all the rage has been lavishly redeveloped to accommodate a futuractive theme park-cum-computer-age emporium of sound, virtual reality and special effects spread over seven storeys.

> Cross to the south side of Piccadilly (St James's Church is described in ST JAMES'S).

Piccadilly★

The shops here display their merchandise with flair: silk, leather, cashmere, tweed; wines and spirits, even rifles and guns. Of the most traditional establishments, it is worth noting no **203** (formerly Simpson's, now Waterstone's) for its fine, elegantly proportioned building (1935); **Hatchard's** (no **187**) established in 1797 and still trading from its original 18C building; the foody wonderland that is **Fortnum and Mason's,** founded 1707; when the clock (1964) above the Piccadilly entrance chimes the hour Mr Fortnum and Mr Mason emerge and bow to one another (see Addresses).

> Cross over to the north side.

The Albany

The harmonious building, designed by **Sir William Chambers,** is named after the Duke of Albany, George III's second son. The prince sold the 18C house to a builder who converted it into 'sets' or 'chambers for bachelors and widowers' which remain to this day. The building, as altered by Henry Holland in 1804, is in the shape of an H; the front, with a forecourt on Piccadilly, is of brick with a central pediment and porch. Its residents have included Gladstone, Byron, J B Priestley, Graham Greene. To preserve the peace, trustees rule that occupants are not allowed to whistle or keep cats, dogs or children under the age of 13!

Burlington House★

The Earl of Burlington's 17C town house was remodelled and refaced in the Palladian style (1715–16) and altered again in the 19C (twice) to its present neo-Italian Renaissance appearance.

The **Royal Academy of Arts** (see Sights) now occupies the main building on the northern side of the courtyard. Note the upper portico of giant columns and the magisterial statues decorating the façade. The adjacent wings of the complex accommodate five learned societies including the Geological Society, the Royal Astronomical Society and the Society of Antiquaries.

The **Burlington Arcade**, built in 1819 along the west side of Burlington House, is a delectable retail experience, with traditional purveyors of luxury goods: table linen, fine antique jewellery, cashmere knitwear, leather and shoes. The arcade is patrolled by beadles; the gates are closed at night and on Sundays.

▷ *Near Old Bond St (&see MAYFAIR) – cross to the south side.*

William Curtis-Green (1875–1960) designed no **160** as a car showroom (1922) for Wolseley Motors and later transformed the interior into a banking hall. The building *(now a restaurant)* is in the 'Big Bow-Wow style of Corinth USA' on the outside and inside, decked in the most sumptuous red, black and gold exotic decoration.

Ritz Hotel

The 135-bedroom hotel was opened on 24 May 1906 by César Ritz, a Swiss waiter turned entrepreneur, at the height of the Edwardian era. It was an immediate success, bordering on the decorous and the decadent! Externally, the early frame structure was fashioned to the French Classical style, while inside all was gilded Louis XVI decoration and marble. Regular patrons have included royalty (the Duke of Windsor and Wallis Simpson), the rich (Aristotle Onassis), the glamorous and showbiz (Rita Hayworth) and the plain famous (Charlie Chaplin, Winston Churchill).

Tea at the Ritz is meant to be the height of the English experience – all cucumber sandwiches, cream scones and Earl Grey, with a harpist in the corner. Book up to six weeks ahead if you wish to indulge.

▷ *Walk on past Green Park towards Hyde Park Corner.*

The west end of Piccadilly is lined by late Georgian houses occupied by a growing number of hotels following the demise of the gentleman's clubs.

No **94**, an 18C town house with a Venetian window beneath the central pediment, was formerly the residence of George IV's son, the Duke of Cambridge (1829–50), and from 1854–65 of Lord Palmerston. No 128 harbours the **Royal Air Force Club**. On the south side of Piccadilly, by the Hyde Park Corner underpass stands a **porters' rest**, a solid plank of wood at shoulder height on which porters could rest their backpacks without unloading them.

SIGHTS
Apsley House★

&(1)*Open Wed–Sun, bank holiday Mon 11am–5pm (Nov–Mar 4pm).* (1)*Closed Good Fri, May Day, 24–26 Dec, 1 Jan.* ⊜*£5.40, no charge 18 June (Waterloo Day). Audioguide (4 languages).* ℘*020 7499 5676. www.english-heritage.org. uk/apsleyhouse.*

Apsley House stands on the site of the old lodge of Hyde Park. As the first house beyond the turnpike, it became known in the 19C as no 1, London.

The present house was purchased by Wellington in 1817, having been designed nearly 40 years before by **Robert Adam** for Baron Apsley. It was subsequently altered by the duke and his architect Benjamin S Wyatt: the exterior was given a pedimented portico and refaced entirely in golden Bath stone; the interior, meanwhile, was rearranged (save the Portico and Piccadilly Drawing Room) and in 1812, extended. The transformation was such as to befit the town residence of the victorious general and national hero (later prime minister). On the ground floor it provided for the Muniment or Plate and China Room to house a priceless collection of treasures and on the floor above, the splendid Waterloo Gallery. In 1947 the 7th Duke presented the house to the nation.

Wellington Museum★ – Most of the objects displayed have significant associations with Wellington himself: orders and decorations include the silver Waterloo Medal, the first ever campaign medal, and 85 tricolours paraded on 1 June 1815 in Paris.

The museum includes his highly personal collection of objects selected as supreme examples of quality and artistry: porcelain and silver, beautiful jewellery, orders of chivalry, field marshal's batons and snuffboxes. Of the paintings by English, Spanish, Dutch and Flemish masters, more than 100 had been appropriated from the Spanish royal collection by Joseph Bonaparte and acquired from him in 1813 following the Battle of Vitoria. The chandeliers are 19C English.

Plate and China – The opulent splendour of the Egyptian (Sèvres: 1810–12), Prussian (Berlin: 1819), Saxon and Austrian porcelain services compares well with the glorious gold and silver plate (Wellington Shield, solid silver candelabra), silver and gilt services (most of several hundred pieces) that would be used for lavish celebratory banquets. Meanwhile, the rich gold, enamelled and jewelled snuffboxes evidently reflect a more personal appreciation for quality.

In the basement are displayed the **Duke's death mask**, his uniforms and garter robes, his and Napoleon's swords from Waterloo, a panorama and a programme, printed on silk, of his remarkable funeral and a commentary on his political career by newspaper cartoonists of the day (1852).

Standing in the staircase vestibule is a Carrara marble (11ft 4in/3.5m) likeness of the Emperor Napoleon Bonaparte, posed like the god Apollo, sculpted by **Canova** – not something that Wellington could very easily hide away! Other portraits of *Napoleon* by Lefèvre and Dabos, of the *Empress Josephine* and *Pauline Bonaparte* by Lefèvre hang upstairs.

Art Collection – On the first floor, the most striking room is the **Waterloo Gallery**. The early Waterloo Day (18 June) reunion dinners, with only the generals present, used to be held in the dining room; but by 1829, with Wellington now premier, the guest list had grown to such an extent that he added the gallery (90ft/27m long). This he had decorated in 18C French style, setting a fashion favoured until the end of the Edwardian era. The windows that once would have had a rural view are fitted with sliding mirrors that would have enhanced still further the already glittering gold decoration, candles, chandelier, silver centrepiece and blue-and-red uniforms with their gold buttons and braid.

The **paintings** are dominated by the portraits of Charles I after Van Dyck, and the Goya portrait of the duke himself in the standard Spanish heroic

Waterloo Gallery, Apsley House

©English Heritage Photo Library

pose on horseback – recent X-rays have revealed that it was painted somewhat prematurely and the head of Joseph Bonaparte had to be overpainted with that of the ultimate victor. Other major masterpieces hung here include works by **Murillo, Rubens,** Reynolds, Ribera, Mengs, Brueghel, **Velázquez**, notably *The Water Seller of Seville* and *A Spanish Gentleman* and the Duke's favourite, *The Agony in the Garden* by **Correggio**. Many of these were seized in 1813 from Joseph Bonaparte, who had in turn stolen them from the King of Spain.

The Yellow Drawing Room is hung with yellow damask resembling that originally in the Waterloo Gallery, while the striped drawing room is devoted to *The Battle of Waterloo* by Sir William Allan (about which the Duke commented 'Good; very good; not too much smoke').

In the Dining Room, the amazing portrait of George IV in Highland dress by Wilkie overlooks the banqueting table set with the silver centrepiece (26ft/8m) from the Portuguese service.

Royal Academy of Arts

Burlington House. &✗◷*Open daily 10am–6pm (10pm Fri), last admission 30mins before closing.* ◷*Closed 24–25 Dec. John Madejski rooms free,* ⊜*£8–£12 according to the exhibition. Restaurant. Café. Shop. Live jazz on Friday evenings in the restaurant.* ✆*020 7300 5760 (recorded information), 020 7300 8000 (switchboard). www.royalacademy.org.uk.*

The Royal Academy of Arts, founded in 1768, is the oldest fine arts institution in Britain. It is universally renowned for hosting some of the capital's finest temporary and touring exhibitions, including the annual Summer Exhibition. The light and versatile Sackler Galleries, designed by Sir **Norman Foster**, were opened in 1991 by the Queen.

The academy's treasures, on permanent display in the lavishly restored John Madeski Fine Rooms include paintings by members (Reynolds, Gainsborough, Constable, Turner), 18C furniture, Queen Victoria's paintbox, **Michelangelo**'s unfinished marble tondo of the *Madonna and Child,* and the famous copy of **Leonardo da Vinci**'s *Last Supper.*

ADDRESSES

⊗ LIGHT BITE

⊜ **The Studio Lounge** – *203 Piccadilly, at Waterstone's (5th floor), W1V 9LE.* ⊖*Piccadilly Circus.* ☎*020 7851 2400.* The Studio Lounge café, on the 5th floor of London's largest bookstore, affords far-reaching views over the rooftops of Westminster. Short eclectic menu features rare roast beef sandwiches, ciabattas and more.

⊜⊜ **Fortnum & Mason** – *Restaurants, 181 Piccadilly, W1A 1ER.* ⊖*Piccadilly Circus.* ☎*020 7734 8040. www.fortnum andmason.co.uk.* This internationally famous purveyor of fine products, established in 1707, operates several restaurants in which to savour the classic institution of afternoon tea. The lower ground floor "Fountain" and the 4th-floor "St James's" with piano music are most popular.

⊜⊜⊜ **The Ritz Restaurant** – 150 *Piccadilly, W1V 9DG.* ⊖*Green Park.* ☎*020 7493 8181. www.theritzlondon. com.* Sheer lavish opulence, the Ritz Restaurant in the legendary hotel is decorated in the style of Louis XVI, and there's always a pianist playing. The menu is traditional, try the classic Dover Sole or Chateaubriand. Jacket and tie – and reservations – required.

⊗ CAFÉS

Mô Tea Room – *23 Heddon St, W1B 4BH.* ⊖*Piccadilly Circus.* ☎*020 7434 4040. www.momoresto.com.* In this small, peaceful alley looking onto Regent's Street, Mourad Mazous's first Moroccan restaurant in London was opened in 1997. Mô, the small adjoining café invites you for a stop in North Africa, with all the trappings, such as pouffes, shining metal trays, mint tea and honey pastries in a very relaxed atmosphere.

The Ritz – *150 Piccadilly, W1J 9BR.* ⊖*Green Park.* ☎*020 7493 8181/0207 300 2345 (tea reservations). www. theritzlondon.com. Tea served daily at 11.30am, 1.30pm, 3.30pm, 5.30pm and 7.30pm (booking essential).* If you fancy joining the illustrious in the English ritual of afternoon tea – Chaplin, De Gaulle, King Edward VII – in the magical Louis XVI lounge, you must reserve your place six weeks in advance.

⊞ SHOPPING

Hatchards Booksellers – *187 Piccadilly, W1J 9LE.* ⊖*Piccadilly Circus.* ☎*020 7439 9921. www.hatchards.co.uk.* This large, traditional bookshop is the official book supplier to Her Majesty the Queen. The five floors cover all ranges except academic.

Lilywhites – *24–36 Lower Regent Street, SW1Y 4QF.* ⊖*Piccadilly Circus.* ☎*0870 333 9600.* Founded in 1863, this famous sports shop is a treasure trove of goods and clothing for every conceivable sport – from football and tennis to ski-ing, squash and rugby.

N Peal – *37 & 71–72 Burlington Arcade, W1J 0QD.* ⊖*Piccadilly Circus.* ☎*020 7499 6485. www.npeal.com. Closed Sun.* Two elegant modern boutiques (one for women, one for men) in this stately arcade selling colourful luxury goods.

Waterstone's Booksellers – *203–206 Piccadilly, W1J 6WW.* ⊖*Piccadilly Circus.* ☎*020 7851 2400. www.waterstones. co.uk.* Occupying 6 floors of an attractive listed 1930s building that was once a department store, Waterstone's is reputedly the largest bookshop in London and possibly in Europe. A good national and international press section. Pleasant café on 5th floor.

Regent's Park★★★

The harmonious composition of the park – orignally known as Marylebone Park – is a unique achievement, combining nature and artistic flair. Bounded by Regent's Canal to the north, the park is surrounded by dazzling terraces and villas.

Visitors young and old enjoy the attractions of the Zoo. The fragrant rose garden, the spirited performances at the open-air theatre and band music in the park are highlights of the summer season. The superb amenities include a boating lake and tennis courts.

A BIT OF HISTORY

The Proposal – In 1811, **Nash** was commissioned to draw up a plan to make use of former royal hunting grounds in the Marylebone area and build a direct route from north central London to Westminster. He devised a tree-landscaped park with a serpentine lake bounded by a road along which, on all except the north side, was to be left open for the view of Primrose Hill and the heights of Hampstead and Highgate. There would be a series of terrace-palaces for the noble and fashionable. Within the park would be a circus, ringed by houses; elsewhere there would be a *guinguette or* summer pavilion for the Prince of Wales, which would be approached along a wide avenue (the Broad Walk) on an axis with Portland Place. Numerous other villas were planned to nestle, half-hidden, among the trees, while the central feature would be the proposed Regent's Canal. All in all, the park would become the most exquisite garden suburb.

The Constraints – Portland Place, a most successful speculation begun by the Adam brothers in 1774, consisted of a private road lined by substantial mansions and closed at the south end by Foley House, whose owner insisted on

▶ **Location:** *Map: Inside front cover (CDV, St John's Wood: BCV, Little Venice: BVX).* ⊖*Regent's Park; Great Portland Street; Baker St.* Regent's Park can also be reached by boat or bus from Camden Town *(*⊖*Camden Town),* famous for its markets, and by boat from Little Venice *(Bloomfield Rd,* ⊖*Warwick Avenue).* To the north and west are the desirable residential areas of Primrose Hill and St John's Wood.

🕐 **Timing:** Allow half a day including 2hr at the Zoo.

👫 **Kids:** The London Zoo, with its Penguin Pool, Elephant and Rhino Pavilion and much more.

an uninterrupted view thereby dictating the street's 125ft/38m width. Between the place and park ran New Road (Marylebone Road), a psychological barrier that bisected the area into two. Portland Place, which Nash greatly admired, would be extended south across Oxford Street and Piccadilly to arrive at Carlton House. The section south of Oxford Circus would be lined with a continuous arcade of shops sheltered by colonnades with balconied houses above.

The Realisation – In essence, the plan survived. The *Guinguette*, or pleasure garden, never materialised, and nor did seven of the planned villas. However, an Inner Circle was laid out as a botanic garden, which has been transformed into the **Queen Mary's Gardens**.

The approach from Portland Place was modified to the open-armed Park Crescent and Park Square. The extension south from Portland Place was given a pivoted turn by the construction of the circular porch of All Souls, and the angle at the south beautifully swept round by means of the Quadrant. The

117

project took eight years to achieve (1817–25). New Street, as it was called at first, was a fashionable success; the houses along the park were snapped up. Nash himself probably designed only a few of the terraces★★, houses and shops, but he set the style sufficiently explicitly for different architects to draw up plans. Giant columns, generally Ionic or Corinthian, are used throughout to articulate the centre and ends of the long façades which, in addition, were usually advanced and sometimes pedimented. Columns of a different order formed arcades; balustrades and continuous first floor balconies of iron or stucco ran the length of the long fronts uniting them into single compositions. In 1828 **London Zoo**★★ opened on the north side of the Park beside the canal.

🐾 WALKING TOUR
Terraces★★

▷ *Start from Regent's Park Station and walk round clockwise.*

The **terraces** are named after the titles of some of George III's 15 children. **Park Crescent** (1821) is characterised by paired Ionic columns in a continuous porch, a balustrade and a balcony which emphasise the classical curve of the Crescent. The **East and West** (1823–24) buildings which flank **Park Square** are embellished by single Ionic columns. Beyond Ulster Terrace lies **York Terrace** (1821; west end now named **Nottingham Terrace**), which is 360yd/329m long or nearly half the width of the park, comprises two symmetrical blocks, York Gate in the axis of St Marylebone Church (⌖*see MARYLEBONE*) and some detached houses.

The attractive **Cornwall Terrace** (1822) has a 187yd/170m front that is marked at either end and in the centre by Corinthian columns and divided into a number of receding planes. Note the lodge with rounded windows and pitched slate roof.

Clarence Terrace (1823) boasts a heavily accented Corinthian centre and angles above an Ionic arcade.

Notable features of **Sussex Place** (1822; **London Graduate School of Business Studies**) include the most surprising, finialled, slim, octagonal cupolas, in pairs, crowning the ends and framing the pedimented centre of the façade.

Hanover Terrace (1822–23) is marked by pediments coloured bright blue as a background to plasterwork and serving as pedestals for statuary silhouetted against the sky. Hanover Gate has a small, octagonal lodge with heavy inverted corbel decoration and niches with statues beneath a pitched slate roof and central octagonal chimney.

The **Mosque** (1977), marked by its minaret (140ft/43m high), white with a small gold coloured dome and finial crescent, stands on the site of one of Nash's villas (Albany Cottage) and was designed by **Sir Frederick Gibberd**. Other new buildings accommodate a school and the Islamic Cultural Centre. **Hanover Lodge,** one of the 18C villas, has a large modern brick addition; note the row of three modern villas alongside and, across the Outer Circle, a neo-Georgian house (1936), **Winfield House**, now the residence of the US ambassador.

The **boating lake**, which curves picturesquely around the Inner Circle, is a popular spot for sport and recreation. There are boats and deckchairs for hire and band music in the summer.

Inner Circle

The **Open Air Theatre** (📞*0844 826 4242; www.openairtheatre.org)* presents a summer season of open-air performances of plays by Shakespeare and other playwrights, and popular musicals. **The Holme** is one of the 18C villas. **Regent's College** is on the site of South Villa and St John's Lodge, rebuilt and enlarged last century in red brick. **Queen Mary's Gardens** were created out of the original Botanic Garden and are a delightful haven. The Rose Garden, filled with heady perfumes in summer, is very romantic.

▷ *Take Chester Rd and walk south down the Broad Walk to the Outer Circle.*

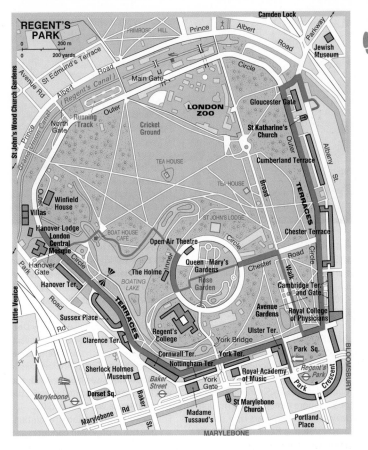

REGENT'S PARK

0   200 m

0   200 yards

Outer Circle

The southern section of the park is flanked by the **Avenue Gardens**, which have been relaid according to the designs prepared by William Andrews Nesfield in 1862. A tesserae-faced building by Denys Lasdun extending squarely forward is the home of the **Royal College of Physicians** (1964).

Cambridge Gate (1875) is a totally Victorian, stone-faced block with pavilion roofs; the adjacent **Cambridge Terrace**, dating from 1825, has been restored.

The longest unbroken façade (313yds/286m) of **Chester Terrace** (1825) has Corinthian columns rising from ground level to emphasise the ends, centre and mid-points between; at either end triumphal, named, arches lead to the access road to the rear.

The Ionic pillars of the façade (267yd/242m long) of **Cumberland Terrace** (1826) recur in the intervening arches. Britannia, science and the arts are represented in the central pediment behind squat vases.

Angle pediments with plasterwork against red-painted tympana and surmounting statues mark the main terrace of **Gloucester Gate** (1827).

▷ *Pass through the gate and make a short detour to Albany St.*

Park Village West – *Albany Street.* This is the most attractive of the two dependent streets to the terraces. The small houses and modest terraces are in Nash's country cottage style, although not designed by him.

Cumberland Terrace

K. Brett/MICHELIN

👤👤 LONDON ZOO★★

🍴🅿♿🕐 *Open daily 13–Feb–17-Jul and 7 Sept–24 Oct 10am–5.30pm; 18 Jul–6 Sept until 6pm; 25 Oct–1 Nov until 4.30pm; 2 Nov–12 Feb until 4pm.10am–5.30pm (4pm Nov–Feb), last admission 1hr before closing.* 🕐*Closed 25 Dec.* 👓*£16.80; child £13.30. Restaurant, refreshments.* 📞*020 7722 3333. www.zsl.org/zsl-london-zoo.*

The Zoological Society of London, founded in 1826 by Sir Stamford Raffles (of Singapore fame) and Sir Humphry Davy, opened two years later on a site (5 acres/2ha) in Regent's Park with a small collection of animals looked after by a keeper in a top hat and striped waistcoat.

The first big cats came from the menagerie at the Tower of London (closed by William IV); the first giraffes, unloaded in the Docklands, were led through the City to Regent's Park (May 1836). During World War II, the most dangerous animals were destroyed in case the zoo was bombed.

Today, the zoo's objective is to conserve and breed endangered species and research the biology of rare animals. A large proportion of the animals are bred in Regent's Park or at Whipsnade Wild Animal Park.

The zoo gardens were laid out by **Decimus Burton**, who also designed several buildings – of which the Ravens' Cage, Clock Tower and East Tunnel remain.

The **Aquarium**, was built in 1853, and was the first of its kind in the world; the **Reptile House** was built in 1902.

Following Hamburg Zoo's revolutionary practice of providing paddocks and surrounding enclosures with moats and ditches, the **Mappin Terraces** were built in London (1914) and Whipsnade created on derelict Bedfordshire farmland (1931). The Zoo has commissioned some innovative architecture. Berthold Lubetkin designed the original Great Apes Breeding Colony (1933), the primates are now housed in the new £5.3m **Gorilla Kingdom**. He also designed the **Penguin Pool** (1934) with its intersecting

TOURING TIP: ACTIVITIES

The programme of **daily events** includes animal **feeding times**, bath time for the elephants, animals in the **Amphitheatre** and **animal encounters** in which the keepers introduce the animals in their charge. The Society's latest conservation, scientific and veterinary work is presented in the **Lifewatch Centre**, where the **London Zoo Experience** brings the history of the zoo to life. The **Discovery Centre** enables visitors "to walk like a camel, hear like an elephant, fly like a bird and see like a giraffe."

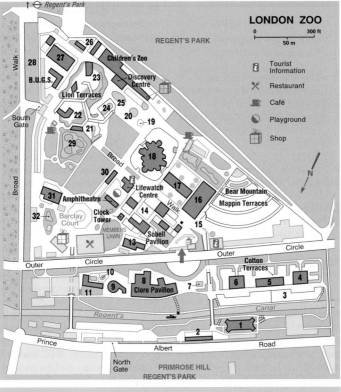

LONDON ZOO

0	300 ft
50 m	

i — Tourist Information
✕ — Restaurant
☕ — Café
◐ — Playground
🎁 — Shop

REGENT'S PARK

Regent's Park

26
28
27
Children's Zoo
B.U.G.S.
23
Discovery Centre
Lion Terraces
25
22
24
20 — 19
21
29
Broad
18
30
Lifewatch Centre
17
Amphitheatre
31
16
Bear Mountain
Mappin Terraces
32
Barclay Court
Clock Tower
14
MEMBERS LAWN
15
13
Sobell Pavilion
Outer
Circle
Outer
Circle
Cotton Terraces
10
8
Clore Pavilion
7
6
5
4
11
9
3
Regent's
Canal
2
Prince
Albert
Road
North Gate
PRIMROSE HILL
REGENT'S PARK
South Gate
Broad
Walk
1
Snowdon Aviary

REGENT'S PARK-LONDON ZOO					
		Camels	19	Reptiles	16
		Flamingos, Pelicans	29	Reptiliary (summer only)	7
African Bird Safari	17	Gibbons	30	Small mammals	8
Anoa, Okapi	5	Giraffe, Zebra	4	Snowdon Aviary	1
Anteaters	28	Gorilla Kingdom	14	Spider Monkeys	22
Aquarium	15	Invertebrates	11	Tapirs	6
Arabian Oryx	3	Lions	23	Tigers	21
Birds	20	Lubertkin Pool	25	Vultures	13
Blackburn Pavilion		Meerkats	9	Water birds	24
(Exotic birds)	27	Meet the Monkeys	26	Zoo World	18
B.U.G.S!	33	Otters	10	*Children's Zoo on map is now	
Butterfly Paradise	31	Owls	2	called Animal Adventure	
		Penguins	32		

spiral ramps, the first example of such use of pre-stressed concrete (birds now housed elsewhere).

Popular zoo exhibits include **Into Africa**, with giraffes, zebras, camels, horses, cattle and antelope. The zoo's elephants have now been transferred to Whipsnade.

The **Lion Terraces**, planted with trees and bushes from which the big cats survey lesser mortals, date from 1976.

At the other end of the food chain, domestic animals are presented at close quarters in the revamped children's zoo, **Animal Adventure**, which also has underground and water zones. Children love the high jinks in the **Meet the Monkeys** area and the **Meerkats**, next to the **Clore Rainforest Lookout**, a South American rainforest through which visitors can wander at canopy and floor level.

The **B.U.G.S** exhibit is devoted to biodiversity and conservation of invertebrates. Other recent additions include two walk-through exhibits; the **Butterfly Paradise**, with clouds of free-flying butterfly species, and the tropical birds

A Valued Trophy

The Ashes urn contains the ashes of a pair of wicket bails. It is competed for in a series of test matches biennially between Australia and England but remains at Lord's irrespective of the winner. It was first awarded to the England's Hon Ivo Bligh in 1883.

in the restored Victorian bird house, the **Blackburn Pavilion**.

Danish Church

Open Tue–Fri 9am–1pm, 6.30–9pm (except Fri), Sat–Sun noon–5pm. Keys available at 5 St Katherine's Precinct, Regents Park. 020 7935 7584. www.danskekirke.org.
The neo-Gothic church (1829) in stock brick, built for the **St Katharine Royal Hospital Community** (*see Suburbs: DOCKLANDS*), was taken over in 1950 by the Danish community, whose own building in Limehouse had been bombed. Inside are a coffered ceiling and, beside the modern fittings, John the Baptist and Moses, two of the four figures carved in wood by the 17C Danish sculptor **Caius Cibber** for Limehouse. Outside to the right is a replica of the Jelling Stone.

EXCURSIONS
ST JOHN'S WOOD

West of Regent's park (take Park Rd and St John's Wood Rd).

It developed rapidly in the first half of the 19C as a residential district following the expansion of Marylebone and Nash's development of Regent's Park. Its rural character was swept aside as Italian type villas, broad-eaved and often in pairs, were erected.
As it was within three miles of the City and Westminster, it was a perfect place for wealthy Victorians resident in Belgravia to keep their mistresses; by 1824 a colony of artists had begun to gather.

St John's Wood Church

Lord's Roundabout. Open daily 9am–5pm. Concerts. 020 7586 3864.
The church is of the same date, 1813, and by the same architect, **Thomas Hardwick**, as **St Marylebone** Parish Church (*see MARYLEBONE*) and, like it, has a distinctive, cupola-topped turret.

Lord's Cricket Ground

St John's Wood Road. Guided tour (including museum) Mon–Sun at noon and 2pm, Sat and Sun also at 10am. Telephone for exact schedule. Closed during test matches, cup finals, preparation days and certain public holidays. £14. Museum only: Open match days to match ticket holders only. 020 7616 8500/8656. www.lords.org.
Marylebone Cricket Club, which owns Lord's Cricket Ground, began life in 1787, and is now a private members' club. The best introduction to the ground is by guided tour through the famous Long Room in the Pavilion, the "real" tennis court, the adjacent **MCC Museum** founded in memory of all the cricketers who lost their lives in World War I and that displays the famous **Ashes**, portraits and cartoons, cricketing dress, memorabilia from batting lists to snuff boxes, the Lord's shop and the award-winning Mound Stand. The Library is perhaps the world's most important Cricket archive.
The first match MCC played at the original Lord's ground (Dorset Fields) was against Essex on 1 June 1787. The present ground was inaugurated with a match against Herts on 22 June 1814. The first test matches at Lord's were played in 1884. The main gates were erected in memory of **Dr WG Grace** (d. 1915) in 1923; Father Time, removing the bails, was placed on the grandstand in 1926.
The much acclaimed **Mound Stand** combines various building techniques used between 1898 and 1987. The futuristic design of the Media Centre (1999), an elliptical aluminium structure, breaks new ground.
Just around the corner from Lord's and up Grove End Road beyond the junction

with **Abbey Road** is the particular zebra crossing immortalised by the Beatles album called Abbey Road and recorded at the EMI studios nearby. Nostalgic fans continue to come here to read the penned inscriptions and graffiti.

LITTLE VENICE

Bloomfield Rd west of Edgware Rd.
The attractive triangular canal basin, shaded by weeping willows and over-looked by Georgian houses, modern flats and the Canal Office (formerly a toll house) is known as Little Venice.
For canal cruises and the Waterbus, see Planning Your Trip. The canal linking the Grand Junction Canal (from Brentford to Uxbridge) to Paddington was built between 1795 and 1801.
The **Regent's Canal** *(towpath Open 9am–dusk)*, begun in 1812, runs for 8mi/13km from Little Venice to Lime-house docks and the Lee Valley (*see DOCKLANDS*), passing through Maida Tunnel – where the boat crews legged

Picturesque houseboats moored on the Regent's Canal at Little Venice

A. Taverner/MICHELIN

their barges along lying on their sides or backs and pushing against the tunnel roof with their feet, under Macclesfield Bridge, between the animal houses of London Zoo, through **Camden Lock** and on to Islington Tunnel. A flight of 12 locks carries the canal down 86ft/26m to the Thames.

Soho★

Soho is the beating heart of the West End, one of the greatest theatre centres in the world ("Theatreland"). By day it is the hub of London's crea-tive advertising and film industry: by night the place takes on new life as lights flicker in the windows of the various clubs, bars, restaurants (French, Italian, Greek and Chinese), jazz venues, nightclubs, cinemas and theatres, thronged with night owls. Soho has its louche side, with risqué shows and shops, but it has a solid core of loyal residents among its otherwise transient population; its Bohemian appeal has always attracted artists, writers and foreign immigrants. Soho is the centre of the book trade with famous bookshops lining Charing Cross Road, immor-talised in Helene Hanff's novel *84 Charing Cross Road*. Centred on Ger-rard Street, just north of Leicester Square, is London's Chinatown.

> ▶ **Location:** *Map Inside front cover (DEX).* ⊖*Leicester Square; Piccadilly Circus; Tottenham Court Road.* Extending north from Piccadilly Circus and Leicester Square, the area is bounded by Oxford Street, Charing Cross Road, Regent St and is to the west of Covent Garden. It is London's theatre and cinema heartland.

> ⊙ **Timing:** You can spend anything from 1hr to a day here. Window-shop along stylish Regent St then make your way to Soho in the early evening where you can: have a meal in Chinatown, see a film or a play, or just join the crowd in one of the many bars and clubs.

A Roll-Call of Luminaries

William Blake was born in Soho (1757), Hazlitt died there (1830); Edmund Burke, Sarah Siddons, Dryden, Sheraton lived there; Marx, Engels, Canaletto, Haydn lodged there; Mendelssohn and Chopin gave recitals at the 18C house in Meard Street of Vincent Novello, father of Ivor and founder of the music publishers. John Logie Baird (1888–1946) first demonstrated television in Frith Street in 1926.

A BIT OF HISTORY

In the Middle Ages Soho was a chase, named after the cry of the Medieval hunt, which was often found in the vicinity of St Giles-in-the-Fields (see COVENT GARDEN).

Street names (Brewer St, Glasshouse St) reflect the area's early activities. By the mid-19C (after a fashionable spell in the 17C–18C), Soho included the worst slums in the capital. The building of Regent Street divided the West End from its disreputable neighbour and two new streets were built to penetrate the foetid tangle: Charing Cross Road (1880) and Shaftesbury Avenue (1886).

People of All Nations – Refugees began to arrive in the 17C: Greeks fleeing the Ottoman Turks; persecuted Huguenots after the revocation of the Edict of Nantes (1685); Frenchmen hounded by the Revolution and later by political changes – these established French restaurants and cafés (**Wheeler's** at 19 Old Compton Street, founded by Napoleon III's chef; the **York Minster** pub at 49 Dean Street). Waves of Swiss, Italian and Spanish immigrants followed. Then came the Chinese from Hong Kong, Singapore and the docks to transform Gerrard Street into a **Chinatown**★.

Commerce – The southern end of Shaftesbury Avenue is known for its theatres; the area around Golden Square is dominated by the film industry, television production companies, cinema advertisers, photographers; sleazy parts boast peep-shows and sex shops below lurid neon signs; this is also the home of London's mainstream jazz

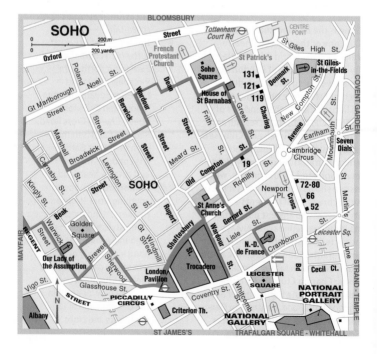

scene – instruments, specialist music shops and clubs pepper Shaftesbury Avenue, Charing Cross Road, and Denmark Street.

☜ WALKING TOUR
Leicester Square★
The square, now a pedestrian precinct surrounded by cinemas and eating houses, is one of the busiest meeting places in London, with some 22 million visitors each year. At the centre stands the Shakespeare Memorial Fountain (1874) facing a statue of **Charlie Chaplin** *(north side)* by John Doubleday (1980), while around the railings sit busts of famous local residents – Reynolds, Newton, Hunter, Hogarth; panels tell the history of the square from Leicester Fields to the building of the **Empire**. Around the edge of the central gardens the **handprints** of many famous actors and movie stars are set into the pavement. The square is also a traditional site for royal and red-carpet premieres, where film stars meet, greet and pose for assembled crowds of onlookers.

On the south side of the central garden is the popular **Half-Price Ticket Booth** (☾ *see YOUR STAY IN THE CITY – Entertainment, Theatre*).

▷ *Cross Cranbourn St to Leicester Pl.*

Inside the circular Roman Catholic church of **Notre-Dame de France**, an Aubusson tapestry hangs above the altar; mosaic ornaments and paintings by Jean Cocteau on the walls (☾ *open daily 9.30am–8pm; brochure (2 languages); ℘020 7437 9363; www. notredamechurch.co.uk*).

▷ *Turn right into Lisle St, then left into Newport Pl to Gerrard St.*

Chinatown★
Gerrard Street is the centre of this colourful area marked by oriental gates, which abounds in restaurants, supermarkets selling exotic foodstuffs, oriental medicine centres etc. It is the scene of great festivities at Chinese New Year (a moveable feast in Jan or Feb) celebrated in traditional and colourful fashion.

▷ *Walk up Gerrard Pl; across Shaftesbury Ave; up Dean St to Old Compton St.*

Old Compton Street, at the heart of Soho, is lined with pubs, eating places, wine merchants, pastry shops, Italianfoodstores, and frequented by a spirited gay crowd.

▷ *Proceed east; left on Greek St.*

House of St Barnabas
1 Greek Street. ☾*Check times before visiting.* ☾*Closed Easter and Christmas.* ☜*Donation appreciated.* ℘*020 7437 1894. www.hosb.org.uk.*
The House of Charity was built c. 1750. The exterior is plain except for two obelisks at the entrance; the interior, one of the finest in Soho, has beautiful plasterwork ceilings and walls, and an unusual crinoline staircase. The proportions of the small chapel, built in 1863 in 13C French Gothic style, are unique.

Soho Square
The pleasant square laid out in 1680 between Greek Street and Frith Street, is adorned by a fountain topped by a statue of Charles II. Two churches stand to the east and north-west.

▷ *Leave by Carlisle St, cross Dean St, continue to Great Chapel St and turn left into Sheraton St to Wardour St.*

Wardour Street and its immediate vicinity (Beak Street, Dean Street and Soho Square) conjure up the **film industry** from the creators of blockbuster movies and catchy commercials.

▷ *Walk south and turn right into Broadwick St, cutting across Berwick St.*

Many of the houses along Berwick Street are 18C. The **Berwick Street Market**,

Mock Tudor façade of Liberty

©Kate Duffell/Bigstockphoto.com

which dates from 1778, is one of the finest fresh produce markets in central London; the surrounding shops include Aladdin's caves of extravagant fabrics used by couturier designers and the frills and fantasy of theatrical costumiers.

▷ *Continue to Carnaby St.*

The largely pedestrianised area in and around **Carnaby St**, which was a high spot of the Swinging Sixties, has now reinvented itself as a centre of stylish shops, trendy bars, eateries and clubs.

▷ *Walk up to Great Marlborough St and turn left towards Regent St (for the beginning of Regent St, see map under MARYLEBONE).*

Regent Street★★

Liberty, Jaeger, Hamleys Toy Shop, Aquascutum, the Café Royal and Austin Reed all line this elegant street sweeping southwards to Piccadilly Circus and the heart of the West End.

Liberty★★ (see Addresses) was founded by Arthur Liberty in 1875. It soon acquired the dignified title of "Emporium" stocking broad ranges of exotic silks imported from the East, Japanese porcelain, wallpapers and fans, and became associated with the Aesthetic Movement. Furniture, made in workshops in Soho, supplemented the imported ranges. Own brand fabrics were made to different weights after traditional Indian prints and from designs by artists sympathetic to the Aesthetic and Arts and Crafts movements.

The Liberty jewellery came from the Continent, where art nouveau was flourishing and from where furniture was imported. The success of the art nouveau style lasted until the outbreak of war in 1914, after which furniture manufacture reverted to Queen Anne and Tudor styles. Liberty fabrics and jewellery, however, continue much in the same traditional vein.

Note the splendid **pediment** on the Regent Street façade. The **Tudor Building** (1922–24) in Great Marlborough Street was built from timbers taken from the Royal Navy's last two sailing ships.

▷ *Proceed down Regent St, turn left into Beak St and right into Warwick St.*

Tucked away off Regent Street, stands **Our Lady of the Assumption,** a plain church (1788) with only a pediment as decoration (Open daily 7am (10am Sat-Sun) to 6pm; 020 7437 1525).

▶ *Turn left into Brewer St and left again into Lower John St.*

The attractive **Golden square** with gardens enclosed by railings is the preserve of the media and fashion industries.

ADDRESSES

✗ LIGHT BITE

🍴 **Bar Italia** – *22 Frith St, W1D 4RT.* ⊖*Leicester Square.* ✆*020 7437 4520. www.baritaliasoho.co.uk.* Open round the clock. Regulars and visitors of all styles spill onto the pavement terrace sipping first-rate espresso or munching a filled ciabatta. It's all old-fashioned Italian: note the poster of Rocky Marciano behind the counter.

🍴 **Busaba Eathai** – *106–110 Wardour St, W1F 0TR.* ⊖*Tottenham Court Road.* ✆*020 7255 8686. www.busaba.com.* Great ambience, sharing tables and good value Thai food in a buzzing atmosphere. No booking, but you'll have to queue to get in and have a quick bite.

🍴 **Café Bohème** – *13–17 Old Compton St, W1D 5JQ.* ⊖*Leicester Square.* ✆*020 7734 0623. www.cafeboheme.co.uk.* A friendly place for a snack or a larger meal, in the very heart of Soho. The small bar gets very busy at weekends, when there is also live jazz.

🍴 **Wagamama** – *10A Lexington St, W1F 0LD.* ⊖*Piccadilly Circus.* ✆*020 7292 0990. www.wagamama.com.* Despite its success, this stylish Asian eaterie serves some of London's best fast food. It's healthy, cheap and delicious. Don't be discouraged by the long queues; the friendly and efficient service keeps things moving. A good choice for families. Other central locations: Harvey Nichols (👜*see KNIGHTSBRIDGE*), 1 Tavistock St (👜*see COVENT GARDEN*) and 4 Streatham St in Bloomsbury.

🍴 **French House** – *49 Dean St, W1D 5BE.* ⊖*Leicester Square.* ✆*020 7437 2477. www.frenchhousesoho.com.* This true Parisian bistro was founded at the beginning of the 20C. During the war, De Gaulle made it the Free France House. Maurice Chevalier, George Carpentier and Salvador Dalí were all regular customers. Now under British management, it is a popular haunt for a mixed crowd of regulars and tourists. Lively atmosphere.

🍴 **L'Escargot** – *48 Greek St, W1D 4EF.* ⊖*Leicester Square.* ✆*020 7437 6828. wwwlescargotrestaurant.co.uk.* Opened in the 1920s, this classic Soho restaurant is usually busy early in the evening with pre-theatre goers. The menu is upmarket and elaborate; expect luxury ingredients such as seared scallops and smoked foie gras, and the eponymous snail is usually found in one guise or another on it.

🍺 PUB

Argyll Arms – *18 Argyll St, W1F 7TP.* ⊖*Oxford Circus.* ✆*020 7734 6117.* Almost 300 years old, this popular two-floored pub is a typical Victorian gin palace with decorative mirrors.

☕ NIGHTLIFE

Lab – *12 Old Compton St, W1D 4TQ.* ⊖*Leicester Square; Tottenham Court Road.* ✆*020 7437 7820. www.lab-town-house.com.* The Lab has a reputation for original cocktails prepared by true specialists. Sit back and enjoy them in a 1970s leather and Formica atmosphere, spread over two floors (look out for the transparent glass floor). Young and mixed crowd in the heart of London's gay area.

🛒 SHOPPING

Algerian Coffee Stores – *52 Old Compton St, W1D 4PD .* ⊖*Leicester Square.* ✆*020 7437 2480. www.algcoffee. co.uk. Closed Sun.* The name honours the first foreign owners, who opened the shop in 1887. Choose from 100 different types of the best coffee and 140 types of tea, not to mention the designer teapots and coffee makers.

Berwick Street – *W1.* ⊖*Piccadilly Circus.* Lively Berwick Street is reputed for its fruit market and specialist record shops (vintage, old and new), particularly the famous Reckless Records at nos 26 and 30. Also check out the two great fabric shops at nos 14 and 16.

Berwick Street Cloth Shop – *14 Berwick St, W1F 0PP.* ⊖*Tottenham Court Road.* ℘*020 7287 2881. Closed Sun.* A treasure trove for fabric enthusiasts, stocked with unusual fabrics, from silks, and organzas, to leather, lycra and faux fur.

Borders Books & Music – *120 Charing Cross Rd, WC2H 0JR .* ⊖*Tottenham Court Road.* ℘*020 7379 8877. www.borders. co.uk.* A large book-shop owned by an American chain, with more than 150 publications, magazines and a café.

Foyles – *113–119 Charing Cross Rd, WC2H 0EB.* ⊖*Tottenham Court Road.* ℘*020 7437 5660. www.foyles.co.uk.* The world's greatest bookshop celebrated its centenary in 2003 with a massive refurbishment, but still specialises in rare books while maintaining a comprehensive general list. It has become an institution, famous for its past eccentric practices and its continuing stimulating literary lunches.

Hamleys – *188–196 Regent St, W1R 6BT.* ⊖*Oxford Circus.* ℘*0870 333 2455. www. hamleys.co.uk.* London's largest toy kingdom, occupying seven floors with wonders such as teddy bears, electric trains and the latest electronic games.

Heals– *196 Tottenham Court Road, W1 7LQ.* ⊖*Tottenham Court Road.* ℘*020 7636 1666. www.heals.co.uk.* This landmark building houses three floors of classic and contemporary home furnishings and designer decoration.

Liberty★★– *Regent Street, W1B 5AH.* ⊖*Oxford Circus.* ℘*020 7734 1234. www.liberty.co.uk.* A fabulous emporium of luxury design, this classic department store has been a favourite with fashionable Londoners since it opened in 1875. Established and avant-garde designers rub shoulders on the racks here. Take time to explore the great toiletries section on the ground floor, which stocks unusual, exclusive and small-name brands beloved of high-fashion magazines such as Vogue.

Milroy's of Soho – *3 Greek St, W1V 6NX.* ⊖*Leicester Square.* ℘*020 7437 2385. www.milroys.co.uk. Closed Sun.* London's most reputed whisky shop with some 700 malt whiskies and many international whiskies as well as bottles for collectors. They run whisky and wine tastings in the cellar below.

Ray's Jazz Shop at Foyles – *113–119 Charing Cross Rd, WC2H 0EB.* ⊖*Tottenham Court Road.* ℘*020 7437 5660. Closed 25–26 Dec.* Popular with jazz fans, Ray's has diversified into blues, folk recordings and world music. Lunchtime and evening events and talks.

St James's★★

St James's is one of London's most exclusive addresses. This elegant area is home to a royal palace and garden, dignified mansions used as royal residences or for official functions, gentlemen's clubs, specialist shops, and theatres. Wander through the warren of alleyways to discover traditional pubs, or pause with office workers lounging on the grass or in deckchairs (for hire).

▷ **Location:** *Map: Inside front cover (DEXY).* ⊖*Piccadilly Circus; Green Park.* The area is hemmed in by Piccadilly, Haymarket and the Mall; Trafalgar Square and Leicester Square are to the east, Mayfair and Belgravia to the west.

⊙ **Don't Miss:** The passages linking King Street and Pall Mall.

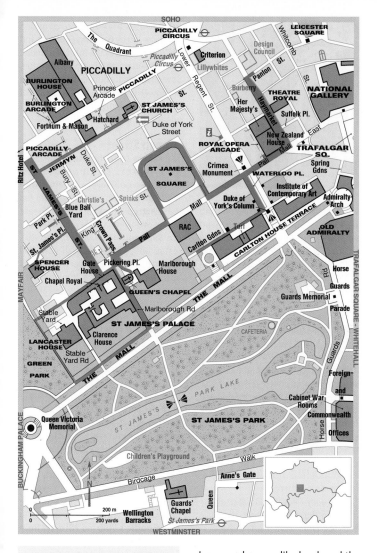

🕐 **Timing**: Allow half a day to stroll through the streets lined with historic mansions and window-shop along St James's St and Jermyn St.

A BIT OF HISTORY

Henry VIII built a palace on the grounds of a former lepers' hospital dedicated to St James the Less of Jerusalem.

The domain was given by Charles II at the Restoration to his loyal courtier, Henry Jermyn, who speedily developed the empty fields into an elegant suburb for members of the re-established court. The founder of the West End, as he has since been described, laid out his estate around a square: to the east was a large market bordered by the Haymarket, to the north lay Jermyn Street, the local shopping street, and in the axis of Duke of York Street stood the church.

At the end of the Stuart monarchy, vacated private houses were taken over by the clubs. The latter had originated in taverns and coffee and chocolate houses

Piccadilly Arcade

D. Chapuis/Michelin

which they finally took over, employing the owner or publican as manager and enhancing the amenities, particularly the food for which many became famous. Numbers grew until by the turn of the 20C there were nearly 200 in the West End; now there are fewer than 30, including eight in St James's St and five in Pall Mall. Their character has also changed from 18C flamboyance, to 19C silence and reserve and now to a modified social function or gaming.

St James's has remained a masculine world of bespoke boot and shoemakers, shirtmakers and hatters, sword, gun and rod makers, antique and 18C picture dealers, wine merchants, cheese vendors, jewellers traditional and modern, fine art auctioneers.

⚓ WALKING TOUR
St James's Church★

🕙Open daily. Recitals: Mon, Wed, Fri at 1.10pm Thu–Sat at 7.30pm. Market: Wed–Sat, 11am–6pm (craft market only), Tue 10am–6pm (antiques also). Lectures, seminars. ℘020 7734 4511. www.st-james-piccadilly.org.

The new parish church designed by Wren in 1676 was a plain basilica of brick with Portland stone dressings and balustrade and a square tower. Plain glass windows line the north and south walls and a Venetian window fills the east end. In the 19C new entrances were made on both sides of the tower.

The galleried interior is roofed with a barrel vault with stucco ornamentation. The organ was donated by Queen Mary, the daughter of James II; its case is

original as is the altarpiece of gilded wood carved by **Grinling Gibbons** and the marble font in the form of a tree of life with Adam and Eve on either side. Several artists are buried here (plaque in vestibule) in what is the parish church of the Royal Academy. The outdoor pulpit against the north wall is from 1902.

Jermyn Street★

The narrow street boasts shirtmakers, pipe makers, antique dealers, antiquarian booksellers, a chemist with real sponges, a provision merchant (no 93) selling countless varieties of cheese over a wooden counter, a perfumer (no 89), modern jewellery (no 80), restaurants (including Wall's original sausage shop, no 113), bars, chambers and the Cavendish, a luxury hotel, on the site of the famous Edwardian rendezvous.

Piccadilly Arcade★, bright with bow-fronted shops, links Piccadilly to Jermyn Street.

St James's Street★

This street was lined with town houses by the end of the 17C, including those of merchants who fled the City after the **Plague** and Great Fire (1665–1666). It retains an atmosphere of quiet elegance with shops, restaurants and clubs.

The most famous buildings (from north to south) include: **White's Club** (no **37**), established in 1693, is the oldest London club and Tory in character; the famous bow window was added in 1811. **Boodle's Club** (no **28**) dates from 1762 and the building from 1765. **The Economist** (no **25**) complex consists of three canted glass towers around a courtyard (1966–68). **Brooks's Club** (no **60** – opposite The Economist) was founded as the rival Whig club to White's in 1764. The house was designed by **Henry Holland,** Robert Adam's rival, in 1778.

The narrow **Park Place** is filled with the buildings of the **Royal Overseas League** (founded 1910; 50 000 members). No **14** was once Pratt's Club.

Next on the right is **Blue Ball Yard**. The far end of the gaslit yard is lined by stables of 1742, now garages, but still with round niches in the walls where iron hay baskets once hung; above are the old tiled cottage quarters.

St James's Place

The L shaped street is lined by 18C houses, some with decorative fanlights and continuous iron balconies.

The Royal Ocean Racing Club (no **20**) is a neat Georgian town house. At the far end is Spencer House (no **27**, *see Additional Sight*).

▶ *Continue down St James's St.*

The **Carlton Club** (no **69** St James's St), founded in 1832 by the Duke of Wellington, is housed in an early 19C Palladian stone building. No **74**, formerly the Conservative Club, was designed by **George Basevi** and **Sydney Smirke** in the mid-19C in modified Palladian style.

Note no **86**, a magnificent Victorian golden ochre stone building (1862).

On the opposite side of the street stands **Byron House** (nos **7–9**), built in the 1960s on the site of the house in which Byron awoke to find himself famous after the publication of his *Childe Harold* (1811). Long-established businesses in the vicinity include **Lobb's** the bespoke bootmaker (no **9**); **Lock's** the firm of hatters (no **6**) since 1700 – the topper in the window is 19C and **Berry Bros & Rudd** (no **3**), the wine merchants 'established in the XVII century'. The half-timbered passage beside the shop leads to **Pickering Place**, a gaslit court

of 18C houses, reputed to be the site of the last duel to be fought in London. At the south end are two buildings by **Norman Shaw** in terracotta brick and stone, with asymmetric gables, friezes and an angle tower.

St James's Palace★★

In 1532 the 'goodly manor' built by **Henry VIII** was converted into a crenellated and turreted palace entered through the **Gate House** at the bottom of St James's Street. The original palace buildings, partly destroyed by the fire of 1809, are of the traditional 16C Tudor red brick with a diaper pattern and stone trim along the line of the crenellations. They surround four courts: Colour, Friary, Ambassadors' and Engine, all lit at night.

Many kings and queens have been born or died in the palace. **Charles I** spent his last night in the guardroom before walking across the park to his execution at the Banqueting House on 30 January 1649. After Whitehall Palace had burned down in 1698, St James's became the chief royal residence and, although no longer so, ambassadors are still accredited to the Court of St James. Today the palace serves as the official residence of the Duke and Duchess of Kent and Princess Alexandra.

Chapel Royal – *Ambassadors Court.* ⏱ *Open for services early Oct to Good Fri, Sun at 8.30am (Holy Communion) and 11.15am (Choral Eucharist/Mattins); also Saints' Days for Evensong.* ℘*020 7839 1377.*

A Traditional Establishment

Pickering's, later known as **Berry Brothers & Rudd Ltd**, has occupied this site, identified as Henry VIII's tennis court, since 1731. The sign of the coffee-mill hanging outside no 3 was put there by the Widow Bourne to mark her grocer's shop (1690s). As the shop was handed down through the generations, business, which had included "arms painting and heraldic furnishings", moved into spices, smoking tobacco, snuff, fine teas and coffee, to become one of the most comprehensive grocer's of the day, judiciously placed for the 18C Beau Monde by St James's Palace. The variously fashionable commodities were carefully weighed from the great brass weighing beams: indeed, a Register of Weights has been kept since 1765. The last remaining stocks of groceries were sold in 1896.

The huge Tudor Gothic window, visible from the exterior to the right of the palace gateway, lights the Chapel Royal and its so-called Holbein ceiling. The choir is famous for its long tradition since the Medieval period and the choristers wear scarlet and gold state coats at services. Several royal marriages have taken here including that of Queen Victoria to Prince Albert (1840).

For security reasons, access to this area is severely restricted.

Clarence House – *Guided tours early Aug–mid-Oct 10am–4pm (3.30pm last admission). Timed ticket and advance booking only. €8. 020 7766 7303. www.royal.gov.uk.* The distinctive white stucco mansion – the former home of Queen Elizabeth, the Queen Mother, and now the residence of the Prince of Wales and Duchess of Cornwall – was built in 1825 by John Nash for the Duke of Clarence, the future William IV. It is best seen from the Mall. The tour takes in five rooms used for official functions, in which the Queen Mother's collection of 20C British art is displayed, with works by John Piper, Graham Sutherland, WS Sickert and Augustus John.

Across Stable Yard stands **Lancaster House**★, the golden Bath stone mansion, designed by Benjamin Wyatt in 1825 for the Duke of York. For many years in the 19C it was the setting for grand balls and soirées; today it maintains that function as the Government's hospitality centre.

The acres now known as **Green Park** were added to St James's Park in 1667 by Charles II, who in the early morning would regularly walk up a path to what is now Hyde Park Corner – hence **Constitution Hill**. From the east side of the park there is a fine view of Spencer House.

Continue towards the Mall for a good view of Buckingham Palace, and turn left to Marlborough Road.

On the corner overlooking the Mall note the life-like relief of Queen Mary, consort of George V, by Reid-Dick and the gaslight lanterns crested with gilded crowns.

Queen's Chapel★

Past a large art nouveau bronze group in memory of Queen Alexandra (1926) is the entrance to the Queen's Chapel, intended for the Infanta Maria of Spain but completed in 1625 for Charles I's eventual queen, **Henrietta Maria** by **Inigo Jones**. It was the first church in England designed completely outside the Perpendicular Gothic tradition.

Marlborough House

While John Churchill, **Duke of Marlborough**, was winning the final victories in the seemingly endless War of the Spanish Succession (Blenheim 1704, Ramillies 1706, Oudenaarde 1708) and the Duchess, one of the Ladies of the Bedchamber to Queen Anne, was supervising the construction of Blenheim Palace (1705–24), Wren designed and completed Marlborough House in two years (1709–11). It was altered in 1771 by **William Chambers** and enlarged in the 19C.

Turn right into Pall Mall.

Pall Mall

The ancient way from the City to St James's Palace gets its name from the game brought over from France early in the 17C and much favoured by the Stuarts.

Crown Passage *(opposite Marlborough House, under 59–60)* is a narrow alley leading past the 19C **Red Lion** pub *(see Addresses)* into King Street where the two world-famous establishments have their headquarters: **Christie's** (no 8), fine art auctioneers, founded in 1766 at the height of the fashion for doing the Grand Tour, and Spinks (no 5), specialists in coins, medals and orders, as well as antiques of all kinds.

Angel Court leads back past the **Golden Lion** *(see Addresses)* gleaming with mirror glass and mahogany, to Pall Mall.

Lord Palmerston founded the exclusive **Oxford and Cambridge Club** (no 71) here in 1830.

The dark red brick exterior of **Schomberg House** (nos 80–82) dates from 1698; Nell Gwynne lived next door (no 79).

The **Army and Navy Club** (no 36, founded 1839) was rebuilt in 1963 – not to be confused with the Naval and Military Club in St James's Square.

The **RAC** (Royal Automobile Club) is a vast building (1911) constructed by the builders of the Ritz.

▷ *Walk up the west side of St James's Square and round clockwise.*

St James's Square★

The square, with a Classical equestrian statue of William III (1807) beneath very tall plane trees, is encircled by modern offices and 19C residences except on the north and west sides where there are still Georgian town houses. Of them the most notable are no 4 of 1676, remodelled in 1725, where Nancy Astor once lived and now the home of the **Naval and Military Club**; no 5 of 1748–51 with 18C and 19C additions; no 13 of 1740 with faked mortar uprights to give an all-header effect to the blackened brick wall; no 15, **Lichfield House,** of 1764–65, **James 'Athenian' Stuart**'s Classical stone façade with its continuous iron balcony; and no 20 built by Adam in 1775 with no 21 its 20C mirror image. No 31, Norfolk House, where George III was born, served as **General Eisenhower's headquarters** in 1942 and 1944.

No 14 (of 1896) is the **London Library** and nos 9–10, Chatham House, the Royal Institute of International Affairs (founded 1920). The houses date from 1736 and no 10, in its time, has been residence of three Prime Ministers: William Pitt 1757–61, Edward Stanley 1837–54 and William Ewart Gladstone, 1890.

▷ *Return to Pall Mall and continue east.*

The **Reform Club** (nos 104–105), which was established in opposition to the Carlton by Whig supporters at the time of the Reform Bill in 1832, is housed in a 19C Italian palazzo building.

The **Travellers' Club** (no 106), also an Italian palazzo building (19C), was founded in 1819 with a rule that members must have travelled a minimum of 500 miles (now 1 000) outside the British Isles in a straight line from London.

Waterloo Place★

Pall Mall is intersected by Waterloo Place, designed by John Nash as a broad approach to Carlton House and demolished in 1829. In the northern half stands the **Crimea Monument**. The beginning of the southern half is marked by two clubs, both planned by Nash, which face each other across the place. The **Athenaeum** (no 107), designed by Decimus Burton, is a stucco block (1829–30) with Classical touches: torches, Roman Doric pillars supporting the porch, the gilded figure of Pallas Athene and the important Classical frieze in deference to the membership of the club, founded as a meeting place for artists and men of letters.

Carlton Gardens is a small grass plot shaded by plane trees and surrounded by four grand houses. No 4 (demolished and rebuilt in 1933) served as the headquarters of the Free French Forces (1940–1945). A tablet is inscribed with General de Gaulle's famous call to arms, broadcast on 18 June 1940.

Carlton House Terrace★

Carlton House (1709), which stood on the south side of Pall Mall, was taken over in 1772 by the Prince Regent. Henry Holland transformed it into the most gorgeous mansion in the land. In 1825, however, five years after his accession to the throne, **George IV** grew tired of the house and transferred his attention to Buckingham Palace.

Carlton House was demolished in 1829, and the government commissioned Nash, who had just re-developed Regent's Park, to design similar terraces here; only two were built. Between the two terraces, at the top of the steps leading down to the Mall is the pink granite **Duke of York's Column,** tall enough according to contemporaries, to place the Duke out of his creditors' reach.

▷ *Turn back up Waterloo Place on the east side to Pall Mall.*

At no 116 stands a building of similar size and style to the Athenaeum opposite, designed by Nash but remodelled by Burton in 1842.

▷ *Cross Pall Mall.*

The delightful row of bow-fronted shops, known as the **Royal Opera Arcade★**, was designed by **Nash** and **Repton** in 1817 as one of three arcades surrounding the then Royal Opera House.

New Zealand House
Haymarket.
Since 1963, the 15-storey tower above a 4-storey podium, 225ft/68m in all, has stood sentinel at the bottom of the street. The bronze statue of George III on horseback in Cockspur Street completes the scene.

▷ *Walk up Haymarket.*

Haymarket is named for its market, which supplied the Royal Mews on what is now Trafalgar Square in the 17C.

Her Majesty's (The King's)
On the corner of Charles II Street is a Victorian, French pavilioned building with an ornate interior plan, constructed by Beerbohm Tree in 1895–97. The theatre now stages major musicals.

Theatre Royal, Haymarket★
John Nash designed the theatre in 1821 to stand, unlike its predecessor of 1720, in the axis of Charles II Street and so enjoy a double aspect. The interior (remodelled) is elegantly decorated in deep blue, gold and white.

ADDITIONAL SIGHT
Spencer House★★
♿🕐⌖ *Guided tour (1hr) Sun (except Jan and Aug), 10.30am–5.45pm (last admission 4.45pm). £9. Children must be accompanied by an adult, no child under 10yrs. Guided tour (7 languages) by arrangement. No photography.*
☎020 7499 8620 (for recorded information). www.spencerhouse.co.uk.
The house was built in 1756–66 for John, 1st Earl Spencer who initially employed the Palladian architect John Vardy. In 1758 Vardy was replaced by James "Athenian" Stuart who was responsible for the Greek detail of the interior decoration (first floor rooms); the house is one of the pioneer examples of the Neoclassical style. In 1942 the house was stripped of original fixtures, with chimney-pieces, panelling, mouldings and architraves being removed to Althorp.
Spencer House has now regained the splendour of its late 18C appearance after a decade of restoration. The eight State Rooms are complemented by a collection of paintings and furniture: *(ground floor)* Morning Room or Ante Room; Library; Dining Room; the Palm Room, designed by Vardy with carved and gilded palm trees framing the alcove; and *(first floor)* the Music Room, Lady Spencer's Room, the Great Room and the Painted Room decorated in Stuart's Greek style.

ADDRESSES

⚒ LIGHT BITE

Balls Brothers – *20 St. James's St, SW1A 1ES.* ⊖*Green Park.* ☎*020 7321 0882 . Closed Sat–Sun.* One of the famous Balls Brothers group, this old-fashioned wine bar is charming, with a great wine list and good plain food.

Caffè Nero – *35 Jermyn St, SW1 6DT.* ⊖*Piccadilly Circus.* ☎*020 7437 9419.* This small café, attached to St James's Church, is an ideal place for a quick sandwich, salad or coffee. In good weather, take a seat on the delightful, tree shaded, brick-paved terrace and watch the world go by.

Davy's – *Crown Passage Vaults, 20 King St, SW1Y 6QY.* ⊖*Piccadilly Circus.* ☎*020 7839 8831. Closed Sat–Sun.* This atmospheric bar recalls bars of old, with its candelit tables and wooden floors strewn with sawdust. It has a great wine list and services classic British food such as fish and chips.

🍺 PUBS

Golden Lion – *25 King St, SW1Y 6QY.* ⊖*Green Park; Piccadilly Circus.* ☎*020 7925 0007. Closed Sun.* This early 18C pub spread over five floors was the annexe of St James's Theatre before its demolition. It has preserved all of its charm owing to such features as the stunning black marble pillars and the glass and mahogany interior.

The Red Lion – *23 Crown Passage off King St, SW1Y 6PP.* ⊖*Green Park.* ☎*020 7930 4141. Closed Sun.* Behind a flowery façade, you will discover a small well-kept pub with a Victorian atmosphere replete with mirrors and mahogany panels. Upmarket clientele.

🛒 SHOPPING

Berry Bros & Rudd – *3 St James's St, SW1A 1EG.* ⊖*Green Park.* ☎*0870 900 4300. www.bbr.com. Closed Sun.* One of the world's oldest wine merchants, founded 1698, and official suppliers of fine vintages to the Royal Family since 1760. Admire the fine early 18C façade.

A wide selection of wines to chose, from old Port to New World vintages. Staff are happy to advise you on wine to suit your purpose or wallet.

Hilditch & Key – *37 Jermyn St, SW1Y 6NP.* ⊖*Piccadilly Circus.* ☎*020 7734 4707. www.hilditchandkey.co.uk. Closed Sun.* Located in Jermyn Street, a bastion of traditional British male fashion, this is the area's oldest shirt shop, with made-to-measure or ready-to-wear shirts, trousers and other accessories. All items are of exceptional quality, with exceptional prices to match, and have won the hearts of such figures as Karl Lagerfeld. Women's section also.

Jermyn Street – *SW1.* A street with a distinctly masculine flavour. Shops include bootmakers, leather workers, hatters, tailors, shirtmakers, shoemakers and pipe and tobacco merchants (Dunhill's at no 48, Davidoff on the corner of Jermyn Street and St James's). Floris the perfumer's (no 89), established in 1730, and the well-known purveyors of cheese and Scottish products, Paxton & Whitfield (no 93).

Paxton & Whitfield – *93 Jermyn St, SW1Y 6JE.* ⊖*Green Park; Piccadilly.* ☎*020 7930 0259. www.paxtonand whitfield.co.uk. Closed Sun.* This institution has been here since 1797, and sells only the finest cheeses, including first-rate Stiltons, Cheddars and a good selection of drinks to accompany the cheese (port, wine, champagne). They offer a mail-order service for their cheeses, too

MUSIC

St James's Church – *197 Piccadilly W1J 9LL.* ⊖*Green Park.* ☎*020 7734 4511. www.st-james-piccadilly.org. Recitals: Mon, Wed, Fri at 1.10pm. Concerts: usually Thu–Sat at 7.30pm.*

🛒 MARKET

St James's Church – *197 Piccadilly W1J 9LL.* ⊖*Green Park.* ☎*020 7734 4511. www.st-james-piccadilly.org. Open Wed–Sat 11am–6pm (craft market only), Tue 10am–6pm (antiques also).*

Strand – Temple★★

Bordering Covent Garden and on the edge of the city, the Strand holds many attractions despite the relentless traffic. Lined with ornate buildings recalling its aristocratic past, it boasts elegant hotels, lively theatres and fabulous art galleries at Somerset House. Fleet Street and Temple are intrinsic parts of entirely different traditions: the former is the national press, the latter is British law.

A BIT OF HISTORY

The Strand was an ancient track, midway between the Thames, London's main thoroughfare, and the highway leading west out of the City.

Only the churches have survived from the Medieval period. Up to Hanoverian times the street was lined with law students' hostels (inns) and provincial bishops' town houses.

After the Dissolution of the monasteries, the palaces and mansions were

- **Location:** *Map: Inside covers (EFX).* ⊖ *Temple; Charing Cross.* Strand is adjacent to Covent Garden, Trafalgar Square and the City. Waterloo Bridge and Hungerford Bridge provide direct access to the South Bank.
- **Don't Miss:** The Impressionism, Post-Impressionism and Fauvism collections of the Courtauld Institute; Temple Church; the spire and crypt of St Bride's Church.
- **Timing:** Allow 2hr to see the Courtauld Institute Galleries, the rest of the day to stroll through the area.
- **Kids:** The ice rink at Somerset House in winter.

purchased by the nobility as local street names testify: Essex Street recalls the House owned by a famous Elizabethan

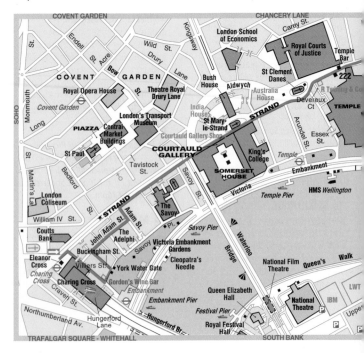

favourite and Arundel Street the great house of the Howards.

In 1624 **James I** presented York House, one-time palace of the Archbishop, to George Villiers, Duke of Buckingham, an event recalled by York Place and Villiers Street. Between the big houses and down the side lanes were hundreds of small houses, ale houses, brothels, coffee houses and shops. The **New Exchange** (1609–1737) was an arcade of shops, mostly milliners and mercers, patronised by royalty and later by **Pepys**. The Grecian, later the Devereux public house and a favourite with Addison, is now the Edgar Wallace with an Edwardian decoration and interesting mementoes.

In the late Victorian and Edwardian era, the Strand was known for its restaurants and hotels – the Cecil (now Shell-Mex) had 1 000 bedrooms, the Metropole, the Victoria and the Grand, and for its theatres: a popular 19C music hall song was *Let's all go down the Strand.*

Temple – The Order of the Knights **Templars** was founded in 1118 to

Fountains in the courtyard of Somerset House

J. Malburet/MICHELIN

protect pilgrims on the road to the Holy City of Jerusalem and welcomed to England by Henry I. They settled by the river where they began building their church in 1185. In 1312 the Templars were suppressed and their property assigned to the **Hospitallers** who, in turn, were dispossessed by **Henry VIII.** The church reverted to the crown; the outlying property was granted to the lawyers, together with the safekeeping of the church, by **James I** in 1608. The lawyers early formed themselves into three Societies: the **Inner Temple** (being within the City; emblem a Pegasus), the **Middle Temple** (emblem a Pascal lamb) and the **Outer Temple**, which was on the site of Essex Street but has long since disappeared. Today the area is abuzz with lawyers through the week and a haven of peace at weekends; at night, it is lit by gaslight.

According to Shakespeare, the origin of the Wars of the Roses derives from the plucking of a red and white rose from the Temple Gardens in 1430.

WALKING TOURS

> *Start from Charing Cross Station.*

STRAND★

Today the Strand links Trafalgar Square to Fleet Street and the City. The elegant open glazed building of **Coutts Bank** (no 440) was designed by **Sir Frederick Gibberd** to be sympathetic to its 19C neighbours in the style of John Nash. The bank was transferred to this address in 1904 by Thomas Coutts.

Across the Strand, down Craven St, on the west side of Charing Cross Station, is

the **Benjamin Franklin House**, in which the statesman, scientist and inventor (1706–90) lived between 1757 and 1775. An actress in period dress conducts guided tours that recall Franklin's busy social life in 18C London and his role as mediator between Britain and America in the years that preceded the Declaration of Independence *(36 Craven St; ⌁ Guided tours Mon at noon, 1pm, 2pm, 3.15pm and 4.15pm; ⌕£3.50; The Historic Experience Show (tour) Wed–Sun noon–5pm. ⌕£7. ☏020 7925 1405 or 0207 839 2006; www.benjaminfranklin house.org).*

Charing Cross Station

The street frontage is scaled to pleasing proportions alongside EM Barry's neo-Gothic **Charing Cross Station Hotel** (1863–64). The modern station buildings conceived by Terry Farrell (1990) as part of a larger project spanning both banks of the Thames feature a great white arch over and beyond the station viaduct. This giant glazed railway "hangar" is lodged between four granite-faced corner service towers.

In the forecourt of Charing Cross Station stands a reproduction, designed by EM Barry, of the original **Eleanor Cross**, which stood in Trafalgar Square.

▷ *Walk down Villiers St.*

Hungerford Bridge

As one of London's Millennium projects, the old rail bridge, a plain lattice girder structure (1862), has been sandwiched between two pedestrian suspension bridges designed by Lifshutz Davidson, their soaring cobweb of struts and cables beautifully lit at night to provide easy pedestrian access to the South Bank.

▷ *Take Savoy Place to Buckingham St.*

Buckingham Street

(River side). 17C and 18C brick houses still line both sides (nos 12, 17, 18, 20 date from the 1670s) down to Victoria Embankment Gardens. Pepys lived at no 12 in 1679–88. At the south end stands **York Water Gate,** a triple arch of rusticated stone, decorated with the Villiers arms and a scallop shell, built in 1626 at the water's edge by Nicholas Stone, master mason to George Villiers, 1st Duke of Buckingham.

▷ *Return to the Strand to view the ornate façades on both sides of the street, then go down the steps to John Adam St and walk round.*

The Adelphi

The riverfront retains the name although the Royal Adelphi Terrace erected by Robert Adam in 1768–72 was demolished in 1937. The Adam brothers – *adelphi* is the Greek word for brothers – transformed the area by the construction along the foreshore of a towering embankment arcade, the Adelphi Arches, supporting a terrace of 11 houses. The end houses were pedimented and decorated to form advanced wings to the terrace. It was the first and possibly finest of Thames-side concepts; now only a few houses remain to give an idea of how the quarter must have looked in the 18C. George Bernard Shaw (1896–1927) lived at no 10a.

John Adam Street: no 8 was built for the **Royal Society of Arts** in 1772–74 by Adam with a projecting porch surmounted by a giant order of fluted columns. The RSA was founded in 1754 "to embolden enterprise, to enlarge science, to refine art, to improve our manufacture and extend our commerce."

Adam Street: the east side has a run of houses beginning with no 10, Adam House, neat and compact with a rounded corner and curved ironwork; 9 and 8 are the street's standard with attractive pilastered doors; no 7, in the axis of John Adam Street, is a typical example of the Adam decorative style including his favourite acanthus leaf motif applied to pilasters, cornice and ironwork.

▷ *Return to the Strand.*

The Savoy

The Savoy is now a precinct that comprises a chapel, a **theatre**, the first public building in the world to be lit throughout by electricity, and a grand **hotel**, built by D'Oyly Carte in 1889. The name dates from 1246, when Henry III granted the manor beside the Thames to his queen's uncle, Peter of Savoy. The estate then passed to the Dukes of Lancaster and as "the fairest manor in England" became, until his death, the "lodging" of King John of France, captured by the Black Prince at Poitiers (1356). The **Savoy Hotel** (currently undergoing a £100million renovation), is one of the most famous in London, while the theatre was the original home of the D'Oyly Carte Opera Company who first staged all Gilbert and Sullivan's much loved operettas. The little access road at the front of the hotel is the only road in Britain on which you drive on the right.

▷ Walk down Savoy Hill to Savoy Pl and Victoria Embankment Gardens.

The Queen's Chapel of the Savoy (Chapel of the Royal Victorian Order)

Savoy Hill. ◷Open (services permitting) Oct–Jul Tue–Fri 11.30am–3.30pm.
The chapel was largely rebuilt after the war and dates back to the construction of a hospital for 100 "pouer, needie people" in 1510–16. The hospital was dissolved in 1702, but the chapel and burial yard survived to be made into the Chapel of the Royal Victorian Order in 1937.
Savoy Hill is famous as the site of the BBC's first studios and offices from 1923 to 1932 (plaque on the Embankment façade of no 2 Savoy Place).
The **Victoria Embankment Gardens**★, complete with their bandstand for summer concerts, were created in 1864. Opposite the gardens on the river front, flanked by great bronze lions stands **Cleopatra's Needle**, erected after a long saga in 1878. One of two great Egyptian obelisks covered in hieroglyphs uncovered at Heliopolis (c. 1450 BC),

it was first offered to George IV by Mehemet Ali of Egypt. Similar obelisks stand in Paris (Place de la Concorde) and New York. Note the dolphin lamp standards and decorated bench ends.

▷ Walk back to the Strand and cross Lancaster Pl.

Simpson's in the Strand restaurant replaces a coffee house – The Grand Cigar Divan founded by Samuel Reiss in 1828 (⟨ see YOUR STAY IN THE CITY – Where to Eat).

Somerset House★★

The present building was erected enduringly in Portland stone in 1776–86 to the designs of **Sir William Chambers** on the site of the palace begun by Protector Somerset in 1547 and still incomplete when he was executed in 1552. The narrow Strand façade of Somerset House, inspired by Inigo Jones' Palladian riverside gallery, has a triple gateway and giant columns beneath a balustrade decorated with statues and a massive statuary group by Bacon.
Through the arch is a vast courtyard surrounded by ranges of buildings treated like rows of terrace houses round a square. A continuous balustrade punctuated by vases unites the fronts. The riverside front stands on a continuous line of massive arches which, in the 18C, were at the water's edge.
The Strand block of Somerset House, is the most elaborate and has two advanced wings. It contains the so-called **Fine Rooms**, which are notable for their pleasing proportions and handsome plasterwork. These were originally designed for three learned societies. Somerset House now houses major art collections, including The Courtauld Collection (⟨ see The Courtauld Institute Galleries), and a variety of temporary exhibitions, workshops and events.
👥Fountains adorn the grand piazza, which is used for public entertainment throughout the year, including musical performances and a full-scale open-air cinema with a giant screen and surround-sound in the summer (advance

booking necessary). An open-air ice rink takes up residence each winter (advance booking necessary), offering timed skates, Christmas music and a café with mulled wine and hot chocolate.

At any time of the year, fine **views**★★ of the Thames may be enjoyed from the riverside façade (*020 7845 4600; www. somersethouse.org.uk).*

St Mary-le-Strand

Open Mon–Fri 11am–4pm, Sun 10am–3pm. 020 7538 5758 (church warden). www.stmarylestrand.org.

This compact, Baroque miniature (1714–24) was the first commission to be undertaken by **James Gibbs**. It is sober and ordered: a simple apsed space that is light and harmoniously proportioned.

The tower rises in four tiers over the rounded porch and first floor pediment to a gilded weather vane. Fine carvings decorate the exterior, but it is perhaps the Italianate plasterwork ceiling which is particularly worthy of note: executed by English craftsmen, the stylised flower heads are especially delicate. It is known as the "Cabbies church".

King's College

King's College, founded in 1829, was housed from its earliest days in the east extension of Somerset House; the Strand front (1970s) is in an unrelated, modern style. The courtyard, long and narrow, is terminated by the colonnaded pavilion which completes the Somerset House river front.

Aldwych

The sweeping semicircle was laid out in 1905. The huge half-moon island on the Strand is occupied by massive buildings: Australia House, India House (reliefs) and, in the centre, the 1925–35 **Bush House**, base of the BBC External Services. Above the lintel the motto 'To the friendship of English speaking people' is inscribed. Today BBC World Service, nearing its 80th year in operation and broadcasting all round the world in 32 languages (including English), is seen as a lifeline to many living under repressive regimes.

St Clement Danes★

Open daily 9am–4pm. Oranges and Lemons carillon operates daily at 9am, noon (except Sun), 3pm (except Sun), 6pm. Leaflets (6 languages). 020 7242 2380.

St Clement's was designed by **Wren** in 1682 on the site of a 9C church built by Danish merchants married to Englishwomen. The building, featuring an open spire in three diminishing pillared stages – the steeple was added by **James Gibbs** (1719) – was burnt down on 10 May 1941 and rebuilt as the RAF church in 1955–58. The dark oak panelling, first floor galleries beneath a richly decorated vault and plasterwork Stuart coat of arms conforms to Wren's original design, now embellished with Air Force mementoes that include badges carved in Welsh slate and inlaid in the pavement, memorials of the Commonwealth air forces and the Polish squadrons, a USAAF and other shrines. The grand pulpit is the original one by Grinling Gibbons.

"Oranges and lemons say the bells of St Clement's" refers to the boats that came up the Thames to land fruit for sale in Clare Market (on the site of Kingsway) and paid a tithe in kind to the church; the carillon rings out the **nursery rhyme** four times a day.

At the east end stands a statue of Dr Samuel Johnson, a worshipper at the church, who lived nearby.

No 216 **Twinings** (*see Addresses)* is a very old tea shop. Several generations have witnessed changes in tea trading over the last centuries. Today Twinings manufacture over 150 blends of black tea, herb and fruit infusions.

Lloyd's Law Courts Branch

No 222. The **Palsgrave Tavern**, as frequented by the dramatist Ben Jonson, was named after Frederick Palsgrave, later King of Bohemia, who married Elizabeth, daughter of James I. All three figures are commemorated in the singular glazed earthenware decoration supplied by Royal Doulton. Inside, the building, a branch of Lloyds bank since 1895, is panelled with American walnut and sequoia, inset with tiles.

Nos 229/230 Strand. The building of the famous **Wig and Pen Club**, which survived the Great Fire (1666), now comprises two narrow 18C town houses with dark wood panelling. The club has now closed.

Royal Courts of Justice

The Law Courts date from 1874–82. The centrepiece inside is the Great Hall, a vaulted arcade decorated with foliated doorways, blind arcades, diapering and a seated statue of the architect. The early courtrooms (there are still more than 20) lead off the hall which is marked outside by a needle spire, offsetting the long arched façade, the heavy tower and polygonal west end. There is a small exhibition of legal costumes.

At this point, the Strand gives way to Fleet Street enclosed within the confines of the City of London: the boundary is marked by the Temple Bar.

TEMPLE BAR TO LUDGATE CIRCUS

See CITY OF LONDON map (AY)

Fleet Street

Named after the **River Fleet**, which flows south from Hampstead to drain into the Thames at Blackfriars, Fleet Street links the City with Westminster. Once synonymous with the press, the street has changed in character since the age of technology has ousted all the national newspaper publishers to offices in Docklands *(The Times, Daily Telegraph)* or south of the river *(Daily Express, Financial Times)*. It is lined with imposing buildings in a variety of styles, such as **Child & Co** (no 1), one of the country's oldest banks *(now Royal Bank of Scotland)* "at the sign of the Marigold" *(see OSTERLEY PARK)* .

▶ *Pass through Inner Temple Gateway (between nos 16 and 17 Fleet Street).*

Temple Bar

It has been the City's western barrier since the Middle Ages; the sovereign pauses here to receive and return the Pearl Sword from the Lord Mayor on entering the City. The present memorial pillar with statues of Queen Victoria and the future Edward VII surmounted by the City griffin, dates from 1880. It replaced the "bars" that had developed from 13C posts and chains and at various times constituted a high, arched building, a prison (thrown down by **Wat Tyler** in 1381) and finally an arch of Portland stone designed by Wren in 1672 and used in the days of public execution as a spike for heads and quarters. It was dismantled in 1870 and removed to Theobald's Park near Waltham Cross.

Temple★★

Inner Temple – The three-storeyed **Inner Temple Gateway**, dating from 1610 (reconstructed 1906), leads into the lane, past 19C buildings and the house *(right)* where Dr Johnson lived from 1760 to 1765, to the church.

Temple Church★★ – *For visiting hours contact the verger or check online. Guide book. ☎020 7353 8559. www.templechurch.com.*

This special church is one of the most historic and beautiful in London, with over 800 years of history that dates from the 12C Crusaders onwards.

The round church, originally built in 1160–85, was modelled on the Church of the Holy Sepulchre in Jerusalem and, as such, sought to recreate the sanctity of that most sacred building.

In 1185 it was consecrated by Heraclius, Patriarch of Jerusalem in the presence of King Henry II, and from then on it acted as the headquarters of the Knights Templar in Britain. Today it remains a private chapel under the jurisdiction of the Sovereign as Head of the Church, who appoints the Master of the Temple.

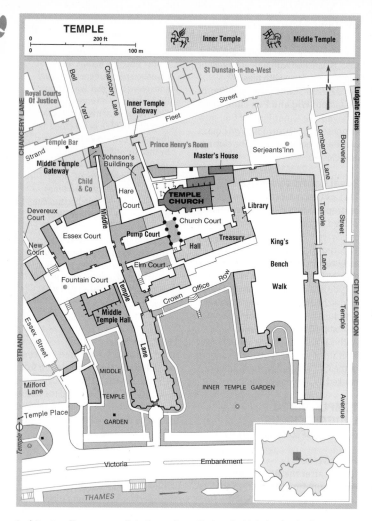

TEMPLE

Inner Temple   Middle Temple

St Dunstan-in-the-West
Royal Courts Of Justice
Bell Yard
Chancery Lane
Inner Temple Gateway
Fleet Street
Lombard Lane
Bouverie
Ludgate Circus
CHANCERY LANE
Temple Bar
Strand
Prince Henry's Room
Serjeants' Inn
Middle Temple Gateway
Johnson's Buildings
Master's House
Child & Co
Hare Court
TEMPLE CHURCH
Library
Temple Street
Devereux Court
Essex Court
Church Court
Pump Court
Treasury
King's
New Court
Hall
Temple Lane
Fountain Court
Elm Court
Bench
Crown Office Row
Walk
STRAND
Essex Street
Middle Temple Hall
Temple Avenue
Milford Lane
MIDDLE
INNER TEMPLE GARDEN
TEMPLE
Temple Place
GARDEN
CITY OF LONDON
Victoria
Embankment
THAMES

Architecturally, a sense of clarity and order is enhanced by the stylised capital decoration and the polished ringed shafts of Purbeck marble, the first free-standing Purbeck columns ever cut, that soar up to the conical roof. On the stone floor lie ten 10C–13C effigies of knights in armour. To be buried here in the Temple Church was highly desired by the knights, as to be 'buried in the Round' was to be buried 'in Jerusalem'. These effigies were created not as memorials, but as symbols of what was to come. The knights eyes are open, ever alert and ready for battle, and all are portrayed in their early 30s, the age at which Christ died, and which the dead will rise on his return. The traditional flexed posture of some of the effigies may indicate these knights took part in the crusades.

In the chancel (1220–40), slender Purbeck columns rise to form the ribs of the quadripartite vaulting. Behind the 16C monument of Edmund Plowden on the north side, a door leads to the penitential cell dating back to Templar times. The oak reredos designed by Wren was carved by **William Emmett** in 1682.

In the graveyard (north side) lies **Oliver Goldsmith**, a contemporary of Dr Johnson. To the northeast of the church

Middle Temple Hall
©Sam Shapiro/Fotolia.com

stands the **Master's House** rebuilt in 17C style.

The Temple Church survived the Great Fire but was badly damaged in the Blitz (1941). "The two learned and honourable Societies of this House" are the four Inns of Court, the Inner and Middle Temples.

The **Inner Temple Hall**, Treasury and Library were all rebuilt after the war.

The northern of the two ranges overlooking **King's Bench Walk** *(accessible through a passageway to the east)* dates from 1678 and is by **Wren** (no 1 rebuilt).

Middle Temple lies on the west side. The cloisters between Church Court and Pump Court and the south side of Pump Court have been rebuilt (Edward

Associations

It is St Bride's associations, however, rather than its architecture, that make it unique to many: **Thomas Becket** was born close by; **King John** held a parliament in the church in 1210; **Henry VIII**, advised by **Thomas Wolsey**, built Bridewell Palace nearby between the church and the river, and received Charles V there in 1522; high-ranking churchmen unable to pay for lodgings within the City walls built town houses in the neighbourhood (Salisbury Square) and since the clergy were the largest literate group in the land it was only natural that when **Wynkyn de Worde** acquired his master's press in 1491, he should remove it from Westminster to St Bride's and Fleet Street (Caxton had been wealthy enough not to have to depend upon the press for his livelihood, unlike his apprentice). By the time Wynkyn died in 1535 (he was buried in St Bride's), the parish boasted several printers, including Richard Grafton, who printed the first English-language Bible in 1539. The church was the first to use the Book of Common Prayer, while its neighbouring taverns and coffeehouses were frequented by Chaucer, Shakespeare, Milton, Lovelace, Evelyn, Pepys (born nearby and, like all his family, christened in the church), Dryden, Izaac Walton, Edmund Waller (poet), Aubrey, Ashmole, John Ogilby (mapmaker), Thomas Tompion (father of English clock and watchmaking), Addison; in the 18C by Johnson and Boswell, Joshua Reynolds, Goldsmith, Garrick, Burke, Pope, Richardson (coffin in the crypt) and Hogarth; in the 19C by Charles Lamb, Hazlitt, Wordsworth, Keats, Hood, Leigh Hunt, Dickens. Today modern pew backs are labelled with the names of contemporaries, for St Bride's remains the printers' church, the Cathedral of Fleet Street.

Maufe); the north (except for the 19C Farrar's Building) is late 17C.

Middle Temple Hall★★ – ♿ ⏱Open Mon–Fri 10am–4pm. ⏱Closed bank holidays and during law vacations. ✆020 7427 4800. www.middletemple. org.uk.

The Elizabethan great hall has a double hammerbeam roof (1574), arguably the finest of the period. Medieval law students not only ate here, but attended lectures and even slept in the hall (100ft/30.5m × 40ft/12m). According to tradition, Queen Elizabeth I watched the first performance of Shakespeare's play *Twelfth Night* (1602) here in the company of the benchers in the hall. When the spectacular 16C carved screen at the hall's east end was shattered by a Second World War bomb, the splintered pieces were painstakingly reassembled.

Up the steps from Fountain Court (immortalised by Dickens in *Martin Chuzzlewit)* is **New Court**, with its Wren building of 1676.

Middle Temple Gateway and Lane

– The pedimented gateway with giant pilasters was erected only in 1684 although the lane is referred to as early as 1330 since it used to end in stairs on the river, affording a short cut by water to Westminster.

▷ *Return to Fleet St and proceed east.*

On the south side of Fleet Street stands the **Cock Tavern (Ye Olde Cocke Tavern)** (♿ *see Addresses).* At no 17 is **Prince Henry's Room**. Its upstairs tavern room with Tudor panelling and a Jacobean ceiling is crammed with Samu el Pepys mementoes. ⏱*Open Mon–Fri 11am–2pm.* ⏱*Closed bank holidays.*

St Dunstan-in-the-West

⏱*Open Tue 11am–3pm, otherwise by appointment.* ✆*020 7405 1929. www.stdunstaninthewest.org.*
Built in 1833 by John Shaw within the City boundary, this church was badly bombed in 1944.

The exterior, apart from the neo-Gothic tower and openwork octagonal lantern, is chiefly remarkable for the additions that associate the church with Fleet Street: the bust of **Lord Northcliffe** (1930), the public **clock** complete with its giant oak jacks; the **statues** from the 1586 **Lud Gate** include that of Queen Elizabeth I modelled during her lifetime, while to the right stand the figures of the mythical King Lud and his two sons (1586). Corbels at the main door are carved with the likenesses of Tyndale *(west)* and John Donne *(east)* who were both associated with St Dunstan's.

St Dunstan's, dedicated to the patron of goldsmiths, jewellers and locksmiths, is octagonal in plan with a high, star vault.

Beyond Fetter Lane and still off the north side of Fleet Street is a series of narrow alleys known collectively as "**the Courts**", which, alas, have been substantially redeveloped, their names providing the sole vestige of interest.

▷ *Turn into Hind Court to Gough Sq.*

Dr Johnson's House★

17 Gough Square. ⏱*Open Mon–Sat 11am–5.30pm (5pm winter).* ⏱*Closed bank holidays.* ⬭*£4.50. Guide book (4 languages).* ✏*Guided tour by appointment (50min)* ⬭*£3.50.* ✆*020 7353 3745. www.drjohnsonshouse.org*
This unremarkable house so typical of the late 17C was home to the great scholar and lexicographer between 1748 and 1759. Modest in size and proportion, it was chosen by **Johnson** (1709–84) almost certainly for its large, well-lit garret, where he worked with his five secretaries to complete his *Dictionary* published in 1755. The small rooms on each floor are sparsely furnished with 18C oak gate-leg tables and chairs, period prints, mementoes and a collection of books on the impecunious essayist's life and times, including his biography by James Boswell.

The work completed, he moved to chambers in the Temple, in 1765 to no 7 Fleet Street (known purely coincidentally as Johnson's Court), and finally to Bolt Court, where he died in 1784.

▷ *Return to Fleet St, past Shoe Lane then cross to the south side.*

In Wine Office Court is the **Cheshire Cheese** pub and restaurant.
The **Express** group building at nos 121–8 remains a landmark, its bold 1931 black and clear glass panels set in chromium; at no 135 stands the **Daily Telegraph** building (1928) boasting a ponderous mixture of styles. The Express and the Telegraph have both moved out.

St Bride's★

🕐*Open Mon–Fri 8am–6pm, Sun 10am–1pm, 5pm–7.30pm.* 🕐*Closed Sbank holidays. Recitals: certain days (except Aug, Advent, Lent) at 1.15pm. Brochure.* 📞*020 7427 0133. www.stbrides.com.*
The famous white **spire**★★of St Bride's, Wren's tallest and most floating steeple, rises by four open octagonal stages to a final open pedestal and tapering obelisk that terminates in a vane (226ft/69m above ground). When the spire was newly erected, a baker used it as a model for wedding cakes; he made a fortune and inaugurated a lasting tradition; his wife's silk dress is displayed in the museum in the crypt.
In 1940 Wren's church was gutted by a ravenous fire that left only the steeple and calcined outer walls standing. During rebuilding the crypt was opened; subsequent excavations revealed a Roman ditch, walls, a pavement and the outlines of church buildings on the site dating to Saxon times at least. Inside, Wren's design of a barrel-vaulted nave and groined aisles has been retained. The decoration is 17C.
The **St Bride Printing Library** and Bridewell Theatre are located nearby as is the **Punch Tavern**, named after the magazine which had premises there.

▷ *Continue along Fleet St to Ludgate Circus.*

COURTAULD GALLERY★★

Somerset House. ♿🕐*Open daily 10am–6pm (last admission 5.30pm); 24 Dec 10am–4pm.* 🕐*Closed 25–26 Dec.* 💷*£5; no charge Mon 10am–2pm (except public holidays).* 📞*020 7848 2526. www.courtauld.ac.uk/gallery.*
This fine collection includes recognised masterpieces from a wide range of periods stretching from the Gothic to Modernism. The highlights are presented from a collection which totals around 530 paintings, 6 000 drawings, 20 000 prints as well as sculpture and decorative arts.

COLLECTIONS

Allow about 1hr15min.
The interior colour schemes throughout the galleries conform, where possible, to William Chambers' original specifications. Works are grouped by benefactor to give a clearer idea of the mind of each collector.

Gallery 1: *Ground Floor.*
Between 1830 and 1870 **Thomas Gambier-Parry** (1816–88) collected 14C Italian Primitives whose simplicity he greatly admired. Displays in Gallery 1 include a Crucifixion polyptych by Bernardo **Daddi**, a limestone statue of the *Vigin and Child* attributed to André **Beauneuveu** and three **Fra Angelico** *predella* panels.

Galleries 2–4: *First Floor.*
Samuel Courtauld began collecting Impressionist and Post-Impressionist paintings in 1923. His perceptive eye and discerning taste selected some of the most famous expressions of the modern masters.
Light is the main preoccupation of the 19C French landscape painters at Barbizon and their followers the Impressionists. Bonnard, Boudin *(Deauville)*, Cézanne *(The Lac d'Annecy)*, Pissarro, Sisley *(Boats on the Seine)*, Seurat *(The Bridge at Courbevoie)*, Monet *(Autumn Effect at Argenteuil)* and Renoir all explored landscapes with stretches of water.

A Bar at the Folies-Bergères (1882) by Edouard Manet

Samuel Courtauld Trust, The Courtauld Gallery, London

Of particular interest in **Gallery 2** are *La Loge* by **Renoir**, which was exhibited in the first Impressionist exhibition in 1874; and *Antibes* by Claude **Monet**, who was influenced by Japanese prints and photography, and liked to experiment with viewpoints.

In **Gallery 3**, **Manet**'s sketch for *Le Déjeuner sur l'Herbe* (final version in Musée d'Orsay) was intentionally controversial: while being "modern," Manet desperately hoped to earn respect from the Salon establishment. *A Bar at the Folies-Bergère*, his last major work, is presented as a bold portrait of a young working woman; the wealthier members of the audience reflected in the mirror behind her seem oblivious of the trapeze artist wearing green pumps suspended in the top left corner.
Cézanne on the other hand, who is considered as the "father of modern art," builds a suggestion of space and depth into still-life *(Still-life with Plaster Cupid)* and landscape *(Montagne Sainte Victoire)* by means of colour (blues and greens give depth, whereas reds and oranges give relief) and form arranged in the foreground, middle ground and background. His figures *(The Card-players)*, meanwhile, are strong and direct studies of personality.
Nevermore and *Te Rerioa*, painted at the height of **Gauguin**'s Tahitian period, in

which naturally posed figures are shown in harmony with a primitive way of life, contrast with *Haymaking*, his bucolic Breton landscape.

Gallery 4 is devoted to Post-Impressionism. Two examples of **Van Gogh** are on display: *Peach blossom in the Crau* works in the mainstream Impressionist manner where fractured light is boldly captured by strong brushstrokes of thick paint. In his world famous *Self-portrait with Bandaged Ear* the artist is dressed in a greeny-blue coat, which gives his eyes a haunting look. Georges-Pierre **Seurat** mechanically painted in dots of colour, a technique known as pointillism, which if seen from a distance merge into tonal values. This accentuates the dusty interior scene of *Young Woman Powdering Herself*. Amedeo **Modigliani**'s *Female Nude* uses influences from Egyptian with her elongated face and early Italian art in the flat surface of the painting.

Gallery 5: Viscount Lee of Fareham, having given his first collection and Elizabethan manor house "Chequers" to the Nation in 1917 for use as a country retreat for Prime Ministers in office, began building his second collection after retiting from politics in 1922. Italian Renaissance paintings including **Botticelli**'s *Holy Trinity* (the central panel of a large altarpiece);

Giovanni **Bellini**'s *Assassination of St Peter Martyr*; Paolo **Veronese**'s *Baptism of Christ* (note the play of light on the figures and landscape); **Parmigianino**'s *The Virgin and Child* (the elegance and poise of the Virgin is characteristic of the artist's refined idea of beauty).

Galleries 6–7: Count Antoine Seilern (The Princes' Gate Collection) was Austrian by extraction but British by birth. As he had undertaken research into the Venetian sources of Rubens' ceiling pictures while in Vienna, 32 paintings and over 20 drawings by the master make up the bulk of his important donation.

In **Gallery 6**, several works by **Rubens** demonstrate the master's ability to treat historical and religious subjects, portraits and landscape with equal adeptness. Strong contrasts of light and texture, gesture and emotion characterise the colourful and restless compositions. The *Portrait of Baldassare Castiglione* is copied from an original painting by Raphael in the Louvre. The intimate scene depicted in *The Family of Jan Bruegel the Elder* has great impact. The *Landscape by Moonlight* is more contemplative in nature.

The early tradition of Netherlandish painting is represented by Pieter **Bruegel the Elder**: religious subjects set in vast landscapes, balanced composition, bands of colour to emphasise spatial recession *(Landscape with the Flight into Egypt)*, austere composition and monumental figures *(Christ and the Woman Taken in Adultery)*. *Adam and Eve* (1526) provides **Lucas Cranach the Elder**, friend and ally of Luther, with an opportunity to represent nude figures. **Gallery 7** is devoted to 18C portraits and to Tiepolo. Portraiture became an important genre in the 17C with **William Dobson** and **Sir Peter Lely** emerging as masters of a style pioneered by Van Dyck and providing modern viewers with a strong idea of dress and attitude.

In the 18C portraiture became an uncontroversial subject matter in which English artists achieved new heights: **Gainsborough**, **Reynolds**, **Raeburn**, and **Romney** *(Portrait of Lady Grenville)* sought to preserve natural likenesses of the leading thinkers, intellectuals, leaders and the gentry of the Age of Enlightenment.

Sketches for altarpieces and ceiling frescoes in luminous colours reveal Giovanni Battista **Tiepolo**'s (1696–1770) technical mastery and deep, religious feeling.

The gallery also contains the **collection of silver** (1710–80) made by three generations of the Courtauld family, who who fled religious persecution in France due to their Protestant beliefs. The service is arranged according to their use and includes tea and coffee sets, dining silver and display silver.

Gallery 8: *Second Floor*
Thsi gallery isplays small bronzes by **Degas** along with his *Two Dancers on Stage*, an example of his famous depictions of ballet . Note also *Woman at a Window* and his pastel *After the Bath*. **Toulouse-Lautrec** uses paint as if it were pastel, faces are lit and even distorted by artificial light *(Tête-à-tête Supper)* and volumes are flattened. In *Jane Avril at the Entrance to the Moulin Rouge, Putting on her Gloves*, Jane's fur-collared coat is defined as economically as the hat and coat hanging from the peg behind her.

Galleries 9–14: *Second Floor*
20C collections. Informality seems to pervade the layout of the early 20C collections. **Gallery 9** is devoted to **Matisse** *(Woman in a Kimono)* and Fauvism. Matisse and others such as André **Derain** and Maurice **de Vlaminck** used vivid colours in their landscapes. **Gallery 10** displays French Painting from the early 20C, such as Pierre **Bonnard**'s unconventional *The Seine in Paris: The Pont du Carrousel*.

Galleries 11a and **11b** house the Roger Fry Collection. **Roger Fry** (1866–1934) was an emminent art historian, critic and painter who collected contemporary works by Duncan Grant (*Lily Pond* four-fold screen), Vanessa Bell associated with the **Bloomsbury Group** and the Omega Workshop during the 1930s (*see INTRODUCTION TO LONDON – Painting*). His personal taste was for Bonnard (*Young Woman in an Interior*, a portrait of the artist's mistress and subsequent wife Marthe Boursin), Derain, Friesz, O'Connor, Rouault and Sickert. Domestic interiors provide recurrent subjects for Walter Sickert, Roger Fry and Vanessa Bell. This collection of works by British artists should be considered as a selection made by individuals for their own personal pleasure rather than for a major public museum, and as such modern art is presented as highly approachable. Following on in 11b, is a display of sketches by Seurat in his pointillist style.

Galleries 12 is devoted to a series of drawings and prints. **Galleries 13** and **14** deal with **Expressionist Art** and **Modernism** with works by German artists such as Max Pechstein, Alexej von **Jawlensky** (*Blue Cap*) and above all Russian-born Wassily **Kandinsky**, who moved to Munich at the age of 30.

Gallery 15 houses temporary exhibitions which change every few months.

ADDRESSES

◉ PUBS

Cock Tavern (or Ye Olde Cocke Tavern) – *22 Fleet St, EC4Y 1AA .* Blackfriars. *Closed Sat–Sun.* The décor is in the 17C style with a panelled bar counter. The restaurant rooms on the first floor were used for meetings of the Dickens and Thackeray Associations.

Punch Tavern – *99 Fleet St, EC4Y 1DE.* Blackfriars. *020 7353 6658. Closed Sun.* The drawings decorating the walls remind us that this was the birthplace of the celebrated satirical magazine. Admire the superb mosaics in the entrance. Excellent beer.

Cock Tavern

Gwen Cannon/MICHELIN

The Devereux – *20 Devereux Court, Essex St, Strand, WC2R 3JJ.* Temple. *020 7583 4562. Closed Sat–Sun.* The Devereux, one of the best pubs in the area, with a flower-decked façade, excellent beer and a restaurant upstairs, is always packed at peak times.

The Sherlock Holmes – *10–11 Northumberland St, WC2N 5DA.* Embankment; Charing Cross. *020 7930 2644.* The former Northumberland Hotel was renamed The Sherlock Holmes in honour of author Sir Arthur Conan Doyle. Upstairs you can see a reconstruction of the Holmes and Watson study and a host of associated objects objects. It is less touristy than you might think, a pleasant pub with a regular clientele.

Ye Olde Cheshire Cheese – *145 Fleet St, EC4A 2BU.* Blackfriars. *020 7353 6170.* A huge labyrinthine 17C pub with small beamed rooms and coal fires on three floors; three rooms are restaurants. A Fleet Street institution.

The Coal Hole – *91–92 Strand, WC2R 0DW.* Temple. *020 7379 9883. Closed Sat–Sun.* Built into a corner of the Savoy Hotel complex, this popular haunt dates from 1904. Inside, dark Medieval-style décor and stone flag floors contrasts with a lively ambience, and a clientele largely composed of office workers and tourists.

AFTERNOON TEA

Swissotel The Howard – ⊖*Temple. Temple Place, WC2R 2PR*. Take traditional Afternoon Tea between 2.30 and 5.30pm daily.

🎭 NIGHTLIFE

American Bar-Savoy Hotel – *Strand, WC2R 0EU.* ⊖*Charing Cross; Embankment.* The American Bar has been a stylish meeting place since the 1890s. Listen to the pianist and enjoy the tradition of new cocktails invented for special occasions, started in the 1920s by the famous American barman, Harry Craddock, inventor of the White Lady and Dry Martini.

Gordon's Wine Bar – *47 Villiers St, WC2N 6NE.* ⊖*Embankment.* ☏*020 7930 140. www.gordonswinebar.com.* A bar with

a soul! A narrow staircase leads to the bar and the dark dusty place is always packed with Londoners. Wine has been served here since 1364. As you savour the atmospheric bouquet, enjoy excellent cheese and good food at reasonable prices.

🛒 SHOPPING

Twinings – *216 Strand, WC2R 1AP.* ⊖*Temple, Charing Cross.* ☏*020 7353 3511. www.twinings.com. Closed Sun.* Two Chinamen flanking the Twining lion over the door identify this very narrow shop. The famed tea merchant has been located here since 1706. It offers a large selection of teas to fill your pot with, and for some background to your 'cuppa' there is also a small museum that traces the history of Twining.

Trafalgar Square – Whitehall★★

Trafalgar Square's famous column, imposing bronze lions and gentle fountains are overlooked by the imposing National Gallery at the culmination of Whitehall, which connects with the Palace of Westminster. Since its pedestrianisation it has lost most of the traffic, but continues to serve as a congregation point in times of strife or joy: political rallies, at Christmas around the Norwegian Christmas tree, or for the traditional New Year's Eve street party.

A BIT OF HISTORY

Trafalgar Square – The square celebrates Britain's naval prowess following Nelson's victory at the Battle of Trafalgar (20 October 1805) and the full glory of her Colonial Empire.
To the north stretches the length of that glorious institution, the **National Gallery** (📖*see NATIONAL GALLERY);* to the east stands **South Africa House**

▷ **Location:** *Map: Inside front cover (EX).* ⊖*Charing Cross; Westminster.* Several main arteries radiate from Trafalgar Square, with buses running to St Paul's and the City, to Waterloo and the South Bank, to Oxford St and Marble Arch, and to Victoria and Chelsea. Leicester Square, Covent Garden, the Mall and Buckingham Palace are easily accessible.

🐾 **Don't Miss:** History buffs will want to visit the Churchill Museum and Cabinet War Rooms; visitors interested in interior design should see Banqueting House.

🕐 **Timing:** Start from Trafalgar Square in the morning, have lunch, then take time to visit at least one sight.

👫 **Kids:** The Horse Guards, particularly a mounting or dismounting ceremony.

designed by Herbert Baker in 1933 where pickets rallied for the release of Nelson Mandela and an end to apartheid; opposite sits **Canada House**, a Neoclassical building of golden Bath stone (1824–27) conceived by Sir Robert Smirke in fact for the Royal College of Physicians. **Admiralty Arch**, built across the Mall (the central gateway being the Sovereign's Gate) by Sir Aston Webb in 1906–11 takes its name from the Admiralty buildings that sit on the south side of the square.

Palace of Whitehall – In 1529, Henry VIII confiscated Cardinal Wolsey's London palace dating back to the mid-13C. Wolsey made it his personal property, rebuilding, enlarging and enriching it. Henry VIII continued building and increased the royal precinct until it extended from Charing Cross to Westminster Hall, from the river to St James's Park. In 1996 archaeologists confirmed the discovery, below the Ministry of Defence, of a sophisticated type of Turkish bath, fitted with a 12ft/3.5m stove and lined with British-made tiles.

The early owners of Whitehall had shown respect for a parcel of land known as Scotland, which until the 16C had been the site of a Scottish royal palace. When it was eventually built over, the streets were named Little, Great **Scotland Yard** etc. The newly formed Metropolitan Police, given an office there in 1829, became known by their address and retained it when they moved along the Embankment in the 1890s and later, in 1967, to Victoria Street.

William and Mary disliked Whitehall Palace and, after a disastrous fire in 1698, did nothing to restore it. All that remains are the Tudor walls and windows behind the Old **Treasury** (visible from Downing Street), the end of Queen Mary's Terrace, a riverside quay and steps that were built in 1661 by Wren (NE corner of the Ministry of Defence) and the highly decorative Banqueting House (*see Additional Sights*).

🐾 WALKING TOUR
Trafalgar Square★★

The square was laid out by **John Nash** in 1820 as part of a proposed north-south route linking Bloomsbury to Westminster. The granite **fountains**, with their mermaids and dolphins, were added in 1845 and remodelled in 1939 by Lutyens. The square was completed at the turn of the 20C by **Sir Charles Barry**, who also constructed the north terrace in front of the National Gallery. Major improvement plans have created a majestic piazza with steps sweeping down from the National Gallery.

Nelson's Column rises from a pedestal, decorated with bronze reliefs commemorating the Battles of St Vincent, Aboukir, Copenhagen and Trafalgar cast from French cannon, via a fluted granite column, to a bronze Corinthian capital supporting the admiral – a full 185ft/56m overall. **Landseer**'s four magnificent bronze lions (20ft/6m long, 11ft/3m high) were mounted in 1867.

Against the north terrace wall are **Imperial Standards of Length** (1 inch, 1 foot, etc.) and busts of 20C Admirals; the north-east pedestal is occupied by a bronze equestrian figure of **George IV**, originally commissioned by the king for Marble Arch; on the south corner plinths are mounted two 19C generals. The fourth plinth was originally meant for an equestrian statue, but laid empty for years, It is now topped by temporary specially commissioned sculpture.

On the outside of the square, before and behind the National Gallery are figures of **James II** by Grinling Gibbons, **George Washington** after Houdon and Henry Irving. On the island (NE) is Nurse **Edith Cavell**.

St Martin-in-the-Fields★

⚒ 🕐*Open daily 8am–6pm. Brochure (6 languages). Lunchtime recitals: Mon–Tue and Fri 1pm; evening concerts: Thu–Sat 7.30pm; jazz nights Wed 8pm and 9.10pm in the Café in the Crypt, tickets available from Crypt box office (Mon–Sat 10am–5pm) or by telephone. 👝£8. Market daily. 📞020 7766 1100.*

The church is famous not only for its architecture – particularly its elegant spire – and, since the 1930s, as a shelter for the homeless, but also for giving its name to the world-famous chamber orchestra the **Academy of St Martin-in-the-Fields**, which maintains the church's long-standing tradition for classical music with recitals and concerts. The present edifice was designed by Gibbs in 1722–26. The steeple rises in five stages to a pillared octagonal lantern and concave obelisk spire. The triangular pediment crowning the Corinthian portico bears the royal arms; this is justified by the fact that Buckingham Palace stands within the parish boundary. The spacious galleried interior is barrel vaulted; the stucco work by the two Italians Artari and Bagutti; the pulpit is by Grinling Gibbons.

In the vaulted crypt is the **London Brass Rubbing Centre**, which has replicas of brasses from churches in all parts of the country and from abroad, including some Celtic engravings (⏰open daily 10am–7pm; 🚫closed Good Fri, 25 Dec; Brass rubbings including all materials according to size 👓from £4.50; 📞020 7766 1122).

In the courtyard is a lively arts and crafts **market**, and in the alley behind the market, Maggie Hamblyn's (1998) bronze commemorates **Oscar Wilde**.

▶ *Walk up to St Martin's Lane.*

Beyond the Post Office stands the striking Edwardian **Coliseum**, home to the English National Opera (*see Your Stay in the City: Entertainment*).

▶ *Retrace your steps to the top of Whitehall and cross to the west side noting Charles I's statue on the island.*

Hubert Le Sueur's equestrian statue of **Charles I** was cast in Covent Garden in 1633; in 1655 it was discovered in the crypt of St Paul's by Cromwell's men, who sold it to a brazier making a fortune from its supposed "relics". Eventually it was purchased by Charles II and set up

Nelson on his column looks down on Trafalgar Square, a rallying point

H. Le Gac/MICHELIN

A National Hero

Horatio Nelson, 1st Viscount (1758–1805), was the son of a Norfolk clergyman. He went to sea aged 12 and rose through the ranks to become captain in 1793. During various French revolutionary actions, he lost his right eye (1794) and his right arm (1797) before defeating the French at Aboukir Bay (1798), and destroying their fleet at Trafalgar. It was during this final campaign that he died from a musket wound to the shoulder (the ball is conserved at the National Maritime Museum in Greenwich, as are many letters, personal possessions and memorabilia). His ship, HMS *Victory*, on which he died, is at the Historic Dockyards in Portsmouth.

in 1675 overlooking the execution site (wreath-laying 30 January at 11am by the Royal Stuart Society). From this point mileages from London are measured (*plaque in pavement behind statue*).

WHITEHALL★★

Whitehall, formerly known as King Street, and Parliament Street are lined by government offices (*see INTRODUCTION TO LONDON – London Today*).

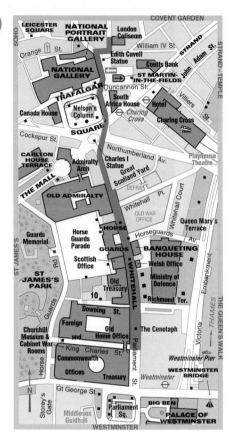

Horse Guards★★★

⏱**Ceremonial mounting of the Queen's Life Guard**★★★ *daily by the Household Cavalry at 11am (10am Sun) on Horse Guards Parade, dismount ceremony daily 4pm in the Front Yard of Horse Guards. The Cavalry rides along the Mall between Horse Guards and their barracks in* **Hyde Park**★★★. *℘020 7414 2353. www.army. mod.uk*

The low 18C stonefaced edifice, designed symmetrically by **William Kent** around three sides of a shallow forecourt, is pierced by a central arch and marked above by a clock tower. The plain building acts as the official entrance to Buckingham Palace and as such is where all dignitaries of State on an official visit are greeted. To this end it is guarded by mounted sentries. When the Queen is in London this comprises an officer, a corporal major to bear the standard, two non-commissioned officers, a trumpeter and 10 troopers (Long Guard); otherwise there are two non-commissioned officers and 10 troopers only (Short Guard). Sentry duty alternates between the Life Guards in scarlet tunics and white plumed helmets, and the Blues and Royals in blue with red plumes. The west front *(through the arch)* overlooks the parade

Old Admiralty★

The Old Admiralty of 1722–26 was, in Horace Walpole's phrase "deservedly veiled by **Mr Adam's** handsome screen", a Classical portico erected in 1759–61.

Hidden History of the Square

A Noble Emblem – In the south-east corner of Trafalgar Square was the early 17C Northumberland House (demolished in the 19C to make way for Northumberland Avenue), identified by the Northumberland lion, now at Syon (*see SUBURBS – SYON HOUSE*), which stood above the gate.

Eleanor Cross – In 1290 Edward I erected 12 crosses to mark the route taken by the funeral cortege of his queen on its journey to Westminster. It was here, in Trafalgar Square that the last of the solid-looking octagonal structures of marble and Caen stone was placed; it was destroyed by the Puritans but a 19C reproduction now stands in the forecourt of Charing Cross Station. A mural in the Underground station (Northern Line) shows the Medieval cross being built.

Death of a King

After his defeat by Cromwell and the Parliamentary troops Charles I had been brought to trial on 20 January in Westminster Hall on a charge of high treason and "other high crimes against the realm of England" before a specially constituted high court of justice, which he refused to recognise on the grounds that "a King cannot be tried by any superior jurisdiction of earth." He maintained that he stood for "the liberty of the people of England" and refused to plead. On 27 January he was sentenced to death as a "tyrant, traitor, murderer and public enemy." He claimed that he was a martyr for the people. He was buried a week later at Windsor.

ground where the Colour is Trooped in June. Among the statues and memorials is a huge French mortar from Cadiz (1812) and the **Guards' Memorial** (1926) *(on the far side)* backed by St James's Park (*see BUCKINGHAM PALACE*).

Cross for Banqueting House.

The 18C **Dover** and **Gwydyr Houses**, both named after 19C owners and facing each other across Whitehall, are home to the **Scottish and Welsh Offices**.

Ministry of Defence
In front of the monolithic building stands the small, jaunty, bronze of **Sir Walter Raleigh**, who was beheaded nearby. Next to him stands '**Monty**', a 10ft/3m solid bronze statue of Field Marshal Lord Montgomery of Alamein by Oscar Nemon, unveiled in 1980.
The façade of **Richmond Terrace**, dating from 1822, has been restored to its original design.

Cross the street again.

Treasuries have stood on the site since the 16C. The present one of 1845 by Barry, used the columns from the previous building by Soane.

Downing Street
No 10 has been the residence of the Prime Minister since 1731 when Sir Robert Walpole accepted it *ex-officio* from George II. The row of four or five very large houses, erected in the 1680s by Sir George Downing, was rebuilt in the 1720s. No 10 contains the **Cabinet**

Room and a staircase, on which hang portraits of each successive resident. The Chancellor of the Exchequer lives at No 11.

The Cenotaph
The slim white monument by **Lutyens** (1919) is the country's official war memorial. A service is held on Remembrance Sunday *(the Sunday nearest to 11 November)* in the presence of the Queen.
The two Victorian-Italian palazzo style buildings on either side of King Charles St are best known for the Treasury door on Great George Street, from which the Chancellor goes to the House on Budget Day, and the former Home Office balcony, from which members of the Royal Family watch the Remembrance Day service.

At the far end of King Charles St are the Cabinet War Rooms (see Additional Sights; for description of Parliament Square, see WESTMINSTER).

ADDITIONAL SIGHTS
Banqueting House★★
Open (Government functions permitting, check by phone) Mon–Sat, 10am–5pm. Closed bank holidays, 24 Dec to 1 Jan. £4.50 (including audio guide). 020 3166 6154/5. www.hrp.org.uk.
The palladian-style hall, all that remains of Whitehall Palace, has been called a memorial to the Stuarts. It was built by Inigo Jones for James I (1619–22); Charles I then had the sumptuous ceiling paintings done by Rubens in

©Richard Lea-Hair/Historic Royal Palaces/NTI

Ceiling paintings by Rubens,
Banqueting House

1629 and stepped on to the scaffold in Whitehall through one of its windows on 30 January 1649; 11 years later, Charles II received the Lords and Commons in the hall on the eve of his restoration.

Although the exterior has been refaced in Portland stone (1829 by Soane) and a new north entrance and staircase were added by Wyatt in 1809 (lead bust of Charles I over the door and bronze of James I by **Le Sueur** inside) and although the interior was used as a chapel and a museum from the 18C to the 20C, it now looks as splendid as it might have done in the 17C and still

serves superbly beneath the chandeliers for occasional official functions.

Inside it is a single empty space, conceived as a double cube 110ft/33.5m x 55ft/17m x 55ft/17m with a balcony supported on gilded corbels on three sides; above, richly decorated beams quarter the ceiling decorated with Rubens' flamboyant **paintings** in praise of James I.

Churchill Museum and Cabinet War Rooms★★

Clive Steps, King Charles Street.
&.*Open daily 9.30am–6pm (last admission 5pm). Closed 24–26 Dec. Audio guide (8 languages). £12.95. Cafeteria. 020 7930 6961. www.iwm.org.uk.*

The underground emergency accommodation provided to protect **Winston Churchill**, his War Cabinet and the Chiefs of Staff of the armed forces from air attacks, was the nerve centre of the war effort from 1939 to 1945. The 19 rooms on view include the Cabinet Room; the Transatlantic Telephone Room (for direct communication with the White House); the Map Room decked with original maps marked with pins and coloured strings; the Prime Minister's Room, and the room from which Churchill made direct broadcasts to the nation. Also in situ are the wedged

Sir Winston Leonard Spencer Churchill (1874–1965)

Churchill was perhaps Britain's most charismatic leader: his speeches – broadcast worldwide by the BBC – rallied military troops into action, civilians at home and in occupied Europe, prisoners, spies, friends and foes. He is still remembered for his bursts of anger and impatience by those who knew him, but is respected for his brilliance, staunch patriotism and remarkable use of the English language. His school report (aged nine) describes him as "very bad… a constant trouble to everybody and is always in some scrape or other" – a far cry from the man who was to rise through Harrow, soldiering, to the war premiership, and become an elder statesman through the Cold War crisis.

He was a creature of habit, on the whole. He would wake at 8.30am, hold court from his bed throughout the morning until it was time for his bath (mid/late morning); he would then lunch, take a nap and maybe another soak before going out to dinner and dealing with business late into the night; meals were preferably accompanied by champagne, and punctuated by a dozen or so cigars smoked throughout the day. His presence lives on in the Cabinet War Rooms while his distinctive silhouette watches over the House of Commons from Parliament Square.

wooden supports that were installed by the Naval team assigned to reinforce the premises against collapse during shelling.

Within his private quarters is now a **museum**. It tells a surprisingly intimate tale of the man in five sections: Young Churchill (1874–1900); Politician to Statesman (1900–1929); Wilderness Years (1929–1939); War Leader (1939–1945); and Cold War Statesman (1945–1965 and legacy). A 50ft (15m)-long, interactive **Lifeline**, using documents, photos, film and sound archives is matched by some 150 original objects including Churchill's baby rattle, a red velvet siren suit and painting materials.

Cabinet Room, Churchill Museum and Cabinet War Rooms

Churchill Museum and Cabinet War Rooms

ADDRESSES

✗ LIGHT BITE

Café in the Crypt – *Duncannon St, St Martin-in-the-Fields, WC2N 4JJ.* ⊖*Charing Cross.* 𝄞*020 7766 1158. www. stmartin-in-the-fields.org.* The self-service installed in the lovely 18C vaulted crypt is one of the best places in the area for a quick, inexpensive snack; all proceeds go to the famous church.

CONCERTS

St-Martin-in-the-Fields – *Evening concerts: Tue, Thu–Sat at 7.30pm; tickets available from the Crypt box office (Mon–Sat 10am–5pm) or by telephone. 𝄞020 7766 1100. www.stmartin-in-the-fields. org.* Candle-lit evening concerts held here make for a highly romantic experience.

Westminster★★★

Westminster resonates with royal and political history: the coronation ceremony and other prestigious royal events at Westminster Abbey, the state opening of Parliament with elaborate pageantry, and state visits when royal personages and other dignitaries process in glittering carriages with the mounted cavalry in attendance. The Palace of Westminster, Big Ben and Westminster Abbey are the undisputed highlights, but there are also elegant enclaves to admire.

A BIT OF HISTORY

Westminster embodies two important institutions of state: Westminster Abbey *(listed separately)*, where coronations

▶ **Location:** *Map: Inside front cover (DEY).* ⊖*Westminster; Victoria.* The South Bank is over Westminster Bridge and for Tate Britain, follow the river upstream on the north bank. St James's Park and Buckingham Palace are within walking distance. For excursions on the Thames, visit Westminster Pier.

🕐 **Timing:** Allow 2hr for Westminster Palace and Abbey; 1.5hr to stroll around the area.

and royal weddings are held, and the Palace of Westminster, the seat of both Houses of Parliament.

The district acquired its name meaning "the minster in the west", as opposed to St Paul's Cathedral, "the minster in the east", when Edward the Confessor rebuilt the abbey church on Thorney Island; he also built a royal palace and the parish church of St Margaret next to the abbey precincts.

Royal Palace

King William I built much at his palace, for, according to Stow, he found the residence of **Edward the Confessor** "far inferior to the building of princely palaces in France." Unlike the Tower, William's palace at Westminster was never strongly fortified but remained intact for centuries. Hemming in the palace on all sides were houses for members of the court who, as representatives of local communities or commons, began from 1332 to meet apart as the House of Commons.

The **opening ceremony of Parliament** took place then, as it does now, in the presence of the monarch, but in those days it was held in a richly ornamented hall known as the Painted Chamber. The Lords then adjourned to the White Hall, while the Commons remained or adjourned to the Westminster Abbey Chapter House (*see WESTMINSTER ABBEY*) or to the monks' refectory. After the fire

of 1512 the old palace was not rebuilt and **Henry VIII** had no royal residence in Westminster, until he confiscated York House from Wolsey in 1529. In 1547 St Stephen's Chapel was granted by **Edward VI** to the Commons as their chamber where they continued to sit until the 19C.

The Lords, so nearly blown up in the **Gunpowder Plot** (1605), continued to meet in the White Hall until the night of 16 October 1834 when a devastating fire swept through Westminster Palace; the only buildings to survive were Westminster Hall, St Stephen's Crypt, St Stephen's cloister and the Jewel Tower.

The new Parliament buildings designed by **Charles Barry** and **Augustus Pugin** by innermost fervour were completed in 1860; there were over 1 000 rooms, 100 staircases and 2mi/3km of corridors spread over 8 acres/3mi.

HOUSES OF PARLIAMENT (PALACE OF WESTMINSTER)★★★

Guided tours (75min) available. Call or see website for details. ℘0870 906 3773. www.parliament.uk.

Barry's ground plan is outstandingly simple: two chambers are disposed on a single, processional north-south axis so that the throne, the Woolsack, the bars

Houses of Parliament

©David Joyner/iStockphoto.com

The Gunpowder Plot

Robert Catesby, Thomas Winter, Thomas Percy and John Wright intended to blow up the House of Lords, the king and queen and heir to the throne. They rented a cellar extending under Parliament and enlisted **Guy Fawkes**, a little-known mercenary from York, just returned from war abroad, to plant the explosive in the cellar: at least 20 barrels of gunpowder camouflaged with coal and faggots. Seeking to recruit additional support, Catesby approached Francis Tresham, who warned Lord Monteagle, his brother-in-law, not to attend Parliament on the fateful day. Monteagle alerted the government and Guy Fawkes was discovered in the cellar late on 4 November. Under torture on the rack he revealed the names of his fellow conspirators. Catesby and Percy were killed while resisting arrest. The others were tried, hanged, drawn and quartered on 31 January 1606. Guy Fawkes Day is celebrated every 5 November with fireworks.

of the two chambers and the Speaker's chair are all in line. At the centre is a large common lobby. Libraries, committee rooms and dining rooms, parallel to the main axis, overlook the river. Above the central lobby rises a lantern and slender spire (originally part of the ventilation system). The ends of the complex are marked by dissimilar towers: the Victoria Tower over the royal entrance, the other housing a clock.

The long waterfront is articulated from end to end with Gothic pinnacles and windows and decorated with medieval tracery, carving, niches and figures, individually designed by Pugin in Perpendicular Gothic.

Royal Entrance and Staircase

On ceremonial occasions, such as the Opening of Parliament, the sovereign is met by high officers of state at the entrance to the Victoria Tower; members of the Household Cavalry line the flight of stairs leading up to the **Norman Porch**, which is square in shape and Perpendicular in style with gilded vaulting.

Robing Room★

Here the sovereign assumes the Imperial State Crown and crimson parliamentary robe. The room, like the Lords' Chamber, presents Pugin's most remarkable concentration of decorative invention: note in particular the elaborately ornamented panelled ceiling.

Royal Gallery

The gallery (110ft/33.5m), the sovereign's processional way, is decorated with frescoes by Daniel Maclise, gilt bronze statues of monarchs from Alfred to Queen Anne and portraits of all the sovereigns and their consorts since George I. In the following **Prince's Chamber** are representations of the Tudor monarchs and their consorts, including all six wives of Henry VIII.

House of Lords★★

The "magnificent and gravely gorgeous" chamber is the summit of Pugin's achievement; a symphony of design and workmanship in scarlet, gilding and encrusted gold. At one end of

House of Lords
© Peter Aprahamian/Corbis

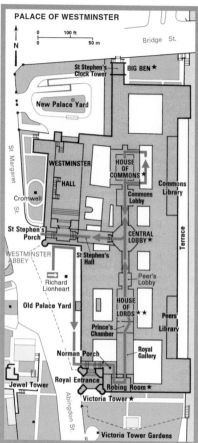

PALACE OF WESTMINSTER

N

0   100 ft
0   50 m

Bridge St.

St Stephen's
Clock Tower

BIG BEN ★

New Palace Yard

St Margaret

WESTMINSTER

HALL

HOUSE
OF
COMMONS ★

Cromwell
St.

Commons
Library

Commons
Lobby

St Stephen's
Porch

WESTMINSTER
ABBEY

St Stephen's
Hall

CENTRAL
LOBBY ★

Terrace

Richard
Lionheart

Peer's
Lobby

Old Palace Yard

HOUSE
OF
LORDS ★★

Peers'
Library

Prince's
Chamber

Norman Porch

Royal
Gallery

Jewel Tower

Royal Entrance

Abingdon St.

Robing Room ★

Victoria Tower ★

Victoria Tower Gardens

the chamber on a stepped dais stands the throne beneath a Gothic canopy. The Woolsack, symbol of England's Medieval wealth, is said to be "most uncomfortable". The benches are covered in red buttoned leather;

the one with arms is for the bishops. The cross benches are between the clerk's table and the bar of the house, behind which the members of the House of Commons stand when summoned by Black Rod to hear the speech from the throne at the State Opening of Parliament in November. Between the windows are statues of 18 barons who witnessed King John's assent to **Magna Carta**.

Central Lobby★

The octagonal lobby (75ft/23m high) is the hub of the building, where constituents waiting to see their MP may spot many well-known political figures. Every element of the design is by Pugin: Perpendicular arches framing the windows and entrances, decorated with English sovereigns, life-size 19C statesmen, mosaics over the doors, gilded and patterned roof ribs and the chandelier.

When the **Commons Lobby**, destroyed in an air raid in 1941, was reconstructed, stones from the original fabric were incorporated in the **Churchill Arch**; it is flanked by his statue in bronze by Oscar Nemon and a statue of Lloyd George.

House of Commons★

The chamber, also destroyed in the 1941 raid, was rebuilt without decoration. The parallel benches in the traditional green hide provide seating for 437 of the 651 elected members. At the end is the canopied Speaker's chair; before it are the seats of the Clerks and the table of the house bearing the mace and the bronze-mounted despatch boxes. The red stripes on either side of the green carpet mark the limit to which a member may advance when addressing the house. The government sits to the Speaker's right, the Prime Minister opposite the despatch box. When a division is called, members leave for the tellers' lobbies past the Speaker's right for Aye and through the far end for No.

The **libraries**, overlooking the river, are oases of silence. The Lords' library, decoration by Pugin, contains the warrant for the execution of Charles I signed by Cromwell and the council.

The **terrace** is reserved for Members of Parliament and their guests, a very special place to take tea.

St Stephen's Hall

The long narrow hall, the public entrance to the Central Lobby, was constructed by Barry to look like the 14C St Stephen's Chapel. At the end are two superimposed arches, the upper filled with a mosaic of St Stephen between King Stephen and Edward the Confessor. The brasses on the floor mark the limit of the old Commons chamber (60ft/18m x 30ft/9m).

Westminster Hall★

The hall was added to William I's palace by his son, **William Rufus**, in 1097. Throughout the Middle Ages it was used for royal Christmas feasts, jousts, ceremonial events and as a place of assembly. **Sir Thomas More** (1535), **Somerset** (1551), **Northumberland** (1553), Essex (1601), **Guy Fawkes** (1606) and **Charles I** all stood trial in the hall. Westminster Hall was later appointed the permanent Seat of Justice until the Royal Courts of Justice (◉ see STRAND) moved to the Strand in the 1870s. During this century monarchs and Churchill have lain in state there.

The superb **hammerbeam roof★★★**, probably the finest timber roof of all time, was constructed by Henry Yevele, master mason, and Hugh Herland, carpenter, at the command of **Richard II** in 1394. The roof rises to 90ft at the crest and depends on projecting hammerbeams. The beams, now reinforced with steel, are carved with great flying angels.

The hall (238ft/69.5m x 70ft/21m) is lit by Perpendicular windows at each end. The south window was removed

Facts and Figures

Measuring 9ft/3m in diameter and 7ft/2m in height, **Big Ben** weighs in at 13tons 10cwts 3qtrs 15lbs, it also has a 4ft/1m crack, which developed soon after being installed.

The **clock** mechanism weighs about 5 tons. The dials of cast-iron tracery (diameter 23ft/7m) are glazed with pot opal glass; the figures are 2ft/60cm long; the minute spaces are 1ft/30cm square; the 14ft/4m long minute hands are made of copper, weigh 2 cwts and travel 120mi/193km per year.

to its present position in the 19C by Barry; beneath the resulting arch, now flanked by six 14C statues of early English kings, Barry inserted a dramatic flight of steps rising from the hall to **St Stephen's Porch**.

St Stephen's Crypt (St Mary's Chapel)

The domestic chapel built (1292–97) by Edward I was on two levels, the upper being reserved for the royal family. After St Stephen's had been granted to the Commons, the lower chapel was used for secular purposes until the 19C when the Medieval chamber was redecorated as a chapel.

Big Ben's Clock Tower★

St Stephen's clock tower (316ft/97m) was completed by 1858–59. Inside is a luxurious prison cell in which the leader of the militant movement for women's suffrage, Emmeline Pankhurst, was detained in 1902.

The name **Big Ben** applied originally only to the bell which was cast at the Whitechapel Foundry. The clock with an electrically wound mechanism proved reliable until it succumbed to metal fatigue in 1976, and subsequently required major repairs. Big Ben's chimes were first broadcast on New Year's Eve in 1923. The Ayrton light above the clock is lit while the Commons is sitting.

New and Old Palace Yards

In **New Palace Yard** is the Jubilee Fountain inaugurated by the Queen in May 1977. Farther south a plinth supports the statue of **Oliver Cromwell**; opposite, above the small north-east door of St Margaret's Church is a small head of Charles I. Meanwhile, **Richard the Lionheart** patiently sits astride his horse in Old Palace Yard.

Victoria Tower★

&♿ ⏱Open Mon–Fri 9.30am–5pm, preferably by appointment. ⏱Closed certain public holidays and last two weeks of Nov. Leaflet. ✆020 7219 4272. www.parliament.uk

The Victoria Tower (336ft/102m), taller than the clock tower, was designed as the archive for parliamentary documents. The **House of Lords Record Office** now contains 3 million papers including journals of the House of Lords from 1510 and of the Commons from 1547, records of the **Gunpowder Plot**, etc. The statuary in the **Victoria Tower Gardens** includes a cast of the great bronze group by Rodin, **The Burghers of Calais**, who ransomed themselves to Edward III in 1347 as well as a slim statue of the emminent suffragette movement leader **Emmeline Pankhurst**.

Jewel Tower

⏱Open daily 10am–5pm (4pm Nov–Mar). ⏱Closed 24–26 Dec, 1 Jan. 💷£2.90. ✆020 7222 2219. www.english-heritage.org.uk

The L-shaped tower with a corner staircase turret, dates from 1365 when it was built as the king's personal jewel house and treasury and surrounded by a moat. There is a brick vaulted strongroom on the first floor with a later iron door (1612). When Westminster ceased to be a royal palace, the tower became the archive for parliamentary papers and subsequently the weights and measures office.

Adjoining the Jewel Tower in Abingdon Garden stands the sculpture *Knife Edge to Edge* by Henry Moore (1964).

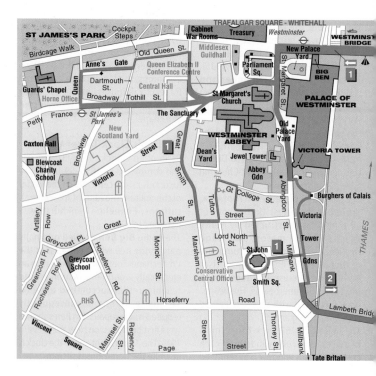

🐾 WALKING TOUR

▷ *Start from Westminster Bridge, then cross to Parliament Square.*

Westminster Bridge★

The stone bridge (1750), where Wordsworth composed his sonnet (1807), was the second to be built, after London Bridge. It was replaced in 1862 with a flat stone structure by Thomas Page, comprising seven low arches. From the bridge there is a fine view of the terrace and riverfront of the Houses of Parliament. At the bridge foot is a sculpture of **Boadicea** heroically riding in her chariot during her campaign against the Romans.

Parliament Square

The square and Parliament Street, which were laid out in 1750 at the time of the building of the first Westminster Bridge, were redesigned in 1951. There are bronze statues of Victorian statesmen such as **Lord Palmerston, Benjamin Disraeli** and **Robert Peel**, but one's attention is inevitably drawn to the powerful statue of **Churchill** by Ivor Roberts Jones.

▷ *Cross the square to the south and walk past St Margaret's Church (👁see Additional Sights) and Westminster Abbey (👁see WESTMINSTER ABBEY).*

The Sanctuary

In the monastery's day, the right of sanctuary extended over a considerable area. The quarter became so overbuilt with squalid houses and the right was so abused by vagabonds, thieves and murderers that it was first restricted and finally abolished, in all but name, under James I.

The Gatehouse in which **Sir Walter Raleigh** spent the last night before his execution and **Richard Lovelace** penned the line "stone walls do not a prison make nor iron bars a cage" was demolished in 1776; on the site stands a red granite column erected in memory of former pupils of Westminster School who died in the Indian Mutiny and the Crimean War.

The Sanctuary buildings, designed by Sir Gilbert Scott with an archway through to the Dean's Yard (👁see WESTMINSTER ABBEY), are in marked contrast with the 1970s **Queen Elizabeth II Conference Centre** and **Central Hall** opposite, designed as a Wesleyan church with the third-largest dome in London by Rickards and Lanchester in 1912 and now used as an examination hall or hired out for public events.

▷ *Walk up Storey's Gate and turn left into Old Queen St lined with several 18C houses (note no 28).*

Cockpit Steps now lead to Birdcage Walk and St James's Park (👁see BUCK-INGHAM PALACE) but in the days of Whitehall Palace they led down to a cockfighting pit.

Flanked by the Home Office buildings on the left, is **Queen Anne's Gate**, an L-shaped street of substantial three-storey terraced houses dating from the reign of Queen Anne (1704). Several pilastered

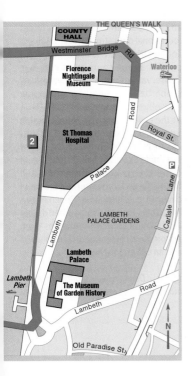

doorways are protected by flat wooden hoods, decorated with rich carving and hanging pendants. The street's hallmark is the white satyr's mask set in place of a tablet stone above the ground and first floor windows of every house.

▷ *Take Broadway and Tothill St to the top of Victoria St.*

Victoria Street

The street was cut through the Georgian slums to link Parliament to Victoria Station in 1862. It is now lined with 20C buildings – tower blocks in steel and brown glass, faced in marble, stone and concrete, providing offices for government ministries and international companies.

Buildings of interest include: **New Scotland Yard** (1967); **London Transport's** headquarters (1927–29) by Charles Holden with decorative statuary groups by **Jacob Epstein** and reliefs by **Eric Gill, Henry Moore** and others; **Caxton Hall** (1878), once famous for register office weddings; the old **Blewcoat Charity School** (*Buckingham Street*), a delightful square red-brick building erected in 1709 to house the school, which was founded in 1688 and is now the property of the National Trust (*National Trust Shop and Information Centre:* ◷*open Mon–Fri 10am–5.30pm (Thu 7pm);* ◷*Closed 25 Dec–1 Jan and bank holidays;* ✆*020 7222 2877).* At the west end of the street stands **Little Ben**, a model (30ft/9m high) of Big Ben. **Victoria Railway Station** was built in the 1870s, but the present buildings are from the 1900s.

▷ *Walk back to Westminster Cathedral piazza, turn right into Ambrosden Ave, walk up Francis St and make for the north side of Vincent Square.*

Vincent Square

The large square was laid out in 1810 to provide playing fields for Westminster School (ⓖ*see WESTMINSTER ABBEY).* On the north-east side is the **Royal**

Horticultural Society (f. 1804), a square brick building with the New Horticultural Hall (1923–28) at the back where monthly flower shows are held *(open to non-members).*

▷ *Proceed along Elverton St and take Horseferry Rd.*

Greycoat School

Greycoat Place.

The grey uniform of this Westminster Charity school, founded in 1698, can be seen on the small wooden niche figures, contrasting puritanically with the bright royal coat of arms set between them on the pedimented stucco; it is now a girls' school.

▷ *Proceed along Great Peter St and turn right into Lord North St.*

Smith Square

The square, the four streets midway along each side, and the streets to the north, include many original Georgian houses: nos 6–9 Smith Square, all Lord North Street except at the northern end and at the south end of Cowley Street (occasional date stones 1722, 1726).

Today, the square is associated with politics; in the south-west corner is **Conservative Central Office** while many properties all around accommodate MPs' offices or lodgings.

At the centre stands **St John's, Smith Square**, a tall Baroque church (1714–28), designed by Thomas Archer, now serving as a concert hall. Its four ornate corner towers having been compared by the queen to an upturned footstool gave rise to its nickname "Queen Anne's Footstool." It was badly bombed during World War II but the interior has been restored with giant Corinthian columns and an 18C chandelier.

▷ *Take Dean Stanley St and turn left into Millbank to return to Parliament Sq.*

WESTMINSTER CATHEDRAL★

&♿ *Open daily 8am–7pm (5.30pm bank holidays).* ✆ *020 7798 9055. www.westminstercathedral.org.uk.*

Set back from Victoria Street and graced by a modern piazza, towers the remarkable neo-Byzantine Roman Catholic cathedral. Cardinal Manning and his successor Cardinal Vaughan determined on early Christian inspiration for the architecture of the new cathedral. The architect **JF Bentley**, travelled widely in Italy before producing (1894) plans for an **Italianate-Byzantine** building; construction started promptly in 1895 and was completed so far as the fabric was concerned by 1903. The brick building (360ft/109m long x 156ft/47m wide) is distinguished by a domed **campanile** (273ft/83m high).

Interior

The initial impression is of vastness and fine proportions. The nave, the widest in England, is roofed by three domes. The decoration is incomplete; above the marble and granite lower surfaces and piers rise unpointed brick walls, awaiting mosaics. The altar, beneath its baldachin supported on yellow marble columns, is dominated by a suspended crucifix. On the main piers are the 14 Stations of the Cross.

The body of the English martyr, John Southworth, hanged, drawn and quartered at Tyburn in 1654, lies in the second chapel in the north aisle. The south transept contains an early 15C alabaster statue of the Virgin and Child, carved by the Nottingham school, which originally stood in Westminster Abbey but was removed to France in the 15C and returned in 1955; there is also a bronze of St Teresa of Lisieux by Giacomo Manzù and a Chi-Rho, executed in flat-headed nails, by David Partridge.

St Margaret's Church★

⏰ *Open daily.*

The Parish and Parliamentary Church built by Edward the Confessor to serve local parishioners was rebuilt in the mid- 14C. A third reconstruction (1488–1523), scarcely completed at the time of the Reformation, would have been demolished had not the parishioners "with bows and arrows, staves and clubs and other such offensive weapons... so terrified the workmen that they ran away in great amazement." Much of the church's present late Perpendicular appearance derives from the radical restoration undertaken by Sir George Gilbert Scott in the mid-19C.

St Margaret's is the church of the House of Commons, not only because the Palace of Westminster lies within the parish but by a tradition inaugurated on Palm Sunday 1614 when the Commons met for the first time for corporate communion and, being mostly Puritans, preferred the church to the abbey.

Each year in November a **Garden of Remembrance**, composed of commemorative Flanders poppies, blossoms in the churchyard.

Interior

The interior presents Tudor monuments: Blanche Parry, Chief Gentlewoman of Queen Elizabeth's privy chamber (to the right side of the porch on entering), a Yeoman of the Guard (d. 1577 at 94), Richard Montpesson, kneeling by his wife's tomb. There are two plaques *(by the east door)* and fragments of a window *(north aisle)* as memorials to **Caxton**, buried in the old churchyard; **Walter Raleigh** executed in Old Palace Yard on 29 October 1618 and buried beneath the high altar is commemorated in a tablet near the east door and in the west window, presented in the late 19C by citizens of the USA. The carved lime-wood reredos (1753) is based on Titian's *Supper at Emmaus*. The east window is special, having been made in Flanders in 1501 at the behest of Ferdinand and Isabella of Spain to celebrate the marriage of their daughter Catherine to Prince Arthur; by the time it arrived Arthur was dead and the princess affianced to the future Henry VIII. The window was despatched outside London and retrieved only in 1758 when the House of Commons purchased it for 400 guineas and presented it to the church.

Westminster Abbey★★★

The Collegiate Church of St Peter at Westminster – better known as Westminster Abbey – is as rich in architectural splendour as it is in history and culture. Moreover, its potent historical associations make it a most glorious monument. For centuries it has hosted the funerals and weddings of statesmen and royalty, witnessed the coronation of many kings and queens, and today hosts cultural events, concerts and festivals. The abbey has a strong musical tradition and the carol concerts are an enjoyable feature of the Christmas period.

A BIT OF HISTORY

Westminster Abbey, for centuries a royal mausoleum, became a national shrine owing to its situation next to the Palace of Westminster, once the Sovereign's residence and now the seat of Parliament.

Since the coronation of William I on Christmas Day in 1066, all but two of the kings and queens of England have been crowned here. In more recent times, it hosted the marriage of the future George VI to Elizabeth Bowes-Lyon (1923), Prince Andrew to Sarah Ferguson (1986) and the funeral of Diana, Princess of Wales (1997).

A Saxon monastery stood on the site in the 6C. **Edward the Confessor** built anew Norman-style abbey church, which was consecrated on 28 December 1065. In 1220, inspired by the Gothic style of Amiens and Rheims, the Plantagenet king, **Henry III**, began to rebuild the church.

By the late 13C, the east end, transept, choir, the first bay of the nave and the chapter house were complete; work then came to a halt and another two centuries passed before the nave was finished.

Henry VII's Chapel (1503–19), built in Perpendicular Gothic style, is the jewel of its age, more delicate, with finer

▷ **Location:** *Map: Inside front cover (EY) and area map under WESTMINSTER.* ⊖*Westminster.* The abbey, at the heart of Westminster, is close to many important tourist sites. The area is on several bus routes from Victoria Station and Trafalgar Square.

⊜ **Don't Miss:** There are 12 bells that ring out, generally between noon and 1pm, on great occasions and on some 25 days of festival and commemoration including 25, 26 and 28 December, 1 January, Easter and Whit Sundays and the Queen's official Birthday. Try to be in the area when they ring.

🕘 **Timing:** The Abbey can easily be visited in under an hour as part of a tour of the whole area of Westminster.

niches and pinnacles than any other part of the abbey.

Later additions, notably the upper parts of the west towers (1722–45) by **Wren** and **Hawksmoor**, and repairs by Sir George Gilbert Scott and others have echoed the Gothic theme. Recent additions (1998) on the west front are limestone statues of modern Christian martyrs (Grand Duchess Elizabeth of Russia, Maximilian Kolbe, Martin Luther King and Oscar Romero among others) placed in niches above figures depicting truth, justice, mercy and peace.

Royal Peculiar – When Henry VIII ordered the Dissolution of the monasteries in 1540, the abbey's treasures were confiscated but the buildings were not destroyed. The 600-year-old Benedictine community was disbanded and the abbot dismissed. In 1560 Elizabeth I established the Collegiate Church of St Peter, with a royally appointed dean and chapter of

12 prebendaries (canons), and also the College of St Peter, generally known as Westminster School, which replaced the monastic school.

VISIT

♿🕒 *Open 9.30am–4.30pm (abbey). Sun services only. Pyx Chamber, Chapter House and shop 10.30am–4pm. Cloisters open daily 8am–6pm; museum open daily 10.30am–4pm. £12, museum free with main ticket. Leaflet (8 languages). Audio-guide. Verger guided tours £3. Free organ recitals every Sun 5.45pm, plus regular programme of concerts throughout the year; some sung services. 020 7222 5152. www.westminster-abbey.org.*

▶ *Enter by the north door.*

The **monuments** to national figures, which crowd the abbey, date from the early Middle Ages. The older monuments, the figures on the ancient tombs, are mostly in the chapels east of the high altar. In the 18C and 19C there was a surfeit of monuments sculpted by the great artists of the day: Roubiliac, the Bacons, Flaxman, Le Sueur, Westmacott, Chantrey. Permission to be buried in the abbey or for a memorial to be erected is granted by the Dean.

Nave – The soaring vaulting retains its original beauty; the carving is delicate, often beautiful, sometimes humorous. At the west end of the nave is the memorial to the **Unknown Warrior (1)**, set in the pavement and surrounded by red Flanders poppies.

Against the first south pier is the **painting of Richard II (2)**, the earliest known painting of an English sovereign. In the north aisle, low down, is the small stone that covered the upright figure of the playwright "O rare Ben Johnson" **(3)** (misspelt).

On the north side, along Musicians' Aisle, you can see the graves and memorials of famous musicians including **Henry Purcell**, a former organist of the Abbey.

The **North Transept**, known as Statesmen's Aisle, contains the graves and memorials of famous national figures.

Choir – The choir screen, which faces the west door, is a 13C structure of stone, with lierne vaulting under the arch.

Sanctuary – This is where the monarch is crowned and receives the peers' homage in the **coronation** ceremony. The floor is laid with a 13C Italian pavement of porphyry and mosaic. Behind the altar is the 19C high altar screen. To the right is a large 15C altarpiece of rare beauty. Beyond is an ancient 13C sedilia painted with full length royal figures (Henry II, Edward I). On the left are three tombs, each a recumbent figure: Aveline of Lancaster (**4**; d. 1274), renowned for her beauty; Aymer de Valence, Earl of Pembroke (**5**; d. 1324), cousin to Edward I; Edmund Crouchback (**6**; d. 1296), youngest son of Henry III, Aveline's husband.

North Ambulatory – On the left is the chapel of Abbot Islip, known for its rebus – an eye and a slip or branch of a tree clasped by a hand.

The **Chapel of Our Lady of the Pew**, in the thickness of the wall, contains a modern alabaster Madonna and Child, modelled on the original which is now in Westminster Cathedral.

Queen Elizabeth Chapel – In the north aisle of Henry VII's Chapel is the tomb of **Queen Elizabeth I (7)** in white marble; beneath is the coffin of Mary Tudor

Westminster Abbey

©Galen Goyer/iStockphoto.com

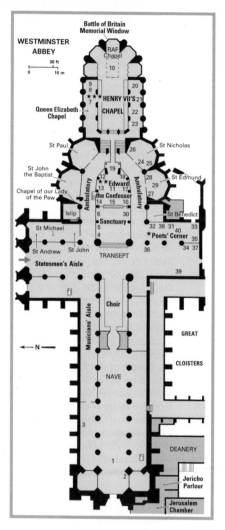

WESTMINSTER ABBEY

Battle of Britain Memorial Window

30 ft
0   10 m

RAF Chapel 10

Queen Elizabeth Chapel

HENRY VII'S CHAPEL

St Paul
St Nicholas
St John the Baptist
St Edmund
Chapel of our Lady of the Pew
Edward the Confessor
Islip
St Benedict
St Michael
Sanctuary
St Andrew St John
Poets' Corner
Statesmen's Aisle
TRANSEPT
Ambulatory

Choir
GREAT CLOISTERS
Musicians' Aisle
NAVE
← N —

DEANERY
Jericho Parlour
Jerusalem Chamber

for the knights' installations in 1725 when George I reconstructed the order.

At the east end is the tomb of Henry VII and Elizabeth of York **(10)**. Beyond, in the **RAF Chapel**, is the **Battle of Britain Memorial Window** (1947), a many-faceted, brightly coloured screen containing the badges of the 68 Fighter Squadrons that took part.

The great double gates at the entrance are decorated with the royal emblems of Henry Tudor and his antecedents: the roses of Lancaster and York, the leopards of England, the fleur-de-lys of France, the falcon of Edward IV, father of Elizabeth, Henry's queen.

Chapel of Edward the Confessor★★ – The chapel contains the tombs of five kings and three queens around the **Confessor's Shrine (11)**. Against the north wall are **Queen Eleanor of Castile (12**; d. 1290), in whose memory the Eleanor crosses were erected (⊙ see TRAFALGAR SQUARE – WHITEHALL) by the master goldsmith William Torel; Henry III **(13**; d. 1272), builder of the chapel; **Edward I**, Longshanks **(14**; d. 1307), the first king to be crowned in the present abbey (1272) and the Hammer of the Scots, who brought south the Scottish regalia and the stone of Scone in 1297.

The carved **stone screen**, which closes the west end of the chapel, was completed in 1441. At the centre stands the **Coronation Chair (15)**; for coronations the chair is moved into the sanctuary.

Against the south wall are Richard II **(16)**; the gilt bronze figure of Edward III **(17**; d. 1377), surrounded by the bronze representations of his children, and his queen Philippa of Hainault **(18**; d. 1369) who interceded for the Burghers of

without any monument. At the east end are memorials to two young daughters of James I **(8)** and, in a small sarcophagus, the bones found in the Tower of London presumed to be those of the Little Princes **(9)**.

Henry VII's Chapel★★★ – Note the superb fan-vaulted roof and the banners of the Knights Grand Cross of the Order of the Bath, hanging still and brilliant above the stalls, which are crowned with pinnacles, helmets and coifs; the witty and inventive misericords date from the 16C to 18C. The chapel was first used

Calais. At the east end is the oak figure of the young Henry V (**19**; d. 422).

South Aisle of Henry VII's Chapel – Here are buried, in a royal vault (**20**), Charles II, William III and Mary, Queen Anne and her consort, George of Denmark. Three grand tombs occupy the centre: Lady Margaret Beaufort (**21**; d. 1509), a masterpiece by **Torrigiano** in gilt bronze; **Mary Queen of Scots (22)** in white marble; Margaret Douglas, Countess of Lennox (**23**; d. 1578), niece of Henry VIII, mother of Darnley and grandmother of James I, a beautiful woman carved in alabaster.

South Ambulatory – St Nicholas' Chapel contains the tomb of Philippa, Duchess of York (**24**; d. 1431) ; the vault of the Percys (**25**); the tomb of Anne, Duchess of Somerset (**26**; d. 1587), widow of the Protector. In St Edmund's Chapel are the tomb of William de Valence (**27**; d. 1296), half brother of Henry III, and the marble effigy of John of Eltham (**28**; d. 1337), second son of Edward II. In the centre, on a low altar tomb, is the abbey's finest **brass** of Eleanor, Duchess of Gloucester (**29**; d. 1399) beneath a triple canopy. On the north side of the ambulatory are Sebert's tomb (**30**) and the sedilia painting of the Confessor.

Poets' Corner★ – This famous corner in the south transept contains the tomb of Chaucer (**31**); statues of the court poets Dryden (**32**) and Ben Jonson (**33**), William Shakespeare (**34**), John Milton (**35**), William Blake (**36**) (bust by Epstein, 1957), Robert Burns (**37**), Longfellow (**38**), Joseph Addison (**39**). Plaques and stones are now more the order of the day: Thomas Hardy, Dylan Thomas, Lewis Carroll (**40**). Oscar Wilde, who died in Paris, is honoured with a window.

Great Cloisters

Preserved in the abbey's precincts are a number of historical buildings.

Chapter House – The octagonal chamber (1248–53), features a fine vault supported by a central pier braced with shafts of Purbeck marble. Under Edward I the Chapter House became the **Parliment House of the Commons** and continued after the Dissolution. By the 19C it had become an archive for the state papers. When the damage caused during World War II was repaired the windows were reglazed with clear glass, decorated with the coats of arms of sovereigns and abbots and the devices of the two Medieval master masons who designed and built the Abbey.

Chapel of the Pyx – The 11C chamber became the monastery treasury in the 13C–14C. At the Dissolution it passed to the Crown and was used as the strongroom in which gold and silver coins were tried against standard specimens kept there in a box or pyx. Today it is used to display church plate from the abbey and from St Margaret's Church (&see WESTMINSTER).

Westminster Abbey Museum – The museum is housed in the low 11C vaulted Norman undercroft. It contains historical documents, gold plate and a number of unique wax and wood funeral effigies. Edward III and Katherine de Valois, both full length, are of wood. The wax figure of **Charles II** in his Garter robes is unforgettable. **Nelson** was purchased by the abbey in 1806 in an attempt to attract the crowds away from his tomb in St Paul's Cathedral.

Among the museum's collection of treasures are the saddle, sword, helm and shield of Henry V that was carried at his funeral in 1422, Mary II's coronation chair, replicas of the coronation regalia that were used for coronation rehearsals and the armour of General Monck, which was carried at his funeral in 1670.

Dean's Yard – The yard, the old heart of the Abbey precinct, is now a tree-shaded lawn. A low arch through the eastern range, is the entrance to **Westminster School** *(private)*. The south side of Dean's Yard is filled by **Church House** (1940), containing the circular Convocation Hall, where the General Synod of the Church of England meets, and the Hoare Memorial Hall, where the Commons sat during the war.

CITY OF LONDON

The City of London, also known as the Square Mile, is a compact area on the north bank of the Thames, now identified with finance. Animated by a commuting workforce on weekdays, at night and weekends it is left silent and eerie, enjoyed only by its tiny population of Barbican residents and, more recently, nightclub-goers. As Docklands to the east makes its mark as a potential rival in the business world, the City continues to expand and reinvent itself, with a skyline of high-rise buildings in modern architectural styles, all set between historic architecture and a plethora of churches.

Highlights

1 Wren's masterpiece, with its iconic dome **St Paul's Cathedral** (p201)

2 World-class theatre and music **Barbican Arts Centre** (p189)

3 Entertaining, fascinating story of London **Museum of London** (p196)

4 Bustling food market in a historic hall **Leadenhall market** (p177)

5 Modern architecture by Richard Rogers **The Lloyd's Building** (p177)

Geography – The boundaries of the City of London have remained largely unchanged since the Middle Ages, and still cover the eponymous "square mile" to the east of the City of Westminster and north of the River Thames. *Take a detailed map to explore the area, as the Medieval street layout can be confusing.*

History – This is the oldest area of London – the original city stretching back to Roman times and earlier. Between and beneath the modern buildings are traces of Celtic and Roman settlements including sections of the city wall (the areas of Aldgate, Ludgate, Bishopsgate and Moorgate indicate where the main gates once were). Historic medieval and Wren churches, rare and tiny gardens and a Victorian market are juxtaposed against modern office buildings. Here, rather than elsewhere in London, vestiges of the old city and her trades and traditions survive, as does the medieval network of narrow courts and alleys, yards and steps steeped in local history.

Today – The City is governed by the City of London Corporation and has a city status – and a police force – of its own. Here you'll find a multitude of old pubs, smart wine bars, expensive restaurants and elegant shops. The arts flourish at the Barbican Centre as well as at small theatres. Visit one of the numerous churches here, the most famous being St Paul's Cathedral.

Traditions – The royal carriage still halts at Temple Bar when the sovereign enters the City; the Prime Minister makes an annual major policy speech at the Lord Mayor's Banquet; on 20 June each year the Guild of Watermen and Lightermen pays a "fine" of one red rose to the Lord Mayor, imposed on Lady Knollys in 1381 for building a bridge across Seething Lane without permission.

The City★★★
The City of London

WALKING TOURS

If visiting the area for the first time, start at **St Paul's Cathedral** (*see ST PAUL'S CATHEDRAL*) before popping into St Mary-le-Bow, walking down past the Bank of England, Mansion House and the Royal Exchange and on to Leadenhall Market and the Lloyd's building. This route will provide an impression of the City's principal institutions and broad range of architectural styles.

1 BANK – BISHOPSGATE
Bank: Cornhill exit.

Bank of England

Seven floors of offices are housed in the Bank, a massive, blank and undistinguished building, designed and erected by Sir Herbert Baker, an associate of Lutyens (1924–39). His version of the Bank of England replaced an earlier building by **Sir John Soane**. The façade sculptures representing Britannia served by six bearers and guardians of wealth are by Sir Charles Wheeler.

The Bank was incorporated under royal charter in 1694 to finance the continuation of the wars against Louis XIV. It acquired its nickname a century later when the institution was forced to suspend cash payments: Gillray drew a caricatur which he captioned "The Old Lady of Threadneedle Street in Danger". The Bank supervises the note issue and national debt and acts as the central reserve. The Governor is appointed by the Crown.

Follow Princes Street and turn right into Lothbury for the Bank of England Museum (see Additional Sights).

St Margaret Lothbury★

Open Mon–Fri 7am–5.15pm.
Closed bank holidays. Organ recitals Thu 1.10pm. Guide book. 020 7726 4878. www.stml.org.uk.
The present building, designed by Wren in 1686–1701, features a slender

Michelin Map: *Map: inside back cover (FGHX).* Bank; Barbican; Moorgate; Liverpool St; Mansion House; St Paul's; Cannon St; Tower Hill; Blackfriars. The City of London extends north from the river between Blackfriars Bridge and the Tower of London, as far as the Barbican.
It is adjacent to the East End and Docklands, and faces Bankside, Southwark and London Bridge across the river.
The heart of the City and the national economy is the Bank of England (**Bank**) and the principal thoroughfares radiate from here.

Info: City of London Information Centre, St Paul's Churchyard, EC4M 8BX. 020 7332 1456. www.visitthecity.co.uk.

Location: Most of the City institutions do not admit casual visitors for security reasons. The whole area is surrounded by a security system that can close off all the roads instantly to protect one of the world's greatest financial centres from the threat of car bombs.

Don't Miss: The Lloyd's Building (Walk 2), St Mary-le-Bow (4), St Paul's Cathedral, the Museum of London.

Timing: We suggest visits during the week when the streets are lively and churches and pubs are open. Note that some churches are open by appointment only, so it is best to check the opening times in advance.

obelisk **spire**★ balancing a gilded ball and vane. The church is renowned for its magnificent interior. The remarkable **woodwork**★ includes an exquisitely carved **pulpit**★ with massive sounding board, dancing cherubs and a reredos with balustered rails; a wonderful oak **screen**★ dated c. 1689 and one of only two made to Wren's design; at the centre pierced pilasters are surmounted by three broken pediments, the central one supported by a great carved eagle.

The dividing screen and the reredos from St Olave Jewry are particularly noteworthy in the south aisle. The **font**★ is attributed to Grinling Gibbons.

Old Stock Exchange
8 Throgmorton Street.

Trading in stocks and shares originated in this country in the 17C: it took place in the coffee houses of **Change Alley** until the first stock exchange was inaugurated in 1773 in Threadneedle Street. In 1801 and 1971 ever larger buildings rose on the site. In 2004, the Stock Exchange moved to a new home in Paternoster Square, beside St Paul's Cathedral.

▶ *Continue along Broad St past Tower 42 and turn left onto London Wall.*

On your right is **All Hallows London Wall** with its Portland-stone tower topped by a pilastered lantern cupola. Inside, note the fine, snowflake-patterned barrel vault (◐ *open Fri 11am–3.30pm; first Wed of month (except Aug) short meditative service (6pm) followed by discussion (7pm); ℘020 7588 2638; www.allhallowsonthewall.org).*

Finsbury Circus
Mid-19C–20C buildings surround the only bowling green in the City, popular in summer with office workers.

▶ *Continue along Blomfield St.*

Broadgate
This redeveloped area features a variety of architectural styles, open spaces, fountains, monumental modern sculpture and, as its focal point, a circular Arena for open-air entertainment, which turns into an ice rink in winter (℘020 7505 4068; www.broadgateice.co.uk). Smart watering holes and restaurants attract City workers.

Liverpool Street Station, erected in 1875, looks like a vast iron Gothic cathedral with soaring arches. Adjoining it is the Great Eastern Hotel, designed by Charles Barry, son of the Houses of Parliament's architect, Sir Giles Gilbert Scott. Following three years of renovation by Conran & Partners, the hotel reopened in 2000 in the grand 19C railway tradition.

Off Bishopsgate to the right is Middlesex Street, known as **Petticoat Lane** and famous for its **market** (◐ *see YOUR STAY IN THE CITY – Shopping).*

Bank of England (left) and Royal Exchange (middle)

J. Malburet/MICHELIN

Lively scene at the Broadgate Arena

K. Brett/MICHELIN

St Botolph-without-Bishopsgate

🕐 *Open Mon–Fri 8am–5.30pm.*
✆ *020 7588 3388. www.botolph.org.uk.*
The church was rebuilt in 1725–29 on a 13C site. The square brick tower, unusually at the east end, rises directly from the Bishopsgate pavement to support a balustrade, clock tower, turret, cupola and crowning urn. Inside, note the wide coffered ceiling and drum-shaped glass dome, added in 1821. The poet Keats was baptised in the existing font in 1795.

In Bishopsgate Churchyard, the **Old Turkish Bath** (1895) faced with decorative glazed tiling and rosewood panelling is now a restaurant.

Nearby is the site of the Saxon gate, renewed several times and finally demolished in 1760. Note the gilded mitres from the old Bishop's Gate on the walls of **nos 105** and **108** *(first floor, Worm-wood and Camomile St corners RX).* Bishopsgate, one of the longest streets in the City, was the principal road to East Anglia in Roman and Medieval times.

St Helen Bishopsgate★

♿ 🕐 *Open Mon–Fri 9.30am–5pm, via Church office entrance. Guide book.*
✆ *020 7283 2231. www.st-helens.org.uk.*
Behind a patch of grass and plane trees stands the late Gothic church *(Entrance on the south side),* which incorporates a small 12C parish church and a 13C conventual church; both were extensively remodelled to give the double-fronted stone façade surmounted by a 17C white belfry turret. Restoration following damage inflicted by a terrorist bomb has returned the church to pre-Reformation airiness and lightness.

Inside, note the small **Night Staircase** built c. 1500, in the middle of the north wall for nuns attending night services; also noteworthy are the **Processional Entrance**, originally 13C, the canopied carved **pulpit** and the 17C font.

Monuments★★ – In 1874, when St Martin Outwich was demolished, 18 major monuments and brasses were transferred here, including those of Sir John Crosby (d. 1475) and his first wife

St Ethelburga

The early 15C church, which stood on this site until destroyed by a terrorist bomb on 24 April 1993, was the City's smallest church and one of the few medieval buildings to escape the Great Fire (1666) and survive World War II with only slight damage. The church accounts date from 1569. The church has been rebuilt to its original plan as three walls and much of the timber, stone mouldings and fittings have survived; it serves as a Centre for Reconciliation and Peace.

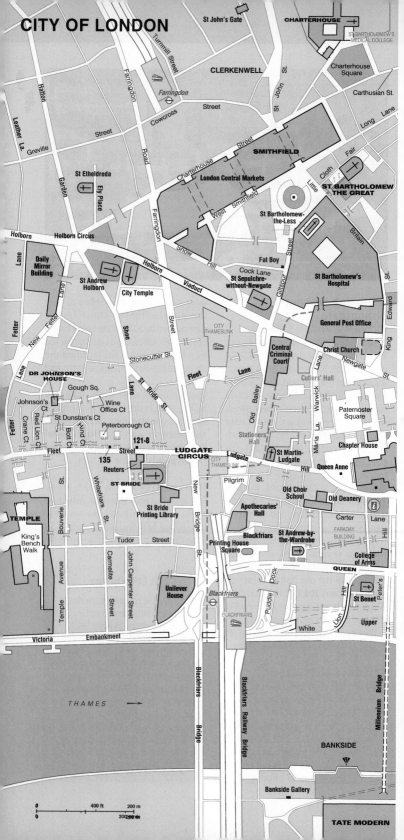

CITY OF LONDON

St John's Gate

CHARTERHOUSE

ST BARTHOLOMEW'S MEDICAL COLLEGE

Turnmill Street

CLERKENWELL

St John St.

Charterhouse Square

Farringdon

Carthusian St.

Farringdon Road

Cowcross Street

Long Lane

Hatton Garden

Greville Street

Street

Leather La.

St Etheldreda

Ely Place

SMITHFIELD

Cloth Fair

Charterhouse Street

London Central Markets

Little Britain

ST BARTHOLOMEW THE GREAT

West Smithfield

St Bartholomew-the-Less

Holborn

Holborn Circus

Daily Mirror Building

Holborn Viaduct

St Andrew Holborn

City Temple

Snow Hill

Farringdon Street

Cock Lane

Fat Boy

St Sepulchre-without-Newgate

Giltspur Street

St Bartholomew's Hospital

Lane

New Fetter Lane

Fetter Lane

Shoe Lane

Stonecutter St.

Fleet Lane

CITY THAMESLINK

General Post Office

Christ Church

Old Bailey

Newgate

King Edward St.

Central Criminal Court

Cutlers' Hall

Warwick Lane

Paternoster Square

Chapter House

DR JOHNSON'S HOUSE

Gough Sq.

Johnson's Ct

St Dunstan's Ct

Wine Office Ct

Peterborough Ct

Red Lion Ct

Crane Ct

Bolt Ct

Hind Ct

121-8

Fleet Street

135 Reuters

ST BRIDE

LUDGATE CIRCUS

New Bridge St.

CITY THAMESLINK

Ludgate Hill

Pilgrim St.

Stationers' Hall

Maria La.

St Martin-Ludgate

Queen Anne

Whitefriars St.

St Bride Printing Library

Old Choir School

Old Deanery

Carter Lane

FARADAY BUILDING

TEMPLE

King's Bench Walk

Bouverie St.

Carmelite St.

Tudor Street

John Carpenter Street

Apothecaries' Hall

Blackfriars

Printing House Square

St Andrew-by-the-Wardrobe

College of Arms

QUEEN

Temple Avenue

Unilever House

Blackfriars

BLACKFRIARS

Puddle Dock

White Lion Hill

St Benet

Peter's Hill

Upper

Victoria Embankment

Blackfriars Bridge

Blackfriars Railway Bridge

Millennium Bridge

THAMES

BANKSIDE

Bankside Gallery

TATE MODERN

0   400 ft   200 m
0   200 m

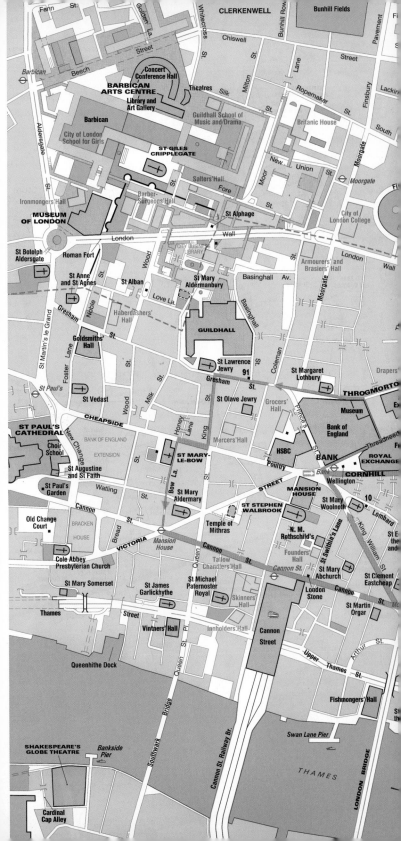

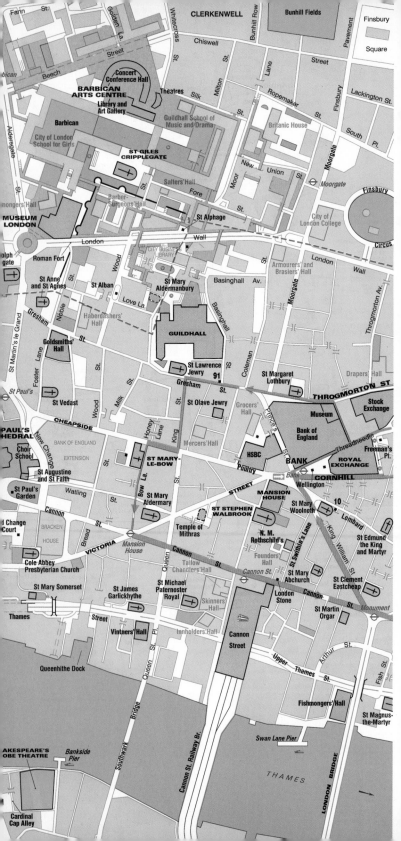

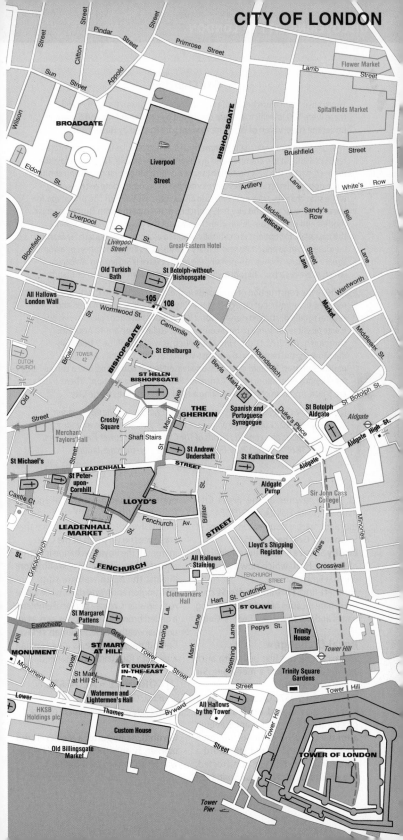

CITY OF LONDON

City Churches

There have been churches in the Square Mile since Saxon times. By 1666, there were 100, of which 87 were destroyed by the **Great Fire** and 51 rebuilt under the supervision of Wren; more were constructed by Hawksmoor.

The City churches are usually symmetrical and rectangular in plan, orientated as far as possible in the cramped and awkward sites available. The choir played a reduced part in the new Protestant service, which hinged more on long sermons: large open galleries were therefore provided to accommodate extra seating, while side chapels, transepts and side aisles were eliminated. The prototype for these light, spacious and airy hall-churches derived partly from Dutch Calvinist models and partly from Jesuit churches, where the altar was placed against the east wall. Exceptions are centrally planned as a cross in a square (St Martin Ludgate; St Anne and St Agnes; St Mary at Hill), as a vaulted octagon or a domed square (St Mary Abchurch) – perhaps the most original is St Stephen Walbrook, which achieves a truly Baroque spirit hitherto unknown in Puritan England.

By 1939 the construction of new roads in the 19C and 20C had drastically reduced the number of churches in the City. Nearly all were damaged and several totally destroyed during World War II, but as the floor plans survived, it was possible for some to be reconstructed. Today there are 40 Anglican churches in the City: 11 pre-Fire; 23 by Wren as well as 6 of the 9 free-standing towers; the remaining 6 are post-Wren (18C–19C). Twenty-four are parish churches; 12 guild churches; one leased to the Lutherans; one a centre for religious education; one a "Centre for Peace and Recociliation". There are 5 non-Anglican churches, making a total of 45 churches in the City.

Apply to the City Information Centre (St. Paul's Churchyard, The City, London, EC4M 8AE; ☎020 7332 1456) or enquire at the churches. To provide voluntary help or contributions, contact Friends of The City Churches, Lower Thames Street, London EC3R 6DN. ☎020 7626 1555. www.london-city-churches.org.uk.

(d. 1460), owner of the great City mansion Crosby Hall (*see CHELSEA*) and the black marble slabbed tomb chest of Sir Thomas **Gresham** (d. 1579).
Crosby Square records the original site of **Crosby Hall**, which now stands on Chelsea Embankment.
Turn left into **Threadneedle St** past the ornate façades of buildings housing banks and the Merchant Taylors' Guild.

Royal Exchange★

The exchange was first built with brick at the sole charge of a merchant, **Sir Thomas Gresham**.
On 27 January 1571 **Queen Elizabeth** came to view it and caused it to be proclaimed the Royal Exchange. Rebuilt after the Great Fire of 1666, it burned down again in 1838 and afterward a third, larger building was constructed. The wide steps, monumental Corinthian portico and pediment with allegorical figures (10ft/3m tall), provide an impressive entrance to an edifice that was once the very hub of the City.
in front of the Royal Exchange is a large equestrian bronze statue of **Wellington**; against the north wall are statues of Whittington and Myddelton, while at the rear, Gresham, whose personal emblem, a gilded bronze grasshopper, acts as an unusual weathervane. **Freeman's Place**, behind the Exchange, is a pedestrian area, with fountains at either end.

② CORNHILL – ALDGATE

⊖ *Bank: Cornhill exit or start from*
⊖ *Aldgate and do the tour in reverse.*

Cornhill, named after a Medieval corn market, is one of the two hills upon which London was first built.

St Michael's

🕐 *Open Mon–Fri 8am–5.30pm. Organ recital: Mon (except bank holidays) at 1pm. ☎020 7248 3826. www.st-michaels.org.uk.*

The four-tiered tower (1718–24) was designed by **Hawksmoor** to replace the one that had survived the Fire but that had become unsafe. The church was extensively remodelled by **Giles Gilbert Scott** (1857–60), but Wren's vault resting on tall Tuscan columns (1670–77) has survived; don't miss the large 18C wooden pelican.

Walk along the alleys south of St Michael's and discover **former coffee houses**: the **Jamaica Wine House**, dating from 1652, and the 600-year-old **George and Vulture**, twice destroyed by fire.

St Peter-upon-Cornhill claims to stand on the highest ground and on the oldest church site in the City. The present building (1677–87) was designed by Wren *(Entrance from St Peter's Alley;* 🕐 *open by appointment;* ☎*020 7283 2231; St Helen's Bishopsgate Church Office).*

The unusual vane, in the form of a key, flying at the top of the spire, is visible only from the churchyard *(south)* and Gracechurch Street *(east).*

Inside, one's eyes are drawn to the oak **screen**★, one of only two to survive in Wren's churches (👁️*see INTRODUCTION – Architecture).* The **organ gallery**, which is meant to have accommodated Mendelssohn on at least two occasions, is original, as are other furnishings including the pulpit and the font.

Leadenhall Market

Gracechurch Street.

Leadenhall, a bustling food market specialising in game is at its most spectacular at the start of the shooting season and at Christmas. The glass and ironwork market hall is an architectural delight. The **Lamb Tavern**, with its early 20C décor, is frequented by market traders.

There has been a market on this site since Roman times. The market takes its name from the house's lead-covered roof; burned down in the Fire, the market buildings were re-erected then, and again to their present form in 1881.

Lloyd's★★

🕐 *Opens once a year as part of London's Open House day; call for details.* ☎*020 7327 1000. www.lloyds.com.*

The trading activities of Lloyd's, the biggest insurance corporation in the world, are conducted in a striking steel and glass building (1986) designed by **Sir Richard Rogers**, one of the architects of the Pompidou Centre in Paris with which it bears striking similarities.

Six towers enclose a central atrium that rises 200ft/61m to a glass barrel vault. Great long escalators link the storeys with the ground level featuring an open-plan environment; glass lifts travel up the exterior of the building. Ventilation shafts, power ducting and water conduits are also streamlined along the outside.

The company's **history** goes back to 1691 when Edward Lloyd took over Pontaq's at 16 Lombard Street *(plaque on Coutts' Bank)*, a French-owned eating house. The house became the favourite meeting place of merchants, shippers, bankers, underwriters, agents and newsmen. Edward Lloyd inaugurated the still current system of

Lloyd's Building

©PhotoDisc, Inc.

Lloyd's Institutions

The **Lutine Bell** was retrieved from *HMS Lutine*, a captured French frigate that was sunk off the Netherlands in 1799 with gold and specie valued at nearly £1.5 million and insured by Lloyd's. Its bullion was partly salvaged in 1857–61. The bell is struck to mark the end of a crisis involving an overdue vessel: once for a loss, twice for a safe arrival.

A reminder of coffee house origins is provided by the **liveried doormen**, resplendent in red frock coats with black velvet collars and gilt-buckled top hats.

The Lloyd's Marine Intelligence Unit (*www.lloydsmiu.com*) keeps details of some 117 000 vessels, 163 500 shipping companies and 3.6 million shipping movements a year.

posting notices and lists of port agents, transport vessels, cargo shipments agents and other such shipping intelligence. He died in 1713 *(plaque in St Mary Woolnoth)* and, in 1774, Lloyd's transferred to more spacious quarters at Cornhill, where it remained until 1928 when the first insurance offices opened in Lime Street.

▷ *Make a short detour to St Mary Axe.*

The Swiss Re Building

The 40-storey Swiss Re Building, better known as "the Gherkin", designed by the UK's other architectural superstars, Sir Norman Foster and Partners, opened in 2004. Circular, bulging in the middle and tapering as it soars into the sky, it is Britain's first environmentally sustainable high-rise, making maximum use of recycled materials, natural air and light, while the building's second skin manages temperature control.

St Andrew Undershaft

The 16C church of **St AndrewUndershaft** is named after the maypole shaft that stood in front of it until 1517

(⊙*open by appointment; ℘020 7283 2231, St Helen's Bishopsgate Church Office; www.st-helens.org.uk).* A staircase turret breaks the square outline of the ancient stone tower, part of which is probably early 14C. The interior boasts a late 16C–17C west window depicting Tudor and Stuart sovereigns, a Renatus Harris organ and altar rails fashioned by **Tijou** (1704).

The most famous of St Andrew's **monuments**★ is **Nicholas Stone**'s half-length carved alabaster ruffed figure of **John Stow** (1525–1605), the antiquarian whose *Survey of London and Westminster* was published in 1598. The quill pen poised to "write something worth reading about" is renewed annually by the Lord Mayor.

▷ *Continue along Leadenhall St.*

St Katharine Cree

⊙*Open Mon–Fri 10.30am–4pm.* ℘*020 7283 5733.*

The present compact, light and airy church, thought to be the third on the site, survived the Great Fire of 1666.

The ragstone corner tower rises to a parapet and small white-pillared turret. Inside the nave, giant Corinthian columns support a series of decorative round arches below the clerestory. High up, above the plain reredos, is a traceried rose window glazed with 17C glass; the central ridge of the lierne vault is decorated with a row of brightly coloured bosses bearing the badges of 17 City Companies. Note the early 17C alabaster font, 18C pulpit and altar table.

Aldgate

The name derives from the Anglo-Saxon *aelgate* meaning free or open to all. The Romans built a gate here on the road to Colchester. In the 14C Chaucer leased the dwelling over the gate, and in the 16C Mary Tudor rode through after being proclaimed queen. The gate was demolished in 1761. The **Aldgate Pump** still stands at the west end of the street.

St Botolph Aldgate

Open Mon–Thu 10am–3pm. ✆*020 7283 1670. www.stbotolphs.org.uk.*

The site on the outer side of the gate had been occupied by a church for over 1 000 years when **George Dance the Elder** came to rebuild it (1741–44). The stone steeple stands on a four-tier brick tower trimmed with stone quoins. Dance's interior was remodelled in the 19C: note in particular the plasterwork frieze decorating the coved ceiling.

▷ *Walk up Duke's Place to Bevis Marks.*

The street name, a corruption of Buries Marks, recalls the site of the 12C mansion of the abbots of Bury St Edmunds.

Spanish and Portuguese Synagogue

Open Mon–Fri 11am–1pm, Sun 11am–12.30pm. ✆*£2.* ✆*Guided tour at noon.* ✆*020 7626 1274.*

The synagogue is the oldest in England (1701) and the only one in the City of London. Set back from the street, the building is plainly functional except for the seven splendid brass chandeliers, which hang down low and are lit for all festive occasions. Also noteworthy is the Ark containing the handwritten Scrolls and the raised Tebah surrounded by twisted balusters.

③ MONUMENT

⊖*Bank: Cornhill exit. Take King William St and Lombard St.*

St Mary Woolnoth of the Nativity

Open Mon–Fri 9.30am–4.30pm. *Closed bank holidays.* ✆*020 7626 9701.*

The church, built in stone by **William the Conqueror**, was damaged in the Great Fire and replaced by the present English Baroque structure (1716–27) designed by **Nicholas Hawksmoor**. The rusticated stone tower rises to Corinthian columns and twin turrets, linked and crowned by open balustrades. Inside, massive fluted Corinthian columns in threes mark each corner of the square nave and support a heavily-ornamented cornice with semi-circular clerestory windows above. The reredos is also by Hawksmoor, with its twisted columns and inlaid pulpit.

Lombard Street

The name derives from the late 13C Lombard merchants, moneychangers and pawnbrokers who settled there. The street, now synonymous with City banking, is lined with 19C and 20C buildings. Note the brightly painted bank signs overhanging the pavement, including Lloyd's horse of 1677, a grasshopper, 1563, formerly Martins, a cat and fiddle *(by Nicholas Lane)* and a massive Barclays eagle in stone.

The Clearing House *(10 Lombard Street)* has its origins in the 18C when bank clerks, known as "clearers," met in the street to exchange and settle for cheques payable at their respective banks. The first Clearing House was built on the site in 1833. The present building is post-war.

Further on, **St Edmund the King and Martyr** is another of Wren's churches, its distinctive black (lead-covered) octagonal lantern and stout **spire**★ending in a bulb and vane, rising from a square stone belfry. The interior was altered in the 19C but is remarkable for its woodwork (*open Mon–Fri 10am–6pm; closed bank holidays;* ✆*020 7621 1391*).

▷ *Walk down St Clements Lane.*

St Clement Eastcheap

Open Mon–Fri 9am–4pm. ✆*020 7626 4481.*

Rebuilt to Wren's design, the church features a brick tower with stone quoins and a balustrade.

Inside, note the very ornate **pulpit**★★, the finely carved organ cases (Purcell played on the organ) and the gilded altarpiece showing the Virgin and an angel with St Martin and St Clement.

▷ *Continue to the main crossroads and into Eastcheap; turn first right into Fish St Hill.*

Monument: engraving of 1680

Monument★

🕐 *Open daily 9.30am–5.30pm.*
🕐 *Closed 24–26 Dec, 1 Jan.* ⌖ *£3.*
📞 *020 7626 2717.*

The fluted Doric column of Portland stone, surmounted by a square viewing platform and gilded, flaming urn, was erected in 1671–77 in commemoration of the Great Fire.

The hollow shaft stands 202ft/62m tall and 202ft/62m from the baker's in Pudding Lane where the Fire began, right on the route between London and Southwark until the construction of Blackfriars Bridge (1769). The relief of Charles II before the City under reconstruction (on the west face of the pedestal) is by Caius Cibber.

A later inscription blaming the papists for the Fire was finally effaced in 1831. The **view**★ from the platform (up 311 steps) is now largely obscured by the

A Quaint Verse

To remember the dates of the **Great Plague** and the **Great Fire**, children once were taught:
'In sixteen hundred and sixty five, scarce a soul was left alive. In sixteen hundred and sixty six, London burned like rotten sticks.'

towering office blocks that also mask the column at ground level.

▷ *Return to Eastcheap and turn right.*

Off Eastcheap to the left is yet another Wren church, **St Margaret Pattens**, its slender hexagonal lead-covered **spire**★ sharpening to a needle point on which a gilded vane balances (🕐 *open Mon–Fri 8am–4pm;* 🕐 *closed bank holidays;* 📞 *020 7623 6630).* The outstanding **woodwork**★ includes the 17C reredos, framing a contemporary Italian painting, carved with fruit, a pea pod and flowers; in front, turned balusters support the communion rail; note a finely carved eagle lectern and the only two canopied pews in London.

▷ *Walk down St Mary-at-Hill opposite.*

St Mary-at-Hill★★

Entrance located between 6 and 7 St Mary-at-Hill. 🕐 *Open Mon–Fri 10am–5pm.* 📞 *020 7626 4184 (office).*

The Wren **plan**★ (1670–76), almost square, is divided into 3 x 3 bays beneath a shallow central dome, supported on free-standing Corinthian columns.

The interior was damaged by fire in 1988 and not all the **woodwork**, for which St Mary's was known, was restored: note the font cover (late 17C); great oak reredos, communion table, altar rails (early 18C); organ gallery (musical trophies), lectern and turned balustrade, pulpit garlanded with fruit and flowers beneath a massive sounding board and approached by a beautiful curved staircase by **William Gibbs Rogers** (19C); box pews.

Turn left to admire the ruins of **St Dunstan-in-the-East**★ with its four-tier **tower**★ surmounted by an elegant Portland stone steeple.

In the early Middle Ages, **Thames Street** ran the length of the river wall; by the 17C, it would have been lined by eight churches and provided rear access to castles and mansions, quays, warehouses and markets. Today Upper and Lower Thames Street are separated by London Bridge.

The Great Fire

The Monument was erected near to the point where the Great Fire began in the king's baker's house in Pudding Lane near London Bridge; it ended at Pie Corner, near Smithfield. The flames, fanned by a strong east wind, raged throughout Monday and part of Tuesday; on Wednesday the fire slackened and on Thursday it was thought to be extinguished. When it burst out again that evening at the Temple; adjoining houses were demolished with gunpowder to prevent it spreading further. People escaped with what they could carry by boat or on foot to Moorfields or the hills of Hampstead and Highgate. The most vivid account is told in the Diary of **Samuel Pepys** (2 September 1666):

So near the fire as we could for smoke; and all over the Thames, with one's face in the wind, you were almost burned with a shower of fire-drops ... When we could endure it no more upon the water, we to a little ale-house on the Bankside ... and there staid till dark almost, and saw the fire grow; and as it grew darker, appeared more and more; and in corners and upon steeples, and between churches and houses, as far as we could see up the hill of the City, in a most horrid, malicious, bloody flame, not like the fine flame of an ordinary fire ... The churches, houses, and all on fire, and flaming at once; and a horrid noise the flames made, and the cracking of houses at their ruine. So home with a sad heart, and there to find every body discoursing and lamenting the fire ...

The present **Custom House** (1813–17), with five lanterns as sole decoration, is the sixth to stand on this site.

Across Lower Thames and up St Mary-at-Hill on the left *(no 18)* is the small **Watermen and Lightermen's Hall** (1780), which belongs to an ancient City Guild dating back to Tudor times.

Old Billingsgate Market

There was a market on this site from 1297 to 1982, when the wholesale fish market moved to new premises in the West India Docks on the Isle of Dogs. The building (1876) with Britannia presiding over two dolphins on its decorative roof, was converted into offices in 1990.

St Magnus-the-Martyr

Lower Thames Street. ♿🕐*Open Tue–Fri 10am–4pm, Sun 10am–1pm. Brochures. Guide sheets.* ✆*020 7626 4481.*
The massive square stone **tower**★ rises to an octagonal belfry, a leaded cupola, lantern and obelisk spire surmounted by a golden vane. St Magnus stood as a stone sentinel on an ancient Roman wharf at the foot of London Bridge from 1176. Wren rebuilt it on the same site. The interior, remodelled in the late 18C features a barrel-vaulted nave

supported by fluted Ionic columns and oval clerestory windows.

However, much remains from the 17C. Note the iron **sword rest**★dated 1708, 16C–17C shrine (right of the altar), altarpiece and rails, font (1683) and pulpit.

London Bridge★

London Bridge was the only crossing over the lower Thames until 1750, when Westminster was constructed. The Romans probably built the first bridge; the Saxons later erected a wooden structure that had to be repeatedly rebuilt. Between 1176 and 1209 a stone bridge was constructed on 19 pointed arches rising from slender piles anchored onto wood and rubble piers which considerably reduced river flow.

In winter, ice would form so that, when at last the river froze over, great **Frost Fairs** could be held (the most famous being between 1683 and 1684). The bridge itself was lined with houses, shops and even a chapel; it was here that traitors' heads were exposed: Jack Cade (1450), Thomas More (1535).

In 1831 John Rennie constructed a robust granite bridge 60yd/55m upstream. In 1973 it was replaced by the existing sleek crossing; Rennie's bridge was sold for £1 million and removed to Arizona, USA. London legend has it that the American purchaser thought he was buying Tower Bridge.

On the west side of London Bridge sits **Fishmongers' Hall**, a neo-Greek building (1831–34) with a rich interior gold leaf decoration (restored post-war).

> ○ *Cross to Arthur St and Martin Lane.*

Ye Olde Wine Shades is a colourful double-fronted pub (1663) with painted boards outside. It claims to be the oldest wine house in London. Presently it is surrounded by the spiky marble and glass buildings of Minster Court.

The square brick and stucco tower (19C) marks the site of the medieval church of **St Martin Orgar.**

> ○ *Proceed west along Cannon St and cross to the north side.*

St Mary Abchurch★

○*Open Mon–Thu 10.30am–2.30pm.*
The Fire consumed "a fair church," last of a line dating back to the 12C. The site was minute, some 80ft/24m square, and Wren decided to cover the new church with a painted **dome**★, approximately 40ft/12m in diameter. Inside, it rises from arches springing directly from the outer walls. There are no buttresses and only one interior column.

Note Robert Bird's original gilded copper pelican weathervane (removed as unsafe in 1764) over the west door and the pulpit with garlands and cherubs' heads. Authenticated by bills and a personal letter from **Grinling Gibbons** himself, is the **reredos**★★, massive in size, magnificent in detail and delicacy. The **tower and spire**★ are on the same small scale as the church: red brick with stone quoins, surmounted by a cupola, lantern and slender lead spire.

Cannon Street Station stands on the opposite side of the street (○*For description see walk no*④). Turn right onto **St Swithin's Lane**. The street is synonymous with the prestigious merchant bank NM Rothschild's. The clean-lined building is post-war; the lane remains old and narrow, and is often blocked from end-to-end with waiting Rolls-Royces, Bentleys and Jaguars.

④ MANSION HOUSE

⊖*Bank: Cornhill exit*

Mansion House★

Until the mid-18C, lord mayors remained in their own residences during the years of their mayoralty. The Palladian-style mansion in Portland stone (1739–52), designed by **George Dance the Elder**, features a raised portico of six giant Corinthian columns, surmounted by a pediment decorated with an allegory of the splendour of London.

The **Lord Mayor** is Chief Magistrate of the City and on the ground floor on the east side is a Court of Justice, with cells below.

> ○ *Proceed along Walbrook Ct.*

St Stephen Walbrook★

○*Open Mon–Fri 10am–4pm (3pm Fri). Services Thu at 12.45pm (Sung Eucharist – Monteverdi, Lassus, Byrd, Palestrina). Organ recital: Fri, 12.30–1.30pm. ℘020 7626 9000. www.ststephenwalbrook.net*
The most striking feature is Wren's **dome**★; it undoubtedly served as a model for St Paul's, which it pre-dates: the slightly off-centre cupola rests on eight circular arches; the bays are delineated by free-standing Corinthian columns grouped to produce unexpected perspectives. Below the dome and raised on two communion steps sits **Henry Moore's** monumental altar of golden travertine (1986).

Ornate pulpit and cupola of St Stephen Walbrook

K. Brett/MICHELIN

London Stone

A block of limestone *(set into the wall of 111 Cannon Street)*, "its origin and purpose are unknown," may have been a milestone or milliary or, according to legend, may be a fragment of an altar erected in 800 BC by Trojan, the mythical founder of Britain.

▶ *Continue along Cannon St west and turn left into College Hill.*

St Michael Paternoster Royal

🕐 *Open Mon–Fri 9am–5pm.*
📞 *020 7248 5202. www.missionto seafarers.org.*

The "fair parish church", as Stow described it, "new built by Richard Whittington," was destroyed in the Fire, rebuilt by Wren and again badly damaged in July 1944. The **spire**★, added in 1715, takes the form of a three-tier octagonal lantern, marked at each angle by an Ionic column and urn.

Inside, the most remarkable features are the post-war stained-glass windows, which include *(south-west corner)* young Dick Whittington with his cat. **Whittington** (🚶*see WALK No* ⑦), who lived in an adjoining house, founded an almshouse, also adjoining, and on his death in 1423, was buried in the church.

Cannon Street

In the Middle Ages Candelwriteystrete was the home of candle makers and wick chandlers – hence the presence on Dowgate Hill of the **Tallow Chandlers' Hall**, rebuilt in 1670–72 and Italianised in 1880, and **Skinners' Hall**, a late 18C building accommodating a fine staircase and a hall decorated by Frank Brangwyn (1904–10).

All that remains of the mid-Victorian **Cannon Street Station** building are two monumental towers, adorned with gilded weathervanes, flanking the viaduct high above the riverbank.

N M Rothschild and Sons Ltd

The merchant bank Rothschild's earned its status in this country in its early years, under its London branch founder, Nathan Mayer Rothschild (1777–1836). It acquired at low cost the drafts issued by Wellington, which the government was unable to meet, and renewed them; ultimately they were redeemed at par. NMR increased his fortune, and the government appointed him chief negotiator of future Allied war loans!

His confidence in victory against Napoleon and in his own intelligence service again increased NMR's wealth, it is said, on the occasion of Waterloo, fought throughout Sunday 18 June: on the Monday, when only rumour was circulating, Nathan bought; the market rose; he sold; the market plunged; he bought again and made a fortune as his personal messenger arrived from the battle scene confirming victory; Wellington's despatches only arrived by messenger the following Wednesday and a report was published in *The Times* on Thursday (22nd). Other business included negotiating lucrative textile deals.

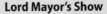

Lord Mayor's Show

This show is for the Lord Mayor's progress to his swearing-in before the Lord Chief Justice, an observance that dates back to the charter of 1215 that required the mayor be presented to the monarch or his justices at the Palace of Westminster. For centuries, the procession was partly undertaken over water when the mayor owned a civic barge (15C). In 1553 full pageantry became the order of the day with men parading their best liveries, trumpets sounding, masques and poems recited along the route. Today, with the judges removed from Westminster, the oath is taken at the Royal Courts of Justice in the Strand; the pageantry, after a decline in the 19C, has returned with floats and the new and old mayors progressing in the golden state and other horse-drawn coaches accompanied by outriders.

The spectacular show on the second Saturday in November, is followed on the Monday evening by the Lord Mayor's Banquet in Guildhall, which by tradition began with turtle soup, and at which the principal speakers are the new Lord Mayor and the Prime Minister. www.lordmayorsshow.org.

St James Garlickhythe

Open usually Mon–Fri 10.30am–4pm. Closed Bank Holiday Mon. Services Sun 10am (Sung Eucharist), Wed 1.15pm. ✆020 7248 7546. www.stjamesgarlickhythe.org.uk.

The church, which owes its name to a flourishing garlic trade during the Middle Ages, is dedicated to St James of Compostella (look out for the saint's emblem, a scallop shell).

It was built to a perfectly symmetrical plan, on an isolated site, and christened "Wren's Lantern" owing to its many windows. The woodwork is principally 17C: note the dowel peg for the preacher's wig. **Sword rests**★, complete with unicorn supporters, recall six Medieval Lord mayors and others.

On the other side of Upper Thames Street stands the **Vintners' Hall**; built in 1671, restored in 1948 and boasting a majestic hall with late 17C panelling. **Queenhithe Dock**, once London's main dock above London Bridge, is beyond. After the footbridge, but before the tunnel, on the north side of Upper Thames Street stands all that survives of **St Mary Somerset**: a slim, square tower (1695), built by Wren and adorned with masks, rises from its garden setting.

▶ *Walk up Lambeth Hill and cross Queen Victoria St (see WALK No 5).*

The square stone tower of **Cole Abbey Presbyterian Church** supports an octagonal lead **spire**★ that rises to **a gilded three-masted ship** weathervane. The church was burned out in 1666 and again in 1941. The stone exterior is pierced by rounded windows beneath corbelled hoods and circled by an open balustrade. Its woodwork is 17C (*open by appointment; www.londonfreechurch.org.uk*).

▶ *At the crossroads, cross over to join Bow Lane.*

Stow tells how the area was once occupied by shoemakers and that the narrow and winding **Bow Lane** was previously known as Hosiers' Lane.

▶ *Turn right into Watling St past an old pub.*

St Mary Aldermary

Open Mon–Fri 10.30am–3.30pm. Guided tours by appointment, Fri. ✆020 7248 9902. www.stmaryalder mary.co.uk.

Corner buttresses, robust pinnacles and gilded finials adorn the tower of St Mary, rebuilt by Wren in the Gothic style at the request of a benefactor.

The beautiful interior retains its fan vaulting and central rosettes, as well as a **Grinling Gibbons** pulpit and rich west doorcase (with a peapod) and, against the third south pillar, an oak **sword rest**, from 1682 carved with fruit and flowers by Gibbons.

Return to Bow Lane.

Williamson's Tavern *(Groveland Court)* is accommodated in a 17C house with a contemporary wrought-iron gate, and once served as a Lord Mayor's residence (1666–1753).

St Mary-le-Bow★★

Open Mon–Wed 7am–6pm (Thu 6.30pm, Fri 4pm), Closed bank holidays. Concerts: Thu in term time at 1.05pm. Brochure (2 languages). 020 7248 5139. www.stmarylebow.co.uk.

The tower contains the famous **Bow Bells** and supports Wren's most famous **spire**★★ (1671–80) in which he used all five Classical orders and the bow (the mason's term for a stone arch) from which the church takes its name. The weather **vane**, a winged dragon (8ft 10in/2.5m long) is poised at the top (239ft/72.8m) with a rope dancer riding on its back.

Built in Portland stone in 1673 and modelled on the Basilica of Constantine in Rome, the church was the most expensive of Wren's Churches. The Norman **crypt** dates from 1087.

Spire of St Mary-le-Bow

Y. Kanazawa/Michelin

The Great Bell of Bow

In 1334 the Great Bell of Bow called people from bed at 5.45am and rang the curfew at 9pm; the practice continued for over 400 years ceasing only in 1874: this sound came to define the limits of the City, giving rise to the saying that "a true Londoner, a Cockney, must be born within the sound of Bow Bells." According to legend it was these bells that chimed out "Turn again Whittington, Lord Mayor of London." During World War I, the 12-bell chime was used as a recognition signal by the BBC and came to mean hope and freedom to millions all over the world, thus deserving the title "the most famous peal in Christendom".

In May 1941 the church was bombed. The exterior was restored to Wren's design, while the interior layout was redesigned. The unique carved rood is a gift from the people of Germany. The bronze sculpture was given by the Norwegians in memory of those who died in the Resistance.

The twin pulpits are used for the famous dialogues where two public figures of opposing views debate moral points.

Turn right into Cheapside (see ST PAUL'S), take Bucklersbury Passage and walk down Queen Victoria St.

Temple of Mithras

The stone temple was erected in the 2C AD when Roman legions were stationed in the City. In 1954, excavations revealed walls laid in the outline of a basilica.

The head of the god Mithras in a Phrygian cap, those of Minerva and Serapis the Egyptian god of the Underworld with a corn measure on his head, together with other retrieved artefacts are now in the Museum of London. The temple itself, removed to enable an office block to rise as planned, was then reconstructed in the forecourt.

5 BLACKFRIARS
⊖*Blackfriars*

The name **Blackfriars** commemorates Blackfriars Monastery, dissolved in 1538, and abandoned until 1576 when a theatre was founded in the cloisters; here a professional children's company would rehearse before performing at court. Twenty years later **James Burbage** converted another part of the monastery into the Blackfriars Theatre for the performance of Shakespeare's later plays and those of Beaumont and Fletcher. The theatre, demolished in 1655, is commemorated in Playhouse Yard.

The **Blackfriars bridges** were both built during the prosperous last years of the 19C and the Millennium footbridge, a century later; it leads directly to the piazza of the Tate Modern on the south bank (&*see BANKSIDE – SOUTHWARK*). The striking structure marks a technical achievement combining sculpture and architecture. On your left is the vast stone building of **Unilever House** (1931) with its rusticated ground floor, pillars and large sculptures in typical 1930s style. **The Black Friar**, a wedge-shaped pub (1896), is fronted by a fat friar.

Queen Victoria Street
The street, the first City street to be lit by electricity, was created in 1867–71 by cutting through a maze of alleys and buildings. Stretching from Bank to Blackfriars, it is lined with a number of widely contrasting ancient and modern institutions.

Printing House Square
The square acquired its name after the Fire, when the King's Printer set up presses and began to publish acts, the King James Bible, proclamations and the *London Gazette* (1666 – as *Oxford Gazette* 1665). The name remained after the printer moved nearer to Fleet Street in 1770.

In 1784 John Walter purchased a house in the square and the following year began publication of the *Daily Universal Register*, altering its title on 1 January 1788 to *The Times*. In 1964 a new slate-and-glass building was constructed for the broadsheet's offices with the old square as forecourt; ten years later they moved to Gray's Inn Road before transferring (1986) to Wapping (&*see SUBURBS – DOCKLANDS*).

&> *The square's history is related on a plaque situated on what is now the Continental Bank house.*

Up Blackfriars Lane stands **Apothecaries' Hall** (1632, rebuilt c. 1670): in the courtyard a pillared lamp stands over the old monastic well.

St Andrew-by-the-Wardrobe
🕐*Open Mon–Fri 10am–4pm. Services: Tue, Wed 12.35pm, Thu 6.30pm, Sun 10am.* ℘*020 7 329 3632. www.stand rewsbythewardrobe.net*
The church takes its name from the Great Wardrobe or royal storehouse, which stood nearby (*plaque in Wardrobe Place*). Church and Wardrobe were destroyed in the Fire; only St Andrew was rebuilt. On 29/30 December 1940, fire again gutted the church leaving just the tower and outer walls. It was rebuilt in 1959–61. The galleried church has attractive vaulting and plaster work. Its square red-brick tower is decorated with irregular stone quoins and a crowning balustrade.

College of Arms
🕐*Open Mon–Fri 10am–4pm.* 🕐*Closed bank holidays, State and special occasions. Brochure. Shop.* ℘*020 7248 2762. www.college-of-arms.gov.uk.*
The college, overlooking a forecourt behind splendid wrought-iron gates, dates from 1671–88 when it was rebuilt after the Fire. The compact red-brick building was truncated when Queen Victoria Street was created.

The interior woodwork is by William Emmett, a contemporary of Grinling Gibbons. The Earl Marshal's Court, the main room, is panelled and furnished with a throne and a gallery.

The College is responsible for granting coats of arms and monitoring their application; it also organises State ceremonies and undertakes genealogical research.

▷ *Cross Queen Victoria St.*

St Benet's Welsh Church
🕐*Open for services (in Welsh) Sun at 11am and 3.30pm; also open by apppointment. ✆020 7489 8754 (church), ✆020 7606 8330.*
Wren designed a small brick church with a hipped roof, rounded windows with carved stone festoons and a general country, Dutch air. The tower of a dark red brick is defined with white stone quoins and rises only two stages before being crowned by a small lead cupola, lantern and spire. The interior is lined with galleries supported on panelled Corinthian columns which rise above the base of the galleries.

▷ *Walk up Peter's Hill, turn left past St Paul's Cathedral (🕯see ST PAUL'S CATHEDRAL) to Ludgate Hill.*

Ludgate Hill
A plaque on the south abutment of the 19C railway states "In a house near the site was published in 1702 the *Daily Courant* first London daily newspaper." Above the bridge stood **Lud Gate**, demolished in 1760: plaque on the wall of St Martin-within-Ludgate.
It was the first curfew gate to be closed at night and was named after the legendary King Lud (66 BC), who is said to have built the first gate on the site. Statues from the 1586 gate were removed to St Dunstan-in-the-West (🕯see STRAND – TEMPLE).

St-Martin-within-Ludgate
🕐*Open Mon–Fri 10am–4pm. Music recitals: Wed 1.15pm. Brochure. ✆020 7248 6054. www.st-martin-within-ludgate.org.uk.*
The church, which stood by the Medieval Lud Gate was burnt down in the Fire. Wren cut off the hill frontage inside by means of stout pillars on which he rested a gallery and thick coffered arches. At ground level beneath the gallery

Baynard Castle
In c 1100 a fort was built on the riverbank, pendant to the Tower downstream, by one "Baynard that came with the Conqueror" according to Stow. When it burnt down in 1428 it was rebuilt by Duke Humphrey of Gloucester; it was here in 1460 that Richard of Gloucester heard that his plans to seize the crown were progressing *(Richard III, 3 vii)*. Henry VII reconstructed a more spacious palace in which Lady Jane Grey received the news that she was to be queen (1553). It finally disappeared in the Fire of 1666.

the bays were filled with three doors, their **cases**★ richly carved by **Grinling Gibbons**. The remaining area is laid out as a square within a square by means of four inner columns on which the groined vault rests, formed by the intersection of barrel vaulting above the nave, chancel and transepts. The woodwork is 17C. The churchwardens' double chair dating from 1690 is unique.
From a lead-covered cupola and lantern, ringed by a balcony, rises a black needle **spire**★, the perfect foil to the green dome of St Paul's Cathedral.

Ludgate Circus
The circus, which was built in 1875 on the site of the Fleet Bridge to Ludgate Hill, includes a plaque (north-west angle) to Edgar Wallace (1875–1932), a Greenwich foundling who became a successful writer of crime novels.

6 GUILDHALL
⊖*Bank: Cornhill exit; St Paul's*

Poultry
The buildings (HSBC) on the north side were designed by Lutyens (1924–39) – high on the corners is a sculpture by Dick Reid of a fat boy driving a goose to the Stocks Market (1282–1737) that was once located nearby and famous for its herbs and fresh fruit. Rent from the stalls was allocated to the maintenance of London Bridge.

▷ *Turn right into Old Jewry.*

The two-stage stone tower of **St Olave Jewry** is topped by a beautiful **weathervane**, a three-master fully rigged. The church, rebuilt by Wren (1670–76), was destroyed in 1940.

Gresham Street

The street bears the name of Sir **Thomas Gresham** (&*see BANK – BISHOPSGATE*), who founded **Gresham College** in his will as a kind of free university in his mansion in Bishopsgate, Gresham House, which fronted on Old Broad Street. The house was demolished in 1768 and the institution re-established in 1843 at no 91 Gresham Street. The college, an independent institution supported by the corporation of London and the Mercers' Company, now occupies premises at **Barnard's Inn** (&*see CHANCERY LANE Walk*). Note the 1956 **Mercers' Hall** in Ironmonger Lane on your left.

St Lawrence Jewry

⊙*Open Mon–Fri 7.30am–1pm. Recitals Mon at 1pm (piano), Tue at 1pm (organ), daily in Aug. Guide book.*
℘*020 7600 9478.*
The church owes its name to the Jewish community that inhabited the district in Medieval times. The stone tower rises to a balustrade with corner obelisks enclosing a lantern.

A lead obelisk spire sits above, from which flies the original gridiron weathervane, now also incorporating a replica of the incendiary bomb that caused the almost total destruction of the church in 1940.

Wren designed a building of modest outward appearance squaring up the interior by varying the thickness of the walls. The restored ceiling, coffered and decorated to Wren's original design with gilded plaster work, emphasises the rectangular plan. The brilliant windows by Christopher Webb contrast with the plain and unassuming modern woodwork. The modern church is the church of the City Corporation.

▷ *Past the Guildhall turn right into Aldermanbury.*

St Mary Aldermanbury

The 12C site is now a garden, with only bases of the perimeter walls and pillars outlining the bombed Wren church (1670). The stones were numbered and sent to Fulton, USA, where the church has been rebuilt to its 17C plan.

▷ *Take Love Lane.*

St Alban

All that remains of Wren's church (1697–98) is the Gothic tower with its slim corner buttresses crowned by a balustrade and crocketed pinnacles.

▷ *Turn left back to Gresham St.*

Goldsmiths' Hall

⊙*Open day tours are held during the year, noon–2pm. Call City Information Office for details ℘020 7332 1456. ℘020 7606 7010. www.thegoldsmiths.co.uk.*
This grand hall in Foster Lane dates from 1835. It is endowed by an exceptional collection of gold and silver plate. Its Baroque interior provides a lavish setting for its annual summer exhibition, plus a number of smaller exhibitions and selling fairs throughout the year; check the website for details.

St Anne and St Agnes

⊙*Open Sun all day, Fri–Tue 10am–6pm. Concerts: Mon (except bank holidays and during Aug) and Fri at 1.10pm. ℘020 7606 4986. www.stanneslutheranchurch.org.*
The church, which was mentioned c. 1200, was rebuilt by Wren (1676–87) to the ancient domed-cross plan within a square, and again after World War II. The exterior is of rose-red brick with round-headed windows under central pediments. The small, square, stuccoed-stone tower is surmounted by an even smaller square domed turret, flaunting a vane in the shape of the letter A. &*For St Botolph Aldersgate, see Barbican, opposite.*

7 BEYOND THE CITY WALL
⊖ Moorgate; Barbican

Moorgate

The street is named after a gate cut in the City wall in 1415 (demolished in 1760) to provide access to Moorfields, the open common on which people practised archery, dried clothes, flew kites; two and a half centuries later it was one of the main exits for thousands fleeing the Great Plague.

The street is today overlooked by the modern office buildings and the **City of London College**, which dates from the rebuilding of London Bridge in 1831.

▶ *Walk south to London Wall.*

St Alphage

14C pointed stone arches in black flint walls mark the west tower of the chapel of Elsing Spital Priory, dissolved by Henry VIII, but revealed by 1940 bombs.

St Giles Cripplegate★

♿ ◷ *Open Mon–Fri 11am–4pm.* ✆ *020 7628 6155. www.stgilescripplegate.com.*
Dwarfed but in no way overpowered by the Barbican, St Giles' tower is built of stone and brick; corner pinnacles guard an open cupola merry-go-round-shaped turret that sports a weathervane (Peal of 12 bells; chiming clock).

During its 900-year history, St Giles' has been scarred by regular acts of destruction and rebuilding – the most recent in 1940. Few memorials, after so many vicissitudes, survive, although signatures recorded in the registers confirm associations with the poet **John Milton** (buried in the chancel, 1674; bust by John Bacon, 1793, south wall), the navigator **Martin Frobisher** (buried in south aisle, 1594), the author of the *Book of Martyrs* **John Foxe** (buried 1587), the mapmaker **John Speed** (buried 1629 below his monument on the south wall), **Oliver Cromwell** (married 22 August 1620), **Sir Thomas More, Ben Jonson, Shakespeare** (at the baptism of his nephew).

Barbican★

The Barbican Project, a residential neighbourhood incorporating schools, shops, open spaces, a conference and arts centre, to be established in the City on the bombed sites of Cripplegate, was conceived in the aftermath of World War I; construction began in 1962. The first residential phase was completed in 1976 and the arts centre finally opened in 1982.

The complex includes 40-storey tower blocks, crescents and mews linked by high- and low-level walkways and interspersed with gardens and sports areas. At the heart of this city within a city, beside the lake with its cascades and fountains, stands St Giles' Church, a vestige of Cripplegate and the only tangible link with the past.

Barbican Arts Centre

Silk Street . ◷ *Open Mon–Sat 9am –11pm, Sun and public holidays noon– 11pm.* ✆ *020 7638 4141 (switchboard); 020 7638 8891 (box office, open daily 9am–8pm). www.barbican.org.uk.*
The centre, of which five out of ten storeys are below ground, contains a concert hall (the permanent home of the London Symphony Orchestra), two theatres, three cinemas, a library, art gallery, sculpture court (on the roof of the concert hall), exhibition halls, meeting rooms and restaurants.

Also incorporated into the concrete maze is the **Guildhall School of Music and Drama** (1977), which is endowed with a canted façade.

▶ *Follow the signs to the Museum of London (* ◐ *see THE CITY – Additional Sights).*

Aldersgate

The original gate was said to have been built by a Saxon named Aldred. As James I entered the capital at this point on his accession, the gate was rebuilt in 1617 in commemoration of his entry, but demolished in 1761.

St Botolph Aldersgate

🕐 Open by appointment.
📞 020 7606 0684.

The church (1788-91), built of dark red-brown brick, is lit by conventional rounded windows. Its small square tower is topped by a cupola with a wooden turret and gilded vane. The building was "improved" in 1829 with the addition of a pedimented east end in stucco. The interior is mainly Georgian with elaborate rosettes in high relief on the white plaster ceiling. The inlaid pulpit stands on a carved palm tree.

Given its situation by a gate in the City Wall, the church is dedicated to the 7C Saxon saint and patron of travellers.

▶ *Take Little Britain, Bartholomew Close and an alleyway to St Bartholomew-the-Great.*

St Bartholomew-the-Great★★

♿🕐 Open Mon–Fri 8.30am–5pm (4pm in winter), Sat 10.30am–4pm, Sun 8.30am–8pm. 🎫£4. Guide book. 📞020 7606 5171. www.greatstbarts.com.

St Bartholomew's was once a great, spacious church of which the present building was only the chancel. It was founded in 1123 by a one-time courtier, **Rahere**, on land granted by **Henry I**. He established both the hospital and an Augustinian priory, of which he became the first prior.

By 1143, when he died, the Norman chancel had been completed; nearly 400 years later the church was 280ft/85m long, the west door being where the gateway on to Little Britain now stands. In 1539 **Henry VIII** dissolved the priory, demolished the church nave and ordained that the truncated building be used only as a parish church. The church fell into disrepair over the next 300 years: the Lady Chapel was "squatted in", became a printers' workshop (where **Benjamin Franklin** was employed in 1724); the north transept was turned into a forge (note the blackened walls) the remains of the cloister became a stable, a thick layer of earth covered the church floor and limewash obscured the walls and murals.

The church was restored between 1863 and 1910.

The Building – The gateway, a 13C arch and the original entrance to the nave, is surmounted by a late 16C half-timbered gatehouse (restored 1932). The path through the churchyard is at the level of the Medieval church. The square brick castellated **tower**, with a small vaned turret, was erected in 1628 off-centre at the west end of the curtailed church. The porch, west front and other exterior flint and stone refacing date from 1839 (restoration by Sir Aston Webb).

The **choir**★ is Norman. An arcade of circular arches springing from massive round piers and plainly scalloped capitals supports a relieving arch and a gallery of arched openings divided into groups of four by slender columns. The late Perpendicular style clerestory, rebuilt in 1405, has survived intact save for the insertion of an **oriel** window in the south gallery in 1520. The Lady Chapel completed in 1336 was all but rebuilt in 1897 so only the end north and south windows are original. 15C oak doors (by the west door) lead to the east walk of the old cloister (c. 1405, rebuilt early this century).

Rahere, the founder, lies on a 16C decorated tomb chest beneath a crested canopy. The **font**, used at Hogarth's baptism in 1697, dates from the early 15C and as such is one of the oldest in the City.

St Bartholomew-the-Less

🕐 Open daily 7am–8pm or later.
📞020 7601 8066.

By the 18C, the 12C hospital church was so derelict as to need repair first by **George Dance the Younger** (1789) and again, in 1823, by **Philip Hardwick**. Monuments date back to the 14C (vestry pavements), while the more modern ones chiefly commemorate hospital personnel. The 15C square tower with a domed corner turret is visible from the market although the church stands within the walls of the hospital.

▶ *Cross the square.*

Smithfield London Central Markets

Smithfield was opened as a wholesale and retail dead meat, poultry and provision market only in 1868. Previously the stock had come in live, driven into the City through Islington. The name, derived from "smooth field" is associated with a stock market in Saxon times, and from the 12C with the Fair of St Bartholomew. The site was also used for executions until the gallows were moved to Tyburn. The livestock market was transferred in 1855 to the Caledonian Market, Islington. The listed buildings, erected in 1868 and since enlarged, are of red brick and stone with domed towers at either end; they extend over 8 acres/3ha, with 15 miles/24km of rails capable of hanging 60 000 sides of beef. After a recent £70 million facelift which has restored the building to its former glory and brought standards of efficiency and hygiene up to modern levels, meat, dairy and delicatessen goods are still traded here (go very early in the morning if you wish to see it in action).

▷ *Return to Giltspur St and walk down.*

Fat Boy

The gilded oak figure, said to mark where the **Great Fire** stopped, stands on a site then known as Pie Corner; hence the saying that the Fire began in Pudding Lane and ended at Pie Corner.

St Sepulchre-without-Newgate

Open Tue–Thu noon–2pm (Wed 11am–3pm). Recitals Wed 1pm, organ recitals 2nd and 4th Tue 1pm, other times various programmes. 020 7248 3826. www.st-sepulchre.org.uk.

The **Church of the Holy Sepulchre** that stands "without the city wall" was of an earlier foundation, renamed at the time of the crusades after the Jerusalem church. The square stone tower (restored) surmounted by four heavy crocketed pinnacles dates from 1450 as does the fan-vaulted porch decorated with carved bosses. St Sepulchre is "the Musicians' Church", its choir central to the emergence of the Royal School of Church Music. Along the north side is the Musicians' Chapel, which contains the ashes of **Sir Henry Wood** (1869–1944), founder of The Proms. The organ (1670) has a superb case that includes the monogram of Charles II, and is reputed to have been played by **Handel** and **Mendelssohn**; it was also where the young Henry Wood aged 14 officiated as assistant organist.

Other mementoes include a stone from the Church of the Holy Sepulchre in Jerusalem; the hand bell rung outside condemned men's cells at midnight in the old Newgate Prison and the colours of the Royal Fusiliers City of London Regiment.

Central Criminal Court, the Old Bailey

Open to the public when the Courts are sitting, Mon–Fri approx. 10am–4.30pm with an adjournment for lunch. Bags, cameras, recording equipment, mobile telephones, food and drink prohibited. Guided tours of the complex are offered by **Old Bailey Insight**. *www.old-bailey.com.*

This is the third Criminal Court to occupy this site. The original trial halls, erected in 1539, were built to protect the judges from "much peril and danger" in the form of sickness and infestation so rife in the gaols – indeed they still carry posies from May to September traditionally to ward off gaol fever.

The Common Council, therefore, passed a resolution "that a convenient place be made... upon the common ground of this City in the old bailey of London": the site chosen was located by New Gate, a gate in the wall built by the Romans for the main road west enlarged in the early Middle Ages, near which a City gaol had been constructed (1180) to relieve the ever overcrowded Fleet Prison.

Remains of a triumphal arch c. AD 200 marking the western entrance to the city have been excavated in Newgate Street.

The Building – The granite structure is dressed in Portland stone, its dramatic entrance emphasised with a broken pediment and allegories of Truth, Justice and the Recording Angel, while the Lady of Justice, a gold figure (12ft/3.5m tall) holding scales and a sword (3ft 3in/1m) stands high above perched on a green copper dome (1907). This dominant feature of the London skyline is cast in bronze and covered in gold leaf (regilded every five years and cleaned every August) – unusually she is neither blindfolded nor blind.

Inside all is marble, a grand staircase sweeping up to halls on two floors decked with painted murals; the four original courts are large. The complex also has 60 cells to accommodate prisoners who are brought daily from Brixton and Holloway Prisons.

▷ *Walk eastwards along Newgate St.*

General Post Office

Plaques on the turn-of-the-19C building indicate the site of Greyfriars (f. 1225) and Christ's Hospital, which occupied the buildings from 1552 to 1902. Outside the main building stands the statue of **Sir Rowland Hill**, who in 1840 introduced the penny post, the uniform rate for a letter sent anywhere in the kingdom.

Christ Church★

The slender square stone tower rises by stages to a slim decorated turret and vane. Christ Church was founded by Henry VIII on the site occupied by the Greyfriars monastery (1225–1538) possibly to serve Christ's Hospital, the second royal foundation nearby, also known as the Bluecoat School (1552–1902). The church, destroyed in the **Fire**, was redesigned by Wren (1667–91)

▷ *Return to the crossroads and walk on.*

Holborn Viaduct

The viaduct was built in 1863–69 to connect the City and West End; previously all traffic had to descend to the level of Farringdon Street and climb up again. The bridge is an example of Victorian cast iron work: strongly constructed and ornate with uplifting statues and lions.

Alongside the viaduct stands the **City Temple** marked by its high square and pillared tower surmounted by a square lantern, lead dome and cross. The church is famous for its preachers. Wartime bombing gutted the sanctuary so that the building now presents the contrast of a Victorian/Palladian exterior and modern interior.

☞*For Holborn, see CHANCERY LANE Walk, below.*

CHANCERY LANE★

Map: inside covers (EFX) and opposite.
➚*Holborn; Chancery Lane. This area lies to the north of Fleet St and on the western boundary of the City of London. Allow half a day to walk around the area, including a pause at Ye Old Mitre pub, off Hatton Garden.*

The character of the area bounded by High Holborn and Fleet Street is defined by the ancient traditions of the Inns of Court. Take the time to wander through the hidden alleyways to discover the fascinating history that underlies modern sites and stresses continuity through the ages. Leafy squares provide a haven from the bustling crowds.

During the Middle Ages, the area around the palace of the **Bishop of Ely** was surrounded by open fields. By the late 16C the four **Inns of Court** and dependent (now defunct) **Inns of Chancery** had been established for nearly 300 years as the country's great law societies. Litigation was a serious business; there were disputes on land entitlement and inheritance, while actions for slurs and insults were also a fashionable pastime. From the 16C there were some 2 000 students dining in the halls.

▷ *From Holborn Station, walk down Kingsway and turn left after a church to Lincoln's Inn Fields.*

Dick Whittington

Whittington was four times Lord Mayor; in 1397, 1397–8, 1406–7 and 1419–20; he died in 1423, in his early sixties. The 3rd son of a Gloucestershire squire, he came to London, entered the mercers' trade, married well and rose rapidly both in trade, from which he amassed a fortune, and in the Corporation where he progressed from ward member to Lord Mayor. He was not knighted, though an important part of his contact with the Crown seems to have been the provision of considerable loans; according to legend he gave a banquet for Henry V at which he burned bonds discharged for the King worth £60 000. His great wealth continued after his death, as in his lifetime, to be devoted to the public cause: permanent buildings for Leadenhall Market, the construction of Greyfriars Library, half the cost of founding the Guildhall Library, the foundation of a college and almshouses at St Michael Paternoster Royal.

Such great personality, wealth and benefactions were embroidered into legend until, in 1605, licence was granted for performances of a play (now lost), *The History of Richard Whittington, of his lowe byrth, his great fortune*. When an engraver, Renold Elstrack, about the same time portrayed him in classic pose with his hand upon a skull, popular protest was so loud that the engraver altered the plate replacing the skull with a cat, which may have given rise to the legend of Dick Whittington and his cat, although an alternative source is a coal barge, known as a catte, since Whittington traded in coal.

Sir John Soane's Museum★★

13 Lincoln's Inn Fields, WC2.
 ♿🕐*Open Tue–Sat 10am–5pm (first Tue of each month 6–9pm). 🕐Closed bank holidays, 24 Dec. 👝Free (£5 late-night opening). 👣Guided tour Sat 11am (£5; no booking). Library and drawings collection available to scholars by appointment. ✆020 7405 2107. www.soane.org.*

On the north side of Lincoln's Inn Fields is Sir John Soane's Museum.

In 1833 Soane obtained a private Act of Parliament to ensure the perpetuation of the museum after his death. His house and collections now offer an insight into the mind of a British collector of that period. Soane acquired **no 12** in 1792 as his town house, **no 13** in 1805 as his museum and he built **no 14** in 1824.

Interior – The rooms are small and passages narrow, but mirrors, skylights, windows on inner courts and domes give an illusion of space and perspective. Fragments, casts and models are displayed throughout the galleries, while below ground are the Crypt, the Gothic Monk's Parlour and the Sepulchral Chamber containing the sarcophagus of the Egyptian pharaoh Seti I

(c. 1392 BC). On the first floor are architectural drawings (8 000 by Robert and James Adam, 12 000 by Soane). Note the painting by Turner in the south drawing room.

On the ground floor is Soane's **collection of pictures★★**, assembled on folding planes in the picture room; it includes drawings by Piranesi and 12 of **Hogarth**'s paintings of the *Election*

Sir John Soane's Museum

Martin Charles/Sir John Soane's Museum

Sir John Soane (1753–1837)

Born the son of a country builder, Soane made his way through his talent: he worked under **George Dance Junior** and **Henry Holland**; he won prizes and a travelling scholarship to Italy (1777–80) while at the Royal Academy where, in later years, he was Professor of Architecture. He held the important office of Surveyor to the Bank of England (1788–1833) for which he executed the most original designs ever made for a bank.

and the *Rake's Progress*. Elsewhere are **Canaletto**, **Reynolds** and **Turner**.

Lincoln's Inn Fields

By 1650 a developer, who had purchased the common fields to the west of Lincoln's Inn 20 years before, had surrounded them on three sides with houses. Of that period, one, **Lindsey House**, remains, probably designed by Inigo Jones. 18C houses in the square include the Palladian style nos 57–58 dating from 1730, and no 66, **Powis House** of 1777, with a pediment marking the centre window. On the north side nos 1–2 are early 18C, 5–9 Georgian, and no 15 mid-18C.

The square's south side is occupied by the neo-Jacobean **Land Registry**, neo-Georgian **Nuffield College of Surgical Sciences** (1956–58), 19C–20C **Royal College of Surgeons**, housing the **Hunterian Museum** dedicated to the study of pathology and anatomy (& ○ *open Tue–Sat 10am–5pm; ℘020 7869 6560; www.rcseng.ac.uk/ museums*).

▶ *Walk through the square and turn right to the porter's lodge.*

Lincoln's Inn★★

Grounds: ○open Mon–Fri 10am– 4pm. ⊘Closed Sat–Sun and bank holidays. Chapel: ○open Mon–Fri noon–2.30pm. Old Hall, New Hall and Library: ↩Guided tour (min. 15 people, ⊜£4 per head with refreshments) on written application to the Assistant Under Treasurer, Lincoln's Inn, London WC2A 3TL. ℘020 7405 1393. www.lincolnsinn.org.uk.

The site belonged to the Dominicans until 1276 before being acquired by the Earl of Lincoln, who built a large mansion which he bequeathed as a residential college, or inn, for young lawyers. The brick buildings with stone decoration date from the late 15C. The main gateway leads to several intercommunating courts and beautiful gardens with an ornate Gothic toolshed.

New Square, surrounded by 17C four-storey buildings, features an archway leading south to Carey Street.

New Hall and Library, Lincoln's Inn

Y. Kanazawa/Michelin

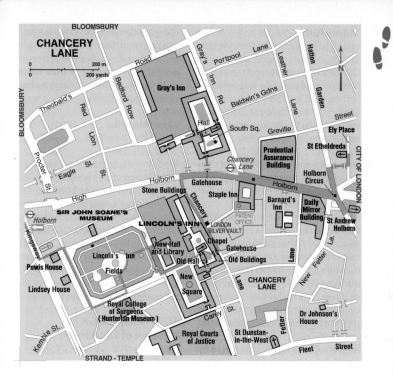

The **Stone Buildings** date from 1775-80. The red-brick mid-19C **New Hall** and **Library** are diapered in the Tudor manner.

The **Old Hall** dates from 1490. The Gothic-style **Chapel** was rebuilt in 1619-23. In the windows, benchers and treasurers are commemorated by their arms and names: Thomas More, Thomas Cromwell, Pitt, Walpole, Newman, Canning, Disraeli, Gladstone, Asquith... The gabled brick buildings immediately south of the court, known as the **Old Buildings**, are Tudor in style (redone in 1609).

The **gatehouse** on Chancery Lane, with its corner towers and original massive oak doors, dates from 1518. Above the arch are the arms of Henry VIII, the Earl of Lincoln and Sir Thomas Lovell.

▶ *Pass through the gate and walk north along Chancery Lane.*

At **no 53** the **London Silver Vaults** present a dazzling array of Georgian, Victorian and modern silver and silverplate. ♿ ⏰*Open Mon–Fri 9am–5.30pm (1pm Sat).* ⏰*Closed bank holidays.* ☎*020 7242 3844. www.thesilvervaults.com*

▶ *In High Holborn turn right, cross the road and pass under a wide arch.*

Gray's Inn★

Gardens: ⏰*open Mon–Fri noon–2.30pm.* ⏰*Closed bank holidays.* *Squares:* ⏰*open Mon–Fri 9am–7pm.* ☎*020 7458 7800. www.graysinn.info.*

Gray's Inn, founded in the 14C and extended in the 16C, was largely rebuilt after the war. The main entrance is through the **Gatehouse** of 1688. **South Square** has at its centre an elegant bronze statue of **Sir Francis Bacon**, the Inn's most illustrious member.

The gardens that so delighted **Samuel Pepys** and **Joseph Addison**, are enclosed by 18C wrought-iron railings. The **hall**, which was burnt out, was rebuilt in its 16C style.

Staple Inn★

Lying just inside the limits of the City, Staple Inn was one of the Inns of Chancery where law students spent their first year studying. The half-timbered houses, built in 1586-96, survived the Great Fire and have retained their overall character. An arched entrance leads to the Inn surrounding a central courtyard.

Once an inn of Chancery, **Barnard's Inn** is now home to **Gresham College** (ⓘ see *The CITY – Guildhall*), an institution that dates back over 400 years.

Across Holborn stands the **Prudential Assurance Building,** a red building designed by Alfred Waterhouse at the turn of the century. On the east side of Barnard's Inn, the former **Daily Mirror Building** is marked by a curtain wall of stone (170ft/52m high), elbowed by taller buildings of glass that extend south between Fetter and New Fetter Lanes (1957–60).

Holborn Circus is now punctuated by a traffic island with a statue of Prince Albert, mounted and with hat aloft.

Just south is **St Andrew Holborn** (ⓘ open Mon–Fri 9am–5pm; ℘020 7583 7394; www.standrewholborn.co.uk) designed by Wren. At the west end, in a recess, is the tomb of **Thomas Coram** (d. 1751), sea captain and parishioner (ⓘ see *BLOOMSBURY – The Foundling Museum*). The font (1804), pulpit (1752) and the case and organ presented to Coram by **Handel** in 1750 are of interest.

▷ *Cross the circus.*

Hatton Garden

Ely Place recalls the Bishop of Ely's town house in Holborn, alluded to by Richard, Duke of Gloucester: "My lord of Ely, when I was last in Holborn, I saw good strawberries in your garden there, I do beseech you send for some of them" (*Richard III*; 3 iv). In 1576 the property was given at Queen Elizabeth's command to **Sir Christopher Hatton**, her "dancing Chancellor" for a yearly rent of ten pounds, a red rose and ten hayloads.

Today, the Garden, built up in the 1680s, is the centre of diamond merchants and jewellery craftsmen. Early history is recalled in the name of **Ye Olde Mitre** (ⓘ see *Addresses*) in Ely Court, a narrow alley off Hatton Garden.

St Etheldreda

ⓘ Open daily 8am–6pm.
℘ 020 7405 1061.

The church was built as a chapel attached to the Bishop of Ely's house. Subjected to neglect and wartime bombing, the 13C building underwent extensive restoration work. New stained-glass windows depict the five English martyrs beneath Tyburn gallows and against the east wall is a carved medieval wood reliquary. The **crypt**,which houses a café (ⓘ see *Addresses*) has bare masonry walls and blackened Medieval roof timbers.

ADDITIONAL SIGHTS

Museum of London★★

150 London Wall, London EC2Y 5HN.
♿ ⓘ Open daily, 10am–6pm. ⓘ Closed 24–26 Dec, 1 Jan. ℘020 7001 9844. www.museumoflondon.org.uk.

This museum, which comprehensively and entertainingly tells of London's turbulent history from 1066 to today, has recently undergone a massive redevelopment, designed by award-winning architects Wilkinson Eyre. Housing over 4 000 items in four new galleries, there are huge, street-level glass windows providing an illuminated showcase for the Lord Mayor's Coach. There is also a modern theatre, state-of-the-art Clore Learning Centre, a coffee shop and The Sackler Hall. Impressive interactive techonology abounds throughout the museum.

By the main entrance of the museum, in Nettleton Court, a monumental bronze leaf stands as a memorial to the Methodist **John Wesley**.

The museum operates a team of archaeologists specialising in urban excavation; this allows sites to be dug with the co-operation of building developers – work is undertaken to restricted time-frames before great concrete foundations are irrevocably sunk through the layers of history. Over the long term, digs have revealed a broad range of artefacts which, classified and compared to other flora, fauna, bone, wood, ceramic, glass or metal finds, provide a reliable record of London and her inhabitants through the ages and ravages of war, fire, flood and plague.

Displays are organised into galleries of bays according to time and theme from prehistory to the present: exhibits include the best Roman wall painting in Britain and the sculptures from the Roman Temple of Mithras, Medieval pilgrim badges, a model of the Rose Theatre based on evidence excavated by Museum of London archaeologists, the Cheapside Hoard of Jacobean jewellery, a diorama of the Great Fire, the doors from Newgate Gaol, 19C shops and interiors, the Lord Mayor's Coach, souvenirs of the women's suffrage movement, the 1930s lifts from Selfridge's department store and a revealing exposition on World War II.

The development of domestic life and public utility services – gas, drainage, the Underground – are illustrated as well as political and fashionable London.

There are regular special events, including walking tours of the surrounding area, and an excellent branch museum: the Museum in Docklands (*see entry p327*).

Bank of England Museum★

Threadneedle Street. ⓓⓒ*Open Mon–Fri 10am–5pm.* ⓒ*Closed bank holidays. Guide (9 languages).* ℘*020 7601 5545. www.bankofengland.co.uk.*

The museum opens with a description of the history of the building in a reconstruction of Sir John Soane's Bank Stock Office. Chronological displays illustrate early banking using goldsmiths' notes; the Charter dated 27 July 1694; Letters Patent under the Great Seal of William and Mary; a £1million note used for accounting purposes only; display of gold bars; paper money and forgeries; the gold standard; silver vessels; minted coins. Interactive touch screens explain modern banking while a modern dealing

Viking weapons, Museum of London

©Museum of London

desk with telephone and screen provide an insight into money dealing.

Mansion House

Guided tour for groups only (15–40min) on written application to the Principal Assistant-Diary, Mansion House, London EC4N 8BH. ⓒ*Closed Easter, Aug and 24–25 Dec.* ℘*020 7626 2500.*

The interior is designed as a suite of magnificent state rooms from the portico leading to the dining or Egyptian Hall. In the hall, giant Corinthian columns forming an ambulatory support the cornice on which the decorated ceiling rests; the walled niches are filled with Victorian statuary on subjects taken from English literature from Chaucer to Byron. The Ball Room is on the second floor.

Plate and Insignia★★ – The Corporation plate, rich and varied, dates from the 17C. The insignia includes much older pieces: the Lord Mayor's **chain of office**, c. 1535 with later additions, suspends from a collar of SS gold links, knots and enamelled Tudor roses; a pendant known as the Diamond Jewel consists of an onyx piece, carved in 1802 with the City arms, and set in diamonds; the **Pearl Sword**, 16C and according to tradition presented by Queen Elizabeth at the opening of the Royal Exchange in

Gog and Magog

Guarding the Musicians' Gallery are the post-war replica giants (9ft 3ins/3m tall) carved in limewood by David Evans after the figures set up in Guildhall in 1708, themselves descendants of 15C and 16C midsummer pageant figures who were said to have originated in a legendary conflict between ancient Britons and Trojans in 1000 BC.

Both images, J. Malburet/MICHELIN

1571; the 17C **Sword of State** and the 18C **Great Mace** of silver gilt and 5ft 3in/1.6m long.

Guildhall★

Gresham Street, EC2P 2EJ.
🕑*Open (civic functions permitting) Mon–Sat 10am–4.30pm.* 🕑*Closed Good Fri, Easter Mon, 25–26 Dec, 1 Jan.* 📞*020 7332 1313. www.guildhall. cityoflondon.gov.uk.*

The City was granted its first charter by **William the Conqueror** in 1067; the first **Mayor** was installed in a building, probably on the present site in 1193; for at least 850 years, therefore, Guildhall has been the seat of civic government. "This Guildhall", Stow quoted in 1598 "was begun to be built new in the year 1411;… the same was made of a little cottage, a large and great house… towards the charges whereof the (livery) companies gave large benevolences; also offences of men were pardoned for sums of money, extraordinary fees were raised, fines… during 7 years, with a continuation of 3 years more… Executors to Richard Whittington gave towards the paving of this great hall… with hard stone of Purbeck". All was complete by c. 1440.

The Great Fire left the outer walls and crypt standing. Rebuilding began immediately and in 1669 Pepys noted: "I passed by Guildhall, which is almost finished". In 1940 history repeated itself. Reconstruction was once more completed in 1954. In the course

of recent building work, excavations have revealed the site of a Roman amphitheatre, traces of the Medieval Jewish quarter and of the 15C Guildhall chapel.

Architecture – Guildhall's 18C façade, a mixture of Classical and Gothic motifs, extends across nine bays, rises to four storeys and culminates, on the four buttresses which divide the face into equal parts, in large and peculiar pinnacles. Crowning the central area are the City arms, which are composed of the Cross of St George, the sword of the patron saint, St Paul, on a shield supported by winged griffins, probably incorporated in the 16C. The **porch**, at the centre, however, is still covered by two bays of Medieval tierceron vaulting.

Inside, the **hall** also is in part Medieval: the walls date back to the 15C and the chamber in which today's banquets are held is the same in dimension (152ft/46m x 49 ft/15m) as that in which Lady Jane Grey and others were tried.

A cornice at clerestory level bears the arms of England, the City and the 12 Great Livery Companies whose banners hang in front; below, the bays between the piers contain memorial statues, notably (north wall) a seated bronze of **Churchill** by Oscar Nemon; Nelson; Wellington; Pitt the Elder by John Bacon. East of the entrance porch in the south wall, behind where the lord mayor sits at banquets, is a canopied oak buffet on which are displayed the City sword and mace and plate; to the west beneath the only remaining 15C window are the Imperial Standards of Length (1878) with the Metric measures (1973) on the right.

Crypt – Guided tours by appointment Mon–Fri. 0207 332 1313.
The crypt comprises two parts: the western pre-15C section with its four pairs of stone columns was vaulted by Wren after the earlier hall above collapsed in the Fire.

The 15C eastern section below the present Guildhall – the largest Medieval crypt in London – survived both 17C and 20C fires: it remains notable for its size and the six blue Purbeck marble clustered piers supporting the vaulting.

Library – Open Mon–Sat 9.30am–4.45pm. Closed bank holidays and Sat preceding Bank Holiday Mon (print room and map section closed Sat). 020 7332 1868/1870.
The library, founded c. 1423, despoiled in the 16C and refounded in 1824, possesses a unique collection of maps, prints, drawings and manuscripts on the history and development of the City and London.

Clock Museum★ – Open Mon–Sat 9am–4.45pm. Closed bank holidays. 020 7332 1868 (Guildhall Library).
The 700 timepieces that make up the Museum of the Worshipful Company of Clockmakers range in size from long case (grandfather) clocks to minute watches, in date from the 15C to the 20C, in manufacture from all wood composition, in movement from perpetual motion (with a ball that rolls 2 522 mi/4 058km a year) and in aesthetic appeal from a silver skull watch, said to have belonged to Mary Queen of Scots, to jewelled confections, enamelled, decorated, engraved and chased. The collection also includes two fine Harrison clocks (see SUBURBS – GREENWICH).

Guildhall Art Gallery – Open Mon–Sat 10am–5pm, Sun, noon–4pm.
Guided tours of the highlights of the permanent collection at 12.15pm, 1.15pm, 2.15pm and 3.15pm. Free.

Closed 25–26 Dec, 1 Jan and special occasions. £2.50 (including amphitheatre entrance). 020 7332 3700 (recorded information). www.guildhall-art-gallery.org.uk.
There is no lift access to the Victorian Galleries until further notice. Access is by staircase only.

A fine modern building, replacing the original gallery (burned down during an air raid in 1941) houses the art collection owned by the Corporation of London: displays of the 250 works in the collection are rotated to explore different themes and allow lesser-seen pictures to come out of storage: the collection's highlights include portraits of dignitaries from 17C–20C (as well as a marble statue of **Margaret Thatcher**), 18C paintings, a remarkable *Salisbury Cathedral* by Constable and works by Victorian painters (Pre-Raphaelites). Take a step back into antiquity and visit the **Roman amphitheatre**, unearthed in 1988 by Museum of London archaeologists, and now subsumed into the Guildhall Art Gallery.

St Bartholomew's Hospital

Guided tour (including St Bartholomew-the-Less, St Bartholomew the Great and Cloth Fair) Fri 2pm.
Closed Good Fri, 24 Dec. £5.
020 7837 0546 . www.stbartsandthe london.org.uk.
The hospital, known as Barts, was founded by Rahere in 1123 as part of an Augustinian priory. Modern blocks now supplement the collegiate style buildings (1730–66), designed by James Gibbs. The north wing includes the great staircase decorated with vast murals by **Hogarth** (1734) and the Great Hall (closed to the public); displays of items (documents, charters, medical paraphernalia) relate the evolution of this historic institution.

The gatehouse from West Smithfield erected in 1702, contains an 18C statue of Henry VIII who dissolved the priory and gave the hospital to the City of London in 1546.

ADDRESSES

✗ LIGHT BITE

🍽 **Café at the Crypt** – *St Etheldreda's Church, EC1N 6RY. ☎020 7405 1061. www.stetheldreda.com/cafe.html. Closed Sat, Sun.* A pleasant place for a break with freshly cooked food and light refreshments.

🍽 **Carluccio's** – *West Smithfield, EC1A 9JR. ☎020 7329 5904. www. carluccios.com.* A long counter links the delicatessen shop to the large restaurant in the rear. Modern décor and Italian cooking using fresh ingredients accompanied by Italian wines.

🍽 **George and Vulture** – *3 Castle Ct, EC3V 9DL. ☎020 7626 9710.* A picturesque establishment serving traditional food.

🍽 **La Grande Marque** – *47 Ludgate Hill, EC4M 7JU. ☎020 7329 6709. www. lagrandemarque.co.uk.* This converted bank retains considerable Victorian charm and stands in the shadow of St Paul's. The menu offers over 110 wines – some by the glass – and light snacks.

🍽🍽 **Simpson's Tavern** – *Ball Court, 38 Cornhill, EC3V 9DR. ☎020 7626 9985. Closed Sat, Sun.* An atmospheric 18C eating house with dark woodwork and polished brass.

🍺 PUBS

Black Friar – *174 Queen Victoria St, EC4V 4EG. ☎020 7236 5474.* Opposite the underground station stands London's only art nouveau pub. It was founded in 1875 and is dedicated to the black monks of the Dominican Priory, which stood on the site between 1279 and 1539. Admire the stained-glass windows, paintings and bronze and copper sculptures. The pub was due to be demolished in the 1960s, but the public, backed by some influential figures, successfully opposed the plans.

Cittie of York – *22-23 High Holburn, Holborn, WC1V 6BS. ☎020 7242 7670. Closed Sun.* This inn, dating from 1667, is a true delight. A pleasant room at the front and the nave of a church at the

back, with tall columns, pointed arches, confession boxes for repentance and a bar to seek sanctuary.

Jamaica Wine House – *St Michael's Alley, off Cornhill, EC3V 9DS. ☎020 7929 6972. Closed Sat, Sun.* This delightful watering hole with historical associations (once frequented by Charles Dickens' Mr Pickwick) is hidden in a small alley.

Lamb Tavern – *10–12 Leadenhall Market, EC3V 1LR. ☎020 7626 2454.* The oldest pub in the centre of Leadenhall Market, the Lamb Tavern has an exceptional interior of stunning marble pillars and a glass roof. The terrace is busy at lunchtime with office workers. The pub is also a popular haunt for film producers.

Ye Old Wine Shades – *6 Martin Lane, EC4A 2BU. ☎020 7626 6303. www. elvino.co.uk. Closed Sat, Sun & bank holidays.* This delightful old pub (1663) is authentically furnished with dark wooden booths, and frequented by business people. It serves excellent wines accompanied in the evenings by a variety of hot and cold bar snacks; at lunchtime traditional English dishes, such as steak and kidney pie and fish and chips, are served in the downstairs restaurant.

Ye Olde Mitre – *1 Ely Court, Ely Place, EC1N 6SJ. ☎020 7405 4751. Closed bank holidays.* This historic, picturesque 16C pub with its irregular shaped rooms was once part of a bishop's residence and is well worth the visit.

The Seven Stars – *53 Carey St, WC2A 2JB. ☎020 7242 8521. Closed bank holidays.* A really charming pub dating from 1602. Large lawyer, musician and young student clientele.

🎭 EVENTS AND FESTIVALS

Lord Mayor's Show – *Second Sun in Nov.* A traditional procession of floats through the City to celebrate the swearing-in of the Lord Mayor of the City of London.

St Paul's Cathedral★★★

The imposing dome of St Paul's has dominated London's skyline for centuries and is one of the city's most enduring sights. The grandeur of the edifice, combined with its harmonious proportions and sheer size, inspires a sense of wonder. There are many surprises in store: discover the Whispering Gallery and its amazing acoustics; climb up to the dome for a close-up view of the frescoes, wonderful perspectives of the interior and a bird's-eye view of the city; explore the crypt with its remarkable monuments to famous men and women; or pause for refreshment in the café and restaurant.

A BIT OF HISTORY

St Paul's is the cathedral of the Diocese of London. It was here on 19 July 1981 that the marriage of HRH Prince Charles to Lady Diana Spencer was celebrated with pomp and glory. It has also seen the funerals of Lord Nelson, the Duke of Wellington and Sir Winston Churchill; and the peace services marking the end of the First and Second World Wars – among many other great occasions.

Ever since the dome of St Paul's first rose out of the ashes of the Great Fire (1666), it has been a talisman for Londoners. In December 1940 when the whole City and docks were set ablaze, the dome soared above the smoke and flames as a symbol of hope and in August 1944 the bells, silent since the start of the war, rang out to celebrate Paris' liberation. After nearly three centuries the glorious dome has lost none of its majesty. Neighbouring **Paternoster Square** (now home to the London Stock Exchange) was recently redeveloped to open up views of the Cathedral, while the creation of the Millennium Bridge offers an uninterrupted view from the river.

Old St Paul's – The present cathedral of St Paul is probably the fifth to stand

Michelin Map: *inside covers (FX) and area map under The CITY.* St Paul's. *For the sights outside the immediate vicinity, see The CITY.*
St Paul's is a focal point in the City of London from which to explore the surrounding area; the Barbican and the Tower of London are within easy access and it's a short walk to the South Bank over the Millennium Bridge.

Kids: A climb up to the dome to discover the fascinating acoustics of the Whispering Gallery and the view from one of the higher galleries.

Don't Miss: The view from the Stone Gallery (378 steps), or if you're ready for even more stairs, the view from the higher Golden Gallery (530 steps).

Timing: Guided tours last an hour-and-a-half to two hours. Allow time to enjoy the garden and, for a sit-down break, have a snack or sandwich in the Crypt Café.

St Paul's Dome (cross section)

MICHELIN

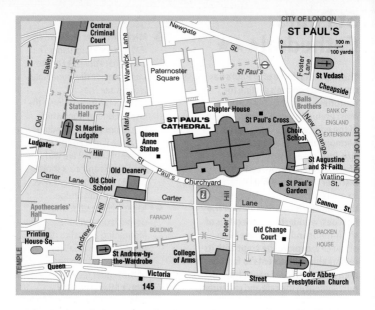

Central Criminal Court

Newgate

Warwick Lane

St.

St Paul's

Foster Lane

St Vedast

Cheapside

Paternoster Square

Old Bailey

Stationers' Hall

Ave Maria Lane

Chapter House

Balls Brothers

BANK OF ENGLAND

EXTENSION

St Martin-Ludgate

ST PAUL'S CATHEDRAL

St Paul's Cross

New Change

CITY OF LONDON

Ludgate

Hill

Queen Anne Statue

Choir School

Carter Lane

Old Deanery

St Paul's Churchyard

St Augustine and St Faith

Watling St.

Old Choir School

Carter Lane

St Paul's Garden

Apothecaries' Hall

Peter's Hill

Cannon St.

Printing House Sq.

FARADAY BUILDING

Old Change Court

BRACKEN HOUSE

St Andrew's Hill

TEMPLE

Queen

St Andrew-by-the-Wardrobe

College of Arms

Victoria

Street

Cole Abbey Presbyterian Church

145

on the site. Records document a church founded here in AD 604. After the 1087 fire destroyed the third building, the next cathedral, planned on a grand scale, featured a massive tower above the central crossing, embellished with a lead-covered 514ft/156m steeple (in 1561 this was struck by lightning and never replaced). In 1258–1314 the chancel was replaced by a longer decorated choir so that the building measured 620ft/189m from east to west.

During the next three centuries, Old St Paul's was neglected and gradually decayed. In the early 17C, it was partly repaired and **Inigo Jones** added an outstanding **Classical portico**★.

Unfortunately, the Civil War brought, in Carlyle's words, "horses stamping in the canons' stalls" and "mean shops squatting in the portico". A commission, which included **Christopher Wren**, then 31 and untried as an architect, was appointed in 1663 "to survey the general decays". Before it had time to report, the Great Fire swept through the cathedral, leading Wren to write, "St Paul's is now a sad ruin and that beautiful portico now rent in pieces".

Wren's Cathedral – Wren's first two designs were rejected by the church authorities. However, having been appointed Surveyor General to the King's Works in 1669, he resolved to go ahead "as ordered by his Majesty".

In 1708, after 32 years of unceasing work, Wren saw the final stone, the topmost in the lantern, set in place by his son; Wren was 75. Fifteen years later (1723) he died and was buried within the cathedral walls.

In 2008, on its 300th anniversary, the cathedral underwent a multi-million pound cleaning and restoration project, inside and out, which included improving access and facilities for people with disabilities, increasing educational facilities, the relighting of the Nelson and Wellington Chambers and the opening of the Triforium Gallery to the public.

VISIT

&⊘*Open for visitors Mon–Sat 8.30am–4pm (last admission), Sun for services only. Galleries: 9.30am–4.15pm.* ⊚*£11.* ➤*Guided tours (90–120min) 10.45am, 11.15am, 1.30pm, 2pm.* ⊚*£3. Regular organ recitals. Audio guide (6 languages)* ⊚*£4. Leaflets (8 languages). Guide book (6 languages).* ☏*020 7246 8357. www. stpauls.co.uk.*

Exterior

The building is dominated by its **dome** ★★, which rises from a drum to a stone lantern crowned by a golden ball and cross. The exterior of the drum is divided into two tiers, the upper tier being recessed so as to provide a circular viewing gallery, the **Stone Gallery**★.

Unlike the dome of St Peter's Basilica in Rome, which influenced Wren, the dome of St Paul's is not a true hemisphere. In fact it consists of three structures (◐*see illustration*): the outer lead-covered timber superstructure designed to satisfy purely aesthetic considerations, an invisible inner brick cone that supports the weight of the lantern (850 tons); and the inner brick dome that opens at the apex (20ft/6m diameter) into the space beneath the lantern.

At the **west end**, the two-tier portico is flanked by the west towers, Wren's most Baroque spires. The shallow **transepts** terminate in semicircular, columned porticoes surmounted by triangular pediments crowned by statues.

The carving and texture of many features are emphasised by floodlighting : statues, reliefs, figures by **Caius Cibber** and Francis Bird; garlands, swags, panels and innocent cherub heads in stone by **Grinling Gibbons**.

Interior

The greatest impact is the size and scale of the building, its almost luminescent stone flattered by gold and mosaic. After 1790, when the figures of four national benefactors Joshua Reynolds, the penal reformer John Howard, Dr Johnson and the orientalist Sir William Jones were placed by the dome piers, marble statuary proliferated.

Nave – At the west end of the aisles are the chapels of St Dunstan (*left*) and St Michael and St George (*right*), each preceded by a finely carved wooden screen (17C–18C) .

The **Wellington** monument **(1)**, completed in 1912 and featuring a full-size equestrian statue of the duke, occupies the entire space between two piers in the north aisle.

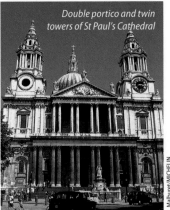

Double portico and twin towers of St Paul's Cathedral

J. Malburet/MICHELIN

In the pavement are the Night Watch memorial stone (cathedral guardians 1939–45) and the inscription commemorating the resting of Sir **Winston Churchill**'s coffin in the cathedral during the state funeral on 30 January 1965. Beneath the dome is Wren's own epitaph in Latin: "Reader,

Facts and Figures

The cost of the cathedral, recorded as £736 752 3s 3¼d, was met, together with the cost of rebuilding the City churches, by a tax levied on all sea coal imported into the Port of London. Wren was paid £200 a year during the construction of the cathedral.

The cathedral's overall length is 500ft/152m; height to the summit of the cross 365ft/111m; height of the portico columns 40ft/12m; height of the statue on the apex of the pediment 12ft/3.7m; length of the nave 180ft/55m, width of the nave, including the aisles, 121ft/37m; width across the transept 242ft/74m; internal diameter of the dome 110ft/33.5m; height of the nave 92 1/2ft/28m; height to the Whispering Gallery 100ft/30.5m; height to the apex of the internal dome 218ft/66.5m; total surface area approximately 78 000 sq ft/7 200sq m.

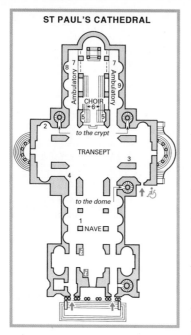

ST PAUL'S CATHEDRAL

to the crypt

TRANSEPT

to the dome

NAVE

Dome – *Entrance in the south transept.* From the **Whispering Gallery**★★ *(259 steps)* there is an impressive perspective of the choir, arches and clerestory far below, and a closer view of the dome frescoes painted by **Thornhill**. A hushed word uttered next to the wall can be heard quite clearly by a person standing diametrically opposite.

The **Stone Gallery** *(378 steps)* provides a good, but less extensive, **view**★★★ of the City rooftops than the one from the **Golden Gallery** *(530 steps)* at the top of the dome.

Choir and Ambulatory – In the east end, the marble high altar is set below a massive post-war baldachin carved and gilded from Wren's drawings. Note the Christ in Majesty in the domed apse.

The dark oak **choir stalls**★★**(6)** are the exquisite work of **Grinling Gibbons** and his craftsmen. Each stall is different from the next ; even the stall backs are carved forming a screen between the choir and the chancel aisles.

The **organ (5)**, a late 17C Smith instrument, together with its Gibbons case, has been divided and now towers on either side of the choir opening.

The iron railing, the gates to the chancel aisles and the gilded screens **(7)** enclosing the sanctuary are by Jean Tijou, wrought-iron smith extraordinaire.

In the north ambulatory, the graceful marble sculpture of the Virgin and Child **(8)** is by **Henry Moore** (1984). In the south ambulatory, against the first outer west pillar, is a statue by **Nicholas Stone** of **John Donne (9)**, the metaphysical poet and Dean of St Paul's (1621-31).

if you seek his monument, look around you."

Crossing and Transepts – The space beneath the dome is emphasised by the giant supporting piers that flank the entrances to the shallow transepts. The north transept features a dish-shaped font carved in 1727 by Francis Bird and a statue of Sir Joshua Reynolds **(4)**. The south transept includes the exceptional portrait statue of **Nelson** by **Flaxman (3)**★ and the beautiful wooden doorcase with fluted columns made up in the 19C from a wood screen designed by Wren and decked with garlands carved by Grinling Gibbons.

The Light of the World

"Behold I stand at the door and knock: if any man hear my voice, and open the door, I will come into him, and will sup with him, and he with me." (Revelations 3:20)

Holman Hunt's best known religious painting **(2)** hangs in the north transept. This large Pre-Raphaelite **Brotherhood** painting is one of three versions of the same subject (Keble College, Oxford and Manchester City Art Gallery) for which Hunt built an outdoor straw hut where he might settle to study and paint the light of a full moon between the hours of 9pm and 5am. It was described by Ruskin as *"one of the very noblest works of sacred art ever produced in this or any other age."*

Crypt – *Entrance in the south transept*. At the east end is the Chapel of the Order of the British Empire (OBE). Grouped in bays, formed by the massive piers which support the low-groined and tunnel vaulting, are the tombs, memorials and busts of men and women of all talents of the 18C, 19C and 20C of British, Commonwealth or foreign origin who contributed to the national life; not all those commemorated are buried here. In the south aisle, east of the staircase, is an area known as **Artists' Corner** honouring, among others, Christopher Wren, beneath a plain black marble stone, William Blake, Ivor Novello, Sir John Everett Millais, JMW Turner, Sir Joshua Reynolds and Holman Hunt.

In the north aisle are commemorations of Sir Arthur Sullivan, Sir Hubert Parry, William Boyce *(on the floor)*, John Constable and Sir Alexander Fleming. Down the steps, **Wellington** occupies the Cornish porphyry and granite sarcophagus; memorials to 10 of the great soldiers of World War II are a more recent addition; beyond, to the south, is a plaque to Florence Nightingale. Below the dome, at the centre of a circle of Tuscan columns lies **Nelson** beneath a curving black marble sarcophagus (originally intended for Cardinal Wolsey and subsequently proposed, but rejected, for Henry VIII). Only a handful of effigies were rescued from Old St Paul's in which Sir Philip Sidney and Sir Anthony van Dyck were buried *(modern plaque)*.

North transept: the **Treasury** displays plate and embroidered vestments. West end: models showing the construction of the Cathedral and dome.

Chapter House

This perfectly proportioned red-brick building was built by Wren (1710–14). The iron hand pump *(west)* was erected in 1819 by the parishioners of St Faith's.

St Paul's Cross

The cross *(site marked on the pavement north of the apse)*, used as a preaching cross in 1256, became the symbol of free speech and so was removed by the Long Parliament in 1643.

Choir School

The modern buildings of the choir school abut the tower of the church of **St Augustine and St Faith** (1680-87), built by Wren and destroyed during World War II. The square tower, tulip-shaped dome and lead spire, were rebuilt after the war to Wren's original design.

St Paul's Garden

The garden is complemented by **George Ehrlich's** sculpture, *The Young Lovers*.

Cheapside

Cheapside, a wide commercial street, takes its name from the Anglo-Saxon *ceap*, meaning to barter. The names of the side streets, Milk Street, Bread Street, Honey Lane, indicate the commodities sold there; other streets were inhabited by craft and tradesmen.

The street was also the setting for many a Medieval tournament, with contests being watched from the upper windows by householders and royalty alike; the Lord Mayor and aldermen watched from a balcony in the tower of St Mary-le-Bow, rebuilt after the Fire.

St Vedast's

Foster Lane. ◐*Open Mon–Fri 8am–6pm.* ◐*Closed bank holidays. Sung Mass Sun 11am, Mon–Fri 12.15pm. Guide book (3 languages).* ℘*020 7606 3998. www.vedast.net*

This Wren-designed church (1670–73) is dedicated to the beatified Bishop of Arras. The **tower and spire**★ consist of a square stone tower on which Wren later (1697) set a lantern below the ribbed stone spire surmounted by a ball and vane. The exterior is almost unnoticeable from Foster Lane. The interior is entirely new: the black-and-white marble floor; pews aligned collegiate style beneath the **ceiling**★, reinstalled to Wren's design.

The East End, an integral part of London, prides itself on its Cockney tradition; a tradition that has been enriched by wave after wave of immigrants over the centuries. The vibrant multicultural scene is in sharp contrast to the business atmosphere of the City, which sits to the west, and the modernistic Docklands development to the south and west. Since London won the bid for the 2012 Olympic Games the area has become a sea of redevelopment. The Olympic Village is to be sited at Stratford, bringing vital regeneration to the area.

Highlights

Geography – The East End stretches from the City to Stratford, West Ham and as far as the River Lee, and includes the riverside communities on the north bank. Major roads cut across the East End: A 11, A 12, A 406 and A 13.

The Docklands Light Railway and the Jubilee Line have opened up many areas of the East End.

History – Urbanisation of the area began in the 12C. In the first instance, the population swelled with the arrival of English craftsmen, then 10 000 freed slaves who worked as dockers. In the 16C Dutch traders and craftsmen began to settle, including leatherworkers, nail- and locksmiths. The overcrowding was further exacerbated by waves of refugees: Dutch and French Huguenots, Irish, Jews and Chinese. From the 16C–19C houses were used as workshops and dwellings; conditions were appalling. Spitalfields, Whitechapel, Stepney, Mile End and Bethnal Green became synonymous with poverty. In the 20C many slums were replaced by modern low-cost housing, inhabited by immigrants from the West Indies, India, Pakistan and Bangladesh. Several famous philanthropic institutions were born in the East End of London. These include **Dr Barnardo's** first children's home (1874) in Stepney and the **Salvation Army**, founded in 1765, which began on Trinity Green in the Mile End Road.

Today – The past decade has seen an influx of creative types drawn to the East End's vibrancy; particularly around the Whitechapel Gallery and Hoxton. As a result, Hoxton Square, Old Spitalfields Market and Brick Lane have been regenerated into fashionable areas. Regeneration has also been kick-started by the 2012 Olympics, including an Olympic Park in development on former industrial land around the River Lee. However, many areas of the East End still remain among the poorest in Britain.

Tower of London★★★

The romantic outline of the Tower of London is evocative of scenes of horror, of royal pageantry and of the, sometimes brutal, politics of Great Britain's past. The Tower is an essential experience, for its fraught history, dazzling Crown Jewels and the dramatic tales of its entertaining Yeoman Warders in their traditional attire. Tower Bridge is also a fascinating experience, with a memorable bird's-eye view of the City enjoyed from its regal elevated walkway.

A BIT OF HISTORY

Tower of London – This royal residence, now a UNESCO World Heritage Site, was established by William I (the Conqueror) primarily to deter Londoners from revolt in the immediate aftermath of the Norman Conquest; additionally its vantage point beside the river gave immediate sighting of any hostile force approaching up the Thames. The first fortress of wood (1067) was replaced by a stone building (c 1077–97) within the Roman City Wall, of which a piece still stands (A). Norman, Plantagenet and Tudor monarchs extended the fortress until it occupied 18 acres/7ha. Excavations have revealed part of a 13C perimeter wall and the Coldharbour Gate (B); St Peter's Church was incorporated within the Tower, a second fortified perimeter wall was built, the moat was excavated, barracks were erected. The last sovereign in residence was **James I**. The palatial buildings were demolished under Cromwell. The Tower was opened to the public in Victorian times, drawing large crowds who were intrigued by lurid tales from Romantic literature.

Royal Stronghold – The reputation of the Tower rests mainly on its role as a prison and place of execution for traitors. Among unwilling inmates were individuals captured in battle or suspected of intrigue: **King John**

> **Location:** *Map: Inside back cover (GHXY).* ⊖*Tower Hill; DLR Tower Gateway.* The tower marks the boundary between the City and Wapping; it is well served by buses. Boats call at Tower Pier on the way from Westminster to Greenwich.

> **Don't Miss:** the Jewel House, where the Crown Jewels are on display.

> **Timing:** Start in the morning: allow three hours to visit the Tower, then cross Tower Bridge, taking in the views from the high-level footbridges. On the south bank, east of Tower Bridge, is the riverside Design Museum and the restaurants of Bermondsey, where you can enjoy a well-deserved meal.

> **Kids:** The Royal Armouries Collection as well as the reconstructions, activities and events scheduled at the Tower; the top of Tower Bridge.

of France (1356–60) captured at Poitiers; **Richard II** (1399); **Charles Duke of Orleans** (1415–37) captured at Agincourt; **Henry VI** (1465–71); the **Little Princes** (1483–85), Edward V and Richard of York, who, according to legend, were murdered in the Bloody Tower; **Thomas More** (1534–35); **Anne Boleyn** (1536); **Lady Jane Grey** (1554); **Sir Walter Raleigh** (1603–16); **Guy Fawkes** (1605); **Roger Casement** (1916) and **Rudolf Hess** (1941).

Following the restoration of the monarchy in 1660, when Charles II returned from exile, the Tower was remodelled and a permanent garrison was posted within the precincts equipped with a battery of weaponry. From 1300 to 1812 the Tower housed the **Royal Mint**. Because of its impregnability it became the **Royal**

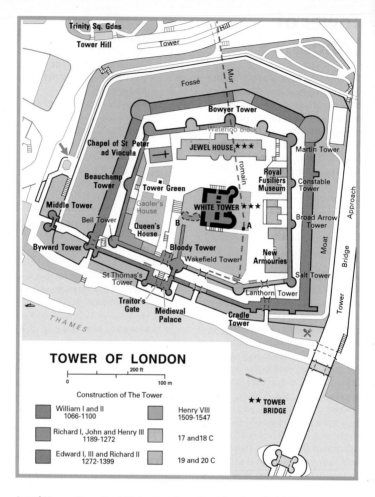

TOWER OF LONDON

200 ft / 100 m
0

Construction of The Tower

- William I and II 1066-1100
- Richard I, John and Henry III 1189-1272
- Edward I, III and Richard II 1272-1399
- Henry VIII 1509-1547
- 17 and 18 C
- 19 and 20 C

★★ TOWER BRIDGE

Jewel House. From the 13C the **Royal Menagerie** was kept in the Lion Tower (demolished); it was closed in 1834 by the Duke of Wellington.

The **Royal Armouries** collection, started by **Henry VIII**, was redistributed by **Charles II** between Windsor Castle and the Tower. A considerable part is now housed in the purpose-built Royal Armoury Museum in Leeds (⊙ see The Green Guide GREAT BRITAIN).

Ceremony and Tradition – The 40 **Yeoman Warders** (including Gaoler and Chief Warder) are former long-serving non-commissioned officers from the Army, Royal Marines or Royal Air Force holding the Long Service or

Good Conduct Medal. They wear Tudor uniform (dark blue and red "undress" for every day; scarlet for ceremony), embroidered with the sovereign's monogram and may be seen on parade in the Inner Ward (daily at 11am).

The **Ceremony of the Keys**, the ceremonial closing of the Main Gates, takes place every night (at 10.05pm; admission on written application only). After the curfew a password, which is changed daily, is required to gain admission.

Every third year at Rogationtide (the three days before Ascension Day) the 31 boundary stones of the Tower Liberty are beaten by the choirboys of St Peter ad Vincula, armed with long white wands, the Governor and Warders in procession (2008, 2011...).

Royal Salutes are fired by the Honourable Artillery Company from four guns on the wharf *(at 1pm)*, 62 guns for the Sovereign's birthday, accession, coronation; 41 guns for the State Opening of Parliament or birth of a royal child.

Tower Hill – Over the centuries the area has preserved its traditional role as a place of free speech and rallying point from which marchers set out, usually to Westminster. In 1380 **Wat Tyler** and the Kentish rebels summarily executed the Lord Chancellor and other prisoners.

VISIT

&⏲*Open Mar–Oct Tue–Sat 9am–5.30pm, Sun–Mon 10am–5.30pm; Nov–Feb Tue–Sat 9am–4.30pm, Sun–Mon 10am–4.30pm; last admission 30min before closing.* ⏲*Closed 24–26 Dec, 1 Jan.* ﹩*£17, discounts for tickets booked online or for joint tickets with Hampton Court and Kensington Palace. Advance booking recommended in high season.* **Guided tour (1hr) by Yeoman Warders** *from the Middle Tower (exteriors only).* ﹩*No charge. Twilight tours Jan–Mar Weds 7pm–8.30pm.* ﹩*£25. Audio guide (Prisoners' Trail – 5 languages)* ﹩*£4. Guide book and leaflet (7 languages). Royal Fusiliers Regimental Museum:* ﹩*50p.* ☏*0844 482 7777. www.hrp.org.uk.* ☺*There are regular special exhibitions, costumed re-enactments, concerts and other activities, together with children's events at half-term and in school holidays.*

Landward Entrance

The Lion Tower (demolished; position marked by stones in the pavement) took its name from the Royal Menagerie introduced by Henry III (1216–72) which included an elephant donated by Louis IX of France in 1255, three leopards given by the German Emperor and a polar bear from the King of Norway. The **Middle Tower** (13C; rebuilt in the 18C) stood between the second and third drawbridges. The moat was drained and grassed over in the 19C.

Pass through the **Byward Tower** (13C) and continue straight on before turning left through the Bloody Tower uphill into the main enclave.

On your left is the **Bell Tower** where **Elizabeth I**, among others, was confined by her sister Mary; she took exercise on the ramparts beyond.

Traitor's Gate

The gateway (13C) served as the main entrance to the Tower when the Thames was London's principal thoroughfare. Later on, it was used for delivering prisoners unseen by prying eyes, hence its name.

The Medieval Palace

St Thomas' Tower contains the Great Chamber where **King Edward I** slept. Meticulous archaeological research has allowed this Magna Camera to be re-created. He ruled as an absolute monarch and extended English power across to France. The end room or Aula was where the king played chess and took his meals.

The octagonal Throne Room in the **Wakefield Tower** (1240) served as the main official government chamber. Its furniture includes a reproduction of the Coronation Chair in Westminster Abbey. The corner turret accommodates a small oratory where Henry VI is thought to have been murdered while at prayer, on the orders of Edward IV.

Bloody Tower

The former Garden Tower acquired its lurid name in the 16C, probably because the Little **Princes** were last seen alive there or after the suicide of Henry Percy, 8th Earl of Northumberland. It was once the main watergate and the portcullis can be seen in the lower storey. The study, which is paved with the original tiles (protected by matting), is furnished as in the time of **Sir Walter Raleigh**, the longest and most famous "resident" who wrote his *History of the World* while imprisoned there (1603–16).

White Tower

Ph. Gajic/MICHELIN

White Tower★★★

The White Tower was begun by William I in 1078 and completed 20 years later by **William Rufus**. The high walls (100ft/30m) of Kentish rag stone (Blue stone) dressed with Portland stone form an uneven quadrilateral, defended at the corners by one circular and three square towers. It became known as the White Tower in 1241 when **Henry III** had the royal apartments and exterior whitewashed.

Chapel of St John the Evangelist★★ – Entrance from south side.

The second floor Caen stone chapel has changed little since its completion in 1080, although the interior painted decoration and rood screen have gone. The nave is divided from the aisles and ambulatory by an arcade of 12 great round piers (known as the 12 Apostles) with simply carved capitals rising to typical Norman round-headed arches, a tribune gallery and tunnel vault.

The Royal Armouries Collection

– The early organisation of a Royal Armoury begins with **Henry VIII**, his personal armours and private arsenal. Between the 15C and 19C, the nation's arsenal depended upon the Office of Ordnance which supervised the design, manufacture, and trial of arms for service on land and sea, while maintaining fortifications of the realm and its garrisons. A large number of paintings, engravings and documentation are used to complete the exhibitions. Smaller arms, several more gruesome weapons allegedly captured from the Armada (1588) and larger trophies retrieved from various battlefields are also on display. The **Line of Kings** reunites a series of 17C life-size portraits of the kings of England dressed in personal attire or suits of armour.

Tower Green

The square was the site of the scaffold where executions took place. A plaque bears the names of the seven noble victims who were privileged to be beheaded within the Tower (the last was the Earl of Essex in 1601), with an axe except Anne Boleyn, who was executed by the sword. Commoners, on the other hand, were hanged publicly on Tower Hill.

Chapel Royal of St Peter ad Vincula

The chapel takes its name from the day of its consecration in the 12C: the feast of St Peter in Chains. It is the burial place of "two dukes between the queens, to wit, the Duke of Somerset and the **Duke of Northumberland** between Queen Anne and Queen Catherine, all four beheaded," to whom Stow might have added Lady Jane Grey, Guildford Dudley, her husband, Monmouth and hundreds more. Note the Tudor font and the carvings by **Grinling Gibbons**.

Beauchamp Tower

The three-storey tower (pronounced Beecham), which served from the 14C as a place of confinement large enough to accommodate a nobleman's household, is probably named after Thomas Beauchamp, 3rd Earl of Warwick (imprisoned 1397–99). The main chamber (first floor) contains many graffiti carved by the prisoners.

The timber-framed **Queen's House** (closed to the public) was built by Henry VIII on the south side of Tower Green as lodgings for Anne Boleyn before her coronation in 1533.

The Ravens

Ravens are usually regarded as birds of ill-omen, feeding as they sometimes do on carrion. It is their absence from the Tower, however, that is feared, as legend has it that this would portend disaster. The practice of having six ravens at all times was decreed by Charles II, two extra are kept in reserve. To prevent them from flying away, they have one wing clipped by the Raven Master. This is a painless operation and by imbalancing their flight, the birds do not stray far. Each is identified by a coloured leg ring. The oldest resident, Jim Crow lived to the great age of 44, and occasionally ravens

Ravenmaster

©Natasha Marie Brown/HRP/ News Team International

have been dismissed for "unbecoming behaviour" – Raven George was sent to the Welsh Mountain Zoo for consistently perching up on TV aerials. Since 1987 several clutches have successfully been reared.

Jewel House★★★

The antechamber, bearing the armorials of every ruling monarch from **William the Conqueror** to **Queen Elizabeth II** serves as a rightful reminder of the long tradition associated with the Crown jewels. For the most part, the priceless gems are real, and the coronation regalia is still used for formal occasions such as the opening of Parliament.

Visitors pass in front of the sparkling displays on **moving walkways** that allow just a few seconds' viewing.

The engraved **Anointing Spoon** is the oldest piece of regalia having been made for Henry II or Richard I (the Lionheart). Otherwise, most of the **Crown Jewels,** which consist of crowns, orbs and rings, date in fact from the Restoration (1660) as the earlier regalia was sold or melted down on the orders of Cromwell.

St Edward's Crown, so named because it may have belonged to Edward the Confessor, was remodelled for the coronation of Charles II and is worn at every coronation. The **Imperial State Crown** made for **Queen Victoria** in 1838 is worn on state occasions such as the Opening of Parliament. It contains a total of 3 733 precious jewels, including a ruby said to have been given to the Black Prince by Pedro the Cruel after the Battle of Najera in 1367 and a diamond,

the second largest of the Stars of Africa cut from the **Cullinan diamond** and presented to Edward VII in 1907. The famous **Koh-i-Noor diamond** (Mountain of Light) is incorporated in the crown made for Queen Elizabeth the Queen Mother for the coronation in 1937. The **Royal Sceptre** contains the **Star of Africa**, the biggest diamond (530 carats) in the world.

On a more modest scale note **Queen Victoria's small crown**, familiar to every stamp collector. To the right of Jewel House is the **Royal Fusiliers Regimental Museum** *(separate entrance charge),* which presents the history of the regiment from its formation in 1685 to the present day.

Cradle Tower – A watergate, was created here (1348–55) as a private entrance for the king.

East Wall Walk

The walk starts in the **Salt Tower** (1240), passes through the **Broad Arrow Tower** (1240) furnished as a knight's lodging in the 13C, through the **Constable Tower** (1240, rebuilt in the 19C) and ends in the **Martin Tower,** which houses the exhibition entitled **Crowns and Diamonds**, presenting additional royal crown frames that would have been

Royal Armour

Henry VIII had one suit of armour made in 1520, when the Tudor king was 29; it weighed 49lb. A larger suit was made in 1540, silvered and engraved for the king and his horse. Some suits were made in Greenwich, including examples tailored to Robert Dudley (c. 1575) and for Worcester (110lb). Note also the armour made in France in 1598 for the Earl of Southampton (1573–1624), the only acknowledged patron of William Shakespeare; a ¾ gilt suit with helmet and cuirass, probably made for **Charles I** as a boy (c. 1610); the ornate Stuart royal armours (c. 1625–30).

temporarily fitted with cut diamonds and precious stones .

⚓ WALKING TOUR
▷ *Start at Tower Hill Station.*

Trinity Square Gardens

The gardens include the site *(railed area)* of the permanent **scaffold and gallows** erected in 1455; the last execution took place in 1747.

On the north side stands **Trinity House**, the seat of the Corporation, founded in the 13C, responsible for the maintenance of automatic lighthouses, lightships, navigation buoys and beacons.

On the south side are the **Mercantile Marine Memorials** (1914–18) designed by Edwin **Lutyens** and (1939–45) by Edward Maufe.

Farther east are a section of the **City Wall**, part Medieval and part Roman, a monumental Roman inscription (original in the British Museum) and the remains of a 13C gate tower.

▷ *Walk up Cooper's Row and turn left into Pepys St.*

St Olave's★

🕐*Open Mon–Fri 9am–5pm.* **Holy Communion** *11am 1st and 3rd Sunday of every month, and 12.30pm every Tue.* **Concerts** *Wed and Thu at 1.05pm.* 📞*020 7488 4318.*

The church was restored in 1953 after severe bomb damage in 1941. The dedication to **St Olaf**, who, in 1013, helped **Ethelred** against the Danes remains, vivid in the new Norwegian flag. A bust (19C) of Samuel **Pepys**,

diarist and founder of the modern Navy, blocks the former south doorway.

The churchyard gateway on Seething Lane, decorated exclusively with skulls, is dated 1658.

The church porch, into which one descends, is 15C, like the major part of the church. The interior is divided into a nave and aisle of three bays by quatrefoil marble pillars, probably from a former, 13C, church. The monuments, which, incredibly, survived the Fire, include tablets, brasses, natural and polychrome stone effigies. Note, in an oval niche high on the sanctuary north wall, the 17C bust of **Elizabeth Pepys**, who married at 15 and died aged 29.

The **crypt** *(steps at west end)* of two chambers with ribbed vaulting, is built over a well and is a survival of the early 13C church.

▷ *Take Hart St west, walk down Mark Lane to Tower St and cross the busy main road.*

All Hallows-by-the-Tower

🕐*Open Mon–Sat 10.30am–4.30pm (between 12.30pm–2pm the church may be closed for recitals or services). Undercroft museum. Organ recital: Thu 1.10pm. Guide book. Brass rubbing Mon–Sat 2–4pm.* 💷*£5 per brass.* 📞*020 7481 2928. www.allhallowsbythetower. org.uk.*

Four churches have stood on the site since the late 7C, the last rebuilding dating from 1957. The square brick tower was built in the 17C. The lantern, encircled by a balustrade and supporting a tapering green copper spire, was added after World War II, making it the only shaped spire to be added to a City Church since Wren. The tower is the one climbed by Pepys on 5 September 1666 when he "saw the saddest sight of desolation that I ever saw" during the Great Fire of London.

Inside, the south wall of the tower is pierced by the only Anglo-Saxon arch (AD 675) still standing in the City; in the baptistery is an exquisite wooden **font cover**★★, attributed to Grinling Gibbons. Note also 18 exceptional **brasses**★ dating from 1389–1591 (of which eight may be rubbed – *by appointment only*).

◐ *Walk down Tower Hill towards Tower Bridge and across the river to Bermondsey.*

Bermondsey

Until the Reformation, Bermondsey was known for its famous Cluniac monastery, Bermondsey Abbey, founded in 1082. In the 18C the area became fashionable as a spa famous for its spring water.

Situated on the south bank of the Thames extending east of Tower Bridge, the area has undergone extensive redevelopment and the riverfront is alive with people enjoying the restaurants, bars and wonderful river views.

For details of the Friday Bermondsey or New Caledonian Market, ⓒsee YOUR STAY IN THE CITY – Shopping.

Butler's Wharf

Presently listed as a conservation area, this part of London is slowly developing its own resident population and commercial interests; fine restaurants and designer bars line the waterfront, and there are interesting specialist shops.

TOWER BRIDGE★★

♿🅿🕐*Open daily Apr–Sept 10am– 6.30pm; Oct–Mar 9.30am–6pm.* 🕐*Closed 25 Dec.* ⬤£6. *Guide book (5 languages). Parking at Tooley Street and Lower Thames Street.* ℘*020 7403 3761. www.towerbridge.org.uk.*

The bridge was designed by Sir John Wolfe Barry and Horace Jones to harmonise with the Tower of London and was built between 1886 and 1894. The familiar Gothic towers are linked by high-level footbridges, encased in steel lattice-work, which provide **panorama views**★★★ of London and a display entitled the 🚶🚶**Tower Bridge Experience**.

The bridge had to allow for the passage of road traffic without impeding the river traffic, hence the bascules (1 100 tonnes) raised by hydraulic pumps powered by electricity since 1976.

New displays include a simulation in the Engine Room of how the opening of the bridge looks if you are underneath it.

China Wharf

Beyond the Design Museum, **Cinnamon Wharf** (the first residential warehouse conversion on Butler's Wharf) and **St Saviour's Wharf**, stands China Wharf facing conspicuously onto the river. Completed in 1988, this striking, orange-red, scalloped building sitting in the river has won its architects CZWG several awards. The unit consists of 17 two-bedroom apartments designed to fill a gap between the existing **New Concordia** and **Reed** Wharves. Note the front entrance balcony named The Great Harry.

Other inventive warehouse conversions include the glazed design-studio-cum-residential **David Mellor Building** (*22–24 Shad Thames*), the modernist **Saffron Wharf** (*18*) and the untreated Iroko timber-clad **Camera Press** (*21/23 Queen Elizabeth St*). The four gently curved blocks that make up **The Circle** (*Queen Elizabeth St*), faced with glazed cobalt-blue tiles, replace the Courage Brewery stables; its balconies swirl in a great spiralling sweep – a far cry from Jacob's Island, the inspiration for Bill Sykes' abject den of vice and poverty described in Charles Dickens' *Oliver Twist*.

Tower Bridge

R. Besse/MICHELIN

Design Museum
Shad Thames. &🕐*Open daily 10am–5.45pm (last entry 5.15pm)* ⊗*£8.50. Café.* ✆*0870 833 9955. www.designmuseum.org.*
The museum opened in 1989 to popularise, explain, analyse and criticise past and present design, and speculate about design in the future. True to the Conran empire ethic, the complex has been summed up as "modest, clean, spacious and white."

The **Review Gallery** on the first floor displays a selection of state-of-the-art products from around the world.

The main space is dedicated to temporary (six monthly) exhibitions of product or graphic design and architecture. Early designs and manufacture are compared and contrasted with current fads and fashions produced by different industrial processes.

The airy top-floor space is reserved for the museum collection of household appliances, television sets, cameras, spectacles, furniture, cars, bicycles...

Church of St Mary Magdalen
Junction of Tower Bridge Rd and Long Lane. &🕐*Open Mon–Fri 9.30am –noon.* ✆*020 7357 0984*
The parish church founded in 1290 retains 12C carved capitals (from Bermondsey Abbey, once on the same site), 17C woodwork, three hatchments vividly painted with armorial bearings and tombstones in the aisle pavements giving a sobering insight into 18C infant mortality.

ADDRESSES

✗ LIGHT BITE

Konditor & Cook – *10 Stoney St, SE1 9AD.* ⊖*London Bridge.* ✆*020 7407 5100, www.konditorandcook. com.* One of the great café/delis in the food-orientated Borough Market, it buzzes all day with people buying takeaways or stopping for coffee and cake and watching the world go by.

M Manze's – *87 Tower Bridge Rd, SE1 4TW .* ⊖*Tower Hill.* ✆*020 7407 2985. www.manze.co.uk.* You'll get a real taste of old London at this great eel and pie shop, which has been serving the residents and workers of the area since 1902. The décor is beautiful and hearkens back to yesteryear; The owners provide a warm welcome.

🍺 PUB

Royal Oak – *44 Tabard St, SE1 4JU.* ⊖*Borough.* ✆*020 7357 7173.* The place to go for some excellent ales that you can't get elsewhere. It's a friendly, local pub, serving good, above average pub grub.

Skinkers – *42 Tooley St, SE1 2SV.* ⊖*London Bridge.* ✆*020 7407 7720. www.davy.co.uk. Closed weekends.* One of the excellent Davy's group, it's old-fashioned looking and full of city types. Go for the hearty food.

The East End

SHOREDITCH
⊖Old Street

The first English playhouse, **The Theatre**, was founded in Shoreditch in 1576 by **James Burbage** (d. 1597) a joiner by trade; he also founded the **Little Curtain**, named after the curtain wall of the enclosure. In 1597 The Theatre in Shoreditch was pulled down on the orders of the Privy Council, and the materials were used by James's son **Cuthbert** (d. 1635) to build the **Globe** (*see BANKSIDE – SOUTHWARK*) on the South Bank in 1599; his other son **Richard Burbage** (d. 1619) was the first actor to play Shakespeare's Richard III and Hamlet – all three Burbages are buried in St Leonard's Church.

▶ *Proceed east along Old St to the junction with Kingsland Rd (see Geffrye Museum and Hackney Rd).*

St Leonard's Church
119 Shoreditch High Street. &⊙Open by appointment only. ℘020 7739 2063.
This mid-18C building boasts a 192ft/58.5m spire. Within its precincts were buried one of Henry VIII's court jesters, William Somers (d. 1560); **James Burbage** (d. 1597) and his sons **Cuthbert** and **Richard** and Gabriel Spencer (d. 1598), a player at the Rose Theatre who was killed by **Ben Jonson** (*see WESTMINSTER*).

Hoxton Square
This working-class district has gained a certain notoriety as artists, musicians and other creative types move in and set up their studios. Consequently there are now a number of sleek bars, restaurants and art galleries set up around the small grassy square, which attract Bohemian and increasingly trendy crowds.

SPITALFIELDS
⊖Shoreditch; Liverpool Street.
In 1991 London's largest wholesale fruit and vegetable market was moved to Leyton. The eastern part of the Victorian structure is all that remains of **Old Spitalfields Market**★ (*along Commercial Street, see YOUR STAY IN THE CITY – Shopping*). Today, the market is a vibrant and popular destination for tourists and locals browsing fashion, jewellery, antiques and organic produce. At its busiest on Sundays when all the stalls and all the surrounding shops are open.

Across the street stands **Christ Church**, built by Hawksmoor in 1714–30, its spire rising above a Classical west portico; at the east end a Venetian window is framed by paired niches beneath a pediment (&⊙*open Sun 1–4pm, Tue 10am–4pm; also Mon and Fri 11am–4pm*

Spitalfields Market

Y. Kanazawa/Michelin

Georgian houses on Fournier Street, Spitalfields

©Marko Beric/Bigstockphoto.com

if church not in use; ℘*020 7859 3035; www.christchurchspitalfields.org).*

The church holds a number of events in the area during the year, including the **Spitalfields Festival** (℘*020 7377 6793; www.spitalfieldsvenue.org).*

As you walk along **Fournier Street** to Brick Lane, note the handsome Georgian houses (1718–28), once occupied by silk weavers and merchants.

Right next to Spitalfields is **Petticoat Lane Marke**t: here you can find some o the cheapest items in London as well as touristy souvenirs. ♿*See WELCOME TO LONDON – Shopping.*

Brick Lane

The area is often known as "little Bangladesh", or "Bangla Town". It can be crowded at the weekend and some say it is the victim of its own success, but it is still a great place in London to go for a curry.

The history of the **mosque**, which was built as a Christian chapel in 1743 and

---

😀 A Bit of Advice 😀

There are many competing and sometimes pushy touts keen to convince you that their restaurant on **Brick Lane** is best. As a result you can sometimes haggle for discount, but do double-check that it appears on your bill at the end of the meal.

---

later became a synagogue, reflects the successive waves of immigrants who have lived in the district. The spacious glass-fronted reception area of **Truman's Brewery** (1666) reveals older buildings round a cobbled yard.

On Sunday mornings, a bric-a-brac and second-hand clothes **market** spreads through the district around Bethnal Green Road, Cheshire Street. Just north, along **Columbia Road**, the equally lively flower market also takes place on Sundays.

WHITECHAPEL

⊖*Aldgate East. Walk east along Whitechapel Rd.*

Whitechapel Gallery

♿🕐*Open Wed–Sun 11am–5pm.* 💷*Charges for some exhibitions. Talks, tours and film screenings, telephone for details.* ℘*020 7522 7878 (recorded info), 020 7522 7888 (general enquiries Mon–Fri). www.whitechapel.org.*

The gallery provides exhibition facilities for modern and contemporary art by non-established artists; **Barbara Hepworth** and **David Hockney** first showed their work here. The building (1901), designed by **CH Townsend**, is decorated with contemporary Arts and Crafts reliefs and surmounted by twin-angle turrets.

The **Passmore Edwards Library** was built in the Arts and Crafts style. In the entrance is a panel of decorated tiles depicting the Whitechapel Hay Market which flourished for over 300 years until it was abolished in 1928.

Whitechapel Bell Foundry

The foundry has been on its present site since 1738. It has cast and recast – owing to the 1666 Great Fire and World War II – the bells of St Mary-le-Bow, St Clement Dane's and Big Ben.

Nearby, the **East London Mosque** was built in 1985 by the most recent immigrants who came from the Indian subcontinent.

Mile End Road

⊖*Whitechapel.*

The Trinity Almshouses, (1695) form a terrace of basement and ground floor cottages around three sides of a tree-planted quadrangle.

On Trinity Green, a statue (1979) of General **William Booth** marks the site where he began the work that led to the foundation of the Salvation Army.

BETHNAL GREEN

⊖*Shoreditch, Bethnal Green*

St Matthew parish church was built (1743–46) by George Dance the Elder and the interior remodelled (1859–61) by Knightly. The **Watch House** (1826) stands in the south-west corner of the churchyard.

The west tower of **Sir John Soane's St John's Church** (1825–28), though not high, is an easily distinguished landmark as it rises to a vaned cupola (⊙*Open at*

Whitechapel Gallery – a rare Arts and Crafts building in the East End

J. Malburet/MICHELIN

Mass times and by appointment. ℘*020 87095243. www.stjohnsbythegreen.org*

WEST HAM

⊖*Bromley By Bow*

West Ham developed early into a manufacturing town owing to its position near the confluence of the navigable River Lee and the Thames and its proximity to London. In the 18C Bow Pottery was the largest porcelain factory in England. At the end of the 19C there were about 300 companies in the area engaged in various industries.

Three Mills

Three Mills Island, Three Mills Lane. &⊙*Open Mar–Dec and early May–late Oct 1st Sun in the month 11am–4pm; all other Suns 1–4pm.* ⊠*£3. Leaflet.* ℘*020 8980 4626. www.housemill.org.uk.*

The London Blitz

During the eight-month bombardment, which ceased in May 1941, 190 000 bombs were dropped; 43 000 civilians died; 61 000 were seriously injured; 404 firemen were killed on duty and 3 000 were injured; 1.25 million houses in the London region were damaged. At first people took refuge in Anderson shelters, which were effective but damp and crowded; later they spent the hours of darkness in the Underground stations, where bunks and sanitary facilities were installed; only three Underground stations received direct hits resulting in deaths. St Paul's Cathedral was hit twice: on 12 September 1940 a 1 000lb bomb lodged in the clocktower; it was removed by sappers (Royal Engineers) who were awarded the first George Crosses. The bomb was exploded on Hackney marshes, where it created a crater 100ft/30m in diameter; on 16–17 April 1941 a bomb fell through the north transept and exploded in the crypt.

Jewish East End

The **Jewish community** in the East End grew rapidly in the 1880s with the influx of 100 000 Russian and Polish Jews and about 20 000 German, Austrian, Dutch and Romanian Jews. By 1914 the East End of London contained the largest Jewish community in England. As they became more affluent, they moved to the outer suburbs of London or abroad. Among the few landmarks to survive is the **Brady Street Cemetery** (1761–1858), where **Nathan Mayer Rothschild** is buried.

At the north end of Bow Creek there is an attractive group of early industrial buildings. **The House Mill**, built in 1776, is the largest tide mill known in the country. The original **miller's house** (demolished in the 1950s) has been reconstructed as part of the restored Georgian street front.

Granite setts and flagstones mark the path across to the **Clock Mill**, which dates from 1817. The ornate clock tower, which is earlier, is surmounted by an octagonal turret, containing a bell and a weathervane. The conical caps of the two **drying kilns** are Victorian.

Period room: a drawing room in 1830, Geffrye Museum
Chris Ridley/Geffrye Museum

Abbey Mills Pumping Station

The impressive cruciform building, that houses sewage pumping machinery, was designed (1865–68) by **Sir Joseph Bazalgette** and Vulliamy in the Venetian Gothic style with an octagonal lantern above the crossing.

ADDITIONAL SIGHTS
Geffrye Museum★

Kingsland Road. Plaistow. Open Tue–Sat 10am–5pm, Sun and bank holiday Mon noon–5pm. Closed Good Fri, 24–26 Dec, 1 Jan. Guided tour by appointment. Herb garden and period garden rooms: Open Apr–Oct. Restaurant. Shop. 020 7739 9893, 020 7739 8543 (recorded information). www.geffrye-museum.org.uk.

Housed in almshouses erected in 1712–19 by the Ironmongers' Company, the museum features displays of furniture and furnishings from Tudor times to the 1950s. In the upper gallery, the new rooms take the collection of English domestic interiors up to the present day and include a minimalist loft.

Museum of Childhood at Bethnal Green

Cambridge Heath Road, Bethnal Green. Bethnal Green. Open daily 10am–5.45pm. 020 8983 5200. www.vam.ac.uk/moc.

The museum houses the Victoria & Albert Museum's enchanting collection of toys, dolls, games, puppets, toy soldiers, as well as children's clothing, furniture, paintings, books and other artefacts of childhood.

The building, a pre-fabricated iron and glass construction, was originally erected to contain items from the **1851 Exhibition** (see MAJOR CENTRAL LONDON MUSEUMS – Victoria & Albert Museum); it was re-erected and opened on the present site in 1872.

Sutton House

*2, 4 Homerton High St. Bethnal Green. Open Feb–Dec Thu–Sun 12.30–4.30pm. **Art Gallery:** Open early Jan–late Dec Wed–Sun 1.30–5pm. £2.90. No photography. No dogs.*

London 2012

Following London's successful bid for the 2012 Olympic Games, East London has become a frenzy of activity as plans are drawn up and venues and transport are whipped into shape. At the core of the plan is a 500-acre/202ha Olympic Park in the Lower Lee Valley, which will house the Olympic Stadium, Velopark, Aquatics Centre, Hockey Centre and Olympic Village. News posted regularly on *www.london2012.org* allows people to follow the transformation of one of London's poorest and most rundown areas. Local residents and visitors can see how hosting the Games will transform the Valley, restore a lost ecosystem and provide much-needed facilities for the local community by taking a three-hour "Regeneration Tour" of the area. For more information visit *www.newham.gov.uk*. In addition, a PDF or text version of the Olympic Supplement can be downloaded from the website.

Braille Guide. Café. ℘*020 8986 2264. www.nationaltrust.org.uk.*

The house, dating from c 1535, was originally known as the "bryk place" as most buildings then were timber-framed structures. It was modified through the centuries but the interior contains one of the **original Tudor transom windows**, now in the Lobby. The Parlour is entirely lined with 16C **oak linenfold panelling** and has retained its original stone fireplace, surmounted by an overmantel with typical Renaissance fluted pilasters. The **painted staircase** is decorated with coloured oil painting directly on to plaster and the Little Chamber is lined with 16C **Baltic oak panelling**.

William Morris Gallery

See Suburbs map (UX). ⊖*Walthamstow Central. Lloyd Park, Forest Road, E17.* ♿☾*Open Tue–Sat 10am–1pm, 2–5pm. Leaflet.* ℘*020 8527 3782. www1. walthamforest.gov.uk.*

The museum is accommodated in a house built in 1750, that was home to the Morris family between 1848 and 1856. The displays are connected with the work of **William Morris** (1834–96) and of the firm Morris & Co. (1861–1940), which he co-founded under the definition "Fine Art Workmen in painting, carving, furniture and the metals". Morris tried architecture and painting under the influence of **Ruskin** and the **Pre-Raphaelites** before finding expression for his talents in the decorative arts.

The career of the designer and the history of the firm are illustrated by examples of stained glass, tiles, furniture, wallpapers, fabrics and embroidery; Morris' own work includes his poetry and books published by the **Kelmscott Press**. Two smaller rooms display work produced by members of the **Arts and Crafts Movement** *(ground floor)* and the work of the **Century Guild** *(first floor)*, founded by Arthur MacMurdo, who was influenced by Ruskin and Morris. Etchings and oils by **Sir Frank Brangwyn** are exhibited *(first floor)* with paintings and drawings by the Pre-Raphaelites and their contemporaries.

ADDRESSES

NIGHTLIFE

Great Eastern Dining Room – *54–56 Great Eastern St, EC2A 3QR.* ⊖*Liverpool Street, Old Street.* ℘*020 7613 4545. www. greateasterndining.co.uk. Closed Sun.* One of the smartest bars in the area, frequented by thirty-somethings drawn by the atmosphere and cocktails.

The Light – *233 Shoreditch High St, E1 6PJ.* ⊖*Liverpool Street.* ℘*020 7247 8989 . www.thelighte1.com. Closed Sun, Christmas and bank holidays.* This reconverted electric generating station will surprise you with its sheer size and industrial décor of exposed beams and bricks. It attracts a lively crowd.

CAMDEN AND ISLINGTON

Liberal and elegant, Camden and Islington have historically had a cultured, creative vibe that is still evident today. Bloomsbury, with its literary connections, is a patchwork of genteel garden squares and home to the British Museum. Further north, Clerkenwell is full of urban style and warehouse conversions, whose residents socialise in Upper Street's bars and traditional pubs. Camden Town is a stroll from both Regent's Park and busy markets full of alternative style. Geography Camden is in the north of the city, and runs from Bloomsbury to Hampstead Heath. It is cut through at the north end by the Regent's Canal. Islington, east of Camden, stretches from Highbury Fields to Islington High Street.

Highlights

1 Modern dance at **Sadler's Wells Theatre** (p226)

2 Learn about the waterways at the **London Canal Museum** (p230)

3 Discover Dickens at **The Dickens House Museum** (p223)

4 Delight in unexpected art works at the **Foundling Museum** (p224)

5 Explore Italian Futurism at the **Estorick Collection** (p228)

History – Bloomsbury's reputation as a bohemian enclave was inspired in the 18C by the Bloomsbury group, which included Virginia Woolf, EM Forster and John Maynard Keynes, who all lived and worked here. Islington became prominent in the 17C as an area to flee to from the City following the Plague and the Great Fire. The Industrial Revolution filled Clerkenwell with warehouses, distilleries and commercial properties, particularly those of the printing industry. Between 1850 and the 1960s it was known for the size of its Italian immigrant population, and dubbed "Little Italy". The 19C saw an expansion of building in Islington, but by the mid-20C intense overcrowding made the area a byword for poverty. However, its fortunes were transformed in the 1960s when Londoners rediscovered elegant Georgian and Victorian terrace housing and gentrification turned the area into a fashionable neighbourhood.

Today – Some of north London's most desirable addresses are found in these boroughs, popular with artists and writers. Upper Street, with its trendy restaurants and bars, is a nightlife hub, while Camden Town remains one of the capital's most visited areas, especially at weekends, when the streets are thronged with thousands of browsers, from the station up to Camden Lock. Here, the biggest of Camden's markets, held in a former timber yard, is a bazaar of market stalls selling clothing, arts and crafts, junk and antiques. At St Pancras the results of a huge regeneration project in the area are evident in the British Library and sleek new international rail terminal that serves the Eurostar rail service direct to Paris.

Bloomsbury★

The area comprises many 18C and 19C squares and is dominated by London University and the British Museum (☚see MAJOR CENTRAL LONDON MUSEUMS). Bloomsbury also contains a concentration of medical institutions, including The Hospital for Sick Children (Great Ormond Street), which is endowed by JM Barry with the royalties of *Peter Pan*.

▷ **Location:** *Map: inside front cover (EFVX).* ⊖*Tottenham Court Road; Goodge St; Russell Square; Holborn.* Bloomsbury is north of Covent Garden and Soho with Euston Rd as the boundary to the north.

A BIT OF HISTORY

The Squares – The development of **Bloomsbury Square** in 1661 introduced a new concept in local planning. The 4th Earl of Southampton, descendant of the Lord Chancellor to whom **Henry VIII** had granted the feudal manor in 1545, erected grand houses around three sides of a square, a mansion for himself on the fourth, northern, side and an innovative network of secondary service streets all around, so ordering, in Evelyn's words, "a little town". His only daughter, Lady Rachel, married the future **1st Duke of Bedford**, uniting two great estates.

The other squares followed in the 19C: **Russell** in 1800, **Tavistock** in 1806–26, **Torrington** in 1825, **Woburn** in 1829, **Gordon** in 1850 (☚see INTRODUCTION – Architecture).

From the late 18C to the early 20C the Bloomsbury district was frequented by artists and writers: Richard Wilson and Constable (**no. 76** Charlotte Street); Madox Brown and **Bernard Shaw**, **Whistler** and **Sickert** in **Fitzroy Square**; Verlaine and Rimbaud in Howland Street; Wyndham Lewis in Percy Street, and David Garnet in Bedford Square.

The most famous residents however, were the **Bloomsbury Group** (☚see INTRODUCTION – Painting) whose members included **Virginia Woolf**, **Vanessa Bell, Roger Fry**, the art critic, who, in 1910 organised the first Post-Impressionist Exhibition in London, Clive Bell, EM Forster, Lytton Strachey – friend and mentor of Dora Carrington – Duncan Grant and Maynard Keynes. In the vicinity of Gordon Square resided Rupert Brooke (war poet), DH Lawrence (novelist), **Bertrand Russell** (Nobel Prize

Fanlights and wrought-iron balconies on the Georgian façades in Bedford Square

Ph. Gajic/MICHELIN

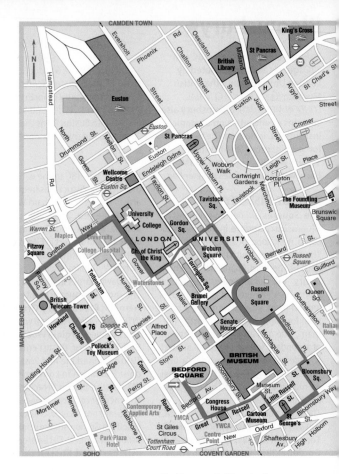

for literature) and his mistress, Lady Ottoline Morrell.

↶ WALKING TOUR
Bedford Square★★
This elegant square was developed to designs by Thomas Leverton.

○ *Proceed along Adeline Pl.*

Great Russell Street
The west end of the street is marked by the YMCA.

○ *Cross Bloomsbury St and turn right opposite the British Museum (⌖see MAJOR CENTRAL LONDON MUSEUMS) into Museum St and left into Bloomsbury Way.*

St George's Bloomsbury
○*Open usually Tue and Thu, 10am–4/5pm, Wed and Fri noon–2pm.* ○*Closed bank holidays.* ☎*020 7580 4101. www.stgeorgesbloomsbury. org.uk.*

Hawksmoor's church (1716–31) has a pedimented portico at the top of a flight of steps. Topping the steeple is a statue of the unpopular George I.

○ *Continue to Bloomsbury Sq and turn left.*

Bloomsbury Square
In the southwest corner are two mid-18C houses; one of them is the former residence of Isaac and Benjamin Disraeli (1818–1826).

ISLINGTON

UNIVERSITY OF LONDON

King's Cross
Thameslink
King's Cross

Gray's

Penton Rise

Percy Street

Cross

Swinton
St.

Acton St.

Wharton
Street

King's Cross Rd

Sidmouth St.

Royal Free Hosp.

UCL Eastman
Dental Institute

Gray's

Margery

Farringon Rd

Mount
Pleasant

Coram's
Fields

Doughty St.

The Dickens
House Museum

Roseberry
Avenue

Goush
St.

Hospital
for Sick
Children

Great Ormond

Lamb's
Conduit

John
St.

Rd

Gray's
Inn

Theobald's

Bedford Row

Red
Lion
St.

Gray's
Inn
Rd

Eagle

Chancery
Lane

High

Holborn

CITY OF LONDON

Row

Kingsway

SIR JOHN SOANE'S
MUSEUM

Holborn

LINCOLN'S
INN

Staple Inn

Lincoln's Inn
Fields

CHANCERY LANE

▶ *Walk down Bedford Pl and through Russell Sq; proceed to Tavistock St past the Percival David Foundation of Chinese Art. Right on Gower St.*

University College

The college houses the **Flaxman Sculpture Galleries**. There are also a number of excellent **museums** *(www.ucl.ac.uk/ museums)* attached to departments such as geology, zoology and archaeology, and the **Petrie Collection** of Egyptian and Sudanese artefacts consists of 80,000 objects housed in galleries so dark you need a torch. This is at the northern end of London's **Museum Mile** *(www.museum-mile.org)* from the British Library down to Somerset House.

▶ *Take Grafton Way.*

Fitzroy Square★

Virginia Woolf lived at **no. 29**.

▶ *Left into Conway St SW of the square; right on Maple St; left on Cleveland St.*

British Telecom Tower

The landmark, originally known as the Post Office Tower, was erected in 1965 to provide an unimpeded path for London's telecommunications system.

▶ *Turn left into Howland St and right into **Charlotte St**, famous for its restaurants. **No. 76** was the residence of Richard Wilson and Constable.*

ADDITIONAL SIGHTS
The Cartoon Art Museum

35 Little Russell Street. ⏰*Open Tue–Sat 10am–5.30pm, Sun noon–5.30pm.* 🎟️*£4. Talks, lectures and events. Shop.* 📞*020 7580 8155. www.cartoon museum.org.*

The Cartoon Trust and its museum collect and exhibit humorous and satirical art works, drawings, engravings, illustrations, advertisements, comic strips and animated films from the time of William Hogarth to the present. The collection comprises some 1 500 cartoons, caricatures and comics, which include evocative names such as Mr Punch, Rupert Bear, The Beano, Dan Dare, Andy Capp, Bonzo the Dog, Captain Pugwash, Fred Bassett, Heath Robinson, HM Bateman, Giles, Calman and Garland. The Heneage Reference Library (⏰*open Wed 10.30am–1.30om; ID required*) contains over 4 000 books on cartoons and 2 500 comics.

The Dickens House Museum

48 Doughty Street. ⏰*Open Mon–Sat 10am–5pm, Sun 11am–5pm.* ⏰*Closed 25–26 Dec, 1 Jan.* 🚶*Guided walks.* 🎟️*£5. Brochure and gallery cards (10 languages).* 📞*020 7405 2127. www.dickensmuseum.com.*

The only surviving London home of **Charles Dickens**, who moved into this late 18C house shortly after his marriage

Charles Dickens (1812–70)

Dickens drew generously on his fertile imagination as well as on his own experiences for his serialised novels: characters were modelled on friends, close relations and acquaintances made in connection with the theatre and the amateur dramatics he so enjoyed, and the philanthropic works he undertook. An early, happy childhood in Chatham was brought to an abrupt end when his father was sent to Marshalsea Prison for debts and he, aged 12, was put to work blacking shoes. As an office boy he studied shorthand and secured a place on the *Morning Chronicle* reporting on debates in the House of Commons. There he developed his acute sense of observation and sharp humour. Close associates and admirers included Thackeray, Wilkie Collins and Hans Christian Andersen. His wife, Catherine Hogarth (1815–79) was a promising young journalist when she married the rising novelist (1835). She bore him ten children (Dora died in 1851). She was persuaded to accept a deed of separation (1858) as Dickens was emotionally involved with Ellen Ternan, a beautiful young actress.

to his "pet mouse" Catherine Hogarth. Dickens lived there with his young family from April 1837 to December 1839, during which time he completed *Pickwick Papers* and wrote *Oliver Twist* and *Nicholas Nickleby*. The house holds letters and manuscripts, copies used for public readings and original illustrations. Original paintings and furniture and authentic décor recreate Dickens' London life here. The museum also holds readings, walks, tours and lectures, as well as special exhibitions about Dickens' life and works.

The Foundling Museum

40 Brunswick Square. ⏰ *Open Tue–Sat 10am–5pm, Sun 11pm–5pm.* ⏰ *Closed 24–27, 31 Dec, 1–2 Jan.* ✑ *£5.* ☎ *020 7841 3600. www.foundlingmuseum.org.uk.*

London's first home for abandoned children was a wholly philanthropic affair, founded by Thomas Coram but backed by artistic luminaries such as Hogarth and Handel, both of whom left substantial bodies of their work (including the original manuscript of Handel's *Messiah*) to the Foundation.

With Hogarth as a fundraiser, the foundation became London's first art gallery, leading to the creation of the Royal Academy of Arts in 1768. The Foundation looked after 27 000 children until its closure in 1953. Coram, next door, now continues the work. Reopened as a museum, its impressive

art collection has works by British artists, notably Hogarth, Gainsborough, Reynolds, Wilson Highmore, Roubiliac and Rysbrack, all of which are displayed in fully restored interiors that aim to provide a similar viewing experience to that had by visitors to the original Hospital in the 1700s.

The museum also houses the Foundling Hospital Archives and the Gerald Coke Handel Collection of manuscripts.

Pollock's Toy Museum and Shop

1 Scala Street. ⏰ *Open Mon–Sat 10am–5pm.* ⏰ *Closed bank holidays.* ✑ *£3.* ☎ *020 7636 3452. www.pollockstoy museum.com.*

This wonderfully eccentric and enchanting museum was founded by Marguerite Fawdry and takes its name from Benjamin Pollock, the last of the Victorian toy theatre printers, whose stock she purchased to make up the initial collection. Here, yesteryear toys are displayed in an atmospheric setting of small rooms, connected by narrow winding staircases. The collection of 19C and 20C toys includes toy theatres, wax, tin, porcelain, peg and spoon dolls, teddy bears, mechanical and optical toys, carved wooden animals, dolls' houses, puppets and board games. Live toy theatre performances are given during the school holidays and there's a toy shop proper on the ground floor.

Clerkenwell

As the fashion for loft living took hold in the 1990s the secluded character of Clerkenwell underwent a radical change. Warehouses and commercial properties were transformed with glass frontages and the trendsetters moved in, soon followed by a range of select eating places and a popular clubbing scene. However, for those in the know it has always been a desirable area, owing to its air of faded gentility and to its convenient location on the edge of the City and a short hop from the West End.

- **Location:** *Map Inside back cover (FGV).*
  ⊖Barbican; Farringdon; Old Street. Clerkenwell is bounded by Bloomsbury, Islington and the City.
- **Don't Miss:** The 16C St John's Gate, once home to the Knights Hospitaller.
- **Timing:** As the sights are spread out it is best to start the first tour from Farringdon and the second from Old Street. Allow half a day.

A BIT OF HISTORY

Clerkenwell recalls in name the Medieval parish clerks who each year performed plays outside the City at a local well-head *(viewed through a window at 14–16 Farringdon Lane).* Finsbury is named after the Fiennes family, the owners of the local manor (bury/burh/burg in Old English) who, in the 14C, gave **Moorfields**, a marsh, to the people of London as its first free open space.

Some open land remains: Finsbury Square, Finsbury Circus, Bunhill Fields and the Honourable Artillery Company Fields, but the outflow of artisans and cottage industry workers from the City, particularly after the Plague (1665) and Fire (1666), caused poor quality housing and tenements to be erected right up to the walls of the Charterhouse, St John's Priory, Bethlem *(in what is now City Road)* and the other hospitals in the district – the only one of which now extant is **Moorfields** Eye Hospital (1805).

The crowded days of home industry in the early 19C are recalled by the Eagle Pub (see Addresses, p231) and the rhyme:

Half a pound of twopenny rice,
Half a pound of Treacle,
Up and down the City Road,
In and out the Eagle,
That's the way the money goes,
Pop goes the Weasel.

Over the centuries, Clerkenwell became the home of groups holding nonconformist or radical beliefs such as Quakers, Chartists and other militant movements. St Peter's Church in Clerkenwell Road, colourful festivals and excellent Italian grocery stores recall the sizeable Italian quarter with street entertainers, ice-cream vendors and craftsmen which grew in the 19C and flourished until fairly recently.

Water Supply – The New River undertaking originated in 1609 when **Sir Hugh Myddelton**, a City goldsmith and jeweller, put up the capital to construct a canal from springs in Hertfordshire to the City. Water was carried down from Clerkenwell to the City in wooden pipes and individual subscribers were supplied with water on tap; the enterprise was eventually taken over by the Metropolitan Water Board (1904–1974).

WALKING TOURS
CLERKENWELL ROAD TO ROSEBERY AVENUE

From Farringdon Station walk up Turnmill St and cross Clerkenwell Rd to Clerkenwell Green.

Clerkenwell Green, the rallying point in the 18C and 19C for workers protesting against the social and industrial injustices of the period, is an appropriate site for the **Karl Marx Memorial Library**, an 18C house (*no 37a*). Cheerful pavement cafés and artists' studios surround the Green.

▷ *Proceed east along Clerkenwell Rd past St John's Gate and Charterhouse (see Additional Sights). Then continue north up St John's St to Rosebery Av.*

Surrounded by the modern buildings of the **City University** *(St John St)* is the original Northampton Institute (1894–96), designed by E Mountford in an eclectic baroque style.

Sadler's Wells Theatre
Rosebery Avenue. 0844 412 4300. www.sadlerswells.com.

The theatre is named after Richard Sadler who opened a music house in 1683 and rediscovered medicinal wells.

The well-appointed new building, opened in 1998, is the sixth theatre on the site; it specialises in ballet but also stages opera performances and welcomes visiting companies (*see YOUR STAY IN THE CITY*).

Also on Rosebery Avenue is the **New River Head** *(Thames Water Authority)*; the neo-Georgian building (now flats) contains a fireplace that is attributed to Grinling Gibbons and pretty plaster ceilings c 1693.

▷ *Make a detour to Myddelton Sq.*

The elegant terraces of **Myddelton Square** were built in the late 1700s on part of the New River Company's estate. Further along Roseberry Avenue is **Mount Pleasant**, now one of the main Post Office inland mail sorting offices and the centre of the Post Office railway.

▷ *Walk down Farringdon Rd past some good restaurants and busy pubs.*

CITY ROAD
▷ *From Old St walk south past Companies House (55–71) towards Moorgate.*

Wesley's House and Chapel
49 City Road. Open Mon–Sat 10am–4pm, Sun 12–1.45pm. Closed Thu 12.45pm–1.30pm, between Christmas and New Year, and bank holidays (except Good Friday). Audioguides, brochures and guidebook. 020 7253 2262. www.wesleyschapel.org.uk.

The charismatic Methodist minister **John Wesley**, who is buried in the churchyard, laid the foundation stone of the chapel in 1777. The interior is notable for the tribune supported on seven jasper columns and the white and gold ceiling by **Robert Adam.** Wesley's mahogany pulpit stands at the centre. A **Museum of Methodism** is housed in the crypt.

Opposite is the entrance to **Bunhill Fields**, used as a burial ground until its closure in 1852. Among the tombs are those of: **William Blake** (1757–1827), **John Bunyan** (1628–88) and **Daniel Defoe** (1661–1731).

Just south are the 18C barracks of the **Honourable Artillery Company**, the oldest regiment in the British army.

ADDITIONAL SIGHTS
Charterhouse★
Guided tours. 020 7251 5002 (tour information); book in writing to: Tour Bookings, Charterhouse, Charterhouse Sq, London EC1M 6AM. Guide book. 020 7253 9503.

At every stage of its history – 14C priory, Tudor mansion, 17C hospital and boys' school, 20C residence for aged Brothers – the buildings of the Charterhouse have been replaced or altered in a variety of materials and architectural styles.

The building comprises the 15C gateway, with its original massive gates and the adjoining house, now the Master's lodging, dated 1716.

On the north side of Master's Court the Tudor **Great Hall**, with hammerbeam roof and 16C screen and gallery remains intact. The Elizabethan **Great Chamber**, is hung with Flemish tapestries. In the tower, to which the belfry and cupola were added in 1614, is the treasury, vaulted in the Tudor period. The present

chapel was created in 1614 out of the monks' Chapter House with the addition of a north aisle and further enlarged to the north in 1824.

St John's Gate

The Order of the Grand Priory, which developed from the First Crusade as a religious order to look after pilgrims visiting the Holy Land, became a military order during the 12C. It left the Holy Land on the fall of Acre in 1291.

In 1540 **Henry VIII** dissolved the **Hospitallers** and in 1546 issued a warrant *(in the museum)* for the buildings to be dismantled but the gate survived. St John's was re-established as a Protestant Order by Royal Charter in 1888.

Gatehouse and Museum – The 16C gatehouse was the Priory's south entrance. In the 20C Tudor-style Chapter Hall, where the Maltese banners hang in the lantern, in the Council Chamber and the Library are displayed pharmacy jars and a rare collection of beaten silver Maltese glove trays and the illuminated Rhodes Missal, on which the knights took their vows. &⊙*Open Mon–Sat,*

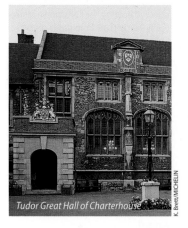

Tudor Great Hall of Charterhouse

K. Brett/MICHELIN

10am–5pm (4pm Sat). ⊙*Closed Sun and Bank Holiday Sat–Mon.* ⟵*Guided tours (1hr) Tue, Fri, Sat at 11am and 2.30pm.* ⊛*Donation.* ☏*020 7324 4005. www.sja. org.uk/museum.*

St John's Church and Crypt – The Grand Priory Church of St John once extended further west into the square where setts in the road mark the site of the round nave. The crypt is 12C, the only original Priory building to survive.

Islington

Islington's elegant Georgian squares, its Victorian terraces, and its proximity to the City of London, ensure its popularity as a residential area. It is a curious mix of gentrification and dilapidation; this is reflected in its smart restaurants, bustling bars, antique shops, art cinema and avant-garde theatres, which do a roaring trade next to its street market and social housing schemes. There are plenty of pleasant discoveries to be made as one strolls about the district.

A BIT OF HISTORY

Islington became a fashionable suburb in the 17C when people fled the City after the plague (1665) and the Great Fire (1666). Taverns marked the stages on the

▷ **Location:** *See SUBURBS map (UX).* ⊖*Angel; Highbury & Islington. Islington is to the north of the City of London with the mainline stations King's Cross, St Pancras and Euston to the west and merges with the East End.*

centuries-old roads from the north, well-trodden by those driving cattle, sheep and swine south to Smithfield (until the coming of the railways). In the 19C, new builder-developers moved into the area, soon inhabited by workers from the new light industries (population: 1801 – 10 000; 1881 – 283 000; 1901 – 335 000). By the 20C Islington and Angel in particular had become a synonym for slums, grime, grinding poverty, the Caledonian Market (Cally Market) and the gaslit glories of Collins Music Hall.

Since World War II restoration and repainting have returned terraces and squares to their precise well-groomed lines – notably **Duncan Terrace**, **Colebrooke Row**, built in 1761, and **Charlton Place**, with their Tuscan column framed front doors and lanterns, or rounded doorways; slums have been largely replaced by four- to eight-storey blocks of brick, reminders of the locality's past as a major London brickfield.

SIGHTS
Angel
Five main thoroughfares converge on the ancient crossroads – named after the Angel Inn that once stood here.

Islington Green
The triangular green has a statue of Sir Hugh Myddelton at its centre.
A plaque marks the site (north side) where, from 1862 until the middle of the last century, **Collins Music Hall** was boisterous with song.

Camden Passage
Upper Street. ◷*Open Wed and Sat.*
www.camdenpassageislington.co.uk.
The quaint old alley, on the east side of Upper Street, is lined with small shops, arcades, restaurants, two Victorian pubs, and the newly built "Georgian Village."
◖*See YOUR STAY IN THE CITY – Shopping.*

Business Design Centre
52 Upper Street. ℘*020 7288 6272.*
www.businessdesigncentre.co.uk.
The former **Royal Agricultural Hall** (1861–62) was used successively for cattle shows, military tournaments, revivalist meetings, bullfighting (1888) and Cruft's Dog Show (1891–1939). After many years of dereliction, it has been restored for trade exhibitions.

CANONBURY
Canonbury is a network of streets and squares lined by early 19C terraced houses, of which **Canonbury**

Square★, once home to George Orwell and Sir Francis Bacon, is the prime example. Minor connecting roads, such as Canonbury Grove with small country cottages overlooking a New River backwater *(towpath walks)*, and others, like Alwynne Road in which later-19C villas and semi-detached houses stand in the shade of plane trees, add to the atmosphere.
◖*See Additional Sights – Estorick Collection of Modern Italian Art.*

Canonbury Tower
A square dark red brick tower (60ft/18m high) is all that remains of the 16C manor, once the country residence of Sir John Spencer, Lord Mayor and owner of Crosby House in Bishopsgate.

HIGHBURY
By the 19C Highbury had fallen into the hands of undistinguished developers except for **Highbury Place** (1774–79), Highbury Terrace (1789) and Highbury Crescent (1830s), where detached and semi-detached villas had been erected for the more affluent.

ADDITIONAL SIGHT
Estorick Collection of Modern Italian Art
39a Canonbury Square. ♿◷*Open Wed–Sat 10am–6pm, Sun noon–5pm. Library: by appointment.* ☜*£5. Café. Shop. Garden.* ℘*020 7704 9522. www.estorickcollection.com.*
Giacomo Balla *(Rhythm of the Violinist)*, Umberto Boccioni *(Modern Idol)*, Carlo Carrà *(Leaving the Theatre)*, Gino Severini *(The Boulevard)*, Luigi Russolo *(Music)* together with the poet Marinetti became fascinated with "universal dynamism". In the words of the Futurist manifesto of 1910, "a clean sweep should be made of all stale and threadbare subject-matter in order to express the vortex of modern life...of steel, fever, pitch and headlong speed." Besides the **Italian Futurists**, Estorick collected works by De Chirico *(The Revolt of the Sage*, 1916), Rosso, Modigliani, Morandi, Marini.

St Pancras – Camden Town

St Pancras is one of London's biggest rail hubs, with three major stations serving the Midlands and the North of Britain. St Pancras is London's Eurostar terminus, providing a seamless railway link between northern Great Britain and Europe for the first time. On the edge of Bloomsbury, the area is home to the British Library in Somers Town and its improving tourist infrastructure includes moderately priced hotels, a trendy club scene and some interesting small museums.
The ever-popular markets, clubs, restaurants and Irish pubs of Camden Town lend a Bohemian atmosphere, especially at weekends.

> **Location:** *Map: inside front cover (EV).* ⊖*King's Cross-St Pancras.* St Pancras is north of Bloomsbury. Euston Road is a busy, major thoroughfare. Camden Town (⊖*Camden Town*) to the north, is well-served by buses; access from Regent's Park.
>
> **Don't Miss:** The Canal Museum and the Camden Town markets.
>
> **Timing**: Allow half a day to stroll round the area and soak up the atmosphere of the up-and-coming St Pancras vicinity.

A BIT OF HISTORY

The area contains three of London's six major railway terminals. To the east stands **King's Cross** (1852); the Great Northern terminus, built by Lewis Cubitt (the clock in the tower was displayed at the 1851 Exhibition *see SOUTH KENSINGTON).*

St Pancras (1864, Medieval Gothic in brick with Italian terracotta), was designed by Sir George Gilbert Scott. **Euston** (1837), the London and North Western terminus, was rebuilt in 1968; a statue of Robert Stephenson, chief engineer of the London Birmingham line (1838) stands in front.

ST PANCRAS
British Library★★

96 Euston Road. &⊙*Open Mon–Sat, 9.30am–6pm (8pm Tue; 5pm Sat), Sun, 11am–5pm.* ⊶*Reading rooms (pass required).* ℘*0870 444 1500. www.bl.uk.*
Eight years behind schedule and three times over budget, the new red-brick premises have earned few compliments, described by the Prince of Wales as "a dim collection of sheds groping for some symbolic significance." In the forecourt stands a powerful statue of Sir Isaac Newton by the British sculptor Eduardo Paolozzi.

The entrance hall in light Portland stone rises the full height of the building and the eye is drawn to the stacks of the King George III Library. The reading rooms are quiet havens. Three exhibition galleries present the library's treasures **(John Ritblat Gallery)** – technology enables visitors to turn the pages of rare books at the touch of a finger. Learn about the story of book production from the Middle Ages to the present time.

The British Library collections include rare manuscripts, Books of Hours, examples of early printing (Caxton and Wynkyn de Worde's books), famous works (Lindisfarne Gospel, Codex Sinaiticus, Gutenberg Bible), handmade books, children's books, postage stamps, George III's library and Henry Davis' Gift (fine bindings). Among the broad range of historical documents (early maps, musical scores, modern calligraphy) are copies of the Magna Carta, Essex's death warrant, Nelson's last letter, Shakespeare's signature and first folio (1623). The core collection is stored on site with the remainder stored elsewhere.

The new precincts now also accommodate the **National Sound**

Archive for discs and tape recordings of music, oral history, documentary material, spoken literature, language and dialect.

St Pancras Parish Church

Upper Woburn Place, Euston Road.
🕐*Open Sun 7.45am–11.30am, 5–7pm, Mon–Thu 9.30am–4pm, Fri 9.30am–12.30pm, Sat 9am–noon (phone ahead to check). Brochure (6 languages). Concert: Thu at 1.15pm; no charge.* 📞*020 7388 1461. www. stpancraschurch.org.*

The church was built in 1819–22 at the time of the Greek Revival, and William Inwood's design, selected from 30 submitted in response to an advertisement, echoes the Erechtheon on the Acropolis in Athens in the caryatids supporting the roofs of the square vestries, north and south. The columned two-stage elevation of the octagonal steeple and front Classical colonnade are modelled on the Tower of the Winds in Athens. Too tall to fit, the caryatid figures had to have their trunks shortened – hence their air of malaise.

Camley Street Natural Park

Camley Stree.
A wildlife haven has been created in a 2-acre/0.8ha park on the banks of the Regent's Canal including ponds, a marsh and reed beds, with the aim of attracting insects, butterflies and birds.

London Canal Museum

12–13 New Wharf Road. ♿🕐*Open Tue–Sun and Bank Holiday Mon 10am–4.30pm (3.45pm last admission), late opening on first Thu of each month until 7.30pm.* 🕐*Closed 24–26 Dec.* 💷*£3.* 📞*020 7713 0836. www.canal museum.org.uk.*

The museum is housed in an old ice house beside the Battlebridge basin on the Regent's Canal which once supplied Carlo Gatti, Victorian London's leading ice-cream maker with natural ice from Norway. An old film, *Barging through London*, illustrates canal life in 1924. The display records the building of canals in England, the construction of the Regent's Canal, the various methods of towing or propelling the barges (horsepower, legging, poling, steam tug, towpath tractors), 20C decline and conversion to leisure use: towpath walk (1970); boating, canoeing, fishing.

CAMDEN TOWN

▷ *From the tube station, walk up Chalk Farm Rd past the markets* (🕐*see YOUR STAY IN THE CITY – Shopping).*

Close to Regent's Park and Primrose Hill, Camden Town, with its delightful village atmosphere, has pockets of elegant houses sought after by artists, writers, actors and media people. In stark contrast to the local terraced houses, the Post-Modernist **TV-AM building**, in Hawley Crescent *(near Camden Lock)*, designed by T Farrell, is of some interest. From Camden Lock it is possible to take a boat trip upstream to the Zoo and Little Venice or downstream to Limehouse.

Roundhouse

Chalk Farm.
The 1840s former locomotive shed, a listed building, was recently converted to provide television, radio and recording studios as well as large and small theatre spaces, a glass-covered restaurant and landscaped garden.

Camden Lock Market

Facing onto the canal, the former timber wharf was renovated in the late 1980s and offered at low rents to young artisans for use as workshops. Once very trendy and upmarket, this has become the centre of street style and cutting edge fashion designers come here for inspiration. On weekends, endless ethnic food stalls open up to cater to the crowds of browsers. The **Regent's Canal Information Centre** presents historical displays relating to the canal development.

Stables Antique Market

The Stables, as their name suggests, were built in the 1840s to accommodate the horses that hauled the barges along the Regent's canal. The present buildings house a large market (𝖈see Addresses): Art Deco artefacts, 1950s and 1960s clothing, period fixtures and fittings and antiques. There are more stalls in the cobbled yard.

Jewish Museum

129–131 Albert St. ✕🕒*Open Sun–Fri.* ℘*020 8371 7373. www.jewishmuseum. org.uk.*

The exhibition space at Raymond Burton House has undergone a huge expansion programme. The museum houses a large number of exhibits including a Welcome Gallery, where visitors can meet Jewish people living in Britain today through an audiovisual display. On the ground floor there is a medieval *mikveh*, uncovered by archaeologists in London in 2002.

There is also an area devoted to history, where you can play the "Great Migration" board game, take part in a Yiddish theatre karaoke session or wander down a 19C East End street. Here visitors can explore how and why Jews have come here from around the world and how they have become part of British life.

In a different gallery, not advised for young children, the Holocaust is uncovered through the eyes of one man, London-born Auschwitz survivor Leon Greenman.

Another gallery explores Judaism, its beliefs and traditions. Explore the Torah, try on a prayershawl, or build your own synagogue. An emphasis is also put on the Jewish Faith today, to what extent it is practised in different areas of Britain, from the occasional bowl of chicken soup to the full Shabbat.

Finally, special exhibitions space will house changing exhibitions, throwing new light on Jewish culture, heritage and identity over the last 4 000 years.

ADDRESSES

✗ LIGHT BITE

Andy's Taverna – *81–81A Bayham St, NW1 0AG.* ⊖*Camden Town.* ℘*020 7485 9718. www.andystaverna.com.* Pretty, local, very well-established Greek restaurant with white-walled courtyard and great interior. The vibe is relaxed, the clientele loyal (including a number of celebrities). Good *meze* and fish.

Smiths of Smithfield – *67–77 Charterhouse St, EC1M 6HJ – ⊖Farringdon. ℘020 7251 7950 . www.smithsofsmithfield.co.uk.* The clever renovation of this former meat warehouse, opposite Smithfields, has been an undisputed success since opening, and the bar can get packed. A great place for a quiet brunch on Sundays though, relaxing in one of its leather armchairs.

🍺 PUB

The Camden Arms – *1 Randolph St, Camden, NW1 0SS.* ⊖*Camden Town. ℘020 7267 9829. www.thecamdenarms. com. Closed Sun.* Trendy lounge and gastro pub serving good Thai food. Excellent array of potent cocktails that are best enjoyed relaxing on leather sofas while listening to the guest DJs.

The Eagle – *159 Farringdon Rd, EC1R 3AL.* ⊖*Farringdon; Chancery Lane. ℘020 7837 1353. Closed bank holidays, 1 week Christmas–New Year.* A large eagle stands sentinel over the green façade of one of London's first gastropubs. The regular clientele enjoys a menu of simple cuisine and a lively vibe.

🛒 MARKETS

Camden Market – *Corner of Camden High St and Buck St. Thu–Sun.*

Camden Lock Market – *Chalk Farm Rd. Sat–Sun.*

Stables Antique Market – *off Chalk Farm Rd. Sat–Sun.*

Genteel and monied, Kensington and Chelsea is one of London's most elegant areas, knitted around a patchwork of squares, dazzling white townhouses converted into flats for central urbanites and mews houses down leafy backstreets, with millionaire pricetags. The area cradles key London attractions, from South Kensington's museums to the shopping hubs of Kensington High Street, the King's Road and trendy Notting HIll, with its bohemian village vibe, café culture and the Portobello Road antiques market every Saturday.

Highlights

1 London's grandest park: **Hyde Park** (p240)

2 Explore the elegance of royal residence, **Kensington Palace** (p243)

3 High-end shopping and coffee on the **King's Road** (p234)

4 Cutting-edge contemporary art at the **Saatchi Gallery** (p238)

5 Find a must-buy at Notting Hill's lively **Portobello Market** (p251)

Geography

Within this west London borough, Kensington's main centre is Kensington High Street. Knightsbridge lies east of Kensington, Chelsea to the south, bordering the River Thames.

History

Traditionally a place for the city's richer residents, two of Henry VIII's wives and Queen Elizabeth I lived in Chelsea, and the King's Road itself was named for Charles II. In the 19C and early 20C the area became a creative and radical crucible: painters Rosetti, Whistler and Singer Sargent lived and worked here, as did writer Oscar Wilde. It rose to prominence again as a "Swinging Sixties" centre, with seminal shops and groovy residents such as Biba and The Beatles on the King's Road (also the birthplace of Punk in the 1970s). The manor of Kensington was mentioned in the Domesday Book, under the tenancy of Aubrey de Vere, later Earl of Oxford. Queen Victoria was born in Kensington Palace, and conferred Royal status on the borough. Later palace residents included Diana, Princess of Wales. Kensington and Chelsea were amalgamated into the Royal borough of Kensington and Chelsea in 1965.

Today Today's Kensington and Chelsea is better known for being a nightlife haunt of young royals than a progressive hotbed. Nevertheless it remains one of the most sought after places to live in the capital. Kensington High Street and the King's Road continue to be enjoyable places to browse, especially at the Duke of York's Square . Nearby, the Saatchi Gallery has brought the creative impulse back to the area, while streams of visitors to South Kensington pack the V&A, Science and Natural History museums (*℅ see CENTRAL LONDON MUSEUMS*).

Chelsea★★

Chelsea is synonymous with a fashionable lifestyle, but its artistic associations still hold fascination. The lively atmosphere, with its dregs of 60s Bohemia, draws those seeking the limelight and the trendy social scene. People-watching is an entertaining pastime and there are plenty of elegant boutiques, antique shops, cafés and restaurants to indulge one's fancy. Explore the King's Road and the residential squares and walk along Chelsea Embankment for views of the Thames, to appreciate the charm of the area.

> **Location:** *Map: inside front cover (BYZ).* ⊖*Sloane Square. Chelsea extends on the north bank of the Thames from Chelsea Bridge west along Chelsea embankment and Cheyne Walk and from Sloane Square to Brompton Cemetery.*

> **Don't miss**: Chelsea Physic Garden for its historic associations, Cheyne Walk for its Georgian terraces and the Kings Road for its boutiques.

> **Timing:** Allow one day to explore the area along the route suggested in the Walking Tour (♿*see below*), soaking in the atmosphere of the Kings Road at the end and taking a well-earned break in one of the local cafés.

A BIT OF HISTORY

The completion of the embankment in 1874 removed for ever the atmosphere of a riverside community: boats drawn up on the mud flats, trees shading the foreshore, people walking along a country road as painted by **Rowlandson** in 1789 *(Chelsea Reach)*, watched in his old age at sunset by Turner, and captured by **Whistler** *(Old Battersea Bridge)*.

Chelsea had royal connections, but the only royal building to survive is the Royal Hospital. Architectural interest lies in the churches, squares, terraces and attractive houses of all periods.

Henry VIII's Palace – The river still served as the main access when the king's riverside palace, a two-storey brick mansion, was built in 1537 near Albert Bridge. Owned by the Cheynes in the 17C , it later belonged to **Sir Hans Sloane** and was demolished when he died in 1753.

Sir Thomas More, Henry VIII's Chancellor, built a house at the water's edge. One regular guest in the 12 years he lived in Chelsea, before sailing downriver to his execution in 1535, was **Erasmus**.

A Fashionable Set – Chelsea has been the setting for many a new or revived fashion: the exclusivity of the Pre-Raphaelites and the individuality of Oscar Wilde's green carnation. The opening of Bazaar in 1955 and the launch of **Mary Quant's** mini skirt: in the 1960s Chelsea was the "navel of swinging London" and the King's Road, a Mecca of the avant-garde. In 1971 **Vivienne Westwood** opened her clothes shop at 430 King's Road; it became the centre of Punk fashion. Today the King's Road has weathered into a well-heeled shopping area.

WALKING TOUR

Sloane Square

The square boasts two very different institutions: **Peter Jones**, the upper-middle-class department store with a stunning exterior (1936); and the **Royal Court Theatre** (✆*020 7565 5000; www.royalcourttheatre.com*), which has assumed a pioneering role since 1956 when the English Stage Co under George Devine presented John Osborne's *Look Back in Anger*.

Holy Trinity

A short way up Sloane Street. Open *Mon–Fri 9am–6pm, Sat, 9.30am–6pm. Concerts.* 020 7730 7270. *www.holy trinitysloanesquare.co.uk.*

The church was rebuilt in 1888 by a leading exponent of the **Arts and Crafts movement**, John Dando Sedding (1838–91). **Burne-Jones** (*see INTRODUCTION – Art and Culture, Decorative Arts*) designed the 48-panel east window with Apostles, Patriarchs, Kings, Prophets and Saints – St Bartholomew by **William Morris**. All decoration is of the period and harmonises with the High Altar marble crucifix and candlesticks. Note also the bronze panels in the choir stalls, the gilded organ case, golden lectern and unusual railings outside on Sloane Street.

▷ *Walk round Sloane Sq to the King's Rd.*

The King's Road

This used to be the private route taken by **Charles II** when calling upon **Nell Gwynne** at her house in Fulham; in fact, the King's Road was only opened to the public in 1830. At the height of the Swinging Sixties, it was the home of Mary Quant and other high fashion designers. It is now famous for its shops selling fashion accessories and antiques, restaurants and pubs, while the small streets around are lined by traditional cottages once built for artisans and now selling for a king's ransom.

▷ *Turn left into Royal Avenue.*

Between the King's Road and the Royal Hospital lies the playing field **Burton's Court,** flanked by **St Leonard's Terrace** – a mid-18C Georgian row (*nos 14–31*). At the centre of the terrace is **Royal Avenue**, planned in the late 17C to extend as far as Kensington Palace but never completed.

The Royal Hospital★★

Open *Nov–Mar Mon–Sat 10am–noon, 2–4pm; Apr–Oct daily 10am–noon, 2–4pm.* **Grounds** open *Nov–Mar 10am (Sun noon)–4.30pm with late closures during summer. Leaflet (8 languages).* 020 7881 5298. *www.chelsea-pensioners.org.uk.*

Chelsea Pensioners have been colourful members of the local community for over 300 years. Inspired by Les Invalides, built by Louis XIV in Paris in 1670, **Charles II,** who had re-established a standing army in 1661, commissioned Sir Christopher Wren to build a veterans' hostel. The architect designed a quadrangular plan with a main court open on the south to the grounds and the river. The main entrance is beneath the lantern-crowned **Octagon Porch** in the north range of the original **Figure Court**, so-called after the Classical statue of Charles II by **Grinling Gibbons** at the centre.

From the Octagon Porch steps rise on either side to the **Chapel and Great Hall**, both panelled beneath tall rounded

Charles II in Classical dress in Figure Court, Royal Hospital

J. Malburet/MICHELIN

Chelsea Luminaries

A varied group of notable people has lived in Chelsea: the famous actresses Nell Gwynne, Dame Ellen Terry, Dame Sybil Thorndyke (who inspired GB Shaw to write *St Joan* for her); Sir Joseph Banks (botanist, explorer and President of the Royal Society); Sir John Fielding (a respected magistrate who was blind from birth), the engineers **Sir Marc Isambard Brunel** and his son Isambard Kingdom; Charles Kingsley (author of *The Water Babies*); Mrs Elizabeth Gaskell (novelist); the **Pre-Raphaelite** poets and painters **Dante Gabriel Rossetti**, his sister Christina, Burne-Jones, William and Jane Morris, Holman Hunt, Swinburne and Millais. Other artists include **William de Morgan**, Wilson Steer, Sargent, Augustus John, Orpen and Sickert. Mark Twain, **Henry James** and TS Eliot are among Chelsea Americans. Smollett lived in Lawrence Street; **Oscar Wilde** at 34 Tite Street; AA Milne at 13 Mallord Street. There were also Hilaire Belloc, the Sitwells and Arnold Bennett.

windows. The Chapel has a barrel vault and, at the end, a domed and painted apse by Ricci. The end wall of the Hall is decorated with an 18C mural of Charles II on horseback before the hospital. The **Council Chamber** (*west wing*) was decorated by both Wren and Robert Adam; Van Dyck painted the portrait of Charles I and his family. The **Museum**, located on the east side, displays Wellington mementoes and illustrates the history of the hospital and its members.

Since 1913 the **Chelsea Flower Show** (🌿*see Addresses*) has been held in the grounds by the **Royal Horticultural Society**. In 1805 the Hospital purchased the celebrated **Ranelagh Gardens** (1742–1805), which offered patrons *alfresco* meals, concerts and spectacles in the Rotunda.

▷ *Walk west along Royal Hospital Rd past the National Army Museum (🌿see Additional Sights).*

Chelsea Physic Garden

66 Royal Hospital Road, SW3 (entrance on Swan Walk). ♿🕐*Open Apr–Oct Wed–Fri noon–5pm, Sun and bank holidays noon–6pm; last admission 30min before closing. Wed in Jul–Aug until 10pm; last admission 8.30pm. before closing.* ⏴£8 Guidebook. No dogs allowed. Plants for sale. Refreshments. ✆020 7352 5646. www.chelseaphysic garden.co.uk.*

The botanical garden, frequented by such leading lights as Linnaeus, was founded in 1673 by the Worshipful Society of Apothecaries of London on land leased from Sir Hans Sloane. His statue by Rysbrack stands in the centre. The record of the garden is remarkable: Georgia's cotton seeds came from the South Seas via the Physic Garden, India's tea from China, her quinine (*cinchona*) from South America and Malaya's rubber from South America.

Cheyne Walk★

The terraces of brick houses standing back from the river front are rich with memories of artists, writers and royalty. Corinthian pilasters mark the entrance to no **4** where **George Eliot** spent her last weeks. Beautiful railings and fine urns distinguish no **5**; no **6** is remarkable for the Chinese-Chippendale gate and railings. The **Queen's House** (*no 16*) was the home of the poet and painter D G Rossetti where the Pre-Raphaelites used to meet. In the gardens opposite stands a fountain bearing a portrait bust of Rossetti, by Seddon. No **18** was the popular Don Saltero's coffeehouse and museum. Nos **19–26** occupy the site of Henry VIII's riverside palace.

For Albert Bridge 🌿*See SUBURBS – BATTERSEA.* 🌿*For Carlyle's House, 24 Cheyne Row, see Additional Sights.*

In **Lawrence Street** flourished the **Chelsea China Works** (1745–84) before being transferred to Derby (🌿*see INTRODUCTION – Decorative Arts*). The **King's Head and Eight Bells** (now a restaurant) dates back to the 17C.

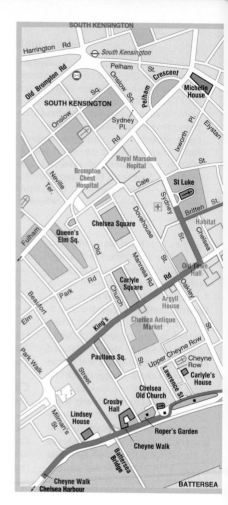

Chelsea Old Church

⊙*Open Tue–Thu 2–4pm, Sun 1.30–6pm.* ℘*020 7795 1019. www.chelseaoldchurch.org.uk.*

The pre-Norman church with a 14C chapel remodelled by **Sir Thomas More** in 1528, was reconstructed after suffering bomb damage. Many monuments were rescued from the rubble: note in particular the 17C altar, rails and small marble font; the **chained books** presented by Sir Hans Sloane; the reclining figure of Lady Jane Cheyne (1699), the massive Stanley monument of 1632 and More's self-composed inscription against the south wall of the sanctuary. The novelist **Henry James** is also buried here, while in the churchyard a **statue** of a sombre, seated black-robed figure with gilded face and hands commemorates Sir Thomas More.

Roper's Garden, once part of More's orchard, is named after his son-in-law. The stone relief of *A Woman Walking against the Wind* is by **Jacob Epstein** who lived in Chelsea (1909–14).

Crosby Hall, the Medieval great hall transferred from the City to Chelsea in 1910 was part of the residence of a 15C wool merchant.

From Cheyne Walk there is a fine view of Battersea Bridge (ⓒ*see SUBURBS– BATTERSEA*). Nos **91–92** were built in 1771 and have several Venetian windows. Nos **93** and **94** date from 1777. Whistler resided at no **96**.

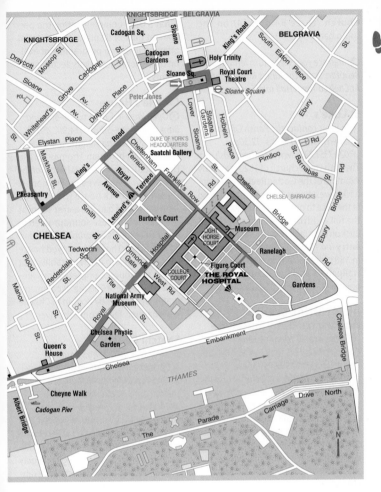

The large **Lindsey House** with mansard roof-storey, built in 1674 on the site of Sir Thomas More's farm and divided later, was home to the Brunels, commemorated in the modern **Brunel House** on the corner at no **105**.

◑ *Continue along the embankment.*

104–120 Cheyne Walk

Several writers and artists lived along this stretch: the essayist anD historian **Hilaire Belloc** (1873–1953), the landscape painter **PW Steer** (1860–1942) and above all **Turner** (1775–1851) who spent his last years at no **119**.
Chelsea Harbour, where barges once unloaded coal, is now a modern river-

Houseboats

Moored on the river are several permanent houseboats: larger and more spacious than a canal barge, these would once have accommodated watermen and river pilots. Today they provide homes for a more Bohemian set of Chelsea residents.

side development organised around a 75-berth marina and comprising a series of elegant and exclusive apartments, offices, a hotel, shops and restaurants: those that face onto the river enjoy fine views across the water to **St Mary's**

Church (&see BATTERSEA) on the south bank.

▶ *Retrace your steps, turn left into Beaufort St, for the King's Road; right. At Chelsea Town Hall take Sydney St.*

St Luke's

&*To view, contact the Parish Office:*
◷*Open Mon–Fri 10am–12.30pm.*
✆*020 7351 7365. www.chelseaparish.org*
The Bath stone church of 1820 is an early example of the Gothic Revival. The pinnacled west tower (242ft/74m) is pierced at the base to provide a porch extending the full width of the west front.
Back on the King's Road, note the **Pheasantry** *(no 152, now a restaurant)* erected in 1881 by the Jouberts to sell French wallpapers and furniture; alas, today only the façade and portico survive.

ADDITIONAL SIGHTS
♟♟**National Army Museum★**

&◷*Open daily 10am–5.30pm.*
◷*Closed Good Fri, May Day Hol, 25–26 Dec, 1 Jan.* ✆*020 7881 2455 (information line),* ✆*7730 0717. www.national-army-museum.ac.uk.*
Visit the National Army Museum and find out how Britain's past has helped to shape Britain's present and future. Discover the impact the British Army has had on the story of Britain, Europe and the world, and see how the actions of a few can affect the futures of many.
Exhibitions – The major exhibition, Conflicts of Interest, examines over three decades of action on the World stage by the modern British Army. it explores the conflicting interests of enforcing peace through violent means, balancing global security with the needs of vulnerable communities and the demands of the job on the personal lives of our troops.
For the family – Win the battle against boredom at the museum's Kids' Zone. There are activities for all ages to enjoy; comfortable seated areas are provided with easy access to the café.
♟♟**For Kids** – Kids will enjoy the Action Zones, featuring quizzes, games and hands-on activities.

What's On – Complementing the permanent gallery displays, the museum offers an inspiring programme of exhibitions, celebrity speakers, lectures and events.

Carlyle's House

◷*Open Wed–Fri 2–5pm, Sat–Sun and Bank hols 11am–5pm.* ⬤*£4.90.* ✆*020 7352 7087. www.nationaltrust.org.uk.*
The Scottish historian Thomas Carlyle (1795–1881) famous for his *History of the French Revolution*, lived in this modest Queen Anne brick house with his wife Jane Welsh and had the garret-room at the top of the house soundproofed in order to write his biography of Frederick the Great. The four-storeyed house contains a wealth of memorabilia that reflect the couple's unpretentious lifestyle. The "Sage of Chelsea" is commemorated in a statue by Boehm in Cheyne Walk gardens facing onto the river.

Saatchi Gallery

Duke of York's HQ, King's Road.
&◷*Open daily 10am–6pm; last entry 5.30pm. Café/Bar. Bookshop.*
⬤*No charge.* ✆*020 7823 2363. www.saatchi-gallery.co.uk.*
Opened at its new location in 2008, this cutting-edge inteactive art gallery in the former Duke of York's barracks HQ showcases contemporary art works by largely unseen young British artists or established International artists unknown in Britain. The vast 70 000sq ft/6 503sq m space with its abundance of natural light holds temporary curated exhibitions; the Project Room is a space for exhibitions of artists featured in the collection, but not in the main exhibition programme. There is also a space, the New Gallery, where Saatchi Online artists can exhibit and sell their works for free, as well as a pleasant café/bar and a bookshop on site.
The gallery operates a free entry policy to all shows and exhibitions, thanks to a corporate partnership with contemporary art auction house Phillips de Pury, as part of its aim to bring Contemporary art to the widest audience possible.

ADDRESSES

🍴 LIGHT BITE

Bluebird Café – *350 King's Rd, SW3 5UU.* ⊖*South Kensington.* 📞*020 7559 1000. www.conran.co.uk.* This informal café is part of Conran's renowned "gastrodome", which also includes a food store, florists and a smart restaurant. Order a croissant, fresh juice or a light meal and a cocktail while watching the world go by along the fashionable King's Road.

Vingt Quatre – *325 Fulham Rd, SW10 9QL.* ⊖*South Kensington, Gloucester Road . 📞020 7376 7224. www.vingtquatre.co.uk.* 24/7/52 is proudly displayed on the canopy as this brasserie is open 24 hours a day, 7 days a week, 52 weeks a year. This lively and popular evening haunt provides an elaborate international café menu. Cover charge from 10.30pm to 7am.

Gordon Ramsay – *68–69 Royal Hospital Road, SW3 4HP. 📞020 7352 4441. www.gordonramsay.com/ royalhospitalroad. Closed Sat, Sun and one week over Christmas.* With just 14 tables, this signature restaurant of the celebrity chef by the same name is an exercise in exclusivity. As such, getting a table is sometimes a bit of a challenge, and it's best to start your bid to book well in advance (two months minimum is required). The reward is fabulous haute cuisine and top flight service.

🍸 BAR

Babushka House – *354 King's Rd, SW3 5UZ. 📞020 7352 0025.* A vodka cocktail bar that is a mixture of 70s kitsch and 'noughties' cool. Relaxed during the day and very busy in the evening with the young Chelsea set.

🍺 PUBS

Chelsea Potter – *119 King's Rd, SW3 4PL.* ⊖*Sloane Square. 📞020 7352 9479.* Ideally located in the heart of one of London's foremost shopping areas, this pub, with a tile décor, is authentic and unpretentious. Full of tourists by day; at night a young crowd takes over.

Admiral Codrington – *17 Glossop St, SW3 2LY.* ⊖*Sloane Square, South Kensington. 📞020 7581 0005. www.the admiralcodrington.co.uk.* A well-established, much-loved local that is packed in the evenings. The small, pleasant dining area at the back has a retractable glass roof.

Phene Arms – *9 Phene St, SW3 5NY.* ⊖*Sloane Square. 📞020 7352 3294.www. phenearms.co.uk.* A friendly and authentic pub in Chelsea with a good selection of beers. The pleasant beer garden to the rear is open all year round and usually packed with locals at weekends.

The Builders Arms – *13 Britten St, SW3 3TY.* ⊖*Sloane Square. 📞020 7349 9040. www.geronimo-inns.co.uk. Closed 25 Dec and 1 Jan.* Comfortably elegant and smartly designed, this pub is located just a stone's throw from the King's Road. The atmosphere is laid-back, bustling and fun. Excellent, hearty, well priced food.

Chelsea Ram – *32 Burnaby St, SW10 0PL.* ⊖*Fulham Broadway. 📞020 7351 4008. Closed 25 Dec and 1 Jan.* A short walk from the King's Road and Chelsea Harbour, this much frequented pub is very pleasant with its scrubbed pine tables and walls packed with books and art. Friendly ambience and good food. Ask for the daily specials.

🛒 SHOPPING

Jo Malone – *150 Sloane St, SW1X 9BX.* ⊖*Sloane Square. 📞0870 192 5121. www. jomalone.co.uk.* Jo Malone's covetable, expensive and very beautiful cosmetics, skin care and home accessories are all available at this delightful shop. Great for presents, and always wonderfully packaged, the shop keeps details of your preferences.

Bourbon-Hanby Antiques Centre – *151 Sydney St, SW3 6NT.* ⊖*Sloane Square . 📞0870 142 3403. www. bourbonhanby.co.uk. Closed bank hols.* A fascinating collection of exhibitors all gathered under the roof of an elegant Victorian building.

General Trading Company – *2 Symons St, SW3 2TJ.* ⊖*Sloane Square. 📞020 7730 0411. www.generaltradingcompany. co.uk.* This unique emporium specialises in home furniture and accessories in contemporary and various ethnic styles. It has a good selection of greetings cards, books, jewellery, and bags as well. Pleasant café.

Manolo Blahnik – *49–51 Old Church St, SW3 5BS.* ⊖*Sloane Square.* ℘*020 7352 8622. www.manoloblahnik.com. Closed bank holidays.* The source of the most desirable shoes in London. Well-heeled women around the world appreciate the creative and ultra-feminine designs of Blahnik's entirely hand-sewn footwear. Men's shoes also available.

Hyde Park – Kensington Gardens★★

The linked green expanses of Hyde Park and Kensington Gardens at London's heart offer many attractions in all seasons and give the capital a special charm. Every day people flock to the parks to walk their dogs, jog, ride, go boating, swim (even if it means breaking the ice on Christmas morning), in-line skate, sail model boats, feed the pigeons, play bicycle polo, football, rounders, tennis, cricket or bowls – even archery is available (Kensington Gardens Archery Club). Concerts and celebrations in the park also attract the crowds.

A BIT OF HISTORY

In Saxon times the acres were part of the Manor of Eia which, until "resumed by the King" in 1536, belonged to **Westminster Abbey**. **Henry VIII** enclosed the area and, having stocked it with deer, kept it as a royal chase. In the 16C and later, the park was used for military manoeuvres and encampments. In 1637 it was opened as a public park and the crowds came to watch horse racing and other sports only to be debarred when it was sold by the Commonwealth to a private buyer who, to Pepys' indignation, charged for admission. At the Restora-

🎭 EVENTS AND FESTIVALS

Chelsea Flower Show – *(&See PLANNING YOUR TRIP – Calendar of Events.* Held in May, this glorious flower show, sponsored by the Royal Horticultural Society, is one of the high points of the summer season. The show ground is full of the latest in garden design, gardening products and gardening trends, as well as some of the most perfect – and fragrant – blooms around. A must for anyone with green fingers.

▷ **Location:** *Map: inside front cover (A-DXY).* ⊖*Marble Arch; Hyde Park Corner; Knightsbridge; Queensway; Lancaster Gate; Park Lane; Knightsbridge.* Kensington Rd and Bayswater Rd mark the boundaries of the two parks.

🕐 **Timing:** This chapter is divided into two walks: one starting from either Hyde Park Corner or Marble Arch and the other from Kensington Palace. Allow one day including a tour of Kensington Palace and/or boating on the Serpentine.

👫 **Kids:** The children's playground and paddling pool at the Lido, on the South bank of the Serpentine.

---

tion the contract of sale was cancelled and the park again became public. The activities of those who frequented and made use of the park were even more diverse in the 18C and 19C than now: the last formal royal hunt was held in 1768; pits were dug to supply clay for bricks to build the new houses of Marylebone and Mayfair; gunpowder magazines and arms depots were sited in isolated parts; soldiers were executed against the wall in the northeast corner; at the same time it was a fashionable carriage and riding promenade first round the road known as the Tour and then **the Ring** (originally a small inner circle) or along the Row **(Rotten Row)**. It was a convenient place for duels and a common spot for footpads.

The **Great Exhibition** of 1851, conceived and planned by Prince Albert, was housed in the **Crystal Palace**, a vast iron and glass structure made of rapidly erected prefabricated unit parts.

Queen Victoria, Wellington and some 6 030 195 others visited the exhibition, which aimed to demonstrate man's inventiveness and 19C British achievement in particular. The profit it made was used to establish the museums in South Kensington (*see KENSINGTON*). The Crystal Palace (*see SUBURBS – DULWICH*) was dismantled and re-erected at Sydenham, where it was destroyed by fire in 1936.

WALKING TOURS

1 HYDE PARK

It was **Pitt the Elder** in the 17C who aptly called the former deer park "the lungs of London". The park is put to many uses: as a place of relaxation and free speech, a rallying ground for parades and royal salutes, and since 1800 a burial ground for pet dogs (at the Victoria Gate).

Marble Arch

At the north-east corner stands a fine triumphal arch of Italian (Seravezza) white marble with three closely patterned bronze gates. Modelled on the Arch of Constantine in Rome by **John Nash** (1827), it was intended to stand before Buckingham Palace, a monument to celebrate the end of the Napoleonic wars, but the central archway was not wide enough to accommodate the Gold Stage Coach.

The arch was dismantled (1837), and in 1851 was rebuilt where the **Tyburn gallows** had stood until 1783.

Speakers' Corner is a relatively modern feature of the park. Anyone may mount their soap box and address the crowds irrespective of creed, colour or persuasion as long as the speaker does not blaspheme or incite a breach of the

Boating on the Serpentine. View east towards the towers of Westminster

A. Taverner/MICHELIN

peace. The best time to join the crowd is on Sunday mornings.

▶ *Walk down Broad Walk.*

At the bottom end of Park Lane stands the **Queen Elizabeth Gate**, erected in 1993 in celebration of Queen Elizabeth, the late Queen Mother's 93rd birthday. The two sets of gates, designed by Giuseppe Lund, provide a cast-iron screen for the central lion and unicorn panels sculpted by David Wynne.

Inside the park is **Richard Westmacott**'s so-called **Achilles** statue (18ft/5.5m), cast from captured cannon and modelled on an Antique horse tamer on the

Tyburn Gallows

The gallows, first a tree, then a gibbet, was finally replaced by an iron triangle for multiple executions. From the Tower or Newgate the condemned were drawn through the streets on hurdles to be hanged (and sometimes drawn and quartered, too) before the great crowds who gathered to hear the last words, see the spectacle and enjoy the side shows. Popular victims were toasted in gin or beer as they passed. A stone in the park railings in the Bayswater Road marks the site.

Quirinal Hill in Rome – it is said to have embarrassed the women who presented it to Wellington by its nakedness.

The riding path through the park, running parallel to Knightsbridge, is known as **Rotten Row** (originally Route du Roi), the first road in Britain with artificial lighting (1690). Today it is used for riding by local stables and cavalry regiments.

Hyde Park Corner

The southeast corner of the park was transformed in 1825–28 by the erection of a triple arched **screen**, crowned by a sculptured frieze, and a **triumphal arch** surmounted by a colossal equestrian statue of the Duke of Wellington. In 1883 the arch was moved to its present position, the statue was transferred to Aldershot and replaced by a quadriga (1912).

▷ *Take the underpass to the central reservation.*

Wellington Arch

🕐*Open 10am–4/5pm.* 🕐*Closed 24–26 Dec, 1 Jan.* 🎫*£3.20.* 📞*020 7930 2726. www.english-heritage.org.uk.*

Hemmed in by the busy traffic, this arch has been restored to its former glory. An exhibition relates the history of the landmark. Go up to the viewing platforms to enjoy views of the parks and of the Palace of Westminster with the London Eye on the horizon. The present **Wellington Monument**, placed before the entrance to Apsley House (👜*see PICCADILLY*), is by Boehm (1834–90); cast from captured guns, it shows the Duke mounted on his horse Copenhagen, guarded by a Grenadier, a Royal Highlander, a Welsh Fusilier and an Inniskilling Dragoon.

▷ *Return to the park and proceed along Carriage Rd.*

From Carriage Road (south side) walk down to Albert Gate, the site of a bridge over the Westbourne. The twin houses flanking the gate were built in 1852; the house on the east side is occupied by the **French Embassy**. Further along, are the **Hyde Park Barracks** and stables

(1970–71). From here the Guardsmen ride down to Horse Guards' when the Queen returns to London.

▷ *Walk through the park, along Serpentine Rd and up a path.*

At the centre of the park is the **Hudson Bird Sanctuary**, marked by the **Jacob Epstein** sculpture *Rima* (1925), where over 90 species have been recorded. The **Serpentine Bridge** (1826–28), designed by John Rennie, spans the Long Water and the Serpentine. It also links Hyde Park to Kensington Gardens and is London's favourite spot for rollerblading. The 👥 **Serpentine** is used for boating and swimming, with a children's paddling pool. If you like to watch people shiver, it's the site of London's traditional New Year open-air swim. There is a café overlooking the water.

Diana Memorial Fountain

🕐*Open Apr–Aug 10am–8pm; Sept 10am–7pm; Mar and Oct 10am–6pm; Nov–Feb 10am–4pm.* 👜*May be closed during extreme cold or severe weather conditions.*

Opened by the Queen in July 2004 and dogged for some time by problems from children slipping on the stones to engineering hiccups that turned the surrounding area into a marsh, this low circular fountain is London's official memorial to Diana, Princess of Wales, who died tragically young in 1997.

② KENSINGTON GARDENS
👜*See Kensington Palace, p243.*

The gardens were at their prime under the Royal Gardeners, **Henry Wise** (portrait in Kensington Palace) and his successor in 1728, Charles Bridgman. An octagonal basin, the **Round Pond**, was constructed facing the State Apartments of Kensington Palace with avenues radiating from it. Other features of the period that persist are the **Broad Walk,** recently replanted, and the **Orangery**★ with a massive stone centrepiece by **Hawksmoor** (1705). Later additions are the Edwardian **sunken**

garden in which pleached limes surround brilliant flower beds and a long canal, the statue of **Peter Pan** (1912) to the west and **The Arch**, sculpted by **Henry Moore** in 1979, from Roman Travertine to the east by the Long Water and the **Flower Walk**, north of the Albert Memorial.

▶ *Take the Broad Walk and continue along the Flower Walk.*

Albert Memorial★

Proverbial as the epitome of mid-Victorian taste and sentiment, the memorial, which stands at the summit of four wide flights of granite steps, was commissioned by a heartbroken Queen Victoria to commemorate her beloved husband Prince Albert, who died of typhoid in 1861. It was designed by **Sir George Gilbert Scott** (1872) as a neo-Gothic spire (175ft/53m), ornamented with mosaics, pinnacles and a cross. At the centre, a brilliantly gilded figure (14ft/4m) of the Prince Consort sits surrounded by allegorical statues. *For details of Royal Albert Hall and surrounding buildings across Kensington Road, see KENSINGTON.*

▶ *Follow the path to the Gallery.*

Serpentine Gallery

Gallery Lawn, Kensington Gardens, W2. ♿🕐*Open daily 10am–6pm.* ☎*020 7402 6075. www.serpentinegallery.org.* This small compact pavilion, shaded by great trees, was formerly a fashionable tea house. It now holds exhibitions of modern art.

Take a diagonal path to view the Statue of Physical Energy and branch right past Peter Pan to the Italian Garden.

Separating the gardens from the Bayswater Road are the railings where artists exhibit their works for sale in an open-air market, and which are very popular with tourists.

KENSINGTON PALACE★★

♿🕐*Open daily Mar–Oct 10am–6pm (last admission 5pm); Nov–Feb 10am–5pm (last admission 4pm).* 🕐*Closed*

Delicate wrought-iron screen against the red-brick façade of Kensington Palace

Historic Royal Palaces/newsteam.co.uk

24–26 Dec. 🍽*Guided tour.* 💷*£12.30, guided tours free. Joint ticket with other Royal Palaces available. Audio-guide.* 📷*No photography.* ☎*0844 482 7777 (info). ww.hrp.org.uk.*

👤 *The State Apartments are on the first floor and there are no lifts. Disabled visitors should telephone in advance to make special arrangements.*

Since its purchase in 1689 by **William III**, Kensington Palace has passed through three phases: the monarch's private residence with **Wren** as principal architect; a royal palace with **William Kent** in charge of alterations; and, since 1760, a residence for members of the royal family, notably the late **Diana**, Princess of Wales.

"Kensington is ready" wrote Queen Mary to her husband, William, in July 1690 and, disliking Whitehall, she moved in. The house grew from an early 17C Jacobean house, rebuilt in 1661, to a rambling mansion around three courts by the early 18C. Throughout, Wren kept to a style befitting a modest house in red brick beneath slate roofs. The only embellishment to the south front was an attic screen with Portland stone vases. The **State Apartments** are approached up the Queen's Staircase, designed by Wren (1691).

The Queen's Apartments

The **gallery** (84ft/25.6m long) is rich in carving, with cornice and door heads by **William Emmett** and sumptuous sur-

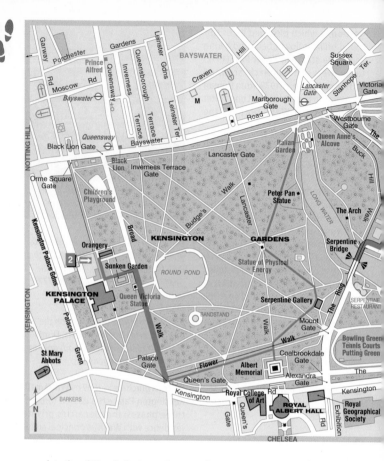

rounds to the gilt Vauxhall mirrors above the fireplace in the gallery by Grinling Gibbons in 1691. Portraits in the rooms are personal: *Peter the Great* in armour by Kneller in commemoration of his visit in 1698, *William III* as King and Prince of Orange, *Queen Mary* by Wissing, *Anne Hyde* by Lely and in the adjoining closet, *Queen Anne* and *William, Duke of Gloucester* by Kneller. In the **Drawing Room** Kneller painted *Queen Anne* in profile and the first Royal Gardener, *Henry Wise*. Note an 18C mahogany cabinet (gallery), 17C–18C Oriental porcelain and a fine Thomas Tompion barometer of c. 1695 (drawing room).

The King's Apartments

The lofty 18C rooms bear William Kent's strong decorative imprint. The **Privy Chamber** has an allegorical ceiling of George I as Mars; the **Presence Chamber**, a red and blue on white ceiling with arabesque decoration by Kent (1724). The **King's Grand Staircase** (Wren, 1689) was altered in 1692–93 when the **Tijou** iron balustrade was incorporated and again in 1696 by Kent who covered walls and ceiling with grand *trompe-l'œil* paintings.

The **King's Gallery** was limited to simpler ornamentation as it was intended to display the greatest pictures in the royal collection.

Although the 19C **Victorian Rooms** were redecorated by Queen Mary, all else belonged to and epitomises **Queen Victoria** and her family: furniture, wallpaper, ornaments, portraits, photographs, toys and doll's house. The **Council Chamber** at the far end of the east front contains mementoes of the

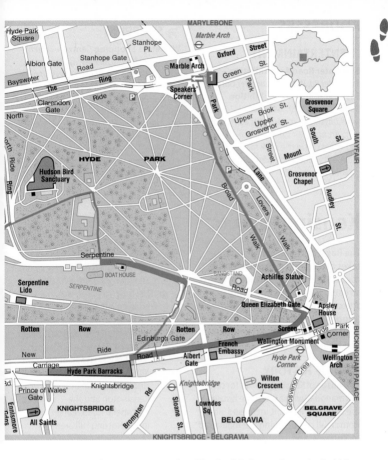

1851 Exhibition and a massive carved Indian ivory throne and footstool. Only the ceiling of arabesques, figures and medallions remains of Kent's Baroque decoration in the **King's Drawing Room**. Queen Victoria was baptized in the **Cupola Room**, high and square with a vault patterned in blue and gold.

The **Red Saloon** where she held her Accession Privy Council in 1837 and the room in which she is said to have been born in 1819 are also on view.

Royal Ceremony

The **Court Dress Collection** traces the evolution of court dress from the 18C to the 20C. Dictated by protocol, elegant dresses and accessories (Orders of Chivalry), court suits and ceremonial uniforms resplendent with gold and silver, lace and embroidery, worn at levées and at court are presented in contemporary settings. More contemporary exhibits include pieces from the Queen's wardrobe, largely designed by the late Sir Norman Hartnell to suit the sovereign's various State functions and dresses belonging to Diana, Princess of Wales.

www.hrp.org.uk/kensingtonpalace

ADDRESSES

🎭 ENTERTAINMENT

Bayswater Road Art Exhibition – *Bayswater Rd, W2 .* ⊖*Lancaster Gate;* **Bayswater Road Art Exhibition** *Queensway.* ☎*020 7641 6000. www.bayswater-road-artists.com. Sun only.* An open-air exhibition of pictures and crafts lining the park railings by the road, variously offered for sale by aspiring artists.

🛒 SHOPPING

Whiteleys Shopping Centre – *Queensway, W2 4YN .* ⊖*Queensway; Bayswater.* ☎*020 7229 8844 . www.whiteleys.com. Various shop closing times apply.* Formerly a grand department store – the first in the UK and supposedly saved from World War II bombs, as Hitler wanted it for his UK headquarters – this is now a wonderful modern shopping mall with smart boutiques, food outlets and a cinema multiplex.

Kensington★★

The Royal Borough of Kensington takes great pride in its aristocratic connections. Elegant residential streets are spacious and white-stuccoed houses boast all the trappings of affluence. It is also famous for its world-class museums and fashionable amenities.

A BIT OF HISTORY

The village of Kensington was for centuries manorial, with a few large houses at the centre of fields. It increased slowly from small houses lining the main road to squares and tributary streets as estates. Before long, separate parcels of land were sold.

Among the famous mansions were Nottingham House – later Kensington Palace, Campden House, Holland House and, on the site of the Albert Hall, Gore House, the home of **William Wilberforce** until 1823 and for 12 years from 1836 the residence of "the gorgeous" Lady Blessington, whose circle included Wellington, Brougham, Landseer, Tom Moore, Bulwer-Lytton, Thackeray, Dickens, Louis Napoleon and other such poets, novelists, artists, journalists and French exiles.

A Visionary Enterprise – When the **Great Exhibition** held in 1851 in Hyde Park was over, **Prince Albert**, its initiator, proposed that the financial profit, a vast £200 000, be spent in establishing a great educational centre in South Kensington.

▷ **Location:** *Map: inside front cover (ABXY).* ⊖*High Street Kensington; South Kensington; Notting Hill Gate; Holland Park.* Kensington and South Kensington are to the south and west of Kensington Gardens.

⊘ **Don't Miss:** The Science Museum and the Natural History Museum in South Kensington and the Portobello Road Market in the Notting Hill area. *See MAJOR CENTRAL LONDON MUSEUMS.*

🕐 **Timing:** Wander through the Portobello Road Market on a Saturday morning, then spend the afternoon in one of the museums. Allow another half a day to explore the leafy avenues and elegant squares lying south of Kensington High Street.

👥 **Kids:** The adventure playground in Holland Park.

The money was used to buy the land on which the world famous museums and colleges, including the Natural History and Science museums, are to be found today (*see MAJOR CENTRAL LONDON MUSEUMS*).

🔍 WALKING TOURS
1 KENSINGTON VILLAGE
Kensington High Street

In 1846 when **Thackeray** and his daughters moved into a house in Young Street, the eldest described Kensington High Street as "a noble highway, skirted by beautiful old houses with scrolled iron gates." Within a few years the population was to multiply from 70 to 120 000; shops spread along both sides of the High Street.

Down Young Street is **Kensington Square**, with houses dating from the 17C-19C, as varied in design as the people who have lived in it: Sir Hubert Parry *(no 17)*, John Stuart Mill *(no 18)*, Mrs Patrick Campbell *(no 33)*. The two oldest houses are nos 11 and 12 in the southeast corner; a cartouche over the door mentions previous owners including the Duchess Mazarin (Henrietta Mancini, niece of the Cardinal) 1692–98.

The **Roof Garden** at no 99 Kensington High Street *(entrance in Derry Street)*, was laid out in the 1930s, and has mature trees, grass and flamingos high up above the bustle of High Street Kensington. ♿🕐*Open (private functions permitting) daily 11am–5pm by appointment.* ☎*020 7937 7994. www.roofgardens.com.*

On the corner of **Kensington Church Street** and the High Street, an unusual vaulted cloister leads to the neo-Gothic parish church of **St Mary Abbots**, which boasts an unusually tall spire (278ft/85m high).

Commonwealth Institute
Kensington High Street.
The unique tent-shaped building, with its four peaked, green copper roofs supported on glass curtain walls, was opened by the Queen in 1962 to replace the former Imperial Institute, opened in 1893 by Queen Victoria, of which only the imposing Queen's Tower survives. This modern complex is dedicated to celebrating the different cultures of the 50 Commonwealth countries.

▶ *Take Holland Walk.*

Holland Park
🕐*Open daily 8am–8pm (dusk in winter); open-air opera, Jun–Aug; Brochures; Café; Sports facilities (golf range, tennis courts, cricket pitch and nets, football pitch);* ☎*020 7471 9813 (enquiries); 0845 230 9769 (opera);* ☎*020 7602 2226 (sports bookings).*
It is nearly 400 years since Holland House was built by the City merchant and courtier Sir Walter Cope in the scattered village of Kensington. The mansion soon became a place of entertainment for king and court. Advanced wings on either side of the central range were added by Cope's daughter, whose husband, in 1624, was made Earl Holland.
In the mid-18C Holland House was acquired by the politician Henry Fox, who was also created Baron Holland. He was rich, knew everyone and entertained lavishly; his grandson, 3rd Baron Holland, politician, writer, literary patron, was the last great host of Holland House. Among those who dined and visited frequently were the Prince Regent, Sheridan, Byron, Talleyrand, Louis Napoleon, William IV and, almost the last visitor, Prince Albert.
Today, the restored east wing and George VI Hostel serve as a youth hostel. In summer the forecourt is canopied to accommodate open-air performances of opera and dance. A restaurant occupies part of the 17C stable block; the Ice House and Orangery, meanwhile, are used for functions and exhibitions. The woodland has been re-established and the gardens replanted after long neglect; peacocks flaunt their plumages in the gardens and water tinkles through the Japanese garden.

▶ *Continue down Ilchester Place and Melbury Rd, cross the high street and walk to Edwardes Sq.*

Edwardes Square
Tucked away behind the Odeon Cinema and the uniform brick range of large houses known as Earl's Terrace (1800–10) is this elegant square. The east and west ranges are composed of more modest three-storey houses (1811–20)

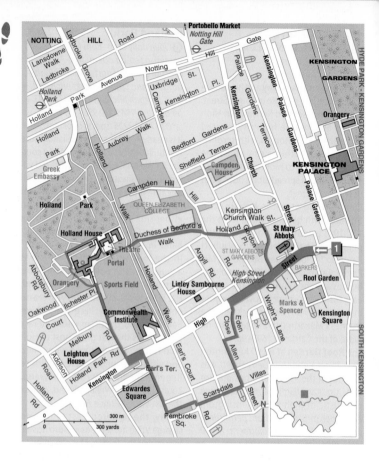

complete with balcony, garden and square ironwork. In the southeast corner stands the **Scarsdale Arms**, a Victorian pub bedecked with flowers established in 1837 (⌖see Addresses). To the south is **Pembroke Square**, lined on three sides with Georgian ranges, matching iron balconies and, in the south-east corner, its pub.

② SOUTH KENSINGTON

The **Royal College of Art**, with eight floors of studios and workshops, dates from 1961. The college evolved from a fusion of the Government School of Design and the National Art Training School (1896) and has nurtured many eminent artists, architects, sculptors and industrial and fashion designers.

In contrast, the elaborately decorated building next door is the former home of

the **Royal College of Organists** (1875); note the frieze of putti carrying musical instruments and garlands incorporating the VR monogram around the door.

Royal Albert Hall★

Kensington Gore, SW7. ↜Guided tours Thu–Tue 10.30am–3.30pm. ⊛£8. ℘020 7838 3105 (tours) 020 7589 8212 (box office). www.royalalberthall.com.

The round hall, almost 1/4 mile (0.4km) in circumference, built of red brick with a shallow glass-and-iron dome, is the foil in shape and ornament to the Albert Memorial (⌖see HYDE PARK – Kensington Gardens) opposite, since its only decoration is an upper frieze of figures illustrating the Arts and Sciences.

Reunions, pop and jazz sessions, exhibitions, boxing, political meetings, conferences and concerts, particularly the eight-week summer series of **Promenade Concerts** (known as "The Proms"), fill the hall with up to 7 000 people at a time. The refurbishment of the interior and of the South Steps was completed in 2004. Behind the Albert Hall stands a monument to Prince Albert, a driving force behind the 1851 Great Exhibition.

Virtually next door, the **Royal Geographical Society** founded in 1830, has been a cornerstone of Britain's exploration of the world ever since. Statues of explorers Shackleton and Livingstone adorn the outer wall. The collections contain many objects linked to the great explorers, from HM Stanley's boots to Livingstone's compass. The Map Room contains 30 000 old and historic maps. *Map Room and Library:* &. ○ *open Mon–Fri 10am–5pm. Picture Library* ○ *open Mon–Fri 10am–5pm by appointment.* ℘ *020 7591 3000. www.rgs.org.*

To the south, in Prince Consort Road, stands the dark-red brick **Royal College of Music**, built in 1893 in neo-Gothic style. Inside is the highly prized **Museum of Instruments**, which has over 600 items, including a spinet played by Handel, and Haydn's clavichord. ○ *Open in term time (except Jan) Wed 2–4.30pm.* ☞£5. ℘ *020 7589 3643. www.rcm.ac.uk.*

Imperial College of Science and Technology extends from either side of the Royal College of Music in Prince Consort Road south to the Science Museum, apart from the small enclaves occupied by Holy Trinity Church (1909), the Edwardian Post Office Building and the Underground exit. With the exception of the neo-Georgian 1909–13 **Royal School of Mines**, the vast, clean-lined buildings date from the mid 50s. In their midst, guarded at its foot by a pair of lions, rises the old **Queen's Tower** (280ft/85m high), last relic of the Imperial Institute (1887–93), erected following the Colonial Exhibition of 1886. Opposite, the Sir Alexander Fleming building with a stepped double-glazed roof designed by **Sir Norman Foster** combines architectural flair and high technology.

Hyde Park Chapel
Exhibition Road.
The stylish Mormon chapel, dating from 1960, is surmounted by a needle spire of gilded bricks.

▷ *Continue past the Science Museum, the Natural History Museum (and the Victoria and Albert Museum; cross Cromwell Rd.* ◐ *See MAJOR CENTRAL LONDON MUSEUMS.*

The distinctive modern **Ismaili Centre**, faced in grey-blue marble and adorned with slim windows serves as a religious and cultural centre for Ismailis.

▷ *Walk along Cromwell Rd.*

The buildings of the **Institut Français**, founded in 1910, although in art nouveau style, date only from 1938. Many of the students enrolled here and at the nearby Lycée are English.

▷ *Retrace your steps and turn right into Cromwell Pl. to Thurloe St and past the station take Pelham St to the left.*

Michelin House
The 1910 purpose-built building, the first in Britain to be constructed with a reinforced-concrete frame, is the former UK headquarters of Michelin Tyre PLC. Its original *art nouveau* **decoration**★has been restored and tiled tyre-fitting bays preserved, despite considerable internal changes (◐ *see Addresses*).

Michelin House in art nouveau style

K. Brett/MICHELIN

249

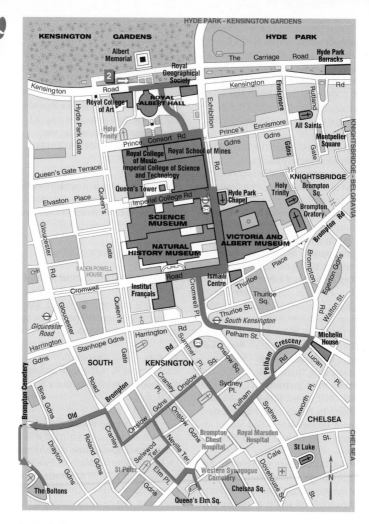

▷ *Walk along Fulham Road beyond Pelham Crescent and two hospitals.*

The Tudor style of **Queen's Elm Square** reflects the story that **Elizabeth I** sheltered here under an elm during a storm.

There are 19C artisan cottages in **Elm Place** *(across Fulham Rd and on the right)* and its immediate vicinity. Turn right past a pleasant pub, then left to **Onslow Gardens**, a mid-19C development of stuccoed houses with pillared porches.

▷ *Cranley Gdns leads to Old Brompton Rd; turn left.*

Bolton Place, on the left, leads to **The Boltons**, where fine white-stuccoed houses are laid out in a mandorla crescent. Further on along Brompton Road is the entrance to **Brompton Cemetery**, a vast 19C necropolis containing neo-Gothic, Egyptian and Baroque style tombs.

HOUSES AND MARKET
Linley Sambourne House★
18 Stafford Terrace. ⊘*Open Mar–Sept.* ☙*Guided tours Sat–Sun 11.15am (conventional guide), 1pm, 2.15pm and*

3.30pm (costumed guide). £6. *020 7602 3316. www.rbkc.gov.uk/linley sambournehouse.*

Edward Linley Sambourne, a leading Punch cartoonist and book illustrator, moved into this Victorian town house in 1874. The original wall decoration by William Morris and the furniture have survived largely unaltered. Cartoons by Sambourne and his contemporaries line the stairs.

Leighton House★

12 Holland Park Road. Call or see website for times. *020 7602 3316. www.leightonhouse.co.uk.*

The Victorian painter **Lord Leighton** (1830–96), President of the Royal Academy, remains most originally reflected in the house that he built for himself in 1866. The **Arab Hall** is covered with panels of glazed tiles imported from the Middle East. A mosaic floor spreads around a bubbling, cool fountain.

To the north of Kensington, the fashionable residential area of **Notting Hill**, which boasts many excellent restaurants and bars, has seen its appeal greatly enhanced since the film, *Notting Hill.*

Portobello Road★

This sleepy winding road, once a cart-track through the fields from the Notting Hill turnpike, comes to life on Saturdays with one of London's finest markets; a symphony of antiques and bric-a-brac. The road hosts part of the **Notting Hill Carnival** in August, Europe's largest street carnival (*see Addresses*).

ADDRESSES

✕ LIGHT BITE

Tom's Delicatessen – *226 Westbourne Grove, Notting Hill, W11 2RH.* Notting Hill. *020 7221 8818.* The eponymous owner, son of Terence Conran, has his father's eye for style and design. Half-deli, half-café with framed vintage posters and an impressive cake display. Popular spot with the fashionable Notting Hill crowd.

The Orangery – *Kensington Palace Gdns, W8 3UY.* Kensington High Street. *020 3166 6311. www.hrp.org.uk. Closed for dinner service.* This delightful orangery, built for Queen Anne in 1704 in the grounds of Kensington Palace, affords charming views of the gardens and park through the vast windows. It is the ideal spot for morning coffee, a light lunch or afternoon tea. Perfect on a summer's day.

Ottolenghi – *63 Ledbury Rd, W11 2AD.* Notting Hill Gate. *020 7727 1121. www.ottolenghi.co.uk.* Café, deli and great restaurant serving a mix of fashionable dishes with lots of Asian spices is a great hangout for trendy 'Notting Hillbillies', as the inhabitants of Notting Hill are generally known.

▯ PUBS

Churchill Arms – *119 Kensington Church St, W8 7LN.* Notting Hill Gate. *020 7727 4242.* An eclectic collection of wicker baskets, photographs, butterflies, tankards and Churchill memorabilia adorn the ceiling and walls of this large cosy pub. Thai cuisine is served under the veranda in a jungle setting.

Ladbroke Arms – *54 Ladbroke Rd, W11 3NW.* Holland Park; Notting Hill Gate. *020 7727 6648.* A country style pub with a meticulous décor in the middle of the residential district of Notting Hill. Large terrace for the summer.

The Cow – *89 Westbourne Park Rd, Notting Hill, W2 5QH.* Royal Oak; Westbourne Park. *020 7221 0021. www.thecowlondon.co.uk.* A popular Notting Hill pub, with a gastro side to it, serving oysters and Guinness as well as other modern British dishes. The small space is often packed. Excellent drinks.

The Westbourne – *101 Westbourne Park Villas, Notting Hill, W2 5ED.* Royal Oak, Notting Hill Gate. *020 7221 1332. www.thewestbourne.com.* Well renovated, with large windows and sun-drenched terrace, the Westbourne is a very popular pub with the locals, who also enjoy its cuisine.

♀ BAR

Julie's Wine Bar – *135 Portland Rd, Notting Hill, W11 4LW.* ⊖*Holland Park.* ☎*020 7229 8331. www.juliesrestaurant. com.* This bar offers an intimate setting and a good selection of European and New World wines. When the weather is good you can enjoy the terrace.

🛒 SHOPPING

Kensington High Street – *Kensington High St, W8.* ⊖*High Street Kensington. Individual shop closing times apply.* A street of boutiques and shopping arcades with many high street names, including some of the wackier ones. Take a stroll through the labyrinth of Kensington Market, across the street, to view a host of exotic and trendy clothes.

The Conran Shop, **Michelin House** – *81 Fulham Rd, South Kensington, SW3 6RD.* ⊖*South Kensington.* ☎*020 7589 7401. www.conran.com.* Smart decoration shop with furniture and stylish accessories for the home and garden. Situated in the old Michelin offices; the shop's famous trend-setting owner, Terence Conran, has wisely preserved the superb art nouveau stained-glass windows depicting, "Bibendum"

(aka the Michelin Man), which make this one of the most distinctive London shopfronts. For a quiet bite there is a downstairs coffee shop in the entrance.

Travel Bookshop – *13 Blenheim Crescent, Notting Hill, W11 2EE.* ⊖*Ladbroke Grove.* ☎*020 7229 5260. www.thetravelbookshop. co.uk. Closed Sun occasionally.* Catapulted into celebrity by the film "Notting Hill", this travel bookshop, in a road full of small specialist shops, has a fine selection of maps and guidebooks. Don't expect to see Hugh Grant though.

🎭 CARNIVAL

Notting Hill Carnival – Revellers throng the streets on the last weekend in August for the capital's premier carnival. ☀*See PLANNING YOUR TRIP – Calendar of Events.*

🛒 MARKET

Portobello Road – Browse for antiquities, Victoriana, later silver, chinaware, stamps, and small items in this atmospheric market held every Saturday along a two-mile-long winding road in Notting Hill. Leave plenty of time to browse. ☀*See YOUR STAY IN THE CITY – Shopping.*

Knightsbridge – Belgravia★★

Knightsbridge and Belgravia are the most exclusive residential districts in the capital, and the fashionable emporia and designer shops along Brompton Road, Sloane Street and Beauchamp Place are temples of delight. It is a pleasurable pastime to mingle with the leisured classes and to admire the stylish displays. The area also boasts some of the finest hotels and restaurants.

A BIT OF HISTORY

Until the end of the 18C **Knightsbridge** was an unkempt village outside London and on a major highway, with its fair share of cattle markets, slaughterhouses, taverns and pleasure gardens.

▷ **Location:** *Map: inside front cover (CDY).* ⊖*Knightsbridge; Hyde Park Corner; South Kensington.* This area is bounded by Hyde Park to the north, the museum district of South Kensington to the west, and Buckingham Palace Gardens to the east.

⊚ **Don't Miss:** Belgrave Square, Harrods, the neo-Baroque Brompton Oratory.

🕐 **Timing:** Allow half a day to stroll through the area, more if you decide to browse through Harrods or visit the Victoria and Albert Museum (☀*see MAJOR CENTRAL LONDON MUSEUMS – Victoria & Albert Museum).*

In 1813 Benjamin **Harvey** opened a linen draper's (Harvey Nichols); in 1849 Henry **Harrod** took over a small grocer's shop. These stores, which over the years have become household names for luxury shopping, attract an elegant and wealthy clientele.

It was probably **George IV**'s decision to transform Buckingham House into Buckingham Palace that provided the impetus for the development of **Belgravia**, part of the Grosvenor estate. By 1827 **Wilton Crescent**, **Belgrave Square**, Eaton Place and **Eaton Square** had been erected. Basevi (the architect) and Cubitt (the builder) were probably responsible for the adjoining square and streets: Chester Square, Belgrave Place and Upper Belgrave Street.

ᐳ WALKING TOUR
ᐳ *Start from Hyde Park Corner. For Apsley House ⌾see PICCADILLY.*

Lanesborough Hotel
This handsome building (1827–29) on Hyde Park Corner, originally designed by William Wilkins to house St George's Hospital, has a central porch with square columns flanked by two wings.

ᐳ *Walk down Knightsbridge and turn left into Wilton Pl.*

The 17C brick terraces of **Wilton Place** predate St Paul's Church by a century, erected in 1843 on the site of a Guards' barracks, still recalled in local street and pub names. **Wilton Crescent** is lined by stuccoed terraces.

ᐳ *Make a short detour to Wilton Row to visit the Grenadier pub (⌾see Addresses), then return to Belgrave Sq.*

Belgrave Square★★
The square (10 acres/4ha) is bordered by twinned, but not identical, ranges consisting of three-storeyed, white-stuccoed houses. The centres and ends are in the Corinthian style with urns and balustrades, pillared porches and an attic screen decorated with statues; there are detached houses in three of the corners. The ironwork matches the fence enclosing the central garden; a bronze statue of Simon Bolivar stands at the south-east corner. Seaford House was the residence of the statesman, Lord John Russell. Today the square is home to several embassies.

St Peter's Church, at the north-eastern end of Eaton Square, was erected in 1827 in the Classical style, as part of the original development project. The interior was refurbished after a fire in 1988.

ᐳ *Proceed along Eaton Sq and Belgrave Pl. then turn left into Chesham Pl., through Belgrave Mews to Halkin Pl. and West Halkin St.*

Pantechnicon
The august Doric-columned warehouse dates from 1830. On either side and in West Halkin Street and Halkin Arcade are a number of small shops dealing in luxury goods.

Just north along Lowndes Street is **Lowndes Square**, developed separately in the mid-19C and largely rebuilt in the 20C.

ᐳ *Walk back and turn right into Cadogan Pl. towards Sloane St.*

Sloane Street
The street, first developed in 1773 to link Knightsbridge to Chelsea and the river, has been rebuilt piecemeal. The **Danish Embassy** (1976–77) was designed by Ove Arup. The area west of Sloane Street, known as **Hans Town,** dates from the late 18C. The tall red brick buildings date mainly to the Cadogan Estate.

ᐳ *Turn right into Pont St.*

On the right is **Hans Pl**, a pleasant residential area.

On the left is **St Columba's**, the London Church of Scotland (1950–55), designed by **Edward Maufe** with a square stone tower capped by a green cupola (⌾open Mon–Fri 9.30am–5pm; ℘020 7584 2321; www.stcolumbas.org.uk).

In the late 19C the area around **Cadogan Square** and Cadogan Gardens was

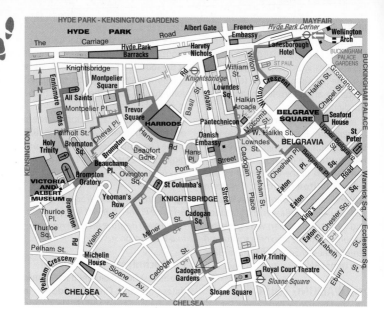

rebuilt in unfading red brick, nicknamed "Pont Street Dutch".

▶ *Right on Walton St; left on Hans Rd.*

Harrods

Since 1905 this shop, which claims to sell everything, has been housed in the familiar terracotta building with towers and cupolas; the lofty **food halls** are decorated with art nouveau wall tiles (☞*see YOUR STAY IN THE CITY – Shopping*). It is still regularly voted the world's finest department store. Owned by Mohammed al Fayed, there is a memorial to Princess Diana and Dodi al Fayed on the ground floor.

▶ *Cross Brompton Rd and follow the map to explore the charming streets and squares, past the following:*

Brompton Road

The triangle between Kensington Road and Brompton Road developed as a residential district in Georgian fashion around a series of squares: **Trevor Square** (1818), **Brompton Square** (1826), **Montpelier Square**★ (1837); the houses have stucco ground floors

and basements with brick upper storeys and balconies. Narrow streets link the squares, with mews and closes lined by colour-washed cottages with handker-chief-sized front gardens.

Oratory of St Philip Neri (Brompton Oratory)

&⊙*Open daily 7am–6pm. ✆020 7808 0900. www.bromptonoratory.com.*

The main body of the church was designed (1881) by Herbert Gribble in the Italian Baroque style in Portland stone, the dome and lantern, meanwhile, was planned by George Sherrin (1895–96) so as to span the exceptionally wide and lofty nave.

The 18C Italian Baroque statues of the Twelve Apostles by Giuseppe Mazzuoli (1644–1725) used to stand in Siena Cathedral. The Baroque pulpit and much of the mosaic decoration are by Commendatore Formilli. The inlaid wooden floor and carved choir stalls inlaid with ivory date from the previous church. The altar is early 18C Flemish Baroque.

Hidden behind Brompton Parish Church is the attractive garden of the early 19C **Holy Trinity Church**.

ADDRESSES

⚘ LIGHT BITE

Wagamama – *At Harvey Nichols, Knightsbridge, SW1X 7RJ.* Knightsbridge. *020 7201 8000. www.wagamama. com.* Wagamama's presence in this chic department store is proof of the mini-chain's popularity among Londoners. The winning formula: minimalist décor, long refectory tables, carefully prepared and healthy Asian dishes and reasonable prices. Generally crowded and good for kids.

The Knightsbridge Café – *5–6 William St, Knightsbridge, SW1X 9HL.* Knightsbridge. *020 7235 4040. Open for breakfast, lunch and dinner.* Just a credit card's throw from Knightsbridge's designer shops, a café with smart modern décor, slick and eager-to-please service and a wide range of salads, sandwiches and pastries. Attractive pavement terrace.

Harrods – *Brompton Rd, Knightsbridge, SW1X 7XL.* Knightsbridge. *020 7730 1234. www.harrods. com.* London's most famous emporium presents an array of restaurants and cafés to suit all palates. In the food hall are a rotisserie, oyster bar, seafood grill and deli. For a traditional tea, make for the 4th-floor Georgian Restaurant. The Green Man Pub offers a pub lunch and a pint of Harrods Ace.

Harvey Nichols – *Fifth Floor Café – 109–125 Knightsbridge, SW1X 7RJ.* Knightsbridge. *020 7235 5000. www.harveynichols.com.* The well-heeled Knightsbridge shoppers enjoy a pot of tea or a glass of champagne in the informal atmosphere of this airy, clean-lined café-bar. There's a smart restaurant for light meals as well.

🍺 PUBS

Grenadier – *18 Wilton Row, Belgravia, SW1X 7NR.* Knightsbridge; Hyde Park Corner. *020 7235 3074.* This area has been haunted since one of the Duke of Wellington's officers was mysteriously murdered here when the pub was used as a mess. According to the landlord, the officer's ghost is now a good friend, who may be seen wandering around the pub and down the alley (one of London's most picturesque). The ghost has an excellent home as the pub is friendly and cosy. Upmarket clientele. Good selection of whiskies. Restaurant service.

The Bunch of Grapes – *207 Brompton Rd, Knightsbridge, SW3 1LA.* Knightsbridge. *020 7589 4944.* This Victorian pub has many of the hallmarks – a mahogany interior, engraved glass sides and a wrought-iron balcony. Its location near Harrods makes it a popular tourist spot. Restaurant upstairs.

The Nag's Head – *53 Kinnerton St, Knightsbridge, SW1X 8ED.* Knightsbridge, Hyde Park Corner. *020 7235 1135.* A country setting just five minutes from Harrods. Follow the picturesque road, which appears to be a dead-end, to this friendly pub. At the counter you can order homemade sausages before chatting with the landlord or a guest by the fireplace. As friendly a welcome as you'll receive anywhere in London.

♟ BAR

Library Bar – *Lanesborough Hotel – 1 Lanesborough Place, Hyde Park Corner, SW1X 7TA.* Hyde Park Corner. *020 7259 5599.* This hotel serves the best Martinis in town and has a refined atmosphere. The Library (great for fish and chips, if a little pricey) has large sofas and a fashionable clientele.

🛍 SHOPPING

Harvey Nichols – *109–125 Knightsbridge, SW1X 7RJ.* Knightsbridge . *020 7235 5000.* This vast department store opposite the Tube station has floors of designer clothing and a ground floor dedicated to costly cosmetics and beauty products.

Philip Treacy – *69 Elizabeth St, Belgravia, SW1W 9PJ.* Sloane Square. *020 7730 3992. Closed Sun.* This hat master is always in the public eye, at Ascot and in lifestyle and fashion magazines. He makes all sorts of headwear from the classic to the extravagant, and from Navy blue to fuchsia.

Beauchamp Place, **Halkin Arcade**, **Brompton Rd** and **Sloane St** are lined with elegant specialist shops where it is pleasant to browse for distinctive items.

Stretching along the central south bank of the River Thames, opposite the City and Westminster, Southwark and Lambeth bustle with vibrancy and creative innovation. This is the perfect day out for culture vultures, whether enjoying a play at the South Bank Centre or installations at Tate Modern, leafing through second-hand bookstalls during a riverside walk or shopping for gastronomic treats at Borough Market. Further upstream, Battersea Park in leafy Wandsworth is a hidden gem with open-air jazz evenings, festivals and a children's zoo.

Highlights

1 Test your nerves at the **London Dungeon** (p265)

2 Watch Shakespeare plays like an Elizabethan at **Shakespeare's Globe Theatre** (p258)

3 Fresh produce at London's oldest market, **Borough Market** (p258)

4 Get the best view in the city from the top of **The London Eye** (p272)

5 Be inspired by performances at the **National Theatre** (p274)

Geography – These three boroughs sit to the south of the meandering River Thames. London Bridge and next to it, Bankside, is in Southwark. Lambeth is further along the river to the west, and the next borough along is Wandsworth. The South Bank stretches 2sq mi/5sq km along the Thames and straddles both Southwark and Lambeth.

History – Lambeth and the South Bank sit on the ancient site of Lambeth Marsh, where the horse ferry operated to Westminster and the City of London in the Middle Ages. Urban post-war regeneration began here in 1951 with the Festival of Britain, for which the Royal Festival Hall was built. Additions in the 1960s and 70s resulted in the iconic concrete South Bank Centre complex, echoing neighbouring Bankside's history as an 16C entertainment district where Shakespeare presented his plays at venues such as the Globe and Rose Theatres. Neighbouring Southwark, by London Bridge has been known as "The Borough" since the 1550s, to distinguish it from the City of London, and looming Southwark Cathedral is a pious architectural reminder that much of this area belonged to the church for centuries.

Today – The South Bank and Bankside are London's cultural crucible, with numerous theatres, concert halls and galleries. The area buzzes with visitors enjoying al fresco coffee and riverside walks up to the Millennium Bridge, which links Bankside with the City and St Paul's Cathedral. Up near London Bridge, Borough market still trades as it has done since the 13C. East along the river from the South Bank Centre, County Hall, former seat of the Greater London Council, is now overlooked by The London Eye, while upstream past Chelsea Bridge, Battersea is a leafy residential area popular with young professionals.

Bankside★ – Southwark★

The Globe and Tate Modern are two potent symbols that combine history and modernity on Bankside, while the bustling London Bridge City and Hay's Galleria east of London Bridge, highlight the vitality of the borough of Southwark, which extends south from the Thames to Crystal Palace. After years of neglect and dereliction, the area is now becoming one of the trendiest in London, full of fashionable loft apartments, theatres, museums, trendy bars and restaurants – and a relaxed atmosphere that invites visitors to stroll and enjoy wonderful river views and those of the City skyline dominated by St Paul's on the north bank.

A BIT OF HISTORY

The Roman Invasion to the Dissolution of the Monasteries – The construction by the Romans of a bridge and the convergence at the bridgehead of roads from the south of England attracted settlers to the fishing village already established on one of the few sites relatively free from flooding on the low-lying marshlands of the Thames' south bank.

By Anglo-Saxon times the bridge had become a defence against ship-borne invaders and the village, the *sud werk* or south work, against attacking land

> **Location:** *Map: inside back cover (FGXY).* ⊖*Southwark; London Bridge; Blackfriars.* Bankside and Southwark extend from Blackfriars Bridge to Tower Bridge on the south bank of the Thames. Explore the last section of the Millennium Mile from Blackfriars, beyond Southwark Cathedral to Tower Bridge and Bermondsey *(allow 90min between Bankside and Rotherhithe).*

forces: **Olaf of Norway**'s rescue of Ethelred from the Danes is commemorated locally in Tooley Street; the Conqueror fired Southwark before he took London by encirclement. In the **Domesday Book**, Southwark was described as having a strand where ships could tie up, a street, a herring fishery and a priory.

Southwark people were also fishermen and boatmen. Industries developed such as mortar making, weaving, brewing (by refugees from the Low Countries), glassmaking and leather tanning.

The Dissolution to the 20C – Henry VIII rapidly sold off the monastery estates. The City increased its interests in Southwark, but it never acquired jurisdiction over the Clink prison or Paris Garden.

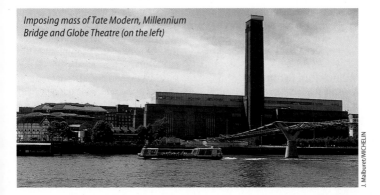

Imposing mass of Tate Modern, Millennium Bridge and Globe Theatre (on the left)

J. Malburet/MICHELIN

William Shakespeare (1564–1616)

England's greatest poet and playwright (38 plays) was born the son of a glove-maker; he married Anne Hathaway in Stratford-upon-Avon before coming to London to find success and fame; he had three children, and died on his 52nd birthday. His popularity is rooted in the rich use of colloquial language, humour that sometimes verges on the bawdy, and a timeless portrayal of human nature. Although there are no autographed copies, a total of 18 plays were printed in his own life time, 36 followed in a folio, the first collected edition, published in 1623. He also wrote 154 sonnets and four long poems.

As the Industrial Revolution kicked in, the area close to the river, largely owned by the City and known as the Borough of Southwark, which time has shortened to **Borough**, became heavily industrialised, following the building of the bridges, the 19C expansion of the docks and the coming of the railway.

By the late 19C the last prisons had been demolished: the **Clink** in 1780; the **Marshalsea** in 1842; King's Bench in 1860 and Horsemonger Lane Jail in 1879. World War II caused devastation to the area, and Southwark is an amalgam of historical and post-war construction.

Borough Market – The Borough Market, London's oldest (13C), was formally established in 1756 and the profits go to rates relief. The market has excellent restaurants and, on Fridays and Saturdays, it serves as one of London's best farmers' market. ⚹See box p253.

♣ WALKING TOUR
1 ALONG THE RIVERSIDE

⊖Southwark; Blackfriars (on the other side of the bridge).

▶ From Blackfriars Bridge take Queen's Walk past the Bankside Gallery and Tate Modern.

Millennium Bridge

A remarkable architectural and technical achievement, the steel suspension bridge (320yd/338m long), designed by Sir Anthony Caro and Foster & Partners, has curving balustrades that form "a blaze of light" spanning the Thames at night. After initial problems, when its swinging gave it the nickname 'wobble

bridge', it now provides a pedestrian link, with fabulous views, between St Pauls and the Tate Modern.

Old Houses

Turn right into **Cardinal Cap Alley**. On either side are two 18C houses. The first (no **49**), the oldest house on Bankside, was built on the site of the Cardinal's Hatte, some 50 years after the Great Fire (1666). The reference to Catherine of Aragon on the plaque is therefore questionable, as is the tradition that Sir Christopher Wren lived there during the building of St Paul's Cathedral.

Shakespeare's Globe★★

Bear Gardens. ✗⚹⚹⚹⚹Open daily 9am–12.30pm (Exhibition and theatre tour every 30min), noon–5pm (Exhibition and Rose Theatre tour); mid-Oct–Apr 9am–5pm (tours and exhibition). Theatre season Apr–Oct. ⚹Closed 24–25 Dec. No access to the theatre during performances. ⚹£10.50 (tour), theatre tickets from ⚹£5 standing and ⚹£12 seated. Restaurant and café. ℘020 7902 1400; Box office ℘020 7401 9919. www.shakespeares-globe.org.

In 1597, the Privy Council threatened all theatres with closure for sedition; the following year, the Chamberlain's Men's lease of the Shoreditch Theatre ran out. The company, which included Richard Burbage and Shakespeare, tore down the theatreand moved the whole thing across the river to Southwark, rebuilding it as the Globe – close to the site of the modern Globe.

The idea for instigating a centre dedicated to encouraging the study and dramatic interpretation of Shakespeare's work came from the late American actor-director Sam Wanamaker. Funding such a dream was arduous, and included supporters paying for individual bricks. The result is a runaway success.

Globe Theatre – The "Wooden O" *(33ft/10m high, 100ft/30.5m in diameter and 300ft/91.5m in circumference)* has been modelled on surviving documentary evidence of the original theatre, pulled down in 1644, and from archaeological excavations of the original Globe (& *see EAST END – Shoreditch*) around the corner. Wherever possible, similar materials (unseasoned "Green" oak, reed thatch) and building methods have been used to re-create the half-covered theatre. Performances *(Apr–Oct)* are held during the afternoon, much as in Shakespeare's day, without the use of artificial stage lighting – and subject to fine weather! The audience can sit on hard benches (☺*use a cushion*) or stand in the pit for the whole performance.

Inigo Jones Theatre – Alongside the main open-air theatre is this small playhouse, built according to Jones' drawings and adapted for concerts and productions all year round.

▶ *Turn right into New Globe Walk and left into Park Street.*

The Playground of London

In the 16C, permission was accorded by the authorities for two theatres to be set up in the old monastery cloisters north of the river in Blackfriars, and the area became known as the playground of London. The reign of the **Rose** (1587), the **Swan** (1595/6), the **Globe** (1599) and the **Hope** (1613) theatres was, however, brief: those that had not already reverted or become bull and bear baiting rings were closed finally under the Commonwealth by the Puritans in 1642.

The Globe Education Centre includes an undercroft UnderGlobe **exhibition** area, a cinema and lecture hall, audiovisual archive and library. The staff also run ☞guided walking tours.

The Rose Theatre Exhibition
56 Park Street. ☞*Guided tour for pre-booked groups only in summer.* ℘*020 7261 9565(Shakespeare's Globe). www.rosetheatre.org.uk*
An imaginative light and sound show brings to life the history of the Rose Theatre, the first theatre on Bankside. Excavations have revealed the remains of the building, now covered by a pool of water because of lack of funds.

Globe Theatre

Pawel Libera/Shakespeare's Globe

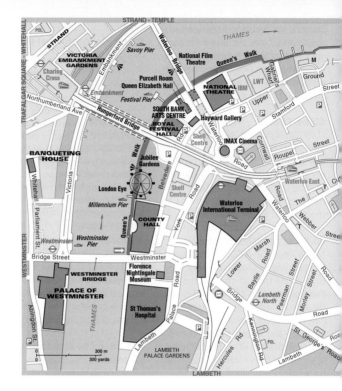

Southwark Bridge

Rennie's bridge (1815–19), referred to by Dickens in *Little Dorrit* as the Cast Iron Bridge, was replaced in 1919 with the iron structure by Ernest George. **Excavations** in the Park Street area have revealed Roman warehouse ruins.

▶ *Cross the street to view the ground plan of the original Globe theatre clearly marked on the site of a former brewery. Continue to the end of the street and turn left to the riverfront.*

The Anchor (◐ *see Addresses*) is an historical tavern erected in 1770–75 on the site of earlier inns.

▶ *Continue past Clink Exibition.*

Winchester Palace

At the heart of a large modern development stands the old ruin comprising the screen wall of the 12C **great hall** pierced by a **rose window** (14C) of Reigate stone and three archways that once would have led to the servery and kitchens.

A Great Adventure

In 1577 Francis Drake (c. 1540–96) set sail on the *Pelican* into the unknown: he returned three years later from the Pacific having laid claim to Nova Albion (California) and the Port of Sir Francis Drake (San Francisco) on the *Golden Hinde*, his ship having been renamed as she approached the Straights of Magellan. Drake chose the name after the symbol of a golden passant hind representing the armorial of the expedition's sponsor, Sir Christopher Hatton (◐ *see INTRODUCTION – History*). On arrival, the vessel was moored at Deptford (◐ *see GREENWICH*) and visited by Queen Elizabeth I who took the opportunity to knight Drake there and then.

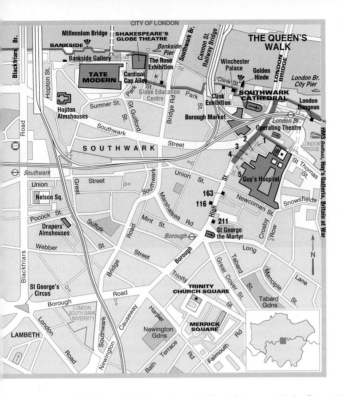

The precinct of the Bishop of Winchester's Palace contained a prison for errant clergy and nuns, which lay below the water level at high tide. From the 15C it was known as the **Clink Prison**, from which is derived the expression "to be in the clink": between 1630 until its closure in 1780 it was used for poor debtors. The museum in Clink Street can be booked for private events.

St Mary Overie Dock

The full-scale galleon replica of Sir Francis Drake's **Golden Hinde** is made of African iroko hardwood and caulked with oakum in the traditional way; she was built in Appledore, Devon and launched on 5 April 1973 with a bottle of mead.

When not away at sea (she has already undertaken several transatlantic journeys and at least one circumnavigation), the *Golden Hinde* is open for tours of her cabins and quarters, galley and hold. ⏱ *Open daily 10am–5pm/5.30pm, telephone ahead to confirm availability.*

Self-guided tour with leaflet ⊜£5.75. Overnight stays, Pirate Parties for children, weddings, corporate functions. ✆08700 118 700 (bookings), 020 7403 0123. www. goldenhinde.org

A riverside **viewing panel** identifies the buildings on the north bank: the twin pavilions at the north end of **Cannon Street Railway Bridge** were built at the same time as the bridge (1866) by J W Barry and J Hawkshaw.

Southwark Cathedral★★ (St Saviour and St Mary Overie)

✕ & ⏱ *Open daily 8am (Sat, Sun 9am)–6pm. Donation ⊜£4. Audio tours £2.50. Exhibition. £3.* ✆020 7367 6700. www.southwark.anglican.org.

The site's history is a progression from Roman building to Saxon minster, from Augustinian priory (1106) to parish Church of St Saviour (1540) and, finally, to Cathedral (1905). The name, according to the historian Stow, derived from the convent being endowed with "the profits of a cross-ferry" from which

West front of Southwark Cathedral

Y. Kanazawa/Michelin

the church came to be known as "over the river" or St Mary Overie.

Interior – Immediately to the left is the Gothic arcading of the church, rebuilt after a fire in 1206. Against the west wall at the end of the north aisle are 12 ceiling **bosses** rescued from the 15C wooden roof when it collapsed in 1830: the pelican, heraldic sunflowers and roses, malice, gluttony, falsehood, Judas being swallowed by the devil. The **nave** was rebuilt in neo-Gothic style in 1890–97 to harmonise with the 13C chancel. There are fragments of a Norman arch in the north wall.

The **north transept**, with 13C Purbeck marble shafts set against 12C base walls, includes the allegorical Austin monument of 1633 showing a standing figure, Agriculture, between girls in sun hats asleep in the harvest field; also the reclining figure, with gaunt face of the quack doctor, Lionel Lockyer (1672).

From the nave near the transept crossing there is an uninterrupted view of the intimately proportioned 13C chancel. The Gothic **altar screen** (1520, the statues added in 1905) is sumptuous. Funeral pavement stones commemorate the church burial of Edmund (d. 1607), brother of William Shakespeare, and the Jacobean dramatists, John Fletcher (d. 1625) and Philip Massinger (d. 1640). Adjoining the arch is the **Harvard Chapel,** dedicated to the founder of

Harvard University in the USA. **John Harvard** was born on Borough High Street and baptised in the church in 1607 (emigrated 1638).

The 13C retrochoir is divided into four chapels by piers; from 1540–1617 it served as prison, billet, sty and bakery. In the **south chancel aisle** near the altar is the free-standing tomb of Lancelot Andrewes (d. 1626), Bishop of Winchester. In the **south transept**, mainly 14C and early 15C, with early Perpendicular tracery in the three windows, are to the left, the red painted arms and hat of Cardinal Beaufort, 15C Bishop of Winchester, and on the right, a recumbent effigy of William Emerson (d. 1575), above, John Bingham (d. 1625), saddler to Queen Elizabeth. Note the tessellated paving from a Roman villa at the chancel step. Against the wall of the south aisle is a memorial to Shakespeare.

Visitor Centre – *Access from the north aisle or from the north door into Lancelot's Link.*

Discover the history of the cathedral through artefacts uncovered during excavations and using interactive cameras. A 360 degree view is reflected in a smooth dish.

A 1C Roman road, vestiges of the Norman church, the Medieval priory and 17C–18C pottery kilns can be viewed from the glazed link.

▷ *Pass under London Bridge (⬦see The CITY).*

London Bridge City

The sleek granite surfaces of No **1 London Bridge** are in sharp contrast to **St Olaf House** (Hay's Wharf). The latter is built in Portland stone in Art Deco style; fine gilded faience relief panels designed by Frank Dobson provide a central motif on the Thames front.

Hay's Galleria and City Hall

The original Hay's Dock has been sealed over: the Galleria now boasts a 90ft/27m high glass barrel vault.
Pride of place is given to a monumental kinetic sculpture *The Navigators* by David Kemp. The converted warehouses now house shops, bars and restaurants.

▷ *The walk can continue along the riverside (Queen's Walk).*

Past *HMS Belfast*, opposite the Tower of London, on a site where archaeological excavation has identified the precincts of **Edward II**'s 14C Rosary Palace, sits London's **City Hall**, home of the Mayor's office and Greater London Assembly. Every aspect of this building, designed by **Sir Norman Foster** and partners in the shape of a ten-storey glass dish around a central spiral corridor, was created to be environmentally friendly (⬦*Open to the public Mon–Fri 8am–8pm*).

Borough Market

Y. Kanazawa/Michelin

② BOROUGH

▷ *Start from London Bridge train station main exit by the taxi rank and walk down to the main road.*

Borough High Street

The Borough, kernel of London south of the Thames, is a vibrant area, full of historic street and inn names. It's currently looking a bit neglected as buildings are being demolished to make way for the planned London Quarter Development. Highlights include **Borough Market** (⬦*see box*) and The George Inn (⬦*see Addresses*).

▷ *Turn left into St Thomas Street. Continue past the Old Operating Theatre (⬦see Additional Sights).*

Hay's Galleria

J. Malburet/MICHELIN

Borough Market

8 Stoney St, Borough High St.
⊖*London Bridge.* ℘*020 7407 1002.*
www.boroughmarket.org.uk. Open Thu 11am–5pm, Fri noon–6pm, Sat 8am–5pm.
This huge, old, traditional food market is full of the best organic and farm produce. The place teems with people, fresh fruit & veg, hot takeaway dishes made in front of you, fresh fish, wheatgrass drinks, ciders and lots more!

Guy's Hospital

The complex retains its 18C railings, gateway and forecourt. The court is flanked by brick wings, leading to the centre range with a frontispiece decorated with allegorical figures by Bacon. In the court stands a bronze statue by Scheemakers of Thomas Guy (1644–1724), son of a Southwark lighterman and coal dealer, who began as a bookseller (Bibles), gambled successfully on the South Sea Bubble and then became a patron of medical institutions. In the chapel (centre of the west wing) is a full-size memorial by John Bacon of Guy. In the rear quadrangles are a statue of Lord Nuffield, a 20C philanthropist, and a mid-18C alcove from old London Bridge.

◯ *Return to the High Steet.*

The Yards and the Inns of Southwark

Several narrow streets and yards off Borough High Street, south of St Thomas Street, mark the entrances to the old inns, the overnight stops of people arriving too late at night to cross the bridge into the capital. These inns were also the starting point for coach services to the southern counties and the ports.

King's Head Yard [1]: the King's Head, known as the Pope's Head before the Reformation, now a 19C building, sports a coloured effigy of Henry VIII.

White Hart Yard [2]: the pub (no longer in existence) was the headquarters of Jack Cade in 1450 and where Mr Pickwick first met Sam Weller.

George Inn★ [3] (◯ *see Addresses*): the **George Inn**, when rebuilt in 1676 after a fire, had galleries on three sides, only part of the south range remains. There are tables in the cobbled yard in summer and open fires in winter. Note the Act of Parliament clock constructed in 1797 when a tax of five shillings (25 pence) made people sell their timepieces and rely on clocks in public places; the act was repealed within the year.

Talbot Yard [4]: recalled by **Chaucer** in the Prologue: "At the Tabbard as I lay,

At night was come into that hostelrie Wel nyne and twenty in a compagnye of sondrye folk... and pilgrims were they alle That toward Canterbury wolden ryde."

Queen's Head Yard [5]: site of the Queen's Head (demolished: 1900) sold by John Harvard before he set out for America; Newcomen Street: the **King's Arms** (1890) takes its name from the lion and unicorn supporting the arms of George II (not George III as inscribed), a massive emblem that originally decorated the south gatehouse of old London Bridge (◯ *see Addresses*).

A plaque at no. **163** indicates the first site of **Marshalsea Prison** (1376–1811), the notorious penitentiary of which only one high wall remains on the later site (*no 211*). No. **116** marks the location of the 16C palace of the Duke of Suffolk, who married a daughter of Henry VII.

St George the Martyr

♿◯*Open Sun 10am–4pm, Wed noon– 1.30pm, Thu (except holiday periods) 12.30–2pm. Induction loop. ✆07906 695 571. www.stgeorgethemartyr.com.* The spire and square tower of the 1736 church on a 12C site mark the end of the first section of the High Street. **Dickens** features the church in Little Dorrit, who is commemorated in the east window. The pulpit is the highest in London.

◯ *Continue to the next crossroads and turn left into Trinity Street.*

Trinity Church Square★

The early 19C square is an unbroken quadrilateral of three-storey houses, punctuated by round-arched doorways. The statue in the central garden is known as **King Alfred**, and believed to be the oldest statue in London.

The church (1824) was converted in 1975 into a studio for use by major orchestras.

Merrick Square★

The early 19C square with elegant lamp standards and modest houses is named after the merchant who left the property to the Corporation of Trinity House.

ADDITIONAL SIGHTS
Bankside Gallery

Open daily 11am–6pm, ring in advance as the gallery closes for a few days between exhibitons. 020 7928 7521. www.banksidegallery.com.

The gallery, which opened in 1980, holds regular exhibitions under the aegis of the Royal Societies of Painters in Water Colours (founded 1804) and of Painter-Etchers and Engravers (founded 1881).

Clink Exhibition

1 Clink Street. Open Mon–Fri 10am–6pm, Sat–Sun 10am–9pm. Closed 25–26 Dec. £5. Guided tour, telephone for details. 020 7403 0900. www.clink.co.uk.

Stairs lead down to a basement on the site of the old Clink jail. The exhibition traces the history of imprisonment and torture and of the Bankside brothels.

Old Operating Theatre, Museum and Herb Garret

9A St Thomas's St. Open early Jan–mid-Dec daily 10.30am–5pm. £5.60. 020 7188 2679. www.thegarret.org.uk

The attic of St Thomas's Parish Church was already in use as a herb garret when, in 1821, it was converted into a women's operating theatre for St Thomas's Hospital (see LAMBETH). The theatre pre-dates the advent of anaesthetics and antiseptic surgery. Its semicircular amphitheatre is ringed by five rows of "standings" for students. Below the operating table was a box of sawdust that could "be kicked to the place where most blood was running".

HMS *Belfast*

Open Mar–Oct daily 10am–6pm, Nov–Feb daily 10am–5pm (last admission half an hour before closing). Closed 24–26 Dec. £10.70. Brochure. 020 7940 6300. www.hmsbelfast.iwm.org.uk.

The Royal Navy light cruiser saw service with the Arctic convoys and on D-Day. It is painted in the original "Admiralty disruptive camouflage colours". Seven decks of the ship are on display; the story of the North Atlantic Convoys in World War II is told on film; the Falklands War exhibition retraces the campaign to recover the islands after the Argentine invasion in 1982.

London Dungeon

34 Tooley Street. Open usually daily 9.30am–7pm, however seasonal variations apply. Check on website in advance. Closed 25 Dec. £21.95 on the door (reduced rate for booking a ticket in advance online). Leaflet (3 languages). Refreshments. 0871 360 2049. www.thedungeons.com.

A gruesome (if rather ham-horror) parade of tableaux that relate scenes of death from disease (leprosy and plague), Medieval torture and various types of execution, as well as early surgery. Not suitable for children or anyone with a nervous disposition (the exhibits have a way of "coming alive"!).

Winston Churchill's Britain at War

64 Tooley Street. Open daily 10am–5pm. Closed 24–26 Dec. £11.45. 020 7403 3171. www.britainatwar.co.uk.

An old London Underground lift provides Tardis-like time travel for visitors to an Underground station fitted with bunks, a canteen and tea urn and a WVS lending library. The exhibition continues with displays of war-time fashion, mementoes of rationing, air raids, an Anderson shelter, a refuge room, evacuation, women at work in factories, the life of Sir Winston Churchill and a reconstruction of simulated air raid damage.

Fashion and Textile Museum

83 Bermondsey Street. Open Thu–Sat 11am–6pm, Wed 10am–8.30pm. £5. Café. 020 7407 8664. www.ftmlondon.org.

Founded and run by flamboyant designer Zandra Rhodes at her Bermondsey studio, this museum to fashion has various temporary exhibitions.

Bramah Museum of Tea and Coffee★

40 Southwark Street. ♿🕐*Open daily, 10am-6pm.* 🕐*Closed 25-26 Dec.* 👓*£4; £10 family. Tea room.* 📞*/Fax 020 7403.* *5650. www.teaandcoffeemuseum.co.uk.* Tracing the history of tea and coffee drinking in England, the teapot collection includes the largest ever made.

ADDRESSES

✗ LIGHT BITE

🍴 **Southwark Cathedral Refectory –** *Southwark Cathedral, SE1 9DA. Southwark, SE1 9AD.* 🚇*Southwark.* 📞*020 7407 5470.* Good hearty fare such as soups, stir-frys and pasta dishes that are reasonably priced.

🍴 **Wine Wharf –** *Stoney St, Southwark, SE1 9AD.* 🚇*London Bridge.* 📞*020 7940 8335. www.vinopolis.co.uk.* Light and airy wine bar that is convenient for the Globe Theatre.

🍺 PUBS

George Inn – *77 Borough High St, Southwark, SE1 1NH.* 🚇*London Bridge.* 📞*020 7407 2056.* Part-17C galleried inn with good food.

Kings Arms – *25 Roupell St, SE1 8TB.* 🚇*London Bridge.* 📞*020 7207 0784.* Traditional local pub perfect for a pre-theatre drink (South Bank, National Theatre).

The Anchor – *34 Park St, Bankside, SE1 9EF.* 🚇*London Bridge.* 📞*020 7407 1577. www.theanchorbankside.co.uk.* This 18C tavern is associated with the prison, and also with Shakespeare, Dr Johnson and Boswell, through their friends, who at one time owned it. Large riverside patio with great views.

🍷 BAR

Vinopolis – *1 Bank End, EC1 9BU.* 🚇*London Bridge.* 📞*020 7940 8300. www.vinopolis.co.uk.* An entertaining audio-visual exhibition to find out more about wine-making, with tastings to test what you've learned! Wine tours from £19.50–£32.50.

Battersea

Battersea, on the south bank, has changed beyond measure from a sedate backwater to a desirable residential area for the overspill from Chelsea. The park, which has a boating lake, gardens, playgrounds and an oriental pagoda, hosts funfairs, concerts and the colourful Easter parade. Development of the riverside is well underway, lining the south bank with glamorous and extremely expensive apartment blocks, while the eventual long-delayed redevelopment of the massive power station, a famous riverside landmark, will give a further boost to the district.

A BIT OF HISTORY

Battersea's transformation from a rural town into an industrial town took just

▶ **Location:** *Map: Inside front cover (CDZ).* Overground rail: Battersea Park from Victoria; Queenstown Road from Waterloo. Chelsea is a short hop on foot over Chelsea, Albert or Battersea Bridge. Excellent views of Chelsea Harbour.

100 years. In 1782, 2 160 souls were engaged in cultivating strawberries, asparagus and vegetables for seed; they sent their produce to Westminster: by 1845 the railway had extended to Clapham (originally Battersea) Junction and the population explosion had begun.

Battersea Power Station

©Claudiodivizia/Dreamstime.com

🚶 WALKING TOUR
▷ *Start from Battersea Bridge and turn right into Battersea Church Rd.*

Battersea Bridge
The present construction was designed by Joseph Bazalgette in 1890. Its predecessor, a wooden bridge (1771) lit first by oil lamps (1799) and then by gas (1824), was the inspiration for Whistler's painting entitled *Nocturne*.

Battersea Old Church, St Mary's
♿🕐*Open Tue–Wed 11am–3pm (ask at the Parish Office), or by appointment. Services: Sun 8.30am, 11am, 6.30pm. Guide book (English).* ℘*020 7228 9648.* *www.stmarysbattersea.org.uk.*
Since Saxon times there has been a church well forward at the river bend. The current building with a conical green copper spire dates from 1775 (portico 1823); the 14C east window encloses 17C tracery and painted heraldic glass. Famous people with local connections include **William Blake**, who married here, and **Turner**, who sketched the river from the vestry window and whose chair now stands in the chancel.

▷ *Continue along Vicarage Cres.*

Devonshire House is an early 18C stucco house of three storeys with a Doric porch and small curved iron balconies and **St Mary's House**, a late 17C mansion. **Old Battersea House**

(no **30**) is a two-storey brick mansion built by Sir Walter St John in 1699.

▷ *At the end of Vicarage Cres, turn left into Battersea High St.*

The Raven, with curving Dutch gables, has dominated the crossroads since the 17C. **Sir Walter St John School**, founded in 1700, was rebuilt in the 19C–20C on the original site in Tudor Gothic style. Note the St John motto surmounted by helm and falcon at the entrance.

▷ *Continue to Battersea Sq and take a bus to Albert Bridge Rd.*

Albert Bridge★
The cantilever suspension bridge, which is most attractive when lit up at night, was designed by RW Ordish in 1873; it was modified by Joseph Bazalgette and reinforced with a central support in the 1970s; spare bulbs are stored in the twin tollmen's huts at either end.

▷ *Take a walk through the park.*

Battersea Park
The marshy waste of Battersea Fields, popular in the 16C for pigeon shooting, fairs, donkey racing and duels, had become ill famed by the beginning of the 19C. In 1843 **Thomas Cubitt** proposed that a park be laid out; a bill was passed in 1846 and the site was built up with land excavated from Victoria Docks.

Today the park is one of London's most charming and interesting, with a boating lake, a garden (*accessible to wheelchair users*), sculptures by **Henry Moore** and Barbara Hepworth, an **adventure playground** and **children's zoo**, a deer enclosure, cafés, and many sports facilities. It has a busy programme of events and is the nesting ground of various birds.

The **Japanese Peace Pagoda** (1985) is one of several instituted by a world peace organisation.

The present **Chelsea Bridge** is a suspension bridge dating from 1934.

Marco Polo House, on Queenstown Road, is a bold building that is clad in hi-tech Japanese panels of Neo-Paries and Pilkington glass.

> *Continue south to Battersea Park Rd and turn left.*

Battersea Power Station
Battersea Pk Rd.

This familiar and iconic industrial landmark with its four white chimneys, overlooking the river, was largely built in 1932–34, and completed by Giles Gilbert Scott after World War II. The power station was shut down in 1983 and it has lain dormant ever since, in increasing stages of dereliction. Proposals of what to do with it are put forward periodically – at present there are plans to convert the massive structure and its 31 acre/12ha site into a shopping and entertainment centre, but nothing has been put in motion as yet.

ADDITIONAL SIGHTS
De Morgan Foundation
38 West Hill. Open Tue–Wed 12pm–6pm, Fri–Sat 10am–5pm. 020 8871 1144. www.demorgan.org.uk.

An imposing white brick building houses a collection of ceramics by **William de Morgan,** who was associated with the Arts and Crafts movement, and paintings and drawings by Evelyn de Morgan Spencer Stanhope, JM Strudwick and Cadogan Cowper.

Battersea Dogs' Home
4 Battersea Park Rd. Open Mon–Fri 1–4pm, Sat–Sun 10.30am–4pm. 020 7622 3626. www.battersea.org.uk.

The UK's premier rescue centre for dogs and cats was established in 1860. The number of abandoned dogs and cats brought in to the shelter annually runs into thousands, particularly in the post-Christmas period.

Lambeth

At the start of the 21C, the property boom has made the south bank very desirable, and as young professionals move in, the signs of change are evident all over the district. With its convenient location, a world-class museum, the London Eye and the South Bank Centre (*see SOUTH BANK*), the future is bright as the regeneration of the south bank progresses apace.

A BIT OF HISTORY
In the Middle Ages the public horse-ferry from Westminster landed at Lambeth, and it was here that the Archbishop of Canterbury obtained a parcel of land on

> **Location:** *Map: inside front cover (EFY).* Lambeth North. This district, wedged between Southwark and Battersea, is the gateway to the southern suburbs and to Kent and Surrey.
>
> **Don't Miss:** The view of the Palace of Westminster from across the River.
>
> **Timing:** Allow 3hr including a tour of the War Museum.

which he built himself a London seat: **Lambeth Palace.** In the mid-18C the building of Westminster Bridge and of

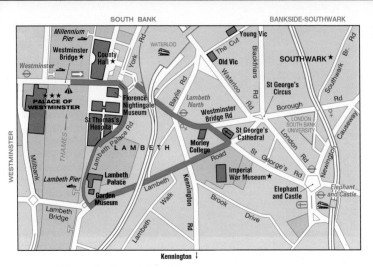

new roads brought about industrial development such as timber yards, dye works, potteries and lime kilns, and the Coade Stone factory.

The population increased and in the early 19C there arose prisons, welfare institutions and asylums. There were also louche taverns and pleasure gardens, which gave the area a dubious reputation. In the late 19C and early 20C St Thomas's Hospital and the **Imperial War Museum** (*see MAJOR CENTRAL LONDON MUSEUMS*) were established and changed the character of this proletarian area.

To the south the streets of Kennington are lined with elegant Georgian houses and terraces and Victorian houses and bay window cottages.

Lambeth Walk, formerly the centre of Old Lambeth, is now lined with grass verges and modern flats. **The Oval**, a famous cricket ground, was a former market garden.

⚓ WALKING TOUR

▷ *From Westminster Bridge (see WESTMINSTER) take Lambeth Palace Rd to the right. For the Florence Nightingale Museum see Sights.*

The red and white buildings of **St Thomas's Hospital** have scarcely changed in outward appearance since being built in 1868–71, in spite of a few 7–14 storeyed buildings dating

St George's Circus

The circus, now a forlorn roundabout, was laid out in 1769 by act of parliament as London's first designed traffic junction, with an obelisk to **Brass Crosby** marking the central island. Five (now six) roads converged at the centre of St George's Fields, long an open area crossed by rough roads where rebels had assembled (the Gordon Rioters), cattle grazed, a windmill turned, preachers roused crowds.

from the 1970s. The **13C Infirmary**, set up in Southwark and dedicated to St **Thomas Becket**, evolved into a hospital endowed by **Dick Whittington** with a lying-in ward for unmarried mothers.

In the 16C it was forfeited, as a conventual establishment, to Henry VIII and closed, only to be rescued in 1552 by the City, which purchased it and re-dedicated it to Thomas the Apostle (Thomas Becket having been decanonised).

The story since is one of expansion, of removal to Lambeth in the 19C, of research and development, of the foundation of the Nightingale Fund Training School for Nurses, and of ten aerial attacks between September 1940 and July 1944, when at least one operating theatre was always open.

The Garden Museum

©Gavin Kingcome/The Garden Museum

Just south of the hospital is **Lambeth Palace**, the London residence of the Archbisop of Canterbury, head of the Anglican (episcopalian) church worldwide. The Medieval red-brick building, boasts an impressive **Great Hall** with hammerbeam roof. The magnificent gateway dates from 1490. Archbishop's Park to the northeast, formerly part of the palace grounds, provides a good view of the palace.

▷ *Walk past the Museum of Garden History and turn left into Lambeth Rd passing the Imperial War Museum.*

St George's Roman Catholic Cathedral

St George's Road. ♿⚲Open daily, 7.30am–7pm. ⚲Guided tour by appointment. Brochure. ☏020 7928 5256. www.southwark-rc-cathedral.org.uk.
The mid-19C cathedral was designed by **AW Pugin** (1812–52), the impassioned advocate of the Gothic Revival. Destroyed by incendiary bombs during World War II, it was rebuilt and reopened in 1958. The **interior** of the new cathedral with an added clerestory is much lighter than the old: fluted columns of white Painswick stone support high pointed arches; plain glass lights the aisles, the only elaborate windows being those at the east and west ends. The new building's sole ornate feature is the high altar with its carved and gilded reredos; statues are modern in uncoloured stone.

Westminster Bridge Road was developed in 1750 when the bridge was built. Note the white spire encircled by red brick bands of Christchurch, built in 1874 with funds from the USA.
On the right is **Waterloo International**, which, in November 2007, after 13 years, gave up its role as the Eurostar Terminal in favour of St Pancras International.

SIGHTS
Florence Nightingale Museum
St Thomas's Hospital, 2 Lambeth Palace Road. ♿⚲Open Mon–Fri 10am–5pm (last admission 4pm). ⚲Closed Good Fri, Easter Sun, 24 Dec–2 Jan. ⚲£5.80. Film (20min). Refreshments. ☏020 7620 0374. www.florence-nightingale.co.uk.
The work of Florence Nightingale (1820–1910), nicknamed the "Lady of the Lamp" by the British soldiers she nursed in Istanbul during the Crimean War (1854–56), has become legendary in pioneering healthcare. Photographs and written panels are supplemented by various personal exhibits, including her medicine chest and copies of her many publications on nursing.

The Garden Museum
Lambeth Palace Road. ♿⚲Open Feb–mid-Dec Tue–Sun 10.30am–5pm. Exhibitions, lectures, courses, outings. ⚲£6. Café. Shop. ☏020 7401 8865. www.gardenmuseum.org.uk
The Garden Museum (formerly the Museum of Garden History) was

founded by the **Tradescant Trust** (1977) in the redundant church of St Mary-at-Lambeth.

The church's graveyard contains the graves of the two John Tradescants, father and son, royal gardeners and importers of exotic plants, who planted the first physic garden in 1628 at their house in Lambeth. The centrepiece in the churchyard is a garden, including a knot garden, created with 17C plants. There is an exhibition of historic garden tools. Lawrence Lee designed the window depicting Adam and Eve and the Tradescants. At their house they also exhibited a collection of "all things strange and rare", which later, under

their neighbour, Elias Ashmole, formed the nucleus of the Ashmolean Museum in Oxford.

ADDRESSES

🍴 PUB

The Waterloo Fire Station – *150 Waterloo Rd, SE1 8SB.* ⊖*Waterloo.* ✆*20 7620 2226.*
This huge scarlet pub in a converted fire station is a lively local institution, which is absolutely packed in the evening. It offers a good selection of beers and wines and there is a restaurant at the rear.

South Bank★★★

Amble along the riverside for classic views of Westminster and live music, then stop for a drink in one of the many restaurants or bars in the modernist environs. Next, browse the second-hand book stalls under Waterloo Bridge, take in a show at the National Theatre, enjoy a concert at the Royal Festival Hall, settle down to some classic cinema at the British Film Theatre or enjoy an exhibition at the Hayward – the choice is yours! The new image of the South Bank as a tourist hot spot is borne out by the crowds of visitors thronging to the attractions built to mark the third millennium. It is a success story that has been enhanced by the complete transformation of the Hungerford Bridge (rail and pedestrian access from the Embankment and Charing Cross) and the ongoing revitalisation of the South Bank complex as London's second home for the arts.

A BIT OF HISTORY

The area on the south bank remained rural until the construction of Westminster and Blackfriars Bridges and their approach roads in the mid-18C. The evolution of public transport developed

▶ **Location:** *Map: Inside covers (EFY).* ⊖*Waterloo; Westminster.* The area known as the South Bank lies opposite Westminster and Charing Cross and past Waterloo Bridge to Blackfriars. The Queen's Walk starting from Westminster Bridge to Southwark, Tower Bridge and Bermondsey runs past most of the attractions of the South Bank. There are several piers for those arriving by boat.

🕐 **Timing:** Allow an afternoon to stroll along the riverside walk, admiring the views and taking a ride in one of the London Eye's glass pods.

👥 **Kids:** The London Eye, one of the most popular attractions in the City *(book in advance)* and the London Aquarium in County Hall.

the area, which finally became a suburb where squares and terraces were erected by **Thomas Cubitt** and lesser men between the major roads.

Benefiting from an ample workforce and easy transport by river, and later by railway, this area has boasted a long list of **industrial works** and plants including the Vauxhall Plate Glass Works (1665–1780), the Coade Stone Factory (18C), Doultons, lead-shot foundries (a shot tower stood at the centre of the 1951 Festival of Britain), as well as vinegar, basket, brush factories, boat yards, breweries, distillers, specialist workshops and potteries, including one producing Lambeth delft.

Bombing during World War II devastated acres of Victorian streets, slums, the Lambeth Walk and factories, making it possible for the authorities to rebuild on a vast scale.

⚫ WALKING TOUR

○ *Start from Westminster Bridge (see description in WESTMINSTER).*

The **South Bank Lion** (13ft/4m long, 12ft/3.6m high), carved out of Coade stone, gazes speculatively from a plinth at the foot of Westminster Bridge. Painted red, it was the mascot in the 19C of the Lion Brewery until placed at the bridgefoot in 1952.

County Hall★

Belvedere Road.
County Hall was the headquarters of the Greater London Council until 1986. It now houses two hotels, some flats, a few restaurants and tourist attractions.
The hall, a colonnaded arc 700ft/213m in diameter, built in 1908, is still one of London's most distinctive buildings. It now houses the **London Aquarium**★ (*see Additional Sights*) as well as an amusement arcade with the latest electronic games and a **Dalí Universe** exhibition (*see Additional Sights*).

👥 London Eye★

♿ ⏱Open Oct–May daily 10am–8pm, Jun and Sept 10am–9pm (Jul–Aug 9.30pm). ⏱Closed 25 Dec and 1 week in Jan. ∞£15.50; fast track £25. Private capsules, champagne flights and even weddings possible. Discounted tickets for a variety of London attractions when

View from Waterloo Bridge - London Eye, Festival Pier and Hungerford Bridge and Palace of Westminster in the background

Y. Kanazawa/Michelin

bought with a ticket for the Eye. Timed tickets. Advance booking essential in high season and recommended at other times. ℘0870 5000 600; 0870 990 8886 (group bookings). www.londoneye.com.
The giant wheel, a triumph of engineering, is a spectacular addition to the landscape of the Thames and one of London's favourite tourist attractions. Designed by husband and wife architects David Marks and Julia Barfield, it is 200 times the size of the average racing bike wheel and, at 443ft/135m high (twice the height of the Prater in Vienna), it is the largest observation wheel ever built and the only cantilevered structure of its kind in the world. Criticisms that it overshadowed the Houses of Parliament have long since been silenced.
Accommodated in closed pods, sightseers (trip 30min), enjoy unparalleled **views**★★★ of London extending 25mi/40km in all directions on a clear

4D Experience at the London Eye

A new attraction opened in August 2009 at the London Eye: the 4D Experience. Wearing 3D glasses, visitors watch a four-minute-long 3D film while experiencing a fourth dimension created by in-theatre effects. These include wind, snow, rain, mist and bubbles.

day, as the wheel rotates to its apex. The glass pods were specially designed to twist with the wheel and allow a 360 degree view at all times. There are also river trips from the pier at the foot of the Eye and regular photographic exhibitions in the office area.

The **Jubilee Gardens**, on the site of the 1951 Festival, were opened in 1977 to celebrate the 25th anniversary of the Queen's accession. The whole area is currently being redeveloped into a first-class park (www.jubileegardens. org.uk).

Southbank Centre★

After the war, the LCC, under Herbert Morrison, cleared bomb-damage debris from the riverside to make way for the 1951 Festival of Britain and a future arts centre. The different parts of the arts complex are connected by elevated walkways (shown in grey on plan).

The riverfront is a lively area for tourists and locals, filled with walkways, shops, bars, restaurants and cafés. Refurbishment of the 1960s arts centres themselves is underway.

Royal Festival Hall★ – The building was planned by the architects Sir Leslie Martin and Sir Robert Matthew, who worked, it was said, from the inside. Design began with the hall: its acoustics, the visibility of the stage capable of holding a choir of 250, comfortable seating for an audience of 3 000 – in that order.

They succeeded both aesthetically and practically in the design of foyers, staircases, concourses, bars and restaurants, managing the space to avoid crowding, and afford views of the river and inner perspectives of the building itself; finally the whole edifice was insulated against noise from nearby Waterloo Station. In 1954 an organ was installed. It now ranks amongst the greatest concert halls in the world. In 1962–65 the river frontage was redesigned to include the main entrance and faced with Portland stone. There are refreshment facilities, book and record shops in the foyer.

The Festival Hall (refurbished with improved acoustics) was reopened 8 June 2007.

Queen Elizabeth Hall and Purcell Room – In 1967 a second smaller concert venue with seating for 1 100 was opened with a third, the Purcell Room, providing a recital room for 370. The exterior is in unfaced concrete; the interior acoustics are superb.

▷ *Go down the east side of the hall, then walk around the Shell Centre.*

BFI IMAX – ℘0870 787 2525. www.bfi. org.uk. The circular structure, run by the British Film Institute, houses a state-of-the-art cinema screening 2D and 3D films. The auditorium has 485 seats, including premium seats. Be prepared for exciting adventures as the camera explores distant horizons and new worlds!

▷ *Return to the riverbank.*

BFI Southbank (formerly known as the National Film Theatre) comprises four auditoriums: NFT1 (450 seats), NFT2 (162 seats), NFT3 (134 seats) and a studio (38 seats). It is one of the world's leading cinémathèques and organises the Times BFI London Film Festival in November each year.

In front of the **National Theatre** stands a statue of Sir Lawrence Olivier as Hamlet, unveiled in September 2007.

The sleek, five-arched concrete structure of **Waterloo Bridge**, faced in Portland stone was designed by GG Scott in 1945; it replaced the original by Rennie that was opened on the second anniversary of the **Battle of Waterloo** (18 June 1817).

On the waterfront is lively **Gabriel's Wharf**, a workplace for craftspeople, which has evolved alongside the gardens and low-cost housing of the Coin Street development (open Tue–Sun 11am–6pm (later bars and restaurants); ℘020 7401 2255; www.coinstreet.org).

Bernie Spain Gardens is a pleasant sunken green space from which to enjoy

The Festival of Britain

The theme *The Land and the People* was presented in pavilions designed in new contemporary styles and materials by a team of young and untried architects and embellished by sculptors and painters. The small site (27 acres/11ha) on the South Bank was dominated by the Skylon, a cigar-shaped vertical feature which appeared to float in mid-air, and the Dome of Discovery (diameter 365ft/111m), a circular pavilion made of steel and aluminium. In 1951, between May and September, 8.5 million people visited the Festival where they learned about British achievement in arts, sciences and industrial design and enjoyed themselves at the **Pleasure Gardens** in Battersea Park: fireworks, Music Hall shows, a vast single pole tent as a dance pavilion, sticks of Festival rock, the tree walk, the crazy Emmett railway and a Mississippi Showboat on the river.

the ever-changing spectacle on the river and the north bank.

Stamford Wharf is marked by the **OXO tower**, a former beef-extract factory and now housing restaurants and designer studios. The **Bargehouse** houses temporary off-beat exhibitions.

ADDITIONAL SIGHTS
Royal National Theatre★★

✕&⌖*Guided backstage tour daily (75min).* ⊛*£5.90. Booking in advance by telephone or in person at the Lyttelton Information Desk (9.30am–11pm). 'Platforms' (early evening discussions, readings, interviews, debates: 45min) as advertised. Bookshop. Restaurant. Cafés. Bars. Free concerts and performances in Lyttelton foyer.* ℘*020 7452 3000. www.nationaltheatre.org.uk.*

The architect **Denys Lasdun** has incorporated three theatres: the Lyttelton, with proscenium stage and seating for 890; the Olivier, with large open stage and audience capacity of 1 100; and the Cottesloe, a studio theatre with a maximum of 400 seats; workshops, bookshops, bars and buffets, within a spacious construction featuring strata-like cantilevered terraces which 'release' the beautiful view of Somerset House and St Paul's beyond.

The theatre provides superb performance spaces and the National Theatre company, founded by Sir Lawrence Olivier in 1963, is quite simply magnificent with the world's greatest theatrical stars from Dame Judi Dench to Sir Michael Gambon regularly on stage in a varied repertoire including works by Shakespeare, Ibsen, Alan Bennett, Mike Leigh and a host of new writers. Prices are reasonable.

National Theatre

Stephen Cummiskey/National Theatre

♁♁ London Aquarium★

In County Hall, Belvedere Road. ⊙*Open Mon–Fri 10am–6pm (5pm last admission), Sat–Sun 10am–7pm.* ⊙*Closed 25 Dec, reduced hours over Christmas and New Year period.* ⊛*£8.25.* ℘*020 7967 8000. www.londonaquarium.co.uk.*

"A fish cathedral", a monumental aquarium has been built in the basement of the County Hall, reaching two floors below the Thames water level. Highlights include moon jellyfish and friendly rays which come up to have their chins tickled by the children. Plenty of activities for children in school holidays. Directly opposite the Aquarium, across Westminster Bridge on the north side of the river is Westminster Pier, from which boat trips run frequently down river to the **Thames Barrier** at Woolwich (*www. westminsterpier.co.uk*).The stunning, futuristic barrier, with its distinctive stainless steel cowls, was constructed in 1972–82 to protect Central London from the threat of a surge tide.

Dalí Universe Exhibition/ County Hall Gallery

Open Sat–Thu 9.30am–6.30pm, Fri and bank holidays 9.30am–7pm. Closed 25 Dec. £11. *0870 744 7485. www.daliuniverse.com.*
Dedicated to the Spanish Surrealist artist who worked in diverse artistic media and techniques. The fascinating exhibits provide an insight into his creative genius range from sculpture, graphics, jewellery to furniture and watercolours. There is also a collection of small and little-known works by Picasso, while the County Hall Gallery holds regular exhibitions of modern work.

Hayward Gallery

Open daily 10am–6pm (Fri–Sat 10pm). £7 Café/bar. Shop. *0803 800 400. www.haywardgallery.org.uk.*
The gallery, purpose-built to house major temporary exhibitions of painting and sculpture, was opened in 1968. The building, a terrace-like structure of concrete 'works' successfully to provide five large gallery spaces and three open-air sculpture courts on two levels.

ADDRESSES

⚒ LIGHT BITE

Archduke Wine Bar – *Concert Hall Approach, SE1 8XU.* Waterloo. *020 7928 9370. www.thearchduke.co.uk. Closed Sun.* Friendly, welcoming wine bar, well placed for the **South Bank Centre**★, offering everything from salads and sandwiches to hot dishes. Cool jazz in the evenings adds to the atmosphere.

Konditor & Cook – *22 Cornwall Road, Southwark, SE1 8TW.* Southwark. *020 7261 0456. www.konditorand cook.co.uk. Closed Sun.* Photographs from past performances at the adjacent Young Vic line the walls of this unpretentious cafe. You can choose homemade cakes and pastries or soups and salads and vegetarian dishes.

Pizza Express – *The White House, 9A Belvedere Rd, SE1 8YP.* Waterloo. *020 7928 4091.* The Pizza Express chain is consistently good, with light, thin based pizzas and a great choice of toppings. Great atmosphere and décor; very good pit stops for the hungry.

Skylon – *South Bank Centre, Belvedere Rd, SE1 8XX.* Waterloo. *020 7654 7800. www.skylonrestaurant.co.uk.*
Amazing panorama of river views and London Skyline at this fine-dining restaurant, part of the Royal Festival Hall. Good central cocktail bar for a casual drink.

Yo! Sushi – *Unit 3B, County Hall, Belvedere Rd, SE1 7GP.* Waterloo. *020 7928 8871. www.yosushi.com.* Sit and watch the conveyor belt slip past you, and pick off the dishes you want. There's a trendy vibe to the restaurants in the chain, with funky music and with the waiting staff. Good choice of dishes.

🍺 PUBS

White Hart – *29 Cornwall Rd, SE1 8TJ.* Waterloo. *020 7401 7151.* Transformed from a decrepit back street pub to a smart venue, this is worth searching out, with its comfortable décor of sofas and benches, curtains and candles. Good light dishes, and buzzing atmosphere.

Anchor & Hope – *36 The Cut, SE1 8LP.* Waterloo, Southwark. *020 7928 9898. Closed Sun.* Lots of people crowding into this great pub means there's a real buzz here. Along with the chatter, you get excellent food that has won awards for modern British dishes like duck heart on toast! Save room for the desserts.

*British Museum, Imperial War Museum, National Gallery,
Natural History Museum, Science Museum, Tate Britain,
Tate Modern, Victoria & Albert Museum, Wallace Collection.*

From ancient to innovative, grand to eclectic, London's museum and gallery culture is world class. Start with the largest, such as the British, Victoria & Albert, Science, Natural History Museums and National Gallery, for a taste of the sheer scale and quality of the national collections. The modern world gets a lively take with Tate Modern's displays of contemporary art, while the Science Museum takes a cutting-edge look at the scientific discoveries and questions of our age.

Highlights

1 Mummies and ancient Greek marbles at **The British Museum** (p282)

2 The IMAX at the **Science Museum** (p302)

3 Contemporary installations in the Turbine Hall at **Tate Modern** (p308)

4 The Blitz Experience at the **Imperial War Museum** (p286)

5 The Tudor Galleries at the **National Portrait Gallery** (p293)

Finding the Museums – South Kensington *(www.exhibitionroad.com)* and Bloomsbury *(www.museum-mile.org.uk)* are both notable for the density of museums and galleries in these areas. South Kensington has the three giants, the **Victoria and Albert Museum** (popularly known as the V&A), **Science Museum** and **Natural History Museum**, all within a two-minute walk of each other. Elsewhere, the **National Gallery** and **National Portrait Gallery** are adjacent at Trafalgar Square; the **British Museum** occupies a large site further north in Bloomsbury; the **Wallace Collection** stands facing a leafy residential square in Marylebone, close to Oxford Street; and **Tate Britain** is located in Pimlico, adjacent to Victoria. South of the river, the **Imperial War Museum** and **Tate Modern** are a 20-minute walk from each other, in the areas of Lambeth and Bankside respectively.

Origins of the Collections – The roots of many of London's collections lie in the bequests of private collections from 18C and 19C collectors, including Henry Tate (Tate Britain), Sir Hans Soane (Natural History Museum and British Museum) and Richard Wallace (The Wallace Collection). Others have evolved through necessity or resourcefulness; the V&A was originally built to house the works created for the 1851 Great Exhibition, while in the 20C, the Tate turned a former power station in Bankside into the outstandingly successful display space for contemporary art that is the Tate Modern.

Visiting – With so many museums and galleries to visit in London, you'll be hard pressed to see even a fraction in a typical visit. The national museums have vast permanent collections, constantly invigorated by innovative temporary exhibitions – such as the Science Museum's *Cosmos and Culture* exhibition *(until end 2010)* – and by exhibitions showcasing a part of cultural or historical achievement, thereby shedding new light and debate on a subject. Many major museums and galleries are subsidised and free to visit, carrying on an ingrained tradition of culture; however, donations are appreciated.

For further information on Museums in London, www.culture24.org.uk is an excellent source.

British Museum★★★

The British Museum is undoubtedly one of the finest institutions of the genre, and its treasures represent a vast canvas of the history of civilisation. It is an uplifting experience to view the rare artefacts, which reveal the ingenuity of man from early beginnings to the present day.

A BIT OF HISTORY

Foundation – The final spur to found the British Museum was supplied in 1753 when **Sir Hans Sloane**, the famous naturalist, bequeathed his collection to the nation. Parliament had already stored in vaults in Westminster a priceless collection of medieval manuscripts acquired in 1700. Elsewhere, there were documents collected by the Earls of Oxford, which were made available, and the old Royal Library was added by George II. A lottery raised the money for the purchase of Montagu House, which opened in 1759.

Collections – Important acquisitions include: Sir William Hamilton's collection of antique vases (1772); Egyptian antiquities, including the **Rosetta Stone** (1802, *see p283*); the Townley Vase (1805); and the **Elgin Marbles** (1816, *see p279*).

▷ **Location:** *Map: inside front cover (EX) and area map under* BLOOMSBURY; ⊖*Tottenham Court Road; Russell Square; Holborn.* The main entrance is on the south side off Great Russell Street; the Montague Place entrance is on the north side of the building.

⊘ **Don't Miss:** The Rosetta Stone; the Egyptian Mummies; the Parthenon frieze; the Portland Vase; the Easter Island Statue; the Lewis Chessmen.

◷ **Timing:** Allow half a day for the must-sees across the entire museum. Obtain a floor plan at the Information desk located in the Great Court. Time permitting, join a 40- or 90min guided tour.

⚄ **Kids:** Hands-on desks in 6 galleries; Free Hamlyn family trails; Ford activity backpacks; the Samsung Digital Discovery Centre located on the lower require booking); a Family Audio Tour, narrated by actor Stephen Fry.

Great Court, British Museum

Y. Kanazawa/Michelin

In 1823, George IV presented his father's library of 65 000 volumes, 19 000 pamphlets, maps and charts; in 1824 came the Payne-Knight bequest of Classical antiquities, bronzes and drawings; in 1827 Banks' bequest of books, botanical specimens and ethnography.

Accommodation – In 1824 **Robert Smirke** was appointed to produce plans for a more permanent building that would replace the decayed Montagu House. The new building, with a Greek-inspired colonnaded façade surrounding the Great Court, was completed 20 years later. The Reading Room was added, at the centre of the Great Court in 1857; the natural history departments were transferred to the new Natural History Museum in South Kensington in 1880–83; the Edward VII Galleries were added in 1914; the Duveen Galleries in 1938. Further extensions were built in 1978 and 1991. In 1991 the British Library was moved to new, purpose-built premises in St Pancras (⌖ See ST PANCRAS – CAMDEN TOWN) prompting a massive redevelopment of the museum.

VISIT

Great Russell Street. ♿✕🕐*Open daily 10am–5.30pm (a small selection of galleries are open until 8.30pm Thu and Fri).* 🕐*Closed 1 Jan, 24–26 Dec.* ✎*No charge for main galleries.* ☞*Guided tour (90min) of the highlights (☞£8).* ✆020 7323 8181. *eyeOpener gallery tours (30–40min) and talks available for free. Audioguide (9 languages,* ☞£3.50).

Restaurant, café, shops. Wheelchairs available for hire (✆*020 7323 8299).* ✆*020 7323 8181. www.britishmuseum.org.*

Great Court

The Great Court was an open, rather gloomy courtyard, filled with a huddle of uninspiring buildings until 2000, when the Museum's Millennium project roofed over the Great Court to create the largest covered square in Europe. Its soaring glass-and-steel roof, spanning the space to the Reading Room, is an architectural marvel, designed by Sir Norman Foster. Sculptures displayed in the public areas introduce the great civilisations and the court has become the hub of the museum with cafés, information desks, several shops and a restaurant.

Reading Room

The circular **Reading Room** (1857) was designed to occupy the originally gloomy courtyard at the centre of the building. It was built by the architect **Sydney Smirke**, who used a sketch by librarian Antonio Panizzi. The Reading Room, with its splendid blue-and-gold dome, was restored in 1997. Currently the Reading Room houses world-class temporary exhibitions.

The King's Library

▷ *Room 1, on the Great Court's east wall.*

Built in 1827 to house the personal library of King George III, the King's Library now houses the exhibition *Enlightenment: Discovering the World*

Young visitors looking at Parthenon (Elgin) Marbles

C. Ochterbeck/MICHELIN

in the 18th Century. Works highlight the seven disciplines of the age: natural history, archaeology, decipherment, art history, ethnography, religion and even the surprisingly interesting art of classification.

THE CLASSICAL COLLECTIONS
Ancient Greece and Rome
Prehistoric to Archaic Greece –
A distinctive civilisation flourished in the Cycladic Islands around 3200–1500 BC, which is characterised by marble figurines usually found in graves.

The influence of Minoan Crete spread throughout the Aegean in the Middle Bronze Age *(12)* including the **Aigina Treasure**, which includes an elaborate gold pendant of a nature god. Early Greek vases *(13)* displayed narrative scenes drawn from mythology with geometric and 'orientalising' motifs. Later, red-figured vases *(14)* from Athens depicted daily life and mythology.

5C BC – The bronze head of Apollo *(15)*, known as the **Chatsworth Head**, is a rare Classical statue. The **Temple of Apollo Epikourios** *(16)* depicts a lively battle between the Greeks and Amazons and the Lapiths and Centaurs (420–400 BC) and the reconstructed **Nereid Monument** *(17)* from Xantos in south-west Turkey has noted elegance.

The Parthenon Galleries *(18)* display the famous **Parthenon (Elgin) Marbles**, a collection of classical Greek marble sculptures and inscriptions, which are deemed to be the culmination of Hellenistic art from the 5C BC and which celebrate Athenian power and wealth. The taking of these treasures for display in Britain (1801–12) has always been hotly disputed and in mid-2009, days before the opening of the new Acropolis Museum in Athens, a major dispute erupted over "ownership" when the Athens museum asserted its right to house the artefacts, which came from Greece in the first place. The row was serious enough to involve the Queen and the Duke of Edinburgh (Greek-born)! At time of writing, a resolution had not been reached.

The **Caryatid Room** *(19)* displays sculptures from the Acropolis in Athens (430–400 BC).

4C BC – The **Payava Tomb** from Lycian Xantos (c. 360 BC) *(20)*, on the Mediterranean coast of Turkey, is typical of the local style of funerary monuments. The **Mausoleum of Halikarnassos** *(21)*, one of the Seven Wonders of the World, is the origination of the noun "mausoleum". Admire also the sculpted column *(22)* from the **Temple of Artemis at Ephesos** with striking figured decoration.

Hellenistic art *(23)* is highly theatrical and stresses individual traits; note the sensuous marble statue of Aphrodite.

Greek and Roman architecture and sculpture are displayed in the lower floor galleries reached from *room 21*.

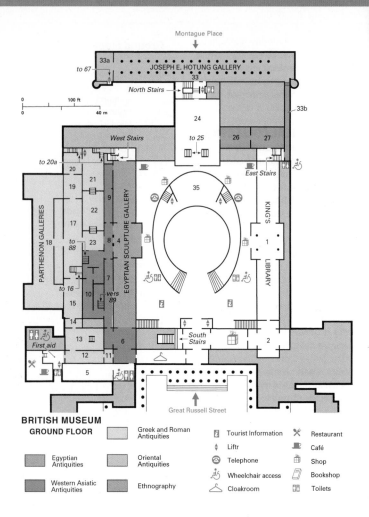

Montague Place

33a
to 67
JOSEPH E. HOTUNG GALLERY
33
North Stairs
33b

0   100 ft
0   40 m

24
to 25
26   27

West Stairs
to 20a
20
19   21
9   35
22
17
18   to   23
88   8   4
7
to 16
10   vers
89
15
14
13   5   6
First aid
12   11
5

PARTHENON GALLERIES

EGYPTIAN SCULPTURE GALLERY

KING'S LIBRARY

East Stairs

1

2

South Stairs

Great Russell Street

**BRITISH MUSEUM
GROUND FLOOR**

Greek and Roman Antiquities

Egyptian Antiquities

Oriental Antiquities

Western Asiatic Antiquities

Ethnography

Tourist Information
Liftr
Telephone
Wheelchair access
Cloakroom

Restaurant
Café
Shop
Bookshop
Toilets

Fragments of ancient Greek and Roman buildings abound *(77)* and inscriptions *(78)*, while *room 82* is mainly dedicated to fragments of the Temple of Artemis of Ephesos.

Rooms 83–84 contain a wealth of Roman sculpture, including the **Townley Vase**. *Room 85* houses Roman portrait sculptures (◦— *rooms 82–85 are closed until further notice*). *Room 69* illustrates Greek and Roman daily life.

▶ *South stairs to the Upper floor.*

Imperial Rome *(70)*

This room spans over a thousand years of Roman history. The bronze **Head of Augustus** is remarkable. Take note of the intentional mutilation on the **Basalt bust of Germanicus**. The **Portland Vase** is a famous cameo-glass vessel.

Pre-Roman Empire Italy *(71)*

The sophistication of the Etruscan world is illustrated by black lustrous ware known as *bucchero*.

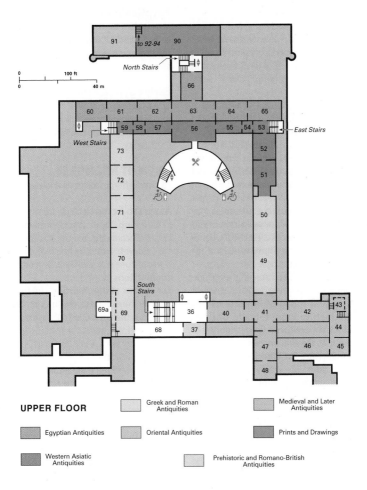

UPPER FLOOR

Greek and Roman Antiquities

Medieval and Later Antiquities

Egyptian Antiquities

Oriental Antiquities

Prints and Drawings

Western Asiatic Antiquities

Prehistoric and Romano-British Antiquities

Cypriot Antiquities *(72)*
A rich collection of artefacts illustrates Cypriot civilisation up until the end of the Roman period: sculptures, gold jewellery and ceramics.

Greek Influences *(73)*
Greek cities established colonies in southern Italy, evidenced by the fine red-figured bowls, bronze figurines (fine bronze horseman c. 550 BC) and funerary artefacts.

COINS AND MEDALS
Room 68 illustrates the development of money and its importance from early 3C BC Aes ingots, 4C Raffia cloth currency to today's plastic cards.

PREHISTORY AND ROMAN BRITAIN
Prehistoric to Celtic Britain
In the Early Bronze Age *(51)* fine pottery with geometric patterns contained rich grave goods in burials such as the **Folkton Drums**.
Celtic art flourished in the Iron Age *(50)*. Note the elegant **Basse-Yutz wine-flagons** (c. 400 BC) from France.

Roman Britain (49)

Highlights include the **Mildenhall Treasure** and the **Hoxne Hoard**, which comprises thousands of coins, jewellery and silver plate, two of the finest treasure troves found in Britain.

MEDIEVAL, RENAISSANCE AND MODERN COLLECTIONS FOREIGN INFLUENCES

Among Anglo-Saxon and Norman antiquities (4C–11C) found in the British Isles (41) is the **Sutton Hoo Ship Burial**, which shows the rich variety of artefacts retrieved from a royal tomb in Suffolk. The mid-12C **Lewis Chessmen** (40), thought to be Scandinavian in origin, consist of 80 pieces carved from walrus ivory; they were found in 1831 in the Outer Hebrides.

Clocks, watches and precision regulators (38–9) trace the evolution of mechanical timekeeping highlighted by the fascinating Prague-made **Galleon Clock** (c. 1585) with figures moving to music as the ship pitches and rolls, and a firing gun. The **Waddesdon Bequest** (45) includes a reliquary for a thorn from Christ's crown made for the Duc de Berry (c. 1400–10).

European Applied Arts

A glittering array (46) illustrates the craft of goldsmithing from 1400–1800: the **Armada Service**, a silver dinner set from the Tudor period; Limoges and Battersea enamels; and Huguenot silver. The 19C (47) is represented by European ceramics such as The **Pegasus Vase**. The Modern Gallery (48) is dedicated to decorative arts of the 20C: examples are continuosly acquired and include work by Marianne Brandt and Eliel Saarinen.

EGYPTIAN ANTIQUITIES

▶ *Start on the Ground floor.*

Egyptian Sculpture Gallery (4)

Pride of place is given to the **Rosetta Stone** (⚫ *see sidebar*). The monumental sculptures are of great historical interest, primarily the enigmatic colossal head of Amenhotep III (c. 1350 BC). The granite bust of Ramesses II (c. 1250 BC) exudes power.

Egyptian Tombs (62–3, Upper floor)

Mummies bandaged in cases and coffins, gilded and painted, include the preserved remains of humans and animals.

Early Egypt & Ethiopia (64–6)

These galleries explore Egypt's relationship with neighbouring Nubia and the introduction of Coptic Orthodox Christianity.

ANCIENT NEAR EAST

▶ *Turn left from the main entrance.*

Assyrian Sculpture (6–10)

Fabled kings built splendid palaces lavishly decorated in Nimrud, Khorsabad and Nineveh. Note the five feet of the Colossal stone statues of human-headed **winged lions** (6).

The **friezes of lion hunting** (10) from the Northern Palace of Nineveh are striking in their depictions of an ancient royal sport.

Arabic World

Antiquities from the Islamic collections range from decorative pottery, carved and mosaic glass carved to inlaid and engraved metalwork. Admire the colourful Damascus and Iznik ceramics (34) and the Damascene geomantic instrument. The South Arabian territories (North and South Yemen) prospered along an important incense trading route. Alabaster sculptures and calcite incense burners are on display (53).

Ancient Iran (52)

The fabulous **Oxus Treasure** (5C–4C BC) attests to the wealth and sophistication of the Achaemenid court. The **Cyrus cylinder** from Persepolis (539–530 BC) records the declaration of the reforms promised by King Cyrus.

Ancient Turkey and Iraq (54)

Antiquities (5500–300 BC) of Anatolia reveal Assyrian influence: note in particular the bronze figure of a winged bull from Urartu.

An Important Find

The **Rosetta Stone** is part of a 6ft (1.8m) block of black basalt found at Rashid, or Rosetta, in the western Egyptian Delta region and retrieved by French soldiers on campaign there during the Napoleonic wars. With the Capitulation of Alexandria in 1801, the French were compelled to surrender the stone to the British, which went on show at the British Museum in 1802. Its significance rests in the parallel transcriptions in Ancient Greek and two written forms of Egyptian of a decree passed on 27 March 196 BC: thereby the French Egyptologist, Champollion, was able to decipher pictorial hieroglyphs in use since the third millennium BC and the linguistics of Demotic texts formalised in 643 BC.

Mesopotamia *(55–56)*

This illustrates the arts and daily life of the Sumerians and Babylonians. The **Flood Tablet** tells a story from the Epic of Gilgamesh.

The Ancient Levant *(57–59)*

Syrian civilisation flourished during the third and second millennium BC. An impressive statue of King Idrimi (16C BC) is in an austere and simplistic style. Ancient Palestine was an important trading centre and the Phoenicians established themselves in the Mediterranean exemplified by a fine collection of ivories includes a delicately carved plaque of a Lion killing a boy (9C–8C BC).

ETHNOGRAPHY

The **Wellcome Trust Gallery of Living and Dying** *(24)* explores how humanity handles life and death. The room is dominated by **Hoa Hakananai'a**, a moai from Easter Island. The quartz **crystal skull** (19C) is fascinating.

Americas

Exhibits in *room 26* illustrate the life of the Native peoples of North America and the effect of European influence. *Room 27* is devoted to important civilisations of Mesoamerica before the Spanish conquest.

Africa *(25, lower floor)*

The collections reflect the vitality and diversity of the continent. Highlights include the magnificent 16C **Benin bronzes**, a brass head, masks and carvings from Nigeria; Asante **goldwork** from Ghana, and 16C Afro-Portuguese **ivories**.

PRINTS AND DRAWINGS *(90)*

This room hosts special exhibitions from the extensive collection of prints and drawings including works by Rembrandt, Michelangelo, Raphael and Goya.

ASIA

▷ *Start on the ground floor.*

China, India, South and Southeast Asia *(33, 33a and 33b)*

Chinese bronzes, exquisite jades and ceramics that became mass-produced and diffused throughout Asia to the West are marks of this collection. Early **Buddhist art** from Gandhara (modern Pakistan) reflects the prolific generation of followers from the 5C BC.

Korea *(67)*

Korea's arts were marked by the Chinese and Buddhist traditions such as the frontispiece of an **Amitabha Sutra manuscript** (1341). From 15C on Confucianism is illustrated through portraiture.

Japan *(92–94, Upper floor)*

Society was strictly regulated and its complexity is reflected in the arts. Note the set of splendid **Momoyama period armour** (late 16C).

Imperial War Museum★★★

The museum is well worth a visit, even for those with no real interest in military history – the social stories are compelling.

A BIT OF HISTORY

The museum, of what Churchill termed the Age of Violence, was founded in 1917, principally through the efforts of **Sir Alfred Mond** who stated in the opening ceremony that the museum "was not a monument of military glory, but a record of toil and sacrifice".

In 1936, the museum was moved to the present building, which stands on the site of a 19C hospital for lunatics known as Bedlam. The white obelisk milestone at St. George's Circus, leading to the museum, commemorates Brass Crosby, Lord Mayor of London in 1771, who refused to convict a printer for publishing parliamentary debates. He was imprisoned in the Tower, but was freed by the populace, and press reporting of Commons' proceedings was inaugurated.

VISIT

Lambeth Road. ⊖Lambeth North. ♿✕⊙Open daily 10am–6pm. ⊙Closed 24–26 Dec. No charge, except for some special exhibitions.

▷ **Location:** *Map: inside front cover (EFY).* ⊖*Lambeth North.* The museum is a short walk from the Tube station and well signposted.

⌖ **Don't Miss:** The sobering Holocaust Exhibition; the intrigue of the life of Spies in the Secret War; the powerful World War galleries.

⊙ **Timing:** Arrive early as there is a lot to see, and leave at least an hour to visit the Holocaust Exhibition alone.

♟ **Kids:** The museum runs regular family events; the interactive Terrible Trenches exhibition *(until end Oct 2010).*

Parking for the disabled. Leaflet (3 languages). Audio-guide £3.50; child £3. Café. ℘020 7416 5000. http://london.iwm.org.uk.

The museum in no sense glorifies war, but honours those who served and looks at the social history surrounding British wars from 1914 to the present day. Two British **15-inch naval guns**, used in action during World War II, command

Majestic Imperial War Museum

K. Brett/MICHELIN

Blitz Experience

© IWM Courtesy Imperial War Museum

the main gate and to the side stands a piece of the **Berlin Wall**.

Military Weapons
(Ground floor)

The wide range of weapons and equipment on display in the **Large Exhibits Gallery** encompass World War I to the present day. Highlights of First World War weapons include a 4-inch gun from the destroyer **HMS Lance**, which fired the first British shot of World War I. The increasing importance of tank development to break the deadlock of trench warfare is exemplified by the **Mark V Tank** (1918).

A **Supermarine Spitfire Mark IA** which saw action in the Battle of Britain represents one of the iconic weapons from World War II. The **Tamzine** is the smallest surviving craft used in the Dunkirk evacuation of May 1940. The intensity of bombing raids on the civilian population can be seen by the enormous **V2 rocket**, over 6 500 weapons of this kind were dropped on London and the V2 could not be intercepted once launched. The **M3A3 Grant tank** was used famously by Field Marshal Montgomery during the Battle of El Alamein *(see Lord Monty p286)*.

The **Submarines** gallery includes interactive displays such as listening to underwater sounds in solar stations and using a periscope.

Of interest to note, is the resplendent **Brough Superior Motorcycle**, owned by TE Lawrence (of Arabia), in front of the **Cinema**.

First World War Galleries
(Lower ground floor)

The focal point of these galleries is **The Terrible Trenches Exhibition**, which uses special lighting, sound and smell effects to recreate the front line of the Somme in 1916 *(until end Oct 2010)*.

The **Origins and Outbreak of the War** looks at the complex shift of power and colliding national ambitions in Europe that led to the conflict.

The **Western Front** includes equipment and personal belongings of the men in the trenches. There is also a model of the front detailing the battlefront and also road signs that were used to name the trenches themselves.

War in the Air explains the growing importance of air reconnaisance and the pilot aces that made a name for themselves.

The **War on Other Fronts** details the conflicts in the Balkans, Turkey, Russia and Egypt.

The **Home Front** details the effects on civilian life that ensued, such as food rationing and the employment of women in industrial jobs.

The **Inter-War Years**, located in the central corridor of this floor, explores the rise of the Nazi Dictatorship in 1933 and the end of Britain's Appeasement policy in 1939.

Lord Monty

Bernard Montgomery(1887–1976), led the Allies to victory at the Battle of El Alamein (1942), one of the turning points of World War II. He inspired loyalty and great belief in his troops. His documents and medals in the exhibition, show how he became one of the great battlefield commanders.

Second World War Galleries
(Lower ground floor)

The Blitz Experience reconstructs an air raid shelter and a a blitzed street in 1940s Britain with sights, sounds and atmospheric effects to evoke the sensation of being caught up in a bombing raid.

The Blitzkrieg highlights the German attacks on Scandinavia and Western Europe and the escape of British and French troops at the Dunkirk evacuation in 1940.

The Battle of Britain details, through archive footage and exhibits, the British victory over the German Luftwaffe which indefinitely postponed Hitler's plans to invade Britain.

The Home Front 1940–45 shows how civilians coped in a world of rationing and bomb shelters through sustained bombing of towns and cities. Exhibits

Secret War

© IWM Courtesy Imperial War Museum

include bomb shelter permits, produce such as powdered eggs that the population had to live on and evocative photographs showing Londoners using undergound platforms to evade the bombs.

The War at Sea 1939–45 describes the conflict between German U-Boats and the Allied merchant shipping that they targeted. Britain's dependence on imports underlined the importance of stopping them.

The Mediterranean and the Middle East gallery chronicles the conflict in North Africa, the Montgomery's victory over Rommel at El Alamein, and the success of Operation Torch, led by Eisenhower.

The Eastern Front 1941–45 shows how Hitler used a Blitzkreig offensive against the Russians and the comprehensive Russian victory at Stalingrad, which drove the Germans out of Russian territory.

Europe under the Nazis recounts the exploitation of conquered territories and how resistance movements carried out a guerrila war against Nazi Germany.

The Bomber Offensive marks out Air Marshal Harris' bombing of German cities to destroy morale and disrupt their porduction lines. This led to the controversial destruction of Dresden, with thousands of civilian deaths.

North West Europe recounts the D-Day Landings, the assault through Normandy and the Low Countries, to the subsequent defeat of Hitler. Exhibits include the signed *Instrument of Surrender* dated 4 May 1945.

The **War in the Far East** outlines the Allied war aginst Japan, which started with the attack on Pearl Harbour in 1941. The turning point came with their defeat at the Battle of Midway in 1942, before the atomic bombs on Hiroshima (6 August 1945) and Nagasaki (9 August 1945) brought about the end of the conflict.

Conflicts since 1945
(Lower ground floor)
This is a gallery dedicated to wars since 1945, encompassing Post War Britain, the Falklands War, the Cold War, right up to the First Golf War. Displays include firearms and uniforms along with audiovisual displays to emphasise the key events from each major conflict, including the Suez Crisis and the Vietnam War.

There is also a permanent exhibition dedicated to the exploits of Field Marshal Montgomery, entitled **Monty: Master of the Battlefield**, opened to coincide with the 60th anniversary of the Battle of El Alamein (&see Lord Monty p286).

Secret War
(First floor)
This compelling exhibition details the clandestine world of Britain's government agencies, MI5 and MI6, as well as the elite special forces such as the Special Air Service and the Long Range Desert Group. Film footage shows reconstructions of operations and training methods undertaken by these groups. Exhibits include SOE sabotage devices and bottles of invisible ink used by Germany during the First World War.

The VC and GC room
(First floor)
This gallery is dedicated to winners of the Victoria Cross and the George Cross, Britain's highest medals for gallantry. These are accompanied by the gallant stories of the people who were awarded and the sacrifices each individual had made. A *13-pounder "Nery" Gun* and the three VCs won by its crew at the Battle of Mons provide a centrepiece for this gallery.

Art Galleries
(Second floor)
The Art Gallery and the nearby John Singer Sargent Room contain paintings and sculptures from the museum's collection of First and Second World War art works. The emphasis is on the individual's lot in war: food queues, people sleeping in tube shelters, the wounded, service life and boredom.

The artists covered are the some of the most well known from their age: **Percy Wyndham Lewis**, **Paul Nash**, **Henry Moore** and **Graham Sutherland**. One of the most well known paintings is *Gassed* (c. 1918) by **John Singer Sargent**, displayed in the Sargent Room. It is a powerful portrayal of war on the front line.

There are also regular special exhibitions covering everything from children at war to 1940s fashion, such as **Breakthrough** *(open until end 2010)*, which will incorporate a major rehang of the museum's art collection.

&Please note, the following two exhibitions are not permitted for children under 11 years old, or recommended for children under 16 years old.

Holocaust Exhibition
(Third floor)
This exhibition uses historical material to recall this sombre part of history, from the rise of the Nazi party and the perversion of Nazi race theory to its full blown Euthanasia policies. Artefacts on display document personal tales of persecution and resistance that are amplified by the silence in the gallery itself. Notable exhibits include a funeral cart from the Warsaw Ghetto, a deportation railcar that visitors can enter and a wagon used to heave labourers in a concentration camp.

Crimes against Humanity
(Fourth floor)
This gallery contains a specially commissioned half-hour film exploring genocide around the world and the common features between these appaling events, from different ages and parts of world history, be it Nazi-occupied Europe, Cambodia or Rwanda. The film is shown continuously throughout the day.

National Gallery★★★

The focal point of Trafalgar Square is the popular National Gallery, one of the highlights of the capital; stand on the portico to enjoy a particularly fine perspective of the square and down Whitehall. The collection is one of the finest in the world and represents the best in all European schools.

A BIT OF HISTORY

Origin – The collection was founded, by parliamentary purchase in 1824, with the intent of offering the wonders of art to all and inspire young artists. The nucleus was 38 pictures assembled by City banker **John Julius Angerstein**, which included works by Titian, Rubens, Rembrandt and Hogarth and displayed at his residence at 100 Pall Mall.

Move to Trafalgar Square – Completed in Trafalgar Square in 1838, the new building designed by **William Wilkins**, on the site of the Royal Mews, provides an architectural climax of the square with the great portico composed of Corinthian columns.

During World War II the collection was evacuated to Wales, but every month one painting was exhibited in London.

▷ **Location:** *Map: inside front cover (EX) and area map under TRAFALGAR SQUARE – WHITEHALL.* ⊖*Charing Cross.* The gallery is well served by public transport and is conveniently situated near Leicester Square, Piccadilly Circus and Covent Garden.

⊙ **Don't Miss:** Leonardo's cartoon of *The Virgin and Child with St Anne and John the Baptist*, Rembrandt's *Self Portrait*, the British School of portrait and landscape painting, the Impressionist Collection.

🕐 **Timing:** *See the Planning Yout Trip box, opposite.* After a visit to the gallery, it is a short walk to the cinemas, theatres and other entertainment venues of the West End.

The **Sainsbury Wing**, designed by Robert Venturi to complement the existing building, was opened in 1991. Between 2004 and 2006, the East Wing Project made the building accessible at street level and restored the ceiling decoration in the Staircase Hall.

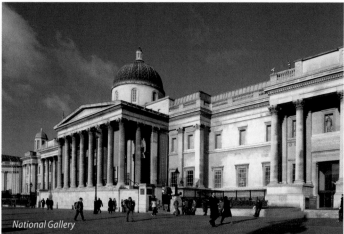

National Gallery

© National Gallery, London

PLANNING YOUR VISIT

Rambling through a large museum is both exhilarating and exhausting. If you are pressed for time, choose a favourite period in history, locate it on the gallery floor plan and explore the art of the times. Because individual pieces in the collection are occasionally rehung, it is impossible to pin-point particular masterpieces. Browsing, however, will allow you to discover unfamiliar images and perhaps provide you with some new 'favourites.'

Gallery Floor plan – Free of charge, this is available from the entrance foyers. If you are pressed for time

Books – The NG has an extensive bookshop selling general and specialist publications on the fine arts, cards, slides and posters.

Website – the Gallery's entire collection is described in the website, with background information on both the artists and their subjects.

Audio Guides – The main audio guide has pertinent information on over 1 000 paintings. Various themed tours covering about 20 paintings each are also available in several languages.

There are also special children's trails (paper and audio).

Special Exhibitions – For the important temporary exhibitions in the Sainsbury Wing Basement, it is sometimes necessary to control the number of visitors with timed tickets.

Special Note – The NG stays open until 9pm on Friday evenings.

Collection – There are now over 2 300 paintings in the collection hung in a loose chronological order from the early Renaissance to French Impressionism.

VISIT

Trafalgar Square. ♿ ✗ 🕐 *Open Sat–Thu 10am–6pm, Fri 10am–9pm.* 🕐 *Closed 1 Jan, 24–26 Dec.* 🚫 *No charge, except for special exhibitions.* 👥 *Guided tour (1hr): daily 11.30am, 2.30pm (and 7pm on Fri), from the Sainsbury Wing Information Desk. Themed Audio guides for hire (6 languages).* 👫 *Children's trails (printed and audio-guides) available. Gallery Floor plan. Restaurant (Sainsbury Wing). Café and Espresso Bar (Getty Entrance). Shops.* 📷 *No photography.* 📞 *020 7747 2885.* www.nationalgallery.org.uk.

13C TO 15C PAINTINGS

Sainsbury Wing

Rooms 51–66 present the development of naturalism and how gilding was used for more stylised depictions.

Giotto is considered as the forefather of Renaissance painting. The *Wilton Diptych* was painted for Richard II by an unknown French or English artist, with examples of elaborate sgraffito gilding contrasting to the ultramarine blues of the Virgin and angels *(53)*. **Masaccio** *(54)* uses light to cast shadows and mould three-dimensional form (*Virgin and Child*).

Uccello *(55)* uses linear perspective to create an illusion of depth in his *Battle of San Romano*. Note also **Fra Filippo Lippi**'s masterly *Annunciation*.

Jan van Eyck *(56)* uses light to convey intimacy and space in the *Arnolfini Portrait*. Note the reflections in the mirror.

Rooms 57–59 display the Venetian **Crivelli** (*The Annunciation, with St Emidius*), a master of perspective in his time, and **Botticelli**, the master of line *(58)*. His *Venus and Mars* is a sensuous portayal of love conquering war. Master of the Umbrian School, **Perugino** *(60)* learned the art of colour from Piero della Francesca and taught **Raphael** (*Portrait of Pope Julius II)* to endow his figures with grace and poise. His style evolved into the epitome of the High Renaissance.

Mantegna *(61–62)* studied the arts of Antiquity; note the construction in his *Agony in the Garden*. Compare this

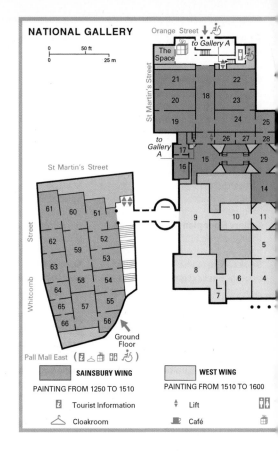

with his brother-in-law **Bellini**'s more realistic work of the same name. He perfected the use of oil paint, using it to capture rich tones of colour and light: *The Doge Leonardo Loredan*.

The Baptism of Christ by **Piero della Francesca** (66) uses composition to emphasise the serenity of the event.

16C PAINTINGS
West Wing

Playful gestures and softness, as in *The Madonna and Child with Saints* by **Parmigianino**, hint at the advent of Mannerism, which eventually degenerates into elongated forms and contorted positions. *Room 2* houses **Leonardo da Vinci**'s *Virgin of the Rocks* (the first version is in the Louvre) and his fragile preparatory 'cartoon' of *The Virgin and Child with St Anne and John the Baptist*, representing two ageless images of motherhood with their young sons.

Holbein's *The Ambassadors* (stand to the right to view the distorted skull) (4) is filled with symbolism. In his *Cupid complaining to Venus*, **Cranach the Elder** aims to convey a moral message: "life's pleasure is mixed with pain".

Distinctive styles are represented by **Michelangelo**'s monumental but uncompleted *The Entombment* and **Raphael**'s *The Madonna of the Pinks* (8). *Rooms 9–10* are devoted to the **Venetian School**. **Titian**'s *Bacchus and Ariadne* depicts Bacchus in mid air, throwing Ariadne's crown to form the constellation of stars.

Lorenzo Lotto's *Family Group* presents an ideal family (12). The intricate detail of **Jan Gossaert**'s *Adoration of the Kings* (14), affirms the message of Christ's birth.

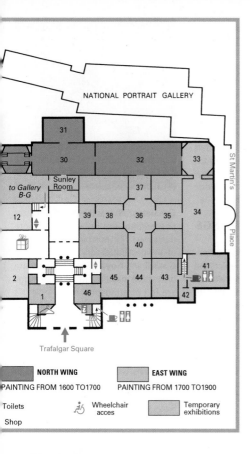

NATIONAL PORTRAIT GALLERY

St Martin's

to Gallery
B-G

Sunley
Room

Trafalgar Square

	NORTH WING		EAST WING
	PAINTING FROM 1600 TO 1700		PAINTING FROM 1700 TO 1900

Toilets   Wheelchair acces   Temporary exhibitions

Shop

17C PAINTINGS

North Wing

Works by **Claude** and **Turner** are exhibited together *(15)*. This was a special concession for Turner who specified in his will that his *Sun rising through Vapour* and *Dido building Carthage* should be hung with *Seaport with the Embarkation of the Queen of Sheba* and *Landscape with the Marriage of Isaac and Rebekah* by Claude.

The *Peepshow* by **Samuel van Hoog-straten** is an interesting curiosity *(17)*.

Claude *(20)* painted peaceful coastal scenes at sunset with mythological subjects. His *Enchanted Castle* is said to have influenced Keats' Ode to a Nightingale.

Poussin's *(20)* Classical style was inspired by the poets of Antiquity, as seen by *Cephalus and Aurora*.

Cuyp's *River Landscape with Horseman and Peasants* is a beautiful example of Dutch landscapes *(21)*. The **Dutch School** also includes **Hobbema** *(The Avenue at Middelharnis)* and **Ruysdael** *(River Scene)* who depict various aspects of the landscape *(22)*.

Several of **Rembrandt**'s classics hang in *Rooms 23–24* such as *Belshazzar's Feast; A Woman bathing in a Stream, Margaretha de Geer,* and *Self-Portrait at the Age of 34.*

Vermeer *(25)* specialised in tranquil domestic scenes bathed in a balmy light: *A Young Woman standing at a Virginal.*

Rubens *(29)* displayed artist's skill in all genres: *Samson and Delilah, Portrait of Susanna Lunden,* and *The Judgement of Paris.*

The master of the **Spanish School** *(30)* was **Velázquez**, who evolves a strong portrait style under Royal patronage. *The Rokeby Venus* and *Philip IV of Spain in Brown and Silver*.

Van Dyck *(31)* is the supreme master of portraiture in a grand confident style: *Equestrian Portrait of Charles I*.

Intense drama animates pictures of the **Baroque**, none more so than **Caravaggio** *(32)*. Intensity comes alive in his use of highlights and shadows *(chiaroscuro)*: *The Supper at Emmaus* depicts a beardless Jesus. Note how the basket of fruit teeters on the edge to represent the early Church.

18 TO EARLY 20C PAINTINGS
East Wing

Drouais' portrait of *Madame de Pompadour at her Tambour Frame*, depicts the famous patron of the **Rococo** style *(33)*, which emphasised curves and delicate colour. *Pan and Syrinx* by **Boucher** is an example of this. Also note *Self Portrait in a Straw Hat*, **Vigée Le Brun**'s take on Rubens, by the famous female painter of the 18C.

The **British School** *(34)* at its height *(📖see Introduction to London – Painting)* is exemplified by *Anne, 2nd Countess of Albemarle* (**Reynolds**); *The Fighting Temeraire* (**Turner**) and *The Hay Wain* (**Constable**). *Whistlejacket* by **Stubbs**, is a wonderfully realistic portrait of a racehorse.

Hogarth's moralising series *Marriage A la Mode* is displayed in *room 35*, along with *Mr and Mrs Andrews* by **Gainsborough.**

Sunflowers (1888) by Vincent van Gogh
©National Gallery, London

Whistlejacket (c. 1762) by George Stubbs
©National Gallery, London

Canaletto *(38)*, was the Venetian master of sparkling landscape painting (note the waves). *The Stonemason's Yard* is one of his finest paintings.

Guardi and **Goya** *(39)* were two quite distinctive masters. Guardi's paintings are full of atmosphere while Goya's portraits are character studies.

Neoclassicism *(41)* was a counter-reaction to the Ancien Régime. **Delaroche**'s *The Execution of Lady Jane Grey* dominates the room.

Wagner's German Romanticism is transposed into paint as exemplified by *Winter Landscape* by **Friedrich** *(42)*.

Depictions of modern life and atmospheric effects are the trademarks of **Impressionism** *(43–44)*. The transient quality of light is carefully explored and captured in outdoor scenes by **Renoir** *(The Skiff)*, **Seurat** *(Bathers at Asnières;* radiant with his pointillist technique*)* and **Monet** *(Bathers at La Grenouillère)*, or in a celebration of industrialisation by **Pissarro** *(The Boulevard Montmatre at Night)*.

In *Room 45*, **Rousseau**'s *Suprised!* combines elaborate patterns with the exotic; **Cézanne**'s *Bathers* inspired Cubism; and **van Gogh**'s *Sunflowers* captivates the room with its thick yellow brushstrokes.

Picasso's *Child with a Dove* experiment with blue in the gallery's last room *(46)* contrasts with the fiery reds of *La Coiffure* by **Degas**.

National Portrait Gallery★★

The fascination of portraits of the great and the good who have wielded power or made a significant contribution in various fields of endeavour throughout the centuries is irresistible as a panorama of British history unfolds. Wander through the gallery at leisure and enjoy a meal in the roof-top restaurant, which gives a wonderful vista over the West End.

National Portrait Gallery

©Colin Streater/National Portrait Gallery

▷ **Location:** *Map: inside front cover (EX) and area map under TRAFALGAR SQUARE – WHITEHALL.* ⊖*Leicester Square; Charing Cross.* The gallery is adjacent to the National Gallery and a short walk from Leicester Square, The Strand and Covent Garden Piazza.

⊙ **Don't Miss:** Elizabeth I and her favourites; Shakespeare, the Romantics; Prince Albert; the Brontë Sisters; Sir Alexander Fleming in his laboratory (1944).

⊙ **Timing:** Allow 3hr for a tour of the gallery.

No charge, except for special exhibitions. Audio-guide (4 languages) £2. Restaurant (third floor; booking recommended ℘0207 312 2490), café (basement). ℘0207 312 2463 (recorded infoline). www.npg.org.uk.

▷ *Take the escalator to the Second Floor from the Main Hall.*

TUDORS TO THE REGENCY
Second Floor
The Tudor Galleries (1–3)
Holbein's fragment of a larger sketch shows **Henry VIII** (1491–1547; Room 1) with his father Henry VII, the founder of the Tudor dynasty; the distorted portrait of Henry's son, **Edward VI** painted by William Scrots (1546) can be viewed in correct perspective from the right.

The statesman and Humanist author **Sir Thomas More** is portrayed with his family: he was executed for opposing Henry VIII's self-appointment as Head of the Church. **Mary I** (1516–58), known as Bloody Mary, sent almost 300 Protestants to their deaths before marrying King Philip of Spain.

The long gallery (2) displays several portraits of **Elizabeth I** (1533–1603). She was an intelligent monarch who saw the Spanish defeated and a flowering of literature. **Sir Francis Drake**, the famous

A BIT OF HISTORY
Founded in 1856 through the efforts of Philip Henry Stanhope, the **National Collection** moved to its present location behind the National Gallery in 1896. Today, over 5 000 personalities are portrayed in various media representing a rich history of Britain.

The permanent collection is presented in chronological order from the top down. The IT Gallery *(located by the Main Hall)* makes the gallery's collections accessible to all.

⊙*Some of the works listed below may have been moved to a different location.*

VISIT
St Martin's Place. ♿✕⊙*Open Sat–Wed 10am–6pm, Thu–Fri 10am–9pm. Closure commences 10min before closing time.* ⊙*Closed 24–26 Dec.*

'Chandos Portrait',
William Shakespeare (c.1610)
attributed to John Taylor

© National Portrait Gallery, London

seafarer who sailed round the world, was a favourite at Elizabeth's court. **James I** (1566–1625; *Room 3*) was crowned King of England in 1603 following the death of Elizabeth I.

The 17C (4–8)

The *Chandos Portrait (4)* is arguably the most famous of **William Shakespeare** (1564–1616), painted at the apogee of his career. The portrait of **Charles I** (1600-49) is by Daniel Mytens *(5)*. The king attracted to his court the diplomat and painter Peter Paul Rubens *(Thomas Howard,)* and Sir Anthony van Dyck *(several portaits hang in room 5)*.

Oliver Cromwell (1599–1658) promoted the king's execution and was appointed Protector of the Commonwealth of England, Scotland and Ireland in 1653.

The Restoration *(7)* is illustrated by **Charles II** (1630–85) portrayed by Thomas Hawker emphasises his libertine reputation.

The portrait of **Nell Gwynn**, his most famous mistress, is by Simon Verelst. **Samuel Pepys** witnessed the Great Plague of 1665, followed in 1666 by the Great Fire which devastated the City, and he related both events in his diaries. Charles' younger brother **James II** (1633–1701; *Room 8*) , painted by Sir Peter Lely *(see panel p293)*, was forced to flee in 1688.

William III (1650–1702; *Room 8*), the grandson of Charles I, and **Mary II** (1662–94), daughter of James II, acceded to the throne in 1688. Their joint rule brought tolerance to the kingdom.

Queen Anne (1665–1714), succeeded her brother-in-law William in 1702. Others pictured include **Isaac Newton** who established the concept of gravitation; and soldier **John Churchill**, victor at the Battle of Blenheim and ancestor of Winston Churchill.

Georgian and Regency (9–20)

The **Kit-cat Club** *(9)* attracted its distinguished members from political and literary circles. They used to meet in a tavern run by Christopher Cat.

The throne passed to the Hanoverian **George I** (1660–1727). Note the fine terracotta bust by Rysbrack *(11)*.

The Arts and Sciences flourished throughout the 18C: **Sir Christopher Wren** *(10)* achieved fame with rebuilding St Paul's Cathedral; **Sir Joshua Reynolds**, depicted in a famous self-portrait *(12)*, promoted the ideal of the imperfect in art; and **Sir Hans Sloane** *(13)* provided the foundation for the British Museum.

Among those who contributed to British expansion during the 18C *(14)* are **Captain James Cook**, who made the first European contact with Australia; and **Robert Clive** of India, who laid the foundations of British power in India.

Britain in the late 18C was shaped by: **William Pitt the Younger** *(20)*; **Horatio Nelson** *(17)*, the victor of Trafalgar, who is portayed next to his mistress **Lady Hamilton**; the **Duke of Wellington** defeated Napoleon at Waterloo (1815) and later became

Lord Byron (1813) by
Thomas Phillips

© National Portrait Gallery, London

Prime Minister. There are several portraits by Sir Thomas Lawrence of **George IV** (1762–1830) painted while he ruled in proxy as Prince Regent. His brother **William IV** (1765–1837), who succeeded him.

The Romantic generation of writers *(18)* includes **William Wordsworth** and **Samuel Coleridge**, who together compiled *Lyrical Ballads*; Scotland's favourite son **Robert Burns**, and **Lord Byron** in his Greco-Albanian costume. **George Stephenson** *(19)*, built the first public railway line.

THE VICTORIANS TO TODAY
First Floor
The Victorians (21–29)
The display starts with portraits of **Queen Victoria** (1819–1901) and **Prince Albert** *(21)*.

The Statesmen's Gallery *(22)* contains portraits and busts of political figures such as **Randolph Churchill** and **Robert Peel**, who created the police force.

The personalities who secured Britain's interests in the world *(23)* include **Sir Richard Burton**, the African explorer; and **Florence Nightingale**, the pioneering nurse.

The Victorian Age *(24)* is epitomised by: the Poet Laureate **Alfred Tennyson**; the writer **Charles Dickens**; and the engineer **Isambard K Brunel** *(27)*.

The world of politics *(25)* is illustrated by portraits by J E Millais of the two great statesmen, **Gladstone** and **Disraeli**. The late Victorians *(28)* include **RL Stevenson** and **Rudyard Kipling**.

The 20C (30–33)
General Officers and *Statesmen* of the Great War *(30)* by John Singer Sargent and James Guthrie respectively, encapsulate the great figures of the time.

Room 31 deals with Britain between 1919–59, exemplified by **Winston Churchill**, and **Viscount Montgomery**.

The artistic environment reflected new ideas in painting, literature and music. Highlights include: the writers **Virginia Woolf**, **EM Forster**, **DH Lawrence** and

Sir Peter Lely (1618–80)
Pieter van der Faes was born in Germany of Dutch parentage. He served his apprenticeship in Haarlem and moved to London in the 1640s. He produced noncontroversial history pictures during the Commonwealth, tailoring his grand and influential manner for the Restoration, succeeding Van Dyck as Principal Painter to Charles II in 1661. His paintings presented ladies of the Court endowed with languid beauty (Nell Gwynne, the king's favourite) and victorious military leaders with masculine dignity.

TS Eliot; the actor **Laurence Olivier**; and the scientist **Alexander Fleming**. The Balcony Gallery *(32)* is devoted to Britain 1960-90: iconic figures from all walks of life illustrate social and political change such as **Her Majesty the Queen** and the **Royal Family**, **Alec Guinness**, **Paul McCartney** and **Margaret Thatcher**.

Britain since 1990 – *Ground Floor*. Portaits and photographs of people in the public eye from all walks of life include: **Richard Branson**, **Ken Loach**, **Harold Pinter**, **Alan Bennett**, **Stephen Hawking** and **Johnson Gideon Beharry**, the first recipient of the Victoria Cross since 1982.

Detail of JK Rowling (2005) by Stuart Pearson Wright
© National Portrait Gallery

Natural History Museum★★

A BIT OF HISTORY

The Natural History Museum is housed in a famous example of Victorian Gothic revival architecture (1873–81) designed by Alfred Waterhouse. It dominates the Cromwell Road and is the centrepiece of "Albertopolis", Prince Albert's vision for a new learning district in London. The foundation for the collection began as the natural history department of the British Museum in Bloomsbury. Richard Owen prompted calls for a move to a separate structure and the museum was opened to the public in 1881. In 1986, the museum absorbed the neighbouring Geological Museum, later to be relaunched as the **Earth Galleries**. The **Darwin Centre** opened on 14 September 2009 and houses the museum's Zoological collections. After more than a century, the museum remains one of the most renowned centres for biological study in the world.

VISIT

Exhibition Road/Cromwell Road ⊖*South Kensington.* ♿✕🕐*Open daily, 10am–5.50pm (5.30pm last admission).* 🕐*Closed 24–26 Dec.* 🚭*No charge except for some exhibitions. Map and guide. Changing programme of special events and children's activities, with additional events during school holidays and half term. Book shop; shop. Restaurant, café, coffee bar, snack bar and picnic area.* 📞*020 7942 5000,* 📞*020 7942 5000 (information). www.nhm.ac.uk.*

The vast neo-Romanesque building expresses the solemn reverence and sense of mission in public education in the 19C. The decoration includes lifelike mouldings of living and extinct species to the west and east wings respectively.

The museum's collections continue to grow by some 350 000 specimens a year, mostly insects. Such increase would not have surprised **Hans Sloane**, who bequeathed his own collection to

▷ **Location:** *Map: inside front cover (ABXY).* ⊖*South Kensington.* The museum is A 5min walk from the Tube station by subway tunnel.

⊛ **Don't Miss:** The fascinating Earth Galleries, the vast blue whale in the Mammals Gallery and the interactive displays in the Human Biology area.

🕐 **Timing:** Get to the museum as early as you can as queues can be long. Expect to spend around 2–3hr on a visit.

👫 **Kids:** The Dinosaur galleries with their skeletons and animatronics, Creepy Crawlies and **Investigate**, the hands-on education centre.

the nation. The museum is divided into **different coloured zones** for ease of touring: Blue and Green (the Life Galleries); Red (the Earth Galleries) and Orange (the Darwin Centre and the Wildlife Garden).

The Blue Zone

On the left of the Central Hall, home to an impressive Diplodocus skeleton, is the **Dinosaurs** gallery which traces the development and extinction of these creatures, including a Triceratops skeleton. A set of animatronic dinosaurs is on display, featuring a Tyrannosaurus rex in a dramatic desert scene.

The **Human Biology** interactive displays explain the how our senses, memories and organs work together in the human body, including interactive experiences on cells, genetics and what a baby experiences in the womb.

The **Jerwood Gallery** hosts some of the museums temporary exhibitions.

An enormous blue whale suspended from the ceiling dominates the **Mammals gallery**; it also offers audio-visual programmes (*3min*), films, sounds, written panels, illustrations and stuffed originals; whales and their relatives are described in the gallery (upstairs), including exhibits on how to make whale noises and the truth about unicorns. Also included is a ferocious skeleton of Smilidon, the extinct sabre-toothed cat.

The gallery on **Marine Invertebrates** displays corals, urchins, crabs, starfish, sponges, molluscs, squid and shells and how pollution effects their marine environment. The black webbed vampire squid with its red eyes and the wonderful display of sea fans are notable exhibits.

The **Fishes, Amphibians and Reptiles** gallery includes exhibits about snakes, tortoises, terrapins, turtles and lizards, crocodilians. Of particular interest, is the sword of a swordfish, the prehisotoric looking komodo dragons and examples of a football fish, which has a light emiting lure that lights up the depths of the ocean.

The Green Zone

On the right side of the Central Hall, **Creepy Crawlies** illustrates the nature and diversity of insects and arthropods, including Chan's Megastick, the world's longest insect.

The **Investigate Centre** down the stairs on the Lower Ground Floor, offers families the chance to handle special exhibits of animal and plants (⏱ *open Mon–Fri 2.30–5pm (11am–5pm during school holidays), Sat–Sun 11am–5pm; 🎫no charge)*. Alongside on the Ground Floor is the **Fossil Marine Reptile** Gallery, containing of the most complete collections of fossilisied sea dinosaurs such as the ichthyosaur.

The **Birds** gallery displays an array of specimens from tiny hummingbirds to a giant ostrich. It also contains a specimen of the extinct Mauritius dodo and the most rare parrot in the world, the kakapo.

The **Waterhouse Gallery** displays temporary exhibitions.

The **Ecology** Gallery traces the impact of man's activities on our living planet, including a dazzling video quadrasphere display on the importance of water. It

Façade of Natural History Museum

©Natural History Museum

also shows an educational guide to conserving our planet's ecology through everyday actions.

At the top of the grand staircase in the Central Hall, is a slice through the trunk of a **Giant Sequoia** felled in 1892 in San Francisco. Note the TREE artwork on theceiling of the mezzanine gallery by Tania Kovats.

The **Primates** gallery includes a skeleton of the extinct giant lemur and a specimen of the howler monkey, the world's loudest land animal.

The parallel **Our Place in Evolution** gallery explores the characteristics humans share with apes.

The World's Largest Cocoon

The **Darwin Centre** is a 213ft/65m, eight-storey cocoon in a glass atrium. It is the largest sprayed concrete, curved structure in Europe and the largest extension to the museum since it opened in 1881. Inside, the building houses over 20 million insect and plant specimens, offering wonderful views of West London. Visitors are able to watch scientists working on research in modern laboratories and partake in interactive exhibitions. The David Attenborough Studio within incorporates interactive films and discussions with leading naturalists about the natural world.

Central Hall

©Natural History Museum

The **Minerals** gallery displays a whole host of raw and cut gemstones, including the reptilianesque snake stone. **The Vault** at the end, displays the museum's most valuable treasures, such as the Nakla Martian meteorite and the Devonshire Emerald, which has a mass of 1 383 carats.

The Red Zone
Accessible via the Birds Gallery on the Ground Floor or through the Exhibition Road Entrance.

The **Earth Hall** contains an elevator rising from the 'molten magma core' to the core of the Earth leading to the second floor where, with sound, vibration and light effects, **The Power Within** demonstrates how earthquakes and volcanoes harness the power of nature.

The **Restless Surface Gallery** examines rock formations transform and shape our planet such as the formation of a stalagmite rock over centuries and an explanation of how the Himalayas were formed.

On the first floor, the **Earth's Treasury** gallery, displays specimens of gemstones, rocks and minerals. Particular highlights are the flourescent minerals, the organic shaped hematite mineral and displays of rare platinum nuggets.

From the Beginning displays a time rail that runs through the gallery, detailing 25 million years of planet life. The fearsome skeleton of a gigantic crocodile is a worthy exhibit.

The **Earth Lab** on the mezzanine level offers users computer and interactive exhibits to compare over 2 000 specimens of fossils, minerals and rocks.

Returning to the Ground Floor, the **Lasting Impressions** Gallery contains exhibits detailing a long-ago event for visitors to appreciate such as the footprints of a Triassic period dinosaur and how to calculate a whale's age from its teeth.

The **Earth Today and Tomorrow** looks at the importance of sustainable development to man and the planet.

The Orange Zone
This zone incorporates the **Darwin Centre** (*open 10am–5.50pm; no charge*) – with a fascinating Cocoon Experience, Climate Change Wall and more – and the **Wildlife Garden** (*open Apr–Oct*), located on the West lawn outside the museum. It re-creates over an acre of British woods, heaths and meadowlands in a living exhibition.

Science Museum★★★

A BIT OF HISTORY

The museum was founded as part of the South Kensington Museum in 1857 under the guiding hand of Bennet Woodcroft, a major figure in the developments of textile manchinery, with exhibits composed from the Royal Society of Arts and items from the Great Exhibition of 1851. The museum in its present location was opened to the public from 1919–28. The Central Block galleries were redeveloped in the sixties to form the backbone of the present layout. Further expansion was undertaken at the end of the century and the resulting Wellcome Wing, with its futuristic decor was opened in 2000 to exhibit technologies of the future.

VISIT

Exhibition Road. ⊖*South Kensington.* ♿✕🕐*Open daily 10am–6pm.* 🕐*Closed 24–26 Dec.* ⬚*No charge except for special exhibitions; IMAX cinema £8; child £6.25. Brochure (6 languages). Bookshop; shop. Restaurant; picnic area.* ✆*0870 870 4868. www.sciencemuseum.org.uk.*

The spirit of the Science Museum, laid out on seven floors, is to encourage initiative and reception in learning and education by presentation, exploration and explanation. There are innumerable objects displayed, constantly updated "Science Boxes", countless working models and interactive computer terminals, while assistants (in orange T-shirts) are on hand throughout the galleries to advise and inform.

The museum galleries are divided into six floors but with constant reinvention of the exhibition space, expect displays to vary from those below.

Basement

Children can enjoy the interactive exhibits of **The Garden**, which make science fun in a multi sensory environment, turning play into learning such principles as floating,

> ▶ **Location:** *Map: inside front cover (ABXY).* ⊖*South Kensington.* The museum is five-minutes walk from the Tube station by subway tunnel.
>
> 🔶 **Don't Miss:** The Secret Life of the Home, Making the Modern World, Exploring Space, Flight ,and the Motionride Simulators.
>
> 🕐 **Timing:** There's a lot to see and do, so split your day between the lower and upper floors, stopping for a picnic or restaurant lunch midway.
>
> 👥 **Kids:** The Garden; Pattern Pod; IMAX cinema; Antenna; Who Am I?; Energy; and Launchpad City.

sinking, shadows and reflections. **The Secret Life of the Home** explain the development of household appliances that we take for granted, from CD players to washing machines. It also shows how applied robotics will develop gadgets for the future.

Ground Floor

Energy Hall celebrates how steam has been the driving force of industry for more than threee hundred years with displays such as the large *Mill engine by Burnley Ironworks Company* (1903), which exemplifies how steam engines became Britain's main power source.

Marine Engineering reveals the fascinating history of marine propulsion, including the oldest surviving marine engine by William Symington.

Rockets, satellites and space exploration are the exciting themes of **Exploring Space** with a fully sized replica of the *Eagle lander,* that took Armstrong and Aldrin to the Moon in 1969.

Above the gallery are suspended two real space rockets, a *British Black Arrow* and a *United States Scout.*

PLANNING YOUR VISIT

Touch-screen Information terminals around the museum display details of exhibitions, events and visitor facilities in six languages, as well as floor plans.

Highlights – For a quick tour consider visiting the sections entitled The Secret Life of the Home *(basement)*; Exploring Space, Making the Modern World *(Ground floor)*; The Challenge of Materials *(First Floor)*; Motionride Simulators; and Flight *(Third floor)*.

Children – Recommended sections include those entitled The Garden *(basement)*; Pattern Pod, IMAX cinema, Antenna *(Ground floor)*; Who am I *(First Floor)*; Energy *(Second Floor)*; and Launchpad City *(Third floor)*.

Interactive learning
– Demonstrations are given in Launchpad and Flight Lab sections: enquire at the information desk for times. Excellent programme of talks, workshops and children's events with additional events during half-term and school holidays; see web site.

Overcrowding – Timed ticketing stops the galleries from being over-run with school-children.

Science Museum Library – The Reference library is now based over two sites in London and Swindon. The archives collection is based in the Swindon facility, where readers can consult original scientific journals and books dating from 1486 onwards. 📞0870 870 4868.

Books – The well-stocked bookshop has technical manuals, documentation, teaching packs and souvenirs.

Shop – An ethical, retro and inventive products shopping haven – one of the best places in the UK to buy presents including games and gadgets for children (also mail order).

Imax – One of two IMAX screens in London; wide variety of films. 📞0870 870 4868.

In **Making the Modern World**, some 150 exhibits including *Stephenson's 'Rocket' locomotive* (1829) and the *Apollo 10 command module* (1969) mark the development of the modern industrial world from 1750 to the present and how these iconic items have framed modern history.

The Ground Floor also has a **Theatre** room, which hosts educational and fun scientific shows *(30min; ⊜no charge)*, investigating the science of heat and temperature, changes of state and the transfer of energy.

Making the Modern World

Science Museum

Science Museum Nights

On the last Wednesday of every month, the museum offers an adults-only evening where guests can explore a funfair atmosphere including interactive science exhibits, pub quizzes and the Launchpad exhibition along with live music and a fully licensed bar in a relaxed atmosphere *(6.45–10pm; ∞no charge)*.

Children (along with accompanying adults) can have a late night of their own by camping in the museum ovenight, after enjoying hands-on workshops and science shows *(on various weekend nights; ∞£30; reservations: ☎0207 942 4777)*.

First Floor

The **Challenge of Materials** gallery explains the various uses of state-of-the-art materials in the modern world. Note the *Steel wedding dress* (1995), made from stainless steel wire . A spectacular glass bridge spans the gallery above the main hall, responding to the visitor with light and sound effects. Original artefacts and interactive exhibits, such as the Three-ring Enigma cypher machine (c. 1930s), illustrate the development of **Telecommunications**.

The **Cosmos & Culture** Exhibition *(open 23 Jul 2009–30 Dec 2010)* explores astronomy through antique instruments from different parts of the world.

A *Massey-Ferguson combine harvester* (1953–62) contrasts with the ancient chinese ploughs illustrating the changing world of **Agriculture**.

The **Time Measurement** gallery explores how people have kept time over the centuries by way of sundials, sandglasses, water clocks to early Rolex designs.

Note the beautiful *Early balance spring watch* by Thomas Tompion (1675–79).

Second Floor

The innovative **Energy Gallery** allows children to think critically about energy through interactive displays, including touch sensitive screens, giant spinning drums and dance-floor footpads. The *Energy Ring*, a huge interactive sculpture suspended in the air, displays the thoughts of visitors who enter answers in the touch screen terminals.

In **Computing and Mathematics** are Babbage's *Difference Engine No 2* and *DEC PDP-8 minicomputer* (1965), the forerunners of the modern computer.

Another fascinating object on show is the *1956 Ferranti Pegasus*, the oldest working computer in the world, which is switched on and run regularly for visitors.

A splendid collection of model ships (including Columbus's *Santa Maria*) and various exhibits are displayed in the **Shipping** gallery.

This nautical theme is amplified further on, in the **Docks and Diving** Gallery, with life-size depictions of deep-sea divers throughout the centuries.

Human identity and the effects of biomedical sciences are the themes explored in **Who am I?** Visitors can morph their face to any age using computers.

They can also search the geneaology of surnames from a century ago.

Third Floor

Everyone from young to old, will delight in the world of aviation, which is brought expertly to life on the third floor. Learn about the principles of flight in the exciting **Motionride simulators** *(£2.50; child £2)*, a highlight of any visit to this museum. Follow the progress of aviation in **Flight**, which displays an extraordinary collection of aircraft, engines and models: a replica of the *Wright brothers' plane* which made the first controlled flight in 1903; Alcock and Brown's *Vickers Vimy biplane*, which made the first non-stop Atlantic crossing in 1919; and a *Gloster-Whittle jet aeroplane* (1941), the first successful British jet aircraft.

Launchpad City, the most popular gallery in the museum, allows children to explore and ask questions about their environment through over fifty

Kids playing in Launchpad City

Science Museum

interactive exhibits. Children will see carbon dioxide turn from solid into a gas and light rays breaking into rainbow patterns.

Health Matters, which relates the history of medicine during the second half of the 20C (kidney machine for home dialysis) and uses interactive exhibits to explore the prevention of ill health. George III's collection of scientific apparatus forms the nucleus of **Science in the 18C.**

Take part in issue-raising games focused on various themes relating to technological developments in **In Future**.

Fourth Floor

Glimpses of Medical History illustrates the history of practical medicine from the Neolithic Age to the modern age with reconstructions and dioramas such as a warship's surgery during the Age of Nelson.

The adjacent **Psychology** Exhibition explores the inner workings of the mind through artworks and audiovisual displays.

Fifth Floor

A social and scientific history of medicine in cultures around the world is presented in **The Science and Art of Medicine**, with over 5 000 objects including: the wonderfully painted

Giustiniani medicine chest (c. 1565); and a mummified Egyptian cat (c. 2 000–100 BC).

Veterinary History illustrates the treatment of animals, a stunning anatomical model of a horse by Louis Auzoux (c. 1850–80) dominates the centre of the gallery.

Wellcome Wing

This modern annexe is devoted to innovative displays on contemporary science, technology and medicine.

Talking Points *(ground floor)* offers thought-provoking displays scattered around the hall questioning the influence of modern science on our way of life. Examples include: Darrell Viner's "Is tall better than small?", which is activated by visitors on the escalator to the IMAX theatre; and a crashed Formula One racing car; and Marc Quinn's 'Eternal Spring (Sunflowers) II', a vase of sunflowers immersed in frozen liquid silicone.

Antenna is a constantly updated exhibition devoted to science news and displays displays a segment of kevlar-rubber tank liner and a enormous Michelin NZG tyre used in the Concorde jet.

An **IMAX cinema** presents spectacular shows. **Pattern Pod** encourages children to study patterns in recurring events.

Tate Britain★★★

On a superb waterfront setting overlooking the Pimlico riverside, this bright, imposing building is a splendid showcase for British Art, and after extensive redevelopment, it boasts modern facilities for innovative displays of its fine collections. The gallery has a strong tradition of well-presented special exhibitions and public events; it also sponsors The Turner Prize, a prestigious, if always controversial, award for the visual arts. Tate Britain is *the* national gallery of British Art from 1500 to the present day.

A BIT OF HISTORY

National Gallery of British Art – Fifty years after the founding of the National Gallery (1824), the nation had acquired a large number of works that were shuffled between the National Gallery, the Victoria and Albert Museum and Marlborough House. In 1889, the sugar broker **Henry Tate**, an astute collector of British art, offered his collection of 67 paintings (including JE Millais's *Ophelia*) to the nation together with £80 000 for a purpose-built gallery dedicated to British art post 1790 on condition that the government provide a site for it. The Tate opened in 1897 on the site of the former Millbank Prison.

National Collection of Modern Foreign Art – In 1915, Sir Hugh Lane died when the *Lusitania* was torpedoed off the south coast of Ireland leaving 39 paintings, including some superb Impressionists, "to found a collection of Modern Continental Art in London". Extensions to the original building were endowed by the son of Sir Joseph Duveen in 1926 and in 1937 to accommodate sculpture. In 1954 the Tate Gallery became legally independent of the National Gallery. Further building was completed in 1979; the Tate then took over the former Queen Alexandra Hospital, before the **Clore Wing** was designed by James Stirling (1987) to accommodate the Turner collection.

▷ **Location:** *Map: inside back cover (FZ).* ⊖*Pimlico.* The gallery is situated along the embankment running from Westminster to Chelsea and near Vauxhall Bridge. Victoria Station is to the west.

⊚ **Don't Miss:** the paintings of John Constable, the works of the Pre-Raphaelites, in particular Millais, those of the American-born Whistler and John Singer Sargent, the Clore Gallery entirely devoted to Turner.

🕐 **Timing:** Allow 3–4hr for a good overall view of what is on display. Obtain a gallery plan from the information desk; the galleries are regularly re-hung as only a small part of the Tate's Collection is on show at any given time. If you intend to visit the collection to see a particular work, contact the Gallery first to check if it is on display.

👪 **Kids:** The Tate organises several family activities for children and adults to do together.

Today, Tate Britain is devoted exclusively to **British Art from 1500 to the Present Day**. The works are presented chronologically with rooms devoted to major artists. The text below traces the main trends and highlights significant paintings.

VISIT

Milbank. ♿✕🕐*Open daily 10am–5.50pm (until 10pm first Fri of month), last entry 50min before closing. Restaurant open daily 10am-5pm. Café.* 👓*No charge except for some special exhibitions.* 🗣*Guided tours Mon–Fri 11am, noon, 2pm, 3pm, Sat–Sun noon, 3pm. Multimedia guide (4 languages)*

£3.50. ✆0207 887 8888 (booking & information), ✆020 7887 8687 (minicom). www.tate.org.uk/britain.

PAINTING IN BRITAIN 1500–1900
Rooms 2–15.
Image and Allegory: English Renaissance
John Bettes painted the earliest English work in the collection. His *A Man in a Black Cap* betrays the influence of Holbein, highlighting the face against a background of mottled brown wall and fur collar, black cap and robe.

Nicholas Hilliard, the famous Elizabethan miniaturist encapsulates an idealised vision of his gracious queen: flat, stylised, linear, exquisite and fragile. *Queen Elizabeth I* is shown holding a rose, a Tudor emblem, red for the House of Lancaster, thornless like that borne by the Virgin Mary, "the rose without thorn": a powerful image full of political allegory.

The prolific **Van Dyck** introduced a change from simple austerity to a celebration of status, painting his figures standing comfortably in space, poised in movement or gesture (*A Lady of the Spencer Family*).

William Dobson's portrait of *Endymion Porter*, executed during Charles I exile in Oxford during the Civil War, shows the artist's concern for capturing the personality of his sitters.

Peter Lely adapted to the delicate political climate. His sitters are shown with elegant informality in uncontroversial poses (*Two Ladies of the Lake Family*). His biblical and mythological subjects meanwhile, verge on the erotic, hitherto unprecedented in the Puritan age.

Hogarth and Modern Life
Hogarth was a perceptive portraitist (*Thomas Herring, Archbishop of Canterbury*) and versatile painter, the patriotic author of "modern moral subjects" and humorous satires that make him the first great commentator of his era (*O The Roast Beef of Old England;* and *A Scene from `The Beggar's Opera' VI*).

The fashion for "conversation pieces," usually representing a domestic interior, were popular with his successors **Francis Hayman** and Joseph Highmore, who exploited the illustrative quality of the genre. Hayman was among the first painter to draw inspiration from Shakespeare (*The Wrestling Scene from `As You Like It'*).

18C: Courtly Portraiture
The term "Grand Style" alluded to art in the manner of the great Italian Renaissance masters (Michelangelo, Raphael, Titian). Subjects were usually drawn from the Bible, classical mythology or literature and thus qualified as 'high art.' **Joshua Reynolds** was quick to recognise that English "history" pictures found little favour with English patrons, and therefore fashioned his own style of portraiture. Sitters were flattered (*Lady Charlotte Hill, Countess Talbot*) and often posed as Classical gods (*Three Ladies Adorning a Term of Hymen*). In contrast, **Gainsborough**'s portraits are full of movement and gesture, colour, light and space (*Giovanna Baccelli*). His patrons were largely country gentry and his sitters often are depicted in Arcadian landscapes.

Landscape and Empire: Aspects of Naturalism, Sporting Art and Genre Painting
The man who most successfully painted landscape in the Grand Manner was **Richard Wilson**, having travelled in Italy for seven years. His topographical landscapes suggest admiration for Claude (*Meleager and Atalanta*) and the Venetians.

George Stubbs adapts the Grand Manner to equestrian pictures (*Horse Frightened by a Lion*), **Joseph Wright of Derby** to modern genre painting and portraiture, such as *An Iron Forge*, where industry is seen as intense and poetic. Watercolour becomes the favourite medium of travellers to the Continent for recording impressions of lofty mountains, avalanches, sun-baked plains and erupting volcanoes.

One room, as well as temporary exhibitions are usually devoted to the great British landscape painter, **John Constable** (Flatford Mill; A Bank on Hampstead Heath; East Bergholt House).

Works on Paper: Watercolours and Prints 1680–1900

William Blake and his followers include the visionary painters Samuel Palmer, Edward Calvert, George Richmond, known as the "Ancients." Blake (1757–1827) pioneered monotype printing methods for his limited edition illustrations of the Creation: pigment was applied to a hard board upon which sheets of paper were laid, each taking a different impression before the colour dried; this image was then worked up separately with pen, ink and watercolour. Romantic subjects were chosen from great literature (Illustrations to Thornton's `Pastorals of Virgil').

Samuel Palmer (1805–81) was profoundly impressed by Blake, not only in the use of woodcut and tempera on a relatively small scale, but also in his mystical view of the English landscape (A Hilly Scene). He was followed by **Richard Dadd** (1817–86) who produced highly individual illustrations (The Fairy Feller's Master-Stroke). In 1843, Dadd murdered his father and was condemned to Bethlem Hospital and Broadmoor Prison where he was able to explore his hallucinatory world of fantasy, visions, fairies and hobgoblins.

Girtin's The White House at Chelsea marks a new departure in watercolour painting from the stained, monochrome drawings of 18C to the luminous, atmospheric "impressions" of the 19C. Great swathes of delicate wash are applied to the absorbent white paper which he favoured, the low horizon a homage to the watercolours and etchings of Rembrandt.

Art and Victorian Society

The Royal Academy School taught technique, its gallery displayed current artistic trends: **Wilkie** (The Village Holiday); **Frith**; and **Edwin Landseer**

A Moral Dilemma

The delicate moral question of infidelity and prostitution was topical at a time when abandoned mistresses and high-society prostitutes used to flaunt themselves on horseback in Hyde Park: in literature the subject treated by Abbé Prévost (Manon Lescaut), Marquis de Sade (Justine, ou les Malheurs de la Vertu), Laclos (Liaisons Dangereuses), Dumas (La Dame aux Camélias), Flaubert (Madame Bovary) was worked in music by Mozart (Don Giovanni) Verdi (La Traviata), Rossini and Massenet. In painting, the cause was publicised with realism by Frith, Millais, Tissot or condoned by the Aesthetes and Decadents with idealisations of exotic beauty (Leighton, Alma Tadema, Russell Flint).

(A Scene at Abbotsford), Queen Victoria's favourite painter who had been an infant prodigy exhibiting his work at the RA from the age of 12 and who learnt to endow his animal subjects with human-like expressions.

Pre-Raphaelites and Symbolists – JE Millais encapsulated the ethic of the Pre-Raphaelite Brotherhood in his painting Christ in the House of His Parents, exhibited in 1849, and full of meticulous realism and elaborate iconography. The carpenter's shop was based on premises in Oxford Street, Joseph's figure and hands are modelled upon those of a real carpenter, his head is a portrait of Millais' father, the sheep were drawn from two heads obtained by the painter from a local butcher's, the still life on the back wall is charged with the symbolism of the Crucifixion (Dove of the Holy Spirit, the triangle of the Trinity, the tools that represent the Passion). The overall effect was new and precipitated controversy. **Rossetti** was the son of an Italian political refugee, living in London. From an early age he showed a fascination for Dante and the dreamy world of Romance, legend, pure love and chivalry that were also to inspire him to write poetry. In 1850 he met Elizabeth Siddal, she became his muse and eventually his wife (1860), only to die two years later from an overdose of laudanum, a derivative of opium. Bereft of his muse, Rossetti became a virtual recluse and eventually died a chloral addict.

In *Ecce Ancilla Domini*, Rossetti beautifully combines realism with religious feeling.

Holman Hunt's *The Ship* shows a moonlit voyage which symbolises his life and religious self doubts, the man at the wheel with his back turned possibly representing himself.

William Frith's *Derby Day* was much admired when it was exhibited in 1858. It is a prize piece of Victorian genre complete with accurate portraits of recognisable people (young and old, rich and poor), realistic vignettes of such an occasion (the gambling, the entertainment, the social scene, lavish picnics and ragged beggary) all set against a meticulously rendered view of Epsom Racecourse, painted from specially commissioned photographs.

Edward Burne-Jones (1833–98) is closely associated with William Morris. His idealised young subjects are bathed in a dreamy soft light *(Sidonia von Bork)*; profiles and textures are carefully contrasted one with another (flesh tones, stone carving, embroidered fabric, metal armour, flora and foliage). A preference for tall compositions may reflect the contemporary use of paintings as decorative panels integrated into more complex interior schemes.

Aestheticism

The movement's call for "art for art's sake" evolved during the 1870s and found its manifesto in Walter Hamilton's *The Aesthetic Movement in England*, published in 1882. Whistler and Albert Moore imported their own ideas from Paris; at home, the handsome, intellectual, well-travelled and charismatic **Lord Leighton** *(The Bath of Psyche)*, elected President of the Royal Academy in 1879, assumed the mantle.

Alma-Tadema, Watts and Poynter, otherwise known as the Olympians, drew inspiration from Hellenistic Greece and the images evoked by the Elgin Marbles. Composition is simplified, colour is carefully blended into harmonious arrangements, form is precisely outlined and defined by texture or surface decoration, the fall of drapery or the perspective of a tiled floor.

British Art and France

The most original painter to digest the current influence and instigate Continental modernism was **Whistler** (1834–1903). Receptive to all the prevailing artistic movements in Paris, Whistler assimilated influences from the Impressionists (overall composition), imported Japanese prints (unusual perspective and muted colour), the writings of established art critics like the Romantic poets Baudelaire and Gautier as well as the spirit of his middle-class Parisian contemporaries Gustave Moreau, Marcel Proust, George Sand, Chopin, Gounod and Berlioz among others. *Symphony in White, No. 2: The Little White Girl* is a wonderfully composed, dreamlike portrait of his lover, enriched with Japanese objects.

John Singer Sargent (1856–1925), an American painter who had worked outdoors with Claude Monet and Camille Pissarro moved to London in 1885 *(Carnation, Lily, Lily, Rose)*.

THE MODERN AGE

British artists reacted to the events of the early 20C in a particular way. The impact of World War I is illustrated in the works of the futurist **Nevinson** *(A Star Shell)* and **Matthew Smith** *(Nude, Fitzroy Street, No. 1)*. In the 1930s **Henry Moore** *(Mask)*, **Barbara Hepworth** *(Figure of a Woman)* and **Ben Nicholson** (*Le Quotidien*, 1932) were pioneers of modernism.

The Destructiveness of World War II was seen through the haunting works of **Paul Nash** *(Flight of the Magnolia)*, **John Piper** *(All Saints Chapel, Bath)* and

Detail of Yacht Approaching the Coast (c. 1840–45) by JMW Turner

© Tate

Graham Sutherland *(Devastation, 1941: East End, Wrecked Public House)*.

The period from 1960 to the present day is illustrated by changing displays. **David Hockney** and **Peter Blake** are leading exponents of Pop art; abstract painting (**Bernard Cohen**, **Richard Smith**) and sculpture (**Anthony Caro**, **Phillip King**) flourished.

Conceptual art which is exemplified by artists such as **Gilbert and George**, **the Living Sculptors** and **Richard Long**, was rejected by the School of London formed by **Howard Hodgkin**, **Lucian Freud** and **Kitaj**. Sculpture became symbolic and allusive as in the works of **Stephen Cox**, **Bill Woodrow** and **Richard Deacon**.

Contemporary art is marked by the YBAs (Young British Artists) whose leading figures are **Damian Hirst**, **Tracey Emin** and **Marc Quinn**. Other artists such as **Tacita Dean**, **Steve McQueen** and the **Wilson twins** explore different media such as film and video.

CLORE GALLERY: TURNER COLLECTION

J M W Turner bequeathed a large portion (100) of his finished paintings to the nation, with the request that they be hung in their own separate gallery. The will was subsequently challenged by his heirs and the Tate received some 300 oil paintings together with 19 000 watercolours and drawings. The Turner Bequest is presently displayed in its purpose-built three temporary and six permanent galleries.

Much research has been undertaken to analyse Turner's genius. Influences include Poussin, Claude, 17C Dutch masters, and Salvator Rosa as he switches from historical subjects *(Hannibal and his Army crossing the Alps)* to Classical *(The Decline of the Carthaginian Empire)* and topographical ones *(London from Greenwich)*. Perhaps it is sufficient to admire them for their evocation of wind and sunshine *(Shipwreck)*, reality or imagination *(Norham Castle, Sunrise)*, artistic talent and technique, and enjoy them for their colour, light, movement and poetic spirit.

Studies and Projects: *Self-Portrait* (1800). The Classical Ideal: works produced in admiration of Claude before Turner's first visit to Italy in 1819. Italy and Venice: *Bridge of Sighs, Ducal Palace and Custom House.* Seascapes: *(Ship and Cutter)*.

Tate Modern★★

A BIT OF HISTORY

The former **Bankside Power Station**, a massive structure (1957–60), known to some as the "cathedral of the age of electricity" with its single chimney (325ft/99m) and Aztec-inspired stepped brickwork, was designed by Giles Gilbert Scott. The oil-fired power station, which closed in 1981, has been converted to house the Tate Gallery's collections of international **20C art**. The wealth of the Tate Modern Art Collection is largely due to the bequests made by Sir Roland Penrose, friend of Picasso and Ernst, and that of Edward James, a patron of Dali and Magritte. Works by 20C British artists are also on view at Tate Britain.

VISIT

&⋏🕒*Open Sun–Thu 10am–6pm, Fri–Sat 10am–10pm (last admission is 45min before closing)* 🕒*Closed 24–26 Dec. Parking for the disabled only; pre-booking essential.* ☜*Guided tours daily (45min) at 11am, noon (on level 3), 2pm, 3pm (on level 5).* ☜*No charge, audio tours £2. Bar/Restaurant (level 7) and café (level 2).* ☎*020 7887 8888 (exhibitions),* ☎*020 7887 8008 (recorded information);* ☎*020 7887 8687 (minicom),* ☎*020 7887 8888 (ticket office); www.tate.org.uk/modern.* **Tate to Tate Boat** *every 40min between Tate Modern and Tate Britain, daily 10.10am–5.10pm.* ☜*£5. www.thamesclippers.com.*

▷ **Location:** *Map: inside back cover (FGXY).* ⊖*Southwark; St Paul's.* The Tate Modern is a 10min walk from the station and well sign-posted. Or approach across the Millennium Bridge, which links Tate Modern with St Paul's on the north bank of the Thames.

◉ **Don't Miss:** The panoramic **views** *(from the top floor)* of the Thames and the city, gigantic sculptures by contemporary artists in the Turbine Hall.

The Museum is split into seven levels. On level one is the **Turbine Hall**, which hosts vast commissions by different artists every six months. On levels three and five are the museum collections which is split into varying themes. Level four is devoted to special exhibitions.

◉ *As the exhibits are rotated according to various themes, the texts below trace the general evolution of genres for a better understanding of the displays.*

France – Primitive Art inspired the 'Sunday' painters **Rousseau** (1844–1910) and **Gauguin** (1848–1903) who stylised form and used patches of flat colour for space within a composition, pattern to

Turbine Hall

Tate Photography

provide texture and relief. The **Nabis** group (1889–99) including Edouard Vuillard, Bonnard, Maurice Denis and Maillol, rejected realism.

Post-Impressionist, **Vincent van Gogh** (1853–90) used pure colour and painted out of doors with strong brushstrokes and impasto technique.

The Neo-Impressionist **Georges Seurat** (1859–91) suggests luminosity by juxtaposed coloured dashes. His pointillist technique has scientific precision.

Henri Matisse (1869–1954) was versatile and prolific: he collaborated with the Nabis, Cézanne, Signac, and Picasso and he was a major exponent of the **Fauves** group(along with André Derain), which emphasised strong colours.

Paul Cézanne (1839–1906) conceived landscape in terms of geometric volumes in which perspective is determined by colour. His portraiture (*The Gardener Vallier*, c 1906) and still-life paintings are also conceived as studies of mass, textured by pattern, moulded by shadow.

Pablo Picasso (1881–1973) draws on the Symbolist use of colour to suggest mood (*Nude Woman with Necklace*, 1968). Picasso, Braque, Modigliani and Brancusi were all greatly impressed by stylised Iberian sculpture and Oceanic carvings. From this artform, each explored eroticism or abstraction.

Cubism (1906–14) was the first truly abstract movement that evolved as a counter-reaction to the visual appeal of Impressionism and Fauvism: Cubism attempted to capture the volume or essence of the subject (form, shape, texture, purpose) as a series of fractured details. In a *Clarinet and Bottle of Rum on a Mantelpiece*, **Braque** presents the instrument as something associated with music (represented by symbols for the clefs). **Léger** (*Leaves and Shell*, 1927), meanwhile, forged his interpretation by highlighting with geometric patterning.

Dada and Surrealism – Dada (1915–22) came from Zurich: a deliberately nihilistic, anti-artform that was intended to shock. Breton, Tzara, **Duchamp** (*The Large Glass*), Arp and Picabia explored the fundamental nature of art by contradicting any established classification or justification with humour. Later, a more intellectual approach was pioneered by the Surrealist writers Apollinaire and Eluard. They were joined in Paris by a wave of foreign artists: **Ernst** (*Dadaville*, c. 1924), De Chirico, **Magritte** (*The Reckless Sleeper*, 1928), **Salvador Dalí** (*Mountain Lake* and *Forgotten Horizon*) , and **Joan Miro** (*Painting*, 1927).

Futurism – "A new art for a new century" was formulated by a group of Italians such as **Balla** (*Abstract Speed – The Car has Passed*), Boccioni, Carra, Severini and **Dottori** (*Expolsion of Red on Green*, 1910) to celebrate modern civilisation. Several main protagonists died during World War I, by which time the movement had fired the **Vorticists**.

German Expressionism – The Expressionists were happy to compromise naturalism by exaggerating form and colour if the end result had a more powerful impact. **Die Brücke** (1905–13) meaning "The Bridge" united Kirchner, Heckel, **Schmidt-Rottluff** (*Male Head*, 1917) and Bleyl in Dresden; soon it included Nolde, Pechstein, Edvard Munch and Der Blaue Reiter, a group that was started in 1911 in Munich by Marc, Kandinsky, Macke, Campendonk and Klee. **George Grosz** (*Drawing for `The Mirror of the Bourgeoisie'*, c. 1925) admitted his "profound disgust for life" before the outbreak of war, intensified by experience: intense themes include prostitutes and bloated businessmen and death. **Beckmann** evolved a brave new style of realism (*Prunier*, 1944).

Abstraction – If form is whittled to its purest outline and most perfect surface, then the subject has forsaken its personality and become abstract. In pursuing abstraction, an artist must

MAJOR MOVEMENTS AND ARTISTS OF THE 20C
Shaded off colours indicate the origin and/or influence of a movement

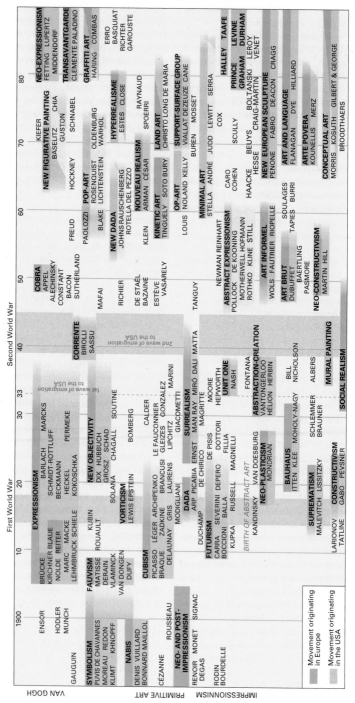

necessarily pare away his character to explore his inner spirituality or religion: Theosophy is the mystical rationale contained in the work of **Kandinsky** (*Lake Starnberg* and *Cossacks*). **Suprematism** was pioneered by **Malevich** (*Composition*, 1912–3) who rejected the "weight of the real world" in favour of a black square, suspended in a void. **Constructivism** originated in Russia out of collages via reliefs and mobiles into abstract compositions of diverse materials. By 1921 the movement was dead, its its concepts transposed to architecture and furniture design.

De Stijl was a Dutch magazine that promoted **Mondrian** (*The Tree A*, c. 1913) and Neo-Plasticism. Born from a graphic medium, the greatest impact was delivered to poster art, packaging and commercial art, but it also left its mark on Gropius and the Bauhaus ideals.

British Abstraction – In Britain, an interest in abstraction can be dated to the conservative Seven and Five Society in 1919, which soon attracted artists such as **Barbara Hepworth** *(Orpheus, Maquette 2)* and **Henry Moore** (*Three Points*, 1939–40); it reformed in 1926 as the Seven and Five Abstract Group and enlisted John Piper.

Realism and traditional values returned after the War, when it was recognised that art had splintered into fractured groups. **Stanley Spencer** (*The Centurion's Servant)* excelled at figurative painting, Lucian Freud evolved his own realism from painting from life, the **Kitchen Sink** school emerged from the Royal College in the 1950s. More violent are the styles of Dubuffet and **Giacometti** (*Venice Woman IX*, 1956), who preceded the trio **Francis Bacon** (*Study for Portrait on Folding Bed* and *Seated Figure*), Sutherland and Henry Moore.

Repercussions – The **Euston Road School** was founded in 1937 as a counter-reaction to the avant-garde, with artists such as Bell, Coldstream, and Rogers. The prospectus stated: "In teaching, particular emphasis will be laid on training the observation ... No attempt, however, will be made to impose a style and students will be left with maximum freedom of expression."

Abstract Expressionism (1942–52) originated in New York, where Ernst, and Mondrian sought refuge during the war, with De Kooning , **Newman** (*Adam*, 1951–2), **Jackson Pollock** (*Naked Man with Knife*; and *Summertime: Number 9A*) and **Mark Rothko** (*Untitled*, c. 1950–2) all exploring similar concepts in different media and styles, often on a large scale: "The familiar identity of things has to be pulverised in order to destroy the finite associations with which our society increasingly enshrouds every aspect of our environment" (Rothko, 1947).

Op and Kinetic Art, which explores the distinction between reality and the nature of illusion, was developed by the Hungarian Vasarely and Bridget Riley. **Pop Art and New Realism** is drawn as its title suggests from popular culture and graphic art. In the 1950s at the ICA, the likes of Paolozzi and Hamilton used collages of mundane objects to capture the spirit of the period. The second phase (1961) emerged from the Royal College with Hockney, Peter Blake, Jones, Boshier, Phillips, **Roy Lichtenstein** (*Whaam!*, 1963), **Claes Oldenburg** (*Counter and Plates with Potato and Ham*, 1961), **Andy Warhol** (*Self-Portrait*, 1967) and Jasper Johns.

Contemporary Art – Auerback, Francis Bacon, Lucian Freud and David Hockney today continue a historic British preoccupation for the representation of contemporary figures in their social context. Artists such as Hirst, Emin and **Cornelia Parker** (*Thirty Pieces of Silver*, 1988–9) are stars of the **Young British Artists** or 'YBAs' working in conceptual media from paint to installations.

Victoria and Albert Museum★★★

The Victoria and Albert Museum is a treasure trove of art objects and is Britain's National Museum of Art and Design. Masterpieces from all over the world create a wonderful hub of decorative arts along town.

A BIT OF HISTORY

The Museum was created to accommodate the contemporary works manufactured for the 1851 Exhibition (◔ See KENSINGTON). In 1857 the collection was moved from Marlborough House to South Kensington. In 1899 it was renamed in honour of Queen Victoria and Prince Albert. The museum now holds a collection of over 4 million objects.

Note also the Morris, Gamble and Poynter rooms (Level A: off 13-15), a pleasant café overlooking the garden, are enhanced with stained glass, ceramics, and elegant furniture.

Redevelopment

The V&A undertook a redevelopment programme, known as **Future Plan**, after celebrating its 150th anniversary. This includes an amazing Cubist-inspired

▷ **Location:** *Map inside front cover* (CY) *and area map under KENSINGTON.* ⊖*South Kensington.* The museum is close to the Brompton Oratory and Knightsbridge.

◔ **Don't Miss:** *Tippoo's Tiger;* The **British Galleries** *(Levels 2 and 4)*, particularly silver and furniture (the Great Bed of Ware); **Constable and Turner** *(Level 3 room 87)*, the lively **Fashion** Gallery *(Level 1, rm 40)*; **Theatre & Performance**; the tranquil Italianate courtyard and reflecting pool of the **John Madejski Garden** and the wonderfully decorated café housed in the **Morris, Gamble and Poynter Rooms**.

◔ **Timing:** For the one-time visitor, it's best to go to the departments of personal interest first, and then meander back through the other sections.

▲▲ **Kids:** Hands-on exhibits, activities, family trails, events, and backpacks.

Ardabil Carpet (c. 1539)

© Richard Waite/Victoria and Albert Museum

structure of a self-supporting spiral clad in ivory-coloured tiles, designed by Daniel Liebeskind.

The museum is divided into four broad themes: **Asia**; **Europe**; **Materials & Techniques**; and **Modern**. The following guide takes you through each section from the ground floor up.

VISIT

Cromwell Road. ⟳⟳*Open Sat–Thu 10am–5.45pm, Fri 10am–10pm.* ⟳*Closed 24–26 Dec. Brochure/map (26 languages).* ⟳*No charge, except for some special exhibitions.* ⟳*Guided tours hourly (1hr) 10.30am–3.30pm from the Grand Entrance; Gallery talks Thu 1pm; Lunchtime Talks Wed 1.15–*

2pm. Photography permitted (☺ no flash, no tripods). Café. Shops. Entrances in Cromwell Road and Exhibition Road. ☎ 020 7942 2000. www.vam.ac.uk.

ASIA
Sculpture *Floor 1: 17–20.*
These rooms explore Buddhist sculpture, detailing Asian conventions in contrast to the adjacent European sculpture.

South Asia *Level A: 41.*
Hindu, **Buddhist** and **Jain India** are represented by stylised figurative works. Note the refined gilt bronze Buddha, with his handsome head crowned like a monarch or conforming to a strict iconography.
The **Mughal** Empire produced fabulous illuminated manuscripts such as *The Akbarnma* and Jahangir's *Memoirs,* as well as carpet weaving. The handle of *Shah Jahan's Jade Cup* is shaped as an expressive wild goat.

South-East Asia *Level 1: 47a-c.*
The Himalayan regions blended Indian, Chinese, Kashmiri, Nepalese and Central Asian designs with Buddhist art.
Nepal was sustained more directly by eastern India. exemplified by the **Newar** community (*Bhairava* sculpture).
Discover the legacy of Angkor in Cambodia, Pagan in Burma, Sukhothai in Thailand and the complex temple communities of central and east Java.

Islamic Middle East *Level 1: 42.*
Spain to Central Asia lands were united under Islam, their arts subjugated to rigorous rules (such as the mosque's orientation towards Mecca) that encouraged alternative embellishment in the form of superlative calligraphy. The *Ardabil Carpet* (c. 1539) is the oldest in the world.

China *Level 1: 44, 47e.*
From 5000BC, this gallery takes in the Bronze Age **Shang** state (1700 BC), when metal signified the greatest wealth and luxury; the **Han** dynasty (206 BC–AD 220) with naturalistic tomb paintings; the **Tang** dynasty (618–906),

GALLERIES
Open at time of press. Levels are in brackets.

Asia:
China (1)
Islamic Middle East (1)
Japan (1)
Korea (1)
Sculpture (1)
South Asia (1)
South-East Asia (1)

Europe:
British Galleries 1500–1760 (2)
British Galleries 1760–1900 (4)
Cast Courts (1)
Europe 1600–1800 (0)
Europe & America 1800–1900 (3)
Medieval 300–1500 (1)
Medieval & Renaissance (0, 1, 2)
Northern Renaissance 1500–1700 (1)
Raphael (1)

Materials & Techniques:
Architecture (4)
Ceramics (6)
Fashion (1)
Glass (4)
Gold, Silver & Mosaics (3)
Ironwork (3)
Jewellery (3)
Leighton (3)
Metalware (3)
Paintings (3)
Photography (1)
Portrait Miniatures (3)
Prints & Drawings (3)
Sacred Silver & Stained Glass (3)
Sculpture (1, 3)
Silver (3)
Tapestries (3)
Textiles (3)
Theatre & Performance (3)

Modern:
20th Century (3)

which produced lavish white porcelain; the **Song** period, witnessing the development of new forms of ceramic and detailed sculpture (*Bodhisattva Guanyin,* c. 1200); the **Yuan** dynasty of

313

the Mongols (1279–1368) which exude political ambition in their art; and finally, the **Ming** dynasty (1368–1644) whose exotic textiles evoke the Forbidden City in Peking.

Japan *Level 1: 45.*

The **Nara** dynasty (645–794) assimilated Chinese Tang influences into ceramic designs. The **Heian** court (794–1185) patronised the arts and culture; this was continued by the **Kamakura** rule (1185–1333) during which time paintings and sculptures of Buddha become more refined.

The **Edo** period (1615–1868) is noted for the production of porcelain and woodblock printing. The Momoyama period (early 17C) six-fold screen depicts the arrival of European traders in Japan.

Korea *Level 1: 47g.*

The main collection dates from the **Koryo** dynasty (918–1392) when the arts strived for perfection, shown in simple and restrained ceramics with harmonious colours.

EUROPE
Europe 17C–18C
Level 0: Rooms 1–7.

Sumptuous objects from Cabinets of Curiosoties reflect ideas of the Baroque and the message of the Counter Reformation.

Medieval & Renaissance
Levels 0, 1 & 2.

These newGalleries, spread over three levels in the east wing, illustrate Medieval and Renaissance Art from 300 to 1600.

Northern Renaissance
Level 1: Rooms 16a, 25–27.

Important artworks from France, Germany and Holand show the transition from the Gothic to Renaissance style including stained glass and textiles.

Medieval 2C–15C *Level 1: Room 46.*

Rich ivory carvings and metalwork are the highlights of this gallery exploring small scale objects.

Cast Courts *Level 1: 46a and 46b.*

The architecture of the courts is typically Victorian. The casts were made for the benefit of art students who could not afford to travel abroad, Illustrating European sculpture through the centuries: *Trajan's Column* (AD 113); statues of *St George* by **Donatello** and of *David* by **Michelangelo**.

Raphael Cartoons *Level 1: 48a.*

These were commissioned in 1515 by Pope Leo X for the Sistine Chapel and illustrate incidents from the lives of the Apostles St Peter and St Paul.

British Collections 1500–1900
Level 2: 52-58; Level 4: 118-125.

The most remarkable single piece from this period is the *Great Bed of Ware* of carved oak *(57)*. Mentioned by Shakespeare, the bed has become legendary since it was made as a tourist attraction for the White Hart Inn, a popular hostelry on the way from London to Cambridge.

Of particular interest is the **18C** collection, with pieces by the great furniture designers **Chippendale** *(see INTRODUCTION – Furniture)*. Re-created interiors include the Glass Drawing Room from Northumberland House (1700s).

The **19C** section is one of the strongest of the furniture collection, many of which were purely ornamental, demonstrating the eclectic tastes of the Victorian Age. Notable pieces include **Pugin**'s armoire; and a painted screen by **Vanessa Bell** reflecting the influence of Matisse.

Europe and America 19C
Level 3: 101. The 19C Collection includes an impressive Gothic Revival bookcase by **Carl Leistler & Son**s and wonderful Art Nouveau objects.

William Morris (1834–96)

Morris epitomises the Victorian age as a well educated, middle class, talented and successful designer, craftsman, poet, conservator and political theorist, endowed with enormous vision, imagination and energy.

Morris went to Oxford to study theology; there he met members of the Pre-Raphaelite Brotherhood (DG Rossetti, Burne-Jones, Ford Madox Brown). He commissioned his friend Philip Webb to design a house in Bexleyheath; when trying to furnish The Red House, Morris discovered how "all the minor arts were in a state of complete degradation" and set about improving the situation.

Morris, Marshall, Faulkner & Co quickly proved successful; major projects included reception rooms at St James's Palace and a new refreshment room for the South Kensington Museum (V & A); in 1875 the company was re-formed as **Morris & Co**, and manufacturing continued until 1940.

Morris employed the services of other like-minded talented technicians and draughtsmen: Webb, Burne-Jones (figurative tapestries and stained glass), George Jack (furniture including the famous Morris chair) and William de Morgan; from embroideries he moved on to wallpapers, stained glass, printed and woven textiles, carpets, rugs, tapestries, furniture, light fittings and ceramics. In 1890 he founded the **Kelmscott Press** for the specialist production of exquisitely printed books modelled on Medieval manuscripts.

Morris upheld the importance of good craftsmanship in the face of mechanisation and industrial processes, the use of the most appropriate materials for functional objects, and the need for good design in even the most lowly, domestic things; his lasting reputation and example have inspired the ethic of 20C industrial design.

MATERIALS & TECHNIQUES

Sculpture Level 1: 21–24.

Many important Italian masters of the Renaissance are represented: **Donatello** (*The Chellini Madonna* 1456); **della Robbia** (*Adoration of the Magi* early 16C); and **Bernini** (*Neptune and Triton*). Perhaps the most highly prized is **Michelangelo's** *Slave*, a wax preparatory model for a figure intended for the tomb of Pope Julius II.

Notable examples of medals include works by the eminent medallist **Pisanello**.

Gilbert Bayes Sculpture Gallery Level 3: 111. Housed in a restored open arcade, this gallery affords extensive views of the superb Cast Courts below.

The gallery displays a history of ivory decorations from early mascots and amulets to exquisite Gothic figures.

Photography Level 1: 38a.

The history of photography is explored through displays and computers deatiling the museum's half a million strong collection of photographs.

Fashion Level 1: 40.

This wonderful collection charts developments in men's, ladies' and children's wear from the 16C. Displays start with Displaying the complicated trimmings and contrivances of the eclectic 18C contrasts to the late 19C and early 20C. Designers include Dior, Chanel, Karl Lagerfeld, **Vivienne Westwood** (*Evening Dress, 1996*) and

© V&A Images

'Watteau' evening dress (1996) by Vivienne Westwood

Pottery

Iznik, in Turkey, produced the finest quality pottery of the Islamic world.
Hispano-Moresque was made in Islamic Spain (8C-1492): colours include green, yellow, white, black and manganese; shapes include albarello drug or water jars.
Delftware or Dutch tin-glazed earthenware was inspired by Italian maiolica (Antwerp c 1584). The commonplace use of underglaze blue was a direct response to Chinese wares imported through the Dutch East India Company founded in 1609.
Lustre is the name given to the iridescent metallic finish: silver oxide provides a brassy yellow colour, copper for a rich red. Pioneered in Baghdad, developed in Spain (Malaga, Valencia) and Italy (Deruta, Gubbio), revived by William de Morgan (19C). Other, less durable gilding methods adopted by Wedgwood included the use of platinum salts for silver, gold for pink, purple lustre.
Cream ware consists of lead glazed stoneware with a cream-coloured body containing flint (silica). Cheap to produce, hard wearing and a lighter alternative to porcelain, it also facilitated intricate open basket work. Its colour was ideally suited to transfer printing.
Slipware suggests the use of diluted clay (slip) for trailed or dripped decoration, sealed with clear glaze.

Catherine Walker (including the *Elvis Dress* worn by Princess Diana). Accessories by Shilling , Vuitton, Ferragamo and Montblanc.

Silver *Level 3: 65-70a.*
England boasts an important silver tradition, exemplified by the Worshipful Company of Goldsmiths (&See *THE CITY*). Note the intricate workmanship of the *Howard Grace cup*, set with pearls and garnets and the Vyvyan salt with its panels of *verre eglomisé*. Also note the wonderful panelling of the **Ceramic Staircase** leading to this gallery.

Gold, Silver & Mosaics
Level 3: 70–73.
The Gilbert Collection (*70–3*) has also been relocated here from Somerset House, and includes gold, silver and micro-mosaics.

Paintings
Level 3: 81, 82, 87, 88, 88a.
A highlight of any visit is *The Daydream* by **Dante Gabriel Rossetti**, an amorous depiction of Jane Morris, the wife of William Morris.
Works in oil and watercolour by **Blake**, **Palmer**, and **Waterhouse** adorn the walls of Room 82.Landscape painting in Britain is displayed through works by **Constable** and **Turner**.

Sacred Silver and Stained Glass *Level 3: 83-84.*
The museum's tall windows illuminate glass from the 12C to today, displayed alongside metalwork.

Prints & Drawings *Level 3: 90.*
The print collection includes artists range from **Rembrandt** (*Virgin and Child with Cat and Snake*) to the post-Impressionist **Kitaj**.

Portrait Miniatures *Level 3: 90a.*
This gallery traces the artform's history from the court of Henry VIII to its heyday in the 19th century.

Jewellery *Level 3: 91–93.*
The exhibits illustrate the history of jewellery from Antiquity to the present day, including sets of exquisite Prussian iron jewellery; pieces designed by the Paris, London and New York famous jewellers; and Oriental jewellery. The *hair ornament* by **Philippe Wolfers** (c. 1905) is inlaid with diamonds and rubies.

Tapestries *Level 3: 94.*
This room is dominated by the detailed *Hunting Tapestries* (c. 1425) made in Arras, Flanders.

Textiles *Level 3: 95–100.*
This collection is a haven for design professionals who can study a vast number of textiles spanning 5 000 years, including Pharaonic linens from Egyptian tombs.

The collections also illustrate the history of printed fabrics including the modern colours and designs of **William Morris** (*see William Morris p315*).

Renowned *"opus anglicanum"* or English medieval ecclesiastical embroidery is also displayed.

Leighton *Level 3: 102, 107.*
These vast frescoes by **Lord Leighton** depict the Arts of Industry as applied to War and to Peace.

Theatre & Performance
Level 3: 103–106.
A gallery focusing on the process of performance from concept to reaction including a smashed *Les Paul Gibson Guitar* played by Pete Townsend and Adam Ant's *Prince Charming uniform*.

Ironwork *Level 3: 113-114e.*
Ranges of wrought-iron grilles and railings illustrate the skill of the blacksmith through the ages.

Metalware *Level 3: 116.*
This is a diverse collection ranging from the 2C BC to today, encompassing a broad selection of items made of metals including platinum and gold.

Architecture *Level 4: 127-128*
A unique guide to architecture from different ages and areas of the world which includes a huge isometric drawing of St Paul's Cathedral.

Glass *Level 4: 129, 131.*
This gallery illustrates the history of glass-making from the impact of Venetian blown glass to the most famous of the English glassmakers.

Ceramics *Level 6: 183–139; 140–145.*
The Ceramic Galleries chart the evolution of pottery ranging from Greek and Roman; tin-glazed earthenware such as **maiolica** from Italy; stoneware including pieces by **Josiah Wedgwood** (1730–95); and enamels from **Limoges**.

MODERN
20th Century *Level 3: 74, 76.*
These rooms show the influence of Modernism and Functionalism throughout the 20C on the design of furniture and objects of daily life.

A Gory Image

Tipu's painted wood tiger represents an Indian tiger mauling a British officer.The tiger's body contains a miniature (possibly French) organ which ingeniously simulates its roar as well as the groans of its victim.
Captured in 1799 at the fall of Seringapatam, during which Tipu the ruler of Mysore was killed, it became a favourite exhibit in the East India Company's London museum. The statue is mentioned in Keats' satirical poem *The Cap and Bells*.

Tipu's Tiger

M. Kitcatt/MICHELIN

Wallace Collection★★★

A BIT OF HISTORY

On the north side of Manchester Square stands **Hertford House**. This imposing mansion was built between 1776–88 for the 4th Duke of Manchester. After being used as the Spanish Embassy, the 2nd Marquess of Hertford acquired the lease and used it as his principal residence to entertain the great and good of London society. In 1900, the Office of Works opened the residence as a public museum. An ingenious remodelling in 2000 has created an airy glass-roofed courtyard, home to an excellent Restaurant and more exhibition space.

Noble patronage – The family art collection was started by the **1st Marquess of Hertford** (1719–94) Ambassador to Paris and Lord Lieutenant of Ireland, increased by his descendants and transformed into one of the world's finest collections of 18C French art by the reclusive **4th Marquess of Hertford** (1800–70), who lived most of his life in Paris and collected old masters and 18C

- **Location:** *Map inside front cover (CDVX).* ⊖*Baker Street.* The Wallace Collection is a few minutes walk from the Tube Station, and 15 minutes from Oxford Circus.
- **Don't Miss:** The famous Laughing Cavalier by Frans Hals, the display of exquisite gold snuffboxes and portraits by Velasquez, Gainsborough and Rembrandt.
- **Timing:** The Wallace collection is a detailed experience and you will need at least 2–3hr to see all of it properly.

paintings (by **Watteau**, **Boucher** and **Fragonard**), tapestries, Sèvres porcelain and the finest French furniture of the 17C and 18C (by **Boulle**, **Cressent** and **Riesener**).

Sir Richard Wallace, the 4th Marquess' son (1818–90, moved the collection to Britain for safety from the Commune uprisings and made substantial additions, specialising in the decorative arts. The collection was bequeathed to the nation by his widow **Lady Wallace** (1897) on condition that the government provide premises in central London for the collection and that objects never be loaned or sold. Hertford House was therefore purchased from the Wallace family heir and transformed into a museum.

VISIT

♿✖🕐*Open daily 10am–5pm. Galleries are undergoing restoration and some may be closed at times. Check website or call ahead for information.* 🕐*Closed 24–26 Dec.* 🎧 *Guided tour (1hr) on an aspect of the collection daily 1pm; general guided tours on Wed, Sat–Sun 11.30am, 3pm. Leaflet. Guide book (3 languages). Wheelchairs are available on request from the cloakroom.* 📞*020 7563 9500. www.wallacecollection.org.*

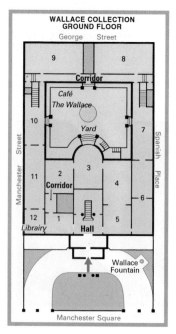

WALLACE COLLECTION
GROUND FLOOR

Ground Floor

Hanging in the **Entrance Hall** is *The Arab Tent* (c. 1865–6) by Sir Edwin Henry Landseer, author of the four lions in Trafalgar Square. Below is a selection of some of the Wallace Collection's most striking exhibits as well as portrait busts of the founders.

The **Billiard Room** (2) is furnished with Louis XIV (1643–1715) and Régence (1715–23) period furniture including a wardrobe and inkstand by Boulle.

The former **Dining Room** (3) displays the fine and applied arts of the Louis XV (1723–74) and Louis XVI (1774–92) periods, including two Venetian paintings by Canaletto. The *Mantel Clock* (1781) by Jean–Baptiste Lepaute is adorned with winged sphinxes based on the Neoclassical style. Note the portrait bust of *Madame de Sérilly* by the renowned French sculptor, Jean Antoine Houdon.

The **Back State Room** (4) contains, among other treasures, a magnificent Sèvres porcelain inkstand (1758) and an oak veneered Gaudreaus and Caffiéri Commodore, which belonged to Louis XV of France.

The **Front State Room** (5) is hung with English 18C and 19C portraits by Joshua Reynolds *('Old Q' as Earl of March)* and Thomas Lawrence *(Margaret, Countess of Blessington, 1822)*, and a gilt bronze vase by Robert Joseph Auguste (c. 1760–65). Note also the lovely miniature by Henry Bone (after Vigée Le Brun) depicting *Lady Hamilton as a Bacchante* (the famous lover of Admiral Nelson and a renowned beauty of the 18C).

The **Sixteenth Century Gallery** contains medieval, Medieval and Renaissance works of art (*St. Catherine of Alexandria,* c. 1502), curiosities from 15C and 16C Italian and Northern School sculpted figures (bronze, boxwood, ivory), wax miniatures to Limoges enamels and Venetian glass.

The former **Smoking Room**, which still retains a sample of its Iznik-style Minton-tile décor, offers displays of Renaissance jewellery, ceramics by the French potter Bernard Palissy (c. 1510–89) and Italian maiolica, a highlight of which is the wine cooler from 1574. The *hand bell of St Mura* from Ireland was said in legend to have descended from heaven ringing loudly.

The Armories

The **Armories Corridor** with its collection of 16C earthenware plates, leads on to the **European Armories Collection** (8, 9, 10), a comprehensive range of muskets, melée weapons and armour from 10C–16C. A notable item in room 8 is the gold and steel dagger of King Henri IV of France, inlaid with mother-of-pearl. The two sets of Gothic style armour depicting knights mounted on horses dominate room 9. Room 10 holds a rare visored helmet (c. 1390–1410) from Milan, which evokes the great battles of Hundred Years War in Europe, such as the Battle of Agincourt in 1415.

The **Oriental Armoury** (11) is devoted to arms set with gemstones, armour and 19C French Orientalist paintings. The 17C Sword of Tipu Sultan, which belonged to the Sultan of Southern India (1782–99) has a hilt decorated with diamonds, rubies and emeralds and inlaid gold inscriptions.

The **Housekeeper's Room** (12) and **Breakfast Room** host the museum shop and cloakroom. They also contain 19C British and French paintings, notably by Richard Parkes Bonnington (1802–28).

Large Drawing Room

Wallace Collection

First Floor

Accessible from the Ground Floor via the Grand Staircase in the Entrance Hall.

The walls of the **Grand Staircase** and the first floor **Landing** are hung with canvases by François Boucher depicting the epitome of the rococo style: *An Autumn Pastoral*, *The Rape of Europa*, *The Rising of the Sun*, *The Setting of the Sun*, *Mercury confiding the Infant Bacchus to the Nymphs*, and a *Summer Pastoral*.

Lady Wallace's **Boudoir** (13) features genre pictures and marble decorations, such as the gilt bronze Chimney-piece (c. 1769–75).

Along the **Gold Box Corridor** is a collection of gold **snuffboxes**★ painted with enamels or lacquered and set with gems.

The **Study** (14) accommodates splendid marquetry furniture by Boulle and portraits by Jean-Baptiste Greuze *(Portrait of a Lady)* and Vigée Le Brun *(Madame Perregaux, 1789)*.

The **Oval Drawing-Room** (15) features 18C portraits such as Vigée Le Brun's *The Comte d'Espagnac (Boy in a red coat)*, Fragonard's charming *A Boy as Pierrot* (c. 1785) and a portrait by Boucher of *Madame de Pompadour*, the mistress of Louis XV and illustrious patroness of the artist. The most famous painting in this room is Fragonard's masterpiece, *The Happy Accidents of the Swing*, symbolising hedonism and the loss of virginity in the rococo era.

Swing (1767) by Jean-Honoré Fragonard

Wallace Collection

The **Large Drawing Room** (16) is hung with *The Toper* by Ferdinand Bol, a student of Rembrandt, and decorated with an oak wardrobe (c. 1700), resplendent with brass and tortoiseshell, and pedestal clock attributed to Boulle.

The **Small Drawing Room** (17) contains French 18C furniture and *Fête Galante* (a sub-genre of rococo depicting scenes of idyllic charm in outdoor settings) paintings Lancret, Pater, and Jean-Antoine Watteau's *Harlequin and Columbine* (c. 1716–18).

The Eastern Galleries

17C Dutch and Flemish easel pictures by Rembrandt, Rubens and their contemporaries deck the the **East Drawing Room** (18).

The 17C paintings of the Dutch Golden Age presented in the **East Galleries** (19, 20, 21) include colourful landscapes by Ruisdael; marine battles and waterside scenes by Willem van de Velde the Younger and Aelbert Cuyp; sketches by Rubens; in contrast to the lively and lustful scenes by Jan Steen. A particular highlight is *The Lace Maker* (1662) by Caspar Netscher in the second room, a genre subject from the painter's earlier years.

The Great Gallery

This leads to the largest display in the museum, namely the **Great Gallery** (22). The clustered nature of the artworks, along with the French and Italian furniture, make the hall all the more intimate and intriguing for the visitor. A lot of the larger 17C pictures and Old Master paintings in the collection can be found on display here: **Titian's** *Perseus and Andromeda* (c. 1554–6); religious paintings by **Murillo** *(The Holy Family with the Infant Baptist*, c 1670*)*; portraits by **Velázquez** *(The Lady with a Fan*, c. 1640, an intense and sober portrait that exemplifies the style of the artist*)*, **Rembrandt** *(Titus, the Artist's Son*, c. 1657, a sympathetic portrait which embodies the relationship between father and son*)*, **Gainsborough** *(Mrs Mary Robinson Perdita*, 1781, who

Promenade Concerts in the Great Gallery

Special promenade concerts are held in the Great Gallery at 2pm on various Tuesdays and Fridays of each month, with music inspired by the collections.

Laughing Cavalier (1624) by Frans Hals

became the mistress of the Prince of Wales, later George IV); and *The Rainbow Landscape* (c. 1636, one of the great landscapes painted by **Rubens**).

Amongst these great paintings, located above one of the chest of draws in the gallery, hangs probably the most famous painting of the museum, **The Laughing Cavalier** by Frans Hals. This baroque portrait was painted in 1624, and despite the title, the sitter is neither laughing nor a cavalier. His opulent jacket is repleted with arrows and lover's knots, suggesting that this was a commission for a betrothal. The bravura technique and lucid colours used by Hals gives this painting its majestic aura.

The Western Galleries

The **Nineteenth Century Gallery** (23) displays 19C French painting and miniatures including works by Delacroix, Géricault, Scheffer and Meissonier(one of the favourite artists of Lord Hertford). The *Temptation of Saint Hilarion* by Dominique Papety (c. 1843–4), is a vivid work on the theme of sexual temptation.

The **West Gallery** (24) was a former dressing room of Sir Richard and Lady Wallace. The room is furnished with fine 18C French furniture by René Dubois, stands out by his use of green velvet and green silk lining. 18C Venetian landscapes line the walls, including works by Francesco Guardi and Canaletto, in contrast to portraiture such as *Innocence* (c. 1790s) by Greuze, which combines childhood innocence with emotional feeling.

The **West Room** (25), which was the bedroom of Lady Wallace, is decorated in a elegant feminine 18C style. Note the exquisite sculpture of Cupid and Psyche by Filippo della Valle and the Mantel Clock attributed to Falconet. Marine paintings by Bonington and Vernet line the walls.

Lower Ground Floor

Accesible from the ground floor via staircases adjacent to the Entrance Hall and European Armoury I.

The **Porphry Court** is the central atrium of this floor and displays French and Italian sculptures (17–18C) and porphyry vases.

The lower ground floor also contains: the Goodison Theatre, which holds special lectures throughout the year; an Education Studio, which hosts workshops *(information and booking available by phoning ✆0207 563 9551)*; the Eranda Visitors' Library *(open by appointment only ✆0207 563 9528)*; and special exhibtion galleries *(check website for the latest exhibitions)*.

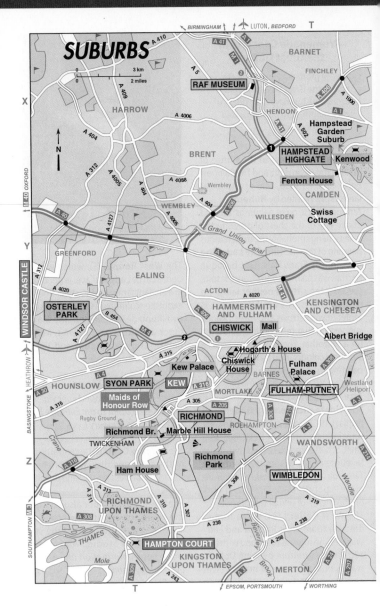

Chiswick★★

The beautiful scenery of Chiswick is a delight, in spite of the thundering traffic of the busy A4. This leafy residential suburb clings to a deep loop of the Thames and has a pretty riverside walk to Hammersmith Bridge past delightful pubs affording fine views of the activity

▶ **Location:** *See Suburbs map (TY).* ⊖*Hammersmith; Turnham Green and Bus no 190 or overground train to Chiswick from Waterloo Station. Chiswick is to the west of the A 4 dual carriageway.*

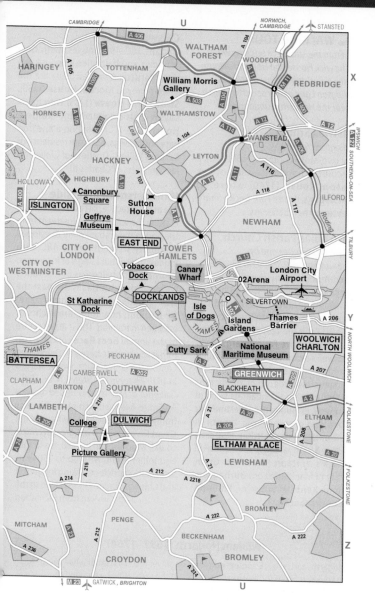

on the river, where keen rowers are out in all weather. Chiswick boasts many artistic and historic associations and a magnificent mansion with splendid gardens.

A BIT OF HISTORY

Chiswick retains something of the country village, which it was until the 1860s; by the 1880s the population had increased from 6 500 to 15 600; in the 20C the motorway (M4) and its feeder flyover divided the riverside from the rest. Georgian houses survive, however, in Church Street and other parallel roads to the river, and in Chiswick Mall overlooking the river and the Eyot.

WALKING TOUR

▶ *From the station or bus stop walk to Chiswick House and Hogarth's House (see Additional Sights) then cross Burlington Lane and proceed to Church St near the Hogarth roundabout.*

Chiswick Square

Burlington Lane.

Low two-storey houses (1680) flank a forecourt in front of the three-storey **Boston House** (1740) where, in **Thackeray**'s *Vanity Fair*, Becky Sharp threw away her dictionary.

St Nicholas Parish Church

🕐 *Open for services and by appointment.* ℘020 8995 4717. *www.stnicholaschiswick.org*

This site was mentioned as far back as 1181. The deceptively broad church has a buttressed and battlemented west tower (1436); the rest dates from the 1880s. Lady Mary Fauconberg, Oliver Cromwell's daughter, was a parishioner of St Nicholas. In the family vault below the chancel are three coffins, the shortest possibly holding the headless body of **Cromwell**, exhumed from Westminster Abbey and rescued from Tyburn in 1661. In the churchyard lie **Hogarth** (enclosed with railings) – under David Garrick's epitaph "Farewell, Great Painter of Mankind"; Lord **Burlington**; **William Kent**; **JM Whistler**; **Philippe de Loutherbourg**.

Chiswick Mall★★

Elegant 18C–19C houses, with bow windows and balconies, overlook the river. Particularly noteworthy are the three-storeyed **Morton House** (1730), **Strawberry House** (1735) with its six bays and attic dormers, and **Walpole House** (16C–17C) boasting a fine iron gate and railings, once the residence of Barbara Villiers, Duchess of Cleveland (and mistress of Charles II).

Hammersmith Riverside

The most attractive part of Hammersmith is along the waterfront. Upstream from the bridge the embankment developed gradually from the early 18C with modest houses built singly or in terraces, adorned with balconies or festooned with purple wisteria; in the past the view included sailing barges making for harbour; now there are yachts or oarsmen in training. This is at the centre of the annual **Boat Race** course, a cut-throat rowing race between Oxford and Cambridge Universities, which started in 1829 (see in PLANNING YOUR TRIP – Calendar of Events). It is rowed along a 4.25mi/6.84km stretch of the Thames from Putney to Mortlake. In October, the **Great River Race** (www.greatriverrace. co.uk), which began in 1988, is a longer and jollier affair, with up to 150 craft from Celtic curricles to Viking longboats and Chinese dragon boats taking to the water for 22mi/35.4km from Richmond to London Docklands.

William Hogarth (1697–1764)

Hogarth started work apprenticed as an engraver to a silversmith while living in Leicester Fields (now Leicester Square). At the same time he enrolled at St Martin's Lane Academy but failed to adopt academic figurative painting in the grand manner. Instead, he developed the "conversation piece" (1729), a more informal type of portraiture representing his middle class sitters in domestic interiors: *Rake's Progress* (1735), *Marriage à la Mode* (1743–45). His acute powers of observation, innate humour and sharp wit animate his narrative pictures, which found a large audience when copied and reproduced as engravings. Admirers recognised their contemporaries lampooned by caricatures. Aware and sensitive to the hardship of life in London as portrayed in his prints (child mortality, alcoholism, prostitution and corruption, cruelty to animals), Hogarth was appointed governor of Captain Coram's charitable institution, the Foundling Hospital in Bloomsbury. His paintings are exhibited at the National Gallery, Tate Britain and Sir John Soane's Museum (see THE CITY – Chancery Lane Walk).

Hammersmith Terrace

The urban terrace of 17 almost identical brick houses of three and four storeys, built as a single unit facing the river, dates from the mid-18C. Philippe de **Loutherbourg**, artist and scenic designer at the Drury Lane Theatre (*see COVENT GARDEN*) in the 18C, once lived at no 13; Sir Emery Walker, antiquary and typographer, who collaborated with Morris at the Kelmscott Press, lived at no 7. At the west end of the Mall are two pubs: the **Old Ship W6** and the **Black Lion** (*see Addresses*).

The **London Corinthian Sailing Club** occupies Linden House (18C, much refurbished); opposite, above the riverside wall, looking like a glassed-in crow's nest, is the race officers' box.

▷ *Make a short detour up South Black Lion Lane to view St Peter's Church.*

North of the Great West Road, the focal point of St Peter's Square is **St Peter's Church** (1829), a yellow stock-brick landmark with pedimented portico and square clock tower.

▷ *Return to the riverside.*

Upper Mall

Kelmscott House, a plain three-storey house, dates from the 1780s. In the 19C it became home to **William Morris** and his family until his death in 1896. Here, Morris drew the illustrations and designed founts for the fine books he printed in the nearby no 14 and published under the imprint of the **Kelmscott Press**. The **Dove** pub has had a licence for 400 years, although the present building goes back only 200 years (*see Addresses*).

Lower Mall

Near the pier is a plaque that indicates the site of the creek and "harbour where the village began".
Among the 18C–19C buildings are the **Blue Anchor** pub; the **Rutland**, a Victorian pub (*see Addresses*); Kent House (*no 10*), which is late 18C with symmetrical bay windows; the

Amateur Rowing Association (*no 6*), which has a canopied balcony over the boathouse entrance.
Hammersmith Bridge is a suspension bridge (1884–7) designed by Joseph **Bazalgette** to replace the first Thames suspension bridge (1827).

ADDITIONAL SIGHTS
Chiswick House★
Burlington Lane (EH)   ♿ 🅿 ✕
House: ⏰ *Open Apr daily 10am–5pm; May–Oct Sun–Wed and bank holidays 10am–5pm; Nov–21 Dec open for pre-booked group tours only.* **Gardens:**
⏰ *Open daily year round 7am–dusk.*
💷*£4.40 house; gardens free.* 🔍*Guided tours by appointment. Audio-guide (3 languages). Tea room, picnic area.*
📞*020 8995 0508. www.chgt.org.uk.*

In 1682 the first Earl of Burlington purchased a Jacobean mansion set in extensive acres at Chiswick. During the 18C, Richard Boyle, the 3rd **Earl of Burlington** (1695–1753), generous host and patron of the arts, transformed the house into a neo-Palladian villa (1725–29) in which to display his works of art and entertain his friends. Much of the interior decoration and the gardens were the work of his protégé **William Kent** (1686–1748). The villa still stands, but nothing remains of the Jacobean mansion nor of additions made in the 18C and 19C by Georgiana, Duchess of Devonshire and her successors, who entertained leading Whigs, Edward VII and the czars.

Exterior – An avenue of terms approaches the villa with its graceful Classical proportion. Paired dog-leg staircases are overlooked by statues of Palladio *(left)* and Inigo Jones *(right)*.
Interior – The lower floor octagon hall, lobbies and library now display material about the design and restoration of the house and garden. From the library the pillared link building leads to the Summer Parlour (1717), originally connected to the Jacobean mansion.
On the first floor *(staircase left of the library)*, intercommunicating rooms are arranged around a central octagon. The **Dome Saloon** has a coffered

Classical symmetry at the heart of Chiswick House

Ph. Gajic/MICHELIN

cupola rising from an ochre-coloured entablature to a windowed drum. The Red, Green and Blue Velvet Rooms have richly gilded coffered ceilings and Venetian windows, the latter having just undergone restoration. The roundels in the Blue Room are of Inigo Jones (by Dobson) and Pope (by Kent). The **gallery** runs along the west front, and consists of three rooms: the apsed, oblong central room communicates through arches to circular and octagonal end rooms. From the octagonal room a passage leads into the upper storey of the link building.

The **gardens** were landscaped mostly by Kent, who planted the giant cedars; temples, obelisks and statues were strategically placed so as to catch the stroller unawares.

Georgiana commissioned Wyatt to build a bridge across the water. The greenhouse was probably the work of Joseph Paxton from Chatsworth. The Inigo Jones Gateway *(northeast of the house)* was a gift from **Sir Hans Sloane** in 1736. The gardens are currently undergoing a £12.1m restoration, involving regenerating statues, paths, monuments and the planting of 1 600 trees, set to be completed in 2010.

Hogarth's House★

Call for opening hours. ☏*020 8994 6757. www.hounslow.info/arts/ hogarthshouse.*

William Hogarth called the three-storey brick house his "little country box by the Thames." The mulberry tree in the small garden grew there in his day. He spent not only the summer, but ever longer periods at Chiswick, entertaining such contemporaries as David Garrick.

Hogarth found fame as a commentator on 18C London life; note in particular: *The Election, London Scenes, The Harlot's Progress and Marriage à la Mode.*

The **Fuller, Smith and Turner Griffin Brewery**, formerly in Chiswick Mall, now stands across the Hogarth roundabout (*guided tours (2hr) Mon and Wed–Fri hourly 11am–3pm. £10 (including tasting session); no admission to children under 14 yrs. Book in advance. ☏020 8996 2063. www.fullers.co.uk.*

ADDRESSES

PUBS

Black Lion – *2 South Black Lion Lane, W6 9TJ. Ravenscourt Park; Stamford Bridge. ☏020 8748 2639.* This attractive pub is set back from the river, behind a garden with a brick arcade from an old riverside factory.

Blue Anchor – *13 Lower Mall, W6 9DJ. Ravenscourt Park; Hammersmith. ☏020 8748 5774.* A bustling pub with a lovely riverside location, which attracts a lively crowd.

The Dove – *19 Upper Mall, W6 9TA. Ravenscourt Park. ☏020 8748 9474.* In the 18C it was a coffee house where

James Thomson is said to have written the words of Rule Britannia in the upstairs room; from 1900 it housed the Dove Press and Bindery. Now it claims to have the smallest bar in the country.

Old Ship W6 – *25 Upper Mall, W6 9TD. Ravenscourt Park. ☏020 8748 2593. www.oldshipW6.co.uk.* A smart, sleekly refurbished pub by the river.

The Rutland Arms – *15 Lower Mall, W6 9DJ. Ravenscourt Park; Hammersmith ☏020 8748 5586.* A Victorian pub in an attractive riverside location. The pub is a good – and traditional – vantage point from which to watch the annual Oxford and Cambridge Boat Race (end March), with plenty of race day atmosphere.

Docklands★

The area opposite Greenwich has undergone a radical change since Canary Wharf was built in the 1980s. Set in a series of great bends in the Thames, this shimmering landmark overlooks a host of award-winning architecture. Arrive by the overhead Docklands Light Railway, or by boat to get a sense of the scale of the redevelopment that heralded the extension of London into the east.

> **Location:** *Map: Inside back cover (HJKL–XYZ).* ⊖*Tower Bridge; Canary Wharf.* Docklands stretches east from Tower Bridge to the Royal Docks in North Woolwich. The area is covered by an overground light train – the Docklands Light Railway (DLR), and the Underground's Jubilee Line.

A BIT OF HISTORY

Under the London Docklands Development Corporation (LDDC) established in 1981, the redundant London docks have been transformed into a modern annexe to the City, thus regenerating the riverside communities: Wapping, Isle of Dogs and Silvertown – some 4942 acres/2 000ha extending 5mi/8km east of Tower Bridge on the north bank, and Bermondsey and Rotherhithe on the south bank.

☙ WALKING TOURS
WAPPING

⊖*Tower Hill. DLR: Tower Gateway; Shadwell.*

Wapping was just a village beside the Thames until the 16C when a continuous riverside sprawl began to develop; there were many stairs (landing places) along the densely populated waterfront cut by alleys, steps, stages and docks, where **Charles Dickens** set several of his novels.

Commercial Docks

Built at the beginning of the 19C, the **London Docks** and **St Katharine Dock**★ finally closed in 1969. The London Docks were infilled and redeveloped as the offices of News International (1986), responsible for publishing *The Times* and *Sunday Times*. Warehouses on the waterfront have been converted into luxury apartments.

St Katharine Dock★ takes its name from the **Hospital of St Katharine by the Tower**. Founded in 1148 outside the City, it sheltered refugees, among them

the English forced to quit Calais in 1558, Flemings, Huguenots and others.

In 1968 the 19C dock basins were converted into a **yacht marina**; Telford's Italianate building, renamed **Ivory house**, was transformed into residential units and arcades of shops; part of a pre-1820 timber brewery was converted into the **Dickens Inn**; the **Coronarium Chapel**, consecrated in June 1977, remembers the Medieval hospice.

New buildings on the dockside accommodate the **World Trade Centre** (*east side*), the **London Commodity Exchange** (*north side*), which trades in cocoa, coffee, sugar, etc., and the **International Petrol Exchange**.

▷ *Take St Katharine's Way and Wapping High St.*

The **Wapping Pierhead** terraces of 18C houses originally flanked the entrance to the docks, housing dock officials.

River Police Boat Yard

The modern building houses the 33 craft of the **Metropolitan Special Constabulary** (Thames Division), which patrols the last 54mi/87km of the River Thames.

The attractive old building, which was originally a **pumping station** providing hydraulic power (1892–1977), is now a trendy restaurant and art gallery.

▷ *Retrace your steps and take Wapping Lane to the Highway.*

St Katharine Docks

B. Pérousse/MICHELIN

Tobacco Dock★

The beautiful brick vaults and cast-iron superstructure of the Skin Floor (1811–13) of the London Docks are of interest. The dock was developed as a chic shopping mall, a sort of East End Covent Garden. Sadly, however, it failed and is largely empty now while decisions are taken on what to do next.

Two historic ships are moored at the rear, on the canal. The *Sea Lark* is an American-built schooner that ran the blockade from 1810–1814 and now tells the classic adventure of *Kidnapped* by RL Stevenson. The *Three Sisters*, a replica of the original, which traded from 1788 to 1854, traces the history of piracy.

St George-in-the-East

Cannon Street Road or Cable Street.
🕐*Open Mon–Fri 8am–5pm, Sat–Sun 9am–5pm; call for group tours.* ✆*020 7481 1345. www.stgite.org.uk.*
The church, designed by **Hawksmoor** and consecrated in 1729, was severely damaged in 1941; a modern church (1964) was built within the 18C shell. The **tower**, with its two-tier octagonal lantern, is a distinctive feature.

▶ *Proceed east along the Highway, past St Paul's Church ('Church of the Sea Captains', including Captain Cook).*

LIMEHOUSE

DLR: Limehouse
Limehouse, named after its lime kilns, was a shipbuilding centre. Its exotic street names and fine Chinese restaurants are a reminder that Chinese immigrants first settled here in the 18C.

Limehouse Basin

From Dunbar Wharf, locally brewed India Pale Ale was shipped to India and Australia. **Regent's Canal Dock**, built in 1820 and subsequently enlarged, used to accommodate barges coming down the Regent's Canal to the Thames or into the Lea Navigation canal system via the Limehouse Cut (1mi/1.6km long).

St Anne's Limehouse

🕐*Open Sun 10.30am–12.30pm.*
✆*020 7987 1502.*
A distinctive square tower marks Hawksmoor's first church in the East End of London (1712–24).

ISLE OF DOGS★

DLR: West India Quay; Canary Wharf; Crossharbour; Island Gardens; Heron Quays; Mudchute; South Quau.
The Isle of Dogs is a tongue of land round which the Thames makes a huge loop south from Limehouse to Blackwall, characterised today by skyscrapers such as One Canada Square (also known as the Canary Wharf Tower), Citigroup Centre, 8 Canada Square. In the 19C the Island developed into a densely

populated industrial district. Since the docks were closed to shipping in 1980, the area has been transformed into a high-tech commercial alternative to the City.

West India Docks

Extensive development of the Island began early in the 19C when the **West India Docks** (1802–06) were built to receive rum and sugar from the West Indies. The docks were enclosed by a high brick wall and patrolled by their own police force. The **City Canal** (1805) was transformed into a dock in 1870.

Canary Wharf★★ – This ambitious project was sponsored entirely by private funding. Development began with the construction of the seven buildings suspended in part over water, enclosing **Cabot Square**. They are dominated by Cesar Pelli's tower block **1 Canada Square** (800ft/244m, 50 floors), also known as Canary Wharf Tower. It is the tallest tower block in London and was the first to be clad in stainless steel to reflect light. Ships belonging to the **Maritime Trust** are sometimes moored in the docks. The development also houses a concert hall, restaurants, pubs, shops, open spaces and the Canada Place and Jubilee Place shopping malls.

The blue-glass South Quay Plaza shimmers with reflections from the still waters. Peterborough House was the editorial office of the **Daily Telegraph**, until its move to Victoria.

Old West India Dock Buildings

At the west end of the old import (north) dock stand the **Cannon Workshops**, now occupied by a number of small businesses. To the north stands the old **Dockmaster's House** (now an Indian restaurant). The north quay of the dock is lined by two large multistorey **warehouses** (1802).

👥 Museum in Docklands★

No. 1 Warehouse, West India Quay, E14 4AL. ⏱*Open daily 10am–6pm (last admission 5.30pm).* ⏱*Closed 24–26 Dec.*

A Philanthropist

The statue by Wyon (1865) on E.India Dock Road shows **Richard Green** seated with his dog, and 19C shipbuilding scenes on the west side of the base: his family owned Blackwall shipyard and were local benefactors.

Whitebait Dinners

Blackwall was associated with the 19C political whitebait dinners. The Brunswick Hotel and Tavern, built in 1835 by the East India Company at Blackwall, was patronised by the Fox Club, followers of **Charles James Fox**; their political opponents, William Pitt the Younger, Gladstone and their Whig followers dined at Greenwich, where the tradition of whitebait dinners still thrives (Trafalgar Tavern).

👝*£5; child £3. Tickets alllow unlimited entry all year.* 📞*020 7001 9844. www.museumoflondon.org.uk/docklands.* This award-winning museum covers every aspect of port activity. Displays of restored working equipment, tugs and barges, *Mudlarks* – an interactive area for children – and *London, Sugar & Slavery*, which reveals the city's involvement in the transatlantic slave trade, make for a fascinating experience. There are costumed re-enactments, a re-creation of 19C riverside Wapping called *Sailortown*, and guided walks along the Thames. The **Billingsgate fish market** moved to its new building in 1982.

Millwall Docks

The 30ft/9m draft of the Millwall Docks (1868) was required in order to accommodate the larger ships bringing cargoes of grain and timber.

Mudchute Park features a riding stable and small urban farm. The name Mudchute recalls how silt dredged from the Millwall docks was deposited here. *Park:* ⏱*Open daily 9.30am–4.30pm.* 📞*020 7515 5901.*

A Fearsome Rascal

Captain Kidd was dispatched by **William III** (1700) to curtail increased pirate activity on the high seas. Bored by long periods offshore, his crew began rioting on board; the captain ended up murdering a man, for which he would have to face the death penalty. He therefore decided to turn his own hand at piracy and raised the Jolly Roger. Captured and repatriated, he was tried on 3 May 1701 and hanged at Execution Dock; the first time the rope stretched and broke, the second time he was less lucky.

The riverside **Island Gardens** (1895), provide a fabulous **view**★★★to Greenwich and the Royal Naval College.

Greenwich Foot Tunnel

Open 24hr.

In the round domed building beside the river a lift (or 100 steps) leads to a foot tunnel beneath the Thames *(10min)* to Greenwich.

The **Island History Trust** maintains an extensive archive of photographs and organises bi-annual festivals of local history, recollection and reunion *(Island House, Roserton Street; open Tue–Wed and 1st Sun of each month 1.30–4.30pm; 020 7987 6041; www.islandhistory. org.uk).*

The blue Dutch-design **lifting bridge** (1969) marks the eastern entrance to the South Dock. The nearby **Gun** pub *(see Addresses)* dates from the 15C;

from time to time Lady Hamilton stayed in the upper room.

BLACKWALL

DLR: All Saints

When Queen Elizabeth granted a charter to the **East India Company** in 1600, it established a shipbuilding and repair yard at **Blackwall**. Houses and inns developed on either side of Poplar High Street. In 1776 the company built **St Mathias Church** (now a nursery), with seven masts supporting the roof, then Brunswick Dock in 1789 (demolished in 1862); in 1806 this dock was incorporated into **East India Docks**.

Early 17C emigrants to America and later mid-19C emigrants to Australia and New Zealand sailed from Blackwall.

The Blackwall yard made its name with fast clipper ships and later with iron ships; in 1943 the East India Import Dock was used for the construction of the Phoenix units of the floating Mulberry harbour used in the 1944 D-Day landings. Today, just above the Blackwall Tunnel, impressive modern buildings accommodate the Town Hall, alongside the **Financial Times printworks**, by Nicholas Grimshaw in 1988.

The Old **Blackwall Tunnel** (1897) carries northbound traffic, the New Tunnel (1963) covers the southbound.

The **Reuters Data Centre** *(Blackwall Yard)*, by **Richard Rogers**, features black glass and, as with the Lloyd's Building, coloured service ducts.

Bow Creek is the name given to the estuary of the **River Lea**.

ADDRESSES

LIGHT BITE

1802 – *1 West India Quay, Hertsmere Rd, E14 4AL.* West India Quay. *0870 444 3886. www.1802docklands.co.uk.* This restaurant is housed within the Museum in Docklands. A nice place to stop for a coffee, drinks, snacks or a large meal, with its exposed brick and original pitch pine beams.

Café Rouge – *29–35 Mackenzie Wlk, 10 Cabot Sq, E14 4PH.* Canary Wharf. *020 7537 9696. www.caferouge.co.uk.* Café Rouge on the waterfront serves good quality French cuisine. Outdoor seating allows you to people watch over a coffee or *croque monsieur.*

PUBS

Prospect of Whitby – *57 Wapping Wall, E1W 3SP.* Wapping. *020 7481 1095.* Built in 1520, this is one of the oldest port-side pubs where mariners came before sailing to the New World. History remains in its original flagstone floor and wonderful pewter bar. It is also one of the most romantic, with a balcony terrace beside the Thames. The pub is nevertheless a victim of its success, with coaches dropping off tourists for lunch and dinner.

The Grapes – *76 Narrow St, Limehouse-Docklands, E14 8BP.* ⊖*Westferry DLR.* ℘*020 7987 4396.* Charles Dickens described this 18C pub under the name of The Six Jolly Fellowship Porters in *Our Mutual Friend.* Well-kept real ales; fish-led bar meals and snacks. Small speciality fish restaurant; booking essential. Tiny outside deck for spectacular

Thames views in a slightly out-of-the-way area near Canary Wharf.

The Gun – *27 Coldharbour, E14 9NS.* ⊖*Blackwall DLR.* ℘*020 7515 5222. www.thegundocklands.com.* This pub looking onto the Thames is named after the neighbouring foundry that produced canons during Nelson's era.

The Town of Ramsgate – *62 Wapping High St, E1W 2PN.* ⊖*Wapping.* ℘*020 7481 8000.* This historic pub, which takes its name from the home town of fishermen who unloaded their catch here, sits by Execution Dock where the bodies of pirates and thieves condemned to death by hanging (Captain Kidd in 1701) were left for the tide to wash over them three times.

Dulwich★

The highlights of Dulwich are its pretty village, fine museums, handsome weather-boarded buildings and elegant houses. The area is also home to a vast park full of magnificent oak trees, and a large lake.

A BIT OF HISTORY

Dulwich Manor, owned by **Bermondsey Abbey** until the Reformation, was acquired in the 17C by Edward Alleyn (◐*see opposite*).
The houses reflect the transition from 17C village to small country town where 18C–19C city merchants and gentlemen chose to reside. Commuter trains and cars have transformed it into a popular London suburb.

✎﹖ WALKING TOUR
◐ *Start at the N end of Dulwich Village and walk down.*

Nos 60, 62 – **The Laurels, The Hollies** – date from 1767. In the 18C the ironwork canopy on iron pillars over the pavement shaded the fare of the village butcher. Nos 97–105 form an 18C terrace, the last two houses date from the mid-1700s.

▷ **Location:** *See Suburbs map (UYZ).* Overground rail: West Dulwich from Victoria, North Dulwich from London Bridge. Dulwich lies to the south of Southwark and is accessible by A 23, A 215 and A 205 (South Circular).

Dulwich College★
Edward Alleyn, one of the greatest actors of the late 16C, bought Dulwich manor and founded the Chapel and College of God's Gift (1619) to serve as almshouses and a school for poor children. The original buildings, at the top of College Road (note the 18C iron gates surmounted by the Alleyn crest), include the chapel where Alleyn is buried.
Dulwich College, one of Britain's top Independent day- and boarding boys' schools, is housed further down College Road.

College Road
The house at no 31, Pickwick Cottage, is said to be where **Dickens** envisaged Mr Pickwick retiring. Bell Cottage (no **23**)

is a rare example of the once-common weatherboarded local cottages.

Pond Cottages (beyond the main road, Dulwich Common) is an 18C group overlooking the Mill Pond, several wholly or partly weatherboarded. The **Toll Gate** is the last in use in the London area.

ADDITIONAL SIGHTS
Dulwich Picture Gallery★

🕐*Open Tue–Fri and Bank Holiday Mon 10am–5pm, Sat–Sun 11am–5pm.* 🔎*Free gallery tours Sat and Sun 3pm.* 🎫*£5 Permanent collection (£9 Temporary Exhibitions and Permanent).* 📞*020 8693 5254. www.dulwichpicture gallery.org.uk.*

Dulwich Gallery, opened in 1814, is the oldest public picture gallery in the country. It was designed by **Sir John Soane** to house a collection of 400 paintings donated by a Frenchman, **Noel Joseph Desenfans**. His friend, **Sir Francis Bourgeois**, and his widow supervised the completion of the project.

Facing the central entrance is the small domed mausoleum of the founders, Sir Francis Bourgeois, Noel Desenfans and his wife. An extension (1999) comprises an elegant cloister in glass and bronze linking the gallery to a new wing.

The Collection – Several landscapes by **Aelbert Cuyp**, three **Rembrandts** including *The Girl at a Window* and *Titus*,

17C and 18C landscapes and pastorals by **Poussin**, Claude, Watteau and Lancret; **Gainsborough** portraits of the Linley family, a **Reynolds** self-portrait and portrait of *Mrs Siddons* are among the collection highlights, which also includes works by **Van Dyck**, Teniers the Younger, Raphael, Tiepolo, Canaletto, **Rubens**, Murillo (peasant boys and *Flower Girl*), Reni, Rosa, Lebrun, Guercino and Veronese; although some may be on temporary loan to other galleries.

👤👤 Horniman Museum★★★

100 London Road, Forest Hill. **Museum:** 🕐 *Open open daily 10.30am–5.30pm.* **Gardens:** 🕐 *Open Mon–Sat 7.30am–dusk, Sun and public holidays 8am–dusk.* 🎫*No charge.* 📞*020 8699 1872. www.horniman.ac.uk.*

In 1901, a Victorian tea trader named Frederick Horniman left his house and collections of curiosities from around the world to the people of London.

The resulting museum, now much expanded, is one of the most original in London, and winner of numerous awards.

The **African Worlds and Centenary Galleries** includes displays from **Africa** (historical and archaeological material, masks), from **America** (Inuit exhibits, pre-Columbian archaeological pieces, Navajo textiles), from **Asia** (carvings of gods, masks and puppets).

The **European** collection concentrates on folk art. The **Pacific** area collection includes material from Polynesia, especially Papua New Guinea. The collections are all backed up by photos, video, film and sound recordings.

The **Musical Instruments Collection** is a fabulous array of 7 000 items from around the world.

Other collections include **natural history**. The gardens, include formal rose gardens and a children's petting zoo, host outdoor concerts in summer.

Horniman Museum

Laura Mtungwazi/Horniman Museum

Eltham Palace★

The vision of discerning art lovers has preserved the remains of Eltham Palace, while creating a refined residence. The wonderful Art Deco interior has been lavishly restored.

A BIT OF HISTORY
South of Eltham High Street, off Court Yard, nestles Eltham Palace, a historical country retreat, documented as being in the possession of Odo, Bishop of Bayeux and half-brother of William the Conqueror in 1086. **Edward II** was the first of several monarchs to live there, preferring it to Windsor. **Edward IV** added the Great Hall in 1479–80; **Henry VIII** met **Erasmus** there, happy to live here until his interest in ships spurred him to move to Greenwich.

The palace gradually fell into ruins and was abandoned during the late 18C and 19C – painted as a Romantic folly by **Turner** and Girtin. In 1931, it was leased to **Sir Stephen Courtauld**, who restored the lovely Great Hall and built his own 1930s country residence. The place is now looked after by English Heritage.

VISIT
🄿✕🕐*Open Mon–Wed and Sun 10am–5pm (Nov–Mar 11am–4pm).*🕐*Closed 21 Dec–31 Jan.* ✆*House and gardens £8, gardens only £5. Guidebook. No dogs.* ✆*020 8294 2548. www.elthampalace.org.uk.*

The house is approached over a fine stone bridge straddling the moat. The **Great Hall** (101ft/31m long, 36ft/11m wide and 56ft/17m to the roof apex) is built of brick, faced with stone. Its chief glory is the sweet-chestnut hammerbeam roof with a central hexagonal louvred section that once would have served to expel smoke from the large open hearth. The windows are placed high in the wall, allowing for heavy tapestry hangings to insulate the lower sections. The wooden reredos was installed in the 1930s. Beyond the dais, reached via the oriels or bay windows, once lay the king's and queen's apartments.

> **Location:** *See Suburbs map (UY). Overground: Eltham or Mottingham from London Bridge.*

Courtauld House
Architects John Seely and Paul Paget redeveloped the site. The five entertainment rooms with the bedrooms above are in the south wing, extending in line with the Great Hall. All "mod cons" pervade the house, including a centralised vacuum cleaner in the basement and underfloor heating. It is, however, the unique quality of the 1930s internal decoration that is particularly remarkable: wooden veneer (flexwood) panelling is fitted in all the main bedrooms.

Notable features include the entrance-hall inlaid panels of Venice and Sweden (Roman gladiator and Scandinavian Viking) and Alice in Wonderland reliefs set between the windows; Lady Courtauld's bathroom with its onyx basin surround, gold-plated taps and mosaic alcove; the dining room with a square-coffered silver-leafed ceiling and 1930s black marble fireplace set with mother-of-pearl ribbon bands and polished Art Deco grate.

The house has been lovingly furnished in Art Deco style based on a detailed inventory and on photographs.

The landscaped **gardens** have mature trees and beds of fragrant flowers (syringa, wistaria, honeysuckle, roses).

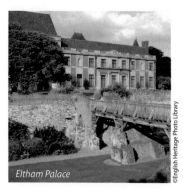
Eltham Palace

©English Heritage Photo Library

Fulham – Putney

These fine residential areas linked by a bridge enjoy a pleasant riverside location. Fulham has become an offshoot of fashionable Chelsea , while Putney with its leafy common land has a rural atmosphere, and is popular with young families.
It is worth taking a stroll to visit the picturesque pubs and enjoy the scenery.

A BIT OF HISTORY

Fulham, Parsons Green and Walham Green were once riverside villages with the odd large mansion in its own grounds running down to the water's edge. Market gardens covered the fertile marshlands. Urbanisation came within 50 years: in 1851 the population numbered 12 000; in 1901, 137 000.

◂•◂ WALKING TOURS
FULHAM

▷ *Start on the N of Putney Bridge.*

Downstream from the bridgehead, **Hurlingham House**, an 18C mansion in its own wooded grounds, is the last of the big houses which once lined the river bank. It is now a private club with extensive tennis courts.

▷ *Walk up Fulham Palace Rd and turn left into Bishop's Av.*

Fulham Palace

The **palace**, which retains the appearance of a modest Tudor manor, was the official summer residence of the Bishop of London from 704 to 1973. The gateway, a low 16C arch with massive beamed doors, leads through to the courtyard (1480–1525) graced by a large central fountain (1885). The chapel (1866), added on the south side, was designed by William Butterfield in Mock Tudor style (◔*see Sight*).
The first magnolia to be grown in Europe and several other exotic species were planted in the grounds by Bishop Compton. The old walled kitchen garden contains some beech hedge screens, a fragrat herb garden and a pretty **wisteria walk**. ◷*Open daily.*
At 210 New King's Road, one disused bottle kiln still stands on the site of the former **Fulham Pottery** established by John Dwight in 1671.

▷ *Return to the bridge and turn right into Church Gate.*

All Saints Church

♿◷*Open Mon–Fri 10am–4pm (Tue 3pm). Guide book.* ℘*020 7736 3264. www.allsaints-fulham.org.uk.*
Fulham parish church has been a landmark at this bridging point of the river since the 14C, its square Kentish stone tower a twin to Putney church on the south bank. Inside there is a rich collection of monuments and brasses. Fourteen Bishops of London are buried in the yew-shaded churchyard.
Close to the church note the 19C **Powell Almshouses** with steep pitched roofs over a single storey.

PUTNEY

The area's transformation was precipitated by the arrival of the railway in the mid-19C. However, the early association with the river remains: rowing clubs still line the Surrey bank.
Putney Bridge, which marks the beginning (just upstream in line with the Universities' Stone by the Star and Garter pub) of the Oxford and Cambridge **Boat Race** *(4.5mi/7km to Mortlake),* was designed in Cornish granite by **Joseph Bazalgette** in 1884.

▷ **Location:** *See SUBURBS map (TY).* ⊖*Putney Bridge.* Fulham and Putney lie to the SW and are bisected by A 308 and A 219, which merge and lead to the A 3 and M 25.

Oxford and Cambridge Boat Race, Putney

K. Brett/MICHELIN

St Mary's Parish Church

&⃝*Open daily 9am–6pm. Leaflet.*
℘*020 8788 4414.*
The church at the approach to Putney
bridge, burnt out in 1973, reopened after
restoration in 1982. The 16C chantry
chapel and 15C tower were preserved
when the church was rebuilt in 1836.

▶ *Take Lower Richmond Rd west.*

Lower Richmond Road winds upriver
past a line of village and antique shops
and small Victorian houses, punctuated
by pubs (late 18C–19C): the **Dukes Head**,
overlooking the river and, just before
the common, the Georgian **Boat and
Dragon** and the gabled **Spencer Arms**
(⃝*see Addresses*).
On the Lower Common is **All Saints
Church** (1874), notable for its Burne-
Jones windows (⃝*open for services*).

▶ *Return to the bridge and walk south.*

The bustling **Putney High Street** has
a Tudor-style, gargoyle-decorated
pub, the **Old Spotted Horse** *(www.
spottedhorse.co.uk)*, half-way along, and
still includes tall 19C house-fronts.
At the start of **Putney Hill**, near the
crossroads, are to left and right, no
11, The Pines, a foreboding tall grey
Victorian House where **Swinburne**
lived and no 28A, a pink-washed
Georgian villa with a firemark set on its
pale wall.

SIGHT

Fulham Palace Museum

Grounds: ⃝ *Open daily dawn until
dusk.* ***Museum:*** &⃝ *Open Mon–Tue
noon–4pm, Sat 11am–2pm, Sun
11.30am–3.30pm. Children under 16
must be accompanied by an adult.
Guided tours 2nd and 4th Sun
in the month at 2pm (except Dec),
otherwise by appointment.* ⃝£5. ℘020
7736 8140. www.fulhampalace.org.
Housed in the east wing, in the Dining
Room and Library (formerly a chapel),
the museum traces the history of the site,
the buildings and the gardens, including
archaeological finds, souvenirs and
portraits of past bishops, ecclesiastical
vestments and stained glass.

ADDRESSES

🍺 PUBS

Dukes Head – *8 Lower Richmond Rd,
SW15 1JN.* ⊖*Putney Bridge.* ℘*020 8788
2552. www.dukesheadputney.com.* This
pub, set in a large traditional buildng,
combines cocktails with Real ales and a
Sunday roast.

Spencer Arms – *237 Lower Richmond Rd,
SW15 1HJ.* ⊖*Putney Bridge.* ℘*020 8788
0640. www.thespencerarms.co.uk.* Sleek
gastropub with plain wooden fittings
in its dining rooms, flooded with
natural light.

The Salisbury – *21 Sherbrooke Rd, SW6
7HX.* ⊖*Parsons Green.* ℘*020 7381 4005.
www.thesalisbury.com.* Smart pub,
much loved by the locals, with a casual
atmosphere and good gastropub food.

Greenwich★★★

The glories of Greenwich are various: a wonderful riverside setting, a vast park, an attractive town with antique shops and a busy market and famous museums. The riverside walk runs past historic pubs and affords superb views of the royal buildings and the modernistic skyline on the north bank. Straddle the Greenwich Mean Time line, the line from which all world time is set. The regenerated Greenwich Peninsula now boasts the Millennium Village and the once-notorious Dome, now converted into the O2 Arena concert venue and exhibition space.

A BIT OF HISTORY

The small town beside the Thames has a worldwide reputation owing to the Greenwich Meridian and Greenwich Mean Time at The Royal Observatory. Greenwich has many associations with the Royal Navy and British maritime history, and its days as a royal residence are recalled in the Queen's House. The area is now a UNESCO World Heritage Site.

Bella Court – Greenwich has been in the royal domain since King Alfred's time. Humphrey, Duke of Gloucester, brother of Henry V first enclosed the park and transformed the manor into

Information: 46 Greenwich Church St, Greenwich, SE10 9BL. ✆0870 608 2000; www.greenwich.gov.uk; www.greenwichwhs.org.uk.

Location: *Map: Inside back cover (KLZ) and Suburbs map (UY).* ⊖North Greenwich; *Overground: Greenwich from Charing Cross; Waterloo; London Bridge; Cannon Street; DLR: Cutty Sark; by boat from Westminster or Tower Bridge.* Greenwich is located on the south bank of the Thames opposite Canary Wharf and the Isle of Dogs. Access by road is by the A 206 or A 2.

Don't Miss: The **antique market** (⊙*see YOUR STAY IN THE CITY*) is well known and there are other shops selling antiques and second-hand books. A footway tunnel *(lift or 100 steps)* leads under the Thames *(10min)* to the Isle of Dogs (⊙*see SUBURBS map*), from where there is a fine **view**★★ of Greenwich, as painted by Canaletto in 1750, whose painting is now in the National Maritime Museum Collection.

Kids: National Maritime Museum; Cutty Sark.

Old Royal Naval College and Queen's House and in the distance, the Royal Observatory

a castle, which he named Bella Court. He also built a fortified tower on the hill from which to spy invaders approaching up the Thames or along the Roman road from Dover. On Duke Humphrey's death in 1447, Henry VI's queen, **Margaret of Anjou**, annexed the castle and renamed it **Placentia** or Pleasaunce.

Tudor Palace – The Tudors preferred Greenwich to their other residences, and **Henry VIII**, born there, enlarged the castle into a vast palace with a royal armoury where craftsmen produced armour to rival the Italian and German suits (*see TOWER OF LONDON*).

Henry also founded naval dockyards upriver at Deptford and downstream at Woolwich. The docks were also accessible by a road skirting the wall, which divided the extensive royal gardens from the park.

Overlooking the thoroughfare was a gatehouse in front of which, legend has it, **Walter Raleigh** threw down his cloak so that **Queen Elizabeth** might cross a mire dryshod.

Palladian House and "Pretty Palace" – Rich as the Tudor palace was, in 1615 **James I** commissioned **Inigo Jones** (*see INTRODUCTION– Architecture*) to build a house for his queen (**Anne of Denmark**) on the exact site of the gatehouse, straddling the busy Woolwich-Deptford road. Based on the principles of the Italian architect,

Palladio (1508–80), it is a compact and well proportioned house despite its "bridge room" over the road.

Work stopped on Anne's death and was resumed only when **Charles I** offered the house to his queen, **Henrietta Maria**. During the Commonwealth the Tudor palace was cleared for use as a barracks and prison. At the Restoration, the Queen's House alone emerged relatively unscathed. In 1665 Charles II commissioned a King's House to be built by **John Webb**, a student of Inigo Jones – now the King Charles Block of the Old Royal Naval College. With the exception of the Observatory, however, construction ceased due to lack of funds before Charles' "pretty palace" was complete.

Royal Hospital to Royal Naval College – Work at Greenwich was resumed in 1694 when **William and Mary**, who preferred Hampton Court as a royal residence, granted a charter for a Royal Hospital for Seamen at Greenwich, founded on the lines of the Royal Military Hospital in Chelsea, appointing **Sir Christoper Wren** as Surveyor of Works. Wren submitted numerous plans before proposing the one we know today.

At Queen Mary's insistence, this incorporated the Queen's House and its 150ft/46m wide river vista, the King Charles Block alongside the construction of three additional blocks, the King William (SW), Queen Mary (SE) and

A. Taverner/MICHELIN

Millennium Dome

©Christopher Steer/iStockphoto.com

Riverside walks, parkland and lakes to attract wildlife have transformed the Greenwich peninsula where the site of a former gas works has been redeveloped to include roads, housing, stores and other amenities for the local population. However, the focal point of the regenerated area is the Millennium Dome with its domed glass-fibre roof designed by Lord Richard Rogers, to mark the third millennium. After the rather disappointing Millennium Experience and years of wrangling over its fate, this controversial structure has now been transformed into the successful **02 Arena**, a concert venue and exhibition space.

Queen Anne (NE, below which exists a crypt, sole remnant of the Tudor palace (o━ *closed to the public).*
To complete the scheme emphasis was focused by projecting cupolas before the refectory and chapel, and the course of the Thames was modified and embanked – the only major vista design by Wren to be properly realised. The project took more than half a century to complete and involved **Vanbrugh**, **Hawksmoor** and **Colen Campbell**.
In 1873 the buildings were transformed into the Royal Naval College, and remained so until 1998. Most are now part of the University of Greenwich. The Queen's House became part of the National Maritime Museum in 1937.

☙ WALKING TOURS
1 EAST OF THE MUSEUM

▷ *Start at Greenwich Pier and walk east along the river past the Old Royal Naval College (ⓒsee Sights) and proceed to Park Row.*

Riverside Downstream
This area is full of historical heritage and elegance.
The **Trafalgar Tavern** (ⓒ*see Addresses),* of 1837, recollects the personalities and events of Nelson's time. In the early 19C the tavern was the setting for the Liberal ministers' **"whitebait dinners"** (ⓒ*see DOCKLANDS – Blackwall).* **Dickens**

used to meet there with Thackeray and Cruikshank. Backing onto Crane Street, is **The Yacht**, a century older.
The **Cutty Sark Tavern** was rebuilt with a great bow window in 1804 on the site of earlier inns (ⓒ*see Addresses),* while at the end stands the four-square Harbourmaster's Office *(no 21)* which for 50 years, until the 1890s, controlled colliers entering the Pool of London.
ⓒ*For Thames Barrier WOOLWICH – CHARLTON.*

▷ *Walk back, turn left into Maze Hill.*

Vanbrugh Castle
The castle, a caricature of a Medieval fortress, stands on Maze Hill. It was built and lived in by the architect and playwright, Sir John Vanbrugh from 1717–26.

▷ *Cross into the park, then return downhill to Park Vista.*

In the park west of the castle, beyond the Roman Villa, is a wilderness with a small herd of fallow deer.

Greenwich Park
Greenwich Park, palisaded in 1433 and surrounded by a wall in Stuart times, is the oldest enclosed royal domain. It extends for 180 acres/73ha in a sweep of chestnut avenues and grass to a point 155ft/47m above the river crowned by

the Royal Observatory and the **General Wolfe** monument. On the slope below the Observatory are traces of the 17C giant grass steps by Le Nôtre.

2 SOUTH OF THE MUSEUM
Greenwich Pier

A pavilion provides access to the **foot tunnel** to the Isle of Dogs *(10min)*.

🧑‍🦽 Cutty Sark★★

🦽➡*The ship itself is closed to visitors, but is expected to reopen end 2010. There is a souvenir shop adjacent to the conservation site where you can also view some of the site work via an observation window.* 🕐*Open daily 11am–5pm.* 🕐*Closed 24–26 Dec.* ☏*020 8858 2698. www.cuttysark.org.uk.*
Launched at Dumbarton in 1869 for the China tea trade, *Cutty Sark* became famous as the fastest clipper afloat. Her best day's run with all 32 000 sq ft/ 2 975sq m or 0.5 acre/0.2ha of canvas fully spread was 363mi/584km. In her heyday she brought tea from China and later wool from Australia, chasing before the wind like the cutty sark or short chemise of the witch Nannie, "a winsome wench" in Robert Burns' poem *Tam O'Shanter*, hence the boat's distinctive figurehead. In 1922 she was converted into a nautical training school and transferred to dry dock at Greenwich in 1954. In May 2007, *Cutty Sark* lost an estimated 5 per cent of the ship's original fabric as the result of fire. The iron hull received little damage, and restoration efforts begun before the fire are scheduled to be completed in summer 2010.

▶ *Continue down King William Walk, turn right into Romney Rd passing near the market to Church St.*

St Alfege Church

🕐*Open Sat 11.30am–4pm, Sun noon– 4pm, other times by appointment. Leaflet (22 languages). Lunchtime recitals Thu at 1pm. www.st-alfege.org.*
This gaunt church (1718) with its Doric portico is by **Nicholas Hawksmoor**, the tower is by John James. Inside the murals *(east end)* are by Thornhill and the carving is by **Grinling Gibbons**.

Crooms Hill

The winding lane was a thoroughfare in the 15C, when the park was enclosed, and became its western boundary.
At the bottom of Crooms Hill is the **Greenwich Theatre** (www.greenwich theatre.org.uk), built in 1968 in the shell of a Victorian music hall.
The Georgian terrace *(nos 6–12)* dates from 1721–23. The Poet Laureate, Cecil Day Lewis lived at no 6 from 1968 to 1972.

▶ *Continue past the Fan Museum (⌂see Sights).*

Gloucester Circus, designed by Michael Searle in the 1700s, has retained original houses on the east and south sides. **The Grange,** an early 17C building with 18C additions, stands on a site recorded as having been given to Ghent Abbey in 818 by a daughter of Alfred the Great; overlooking the park is a 17C **gazebo**. **Heath Gate House** is a relatively low brick mansion with gabled dormers and pilasters supporting the upper floor.

A Famous Name

Cutty Sark is also the name of a pale, delicate Scotch whisky branded by **Berry Bros & Rudd** of St James's. The name was suggested by the clipper, which had just returned to British waters having traded under the Portuguese flag. The whisky, meanwhile, was especially blended for the export market – destined for America and supplied throughout Prohibition (1920–33) via Nassau in the Bahamas – "the real McCoy", a certain Captain William McCoy, was one such bootlegger there. Between 1973 and 2003, the annual *Cutty Sark* Tall Ships' Races (now the Tall Ships' Races) were sponsored by the wine and spirit merchants.

The **Manor House**, two storeys of red brick, is typical of 1697, even to the hooded porch with a carved shell motif.

Macartney House (⊶ *closed to the public; private flats*) was built by Andrew Snape, Serjeant Farrier to Charles I.

▸ *Croom's Hill leads to Ranger's House (see Sights) and Blackheath.*

SIGHTS
🧍🧍 National Maritime Museum★★★

♿✕🕐*Open daily 10am–5pm (last admission 30min before closing); 31 Dec, 1 Jan, London Marathon Day, restricted hours.* ☛*Guided tours (2hr).* 🕐*Closed 24–26 Dec.* ☞*Free; charges for some exhibitions. Planetarium shows £6. Licensed café-restaurant. Play area.* ✆*020 8312 6565 (24hr recorded information;* ✆*020 8858 4422 (administration). www.nmm.ac.uk.*

A fabulous collection of all things maritime (fine art, rare instruments, treasures and mementoes) is displayed by this beautifully organised museum. The development of Britain as a sea power is traced from Henry VIII's Tudor fleet through **Captain Cook**'s travels in the South Seas and Pacific Islands to Sir John Franklin's Polar exploration.

The theme of **Explorers** is the quest of early navigators and explorers. Migration, tourism and transport of goods and mail brought about the age of cruise liners presented in **Passengers**. The style of uniforms and functional outfits (diving and survival suits) is dictated by climate and rank as illustrated in **Rank and Style**. Oceans influence the climate and help to sustain life on earth, and **Planet Ocean** focuses on environmental change.

Maritime London has held a prominent place in international economic and social development and the city's history and growth is bound with the thriving docks and related industries. The first of three new galleries addressing Britain's growth as a maritime power is **Atlantic Worlds**, covering settlement in America, the development of the trans-Atlantic slave trade and its abolition, unrest in the colonies and the move to independence. The galleries planned for the Indian Ocean and the Pacific will follow in 2010.

Horatio **Nelson**'s military campaigns during the French Revolutionary wars and battles with Napoleon are illustrated with contemporary paintings, uniforms, logs, maps and navigational instruments

Atlantic Worlds Gallery, National Maritime Museum

©National Maritime Museum, London

J Harrison's Marine Timekeeper No 1

A Pioneering Clockmaker

John Harrison (1693–1776) was born the son of a carpenter; little otherwise is known of his early life until 1713 when he completed his first pendulum clock made entirely of wood: oak for the wheels and box for the axles (Worshipful Company of Clockmakers Museum. *See CITY – Guildhall*).

In 1722 Harrison installed a unique clock at Brocklesby Park made from lignum vitae, a tropical hardwood; this continues to keep accurate "mean" time today. His next important invention was the bi-metallic gridiron-grasshopper pendulum (1725–27); the grasshopper mechanism provided a friction-free means of clocking the units of time.

At an age of increasing maritime activity, it was critical for sailors to determine longitude in order to accurately chart the oceans that divided land masses. In 1730 Harrison journeyed to London with drawings and calculations for a reliable clock that would be seaworthy: pendulumless, resistant to corrosion or rust and resilient to extremes in weather. There he met the astronomer Dr Edmund Halley. Harrison's No 1 (H-1) was tried on a journey to Lisbon in 1737, the clock proved itself accurate and the Board of Longitude convened for the first time. Described by **Hogarth** in his Analysis of Beauty as "one of the most exquisite movements ever made" (1753), H-1 helped the English roll out colonisation of foreign shores.

and a collection of china memorabilia. Personal artefacts include his bullet-pierced uniform worn at Trafalgar and items from his house at Merton.

Queen's House★★

&⊙*Open daily 10am–5pm (last admission 30min before closing), 31 Dec, 1 Jan, London Marathon Day, restricted hours.* ⊙*Closed 24–26 Dec.* ℘*020 8312 6565 (24hr recorded information).* ℘*020 8858 4422 (administration). www.nmm.ac.uk.*
This Palladian villa (1616), England's first Classical building, was designed by **Inigo Jones** for the wives of James I and Charles I. The ground floor rooms display portraits of the Tudor and Stuart kings and queens and historical paintings of the old Greenwich Palace of Placentia. On the first floor **Art for the Nation** displays 200 paintings, including works by Gainsborough, Lely, Hogarth, Reynolds and Canaletto.

Royal Observatory Greenwich★★

Tour 45min. &✕⊙*Open daily 10am–5pm (6pm summer, last admission 30min before closing, last Planetarium show 4pm), 31 Dec, 1 Jan, London Marathon Day, restricted hours.* ⊙*Free.* ⊙*Closed 24–26 Dec.*
Leaflet (6 languages). Café and restaurant. ℘*020 8312 6565 (24hr recorded information),* ℘*020 8858 4422. www.nmm.ac.uk.*
In 1675 **Charles II** directed **Sir Christopher Wren** to "build a small observatory within our park at Greenwich" for "the finding out of the longitude of places for perfecting navigation and astronomy." Wren, a former astronomer as well as an architect, designed a house of red brick; it is named Flamsteed House after John Flamsteed, the first Astronomer Royal, appointed in 1675.

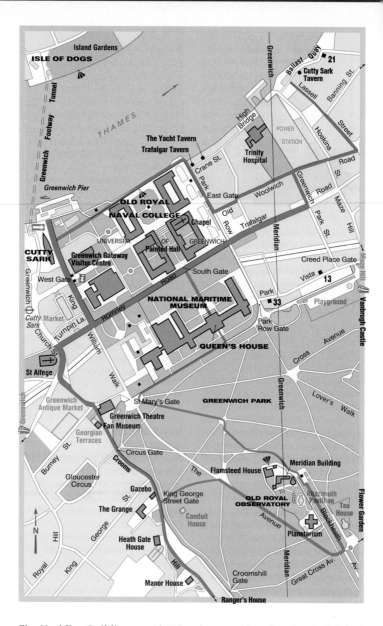

The **Meridian Building**, a mid-18C addition, was built to house the observatory's **collection**★★ of instruments. At the main gate is the 24-hour dial of the Shepherd Gate Clock (1851) clock and British Standard Measures. The **tour** begins in the Meridian courtyard where visitors may record the exact time they stand on the Greenwich Meridian, the brass meridian of zero longitude linked in a line to the north and south poles. On the south face of Flamsteed House are sundials. The red time ball on the roof was erected in 1833 to serve as a time check for navigation on the Thames; the ball rises to the top of the mast and drops at exactly 13 00 hours GMT.

Within **Flamsteed House** the first rooms trace the Observatory's foundation and the evolution of man's understanding of the heavens. Other displays trace the discovery of latitude and longitude, including the standardisation of the Greenwich meridian in 1884 at the Meridian Conference in Washington.

The **Meridian Building** contains the **Quadrant Room**, the Airy Transit Circle through which the meridian passes *(video)*, the Telescope Dome, containing Britain's largest (28in/50cm) refracting telescope *(video of the moon landing)*. Adjacent are the **Peter Harrison Planetarium** and Weller Astronomy Galleries, opened in 2007.

Old Royal Naval College★★

Enter from Cutty Sark Gardens, College Approach, Romney Road Gate, Royal Gate and on Park Row. Painted Hall & Chapel and Greenwich Gateway Visitor Centre (Pepys Building, beside Cutty Sark entrance): ⏰*Open daily 10am–5pm. Grounds:* ⏰*Open daily 8am–6pm.* ☎*020 8269 4747. www.oldroyalnavalcollege.org.*

The college accommodates the University of Greenwich's Maritime Campus.

Painted Hall★

Wren's domed refectory was completed in 1703. In 1805 Nelson lay in state here before his burial in St Paul's.

The hall and upper hall were painted in exuberant Baroque by **Sir James Thornhill**: William and Mary, Anne, George I and his descendants celebrate Britain's maritime power in a wealth of involved allegory. The artist (1708–27) was paid £3 a sq yd/0.8sq m for the ceilings, £1 for the walls.

Chapel★

Wren's chapel was redecorated after a fire in 1779 by "Athenian" Stuart and William Newton in Wedgwood pastel colours. Across the apse is *The Preservation of St Paul after the Shipwreck at Malta* by Benjamin West (1738–1820).

Fan Museum★

Crooms Hill. ⏰*Open Tue–Sun, 11am (noon Sun) to 5pm.* ⏰*Closed Yom Kippur, 24–26 Dec, 1 Jan.* ☞*£4 (no charge for senior citizens Tue after 2pm). Fan-making workshop 1st Sat in every month. Audio-guide. Brochure.* ☎*020 8305 1441. www.fan-museum.org.*

This delightful museum owns 3 500 fans from the 11C to the present day, with strong reference to the 18C and 19C; regular demonstrations on fan-making, conservation and restoration.

Ranger's House★

Chesterfield Walk, West Parkside (EH) ♿🅿⏰*Open Mar–Sept Sun–Wed 10am–5pm, Oct–Dec group access only, Thu (pre-book).* ☞*£5.40. Audio-tour. Parking.* ☎*020 8853 0035. www.english-heritage.org.uk.*

Originally a small brick villa with a stone balustrade. Rounded wings were added during the house's ownership by Philip, 4th Earl of Chesterfield (1694–1733).

The ground and first floors provide a splendid setting for the **Wernher Collection** of European Art, which reflects the eclectic taste of Sir Julius Wernher (1850–1912), a mining magnate and philanthropist instrumental in founding Imperial College (🔍 *see KENSINGTON*).

The collection includes rare early religious paintings (Filippo Lippi, Hans Memling) and paintings by Dutch painters (Metsu, Van Ostade, de Hooch), Renaissance jewellery and Medieval silverware. Also on view are Maiolica ceramics, Limoges plates, Sèvres porcelain and Meissen pottery as well as tapestries and portraits by Sir Joshua Reynolds and George Romney.

ADDITIONAL SIGHTS
Blackheath★

Overground: Blackheath from Cannon Street or London Bridge

The course of the Roman Watling Street between the south coast and London is marked by Blackheath Road, Blackheath Hill and Shooters' Hill, notorious for highwaymen in the 18C.

Rebel forces have used the heath as a rallying ground: **Wat Tyler** (1381); the Kentishmen under **Jack Cade** (1450); the Cornishmen under Audley (1497). In more joyful mood, in 1415 the people greeted **Henry V** on his victorious return from Agincourt; in 1660 **Charles II** was welcomed by the Restoration Army and in 1608, it is said, **James I** taught the English to play golf on Blackheath.

The heath is ringed by stately 18C and 19C **terraces** and **houses**★, when merchants, newly rich from the expanding docks, began to build in the vicinity.

Overlooking the heath from the **south side** are buildings including **Colonnade House** (*South Row*) and **The Paragon**, a late 18C crescent by Michael Searles.

On the **west side** are the early 18C Spencer House and Perceval House.

Blackheath Village

The main street and Tranquil Vale, in reality full of traffic, lead off the heath southwards to modern estates.

DEPTFORD

Overground: Deptford from London Bridge.

The riverside village expanded during the reign of **Henry VIII** as a shipbuilding yard. It was in Deptford Creek that **Queen Elizabeth** boarded the *Golden Hinde* in 1581 to dub **Francis Drake** knight for his globe circumnavigation and where Christopher **Marlowe** was stabbed in a tavern brawl (1593). In the 17C the diarist John **Evelyn** lived at Sayes Court, which he briefly leased to **Peter the Great** in 1698, while the latter learned the art of shipbuilding in the yards. The dockyard closed in 1869.

St Paul's Church

East of Deptford High Street. ○*Open for services or by appointment only.* ✆*020 8692 7449. www.paulsdeptford.org.uk.* Thomas Archer's church (1712–30) has a stone portico and Corinthian columns upholding a sculpted plaster ceiling.

St Nicholas' Church

Corner of Deptford Green and Stowage Lane. ○*Open Mon–Fri 9.15am–2pm, Sat–Sun by arrangement.* ▸*Guided tours by appointment.* ✆*020 8692 2749.* Of particular interest are the reredos by the church's 17C parishioner **Grinling Gibbons** (see *INTRODUCTION – Architecture*).

There is also a weird carved relief by Gibbons, known as the *Valley of Dry Bones*. The Jacobean pulpit is supported on a ship's figurehead.

The skulls on the gateposts were originally above crossed bones, and since so many privateers sailed from Deptford, it is claimed they inspired the skull and crossbones flag. More honourably, the church, associated with **Sir Francis Drake**, has the privilege of flying the White Ensign. **Christopher Marlowe** is buried here.

ADDRESSES

⃟ PUBS

The Cutty Sark Tavern – *4–6 Ballast Quay, Lassell St, SE10 9PD.* ⊖*Greenwich; DLR: Cutty Sark.* ✆*020 8858 3146. www.cuttysarktavern.co.uk.* The Union Tavern, built in 1804, was an important meeting place for fishermen. It was renamed The Cutty Sark Tavern in memory of the famous clipper moored at Greenwich. A truly charming, picturesque pub with great views of the Thames from the Georgian panelled interior and the terrace.

Inc Bar & Restaurant – *7 College Approach, SE10 9HY . DLR: Cutty Sark.* ✆*020 8858 6721. www.incbar.com.* Idiosyncratic, fantastic interior at this two-level cocktail lounge, with suggestive wallpaper and colourful large main bar. The cocktail list is inspiring and innovative; try the apple and melon martini. Good restaurant area on mezzanine with modern cooking.

North Pole Piano Restaurant – *131 Greenwich High Rd, SE10 8JA. DLR: Deptford Bridge; Greenwich.* ✆*020 8853 3020. www.northpolegreenwich.com.*

Trendy venue with bars complete with DJ decks and good upstairs restaurant. Piano player sets the mood; the bar staff are friendly and cheerful.

Plume of Feathers – *19 Park Vista, SE10 9LZ.* ⊖*Greenwich. DLR: Cutty Sark.* ✆*020 8858 1661. www.plume-of-feathers.co.uk.* An old-fashioned pub with a friendly fireplace and nautical ephemera inside and outdoor seating. A separate restaurant area serves fresh, homemade pub favourites.

Trafalgar Tavern – *Park Row, SE10 9NW. DLR: Cutty Sark, Greenwich.* ✆*020 8858 2909. www.trafalgartavern. co.uk.* Since the mid-19C, the Trafalgar has overlooked the Thames from its location near the Old Royal Naval College. Dickens immortalised this pub in his novel *Our Mutual Friend.* Refurbished, it is a delightful, but very busy place with bar food and a separate restaurant, renowned for its whitebait dinners – a historical favourite and now served with a modern twist. Restaurant also serves great roasts at the weekend.

Hampstead★★ – Highgate

High up on a hill is the picturesque village of Hampstead, a maze of alleyways and passages, smart shops and plenty of café society in its bars and restaurants, frequented by affluent residents. Hampstead's glory lies in the rolling woodland and meadows of the Heath, enjoyed by walkers (some even swim in the ponds) and film crews alike for its rural London aspect. Concerts and funfairs are seasonal features. Highgate is also full of character, with some fine houses and pubs.

A BIT OF HISTORY

Hampstead Village developed into a fashionable 18C spa when the chalybeate springs were discovered in what became Well Walk. Builders then began the erection of houses and terraces, which continues to this day. In 1907 came the Underground. Throughout its history this pleasant district has attracted writers, artists, architects, musicians and scientists.

The village, irregularly built on the side of a hill, has kept its original street pattern; between the main roads is a network of lanes, groves, alleys, steps, courts, rises, places... At the foot of the hill lie Hampstead Ponds. On the north side of the Heath is Kenwood (⚒ *see Additional Sights*).

▷ **Location:** *See Suburbs map (TX).* ⊖*Hampstead.* Hampstead lies to the N of Regent's Park, and Highgate is slightly to the NE.

⚒ **Don't Miss:** Fenton House and Hampstead Village, then head for Kenwood on the north side of Hampstead Heath; stop at the Spaniard's Inn on the way.

⚘ WALKING TOURS
1 HAMPSTEAD VILLAGE – WEST SIDE

Flask Walk, which begins as a pedestrian street with a Victorian pub and tea merchant, continues east past Gardnor House, built in 1736, to New End Square and Well Walk beyond. **John Constable** lived at **no 40** Well Walk from 1826 to his death in 1834. Christchurch Hill with its Georgian cottages leads to the mid-19C Church with a soaring spire that's visible for miles.

▷ *Walk back and up Fitzjohn's Ave.*

One flank of **Church Row** is lined by a fine 1720 terrace of brown brick houses with Georgian doors. The range along the north pavement includes cottages, a weatherboarded house and three-storeyed town houses with good ironwork. The 18C Parish Church of **St John** at the row's end boasts a spire

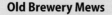

Old Brewery Mews

Off Hampstead High Street on the east side, the former brewery is well protected by a wrought-iron cage and has been converted into offices and a row of modern town houses.

rising from a battlemented brick tower, banded in stone. The interior, with giant pillars, galleries on three sides and box pews, was twice enlarged in the 19C to accommodate the expanding population.

▷ *Detour to Frognal via Frognal Way.*

Frognal

Noteworthy buildings include the neo-Georgian University College School with Edward VII in full regalia standing above the entrance door; **Kate Greenaway**'s house (no **39**) designed in 1885 by **Norman Shaw** in story book style, with rambling gables and balconies; and the Sun House *(no 9 Frognal Way)* by **Maxwell Fry** at his 1935 best.

▷ *Return and turn into Holly Walk.*

Holly Walk

The path north from the church, bordered by the 1810 cemetery extension crowded with funeral monuments, rises to the green- and pink-washed, three-storey houses of Prospect Place (1814) and delightful cottages of Benham's

Hampstead Residents – Old and Young

In the cemetery lie Kate Greenaway, the illustrator of children's books, and Laszlo Biro, the inventor of the ball-point pen. Temporary residents of the neighbourhood have included John Constable, John Keats, Ian Fleming, Agatha Christie, Sting, Boy George, Elizabeth Taylor, Tom Conti, Emma Thompson, Rex Harrison, Peter O'Toole and Johnny Depp.

Place (1813). Holly Place, 1816, is another short terrace flanking **St Mary's**, one of the earliest RC churches to be built in London, founded by Abbé Morel, refugee from the French Revolution, who came to Hampstead in 1796. From the top of the hill a maze of steps and alleys leads down to Heath Street. Overlooking **Mount Vernon Junction** is **Romney's House** (plaque), built of brick and weatherboarding in 1797.

▷ *Walk up Hampstead Grove past Fenton House (&see Additional Sights) and turn left.*

Admiral's Walk

The road leads to Admiral's House, an early 18C mansion with nautical superstructure, named after the colourful Admiral Matthew Burton (1715–95). It was the home of **Sir George Gilbert Scott** from 1854 to 1864. The adjoining Grove Lodge, probably older, was **Galsworthy**'s home from 1918 until his death in 1933 where he wrote all but the first part of the *Forsyte Saga*. Lower Terrace, at the end of Admiral's Walk, is where **Constable** lived from 1821 to 1825 before moving to Well Walk.

▷ *Continue up Lower Terrace to Heath St and the Whitestone Pond.*

Hampstead Heath

Hampstead Heath was the common of Hampstead Manor, an area where laundresses once laid out washing to bleach in the 18C. Since the earliest times it has been a popular place of recreation (vast one-day fairs; *Easter, Spring and Summer Bank holiday Monday*).
Whitestone Pond and the milestone ("Holborn Bars 4 1/2" in the bushes at the base of the aerial) from which it takes its name are on London's highest ground (437ft/133m).

▷ *Short detour down East Heath Rd.*

Vale of Health

The Vale, a cluster of 18C–19C cottages, mid-Victorian and now a few modern houses and blocks, connected by a

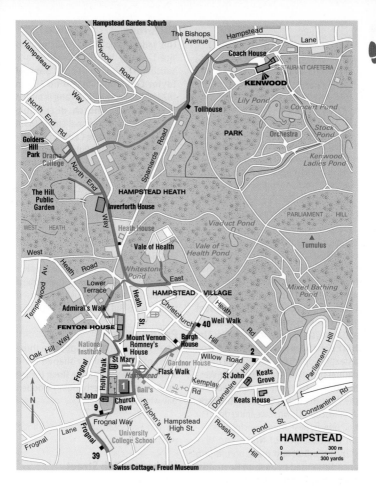

maze of narrow roads and paths, has at various times been the home of Leigh Hunt, DH Lawrence, Edgar Wallace and Compton Mackenzie. The origin of the Vale's name is said to derive from the fact that the area was unaffected by the plague in 1665.

▶ *Return and proceed to North End Way.*

At the crossroads stands **Jack Straw's Castle**, a former inn (now flats) first mentioned in local records in 1713. Almost opposite is **Heath House**, a plain early 18C mansion of brown brick, chiefly remarkable for its commanding position and the visitors received by its 18C–19C owner, the Quaker abolitionist, **Samuel Hoare**; **William Wilberforce**,

Hampstead Garden Suburb

The suburb was conceived by **Dame Henrietta Barnett**, living in what is now Heath End House, as a scheme for rehousing London slum dwellers in the early 20C. Raymond Unwin, the principal architect, designed an irregular pattern of tree-lined streets and closes converging on a central square with its Institute and two churches (one Anglican and one Nonconformist) by Sir Edwin Lutyens. The houses are in varied architectural style. It is now an affluent area.

Spas

In the 18C a number of **London spas** developed round mineral springs ,where people could take the waters in rural surroundings. They were frequented by the less wealthy, who could not afford the elegance of Bath. Among the most popular were Hampstead and Islington and also Sadler's Wells, which offered dancing, pantomimes and rope dancing, accompanied by the consumption of cold meat and wine.

Elizabeth Fry and the leading politicians of the day.

Further up North End Way stands Inverforth House, rebuilt in 1914 and now a residential development. Lord Leverhulme's extensive pergola, sweet with wisteria, rambling roses, clematis and honeysuckle, now forms part of **The Hill Public Garden**, formally laid out on a steeply sloping site and framed by the natural beauty of the trees of the West Heath. Nearby on the northern edge of the West Heath lies **Golders Hill Park**, its landscaped lawns sweeping down to two ponds, past animal enclosures.

On the east side of North End Way stands the Bull and Bush, an old pub once patronised by **Joshua Reynolds**, **Gainsborough**, **Constable and Romney**.

▷ *A path runs east across the heath to Spaniards Rd, which leads N to Kenwood House, past the 18C Tollhouse and the Spaniards Inn.*

2 HIGHGATE

⊖ *Archway; Highgate*

The area began to be developed in the 17C when rich merchants decided it was the place to build their country seats... Today Highgate remains a village in character, centred on pretty Pond Square and the High Street.

▷ *Start from the top of Highgate High St, walk west along Hampstead Lane and turn left into The Grove.*

The Grove

This wide, tree-planted road presents late 17–early 18C rose-brick terrace housing. The poet and critic **Samuel Taylor Coleridge** lived at no 3 from 1823 till his death in 1834 and is buried in **St Michael's Church**, discernable by its tapering octagonal spire (1830) overlooking Highgate Cemetery.

The Flask (1721) on Highgate West Hill corner is a period country pub with outdoor courtyard (see Addresses).

South Grove is lined with various houses: the early 18C Church House (no **10**), the Highgate Literary and Scientific Society (no **11**), Moreton House (no **14**), a brick mansion of 1715, and the late 17C **Old Hall**, with its great bow window.

Bacon's Lane honours the philosopher Francis Bacon, who was a frequent guest (and died) at Arundel House, which used to be where Old Hall now stands.

Pond Square

Small houses and cottages line three sides of the irregularly shaped Pond Square. On the south side **Rock House** *(no 6)* retains its overhanging wooden bay windows (18C).

▷ *Left into South Grove, then continue down the High St.*

Highgate High Street

The **Gate House Tavern** (*see Addresses)* stands on the site of a 1386 gate house to the Bishop of London's park; no **23** opposite, with its straight-headed windows and modillion frieze, and nos **17**, **19** and **21** are all early 18C.

Highgate Hill

Just inside **Waterlow Park** stands **Lauderdale House**, 16C in origin but remodelled in the 18C in small country house style (now a cultural centre).

Highgate Cemetery★★

Swains Lane. ○*Open Mon–Fri 10am– 4.30pm, Sat–Sun 11am–4.30pm (until 3pm daily winter).* ○*Closed funerals and 25–26 Dec.* ☞£3. ☞Guided tours available weekdays (call to book).* ☞Permission needed for cameras.*

An Ancient Land

Highgate Wood (*north of Archway and Muswell Hill junction*) comprises 70 acres/28ha and is classified an ancient woodland, a remnant of the larger Ancient Forest of Middlesex, mentioned in the **Domesday Book**. Archaeological surveys have revealed that potteries were active in the area around the time of the Roman conquest (AD 43). Between the 16C and 18C hornbeam would have been coppiced, while oak would have been grown to provide the Crown with timber for shipbuilding. In 1885, under threat of development, the wood was acquired by the Corporation of London. Today it is protected by an active conservation policy and equipped with children's recreation facilities.

℘020 8340 1834. www.highgate-cemetery.org.

Perhaps an eccentric thing to do, but a guided tour of Highgate Cemetery can be one of the most fascinating days out in London, with a story behind every tombstone and an enormous cast of the great, the good and the howlingly eccentric.

The Eastern Cemetery is still in use; here lie **George Eliot** (1819–80) and **Karl Marx** (d. 1883) – bust (1956) by Laurence Bradshaw. The Western Cemetery (opened 1838) contains some remarkable 19C monumental masonry and the tombs of **Michael Faraday**

(1791–1867), Charles Cruft, who started the dog shows in 1886, and **Dante Gabriel** and **Christina Rossetti** (⌖see MAJOR CENTRAL LONDON MUSEUMS – Tate Britain).

▶ *Walk back to Highgate Hill*

Opposite, high above the road, is **The Bank**, a row of brick houses; nos **110**, **108** and **106** are early 18C, no 104, of now mellow red brick with a solid parapet, is 16C and has an octagonal domed turret (1638).

A short detour along Hornsey Lane leads to the **Archway**, a viaduct built to allow

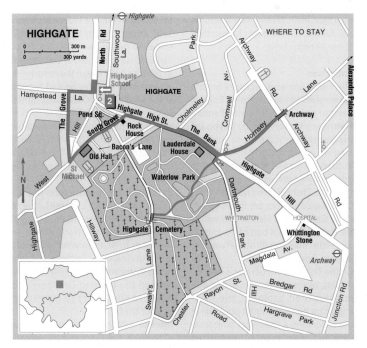

the road north (A1) to pass through the hill 80ft/24m below Hornsey Lane. The original structure by John Nash was replaced in 1897 by a metal construction designed by Alexander Binnie.

The **Whittington Stone** (1821), a marble cat sitting on a stone, marks the spot where, according to tradition, **Dick Whittington** heard Bow bells telling him to "turn again".

ADDITIONAL SIGHTS
Fenton House★★

(NT) ♿🕐*Open Wed–Fri 2–5pm, Sat–Sun and bank holidays 11am–5pm.* 👓*£5.70. Guide book (4 languages). Braille guide.* 🚫*No photography.* ☎*020 7435 3471 or 01494 755 563 (information line). www.nationaltrust.org.uk/main/ w-fentonhouse.*

An iron gate (1707) by **Tijou** gives access to a red-brick house, built in 1693; it is Hampstead's finest, besides being one of its earliest and largest. The original main pine staircase, with its twisted balusters and wide handrail, has survived as well as some doorcases, panelling and chimney-pieces.

In 1793 the house was bought by a Riga merchant, Philip Fenton, after whom it is still named; in 1952 it was bequeathed to the National Trust.

Collection

The furniture and pictures form a background to 18C porcelain – English, German and French – and the Benton-Fletcher collection of early **keyboard instruments**, some 18 in number ranging in date from 1540–1805. The instruments are for the most part kept in good playing order and are accessible to students. There are frequent concerts. On the ground floor are harpsichords (1770 English, 1612 Flemish), as well as the most important part of the English porcelain collection (Bristol, Plymouth, Chelsea, Bow, Worcester).

On the first floor are German figurines, teapots, Worcester apple green porcelain in satinwood cabinets, the most important piece of English porcelain in the collection, a Worcester pink-scale vase and cover probably decorated in London (Drawing Room), 17–18C Chinese blue and white porcelain, 18C English harpsichords, a 16C Italian and an early 18C English spinet, and a 17C virginal; on the top floor 18C square pianos, 17C and 18C harpsichords, 17C and 20C clavichords, and a 17C spinet and virginal. The 17C needlework pictures (Rockingham Room), the bird and flower pictures by the 18C artist Samuel Dixon (Porcelain Room) and the works of Sir William Nicholson (Dining Room) are noteworthy.

Kenwood★★

(EH) ✕🅿♿*Access by bus 210 from Golders Green or Archway.* **House:** 🕐*Open daily 11.30am–4pm.* 🕐*Closed 24–26 Dec, 1 Jan.* 📞*Group tours.* **Grounds:** 🕐*Open daily 8am–dusk. Parking. picnic area.* ☎*020 8348 1286. www.english-heritage.org.uk.*

"A great 18C gentleman's country house with pictures such as an 18C collector might have assembled" – William Murray, younger son of a Scottish peer, acquired Kenwood in 1754, two years before he was appointed Lord Chief Justice and created Earl of Mansfield. In 1764 he invited his fellow Scot Robert Adam to enlarge and embellish the house.

Kenwood was purchased by **Lord Iveagh** in 1925. He filled it with the remarkable collection of pictures he had formed at the end of the 19C and bequeathed to the nation in 1927. Efforts to recover the original furnishings (Adam sidetable and pedestals of 1775 in the Parlour) have been painstaking. The **Suffolk Collection** of portraits is also on display on the first floor.

Exterior – The pedimented portico with giant fluted columns, frieze and medallion was Adam's typical contribution to the north front; on the south front, from which there is a splendid view down to the lake, Adam raised the central block to three floors, refaced the existing Orangery and designed the Library to the east to balance the façade.

Interior – Of the rooms on either side of the hall, the most remarkable are the Music and Dining Rooms (cornice and doorcase related in motif to the preceding enriched columns and entablatures), the Adam Library and Orangery.

Adam Library★★ – The "room for receiving company" as Adam described it, is richly decorated with Adam motifs and painted in blue and old rose, picked out in white and gold. The oblong room, beneath a curved ceiling, leads into two apsidal ends, each lined with bookcases and screened off by a horizontal beam supported on fluted Corinthian columns. Arched recesses, fitted with triple mirrors, flank the fireplace and reflect the three tall windows opposite.

Paintings★★ – A **Rembrandt**, *Self-Portrait in Old Age*, *The Man with the Cane* by Frans Hals, the ringletted young girl *Guitar Player* by Vermeer, and works by Bol, Rubens, Cuyp and Crome hang in the Dining Room. **Van de Velde** seascapes and a Turner, *The Iveagh Seapiece,* are found in the Parlour. Portraits by the English school people other rooms: beautiful **Gainsborough** women, including *Mary, Lady Howe* in pink silk with that special flat hat, *Lady Hamilton* by **Romney**; children's portraits by **Reynolds** *(The Brummell Children)* and Lawrence *(Miss Murray)*. **Gainsboroughs** of unusual character hang in the Breakfast Room and Orangery: *Going to Market, Two Shepherd Boys with Dogs Fighting* and the dramatic *Hounds coursing a Fox.*

Burgh House

New End Square, Hampstead. **House and Museum:** ◷*Open Wed–Sat noon–5pm, Sat by appointment, bank holidays 2pm–5pm.* ◷*Closed Good Fri, Easter Mon, 25 Dec–1 Jan.* **Licensed Buttery** ◷*Open Tue–Fri 11am–5.30pm, Sat–Sun 9.30am–5pm.* ℘*020 7431 0144 or* ℘*020 7794 2905 (Buttery). www.burghhouse.org.uk.*

This dignified, grand 1 listed house, with its south-facing terrace, was built in 1703 when Hampstead was becoming popular as a spa. The house takes its name from the Revd Allatson Burgh, vicar of St Lawrence Jewry in

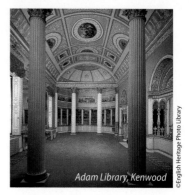

Adam Library, Kenwood

the City, who was so unpopular that his parishioners petitioned Queen Victoria to have him removed.

The panelled rooms are now used for poetry and music recitals, exhibitions by local artists and the Hampstead Museum; one room is devoted to the artist **John Constable**.

2 Willow Road

(NT) 👣*Guided tours (1hr) by timed ticket Thu–Sat at noon, 1pm and 2pm (also 11am on Sat), unguided visits 3–5pm, early Mar to early Nov.* 👓*£5.30, joint ticket with Fenton House £7.70.* ℘*020 7435 6166, 01494 755 570 (infoline). www.nationaltrust.org.uk.*

Erno **Goldfinger** (1902–87) was born in Hungary; in 1920 he went to Paris and studied architecture at the École des Beaux Arts; five years later, he and a number of fellow students persuaded Auguste Perret, a pioneer in the use of reinforced concrete and "structural rationalism", to set up a studio. In Paris he met and married the striking Ursula Blackwell (of the Crosse & Blackwell family), who then began painting under Amédée Ozenfant, a former collaborator of Le Corbusier.

The three houses they built replaced a run-down terrace, but despite causing early controversy, their discreet, modern, functional design is sympathetic to the Georgian brick houses around. Inside, the central block is spacious, airy, light, and full of individual mementoes, as well as art collected by the couple (Ernst, Penrose, Miller, Picasso). A central

A Romantic Poet

John Keats (1795–1821) was the eldest of three sons. From an early age he showed a keen talent for poetry by translating Virgil's *Aeneid* into prose when still at school. In 1810, after losing both his parents (his father in a riding accident and his mother to consumption), he was apprenticed to a surgeon; four years later he transferred to St Thomas' and Guy's Hospitals in Southwark. By 1817, then living in the City, Keats decided to devote himself to the study of Elizabethan literature and to writing poetry, adopting the free form of the heroic couplet. When his brother and sister-in-law resolved to sail for America, Keats travelled to Liverpool to see them off and onwards on an extensive tour of the north (Lancaster, Lake District, Carlisle, Dumfries, Ireland, Ayr, Glasgow); spent by the exertion and exposure, Keats began to display the symptoms of his fatal malady. His other brother died that December and Keats returned to Hampstead, where he met Fanny Brawne not long before he, too, was to die in Rome.

stairwell provides the main axis and access to the three floors.

St John-at-Hampstead

Downshire Hill. ⓞ*Open Mon–Sat 9am–5.30pm, Sun 8am–7pm.* ℘*020 7794 5808. www.hampsteadparish church.org.uk.*
This church marks the Keats Grove fork, white and upright with a domed bell turret. It has a Classical pediment, large name plaque and square portico, and is a chapel of ease dating from 1818.

Keats House

&。ⓞ*Open Tue–Sun 1–5pm (4pm Nov–Mar); call to check.* ↝*Guided tours Sat–Sun 3pm.* ⓞ*Closed 25–26 Dec, 1 Jan.* ≤*£3.50.* ℘*020 7435 2062. www.cityoflondon.gov.uk/keats.*
Two small semi-detached Regency houses with a common garden, known as Wentworth Place, were erected in 1815–16 by two friends with whom Keats

Keats House, Hampstead, celebrates a young poetic genius

K. Brett/MICHELIN

and his brother, in lodgings in Well Walk, soon became acquainted. In 1818, Keats came to live with his friend Brown in the left-hand house; shortly afterwards Mrs Brawne and her children became tenants of the right-hand house. He wrote poems, including the *Ode to a Nightingale*, in the garden; he became engaged to Fanny Brawne but, after falling ill with tuberculosis in September 1820, he left to winter in Italy and died in February 1821.
Records are now assembled, chiefly in the Chester Room added in 1838–39 when the second house was acquired.

Freud Museum

20 Maresfield Gardens. ⊖*Swiss Cottage.* &。ⓞ*Open Wed–Sun noon–5pm.* ⓞ*Closed Easter bank holidays, 24–26 Dec, 1 Jan (call for details).* ≤*£5. Brochure (5 languages). Limited parking. Shop.* ℘*020 7435 2002. www.freud.org.uk.*
The house to which Sigmund Freud escaped from Nazi persecution in Vienna in 1938 and where he lived until his death in 1939 has been turned into a museum devoted to his life and work and to the history and development of psychoanalysis. On the ground floor are his study and working library with his famous couch and collection of books, pictures and **antiquities**★★, kept intact by his daughter Anna.

ADDRESSES

☺ LIGHT BITE

Coffee Cup – *74 High St, Hampstead, NW3 1QX.* ⊖*Hampstead.* ✆*020 7435 7565.* Under its distinctive red and white canopy, this coffee shop makes the ideal pit stop. Inside there's wood panelling and red leather, but outside seats provide people watchers with a good vantage point.

Cafe Rouge – *6–7 South Grove, Highgate N6 6BP. www.cafeouge.co.uk.* ⊖*Highgate.* ✆*020 8 342 9797.* Well-priced French fare at this reliable chain. The restaurant is set on a pretty corner of the high street and offers a great view of Highgate's daily comings and goings, especially from its outdoor tables in summer.

🍺 PUBS

Gatehouse – *1 North Rd, Highgate, N6 4BD.* ⊖*Highgate; Archway.* ✆*020 8340 8054.* A busy pub with elaborate décor and historic associations. The well-regarded theatre upstairs showcases young writers and actors in a regularly changing programme of rep theatre: ✆*020 8340 3488 (box office). www.upstairsatthegatehouse.com.*

Spaniard's Inn – *Spaniards Rd, NW3 7JJ.* ⊖*Hampstead.* ✆*020 8731 6571.* Historic tavern founded in 1585. In 1780, when Gordon's anti-papal rioters were

heading for Lord Mansfield's residence to ransack it, they stopped at the inn to ask the way. The landlord plied them with drinks and held them up until the militia were able to arrive – or so the story goes. Worth a trip out in summer. Take time to read the display of humorous sayings such as: "When a woman marries, she loses the attention of all men and gains the inattention of one."

The Flask – *14 Flask Walk, Hampstead, NW3 1HE.* ⊖*Highgate.* ✆*020 7435 4580. www.theflaskhampstead.co.uk.* A quaint pub with a roaring fire in winter, where Karl Marx was a frequent visitor. Large outdoor space that can get very crowded on sunny days. Good pub food, including Sunday roasts. Get there as close as you can to noon to get served quickly.

The Flask Tavern – *77 Highgate West Hill, N6 6BU.* ⊖*Highgate; Archway.* ✆*020 8348 7346.* Delightful, historic pub with a warren of rooms and an outside courtyard. Great after a walk in Highgate Cemetery. Decent pub food.

Ye Olde White Bear – *Well Rd, Hampstead, NW3 1LJ .* ⊖*Hampstead.* ✆*020 7435 3758.* In a picturesque area of Hampstead, this old pub has been carefully preserved. Comfortable club atmosphere with wooden floorboards and wooden panelling in the two bars. Pub quiz Thu eve.

Hampton Court★★★

One of King Henry VIII's favourite palaces, Hampton Court was the perfect rural retreat for many sovereigns, with its romantic setting by the Thames. The glorious buildings in contrasting styles and the splendid gardens, are enduring symbols of royal power and wealth.

A BIT OF HISTORY

Hampton Court Palace was begun in the 16C, an age of splendour and display, which is reflected in the magnificent and extensive Tudor buildings. It was

▷ **Location:** *See Suburbs map (TZ). Overground rail: Hampton Court from Waterloo. Boat: Hampton Court.* Hampton Court is to the SW of London at the junction of the A 308 and A 309.

extended in the late 17C with two ranges of handsome state apartments designed by **Sir Christopher Wren** for **William** and **Mary**.

Wolsey's Mansion – **Thomas Wolsey**, the son of an Ipswich butcher rose under **Henry VIII** to be Archbishop of York

Hampton Court

C. Ochterbeck/Michelin

(1514), Lord Chancellor (1515), Cardinal (1515) and Papal Legate (1518). Eager to celebrate his wealth and position, he bought the manor of Hampton, enclosed the estate (1 800 acres/ 728ha) and began to construct a fine mansion according to the usual Tudor plan of consecutive courts bordered by buildings: Base Court, Clock Court, Carpenter's Court, hall and chapel (300ft/91m by 550ft/168m overall).

The mansion was richly furnished throughout with painted and gilded ceilings and panelling and tapestries on the walls. It contained some 1 000 rooms, of which 280 were kept prepared for guests. Spring water was brought from Coombe Hill 3mi/5km away and

carried under the Thames in leaden pipes.

The magnificence of Wolsey's mansion outshone the royal palaces and attracted the eye and envy of the king. After 15 years Wolsey fell from power; within months of his disgrace he died (1530). Henry annexed Hampton Court.

Tudor Palace – Despite its magnificence, **Henry VIII** enlarged and rebuilt much of the palace. Major additions included the Great Hall, the Great Watching Chamber, the annexes around the Kitchen Court, the Fountain Court and the tennis court wing. Henry also planted a flower garden, kitchen garden and two orchards.

Edward VI, who was born and christened (1537) at Hampton Court, his two sisters, Mary and Elizabeth, and the early Stuarts resided at the palace in fine weather or when the plague was rife in London.

Hampton Court was reserved for **Cromwell** and was therefore preserved with its contents. At the Restoration, the buildings remained largely unaltered and unmaintained until the late 17C.

Renaissance Reconstruction – Hampton Court entered its third and last phase of construction in the reign of **William and Mary**, who wished to make Hampton Court their main residence outside London. Initial schemes for the total

A Curiosity

The **Astronomical Clock** was made for Henry VIII in 1540 by Nicholas Oursian; on the dial (8ft/2.5m) the hour, month, date, signs of the zodiac, year and phase of the moon are indicated. It predates the publication of the theories of Copernicus and Galileo and the sun therefore revolves round the earth. It was transferred in the 19C from St James's Palace to its present site in the Clock Court, which was the main Court of Wolsey's house.

demolition of the Tudor palace were discarded. Instead **Wren** rebuilt the east and south ranges of the Fountain Court to provide two suites of State Apartments.

The King's Side was in the south range overlooking the Privy Garden, and the Queen's Side was in the east range overlooking the Fountain Garden. Wren also rebuilt the smaller informal royal apartments facing into the **Fountain Court**★ and added a colonnade and a new south range to the Clock Court. The buildings were executed in brick in the classic Renaissance style of the 17C. The rooms were decorated by **Grinling Gibbons** (sculptures) and **Antonio Verrio** (painted ceilings). The Banqueting House overlooking the river was built in the last years of William's reign after the death of Mary.

The decoration and furnishing of the State Apartments continued under **Queen Anne** and was completed under **George II**, the last monarch to reside at the palace, who also commissioned **William Kent** to decorate the Cumberland Suite. When the Great Gatehouse was rebuilt (1771–73), it was reduced in height by two storeys.

In 1838 **Queen Victoria** opened the State Apartments, the gardens and Bushy Park to the public.

VISIT

✗♿**House:** 🕐 Open daily Apr–Sept 10am–6pm (last admission 5pm), Oct–Mar 10am–4.30pm (last admission 3.30pm). **Gardens:** 🕐 Same but one hour later than house. 🕐Closed 24–26 Dec. Orientation leaflet (7 languages). ⤙Guided tours. Family trails. Audioguide. ⊜£14 (House and Gardens); Gardens £4.60. Parking £3.50. Summer – Hampton Court Flower Show, open-air concerts and theatre. Winter – open-air ice-rink and Christmas evenings. ✆0844 482 7777. www.hrp.org.uk.

HIGHLIGHTS
PALACE★★★

The **Trophy Gates** were built as the main gates in the reign of George II with lion and unicorn supporters.

The **moat and bridge** were constructed by Henry VIII; the bridge is fronted by the King's Beasts.

The **Great Gatehouse** built by Wolsey was flanked with wings in the reign of Henry VIII. The **stone weasels** on the battlements are the same period.

The **Arms of Henry VIII** appear in a panel *(renewed)* beneath the central oriel in the Great Gatehouse and also on Anne Boleyn's Gateway (🕐 *see below*). The **terracotta roundels** depicting Roman emperors, which appear on the turrets and elsewhere, were bought by Wolsey for Hampton Court in 1521.

Anne Boleyn's Gateway is so called because it was embellished by Henry VIII during her brief period as Queen. The Base Court side bears Elizabeth I's badges and initials; on the other side are Wolsey's arms and his cardinal's hat.

Clock Court owes its name to the **astronomical clock** made for Henry VIII in 1540.

Tudor Royal Lodgings
30min. Entrance in Anne Boleyn's Gateway.

The **Great Hall (1)** (106ft/32m x 40ft/12mx 60ft/18m), used by Henry's men for dining and sleeping, was built in five years (1531–36). The magnificent hammerbeam roof is ornamented with mouldings, tracery, carving and pendants relieved with gilding and colours. The walls are hung with 16C Flemish tapestries made by Van Orley to illustrate the *Story of Abraham*. At the west end is the Minstrels' Gallery.

The **Horn Room (2)**, from which the stairs led down to the kitchens, was the serving place for the upper end of the hall.

The **Great Watching Chamber (3)** was built in 1535–36 at the entrance to the Tudor State Rooms *(demolished)* with a panelled ceiling set with coloured bosses displaying Tudor and Seymour devices. Note the 16C Flemish tapestries depicting the *Vices and Virtues*.

The **Haunted Gallery (4)**, said to be haunted by the ghost of Catherine Howard (condemned because of her infidelity), looks on to the Round Kitchen

HAMPTON COURT PALACE

FIRST FLOOR

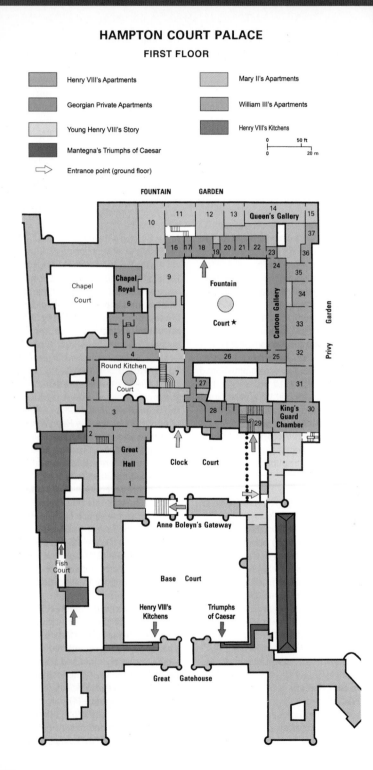

Henry VIII's Apartments

Georgian Private Apartments

Young Henry VIII's Story

Mantegna's Triumphs of Caesar

Mary II's Apartments

William III's Apartments

Henry VIII's Kitchens

Entrance point (ground floor)

FOUNTAIN GARDEN

Queen's Gallery

Chapel Royal

Chapel Court

Fountain Court ★

Cartoon Gallery

Privy Garden

Round Kitchen Court

King's Guard Chamber

Great Hall

Clock Court

Anne Boleyn's Gateway

Fish Court

Base Court

Henry VIII's Kitchens

Triumphs of Caesar

Great Gatehouse

Court. The Flemish tapestries are from Queen Elizabeth's collection.

The **Royal Pew (5)** was designed for Queen Anne with a ceiling by Sir James Thornhill.

The **Chapel Royal (6)** was built by Wolsey but lavishly transformed by Henry VIII. The reredos is by **Gibbons**; it is framed by Corinthian pillars and a segmental pediment by **Wren**.

Queen's State Apartments

45min. Entrance in Clock Court.

The beautiful wrought-iron balustrade of the **Queen's Staircase (7)** is by **Tijou** and the lantern by Benjamin Goodison (1731). The walls and ceiling were decorated by Kent (1735); on the west wall is an allegorical painting by Honthorst (1628) depicting Charles I and Henrietta Maria as Jupiter and Juno, and the Duke of Buckingham as Apollo.

The **Queen's Guard Chamber (8)** contains a monumental chimney-piece carved by Grinling Gibbons.

The **Queen's Presence Chamber (9)** contains a bed and furniture made for Queen Anne (1714). The elaborate plaster ceiling is by Sir John Vanbrugh, the carvings by Gibbons and the paintings by Tintoretto *(The Nine Muses)*, Gentileschi and Vasari.

The **Public Dining Room (10)** was decorated by **Sir John Vanbrugh** c 1716–18 for the future George II and Queen Caroline.

The **Queen's Audience Chamber (11)** is hung with a 16C tapestry illustrating the *Story of Abraham* and contains the canopied Chair of State.

The **Queen's Drawing Room (12)** is decorated with wall and ceiling paintings by Verrio (1703–05) commissioned by Queen Anne. From the central window there is a splendid **view**✶ of the **Fountain Garden**.

The **Queen's Bedroom (13)** contains a state bed, chair and stools (1715–16) in crimson damask and a portrait of *Queen Anne as a child* by **Sir Peter Lely**. The ceiling is **Sir James Thornhill**'s (1715). In the **Queen's Gallery (14)** the mantelpiece was designed by John Nost and the carvings are by Grinling Gibbons. The adjoining chamber **(15)** is decorated with embroidered wall coverings.

Georgian Rooms

30min. Entrance in Fountain Court.

In contrast with the public state rooms, these private apartments are more intimate and comfortable. Most have been restored to recreate interiors from 1737.

The **Queen's Private Chapel (16)** has a domed ceiling with a lantern. Religious paintings by Fetti surmount the doors here and in the following rooms.

The **Bathing Closet (17)** leads to the **Private Dining Room (18)** hung with works by Pellegrini. The large silver service is on loan from a private collector.

The next room is a second **Closet (19)**.

The **Queen's Private Chamber (20)** is hung with paintings by Ruysdael, Brueghel and Van de Velde. The painting of *Friars in a Nunnery* was a particular royal favourite.

The **King's Private Dressing Room (21)** contains a small early 18C bed.

George II's Private Chamber (22) is notable for its 1730 flock wallpaper and a portrait of Cardinal Richelieu by Philippe de Champaigne. A small **lobby (23)** leads to the **Cartoon Gallery (24)** designed by Wren (1699) to display seven of the ten tapestry cartoons drawn by **Raphael** (1515) and depicting scenes from the lives of St Peter and St Paul (now in the Victoria & Albert Museum). The cartoons hanging here are copies.

The **lobby (25)** is hung with a view of Hampton Court in George I's reign and a 17C hunting scene.

The **Communication Gallery (26)**, which links the King's and Queen's Apartments, is hung with the famous **Windsor Beauties** of Charles II's court by Lely; originally it was hung with Mantegna's cartoons, which are now in the **Orangery**.

Wolsey's Closet (27) contains its original furnishings: linenfold panelling (restored); painted wall panels; frieze with Tudor badges, mermaids and Wolsey's motto as a running motif.

The **Cumberland Suite (28)** was designed by **William Kent** (1732) for George II's third son: elaborate plasterwork and chimneypieces; portraits of some of the royal children; paintings by Ricci, Giordano, Vouet *(Diana)* and Le Sueur.

King's Apartments

45min. Entrance in Clock Court.

The **King's Staircase (29)** is decorated with allegorical scenes by Verrio (c. 1700) and a stylised wrought-iron balustrade by Tijou.

In the **King's Guard Chamber (30)** the upper walls are decorated with over 3 000 **arms** arranged by John Harris, William III's gunsmith.

The **First Presence Chamber (31)** contains William III's canopied chair of state. A picture of the king by Kneller (1701) hangs in its original place.

The smaller **Second Presence Chamber (32)** sometimes served as a dining room.

The **King's Audience Chamber (33)**, which contains the state canopy and 17C chair, offers a view of the Privy Garden.

In the **King's Drawing Room (34)** note, above the fireplace, the elaborate carved frame by Grinling Gibbons.

In the **King's State Bedroom (35)** the ceiling was painted by Verrio. The state bed was used only for the formal *lever* and *coucher*.

The king slept in the **King's Dressing Room (36)** which is furnished in yellow taffeta; the ceiling by Verrio depicts *Mars in the Lap of Venus*.

The **King's Writing Closet (37)** was used for formal business, signing important documents.

The **King's Private Apartments** on the ground floor display architectural drawings of the Palace, a silver-gilt toilet service (c. 1670) by Pierre Prévost, Dutch and Italian paintings, furniture.

The **Orangery** provided winter accommodation for the orange trees which grew in tubs and stood outdoors in summer.

The **Oak Room** is furnished with bookcases and a writing table.

The **King's Private Dining Room** is hung with portraits of the **Hampton Court Beauties** (Queen Mary's Court) by Kneller.

Wolsey Rooms and Renaissance Picture Gallery

30min. Entrance in Clock Court.

The Wolsey rooms were probably used by guests rather than by the cardinal himself. They are currently home to a permanent exhibition exploring the lives of Henry VIII, Katherine of Aragon and Cardinal Wolsey using historic paintings from the Royal Collection together with audiovisual and hands-on displays. The exhibition was set up in 2009 to celebrate the 500th anniversary of Henry VIII's accession to the throne. The two **Victorian Rooms** are furnished in the style of the 1840s.

Tudor Kitchens

45min. Entrance in Clock Court.
Audio-guide available.

The 16C kitchens are the largest and most complete to survive from this period. When the court was in residence they served two meals a day to some 600 people and employed about 230 staff. They are laid out as for the preparation of the feast served on Midsummer's Day in 1542. The tour begins in the cellar beneath the Great Hall (**model** of the kitchens), proceeds to the main gates, where the produce entered the palace, and passes through the **Butchery**, the **Boiling House**, the **Flesh Larder** and the **Fish Court** to the **Great Kitchens**, where the meat was cooked on spits, turned by boys known as gallopines, and sauces were prepared over charcoal stoves; the dishes were then dressed or transferred directly to the **Servery**. The Wine Cellar is one of three in which home-brewed ale and imported wine were stored.

GARDENS★★★

The gardens (50 acres/20ha) bear the imprint of their creators: the Tudor, Stuart and Orange monarchs, their designers and great gardeners. Over the years features have changed in

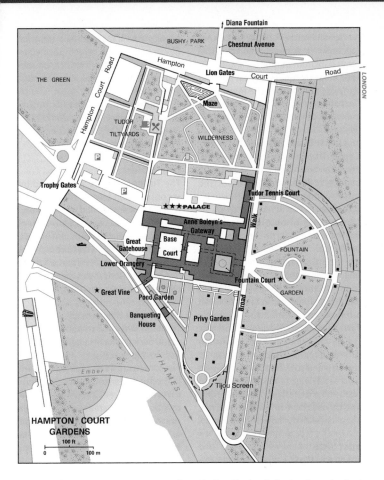

HAMPTON COURT GARDENS

0 100 ft
0 100 m

line with fashion. Henry VIII converted Wolsey's walled flower garden into the Pond Garden and Privy Garden.

The **Privy Garden** began as squares of grass, dotted with heraldic beasts on poles and topiary; a gazebo was erected on a raised mound by the river, with a spiral approach flanked by gaudily painted King's Beasts; there was a watergate to welcome visitors who usually travelled by river in those days. Between 1599 and 1659 the heraldic garden was replaced with four simple grass plots containing fine statuary; the beasts were transferred to stand in the court before the main entrance and the mound was levelled and the soil used to construct the terraces which now flank the Privy Garden.

Under Charles II the land overlooked by the east front was laid out in the fashionable French style practised by Le Nôtre; a vast semicircle of lime trees enclosed three radiating avenues, laid out in a giant goosefoot (patte d'oie); the central claw was represented by a canal, known as the Long Water, which pierced the rows of lime trees.

The layout of the gardens today has been restored to that of 1702, designed largely by William III and Mary.

South Side

The **Knot Garden**, a velvety conceit of interlaced ribands of dwarf box or thyme with infillings of flowers, was replanted this century within its walled Elizabethan site. The royal cipher **ER 1568** appears on the stonework of the bay window in the **South Front** overlooking the Knot Garden; the lead cupola and octagonal turret date from the 16C.

The **Lower Orangery**, a plain building by Wren, now houses the **Mantegna Cartoons** (c. 1431–1506), nine giant paintings depicting *the Triumph of Caesar*.

The **Great Vine**★, planted in 1768 by **Capability Brown** for **George III**, produces an annual crop of 500–600 bunches of Black Hamburg grapes. The massive wisteria, near the Vine House, dates from 1840.

The **Banqueting House** has an important Baroque interior, the *Painted Room* by Verrio.

The **Privy Garden** was reserved for the monarch and his guests. The last major redesign took place under William and Mary when Queen Mary's Bower, a hornbeam alley, and the Queen's Terrace were built; the Tudor Water Gallery was demolished and the garden extended to the river; it was screened from the towpath by 12 wrought-iron panels with English, Welsh, Scottish and Irish emblems designed by **Jean Tijou** The gardens have now been restored, complete with the bowered walkway.

East Side

The **Broad Walk** was planned by Wren and Queen Caroline to separate the Privy Garden from the Fountain Garden.

The **Fountain Garden** was created under William III by retaining the radiating avenues created by Charles II and reducing the Long Water to its present length (0.75mi/1.2km); 13 fountains were installed in a formal scrollwork setting of dwarf box hedges (a Dutch fashion), obelisk-shaped yews and globes of white holly. Under Queen Anne eight fountains at the circumference were removed, the box hedge arabesques were replaced by grass and gravel; in Queen Caroline's time the fountains were reduced to the present singleton. In the late 20C the yews, which grew as they would in the 19C, were trimmed to their

present conical shape to make room for flower beds and to reveal spectacular vistas from the east front. The double semicircle of lime trees was replanted in the 1980s.

The **Tudor Tennis Court** *(for access, ♿see plan)* for real tennis, which is still played on regularly, was built by Henry VIII; the windows are 18C.

North Side

The **Tudor tiltyards**, surrounded by six observation towers, of which one remains, are now walled rose gardens.

The **Wilderness**, now an area (9 acres/4ha) of natural woodland, includes a triangular **maze** *(for access, ♿see plan)* that dates from 1714. The site, originally occupied by Henry VIII's orchard, was formally laid out by William III with espaliers, clipped yews, hollies, box hedges and a circular maze.

The **Lion Gates** were part of Wren's grand design for a new north entrance and front to the palace.

The **Chestnut Avenue** in Bushy Park is another feature of Wren's plan. Four rows of lime trees flank the double row of chestnut trees extending for over a mile/2km. The **Diana Fountain** was commissioned by Charles II from Francisco Fenelli for the Privy Garden. North-west of the fountain is a **Woodland Garden** (100 acres/40.5ha) where rhododendrons and azaleas flourish beneath the trees on either side of the stream, home to a black swan.

HAMPTON COURT GREEN

Opposite the palace gates are houses associated with the court, particularly in the late 17C and 18C, including **Old Court House**, the home (1706–23) of Sir Christopher Wren, and **Faraday House** (18C) where **Michael Faraday** lived in retirement (1858–67). Hidden behind the last two houses is small, square **King's Store Studio**, with white weatherboarding (George III plaque). Facing the Green are the Tudor **Royal Mews**, built round a courtyard.

Kew★★★

The Thames draws a great loop around Kew, an affluent residential area in west London with a village atmosphere. An ideal day excursion out of town brings much enjoyment as one strolls through the splendid gardens with their rare and exotic species, great glasshouses and picturesque dells.

A BIT OF HISTORY
Royal Residence

In 1721 the future **George II** bought **Richmond Lodge** around which his consort, Queen Caroline, laid out elaborate gardens featuring typical 18C ornamental statues and follies.

In 1730, Frederick, Prince of Wales, although on unfriendly terms with George II, leased the **White House** only a mile away. Frederick and his wife Augusta rebuilt the house (known also as Kew House) on a site now marked by a sundial, in which the princess continued to reside after Frederick's death in 1751, devoting herself particularly to the garden.

King George III (1760–1820) and Queen Charlotte found, with a growing family of 15 children, Richmond Lodge and the White House both too small and, in 1773, the **Dutch House** was leased for the young Prince of Wales (the future George IV) and his brother as well as other houses on Kew Green. A new palace, designed by **James Wyatt**, was never completed, but like the White House was demolished, leaving alone of all the cousinhood of royal residences, just the Dutch House or Kew Palace, which was opened as a museum in 1899.

ROYAL BOTANIC GARDENS★★★

Kew Green. &. ✕ **Gardens:** ⏱*Open daily Mon–Fri 9.30am–6.30pm, Sat–Sun and bank holidays 9.30am–7.30pm (last admission 30min before closing); Sept–Mar earlier closing; call or see website.* ⏱*Closed 24–25 Dec.* **Glasshouses, museum and galleries**

Location: *See Suburbs map (TY)* ⊖*Kew Gardens.* Access to Kew to the SW of London is by the A 4 or A 315 and the A205 (South Circular).

*close earlier. The **library and archives** are closed on Mon and Fri Jun–Dec.* 👓*£13. Visitor Centre at Victoria Gate.* ✎*Guided tours from Victoria Gate daily 11am and 2pm. Maps (5 languages). Restaurants. Shops.*

There are regular exhibitions, festivals and events throughout the year including an orchid festival in spring, summer open-air theatre and concerts and a Christmas festival with an atmospheric open-air ice-rink. ✆*020 8332 5655. www.kew.org.*

Kew Gardens are pure pleasure. Colour and the architecture of the trees, singly like the weeping willow and the stone pine, or in groups, delight at all seasons. The layman will spot commonplace flowers and shrubs and gaze on delicate exotics, gardeners check their knowledge against the labels, for this 300 acre/120ha garden is the superb offshoot of laboratories engaged in the identification of plants and plant material from all parts of the world and in economic botany.

The curatorship of the biggest herbarium in the world, a wood museum, a botanical library of more than 100 000 volumes and the training of student gardeners are also within the establishment's province. Declared a UNESCO World Heritage Site in 2003, these are probably the most important – as well as some of the most beautiful – botanical gardens in the world.

Princess Augusta was personally responsible for the inauguration of a botanic garden south of the Orangery and the enlargement of the gardens from seven to more than 100 acres/40ha. **William Kent** rebuilt the White House and landscaped the garden. In 1751, the Dowager Princess of Wales, guided by the Earl of Bute, a considerable botanist, appointed William Aiton as

Palm House, Kew

Ph. Gajic/MICHELIN

head gardener (1759–93) and **William Chambers** as architect (1760).

Under Aiton, a Scot who had worked at the Chelsea Physic Garden, his son who succeeded him (1793–1841), and **Sir Joseph Banks** (d. 1820), voyager, distinguished botanist, naturalist, biologist and finally director, plants began to be especially collected from all parts of the world for research and cultivation. By 1789, 5 500 species were growing in the gardens.

In 1772 on the death of Princess Augusta, George III combined the Kew and Richmond Lodge gardens and had them landscaped by **Capability Brown**.

Gardens

Major plantings and flowering seasons are indicated on the map opposite, colour-keyed to draw attention to flowers in outlying areas. Many fine specimens of trees, some over 200 years old, were uprooted in the great storm of October 1987, but most of the damage has been repaired.

Greenhouses

Palm House★★ – The iron- and-glass structure designed by **Decimus Burton** and the engineer, Richard Turner, as a purely functional building (362ft/110m long, 33ft,10m high in the wings and 62ft/19m at the centre) took four years to erect (1844–48). Inside are tropical plants, both useful (coffee, cocoa) and ornamental. The Chilean runner lizards in residence were given to Kew by the then Customs and Excise after having been smuggled into Britain.

Outside (*west*) a semicircular rose garden; the pond (*east*) is watched over by the Queen's Beasts (stone replicas of those designed by James Woodward to stand outside Westminster Abbey at the coronation in 1953).

Temperate House★ – The house, again by Burton, but 20 years later, epitomises Victorian conservatory construction.

The **Evolution House** recreates the climate of change affecting the Earth.

Alpine House – Beneath a glass pyramid, built in 1981, from which rainwater drains into the surrounding moat, is a rock landscape including a refrigerated bed.

Princess of Wales Tropical Conservatory – In this modern steel and glass diamond-shaped structure ten different tropical habitats are recreated, ranging from the extremes of mangrove swamp to desert – from ferns and orchids to carnivorous and stone plants (*Lithops*), cacti and succulents set against a Mohave desert diorama. In 1996, a titan arum or "corpse flower," which blooms every 30-odd years, attracted great attention: the Sumatran native has flowered at Kew in 1889, 1926 and 1963.

Marianne North Gallery

🕐*Call for opening hours.*
📞*020 8332 5655.*

In a building (1882) designed by her architect friend, James Ferguson, is an exhibition of paintings by Miss North showing plants, insects and general scenes from the many countries she visited between 1871 and 1884.

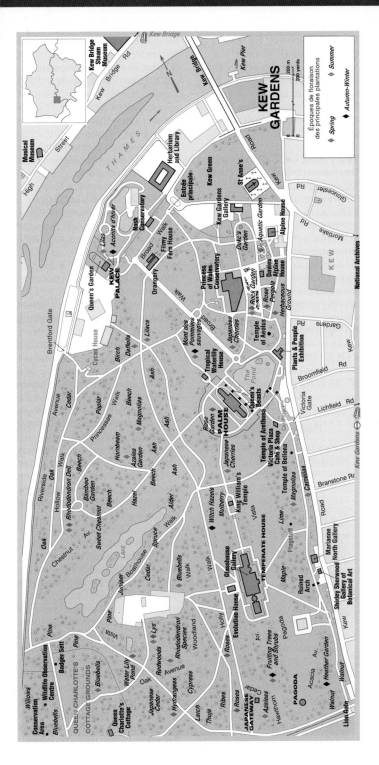

KEW GARDENS

Époques de floraison
des principales plantations

● Spring   ● Summer
● Autumn–Winter

200 m
200 yards

363

Shirley Sherwood Gallery
🕐 *Open daily 9.30am–3.45pm.*
Adjacent to the Marianne North Gallery, this gallery, opened in 2008, is dedicated to botanical art – both from Kew's historic collection, and also the contemporary collection of Dr Sherwood.

Kew Palace★★ (Dutch House)
The terracotta brick building was built by Samuel Fortrey, a London Merchant of Dutch parentage, who commemorated his house's construction in a monogram and the date 1631 over the front door. At the rear is the **Queen's Garden**, a formal arrangement of pleached alleys of laburnum and hornbeam, parterres (formal symmetrical beds), a gazebo and plants popular in the 17C. The 17C nosegay garden has been replanted with contemporary herbs.

The rooms downstairs are all panelled: the King's Dining Room in white 18C style, the Breakfast Room in early 17C style and the Library Ante-Room in re-set 16C linenfold. The Pages' Waiting

Pioneering Work
Kew has practised biological control (Integrated Pest Management) throughout its premises tailored to 40 000 taxa (specific species) of plant and 750 000 specimens of fungi since 1991. Efforts to save some of the world's rarest orchids have led scientists at Kew to evolve a way of germinating plants from seed without the symbiotic fungus required in more natural habitats. Some 5 000 species (about 20% of the total known number) are now propagated at Kew, having been accumulated over the last 200 years. At Kew's Wakehurst Place site, in West Sussex, the Millennium Seed Bank, an international conservation project to safeguard the world's most endangered plants, is currently undergoing an £80 million expansion.

Room houses an exhibition of minor royal possessions: silver filigree rattles, alphabet counters, snuffboxes etc. Upstairs, apart from the white and gold Queen's Drawing Room, formally set out with lyre-back chairs for a musical evening, the rooms are wallpapered and intimate with family portraits by Gainsborough and Zoffany. In the King's rooms note the embossed terracotta paper in the Ante-room.

Queen Charlotte's Cottage
The two-storeyed thatched house, typical of "rustic" buildings of the period (1772) was designed by Queen Charlotte as a picnic house.

Other Buildings and Monuments
Under Princess Augusta, **William Chambers** set about constructing typical 18C garden follies: temples, a ruined arch, an **Orangery**★(1761) and a **Pagoda**★(1761), a garden ornament 163ft/49m and 10 storeys high. Now alas without its gilded dragon finials, this folly had its floors pierced by the RAF during World War II to give them a 100ft/30m vertical drop to test model bombs.
The **Main Gates** are by Decimus Burton (1848, the lion and unicorn on the original gate are now above gates in Kew Road). The **Japanese Gateway**★ was imported for the Anglo-Japanese Exhibition of 1912.

SIGHTS
Kew Green
The most attractive houses on the green are those by the main gates to the gardens. Dominating the north (river) side are Kew Herbarium: 5 million dried plants and library (🕐*open to specialists*), a three-storey Georgian house and extensive annexe, followed by an irregular line of 18–19C brick houses *(nos 61–83)*. On the far side of the gates backing onto the gardens are a line of one-time royal "cottages," including, at no 37, Cambridge Cottage, now the **Wood Museum** and **Kew Gardens Gallery** *(enter from inside the gardens).*

The Domesday Book

The famous register of lands of England, named after *Domus dei* – where the volumes were originally preserved in Winchester Cathedral – was commissioned by William the Conqueror so that he might ascertain the dues owed to him by his subjects, thereby setting the rules by which the monarch, later the government, might levy tax nationwide. As a result we have a comprehensive idea of how the kingdom was divided in 1085–86 both in terms of land holding and popular employment. Lords of the manor held the bulk of the land on a freehold basis, which they tenanted or leased to a complex hierarchy of dependents, villeins or freemen. Land was allocated to agricultural functions (meadow, pasture) in proportion to hunting (woodland) and fishing (ponds, rivers).

The **Little Domesday** (384 pages) records estates throughout latter-day Essex, Norfolk and Suffolk, while the **Great Domesday** (450 pages) surveys the rest of the kingdom with the exception of Northumberland, Cumberland, Durham, parts of Lancashire and Westmorland, which lay outside the king's jurisdiction. The City of London is also omitted, as the conquering king could not have been certain of brokering his rights over the shrewd and powerful business community. A facsimile is displayed at the National Archives in Kew (*see above*).

St Anne's Church

The nave and chancel were constructed. in 1710–14 on the site of a 16C chapel ; In 1770 a north aisle was built George III added the royal gallery in 1805.. **Gainsborough** (d. 1788) and Zoffany (d. 1810) lie in the churchyard.

National Archives

Ruskin Avenue. Open Mon, Wed, Fri 9am–5pm, Tue 10am–7pm, Thu 9am–7pm, Sat 9.30am–5pm. Closed Sun, public hols, bank holiday weekends, Christmas, New Year and Easter. ID required for admission. 020 8876 3444. www.nationalarchives.gov.uk.

The **Domesday Book**, **Shakespeare**'s will, **Guy Fawkes**'s confessions, **Captain Cook**'s charts, Bligh's accounts of the mutiny on the *Bounty* are just a few of the precious historic charters, accounts, maps, seals, reports, registers, government papers and old chests entrusted to the PRO, founded in 1838 and formerly in Chancery Lane. Fragile papers are kept in controlled environments but there are regular exhibitions of documents.

ADDITIONAL SIGHTS
Kew Bridge Steam Museum

Brentford. Entrance in Green Dragon Lane. Open Tue–Sun 11am–5pm. Closed Good Fri, 20–28 Dec, 31 Dec–2 Jan. £9.50 (multi-visit ticket). Children under 16 must be accompanied by an adult. Guide book and brochure (6 languages). Large print Braille guide. Parking. Café. 020 8568 4757. www.kbsm.org.

This museum of water supply demonstrates the development of James Watt's basic idea through over a century of improved efficiency and increased scale. There are six Cornish Beam Engines and the Waddon Engine, the last steam-powered water pumping engine used commercially until 1983.

Smaller steam engines, traction engines and steam lorries, a narrow-gauge railway, a water-wheel (1702), a forge, machine shop and relics connected with London's water supply complete the display. The standpipe tower outside is a local landmark nearly 200ft/61m high.

Musical Museum

399 High St, Brentford. Open Tue–Sun 11am–5.30pm (last admission 4.30pm). £7. Guide book, recordings available. 020 8560 8108. www.musicalmuseum.co.uk.

The museum's collection of some 200 mechanical music-makers – pianolas, organs, a Wurlitzer, is displayed in modern, purpose-built, brightly painted premises.

Boston Manor

⊖*Boston Manor.* **Grounds:** 🕐*Open daily.* **House:** 🕐*Open Apr–Oct, Sat–Sun and Bank Holiday Mondays 2.30–5pm. Guide book.* 📞*020 8583 4463. http://ealing-web.com/boston_manor_house.htm.*

The three-storey red-brick house was built in 1623 for Lady Mary Read, a young widow who remarried soon after into the Spencer family; the magnificent Jacobean plaster ceiling in the Drawing Room is dated 1623. In 1670, East India merchant **James Clitherow** bought the property for £5 136, extended it and

landscaped the grounds with cedars and a lake. It remained in the family until 1924 when it became the property of the local council.

ADDRESSES

🍴 ELEGANT DINING

⊜⊜**The Glasshouse** – *14 Station Parade, TW9 3PZ .* ⊖*Kew Gardens.* 📞*020 8940 6777. www.glasshouse restaurant.co.uk.* A Michelin one-star restaurant not far from Kew Gardens.

Osterley Park★★

This magnificent country mansion surrounded by parkland on the outskirts of London is well worth a visit. The rooms are elegantly furnished and decorated to reflect the tastes of wealthy and discerning owners. Osterley Park is the place to see **Robert Adam** interior decoration at its most complete. Room after room is as he designed it: ceilings, walls, doorcases, doors, handles, carpets, mirrors and furniture down to chairs standing in the exact positions for which they were designed. This is an easy excursion by public transport.

A BIT OF HISTORY

A Country Seat for City Gentlemen – **Sir Thomas Gresham** bought Osterley Manor in 1562 and began an adjoining country house.

When Gresham's mansion was complete, **Queen Elizabeth** honoured her financier with a visit (1576). In 1711 the mansion was purchased by another City grandee **Francis Child**, whose grandchild began transforming the place in 1756, work that continued for more than 20 years.

In 1773 Horace **Walpole**, visiting from nearby **Strawberry Hill**, wrote: "The old house is so improved and enriched that all the Percies and Seymours of Sion must die of envy..." Osterley was

▶ **Location:** *See Suburbs map (TY).* ⊖*Osterley.* West of London by the A 4 (N side) and near the M 4 (Exit 2).

presented to the nation by the 9th Earl of Jersey in 1949.

VISIT

(NT) ♿🅿✕ **House:** 🕐*Open Mar–Nov Wed–Sun 1–4pm (5–20 Dec Sat–Sun 12.30–2.30pm).* 🕐*Closed 25–26 Dec.* **Garden:** 🕐*Open Wed–Sun 11am–5pm (last admision 30min before closing).* 🎟*£8.40; Garden only £3.70.* 📷*No photography. Dogs on lead. £3.50. Tea room. Braille guide; hearing scheme.* 📞*020 8232 5050 (visitor services), 01494 755 566 (infoline). www.nationaltrust. org.uk/osterley.*

Exterior

The square form with corner towers of Sir Thomas Gresham's house remains, though enlarged and encased by new bricks and stone quoins in the 18C by **Sir William Chambers** who reduced the courtyard to provide a hall and completed the Gallery and Breakfast Room.

Robert Adam then added the grand, six-columned portico at the front and, at the rear, a horseshoe staircase with wrought-iron and brass work (1770).

Interior

The wide **Hall** is apsed at either end, the fine ceiling filled with floral scrolls is echoed in the two-tone marble pavement. Classical statues nestle in niches on either side of the curved fireplaces and grisaille paintings, each detail designed by Adam.

◑ Leave the Hall by the N door and walk to the far end of the passage.

The **Breakfast Room** is painted in a strong lemon yellow contrasted with touches of blue that highlight the ornamental detailing. The ceiling is by Chambers; tables and pier glasses, however, were designed by Adam and the lyre-back mahogany armchairs probably by Linnell.

The **staircase**, begun by Chambers, has a fine iron balustrade and delicate stucco decoration added by Adam who also designed the three lamps that hang between the Corinthian columns. The sumptuous ceiling painting is particularly Rubensesque.

◑ At the top, turn right.

The **State Bedroom** or Yellow Taffeta Bedchamber is furnished with painted taffeta curtains and bed hangings, and ornate gilded mirrors. The bed, surmounted by cupped acorns, was designed by Adam (1779).

Beyond the stairhead is the suite of less extravagant rooms designed by Chambers for the Childs: his **dressing room**, the **bedchamber** (note the lacquer dressing-table and French ebony cabinet on a stand) and her **dressing room** (chimney-piece and mirror by Linnell).

◑ Return downstairs; turn right.

The **Eating Room** is an all Adam room: motifs from the pink-and-green ceiling decoration are most typical. According to 18C custom the beautifully carved mahogany lyre-back chairs are set against the wall.

The light and airy **gallery**, boasting a fine view of the garden, was designed by Chambers. Marble chimney-pieces, Classical doorcases, 18C Chinese pieces and lacquered furniture are contrasted by the delicate Rococo-style frieze. Other fixtures are by Adam.

The somewhat over gilded **Drawing Room** is dominated by the low, heavy coffered ceiling. The serpentine sofas and chairs are after the early French neo-Classical style. The pier glasses and perfume burners are French in origin.

In the **Tapestry Room**, one's attention is drawn to the richness of the Gobelins' tapestries, signed and dated by (Jacques) Neilson, 1775, an artist of Scottish origin in charge of the works in Paris from 1751 to 1788.

The **State Bed Chamber** is decked in cool green. The Child crest above the chimney glass features an eagle with an adder in its beak. The gilded chairs, their oval backs supported on reclining sphinxes, are one of Adam's most graceful designs (1777).

The **Etruscan Dressing Room**, which helped to launch a fashion for the style of antiquity, boasts ancient Greek decorative themes that Adam took to be Etruscan. According to surviving inventories from 1782, it was here that the japanned **Chippendale** 1773 lady's writing desk was situated.

The **Stables**, built in 1577 by Sir Thomas Gresham, were refitted in the 18C.

The **Pleasure Grounds** *(west of the house)*, which have been restored according to old maps and prints, contain Chambers' Doric temple to Pan and Adam's semicircular garden house (c. 1780). The grounds erupt in fragrant, colourful blooms between June and September, a perfect time to visit. The cedar trees on the south lawn were planted in the 1760s, as was the large oriental plane tree. The chain of lakes was created in the 1750s; at the head of the Garden Lake there is a brick bridge leading over to a secluded island.

Richmond★★

In an attractive riverside location, the vibrant town of Richmond is complemented by a rural atmosphere, with its leafy parks, woodland and golf courses. Together with neighbouring Twickenham (the home of English rugby), Richmond is a highly desirable area. Fine mansions recall past aristocratic associations when Richmond Palace was a favourite residence of the Tudor monarchs. Richmond has all the amenities of an affluent town: historic pubs, pleasant restaurants, antique shops and select boutiques.

Information: Old Town Hall, Whittaker Avenue, Richmond TW9 1TP. *℘*020 8940 9125. www.visitrichmond. co.uk; The Atrium, Civic Centre, 44 York Street, Twickenham TW1 3BZ.

Location: *See Suburbs (TYZ).* ⊖*Richmond; Overground: Richmond from Waterloo Station and by North London Line.* Richmond lies to the SW of London between the main axes to the A 3 and M 3. It is also accessible by boat from Westminster Pier.

A BIT OF HISTORY

Richmond, possessing what has been called the most beautiful urban green in England, grew to importance between the 12C and 17C as a royal seat and, after the Restoration, as the residential area of members of the court: Windsor, Hampton Court and Kew are easily accessible. In the courtiers' wake followed diplomats, politicians, professional men, dames and their schools, and with the coming of the railway in 1840, prosperous Victorian commuters.

Richmond Palace: Royal Residence Through Six Reigns – The 12C manor house was extended and embellished by **Edward III,** who died in it in 1377, and favoured by **Richard II**, his grandson while his queen was alive but demolished at her death in 1394. A new palace, the second, was begun by **Henry V** but completed only 40 years after his death in the reign of **Edward IV,** who gave it with the royal manor of Shene to his queen, Elizabeth Woodville, from whom it was confiscated by Henry VII; in 1499 it burned to the ground. **Henry VII**, parsimonious where his son was prodigal, nevertheless, "rebuilded (the palace) again sumptuously and costly and changed the name of Shene and called it Richmond because his father and he were Earls of Rychmonde" (in Yorkshire). This palace, the third on the site, was to be the last. **Henry VII, Henry VIII, Queen Elizabeth** and **Charles I** all resided here. The new Tudor palace conformed to standard design: service buildings of red brick, preserved today in the gateway, enclosed an outer or Base Court, now Old Palace Yard, from which a second gateway led to an inner or Middle Court, lined along one side by a Great Hall of stone with a lead roof. The Privy Lodging, which included the state rooms, surrounded another court. Domed towers and turrets crowned the construction, which covered 10 acres/ 4ha and was by far the most splendid in the kingdom, favoured by several monarchs. An art gallery was added to house the extensive collection of royal paintings. At Charles I's execution the palace was stripped and the contents, including the pictures, were sold. By the 18C little remained and private houses were constructed out of the ruins.

🐾 WALKING TOUR

Take a stroll through the town.

Town Centre

On the east side of the main road are reminders of the growing village in the parish **Church of St Mary Magdalene** with its 16C square flint and stone tower, early brasses and monuments (actor

Edmund Kean), 18C houses (Ormond and Halford Roads), 19C cottages (Waterloo Place), the Vineyard dating back in name to the 16–17C when local vines were famous, and the rebuilt almshouses of 17C foundation. In Paradise Road stands Hogarth House built in 1748, where Leonard and **Virginia Woolf**, who lived there from 1915 to 1924, founded the **Hogarth Press**.

Richmond Theatre

Ph. Gajic/MICHELIN

▶ *Cross the High St and pass through charming alleyways to Richmond Green.*

Richmond Green

The Green, once the scene of Tudor jousting, has been a cricket pitch since the middle of the 17C.

Richmond Theatre, which overlooks the Little Green, was extensively refurbished in 1991 in accordance with its late 19C appearance.

The east side of the Green is lined with 17C and 18C houses.

Along the west side is **Old Palace Terrace** (1692–1700), six two-storey brick houses with straight hooded doorways, built by John Powell (who lived in no 32).

Oak House and **Old Palace Place** date back to 1700. **Old Friars** (1687) stands on part of the site of a monastery founded by Henry VII in 1500; the house was extended in the 18C to include a concert room for the holding of "music mornings and evenings."

Maids of Honour Row★★★ – The three-storey brick-built houses, adorned with pilasters and friezes, were erected in 1724 "to serve as lodgings for the Maids of Honour attending the Princess of Wales."

Old Palace and Gatehouse – On the south side are two houses: the first, castellated, boasts a central doorway incorporating brickwork from Henry VII's palace; the second is the original outer gateway of the palace.

The Wardrobe – *Old Palace Yard.* Note the blue diapered Tudor walls incorporated in the early 18C building and the fine 18C ironwork.

Trumpeters' House★ – *Old Palace Yard.* The main front of this house converted c

1701 from the Middle Gate of Richmond Palace, overlooks the garden and can be seen through the trees from the riverside path. The giant pedimented portico of paired columns was formerly guarded by stone statues after which the house is still named.

▶ *Walk down Old Palace Lane.*

Richmond Riverside

Old Palace Lane, lined by modest, wistaria-covered 19C houses and cottages, leads from the southwest corner of Richmond Green to the river.

Asgill House★ – The house, standing at the end of the lane overlooking the river, was built c. 1760 as a weekend and summer residence for the City banker and sometime Lord Mayor, Sir Charles Asgill. In pale golden stone with strong horizontal lines and a tall central bay, it was one of the last of its type to be built overlooking the Thames.

Take the towpath upstream past Trumpeters' House and Friars Lane to Whittaker Avenue. The Old Town Hall houses the Museum of Richmond (⊙*see Additional Sights*).

Richmond Bridge★★ – a classical, stone structure designed by James Paine – was built in 1774 and widened in 1937; tolls were levied until the 19C. There is a milestone-obelisk at the north end.

The towpath continues beyond the bridge as a riverside promenade below Terrace Gardens.

▶ *From Richmond Bridge walk up Richmond Hill.*

Richmond Hill

The **view**★★ gets ever better as one climbs the steep road lined by balconied terraces, immortalised through the ages by many artists, including Turner and Reynolds.

On the west side of the road, **The Wick** (1775) and **Wick House** (1772) – the latter built by **Sir William Chambers** for **Sir Joshua Reynolds** – both enjoy views across the bend in the river towards Marble Hill.

At the top, overlooking the park, stands **Ancaster House**, a brick mansion built in 1722 to designs by **Robert Adam**. The house is now attached to the **Star and Garter Home** for disabled sailors, soldiers and airmen opposite. The park gates that mark the hilltop are dated 1700 and are attributed to **"Capability" Brown**.

Richmond Park★★

The countryside had been a royal chase for centuries when **Charles I** enclosed 2 470 acres/494ha as a park in 1637. It is the largest of the royal parks and is famous for its varied **fauna and flora** – most notably its herds of almost tame red and fallow deer, its majestic **oak trees** and the **spring flowers** (rhododendrons) of the Isabella Plantation.

On a fine day from the top of the Henry VIII mound there is a dramatic **panoramic view**★★★ extending from Windsor Castle to the dome of St Paul's

– look out for Telecom Tower, Battersea Power Station, Canary Wharf…

Among the houses in the park are **Pembroke Lodge** (*cafeteria*) adapted by **John Soane** from a molecatcher's cottage and later used by the philosopher **Bertrand Russell**; and **White Lodge**, built by George II in 1727 as a hunting lodge and since 1955 the junior section of the **Royal Ballet School**.

TWICKENHAM

♿*See Suburbs map (TYZ) Overground: Twickenham; St Margaret's from Waterloo.*

Twickenham nowadays draws visitors to its rugby matches, rather than to its riverside (♿*see YOUR STAY IN THE CITY – Sports*). In the 19C, **Louis-Philippe**, cousin of Louis XVI and future King of France (1830–48), three of his five sons, several descendants and a number of sympathisers all lived with his family in as many as nine houses in Twickenham. Of these, three remain: **Bushy House** was the home of the future William IV; it is now leased by the Crown Estates to the National Physical Laboratory (Teddington). The other two are **Morgan House** on Ham Common, now part of the Cassel Hospital, and **York House**. In the grounds of Upper Lodge is the most complete 18C water garden in London. ♿*See Marble Hill House in Additional Sights.*

York House

Richmond Road.

The Yorke family lived on and worked a farm on the site in the 15C and 16C; successors, who from 1700 altered and rebuilt the house, retained the name including, in the 19C, members of the exiled French royal family and, this century, an Indian merchant prince. Today, the house accommodates Council offices.

Sion Road

The road leading down to the river is joined halfway down by Ferry Road, a close of "two down, two up" cottages. At the end, parallel to the river, is a straggling line of houses of all periods

---

A Ditty

*This lass so neat, with smiles so sweet,
Has won my right good-will,
I'd crowns resign to call thee mine,
Sweet lass of Richmond Hill.*

Leonard Macnally (1752–1820)

---

including a pub. There is a passenger ferry to Ham House (see *Additional Sights*).

ADDITIONAL SIGHTS
Ham House★★
 See Suburbs map (TZ) Overground: Twickenham from Waterloo (NT)
 House: Open Mar–early Nov Sat–Wed and Good Friday noon–4pm.
Garden: Open Sat–Wed 11am–5pm/ dusk. Closed 25–26 Dec, 1 Jan.
 £9.90, garden only £3.30. Braille guide. Sympathetic hearing scheme. Parking. Refreshments. 020 8940 1950. www.nationaltrust.org.uk.

Ham House was at its prime under Elizabeth Dysart, **Duchess of Lauderdale**, "a woman of great beauty but... restless in her ambition and of a most ravenous covetousness."

She lived in dangerous times – her father, William Murray first Earl of Dysart, had literally been youthful "whipping boy" for Prince Charles, future Charles I. Elizabeth, it was said, became for a time the Protector's mistress.

Her second husband, the Earl, later Duke of Lauderdale, favourite of the Stuart restoration, was a learned, ambitious, vicious character.

The Lauderdales, according to their contemporaries, "lived at a vast rate." They enlarged the house, which had been built to the conventional Jacobean plan in 1610, and modified the front to give a continuous roof line with a horizontal emphasis. A family idiosyncrasy for making inventories has enabled the house to be returned to its 1678 appearance when it was described by **John Evelyn** as "furnished like a great prince's." The gardens have been relaid to the 17C plan.

Exterior – The fabric is brick with stone dressings; the building, three storeys beneath a hipped roof with a five-bay centre *(north side)* recessed between square bays and typical, canted Jacobean outer bays. The fine iron gates and piers date from 1671. The present forecourt, with the **Coade stone** figure of **Father Thames** by John Bacon, was laid out in 1800.

Interior – Paintings in this house bring to life the period of Charles II, the Cavalier generals and the women at court. Furniture, doors, doorcases, fireplaces and ceilings display the craftsmanship of the period, frequently Dutch. The remarkable ceilings show the progress from geometrical type plasterwork to garlands and spandrels (compare the original, north and later, south rooms).

Ground Floor – The Great Hall boasts a Round Gallery with a decorated plaster ceiling by Kinsman (1637). **Lely** portraits adorn the gallery, while below are fine portraits of Dysarts (17–18C) by **Kneller and Reynolds.**

The most notable features of other rooms include the gilt leather wall hangings, the 1679 cedar side tables, the grained and gilded panelling and the chimney furniture of silver in the **Marble Dining Room**. In the **Duchess's Bedchamber** are damask hangings; in the **Yellow Bedroom** or Volury Room the bed (note the carved cherub feet) is hung with purple and yellow; in the **White Closet** are an oyster work veneered writing desk and picture of the south front of the house in 1683 *(fireplace)*. The altar cloth of "crimson velvet & gould & silver stuff", held in the chapel, is original.

The **Great Staircase** of 1637, built of oak round a square well and gilded, has a singularly beautiful balustrade.

Upper Floor – Lady Maynard's suite contains 17C Flemish tapestries after Poussin below a wooden frieze and family portraits.

The **Museum Room** displays examples of the original vivid upholstery and contains the 1679 inventory which has enabled the rooms to be arranged as in Elizabeth Dysart's day. The **North Drawing Room** is sumptuous with its plaster frieze and rich ceiling (1637) above walls hung with English silk tapestries (woven by ex-Mortlake workers in Soho), carved and gilded wainscoting, doorcases and doors; furniture is also carved, gilded and richly upholstered; the fireplace is exuberantly Baroque.

Equally opulent is the **Queen's Suite**, rich with late 17C garlanded plaster ceilings; the furniture includes Oriental screens, English japanned chairs, a small Chinese cabinet and 18C tapestries.

In the heavily ornate closet with its painted ceiling and the original satin brocade hangings, note the carved "sleeping chayre."

Marble Hill House★

Across the river from Ham House (foot ferry). ♿🅿✖🕐*Open Mar–Oct Sat 10am–2pm, Sun and bank holidays 10am–5pm, Nov–Dec by appointment only.* 🕐*Closed 22 Dec–Feb.* 👓*£4.10.* ✎*Guided tour (1hr) by appointment. Dogs on leads.* ✆*020 8892 5115. www.english-heritage.org.uk.*

The last of the Palladian mansions that once lined this stretch of the Thames, Marble Hill House was built in 1729 by Henrietta Howard (a mistress of the future George II), with monies settled on her by her royal lover. Plans were sketched by **Colen Campbell**, Architect to the Prince of Wales.

It was 1731, however, before Henrietta, now **Countess of Suffolk** and Mistress of the Robes, could "often visit Marble Hill" and several years more before she took up residence there with her second husband, George Berkeley. She was an active hostess and received politicians, lawyers, and men of letters, including **Alexander Pope** and **Horace Walpole**. The Palladian style, stucco house is three storeys high with the centre advanced beneath a pediment.

The square mahogany staircase leads directly to the Great Room, richly decorated in white and gold with carvings and copies of Van Dyck paintings upon the walls.

Lady Suffolk's bedchamber (*left*), divided by Ionic pillars and pilasters to form a bed alcove, is completed, like the other rooms, by a rich cornice and ceiling decoration. An almost exact reconstruction of the furniture and furnishings has been achieved and some of the original items have been successfully traced. There is also a fine collection of 18C paintings (Hogarth, Wilson, Hayman, Kneller).

A stone staircase leads to the restored second floor (*access on conducted tours only*) with its collection of chinoiserie.

Museum of Richmond

Old Town Hall. ♿🕐*Open Tue–Sat, 11am–5pm.* ✆*020 8332 1141. www.museumofrichmond.com*

Displays relate to the local history of Richmond, Ham, Petersham and Kew: model of Richmond Palace in 1562.

Orleans House Gallery

Riverside; Twickenham. ♿🅿🕐
Garden: Open Apr–Sept daily 9am–dusk. ♿*House: Open Tue–Sat 1–5.30pm, Sun and Bank Holidays 2–5.30pm (Oct–Mar 4.30pm). Guide dogs welcome.* ✆*020 8831 6000. www.richmond.gov.uk/arts.*

Only the **Octagon**, added in 1720, 10 years after the house was first built, remains. This wing by **James Gibbs** has a brick exterior and splendid plasterwork, including fireplace, door pediments, figures and ceiling.

ADDRESSES

🍺 PUBS

Prince's Head – *28 The Green, TW9 1LX.* ⊖*Richmond.* ✆*020 8940 1572.* A pleasant local pub with various draught beers and a good atmosphere.

The Cricketers – *The Green, TW9 1LX.* ⊖*Richmond.* ✆*020 8940 4372.* Situated beside Richmond Cricket ground, this pub is the perfect place to unwind in the sun. It's compact, so arrive early in the evening if you want to get a seat.

The White Swan – *Riverside, Twickenham, TW1 3DN.* ⊖*Twickenham.* ✆*020 8892 2166.* This 300-year-old pub, overlooking the Thames and only 10min from Twickenham stadium, has a rich history. Today rugby paraphernalia cover the walls, the exterior terrace looks onto Eel Pie Island, and the landlord prepares barbecues for match days. A visit to this charming pub is really well worth the detour.

Royal Air Force Museum★★

Magnificent flying machines and simulators inform and entertain enthusiasts and laymen alike at this well-presented museum with over 200 aircraft as well as many smaller exhibits. Events throughout the year help to give an understanding of history to the younger generations.

A BIT OF HISTORY

Affiliated with the Imperial War Museum (🔍see MAJOR CENTRAL LONDON MUSE-UMS), this museum is dedicated to the history of aviation and of the RAF and is presented in several hangars on the historic site of Old Hendon Airfield, where Grahame-White established his flying school before World War I.

VISIT

👥♿🍴(licensed)🅿

Museum: 🕐Open daily 10am–6pm (last admission 5.30pm). **Grahame White Factory:** 🕐Open daily 10am–noon. 🕐Closed 24–26 Dec, 1 Jan, one week in Jan. 🚫Free. Flight simulator £2.75. 🔎Guided tours. Picnic area. Shop. ☎020 8205 2266. www.rafmuseum.org.uk.

The vast collection has over 200 planes, as well as engines, vehicles, weapons and smaller items from logbooks and uniforms to medals.

In addition there are interactive displays, including the Aeronauts Interactive Centre, with 40 hands-on experiments to help visitors learn how an aeroplane flies, and regular special events.

Eurofighter, Royal Air Force Museum

Royal Air Force Museum

> **Location:** See Suburbs (TX). Grahame Park Way. Buses: 226 along Edgware Road; 204 towards Edgware. ⊖Colindale (Edgware branch of Northern Line). Colindale is situated to the NW of London off the A 5 or A 41.

Milestones of Flight

Opened to celebrate the 100th anniversary of powered flight, this fascinating exhibit traces the history of aviation from its earliest beginnings to the present day, with many of the planes on display and an interactive timeline.

Historic Hangars

World War I halls present a unique collection of aircraft in chronological order from a Blériot monoplane through a Supermarine Stranraer flying boat, and a Sikorsky hoverfly to a Lightning Mach 2. The **Flight Simulator** enables visitors to experience the thrill of a flight with the Red Arrows and others.

Bomber Hall

This hall relates the history of aerial bombing from World War I to the present day. Bombers displayed include an Avro Lancaster, a Heinkel He 162A-2, a B17 Flying Fortress and a Vulcan. Note also a replica of the office of Sir Barnes Wallis, who invented the bouncing bomb.

Battle of Britain Collection

A special hall is dedicated to the battle that was fought in the skies of south-east England during the summer of 1940. The forces involved are represented by an impressive array of aircraft: Junkers 87 and 88, Heinkel 111, Messerschmitt against Gloster Gladiators, Tiger Moths, Spitfires and Hurricanes. In addition to the machines are an operations room, uniforms, medals, documents, relics and other memorabilia. There is also a 30min sound and light show.

Syon Park★★

The prospect of this splendid mansion, set in a vast park by the Thames and opposite Kew Gardens, is enchanting. It has been the seat of an aristocratic family since the 16C and is a prime example of the Robert Adam style. Take a stroll through the fragrant rose garden, admire the great conservatory and enjoy the many other attractions in the grounds.

A BIT OF HISTORY

Artistic Patronage – On the walls inside are portraits of the men and women who built up the house and their royal patrons by **Gainsborough**, **Reynolds**, **Van Dyck**, Mytens, **Lely** and by unknown artists of the English 16C school. Two men were principally responsible for the construction: the Lord Protector, **Duke of Somerset**, brother of Henry's queen, Jane Seymour, in the 16C, and Hugh Percy, 1st Duke of **Northumberland**, in the 18C. Somerset was given the former monastery site in 1547 by his nephew **Edward VI** and erected a Tudor mansion in the plan of a hollow square, dined his monarch there in 1550, laid out gardens, including the first Physic garden in England... but in 1552 he was charged with conspiracy and executed.

In 1594, the estate was acquired by the Percy family, who still own it and live in it. Moreover, with the marriage in 1682 of Elizabeth Percy to Charles, 6th Duke of Somerset, Syon returned to a descendant of its earlier owner, who also held office under the Crown. In the 18C the new heirs, the Duke and Duchess of Northumberland, considered the house and grounds were in urgent need of remodelling; they commissioned **Robert Adam** and **Capability Brown** to produce designs.

HIGHLIGHTS

Gardens: ⏱*Open daily 10.30am–5.30pm/dusk.* ♿*House:* ⏱*Open 18 Mar–Oct Wed, Thu, Sun and bank holidays 11am–5pm (last admission*

▷ **Location:** *See Suburbs (TY).* Overground: Syon Lane from Waterloo Station. Syon Park is south of the A 4 and near the M 4 (Exit 2).
👪 **Kids:** Tropical Forest; Snakes and Ladders.

4pm). Audio-guide. Guide book. Leaflet. ⏱*Closed 25–26 Dec.* 🎫*House and gardens £9, gardens only £4.50.* ☎*020 8560 0881. www.syonpark.co.uk.*

The House

The colonnaded east front of Syon House is visible across the river from Kew Gardens, the Northumberland Lion with outstretched tail silhouetted against the sky; a second beast, also from the model by Michelangelo, crowns the Lion Gate and graceful Adam screen on the London Road (A 315).

In the **Great Hall**, Adam is at his most formal: the high ceiling echoes the patterns laid into the black and white marble pavement; in the apses at either end nestle copies of Classical statues – the *Apollo Belvedere*, the *Dying Gladiator*.

The **Ante-room**, by contrast, gleams darkly with heavy gilding, reds, blues, yellows, in the patterned *scagliola* floor, and green marble and *scagliola* pillars (dredged from the Tiber).

The long **State Dining Room** with column-screened apses at either end was the first to be remodelled by Adam: deep niches with copies of antique statues along the left wall were reflected in pier mirrors; frieze, cornice, ceiling, decorated half domes, beautiful doorcases and doors afforded a perfect setting for the banquets given by the Duke and Duchess in the late 18C.

The rich decoration of the **Red Drawing Room** includes scarlet Spitalfields silk, blooming with intricate pale gold roses, on the walls and at the windows, a carpet, signed and dated 1769, woven at Moorfields, door pilasters with ivory panels covered with ormolu, gilded ceiling studded with Cipriani painted

Great Conservatory, Syon Park

K. Brett/MICHELIN

medallions. The room is, however, dominated by its commanding Stuart portraits by Lely, Van Dyck, Vna Honthorst, Mignard, Huysmans... The elegant mosaic-topped side tables are noteworthy.

The **Long Gallery** of the Tudor house was transformed by Adam into a ladies' withdrawing room (136ft/42m long, 14ft/4m wide), lined with grouped pilasters, wall niches and pier mirrors, so arranged as to disguise the length. Much of the furniture was designed by Adam, notably the veneered chest of drawers made by Chippendale.

The furniture in the **Print Room** includes two remarkable walnut, marquetry inlaid cabinets that date to the late 17C; the walls are hung with family portraits, most notably by Gainsborough and Reynolds.

A huge Sèvres vase stands at the foot of the main staircase leading to the **bedrooms**; two of them were refurbished in 1832 for the Duchess of Kent and her daughter, the future Queen Victoria: note the canopied beds, sofa and chairs, all enhanced by the same blue silk.

Gardens★

Capability Brown assisted in designing the gardens, which extend all the way to the river. In 1837 the gardens were world famous for their botanical specimens, and were subsequently opened to the public. A vast fragrant **rose garden** *(separate entrance south of the house)* is in bloom from May to August.

The **Great Conservatory**, a beautiful semicircular building with a central cupola and end pavilions was designed by Charles Fowler in 1820–27. Inside the graceful space are an abundance of cacti and a small aquarium.

Other attractions

The extensive grounds contain a number of other attractions. These include: the **Tropical Forest** (*℘020 8847 4730; www.tropicalforest.co.uk*); **Snakes and Ladders** indoor adventure playground (*℘020 8847 0946; www.snakes-and-ladders.co.uk*); **Syon Park Trout Fishery** (*℘020 8568 6354 or 07956 378138; www.alburyestate.com*); **Wyevale Garden Centre** (*℘08448 008 082; www.wyevale.co.uk*).

ADDRESSES

PUBS

London Apprentice – *62 Church St, Isleworth, TW7 6BG. ℘020 8560 1915.* The pub is said to be named after one of the apprentices who, from the 16C to 19C, rowed up the river on their annual holiday and made the inn their own for a day.

Wimbledon

In addition to its thriving village perched on a hilltop, vast common land including meadows, woods, ponds, a windmill and a golf course, Wimbledon takes great pride in its acclaimed tennis championship, which draws international stars every summer. Two theatres and a stadium offer other kinds of entertainment; a Thai Buddhist temple is an unusual feature in the borough.

> **Location:** *See Suburbs (TZ).* ⊖*Wimbledon,; Southfields; Wimbledon Park; Overground Wimbledon.* The busy suburb of Wimbledon to the SW of London is accessible by the A 3, the main thoroughfare to the south.

A BIT OF HISTORY

The village developed along the High Street and around the church, first coming to prominence in 1588 when Thomas Cecil, **Lord Burghley**, then Lord of the Manor, built a mansion with turrets and gables on a slope north-east of the church. It was unfortunately destroyed in 1720 and the only building surviving from this period is Eagle House (1613) in the High Street, which was built by Robert Bell, a native of Wimbledon and a founder of the **East India Company**. The Manor eventually passed to Sarah, **Duchess of Marlborough**, who built a new house linked to detached servants' quarters by an underground passage.

VISIT
Wimbledon Common

In 1871, after seven years of legal dispute with Earl Spencer, Lord of the Manor, who wanted to enclose the Common and develop 300 acres/120ha for housing, Wimbledon Common was transferred to the Conservators to preserve it. Whereas Lord Spencer asserted that the land was boggy with noxious mist arising from it, Leigh Hunt wrote of the "furze in full bloom making a golden floor of all that fine healthy expanse." The horse racing, duelling and drilling of soldiers of earlier days have given way to horse riding, cricket, rugby and golf. "Every person playing golf" is required by the Conservators "to wear a red outer garment." From 1860 the National Rifle Association held their annual shooting competitions

on the Common, before moving to Bisley in 1889.

The 18C saw several large mansions rise round the Common including **King's College School** (1750) with adjoining Great Hall in Gothic Revival style; **Southside House** (1776) Woodhayes Rd (🔎*guided tours (1hr 15min) Sat before Easter to early Oct, Wed, Sat–Sun and Bank Hol Mon at 2pm, 3pm, 4pm,* 🎫*£5;* 📞*020 8946 7643; www.southsidehouse. c om; Access: by bus 93 to Wimbledon War Memorial);* **Crooked Billet** and **Hand-in-Hand** are 17C public houses *(⚘see Addresses);* **Chester House** (1670) was owned by the Revd John Horne Tooke, whose election to Parliament in 1801 provoked the Act which made the clergy ineligible; **Cannizaro** (1727, rebuilt in 1900) was owned by Viscount Melville from 1887 who laid out the gardens and entertained William Pitt, **Edmund Burke** and **Richard Sheridan** (🕐*open daily 8am (9am Sat–Sun and bank holidays) to dusk (9.30pm at latest).*

Also of interest is the **Round** or **Old Central School** *(Camp Rd),* an octagonal building (1760), now incorporated in a primary school. Wimbledon Village Stage Coaches set out from the **Rose and Crown** and later from the **Dog and Fox** in the High Street, although the road over Putney Heath was infested with highwaymen (⚘*see Addresses).*

St Mary's Church

Church Rd. ♿🕐*Open Mon–Tue, Thu– Fri 9am–4pm, Wed 2.30–4pm.* 🕐*Closed sometimes during school holidays.* 📞*020 8946 2605. www.stmaryswimbledon.org.* Wimbledon church was mentioned in **The Domesday Book**; parts of a 13C rebuilding remain in the chancel. The present 19C nave, tower and spire were designed by Sir George Gilbert Scott. **William Wilberforce**, Sir Theodore Janssen and **JW Bazalgette** are buried in the churchyard. To the north stands the **Old Rectory** (1500) the oldest house in Wimbledon.

ADDITIONAL SIGHTS

Wimbledon Lawn Tennis Museum

Church Rd. &⏱*Open daily 10am–5pm (to 8pm during the Championships).* 👣*Guided tours daily 2–3 times a day. Check website for times and dates. No tours during the Championship.* ⏱*Closed Sun during and Mon following the Championships, 24–26 Dec, 1 Jan. Tour* 💷*£15.50, museum only £8.50. Leaflet (6 languages). Parking. Tea room.* 📞*020 8946 6131. www.wimbledon.org/museum*

Home of the world's premier tennis tournament, Wimbledon is actually a private members' club, the All England Lawn Tennis and Croquet Club. The museum, recently revamped with touch screens and interactive displays, charts the history of tennis and Wimbledon from its earliest years. Additionally, there are enhanced facilities for the disabled. Amongst the new displays, **Get a Grip** compares wooden and contemporary rackets while a section on **fashion** looks at tennis outfits back to 1884. Tours take

Anyone for Tennis?

Wimbledon – The world's longest-running, most prestigious tennis championship – is held at the All England Club every year from late June–early July. every summer. Winning at Wimbledon is every professional tennis player's dream.

in the museum, the courts, the players' facilities and broadcast studios.

Wimbledon Museum

Ridgway. ⏱*Open Sat–Sun 2.30–5pm.* 📞*020 8296 9914. www.wimbledon museum.org.uk.*

The local history museum is housed in the **Village Club**, built in 1858 to provide the working and middle classes with enjoyment and improvement through a reading room, library, lectures and instruction.

Wimbledon Windmill Museum

Windmill Rd. &🅿❌*Open Mar–Oct Sun and bank holidays 11am–5pm, Sat 2–5pm.* 💷*£2. Parking. Café.* 📞*020 8947 2825. www.wimbledonwindmill museum.org.uk.*

The windmill, a hollow post mill built on the Common in 1817, has been converted into a museum illustrating the story of windmills in pictures, models and the machinery and tools of the trade.

ADDRESSES

🍺 PUBS

Crooked Billet – *14 Crooked Billet Rd, SW19 4RQ.* ⊖*Wimbledon.* 📞*020 8946 4942.* A country pub feel, full of oak beams and an open fire. Good real ales, and supposedly a haunted cellar!

Dog and Fox – *24 High St, SW19 5DX.* ⊖*Wimbledon.* 📞*020 8946 6565. www. dogandfoxpub.com.* Landmark pub in Wimbledon Village, close to the All England Lawn Tennis and Croquet Club.

Hand-in-Hand – *6 Crooked Billet Rd, SW19 4RQ.* ⊖*Wimbledon.* 📞*020 8946 5720.* Historic low-ceiling 19C cottage pub with bags of charm.

Rose and Crown – *55 High St, SW19 5BA.* ⊖*Wimbledon.* 📞*020 8947 4713. www.roseandcrownwimbledon.co.uk.* Traditional pub with a nice beer garden.

🎭 ENTERTAINMENT

Polka Theatre for Children – *240 The Broadway, SW19 1SB.* ⊖*Wimbledon.* 📞*020 8543 4888 (box office). Open late Sept–early Aug Tue–Fri 9.30am–4.30pm, Sat–Sun noon–5.30pm.* A full programme of performances and workshops for children; also has a playground, shop and café.

Windsor Castle★★★

On a steep bluff and in a beautiful park setting, the romantic turrets and the massive tower of Windsor Castle rise above the bustling town in the Thames valley. It is a fascinating example of a medieval castle that has evolved into a sumptuous royal residence. The royal association gives great cachet to the pretty town, which boasts a thriving theatre, fine shops, restaurants and tearooms. Over the bridge are the fine buildings of Eton College, which are of great interest.

A BIT OF HISTORY

Windsor Castle is the oldest royal residence to have remained in continuous use by the reigning monarchs, and the largest castle in England. It was originally intended by **William the Conqueror** (c. 1080) as one of several defensive strongholds built around London, and as such was constructed on the only elevated point in that stretch of the Thames valley. Norman castles conformed to a standard plan, with a large tower or keep dominating the complex from an artificially raised earthen mound or *motte*; at Windsor this is flanked by the Upper and Lower Wards. The castle covers an area of 13 acres/5ha.

▷ **Location:** 24 High St. ℘020 7766 7304. www.royalcollection.org.uk. *Overground from London Waterloo or Paddington.* Windsor is to the west of London and is easily accessible by the M 4. Leave the motorway at Junction 6.

🕐 **Timing:** Allow at least half a day to visit the castle, then stroll through the town and across the Thames to Eton.

The castle was used from 1110 onwards by successive monarchs. **Henry II** began building the stone castle as a royal residence with state apartments in the Lower Ward and private lodgings on the north side of the Upper Ward (1165–79). Further expansion was undertaken by **Henry III** (r. 1216–72) and by **Edward III** (r. 1327–77) .

Used by the Parliamentarians during the Civil War as a prison for Royalist supporters, it became **Charles II**'s favourite (defensible) home outside London. In 1673 the architect Hugh May was appointed to manage a series of ambitious renovations mainly concerning the interior: walls were insulated with oak wainscoting and festooned in **Grinling Gibbons** carvings, the ceilings decorated by

St George's Chapel

©Philip Coblentz/Brand X Pictures

the Italian painter **Verrio** and gilded by a French master-craftsman René Coussin.

George III had the Queen's Lodge (1777) designed by **William Chambers**; he modernised Frogmore in Home Park as a retreat for Queen Charlotte. Alterations to provide ever greater comfort were begun by **George IV**. Mock Gothic renovations included the addition of turrets, chimney-stacks and battlements and the heightening of the Round Tower by 33ft/10m, while extensions were remodelled to accommodate the large and complicated extension of the royal family. For this reason, Windsor was popular with **Queen Victoria**, who received endless visits from her extended family in Europe and chose to receive heads of state there (King Louis Philippe in 1844; Emperor Napoleon III in 1855; King Victor Emanuel I of Italy; Emperor William I of Germany). She started the "dine and sleep" practice maintained by Queen **Elizabeth II**, where guests might be invited to spend an evening and stay overnight. The principal change made by Victoria was the creation of a private chapel in honour of **Prince Albert**, who died at Windsor on 14 December 1861.

With the turn of the century came a change in spirit. **George V**'s Queen Mary began careful restoration of the castle, which became the childhood home of HRH The Princesses Elizabeth and Margaret during the war; since then it has remained the Royal Family's principal home. The Court is in official residence throughout April and for Ascot Week in June when the annual Garter Day celebrations are held.

HIGHLIGHTS

♿🕐*Open daily 9.45am–5.15pm (4.15pm Nov–Feb); last admission 30min before closing.* 🕐*Closed 10 Apr, Good Fri, 15 Jun, 25–26 Dec.* ***St George's Chapel:*** 🕐*Open (functions permitting) Mon–Sat 10am–4.15pm (4pm last admission).* ⊜*£15.50 (Queen Mary's Dolls' House, State Apartments and St George's Chapel), reduced rate when the State Apartments are closed.*

---

20 November 1992

The fire which broke out in the Queen's Private Chapel at the northeast angle of the Upper Ward is thought to have been caused by a spotlight on a curtain high above the altar. Major losses included the wooden ceiling of the St George Hall and Grand Reception room. Restoration work was completed in November 1997, six months ahead of schedule, to coincide with the Queen's 50th wedding anniversary. It was the largest project of its kind in the 20C, costing over £37 million and calling on the skills of some of the finest craftspeople.

Call in advance to check. Audiotour. Guidebook (8 languages). **Changing of the Guard**★★★ *takes place () Apr–Jul Mon–Sat 11am; Aug–Mar alternate days.* ***Frogmore House and Gardens:*** 🕐*Open open May and Aug, certain days.* 📞*020 7766 7304 (tickets), 01753 831 118 (information),* 📞*01753 865 538 (St George's Chapel). www. royalcollection.org.uk.*

PRECINCTS

▶ *Enter from Castle Hill and proceed into the Upper Ward.*

Round Tower

Henry II built this impressive section as a main defence feature surrounded by a dry (chalk) moat in c. 1170; it was heightened in the 19C. The Tower, which is in fact oval, now houses the Royal Archives (⊙*closed to the public*). From the North Terrace there is a fine **view** over Eton and the River Thames.

Queen Mary's Dolls' House

Conceived by Sir Edwin Lutyens on a scale of 12:1, it was presented to Queen Mary in 1924. The miniature contents include standard amenities all in working order (water system, electric lights and two lifts), a gramophone, vintage bottles of wine, original paintings and leather-bound books. Wall cases also display a remarkable travelling "trousseau" of designer fashion-wear provided by the French and presented to the Princesses Elizabeth and Margaret after King George VI's official visit to France (1938).

State Apartments★★

When the apartments were remodelled by George IV, Gothic was used for processional spaces (lobbies, halls, staircases) and an eclectic form of Classicism for the main reception rooms.

The **Gallery**, designed to serve as the principal entrance hall to the State Apartments, was cut off when the Grand Staircase was remodelled during the reign of Queen Victoria. Today it accommodates temporary exhibitions of prints, drawings and books. The **China Museum** displays fabulous pieces from services in the Royal Collection: Sèvres, Meissen, Copenhagen, Worcester... still used occasionally at banquets.

The **Grand Staircase** leads up to the first floor. The full-size statue is of King George IV. In the fan-vaulted **Grand Vestibule** various 18C and 19C trophies are displayed, acquired after the Battle of Seringapatam (1799) and the Napoleonic Wars (the lead shot that killed Lord Nelson in the Battle of Trafalgar).

The **Waterloo Chamber**, used to celebrate the anniversary of the **Battle of Waterloo** on 18 June, is hung with a series of portraits by Sir Thomas Lawrence, depicting political and military leaders, who assisted in defeating Napoleon. Today the chamber is used for the annual luncheon given by the Queen for her Knights of the Garter and their consorts, and for balls, receptions and concerts.

The **Garter Throne Room** and the **Ante-Throne Room** are used by the Queen to confer upon her newly chosen knights the Order of the Garter. The **Grand Reception Room** style particularly reflects George IV's personal francophile taste.

Public Rooms – The **King's Drawing Room** was once used by Queen Victoria for private theatrical performances. Note the finely carved dado rail and Grinling Gibbons cornice; the five paintings by **Rubens** and his followers; the beautiful boulle kneehole desk reputedly acquired by William III; the carpet presented to Edward VII by the Shah of Persia in 1903. The porcelain is all Chinese.

The **King's Bedchamber** has been considerably altered through history. The grandiose "polonaise" bed is attributed to the French furniture designer George Jacob and given its furnishings for the occasion of a visit from Emperor Napoleon III and his wife Eugénie in 1855, whose initials appear at the foot of the bed. The early 19C Aubusson carpet was presented to HM The Queen by President de Gaulle in 1960. Note the Canaletto views of Venice.

The **King's Dressing Room** is lined in red damask as intended by George III. On the walls hang a number of **masterpieces★★**: works by Dürer (Portrait of a Young Man), Hans Memlinc, Jean Clouet, Hans Holbein, Andrea del Sarto, Rembrandt (The Artist's Mother), Rubens (Portrait of the Artist), Jan Steen, Van Dyck (Charles I in Three Positions).

The **King's Closet** is furnished with exquisite pieces, mainly French and made of exotic woods (mahogany or satinwood) set with Japanese lacquer panels and bronze mounts.

The **Queen's Drawing Room** was substantially altered by Wyatville in 1834. The room is adorned with early 16C and 17C paintings (Holbein: Sir Henry Guildford, Mytens, Van Somer, Dobson: Charles II, Lely: Mary II) and furniture.

The **Octagon Lobby** is panelled in oak with splendid oval garlands by Gibbons. The **King's Dining Room** retains much of the character imparted to it by Charles II. Verrio's ceiling depicts a banquet enjoyed by the gods, while below, lovely still-life panels illustrate fruit, fish (lobster) and fowl; intricate limewood garlands of fruit and flowers carved by Grinling Gibbons and Henry Phillips tumble down the oak panelling.

The **Queen's Ballroom** or Queen's Gallery serves as a meeting room in which visiting heads of state may greet members of their diplomatic staff. Note

Order of the Garter

The highest order of chivalry in the land is also the oldest to survive in the world. It was established by Edward III in 1348 when England was engaged in the Hundred Years' War with France, and may have been modelled on the legendary story of the 5C King Arthur and his Knights of the Round Table. Not only was the order to reward men who had shown valour on the battlefield, but also to honour those who manifested the idealistic and romantic concept of Christian chivalry. Tradition relates how at a ball fêting the conquest of Calais in 1347, the king retrieved a fallen garter and returned it to its rightful owner, the young and beautiful Joan of Kent, Countess of Salisbury, with the words *"Honi soit qui mal y pense"* 'Shame on him who thinks evil of it' – the emblem and motto of the Order. A more likely derivation is a strap or sword-belt from a suit of armour to denote the bond of loyalty and concord. At its initiation, Edward III nominated 25 English **Companion Knights**, including the Heir Apparent (the Black Prince), thereby providing himself with his own jousting team and one with which to do battle! Today there are still 25 Companion Knights including the Prince of Wales and at least one representative of each force (Navy, Army, Air Force). Additional **"Royal Knights"** may also be appointed by the sovereign following amendments made to the statutes by George I. Stranger, Foreign or **"Extra Knights"** may also be appointed; since 1905 this has been conferred upon regents or monarchs only (including two Sultans of Turkey, two Shahs of Persia and four Emperors of Japan).

the three English cut-glass chandeliers made for George III and the 17C silver pieces of furniture between the windows. On the walls hang portraits by **Sir Anthony van Dyck** – the most notable being *Charles I in Robes of State*. The **Queen's Audience Chamber**, together with the **Queen's Presence Chamber** next door, preserve the skilled artistry of craftsmen employed by Hugh May during the reign of Charles II, in particular Verrio and Gibbons. Note the Gobelins tapestries acquired by George IV in Paris in 1825 and the busts by Roubiliac (Handel) and Coysevox.

The **Queen's Guard Chamber** was remodelled as a museum of British military achievement: replica French banners, the tricolour and the gold fleur-de-lys are presented each year to the Queen by the current Duke of Wellington and the Duke of Marlborough as quit-rents for their estates at Stratfield-Saye and Blenheim, granted to their ancestors on perpetual leases by the grateful nation.

St George's Hall – This long room (180ft/55m) formed by remodelling Charles II's chapel and hall, was decorated by Wyatville in the neo-Gothic style inspired by the novels of Sir Walter Scott, so admired by George IV. Completely gutted in the fire, the hall has been magnificently restored with a hammerbeam oak roof (instead of previous painted plaster ceiling), complete with the 700 coats of arms of past Knights of the Garter.

Quadrangle
The equestrian statue is of Charles II. In the south-east corner is the Sovereign's Entrance, which leads directly to the private royal apartments.

Lower Ward
Much of this section of the Castle precincts is given to the **College of St George** founded on 6 August 1348 by Edward III and comprising a dean, 12 canons, 13 vicars and 26 "Poor Knights" on whom was conferred the Order of the Garter. On the left are the mid-16C lodgings of the Military Knights built by Queen Mary. At the bottom stands the Guard House (1862).

To the right sits St George's Chapel and beyond, a maze of cloisters and buildings attached to the chapel and choir school; the brick and timber-framed Horseshoe Cloister is reserved for the lay clerks (adult choristers).

St George's Chapel★★★

The spiritual headquarters of England's prime order of chivalry, the Most Noble Order of the Garter, is also the final resting place of 10 sovereigns including Charles I, brought here after his execution at Whitehall in 1649.

The building, initiated by Edward IV (1475) and completed in 1528 in the reign of Henry VIII, is a glorious expression of Perpendicular Gothic architecture. Note the **Royal Beasts** (modern replacements) above the flying buttresses of the west end.

Interior – The 1790 Gothic-style Coade stone **organ screen** by Henry Emlyn was installed at the same time as the Samuel Green organ presented by George III. The splendid 75-light **west window** (36ft/11m high and 29ft/9m wide) survives in part from 1479, 1503, 1509 and 1842.

George VI Memorial Chapel was built in 1969, the first structural addition to the Chapel since 1504. The windows were designed by John Piper.

Quire – So called at Windsor to differentiate it from the body of choristers or choir, the Quire is separated from the nave by John Tresilien's magnificent set of wrought-iron gates (1478). The glorious east window (30ft/9m high, 29ft/8.5m wide; 52-lights) commemorates Prince Albert with incidents from his life illustrated in the lower tier, below the *Resurrection* (painted by Benjamin West) and the *Adoration of the Kings*. The carved alabaster reredos was also given by the Dean and Canons in memory of Prince Albert. The woodwork, executed largely by English and Flemish craftsmen, dates from 1478–85.

Garter Stalls – On installation each knight is granted a stall marked with a numbered enamel nameplate (North 1 marks the Prince of Wales' stall), over which he/she will display their banner (5ft/1.5m square of heavy silk bearing the arms approved by the College of Arms in the City of London), crest, helm,

mantling and sword (made of cloth or wood and depicted half drawn in readiness to defend the sovereign) and which they will keep until death when the accoutrements are all removed. Other stalls are reserved for the Military Knights of Windsor (formerly the 24 Poor Knights appointed by Edward III, impoverished by ransoms paid to the French for their freedom).

Memorials – Emperor **Napoleon III** and his wife Eugénie of France, the close friends of Queen Victoria who died at Chislehurst in 1873. Statue of **Leopold I**, King of the Belgians, the uncle of both Queen Victoria and Prince Albert – his first wife, **Princess Charlotte Augusta**, who would have succeeded her father George IV had she not died in childbirth, is commemorated by a sculptural group in the Urswick Chapel where the tomb of **George V** (d. 1936) and Queen Mary (d. 1953) by Lutyens is situated. In the north aisle, but despoiled of its effigy and jewels during the Commonwealth, is the tomb of **Edward IV** and Queen Elizabeth Woodville.

The **Royal Vault** extends from the High Altar to the Albert Memorial Chapel; in it rest George III, George IV, William IV and many of their direct descendants. In a second vault lie **Henry VIII**, Jane Seymour and **Charles I**. In the south aisle are the tombs of Edward VII (d. 1910) and Queen Alexandra (d. 1925) with their dog Caesar; Henry VI, founder of Eton College and King's College, Cambridge.

Albert Memorial Chapel

This was the original chapel of the Order of the Garter; left to decay, it was renovated by Henry VII as a mausoleum for Henry VI and intended by **Cardinal Wolsey** as his ultimate resting place. It was given its magnificent Victorian embellishment by Sir George **Gilbert Scott** after the death of Albert, the **Prince Consort**, at the age of 42; it stands as a supreme expression of the 19C revivalist age complete with Venetian mosaics, inlaid marble panels and statuary. Prince Albert's tomb was later removed to Frogmore.

Home Park

This section outside the Castle precincts but within the private grounds of Windsor Castle includes **Frogmore House**, which was built in 1684 and used by various members of the Royal household, most notably by Queen Charlotte and her unmarried daughters; today it is furnished largely with possessions accumulated by Queen Mary.

Other buildings nearby consist of follies (Gothic ruin, Queen Victoria's Tea House and an Indian kiosk built of white marble) and the **Royal Mausoleum**, built (1862) by Queen Victoria after the untimely death of her husband Prince Albert. In the **Royal Burial Ground** (o—*closed to the public*) at Frogmore rest the Duke (Edward VIII) and Duchess of Windsor.

WINDSOR GREAT PARK★

Open daily dawn–dusk. 01753 435544. www.theroyallandscape.co.uk. This 4 800 acre/1 942ha park, once the hunting ground of Saxon leaders and medieval knights, is today linked to the castle by the **Long Walk** (3mi/5km) planted by Charles II. At the top of the hill stands the **Copper Horse**, an equestrian statue of George III (1831). Nestling in the park are two additional secluded former royal residences: **Royal Lodge** and **Cumberland Lodge**.

Smith's Lawn is a stretch of lawn reserved for polo matches, while beyond stretch the **Valley Gardens**, planted by the Duke of Cumberland with shrubs and trees that extend to **Virginia Water**, an area of 130 acres/53ha arranged around an artificial lake (*open daily 10am–6pm (4.30pm/dusk in winter) via local car park (fee);* 01753 435 544). On the far side of the lake stand the **Ruins** which consist of fragments brought in 1817 from Leptis Magna in Libya.

The Savill Garden (*open daily 10am–6pm (Nov–Feb 4.30pm);* *closed 25–26 Dec;* £7.50 Mar–Oct (£5.50 Nov–Feb); 01753 435544) is another, independent landscaped wooded garden laid out in 1932 and endowed with a fine Temperate House in 1995. The garden is a glorious show in the spring when rhododendrons, azaleas, camellias and magnolias burst into symphonies of colour; highlights include many varieties of lilies and roses in summer.

ETON COLLEGE★★

School Yard, Chapel, Cloister and Museum of Eton Life: *Open daily 10.30am–4.30pm in school holidays and Wed, Fri, Sat–Sun 2pm–4.30pm in term time.* *Closed 10 April, 27 May, 9 Sept.* 01753 671 1177. www.etoncollege.com.

Royal Antecedent

"The King's College of Our Lady of Eton beside Windsor" was founded by **Henry VI** in 1440; a year later he founded King's College Cambridge, where the young men might continue their studies. Along the north side of the **School Yard** (now dominated by a statue of the founder and the 16C **Lupton's Tower**) stands the 15C brick building of **Lower School**. Upper School on the west side was added in the 17C.

Chapel★★

At the heart of the college is the chapel, which was completed in 1482 and endowed with many beautiful and significant works of art.

The oldest are the Flemish-style wall paintings (1479–87), executed by at least four masters, considered to be the finest 15C English murals. On the north side are scenes associated with the chapel's patron the Virgin Mary, the south side ones depict the Medieval story of a mythical empress. In 1940 a bomb landed on the Upper School thereby destroying all the glass in the chapel, save that above the organ. The east window was designed by Evie Hone in 1952 to complement panels by John Piper. Famous pupils have included several kings including **George III**, statesmen, of whom 19 became prime ministers, including **Walpole, Gladstone, Pitt the Elder**, Charles James Fox, **Wellington**, Macmillan and Douglas-Home, and the writers Fielding, Shelley, Thomas Gray, Aldous Huxley and George Orwell.

AD · 1881

Leadenhall Market
©Monica Wells/Pictures Colour Library

Where To Stay

Addresses listed in the Guide are comparable with those in other European cities. London is an expensive place to stay and finding a suitable room in a metropolis with over 27 million visitors annually and an average hotel occupancy rate of 80%, often requires patience. Fortunately, the choice of accommodation is astounding and, with proper preparation prior to your trip, you will undoubtedly find pleasant accommodation in your price range and in your favourite area. *Bear in mind that advance reservation is a must in any season, especially over Christmas, Easter and summer.*

Whether you are looking for a luxury hotel in Mayfair or a modest but pleasant family-run guest house away from the bustle of central London, you should find something to suit in the following listing of hotels, guest houses, B&Bs and youth accommodation that have been carefully chosen for their unique character, convenient location, quality of comfort and value for money. They are grouped in areas covering districts that should be familiar to visitors.

ADDRESSES

SELECTING A DISTRICT

As London is such a large city, it is advisable to decide where to stay according to your budget or what you plan to visit.

The **most elegant central districts** – Mayfair, St James, Strand – are home to world-renowned luxury hotels.

In the Kensington, Notting Hill and Bayswater areas, many attractive 19C terrace houses have been converted into small, often charming, **moderate-to-expensively priced hotels**.

Centrally located Bloomsbury is packed with **small, inexpensive-to-moderate family-run establishments**. Those

travelling on a budget will find **no-frills hotels** and B&Bs in Earl's Court and Victoria. **Young travellers** will be surprised at the choice of decent **youth accommodation** in the city centre. Lodging in the Suburbs is usually less expensive than in the centre. The Suburbs hotels listed in this guide are located near tourist attractions. Particularly well-connected areas to stay in include **Baker Street**, **Liverpool Street** (for The City) and **Victoria**, all of which are major bus, Underground and overground rail hubs. Centrally, Covent Garden, Soho, Kensington and Knightsbridge are well served by bus and Tube lines, although most hotels in Central London will be within a 5min walk of an Underground station.

FOR ALL BUDGETS

Budget accommodations (⊜) include the small, simple but well-maintained establishments charging £90 or less for a double room in high season. Expect basic service and shared bathrooms for the least expensive room.

In the **moderate** range (⊜⊜–⊜⊜⊜) doubles from £90 to £200 in hotels of greater comfort or tastefully converted houses located in attractive neighbourhoods. We recommend booking in advance, as these small establishments usually have a faithful clientele and the few rooms at the lower rates are often booked.

For those in search of a memorable stay, **luxury** accommodations (⊜⊜⊜⊜) tend to be priced at more than £200 for double occupancy. There are a limited number of centrally located upmarket establishments that guarantee a truly unforgettable London experience. Stylistically, these hotels run the gamut from traditional British to minimalist contemporary and, as to be expected, the rates reflect the outstanding quality of the comfort and service.

One person staying in a double room (*Indeed, singles in Central London are often pocket-sized*) will generally be given a reduction on the double rate, except during major events. Please note that prices vary widely according to time of year, and whether it is a weekend or weekday. You may be able to negotiate a good rate if you are coming for a long time, or at a low time of year. Booking via the internet is also usually cheaper, or try the various agencies on the internet. It is advisable to confirm all details, including the inclusion of VAT and breakfast, before making the reservation. Many hotels offer special prices for short breaks – weekends or stays of at least three days. A credit card number will be requested for all reservations.

A note for light sleepers: traffic-clogged Central London is quite noisy by day and night. Enquire about noise levels and remember that in small hotels, rooms at the rear are often quieter.

P Parking in Central London is expensive, frustrating and almost impossible – it's best to leave the car at home. A limited number of luxury hotels offer on-site parking for a fee. Chain hotels are often situated near NCP car parks.

Breakfast – As well as the Continental-style breakfast of coffee and bread and jam, most establishments offer the traditional cooked breakfast, which begins with porridge or cereal and ends with toast and marmalade, accompanied by tea or coffee. The main dish is usually eggs or fish. Breakfast is normally included in the price.

TYPES OF ACCOMMODATION

The terms, "hotel", "guest house" and "Bed & Breakfast", are used loosely – often according to the proprietor's preference – to apply to a wide variety of accommodations. However, traditionally hotels tend to be medium-to-large establishments, with ensuite rooms and a full range of services. The term "guest house" denotes a smaller operation with fewer facilities and generally more appealing to tourists than business visitors; the distinction between hotel, guest houses and **Bed-and-Breakfast** places is often blurred. As individual capacity is low, this type of B&B is not given in our selection but information is available from:

DON'T FORGET THE MICHELIN GUIDE

If you are unable to find a suitable accommodation among the selected establishments described below, consult the red-cover *Michelin Guide London*, an extract from the annually revised *Michelin Guide Great Britain & Ireland*. This reputed guide lists over 250 hotels throughout Greater London.

- **At Home in London**
  70 Black Lion Ln, W6 9BE
  020 8748 1943
  www.athomeinlondon.co.uk
- **London Home-to-Home**
  26 Ascott Avenue, London W5 5QB
  020 8769 3500
  www.londonhometohome.com
- **GB and France Bed and Breakfast**
  PO Box 47085, SW18 9AB
  0871 781 0834.
  www.bedbreak.com
- **London Bed and Breakfast Agency Ltd** 71 Fellows Road, London NW3 3JY
  020 7586 2768
  www.londonbb.com
- **Uptown Reservations**
  8 Kelso Pl, London W8 5QD
  020 7937 2001
  www.uptownres.co.uk

YOUTH ACCOMMODATION

University Residences and **Youth Hostels**, as well as small hotels, guest houses and B&B accommodation in the budget price bracket are worthwhile options for young travellers. University Residences are often available during the vacations and offer good cheap places to stay in a central location *(Bloomsbury)*. For a contemporary take on the youth hostel concept try **The Generator** (www.generatorhostels.com).

Some useful addresses:

- **Venuemasters**
  0114 249 3090
  www.venuemasters.co.uk
- **Central Bureau for Educational Visits and Exchanges**

Seymour Mews House, Seymour Mews, London W1H 9PE
℘020 7930 8466
www.britishcouncil.org

♦ **International Students House (ISH)**
229 Great Portland Street, W1N 5HD
℘020 7631 8310 for students (single, double and dormitory)
www.ish.org.uk

♦ **YMCA, National Council**
640 Forest Road, London E17 3DZ
℘020 8520 5599
www.ymca.org.uk

♦ **YWCA, National HQ**
52 Cornmarket Street, Oxford OX1 3EJ
℘01865 304 200
www.ywca-gb.org.uk

Holders of an **International Youth Hostel Federation** card should contact the International Youth Hostel Federation (www.yha.org.uk). The **Hostelling International /American Youth Hostel Assocation** in the US can be contacted via www.hiusa.org. Contact the **Youth Hostels Association** (℘01629 592700; www.yha.org.uk) for information on youth hostels in the UK.

To book a room in one of the six Youth Hostels in London: ℘01629 592700:

🕿 14 Noel Street, W1V 3PD
℘0845 371 9133

🕿 38 Bolton Gardens, SW5 0AQ
℘0845 371 9114

🕿 Holland House, Holland Walk, Kensington, W8 7QU
℘0845 371 9122

🕿 36 Carter Lane, off St Paul's Churchyard, EC4V 5AB
℘0845 371 9012

🕿 Island Yard, 20 Salter Road, Rotherhithe, SE16 1PP
℘0845 371 9756

🕿 104 Bolsover St, W1N 5NU
℘0845 371 9154

CAMPSITES

There are several campsites within reasonable distance of Central London; it is advisable to book in advance; prices vary according to the season:

♦ **Crystal Palace Caravan Club Site**
Crystal Palace Parade, London SE19 1UF. 8mi/12.8km from Central London. Open all year.
℘020 8778 7155
www.caravanclub.co.uk

♦ **Lee Valley Camping and Caravan Park**
Meridian Way, Edmonton, London N9 0AS. 10mi/16km from Central London. Open all year.
℘01992 702 200. www.leevalleypark.org.uk

♦ **Abbey Wood**
Federation Road, Abbey Wood, London SE2 0LS. 12mi/19.3km from Central London. Open all year.
℘020 8311 7708.
www.caravanclub.co.uk

CHAIN HOTELS

If you are willing to forego charm and personalised service and your budget is limited, a chain hotel might be a suitable alternative.

🏠*For descriptions of areas described in the Chain Hotels section, see the Index.*

Premier Inns
The Travelodge and Premier Inn chains have now merged, and they have many hotels all over London. They offer simple but comfortable rooms, with rates starting from £49 per night.
Service, VAT inc. Central booking ℘0870 242 8000. www.premiertravelinn.com
Locations: Euston, County Hall (Lambeth), Tower Bridge, Putney, Docklands, Beckton, Ilford (E), Croydon (S).

♦ **Travelodges**
These offer similar facilities at a single rate of £26– £80. *VAT inc. Central booking ℘08700 850 950 (freephone). www.travelodge.co.uk*
Locations: Kings Cross, Battersea (SW), City of London, Docklands, Ilford (E) Park Royal (W), Kew Bridge (W), Wimbledon, Kingston (SW).

♦ **Holiday Inn Express**
These offer comfortable rooms at moderate rates from £90. C*entral booking ℘0870 400 9670. www.ichotelsgroup.com*
Locations: Victoria, Southwark, Hammersmith (W), Wandsworth (S), Stratford, Royal Docks (E), Wimbledon. With 11 hotels

in London, this group offers good value and more upmarket accommodation.

HOTEL INFORMATION AND RESERVATION SERVICE
Among the numerous websites worth consulting:

www.visitbritain.com
Official websiteof **Visit Britain**, the national tourist agency, with pages specially adapted according to visitors' country of origin.

www.visitlondon.com
Official websiteof **Visit London**, the capital's tourist agency. Telephone booking service Mon–Fri 9.30am–6pm: ☎08456 44 30 10 (£5 booking fee). Telephone booking service is now available on ☎0870 1566 366.

www.londontown.com
offers hotel information and online reservations for moderate and luxury accommodation in London. Special discounted rates for selected hotels.

British Hotel Reservation Centre, 15 Monck St, SW1P 2BJ; ☎020 7592 3055. www.bhrc.co.uk

Although the lodgings described in this guide have been selected with care, changes may have occurred since our last visit, so please send us your comments: favourable or unfavourable.
The properties described below were selected for their ambience, location and/or value for the money.

INNER LONDON
BLOOMSBURY
Arosfa Hotel – *83 Gower St, WC1E 6HJ. Goodge Street. ☎020 7636 2115. www.arosfalondon.com. 15 rooms.* A small family-run hotel in one of Bloomsbury's busiest thoroughfares, the Arosfa offers simple but impeccably clean and comfortable accommodation at reasonable rates. No ensuite bedrooms. Ask for a quieter room overlooking the small rear garden.

Cavendish Hotel – *75 Gower St, WC1E 6HJ. Goodge Street. ☎020 763 rooms.* DH Lawrence once stayed at this Georgian house, run by the same family for over 40 years. Period furniture adds to the charm.

Coin Ranges Explained
Prices reflect the average cost for a standard double room (two people), not including taxes.
The ☐ symbol indicates that breakfast is included in the rate. If there is a charge for breakfast, it is shown after the ☐ symbol. For other symbols used below, see the Legend on the cover flap.

⊖	**less than £90**
⊖⊖	**£90 to £135**
⊖⊖⊖	**£135 to £200**
⊖⊖⊖⊖	**more than £200**

Crescent Hotel – *49–50 Cartwright Gdns, WC1H 9EL. Russell Square. ☎020 7387 1515. www.crescenthoteloflondon.com. 27 rooms.* This charming hotel, occupying two Georgian houses, has developed a loyal clientele. Pleasant features include a cosy sitting room, the original cast-iron oven in the breakfast room, large communal garden and tennis courts.

The Generator – *Compton Pl. (off 37 Tavistock Pl), WC1H 9SD. Russell Square. ☎020 7388 7666. www.generatorhostels.com. 800 beds.* This industrial-complex-turned-youth-hostel with chrome décor comprises a games room, Internet space and a bar, open late. The spartan dormitories vary in size; the more you're willing to share with, the less you'll pay.

Gresham Hotel – *36 Bloomsbury St, WC1B 3QJ. Tottenham Court Road. ☎020 7580 4232 . www.gresham hotellondon.com. 42 rooms.* Guests at this Georgian house will appreciate the competitive prices and its location near the tube station. Bedrooms are spacious but not all are en suite; those at the rear are quieter.

Jenkins Hotel – *45 Cartwright Gdns, WC1H 9EH. Russell Square. ☎020 7387 2067. www.jenkinshotel.demon.co.uk. 14 rooms.* This hotel in an early-18C Georgian crescent is lovingly maintained by charming hosts. Clean, well-kept and tastefully decorated bedrooms.

⊜ **Premier Inn Euston** – *1 Dukes Rd, WC1H 9PJ.* ⊖*Euston Square.* ☏*0870 238 3301. www.premiertravelinn.com. 220 rooms.* Unbeatable value for central London; it may be a budget chain hotel but the rooms are spotless and spacious with well-lit en suite bathrooms. Rooms at the rear are quieter.

⊜ **Thanet Hotel** – *8 Bedford Pl, WC1B 5JA.* ⊖*Russell Square.* ☏*020 7636 2869. www.thanethotel.co.uk. 16 rooms.* ⊑. Hanging baskets adorn the Thanet's façade in the middle of a Georgian terrace. The personable owners create a relaxing and friendly ambience.

⊜⊜ **Academy Hotel** – *21 Gower St, WC1E 6HG.* ⊖*Goodge Street.* ☏*020 7631 4115. www.theetoncollection.com. 49 rooms.* ⊑. This "boutique" hotel is centrally located, near the British Museum. The Georgian exterior belies the contemporary interior; bedrooms are stylish and comfortable and there is a basement bar and restaurant. Rooms at the back are quieter.

⊜⊜⊟ **Grange Blooms Hotel** – *7 Montague St, WC1B 5BP.* ⊖*Russell Square.* ☏*020 7323 1717. www.grangehotels. com. 26 rooms.* ⊑*£15.50.* Located in a row of Georgian houses flanking the British Museum, Blooms exudes a great deal of charm and intimacy. Individually designed "themed" rooms and a small rear garden.

⊜⊜⊟⊟ **Charlotte Street** – *15 Charlotte St, W1P 1HB.* ⊖*Tottenham Court Road; Goodge Street.* ☏*020 7806 2000. www.firmdale.com. 44 rooms.* ⊑*£19.* This contemporary English hotel is renowned for its charm. The individually appointed rooms have nice touches such as CDs and mobile phones. Visit the hotel's stylish bar and restaurant, **Oscar**. Well located on the Bloomsbury fringes, close to Oxford Street.

⊜⊜⊟⊟ **The Montague** – *15 Montague St, W1C 5BJ.* ⊖*Russell Square.* ☏*020 7637 1001. www.montaguehotel. com.* This charming hotel features friendly staff and elegant rooms with modern conveniences. Spacious grounds, an on-site restaurant and tea service are added benefits.

CHELSEA, EARL'S COURT

⊜ **Amsterdam Hotel** – *7–9 Trebovir Rd, Earl's Court, SW5 9LS.* ⊖*Earl's Court.* ☏*020 7370 5084. www.amsterdam–hotel. co.uk. 19 rooms.* ⊑. Just doors away from the Rushmore, this small hotel has bedrooms with vivid colour schemes and some with balconies. Several suites available. In good weather take advantage of the small garden.

⊜ **Henley House** – *30 Barkston Gdns, Earl's Court, SW5 0EN.* ⊖*Earl's Court.* ☏*020 7370 4111. www.henleyhousehotel. com. 21 rooms.* ⊑*£4.95.* Nestling in a pleasant redbrick square close to Earl's Court Road, this small friendly hotel is good for well-priced and reliable accommodation close to the museums of South Ken.

⊜ **London Town Hotel** – *15 Penywern Rd, Earl's Court, SW5 9TT.* ⊖*Earl's Court.* ☏*020 7370 4356. www.londontownhotel. co.uk. 30 rooms.* Behind the porticoed Georgian exterior, you'll find a modern hotel, cheerily decorated and with thoughtfully equipped and relatively spacious bedrooms. Rooms to the rear are quieter.

⊜ **Merlyn Court Hotel** – *2 Barkston Gdns, SW5 0EN.* ⊖*Earl's Court.* ☏*020 7370 1640. www.merlyncourthotel.com. 20 rooms.* This friendly, family-run hotel near Earl's Court underground station has simply furnished, comfortable bedrooms, some of which overlook a tranquil Edwardian square.

⊜ **Oliver Plaza Hotel** – *33 Trebovir Rd, Earl's Court, SW5 9NF.* ⊖*Earl's Court.* ☏*020 7373 7183. www.capricornhotels. co.uk. 38 rooms.* Small comfortable hotel, with friendly reception and a private car park. All rooms are en suite and have satellite TV.

⊜ **Rushmore** – *11 Trebovir Rd, Earl's Court, SW5 9LS.* ⊖*Earl's Court.* ☏*020 7370 3839. www.rushmore-hotel.co.uk. 22 rooms.* ⊑. This small hotel located close to Earl's Court tube has won a loyal following. Bedrooms are individually decorated and many shapes and sizes. The conservatory breakfast room doubles as a bar.

THE CITY

Travelodge – *1 Harrow Pl, E1 7DB. Aldgate. www.travelodge.co.uk.142 rooms.* Accommodation for the cost-conscious traveller in the financial district. The ensuite bedrooms are spacious and modern. Extra sofa beds and ample workspace in all rooms.

Hoxton Hotel – *81 Great Eastern Street, EC2A 3HU. Old St. 020 7550 1000. www.hoxtonhotels.com. 205 rooms. Restaurant.* Upmarket is the aim of this trendy hotel, opened in 2006, and it has succeeded admirably. Touches such as flat-screen TVs, sleek décor in neutral tones, roaring fires in the lobby and fine linens make this feel far more of an expensive stay than it is. Room prices vary wildly throughout the year; keep an eye on the website for details.

CLERKENWELL, ISLINGTON

Malmaison – *Charterhouse Square, EC1M. Farringdon. 020 7012 3700. www.malmaison-london. com.* Charming and elegant, this hotel, one of a boutique chain, is set on a cobblestone square, close to Smithfield market. The décor is chic, with purples and dove egg blues, and there's a gym, a brasserie restaurant and a rooftop bar to unwind in.

The Rookery – *12 Peters Lane, Cowcross St, Islington, EC1M 6DS. Farringdon. 020 7336 0931. www.rookery.co.uk. 32 rooms. £9.54.* This charming restored 18C house, with wood-panelling, period furniture and open fires, is located a short distance from St Paul's Cathedral. Bathrooms have Victorian fittings, and the suite has a retracting roof over the bedroom.

The Zetter – *Charterhouse Square, EC1M. Farringdon. 020 7324 4455. www.thezetter.com.* Modern, with clean lines and happy staff, The Zetter is youthful and very much in the spirit of the area. Nice touches in rooms include old Penguin paperbacks and hot water bottles. There's a restaurant serving modern Mediterranean food downstairs for when you get peckish.

COVENT GARDEN, SOHO, CHINATOWN

The Fielding – *4 Broad Court, Bow St, Soho WC2B 5QZ. Covent Garden. 020 7836 8305. www.the-fielding-hotel.co.uk. Closed 1 week at Christmas. 24 rooms.* A hotel that enjoys an unrivalled location in a quiet pedestrian street in Covent Garden. Bedrooms are compact but well kept. A rare find for the area.

Hazlitt's – *6 Frith St, Soho, W1V 5TZ. Tottenham Court Road. 020 7434 1771. www.hazlittshotel. com. Closed 24–25 Dec. 23 rooms + VAT. £9.50.* Virtually the only hotel in Soho, the former home of the eponymous essayist still attracts a mix of well-heeled urban travellers. Individually decorated bedrooms, many with antique furniture and plenty of Victorian charm. Continental breakfast.

St Martins Lane – *45 St Martin's Lane, Covent Garden, WC2N 4HX. Charing Cross. 020 7300 5500. www.stmartinslane.com. 200 rooms. £25.* Bearing the signature of French designer Philippe Starck, the St Martins Lane is one of London's most spectacular designer hotels: from the state-of-the-art bedrooms to stylish bars and restaurants.

KENSINGTON, SOUTH KENSINGTON, NOTTING HILL, BAYSWATER, PADDINGTON

Columbia Hotel – *95–99 Lancaster Gate, Bayswater, W2 3NS. Lancaster Gate. 020 7402 0021. www.columbia hotel.co.uk. 103 rooms.* This stately row of five 19C houses was occupied by the US Officers' Club until 1975. Bedroom décor is unremarkable, but half overlook Kensington Gardens and many have balconies.

Garden Court Hotel – *30–31 Kensington Gardens Sq, W2 4BG. Bayswater. 020 7229 2553. www.gardencourthotel.co.uk. 32 rooms.* In the corner of a 19C garden square stands the gleaming façade of this friendly hotel. Family owned and run since 1954, the Garden Court features a cosy lounge and simply furnished rooms, half of which are en suite. Good value.

Gresham Hotel – *116 Sussex Gdns, Paddington, W2 1UA. Paddington. 020 7402 2920. 57 rooms.* Named after the founder of the Royal Exchange, the Gresham has well-equipped bedrooms, bright breakfast room and small wooden-floored bar.

Meininger Hostel– *65–67 Queens Gate. SW7 5JS. South Kensington. 020 7590 6190. www.meininger-hostels. com. 30 rooms. £3.* The first foray into London by this reliable German hostel chain, which provides an experience that is functional, comfortable, stylish and easy on the pocket. Table tennis table, wireless Internet access and a 24hr tea and coffee facilities are welcome extras., while accommodation is in dormitory, twin or single rooms. Great location, opposite the Natural History Museum.

Parkwood Hotel – *4 Stanhope Pl, W2 2HB. Marble Arch. 020 7402 224. www.parkwoodhotel.com. 16 rooms.* In a quiet residential street, this porticoed Georgian hotel is ideally situated for Oxford Street and Hyde Park. Traditionally decorated and well-kept bedrooms and a compact and pretty roof terrace on the first floor.

Pavilion Hotel – *34–36 Sussex Gdns, W2 1UL. Paddington. 020 7262 0905. www.pavilionhotelUK.com. 30 rooms.* This quirky, intimate Victorian house brims with antiques gleaned from auctions and flea markets. Choose from themed bedrooms ("Enter the Dragon," "Honky Tonk").

Abbey Court – *20 Pembridge Gdns, W2 4DU. Notting Hill Gate. 020 7221 7518. www.abbeycourthotel.co.uk. 22 rooms.* An ideal base for antique hunters roaming Portobello Road. This elegant town house has a very personal touch. Bedrooms are individually appointed, and the service is friendly.

Aster House – *3 Sumner Pl, SW7 3EE. South Kensington. 020 7581 5888. www.asterhouse.com. 13 rooms + VAT.* A true home-from-home experience. This pretty Victorian house is within easy walking distance of the Victoria & Albert Museum. Tranquil garden and conservatory.

Byron Hotel – *36–38 Queensborough Terr, W2 3SH. Bayswater. 020 7243 0987. www.byronhotel.co.uk. 45 rooms.* Reasonably priced accommodation in the heart of Bayswater, just steps away from Kensington Gardens. Bedrooms are bright and spacious and all have en suite showers.

Millers Residence – *111A Westbourne Grove, Bayswater, W2 4UW. Bayswater. 020 7243 1024. www.millersuk.com. Closed 24–27 Dec. 8 rooms.* Amid the shops of Bayswater, you'll find this quirky Victorian house, laden with fine antiques. Lavishly furnished bedrooms. Breakfast in the charming sitting room.

Portobello Gold Hotel – *95–97 Portobello Rd, W11 2QB. Notting Hill. 020 7460 4901. www.portobellogold. com. 6 rooms. Restaurant.* Located in Portobello market, this hotel-restaurant-pub offers good value in Notting Hill. Bill Clinton is among the celebrities who have popped in for a drink. Wireless Internet access available. The owner will even drive you in his 1952 Buick convertible for a fee.

Portobello Hotel – *22 Stanley Gdns, North Kensington, W11 2NG. Holland Park. 020 7727 2777. www.portobello-hotel.co.uk. 24 rooms.* Elegance prevails throughout this white 19c terrace town house. Individual bedrooms offer theatrical flourishes: circular beds and deep free-standing Victorian bathtubs.

KNIGHTSBRIDGE, BELGRAVIA, WESTMINSTER, VICTORIA, PIMLICO

Cartref House – *129 Ebury St, SW1W 9QU. Victoria. 020 7730 6176. www.cartrefhouse.co.uk. 11 rooms.* This family-owned and operated B&B in a Georgian house is located between Victoria Station and Sloane Square. A range of tastefully appointed, well-kept rooms to suit all budgets.

Luna & Simone Hotel – *47–49 Belgrave Rd, SW1V 2BB. Pimlico. 020 7834 5897. www.lunasimonehotel.com. 36 rooms.* You'll receive a warm welcome in this family-run hotel, with its porticoed façade. The house has vibrantly decorated bedrooms with thoughtful extras and a well-equipped computer room.

Melbourne House Hotel – *79 Belgrave Rd, Victoria, SW1V 2BG. ⊖Pimlico. ✆020 7828 3516. www.melbourne househotel.co.uk. 17 rooms. ⊑.* A traditional family-run hotel located a short walk from Tate Britain. Most of the simple but immaculately kept bedrooms have ensuite shower rooms. Reserve one of the rear facing rooms; they're quieter.

Melita House Hotel – *35 Charlwood St, SW1V 2DU. ⊖Pimlico. ✆020 7828 0471. www.melitahotel.com. 22 rooms. ⊑.* In a fairly quiet residential street off Belgrave Rd, Melita House offers spacious, modern rooms with fridges and modem points.

Morgan House B&B – *120 Ebury St, SW1W 9QQ. ⊖Victoria. ✆020 7730 2384. www.morganhouse.co.uk. Open all year. 11 rooms. ⊑.* A friendly guest house close to Buckingham Palace and Knightsbridge. The listed Georgian house has individually decorated bedrooms; our favourite is room 8 on the top floor.

Sanctuary House Hotel & Pub – *33 Tothill St, Westminster, SW1H 9LA. ⊖St James's Park. ✆020 7799 4044. www.fullershotels.com. Closed 1 week Christmas. 34 rooms. ⊑ £10.95. Restaurant⊖.* This Victorian hotel, above an English pub, offers good value rooms close to Big Ben and the London Eye. Spacious rooms with air conditioning.

The Diplomat – *2 Chesham St, Belgravia, SW1X 8DT. ⊖Sloane Square. ✆020 7235 1544. www.thediplomat hotel.co.uk. 26 rooms. ⊑.* This reasonably priced hotel occupies an imposing late 19C corner house in the heart of Belgravia. A sweeping staircase leads to the large, well-decorated rooms, all are en suite.

Claverley Hotel – *13–14 Beaufort Gdns, SW3 1PS. ⊖Knightsbridge. ✆020 7589 8541. www.claverley hotel.co.uk. 29 rooms. ⊑.* In a peaceful tree-lined cul-de-sac just a short stroll form Harrods, this hotel has a well-established reputation and spacious rooms, some with four-poster beds. Well-priced singles.

Draycott House Hotel – *26 Cadogan Gdns, Knightsbridge, SW3 2RP. ⊖Sloane Square. ✆020 7730 6466. www.draycotthotel.co.uk. 35 rooms. ⊑. £20.* Country house living minutes away from Harrods. This charming Victorian house is set in a smart residential street and many of the luxuriously appointed bedrooms overlook a tranquil communal garden. Room service.

The Goring Hotel – *15 Beeston Pl, Grosvenor Gdns, Victoria, SW1W 0JW. ⊖Victoria. ✆020 7396 9000. www. goringhotel.co.uk. 68 rooms. ⊑£18. Restaurant.* This stunning landmark hotel has remained in the Goring family for four generations. Elegance and comfort in the best British tradition. The quietier rooms at the rear overlook a private garden.

Knightsbridge – *10 Beaufort Gdns, Knightsbridge, SW3 1PT. ⊖Knightsbridge. ✆020 7584 6300. www.firmdale. com. 44 rooms. ⊑£16.50.* A porticoed town house tucked away behind Knightsbridge. The rooms vary in size but all have mini-bars and safes.

Knightsbridge Green – *159 Knightsbridge, SW1X 7PD. ⊖Knightsbridge. ✆020 7584 6274. www.thek ghotel.com. 16 rooms. ⊑£5.50–£12.50.* Discreet small hotel located in the heart of the famous shopping district. Spacious rooms and reasonable rates for central London. Breakfast served in bedrooms. Suites also available.

The Berkeley – *Wilton Pl, Knightsbridge, SW1X 7RL. ⊖Knightsbridge. ✆020 7235 6000. www.the-berkeley.co.uk. 186 rooms. ⊑£26.50 + VAT.* The Berkeley's discreet charm is evident throughout: in the panelled drawing room, rooftop pool with retracting roof and opulently decorated bedrooms. Restaurants include **Marcus Wareing** and Gordon Ramsay's **Boxwood Café**.

Cadogan – *75 Sloane St, SW1X 9SG. ⊖Sloane Sq. ✆020 7235 7141. www.cadogan.com. 65 rooms. ⊑£20.* This classic English hotel has welcomed such celebrities as Oscar Wilde and Lillie Langtry. The still-charming Cadogan remains a haven of peace, with a wood-panelled lounge that is a favourite afternoon tea spot.

⊜ ⊜ ⊜ ⊜ **Mandarin Oriental –** *66 Knightsbridge, SW1X 7LA.* ⊖*Knightsbridge.* ☎*020 7201 3773. www.mandarinoriental.com. 65 rooms.* ⊑*£25.* Right in the heart of Knightsbridge, opposite Harvey Nichols, this luxury hotel more than lives up to its exalted location with plush amenities and service to match. The Mandarin Bar is a favourite haunt of London's rich, famous or wannabes, and serves great cocktails.

MARYLEBONE, REGENT'S PARK, PRIMROSE HILL, ST JOHN'S WOOD

⊜ **Blandford Hotel –** *80 Chiltern St, W1U 5AF.* ⊖*Baker Street.* ☎*020 7486 3103. www.capricornhotels.co.uk. 33 rooms.* ⊑. Close to Regent's Park, this privately owned hotel has a friendly atmosphere, well-kept rooms and an adjacent car park.

⊜ **Edward Lear Hotel –** *28–30 Seymour St, Marylebone, W1H 5WD.* ⊖*Marble Arch.* ☎*020 7402 5401. www.edlear.com. 31 rooms.* ⊑. This Georgian house was the residence of the Victorian painter and limerick writer. Narrow staircases lead to bright rooms, four en suite. Internet access in the lounge.

⊜ **Hart House –** *51 Gloucester Pl, Marylebone, W1U 8JF.* ⊖*Marble Arch.* ☎*020 7935 2288. www. harthouse.co.uk. 15 rooms.* ⊑. In a busy road north of Portman Sq, this Georgian house once provided refuge to French nobility fleeing the Revolution. It is now a welcoming well-maintained hotel. Rear rooms are quieter.

⊜ **Lincoln House –** *33 Gloucester Pl, W1H 3PD.* ⊖*Marble Arch.* ☎*020 7486 7630. www.lincoln-house-hotel.co.uk. 23 rooms.* ⊑. A family-run hotel in a convenient location, housed in a late 18C townhouse. Rooms on the 1st floor are more spacious.

⊜ ⊜ **Sherlock Holmes Hotel –** *108 Baker St, W1U 6LJ.* ⊖*Baker Street.* ☎*020 7486 6161. www.parkplazasherlockholmes.com. 119 rooms.* ⊑. Rejuvenated from a chintzy hotel to an altogether slicker number by the Park Plaza chain, this central hotel is now full of neutral décor and comfortable touches such as scatter cushions, sauna, bar and organic restaurant.

⊜ ⊜ ⊜ **Durrants Hotel –** *26–32 George St, Marylebone, W1H 5BJ.* ⊖*Bond Street.* ☎*020 7935 8131. www. durrantshotel. co.uk. 88 rooms.* ⊑*£15.* This elegant, quintessentially English hotel is around the corner from the Wallace Collection. Enjoy afternoon tea in the fire-lit lounges or traditional British fare in the wood-panelled dining room.

MAYFAIR

⊜ ⊜ **Flemings –** *13 Half Moon St, W1Y 7RA.* ⊖*Green Park.* ☎*020 7499 2964. www.flemings-mayfair.co.uk. 119 rooms.* ⊑*£18. Restaurant* ⊜*–* ⊜ ⊜. The noted polymath Henry Wagner once resided at this address, close to Green Park. The Georgian architecture is complemented by the traditional interior featuring oil paintings and antique English furniture.

⊜ ⊜ ⊜ ⊜ **Claridge's –** *Brook St, W1A 2JQ.* ⊖*Bond Street.* ☎*020 7629 8860. www.claridges.co.uk.143 rooms.* ⊑*£28.* The hotel has enjoyed Royal patronage to such an extent that a telephone request to speak to the King once required the response "Which one?" Claridge's continues to epitomise English grandeur and is celebrated for its art deco design and luxury.

⊜ ⊜ ⊜ ⊜ **The Metropolitan –** *Old Park Lane, W1Y 4LB.* ⊖*Green Park.* ☎*020 7447 1000. www.themetropolitan. co.uk. 152 rooms.* ⊑*£32.50.* The ultra-minimalist design and hip reputation have made this the favoured haunt of celebrities.

The chic **Met Bar** proves that hotel bars need not be dull, open till late, serving cocktails and snacks. Rooms on the higher floors offer views of Hyde Park. Trendy restaurant **Nobu** (☾*see Where to Eat)* also within the hotel.

PICCADILLY, ST JAMES'S

⊜ ⊜ ⊜ **The Stafford –** *16–18 St James's Pl, SW1A 1NJ.* ⊖*Green Park.* ☎*020 7493 0111. www.thestaffordhotel.co.uk. 75 rooms.* ⊑*£22.* Tucked away in a street beside Green Park, the genteel Stafford is one of London's quietest hotels, with tastefully appointed rooms. Have a drink in the famed "**American bar**".

⊝⊝⊟⊟ **The Cavendish** – *81 Jermyn St, SW1Y 6JF.* ⊖*Piccadilly Circus.* ✆*020 7930 2111. www.cavendish-london.co.uk. 295 rooms.* ⊑*£21.* Across the street from Fortnum & Mason, this large corporate hotel offers all the conveniences of a modern hotel. For great views, ask for a room on one of the top five floors.

⊝⊝⊟⊟ **22 Jermyn St** – *22 Jermyn St, SW1Y 6HL.* ⊖*Piccadilly Circus.* ✆*020 7734 2353. www.22jermyn.com. 18 rooms.* ⊑*£13.* Pure luxury at this boutique hideaway in the heart of St James's, with marble bathrooms, giant plumped up pillows, deep beds and superlative customer service. Central London is on the doorstep and Fortnum & Mason is five minutes away for afternoon tea.

SOUTH BANK, BANKSIDE, SOUTHWARK, BERMONDSEY, WATERLOO

⊝ **Premier Inn London County Hall** – *Belvedere Rd, Waterloo, SE1 7PB.* ⊖*Waterloo.* ✆*0870 238 3300. www.premierinn.com. 313 rooms.* Once home to the Greater London Council, this hotel offers spotless, uniformly fitted rooms.

SUBURBS

NORTH-WEST: HAMPSTEAD, HIGHGATE, SWISS COTTAGE

⊝ **Hampstead Village Guest House** – *2 Kemplay Rd, Hampstead, NW3 1SY.* ⊖*Hampstead.* ✆*020 7435 8679. www.hampsteadguesthouse.com. 9 rooms.* ⊑*£7.* This Victorian house, close to Hampstead Heath, evokes images of writers and thinkers who have settled in the area. Not all rooms are en suite, but all are decorated with antiques.

⊝ **Langorf** – *18–20 Frognal, Hampstead, NW3 6AG.* ⊖*Finchley Road.* ✆*020 7794 4483. www.langorfhotel.com. 36 rooms.* ⊑. Village life within the city. This Edwardian house has a breakfast room that overlooks a walled garde, spacious bedrooms and convenient transport links to central London.

⊝ **Mountview** – *31 Mount View Rd, N4 4SS.* ⊖*Finsbury Park.* ✆*020 8340 9222. www.mountviewguesthouse.com. 4 rooms.* ⊑. An attractively furnished Victorian house in a quiet residential tree-lined street. Bedrooms are individually decorated and two overlook the rear garden.

⊝⊝ **La Gaffe** – *107–111 Heath St, NW3 6SS.* ⊖*Hampstead.* ✆*020 7435 8965. www.lagaffe.co.uk. 18 rooms.* ⊑. Italian hospitality at this small hotel a short walk from Hamstead High Street, which stands on the site of two former shepherds' cottages . Ask for one of the bedrooms at the back, overlooking a tranquil Georgian Square. The adjoining restaurant, also run by the owners, has a menu of traditional Italian cooking.

SOUTH-EAST: GREENWICH, BLACKHEATH

⊝⊝ **Holiday Inn Express London Greenwich** – *Bugsby Way, SE10 0GD.* ⊖*Greenwich.* ✆*0871 423 4931. www.hiexpress.co.uk. 70 rooms.* ⊑. This seven-storey modern hotel, just south of the Millennium Dome, has great panoramic views and a Chinese restaurant.

SOUTH-SOUTH-WEST: FULHAM, PUTNEY, WIMBLEDON

⊝ **Premier Inn,London Putney Bridge** – *3 Putney Bridge Approach, Fulham, SW6 3JD.* ⊖*Putney Bridge.* ✆*0870 238 3302. www.premierinn.com. 154 rooms.* Converted from an office block this chain hotel offers dependable accommodation.

SOUTH-WEST: RICHMOND, KEW

⊝ **Chase Lodge** – *10 Park Rd, Hampton Wick, KT1 4AS.* ⊖*Richmond.* ✆*020 8943 1862. www.chaselodgehotel. com. 13 rooms.* ⊑. A warm welcome is guaranteed at this Victorian property located a short distance from the Thames. Furnishings and decoration vary, but all rooms are comfortable.

Where To Eat

London has become a gourmet's paradise, and the capital now occupies a prominent role on the international culinary scene. The number and variety of eating places reflect the multitude of current cooking styles ranging from traditional British (including fish and chips), to classic French, to popular Mediterranean-style and world cuisine inspired by far-flung places around the globe. Indeed, a tasty legacy of the British Empire's former worldwide ties is the abundance of dishes hailing from South Asia, Africa, the Caribbean and the Near and Far East.

The term "Modern British", coined in the late 1980s, is loosely applied to the wave of innovative cooking that borrows freely from various international sources, highlighting fresh home-grown and locally sourced products and eye-pleasing presentation. In the 1990s, the unofficial ambassador of British style, Sir Terence Conran, further enhanced London's culinary reputation by launching several spectacular "gastrodomes" (Bluebird in Chelsea, for example). In these sprawling "designer restaurants", eating becomes a multi-sensory experience, dazzling the eyes and ears as well as the taste buds.

ADDRESSES

FOR ALL BUDGETS

Budget eateries (⊖) are generally simple, unpretentious places where you can expect to spend less than £25. In the **moderate** range (⊖⊖–⊖⊖⊖), dining spots are slightly more formal, with a meal costing from £25 to £75. The **expensive** restaurants (⊖⊖⊖⊖ – more than £75) are upmarket establishments with a high culinary standard and distinctive ambience.

Coin Ranges Explained

Prices indicate the average cost of a starter, main course and dessert, not including beverage, tax or tip.

⊖	**less than £25**
⊖⊖	**£25 to £45**
⊖⊖⊖	**£45 to £75**
⊖⊖⊖⊖	**more than £75**

Prices indicate the average cost of a starter, main course and dessert. If you are tempted to try a noted pricey restaurant, but your budget is limited, consider the value lunch menus proposed by many of these establishments. Naturally, prices will vary depending on the number of courses and the beverages ordered. Wine can be an expensive item, and consequently the cost of a meal will be substantially higher.

Tax and service are generally included in the restaurant bill. Tipping is optional, but it is common to leave 10% when the service is pleasing. Some restaurants will leave the total open on a credit card slip so that the customer can add a tip to the bill. Restaurants are usually open in the evening from 6.30–10pm (earlier and later if they are serving pre- and post-theatre meals) and also at lunchtime from noon–2.15pm, depending on the district. Many close one day a week. It is advisable to book in the evening, particularly at weekends. A formal evening meal – dinner – consists of three courses, but in many restaurants it is quite acceptable to eat only a starter and a main dish or a main dish and a dessert. Most restaurants offer bottled water – but tap water will be provided if requested.

LIGHTER FARE

Cafés and informal eating places and pubs, which keep flexible hours and can provide a light meal in the middle of the day, are listed under *Pubs* and *Light Bites* in the *DISCOVERING LONDON* section of the guide. An average meal in these places will cost under £15. The following café/restaurant chains have numerous branches throughout Central London and provide consistent value for casual meals: Prêt-à-Manger, Eat, Caffè Uno, Café Rouge, Itsu, Chez Gérard, Wagamama and Giraffe. Church refectories are another good place for light meals; those at Southwark Cathedral and St Martin-the-Fields are particularly notable.

AFTERNOON TEA

Tea roooms, cafés and hotels providing afternoon tea appear in the *DISCOVERING LONDON* section of the guide. The traditional times for the celebrated institution of afternoon tea is 4 o'clock, but in most establishments, it is served between 3pm and 5pm. Order a selection of sandwiches – cucumber is the traditional filling – or a cream tea (scones and jam and clotted cream) or crumpets or muffins with butter, cakes and fruit tarts. Choose from a variety of teas – Indian (Darjeeling) or China (green or perfumed like Lapsang Souchong or Earl Grey).

For the authentic atmosphere of an English tearoom try the Fountain Restaurant in Fortnum & Mason, the Ritz Hotel, Brown's Hotel, the Lanesborough Hotel at Hyde Park Corner as well as other well-known places such as the Dorchester Hotel (dress appropriately) and the Winter Garden in the Landmark London Hotel. Less select but very good are the tearooms in the Richoux chain.

Although the restaurants described in this guide have been selected with care, changes may have occurred since our last visit, so please send us your comments, favourable or unfavourable.

Like the hotel listings, the restaurants described in this guide have been selected for quality, atmosphere, location and value for money. For more informal and inexpensive eating throughout the city, consult the Light Bite *and* Pub *listings within the DISCCOVERING LONDON section of the guide.*

INNER LONDON
BLOOMSBURY, FITZROVIA

Abeno – *47 Museum St, WC1A 1LY. Holborn. 020 7405 3211. www. abeno.co.uk. Closed 25–26 Dec and 1 Jan.* This original Japanese restaurant is close to the British Museum. On your first visit try the delicious house speciality: Okonomi-yaki, pancakes cooked on a hotplate on your table.

North Sea Fish Restaurant – *7–8 Leigh St, WC1H 9EW. Russell Square. 020 7387 5892. Closed Sun.* Drop in to this friendly eatery for genuine fish and chips. Only ground nut or vegetable oil is used; egg and matzo coating also available. Jumbo sizes fried or grilled.

Ristorante Paradiso – *35 Store St, WC1E 7BS. Goodge Street. 020 7255 2554. www.ristoranteparadiso.co.uk.* Founded in 1934, this pizzeria-ristorante with its typical décor of assorted bottles and black and white photos, has retained much of its original atmosphere and serves good pizza.

Tas – *22 Bloomsbury St, WC1B 3QJ. Holborn. 020 7637 4555. www. tasrestaurant.com.* With its colourful flowers cascading outside in large pots this family-friendly restaurant close to the British Museum is incredibly inviting. Menus include mezze and great lamb kebabs. A great find.

CHELSEA, EARL'S COURT

The Ebury – *11 Pimlico Rd, SW1W 8NA. Sloane Square. 020 7730 6784. www. theebury.co.uk.* This is at the posh end of gastropubs, with an elegant upstairs dining room serving accomplished cooking, using seasonal ingredients.

DON'T FORGET THE
MICHELIN GUIDE

For a more extensive listing of restaurants in the London area, consult the *Michelin Guide London*, an extract from the annually revised *Michelin Guide Great Britain & Ireland*. This respected gastronomical guide lists over 375 restaurants throughout Greater London.

Itsu – *118 Draycott Ave, Chelsea, SW3 3AE.* ⊖*South Kensington.* ℘*020 7590 2400. www.itsu.com. No bookings.* Take your pick of the European-style sushi as it passes along the conveyor belt. Dishes are priced according to their colour, and the attentive staff is a buzzer call away. Upstairs, a more formal area with a lively bar.

Bibendum Oyster Bar – *81 Fulham Rd, South Kensington, SW3 6RD.* ⊖*South Kensington.* ℘*020 7581 5817. www.bibendum.co.uk. Closed 1 week Christmas.* The foyer of London's beloved art nouveau gem, Michelin House, provides the setting for an informal meal of light seafood and shellfish specialities. Like many other Conran eateries, the Oyster Bar is often packed.

Racine – *239 Brompton Rd, SW3 2EP.* ⊖*Knightsbridge.* ℘*020 7584 4477.* Dark leather banquettes and large mirrors create a Parisian brasserie atmosphere. The cooking from Henry Harris, however, is far superior, producing regional and classic French dishes.

Bluebird – *350 King's Rd, SW3 5UU.* ⊖*South Kensington.* ℘*020 7559 1000. www.bluebird-restaurant.com.* Sir Terence Conran's Chelsea "gastrodome" comprises foodshop, flower market, café, Bluebird Dining Room and Bluebird, a skylit restaurant and bar. The emphasis here is on seasonal ingredients. Weekend brunch is popular.

THE CITY

Pizza Express –*232–238 Bishopsgate, EC2M 4QD.* ⊖*Liverpool Street.* ℘*020 7247 2838. www.pizzaexpress.com.* Stylish, well-priced pizza chain, serving light, crispy pizzas in sleek, modern surroundings.

1 Lombard Street (Brasserie) – *1 Lombard St, EC2V 9AA.* ⊖*Bank.* ℘*020 7929 6611. www.1lombardstreet.com. Closed Sat, Sun, bank holidays.* A former banking hall provides the grand setting for this brasserie serving modern European fare. A popular venue for City workers and often quite noisy.

Le Coq d'Argent – *No. 1 Poultry, EC2R 8EH.* ⊖*Bank.* ℘*020 7395 5000. www.coqdargent.co.uk. Closed Sat lunch, Sun eve.* This spectacular restaurant on top of one of the City's modern buildings also boasts a terrace. The crustacea bar is terrific, and the modern European cooking sophisticated.

White Swan Pub & Dining Room – *108 Fetter Ln, EC4A 1ES.* ⊖*Chancery Lane.* ℘*020 7242 9696. www.thewhite swanlondon.com. Closed Mon lunch, Sat, Sun.* Choose from two experiences: the traditional pub menu downstairs or the upstairs dining room with fine dining, which has won awards.

CLERKENWELL, ISLINGTON

St John – *26 St. John St, Islington, EC1M 4AY.* ⊖*Farringdon.* ℘*020 7251 0848. www.stjohnrestaurant.com. Closed Sun.* This busy, unpretentious restaurant is housed within a former 19C smokehouse. The bar is a popular after work meeting place, while the menu specialises in offal and a mix of traditional and rediscovered English dishes.

St John

Laurie Fletcher/St. John Restaurant Ltd

Morgan M – *489 Liverpool Rd, N7 8NS.* ⊖*Highbury & Islington.* ℘*020 7609 3560; www.morganm.com. Closed Sat, Mon, Tue lunch, Sun.* Since young Morgan Meunier opened his restaurant in a former pub at the wrong end of Islington, he has been earning all the awards. Terrific classic French cooking.

COVENT GARDEN, SOHO, CHINATOWN

Carluccios – *105 Strand, WC2R 0AA.* ⊖*Charing Cross.* ℘*020 7497 210. www. caluccios.com.* Well-priced Italian chain of restaurants set up by the Italian chef Antonio Carluccio. The delicious menus, using fresh ingredients include pastas, salads, fish and antipasti. Relaxed ambience makes it a popular lunch spot. Airy, modern dining room upstairs.

Fung Shing – *15 Lisle St, WC2H 7BE. Leicester Square. 020 7437 1539. www.fungshing.co.uk. Closed 24–26 Dec and lunch bank holidays.* A long-standing Soho favourite on the edge of **Chinatown★**. Chatty and pleasant service. Lovers of Chinese food will find classics as well as more adventurous dishes.

Porters – *17 Henrietta St, WC2E 8QH. Leicester Square. 020 7836 6466. www.porters.uk.com. Closed 25 Dec.* This well-established restaurant is owned by the 7th Earl of Bradford. The menu specialises in traditional English dishes, and homemade pies. Family friendly, with a separate children's menu; older guests can enjoy the adjacent bar.

Rock and Sole Plaice – *47 Endell St, WC2H 9AJ. Covent Garden. 020 7836 3785. Closed Sun, bank holidays.* This informal fish and chips eatery, reputedly founded in 1871, has portions big enough to satisfy all appetites, and somewhat kitsch aquatic décor.

Smollensky's on The Strand – *105 Strand, WC2R 0AA. Charing Cross. 020 7497 2101. www.smollenskys.com.* A large family-orientated basement restaurant serving American food, and boasting ersatz art deco with booths. Live jazz on Sundays. Good value for the area.

The Admiralty – *Somerset House, Strand, WC2R 1LA. Temple. 020 7845 4646. www.theadmiraltyrestaurant. com. Closed Sun eve, 25–26 Dec.* Interconnecting rooms with bold colours and informal service contrast with its setting within the restored Georgian splendour of Somerset House.

Mon Plaisir – *21 Monmouth St, Covent Garden, WC2H 9DD. Covent Garden. 020 7836 7243. www.mon plaisir.co.uk. Closed 25 Dec, Sat lunch, Sun, bank holidays + VAT.* Francophiles still flock to London's oldest French restaurant. This family-run establishment, founded over 50 years ago, has four dining rooms all decorated with a common Gallic touch.

Rules – *35 Maiden Lane, Covent Garden, WC2E 7LB. Covent Garden. 020 7836 5314. www.rules.co.uk. Closed 4 days Christmas.* Grouse, partridge and woodcock are some of the game on the menu at London's reputedly oldest restaurant, and all from its own estate! Antique cartoons and drawings adorn the walls.

Simpson's in The Strand – *100 Strand, WC2R 0EW. Charing Cross. 020 7836 9112. www.simpsonsinthe strand.co.uk.* An English institution since 1828, Simpsons is the place for splendid breakfasts (try the Ten Deadly Sins) and top traditional cooking. **The Grand Divan** upstairs is the more casual option.

The Ivy – *1 West St, Covent Garden, WC2H 9N. Leicester Square. 020 7836 4751. www.the-ivy.co.uk. Closed eve 24–26 and 31 Dec, 1 Jan, Aug bank holiday.* Once past the liveried doorman and waiting paparazzi, you'll find wood panelling, stained glass and an unpretentious menu. The Ivy is one of London's most coveted "Theatreland" restaurants, so securing a table is challenging. A West End institution.

KENSINGTON, SOUTH KENSINGTON, NOTTING HILL, BAYSWATER, PADDINGTON

L'Accento – *16 Garway Rd, Bayswater, W2 4NH. Bayswater. 020 7243 2201.* L'Accento is a favourite with aficionados of authentic Italian provincial cuisine. Delicious shellfish specialities. Choose from the front room or the rear conservatory with a removable roof.

Costas Fish Restaurant – *18 Hillgate St, W8 7SR. Notting Hill Gate. 020 7727 4310 Closed Sun, Mon.* Greek-Cypriot ingredients meet traditional English fish and chips (and classic mushy peas!) in this jolly venue.

Island Restaurant and Bar – *Lancaster Terr, Lancaster Gate, W2 2TY. Lancaster Gate. 020 7551 6070. www.islandrestaurant.co.uk.* Look out through long windows to Hyde Park and at this airy restaurant and enjoy good modern European cooking.

Kam Tong – *59–63 Queensway, Bayswater, W2 4QH.* ⊖*Bayswater.* ☏*020 7229 6065.* This long-established and smoothly run Chinese restaurant offers a cheaper menu than many in the area. Bow-tied waiters in the dining room supervise the Dim Sum.

Malabar – *27 Uxbridge St, Kensington, W8 7TQ.* ⊖*Notting Hill Gate.* ☏*020 7727 8800. www.malabar-restaurant.co.uk. Closed last week Aug, 4 days Christmas.* Lovers of Indian cooking flock to this restaurant. Choose from an extensive range of good-value dishes, and many vegetarian options.

Raoul's – *13 Clifton Rd, Maida Vale, W9 1SZ.* ⊖*Warwick Ave.* ☏*020 7289 7313. www.roaulsgourmet.com.* Great at the weekend, this smart café/deli with outside seating is the place for classic dishes like croque monsieur and top coffee.

S& M Café – *268 Portobello Rd, Notting Hill, W10 5TY.* ⊖*Ladbroke Grove.* ☏*020 8968 8898. www.sandmcafe.co.uk.* This eatery under a bridge at the far end of the Portobello Road market is fun. Share pine tables with other patrons, and choose various homemade sausages and mashed potato.

Shikara – *87 Sloane Ave, SW3 3DX.* ⊖*South Kensington.* ☏*020 7581 6555. www.shikara.co.uk.* Pretty restaurant that serves excellent Indian food at good prices in a usually expensive neighbourhood. A great find.

The Tenth – *Royal Garden Hotel, 2–24 Kensington High St, Kensington, W8 4PT.* ⊖*High Street Kensington.* ☏*020 7937 8000. www.royalgardenhotel.co.uk. Closed Sun, Sat lunch.* The name refers to the hotel's top floor where this stylish dining room is situated. Spectacular views of Kensington Palace and Kensington Gardens. The lunch menu is a bargain.

Belvedere – *Holland House (off Abbotsbury Rd), Kensington, W8 6LU.* ⊖*Kensington Olympia.* ☏*020 7602 1238. www.belvedererestaurant.uk.* On a summer's day secure a table on the balcony terrace at this 19C orangery in the middle of Holland Park. The menu offers a modern take on classic French and British dishes.

KNIGHTSBRIDGE, BELGRAVIA, WESTMINSTER, VICTORIA, PIMLICO

Jenny Lo's Tea House – *14 Eccleston St, SW1W 9LT.* ⊖*Victoria.* ☏*020 7259 0399. Closed Sun, bank holidays.* It's popular, authentically Chinese and the prices are right. The imaginative menu at this "canteen" informs diners that no MSG is added to dishes. Come early to avoid queues. Cash and cheques only.

Oliveto – *49 Elizabeth St, SW1W 9PP.* ⊖*Victoria.* ☏*020 7730 0074. Closed bank holidays.* Close to Victoria station, Olivetto has an extensive modern Italian menu with fabulous oven-baked pizzas. Advisable to book for lunch.

Café Rouge– *21–31 Basil St, SW3 1BB.* ⊖*Knightsbridge.* ☏*020 7584 2345. www.caferoue.com.* French bistro chain, serving light meals. Good value, especially the Prix Fixe menu daily between noon-5pm.

Swag and Tails – *10–11 Fairholt St, Knightsbridge, SW7 1EG.* ⊖*Knightsbridge.* ☏*020 7584 6926. www.swagandtails.com. Closed 25–26 Dec, 1 Jan, bank holidays.* Tucked down a side street, the Swag and Tails is a handsome pub with daily specials. Good service.

Aubaine – *260–262 Brompton Rd, SW3 2AS.* ⊖*South Kensington.* ☏*020 7052 0100. www.aubaine.co.uk.* The place for summer when the windows roll back. Good bakery at the front, and imaginative food. Friendly, with a large table for people who can share.

Zafferano – *15 Lowndes St, Belgravia, SW1X 9EY .* ⊖*Knightsbridge.* ☏*020 7235 5800. www.zafferano restaurant.com. Booking essential.* Book weeks in advance to secure a table at one of London's finest Italian restaurants. Enjoy robust dishes that reflect the season. Keep space for the wonderful tiramisu.

MARYLEBONE, REGENT'S PARK, PRIMROSE HILL, ST JOHN'S WOOD

Café Bagatelle – *The Wallace Collection, Hertford House, Manchester Sq, W1U 3BN.* ⊖*Bond Street.* ☏*020 7563 9505.* The glass-enclosed courtyard of Hertford House provides a stunning setting for lunch, amid a verdigris fountain and sculptures. A popular spot for afternoon tea.

Chada Chada – *16–17 Picton Pl, Marylebone, W1M 5DE. Bond Street. 020 7935 8212. www.chadathai.com. Closed Sun, bank holidays.* Authentic and delicately spiced traditional Thai dishes as well as some surprises. Good service. The intimate rooms fill up quickly.

Café Rouge – *120 St John's Wood High Street, NW8 7SG. St Johns Wood. 020 7722 8366. www.caferouge.com.* French bistro chain, serving light meals. Good value, especially the Prix Fixe menu daily noon–5pm.

The Engineer – *65 Gloucester Ave, Primrose Hill, NW1 8JH. Chalk Farm. 020 7722 0950. www.the-engineer. com. Closed 25–26 Dec, 1 Jan.* Mingle with the locals in the busy front bar or dine by candlelight in one of the dining rooms. In summer, ask for a table on the attractive terrace. Unhurried service and an appealing modern menu.

The Providores and Tapa Room – *109 Marylebone High St, W1U 4RX. Baker St. 020 7935 6175. www.theprovidores.co.uk.* Sit in the buzzing Tapa Room, open all day, for great breakfasts and tapas. Upstairs the restaurant serves fusion food, using unusual ingredients to great effect.

The Queens – *49 Regent's Park Rd, Primrose Hill, NW1 8XD. Chalk Farm. 020 7586 0408. www.geronimo-inns. co.uk.* One of London's excellent "gastropubs", the Queens serves hearty traditional dishes. Grab a seat on the balcony overlooking Primrose Hill.

The Salt House – *63 Abbey Rd, St John's Wood, NW8 0AE. St John's Wood. 020 7328 6626. www.thesalt house.co.uk. Closed Mon lunch. Booking essential.* After paying homage to the Beatles at the nearby Abbey Road zebra crossing, stop into this gastropub with its lounge or formal restaurant, for modern British cooking.

Union Café – *96 Marylebone Lane, Marylebone, W1M 5FP. Bond Street. 020 7486 4860. www.brinkleys.com/ union.htm. Closed Christmas, New Year, Sun, bank holidays.* This laid-back restaurant is tucked away in a lane near the Wallace Collection. Open plan kitchen and innovative Mediterranean cooking at reasonable prices.

Villandry – *170 Great Portland St, Marylebone, W1W 5QB. Great Portland Street. 020 7631 3131. www.villandry. com. Closed 25 Dec, 1 Jan, Sun eve, bank holidays.* Take a walk around the day-time deli before sampling the freshly prepared dishes in the restaurant to the rear. A relaxed, informal eatery with wooden tables.

MAYFAIR

The Café at Sotheby's – *34–35 New Bond St, W1A 2AA. Bond Street. 020 7293 5077. Open for lunch only. Closed 2 weeks Aug, 2 weeks Christmas, Sat–Sun. Booking essential.* Now you can also eat in the simple dining room in this prestigious auction house located in Mayfair.

Momo – *25 Heddon St, W1B 4BX. Piccadilly Circus. 020 7434 4040. Closed Christmas.* The "in" crowd love this colourful Moroccan restaurant, with its traditional rugs and atmospheric Arabic music. Staff will guide the uninitiated through the menu.

Scotts – *20 Mount St, W1Y 6HE. Bond Street. 020 7495 7309. www. scotts-restaurant.com. Closed 25 Dec.* First opened in 1851 and a favourite haunt of Winston Churchill, Scotts was given a face lift in the 1990s. The upper floor formal room specialises in oysters and modern fish dishes, with snacks in the piano bar downstairs.

Mirabelle – *56 Curzon St, W1J 8PA. Green Park. 020 7499 4636. www.whitestarline.org.uk.* This legendary restaurant still oozes the glamour that made its reputation in the 1930s. Refined cuisine featuring both modern and classic dishes and a notable wine list. Reasonably priced lunch menu.

Nobu – *19 Old Park Lane, W1Y 4LB. Green Park. 020 7447 4747. www.noburestaurants.com. Closed 25–26 Dec and Sat lunch. Booking essential.* At the Metropolitan's (see Where to Stay) ultra-trendy eatery, South America meets Japan to create cuisine that attracts a celebrity clientele. Minimalist décor. Come with a large wallet.

PICCADILLY, ST JAMES'S

Al Duca – *4–5 Duke of York St, St James's, SW1Y 6LA. ⊖Piccadilly Circus. ℘020 7839 3090. www.alduca-restaurant.co.uk. Closed Sun.* Considering its location in pricey St James's, this modern Italian restaurant offers good value, with a relaxed atmosphere.

Benihana – *37 Sackville St, W1X 2DQ. ⊖Piccadilly Circus. ℘020 7494 2525. www.benihana.co.uk. Closed 25 Dec.* Come here to marvel at the Japanese chefs' dexterity as they cook before diners' eyes. Diners are seated in groups around the counters. Reasonably priced set menus available.

Getti – *16-17 Jermyn St, SW1Y 6LT. ⊖Piccadilly Circus. ℘020 7734 7334. www.getti.com. Closed Sun.* Among the shops of London's most renowned tailors, this modern Italian restaurant stands out. An extensive menu of both traditional and contemporary dishes. The "express menu" is good value.

ST PANCRAS, CAMDEN TOWN

Camden Brasserie – *9-11 Jamestown Rd, Camden, NW1. ⊖Camden Town. ℘020 7482 2114. www.camdenbrasserie.co.uk.* For over 20 years this popular brasserie has provided the perfect lunch spot after the market. The specialities are grilled meats and fish.

Wagamama – *11 Jamestown Road, NW1 7BW. ⊖Camden Town. ℘020 7428 0800. www.wagamama.com.* Asian chain, serving light meals of noodles, salads, freshly squeezed juices and soups at long, comunal tables. Fast service and very good value for money. No booking required.

SOUTH BANK, BANKSIDE, SOUTHWARK, BERMONDSEY, WATERLOO

Livebait – *43 The Cut, Southwark, SE1 8LF. ⊖Southwark. ℘020 7928 7211 www.livebaitrestaurant.co.uk. Closed Sun.* With its cosy booths, this seafood restaurant gets lively with the flow of theatre crowds from the Old Vic. Other central London locations: 175 Westbourne Grove (Kensington) and 21 Wellington St (Covent Garden).

Pizza Express – *Royal Festival Hall, The White House, SE1 8YP. ⊖Waterloo. ℘020 7928 4091. www.pizzaexpress.com.* Stylish, well-priced pizza chain, serving light, crispy sophisticated pizzas in sleek surroundings.

Southwark Cathedral Refectory – *Southwark Cathedral, SE1 9DA. Southwark, SE1 9AD. ⊖Southwark. ℘020 7407 5470.* Good hearty fare such as soups, stir-frys and pasta dishes that are reasonably priced.

The Fire Station – *150 Waterloo Rd, Southbank, SE1 8SB. ⊖Waterloo. ℘020 7620 2226 .* Located between the Old Vic and Waterloo Station, this 1910 fire station specialises in Mediterranean-style cuisine. Tiled floor, church pews and an open kitchen contribute to the pleasant atmosphere.

Fish – *Cathedral St, Borough Market, Southwark, SE1 9AL. ⊖Southwark. ℘020 7407 3803. Closed 25 Dec, Sun eve, bank holidays.* Inside this modern glass and metal structure you can choose the fish as well as the cooking method and accompanying sauce.

Blue Print Café – *Butlers Wharf, Design Museum, Shad Thames, Bermondsey, SE1 2YD. ⊖Bermondsey. ℘020 7378 7031. www.blueprintcafe.co.uk. Closed Sun eve.* After visiting the Design Museum, secure a window table in this adjoining restaurant and enjoy the views of Tower Bridge. Personable service and modern European menu.

Oxo Tower Brasserie – *Barge House St (8th floor), Oxo Tower Wharf, Southwark, SE1 9PH. ⊖Southwark. ℘020 7803 8888. www.oxotower.co.uk.* Sharing the 8th floor of a converted factory with the formal restaurant, the brasserie offers terrace dining and the same spectacular city view.

SUBURBS

NORTH-WEST: HAMPSTEAD, HIGHGATE, SWISS COTTAGE

Banners – *21 Park Road, Crouch End, N8 8TE. ⊖Finsbury Park. ℘020 8348 2930.* Trendy restaurant with a lively atmosphere serving a varied menu of world cuisines and daily specials. Good breakfast menu. Eclectic décor, including band posters, motorcycle leathers, blackboards, quirky bric-a-brac and a long aluminium bar.

The Wells – *30 Well Walk, Hampstead NW3 1BX.* ⊖*Hampstead.* ℘*020 7794 3785. www.thewells hampstead.co.uk.* Atractive 18C pub on the edge of Hampstead Heath, with leather sofas to sink into after a walk on the Heath. The upstairs dining room offers classic French cooking, served with charm.

NORTH-EAST: EAST END, HACKNEY, WHITECHAPEL

Café Naz – *46-48 Brick Lane, E1 6RF.* ⊖*Aldgate East.* ℘*0800 389 0722. www.cafenaz.co.uk. Closed Sat lunch.* Brick Lane is renowned for its Indian restaurants, and Café Naz is a contemporary take on the theme. The menu has Bangladeshi specialities. A real "East-End" experience.

Café Spice Namaste – *16 Prescot St, Whitechapel, E1 8AZ.* ⊖*Tower Hill.* ℘*020 7488 9242. www.cafespice.co.uk. Closed Sun, Sat lunch, bank holidays.* This Indian restaurant is a riot of colour, from the bright walls to the flowing drapes. Friendly atmosphere and fragrant, competitively priced food.

SOUTH-EAST: GREENWICH, BLACKHEATH

Chapter Two – *43-45 Montpelier Vale, Blackheath, SE3 0TJ.* ⊖*New Cross.* ℘*020 8333 2666. www.chaptersrestaurants.com.* Located at the upper end of the high street, this contemporary restaurant has a cool yet cosy feel. Well-prepared and well-priced modern European cuisine. Service is formal without being stuffy.

North Pole Piano Restaurant – *131 Greenwich High Rd, Greenwich, SE10 8JA.* ⊖*New Cross.* ℘*020 8853 3020. www. northpolegreenwich.com. Closed 25 Dec and Mon lunch.* It's a short stroll from Greenwich centre to this lively, trendy establishment, with two bars and an upstairs restaurant serving good food in a casual atmosphere.

SOUTH: BATTERSEA

Boiled Egg & Soldiers – *63 Northcote Rd, SW11 1NP.* ⊖*Clapham Junction.* ℘*020 7223 4894. Closed eves.* A bright and jolly café full of mums and children. Try the all day breakfast for a real British treat.

The Food Room – *123 Queenstown Rd, SW8 3RH.* ⊖*Queenstown Road.* ℘*020 7622 0555.* Delightful French restaurant with great food in charming, peaceful room.

SOUTH-SOUTH-WEST: FULHAM, PUTNEY, WIMBLEDON

Light House – *75–77 Ridgeway, Wimbledon, SW19 4ST.* ⊖*Wimbledon.* ℘*020 8944 6338. Closed Sun eve.* Close to Wimbeldon tube, this bright restaurant has an open kitchen and a changing menu of Italian and fusion dishes. Try the risotto specialities.

Pizza Express – *4 Fulham Broadway Development, SW6 1BW.* ⊖*Fulham Broadway.* ℘*020 7381 1700. www. pizzaexpress.com.* Stylish, well-priced pizza chain, serving light, crispy sophisticated pizzas and salads in sleek surroundings.

River Café – *Rainville Rd, Thames Wharf, Hammersmith, W6 9HA.* ⊖*Hammersmith.* ℘*020 7386 4200. www. rivercafe.co.uk. Closed Christmas–New Year, Easter, Sun eve, bank holidays.* Owned and operated by Ruth Rogers and Rose Gray, this restaurant in a converted warehouse has young staff, an open kitchen and first-rate Italian cuisine incorporating the best ingredients around.

SOUTH-WEST: BARNES, RICHMOND, KEW

Ma Cuisine – *9 Station Approach, Kew, Surrey TW9 3QB.* ⊖*Kew Gardens.* ℘*020 8332 1923. www.macuisinekew.co.uk.* This real French "bistro", with gingham tablecloths, is a café by day and in the evenings serves the likes of **boudin noir** and **cassoulet**.

The Glasshouse – *14 Station Par, Kew, TW9 3PZ.* ⊖*Kew Gardens.* ℘*020 8940 6777. www.glasshouserestaurant. co.uk. Closed 25 Dec, 1 Jan, Sun eve.* Beside Kew Gardens Tube station, this restaurant has a glass façade. Inside, the atmosphere, like the cooking, is refined. Attentive service.

Entertainment

London is truly one of the world's top cities for entertainment. From "Theatreland" to the City's diverse nightclubs, the best contemporary music concerts at the Wembley and 02 Arenas to a belly-aching laugh at The Comedy Store, or a quiet pint of ale at one of the capital's historic pubs – London has got it all. A variety of publications – many of them free – offer up-to-date listings for events across the city. *Ask at tourist offices and ticket outlets or accept free fliers handed out as you walk along.*

CINEMAS

Catching the latest film releases in a comfortable cinema is a great way to relax, and West End cinemas offer the latest technology.

BFI LONDON IMAX CINEMA

1 Charlie Chaplin Walk, South Bank, SE1 8XR. ⊖*Waterloo.* ℘*0870 787 2525. www.bfi.org.uk.*
This special cinema shows 2D and 3D films on a 85.3ft/26m-wide screen: from Antarctic adventure to Walt Disney® films.

NATIONAL FILM THEATRE

Belvedere Rd, South Bank, SE1 8XT. ⊖*Waterloo.* ℘*020 7633 0274. www.bfi.org.uk/nft.*
The London Film Festival is held here every year in November.

ODEON CINEMAS

22–24 Leicester Sq, Soho, WC2H 7LQ. ⊖*Leicester Square.* ℘*0871 224 4007. www.odeon.co.uk. Open daily 11am–9pm.*
London's biggest cinema (1 943 seats), where the premieres of prestigious British and Hollywood films are shown.

RITZY PICTUREHOUSE

Brixton Oval, Coldharbour Lane, Brixton, SW2 1JG. ⊖*Brixton.* ℘*0871 704 2065. www.picturehouses.co.uk. £6.50.* This Edwardian cinema shows classics and recent films, and is loved by English producers such as Ken Loach.

COMEDY CLUBS

THE COMEDY STORE

1a Oxendon Street, SW1Y 4EE. ⊖*Picadilly Circus; Leicester Sq. www.thecomedystore.co.uk. Contact* **Ticketmaster** *for tickets (☏ see p405).*
Acts inclunding comedians Andy Parsons and Russell Howard have played here. Seating is not the most comfortable, but the atmosphere makes up for this.

HMV HAMMERSMITH APOLLO

Queen Caroline St, Hammersmith, W6 9QH. ⊖*Hammersmith.* ℘*0844 844 4748. £15–£50.*
This is the place for comedy: some of the best in UK comedians take centre stage at this large venue. Hot 21C favourites such as Frankie Boyle, Michael McIntyre and Reginald D Hunter have played this venue to packed audiences. The Apollo also hosts popular music concerts; come here to see some of the big stars.

NIGHTCLUBS

London's energetic club scene is a major attraction. Venues usually offer special rates in the early evening, but the real action starts later and continues until early morning. In 1990 all-night clubbing was legalised.

CENTRAL LONDON

Bar Rumba

36 Shaftesbury Ave, Piccadilly, W1V 7DD. ⊖*Piccadilly.* ℘*020 7287 6933. www.barrumbadisco.co.uk. Open Mon, Sat 9pm–3.30am, Tue 6pm–3am, Wed 9pm–3am, Thu–Fri 6pm–3.30am, Sun 8.30pm–2am.* In the heart of Soho, the Rumba is one of London's best clubs even if the size of the dance floor is far too small, given the club's popularity. There's always a good atmosphere and the music varies from night to night, ranging from jazz, funk, house, drum n'bass to latino (salsa lessons).

Cargo
83 Rivington St, EC2A 3AY. ⊖Old Street. ℘020 7749 7844. www.cargo-london. com. Open Mon–Thu 6pm–1am, Fri–Sat 6pm–3am, Sun 6pm–midnight. ⊛£5–£13.
Located in a Victorian railway arch, offering a restaurant, bar with lounge furnished with big cushions, and a heaving main room with a band. DJs offer great music from Asian underground to hip hop.

Embassy Bar
119 Essex Rd, N1 2SN. ⊖Angel. ℘020 7226 7901. www.embassybar.com. Open Sun–Wed 4pm–midnight, Thu 4pm–1am, Sat–Sun 4pm–2am. Over-25 years old only.
This club-bar situated just outside the centre of Islington is furnished with red-and-gold flock wallpaper and leather armchairs, giving it a glamorous retro feel. The superb music varies with the days of the week, and the atmosphere is one of the best in London.

Fabric
77A Charterhouse St, EC1M 3HN. ⊖Farringdon. ℘020 7336 8898. www. fabriclondon.com. Open Fri 9.30pm–5am, Sat 10pm–8am. ⊛£12–£16.
Opened in 1999, Fabric is a gigantic club capable of holding 1 500 revellers in three originally decorated halls. The acoustics are exceptional and attract top DJs (Fatboy Slim, Rennie Pilgrem, Backspace) and a mixed 20–30-year-old crowd. The music is predominantly drum n'bass and techno/house.

The Fridge
1 Town Hall Parade, Brixton Hill, Brixton, SW2 1RJ. ⊖Brixton. ℘020 7326 5100. Open Mon 8.30pm–late, Tue–Sun 8.30pm–3.30am (Fri 5am, Sat 4.30am).
This giant club (a converted cinema) with mosaic décor can hold up to 1 000 people. The music is excellent: roots, funk, hip-hop during the week and trance and house at the weekend. Public: 20–30ish.

Heaven
Under The Arches, Villiers St, Strand, WC2N 6NG. ⊖Charing Cross. ℘020 7930 2020. www.heaven-london.com. Open Mon, Wed, Fri–Sat 11pm–6am. Advance bookings only. ⊛£11–£15.
This gay heaven is located under the railway arches. There are three dancefloors and three types of music from disco to techno and a stunning laser show. This place is popular, so get there early.

koko
1A Camden High St, NW1 9JE. ⊖Mornington Crescent. ℘0870 432 5527. www.koko.uk.com. Open Mon–Fri 7pm–11pm (Fri 3am), Sat 10pm–4am. Telephone for details of other nights.
Once a music hall, It's now a splendidly opulent warren of a place with terrific sound.

SUBURBS
Babalou
The Crypt, St. Matthew's Church, Brixton Hill, Brixton, SW2 1JF. ⊖Brixton. ℘020 7738 3366. www.babalou.net. Usually open Wed–Sat 7pm–3am (5am Sat), Sun 7pm–11pm. ⊛£5–£10. Under the vaults of St Mathew's crypt, this is an intimate bar-club with comfy velvet sofas. The music (live or DJ) varies between soul, jazz, funk, blues and hip-hop.

Ministry of Sound
103 Gaunt St, Elephant and Castle, SE1 6DP. ⊖Elephant & Castle. ℘0870 0600 0101. www.ministryofsound.com. Open Wed 10pm–3am, Fri 10.30pm–5am, Sat 11pm–7am. London's best-known nightclub has become an institution in the capital and draws a mixed crowd of revellers (20–35 years old) for house, garage and techno music every weekend. The sound is exceptional, the experience stunning, but behave

yourself if you want to get through the door, and above all be patient.

CABARET (CENTRAL LONDON)
Madame Jo Jo's
8-10 Brewer St, Soho, W1R 3SP.
⊖*Piccadilly Circus.* ℘*020 7734 3040.*
www.madamejojos.com. Usually open Mon–Sat, shows start at 7pm. ⊗*£25–£52.50 (Cabaret tickets).* A warm-hearted cabaret for night owls and a favourite haunt of drag queens. Sometimes bit of a madhouse, the ambience changes from day to day.

PERFORMING ARTS
THEATRE
At all times of the year London offers everything, from top block-busting musicals to serious theatre. Experimental theatre is found in the "fringe" theatres. During the summer, open air venues in Holland Park, Regent's Park and the Globe Theatre offer performances (weather permitting!).

Most of the mid-range theatres are grouped together in the West End in and around Shaftesbury Avenue in Soho, near a wide range of restaurants, many of which offer excellent pre- and post-theatre 2- and 3-course set meals at around ⊗£14–£20.

The theatres listed below are some of the better known ones that feature long-running plays and musicals. For a complete listing of current shows, consult the publications mentioned at the beginning of the chapter.

Tickets for West End theatres and musicals are booked by agents who will charge a fee – either 10% or a flat fee of a few pounds. To avoid paying a surcharge buy seats directly from the theatre box office. Matinée performances are cheaper, although star casts may be replaced by understudies.

⊗Ticket prices vary, but generally range between £15 and £45, though you may pay more for a big musical or a play with top stars performing.

Adelphi
The Strand, Strand, WC2E 7NA.
⊖*Charing Cross.* ℘*0870 906 3838.*
Several of Dickens' novels were adapted for the stage here soon after publication (1837–1845). This theatre is fondly remembered for some great musical productions (*Me and My Girl, Sunset Boulevard*, and recently *Chicago*).

Apollo Victoria Theatre
17 Wilton Rd, Victoria, SW1V 1LG.
⊖*Victoria.* ℘*0870 400 0650.*
www.rutheatres.com.
This former cinema (built 1930) converted into a theatre in 1979, has hosted such famous performers as Shirley Bassey, Cliff Richards and Sammy Davis Jr. Among recent productions are *Starlight Express* and *Bombay Dreams*.

Barbican Arts Centre
Barbican Centre, Silk St, EC2Y 8DS.
⊖*Barbican.* ℘*020 7638 8891.*
www.barbican.org.uk. Box office Mon–Sat 9am–8pm, Sun 11am–8pm.
This arts complex, designed by Chamberlin, Powell and Bon, is a five-floor development housing a concert hall, a cinema, exhibition areas and restaurants. The theatre offers a wide range of productions from experimental cabaret to dance, classical theatre and new plays.

Dominion
268–269 Tottenham Court Rd, W1T 0AG.
⊖*Tottenham Court Road.* ℘*0870 607 7401. www.dominiontheatre. co.uk.* Built as a concert hall in a former leprosarium and brewery, and formerly a cinema, the Dominion is now famous for its musicals such as *Grease,* and *We Will Rock You.*

Duke of York's Theatre
St Martin's Lane, WC2N 4BG.
⊖*Leicester Square.* ℘*0870 400 0650.*
Its name is synonymous with playwrights such as Shaw, Ibsen, Galsworthy and Noel Coward.

Tkts
(Half-Price Ticket Booth)

Run by the Society of London Theatres (SOLT) and based at Leicester Square, **tkts** is the only official Half-Price and Discount theatre ticket organisation. It offers a limited number of half-price tickets to most West End shows on the day of performance. Available on a first-come, first-served basis, cash/credit/debit payment only accepted plus service charge, no returns, maximum four tickets per application. Visitors can also book full-price advance tickets to shows here (half-price and full-price tickets also available at the tkts booth in Brent Cross Shopping Centre, north London). *Open Mon–Sat 10am–7pm, Sun (matinées only) noon–3pm (Brent Cross 6pm). For more information, contact SOLT, 32 Rose St, WC2E 9ET.* 020 7557 6700.

Her Majesty's Theatre
Haymarket, St James's, SW1Y 4QL. Piccadilly Circus. *0870 400 0650. www.rutheatres.com.*
Designed in 1896 by architect C.J. Phills, the theatre seats 1200 people. The musical the Phantom of the Opera has been running here since 1986.

London Palladium
8 Argyll St, Soho, W1F 7TF. Oxford Circus. *0870 890 1108.*
A sumptuous theatre famous for variety shows.

Lyceum
21 Wellington St, Covent Garden, WC2E 7RQ. Covent Garden. *0870 400 0650. www.lyceum-theatre.co.uk.*
The fourth theatre to be built on the site, the Lyceum resembles a Roman temple. Reopened in 1904, it was long a venue for ballets, musicals, and classical plays. Today the theatre produces mega-musicals like the *The Lion King.*

New London Theatre
167 Drury Lane, Covent Garden, WC2B 5PW. Covent Garden. *0870 890 0141. £20–£45.*
Previous theatres on the site included the 1851 Middlesex Music Hall rebuilt by Frank Matcham and renamed the Winter Garden 1919. *Cats* was one of the musicals performed here; today it is used for plays and cabaret-style performances.

The Old Vic
103 The Cut, Lambeth, SE1 8NB. Waterloo. *0870 060 6628 (box office). www.oldvictheatre.com. Pit Bar: Open daytime and evening.*
Former home of the National Theatre, the Old Vic opened in 1818 as the Coburg Theatre. Taken over by Emma Cons in 1880, it was renamed the Royal Victoria Music Hall and Coffee Tavern. After Emma Cons died, in 1912, the "Old Vic", as it became known, was taken up by her niece, Lilian Baylis. Now under the artistic leadership of Kevin Spacey, it offers a range of theatre, including a Christmas pantomime. There are low ticket prices for under-25s.

Open Air Theatre
Inner Circle, Regent's Park, NW1 4NR. Baker Street. *0844 826 4242 (box office Mon–Sun 9am–9pm). www.openairtheatre.org. Performances May–Sept. £12–£40.*
In summer the New Shakespeare Company, founded in 1932, stages productions here, including such favourites as *A Midsummer Night's Dream.* Bring warm clothing, a cushion, an umbrella and a picnic. Barbecue and cold buffet available. A pavilion bar serves hot drinks.

Palace Theatre
Shaftesbury Ave, Soho, W1D 8AY. Leicester Square. *0870 906 3838. www.rutheatres.com.*
Opened as an opera house by Richard D'Oyly Carte, this grandiose building

has retained its Victorian atmosphere. It is now a venue for large-scale musicals: *The Entertainer, Jesus Christ Superstar, Les Misérables* and *The Woman in White*.

Queen's Theatre
Shaftesbury Avenue, W1V 8BA.
Piccadilly Circus. *0844 482 5160.*
After being partially rebuilt by Sir Hugh Casson after bomb damage in the war, this theatre was refurbished in early 1992, hosting musicals like *Stop the World – I Want to Get Off!* Now owned by Sir Cameron Mackintosh's company, there are refurbishment plans. In the meantime it is home to plays such as *Les Misérables*, which transferred from the Palace Theatre in 2004.

Royal Court Theatre
Sloane Sq, Chelsea, SW1W 8AS.
Sloane Square. *020 7565 5000.*
www.royalcourttheatre.com. £8–£25.
The role of the Royal Court is to promote contemporary plays and new English and international talent.

Royal National Theatre
South Bank, SE1 9PX. Waterloo.
Guided tours. *020 7452 3000* (ticket office open Mon–Sat 9.30am–8pm). *www.nationaltheatre.org.uk.*
The National Theatre Company, founded by Sir Laurence Olivier in 1962, has been based since 1976 in this modern building, designed by Deny Lasdun, with three theatres: the Olivier, the Lyttelton and the Cottesloe. Some tickets are reserved for sale on the day of the performance.

Shakespeare's Globe
21 New Globe Walk, Bankside, SE1 9DT.
Blackfriars; Cannon St; London Bridge; Southwark; Waterloo. *020 7401 9919 (box office). www.shakespeares-globe.org.* Box Office open Mon–Sat 10am–6pm, performances May–Sept. £5–£29.
This white building with a thatched roof, on the Thames south bank is identical to the original Elizabethan

theatre, which was brought down by the 17C censure of the Church. It is a museum and a theatre, but as it is open to the elements, plays are summer events.

Theatre Royal
Drury Lane, Covent Garden, WC2B 5JF.
Covent Garden. *0870 890 6002.*
There has been a theatre on this site since 1633. The present building was designed in 1812 by Benjamin Wyatt. Productions over have featured Nell Gwynne, Mrs Jordan, Edmund Keane and the clown Grimaldi. Nowadays it hosts popular musicals (*Oklahoma, My Fair Lady, Miss Saigon* and Mel Brooks' *The Producers*).

OPERA AND BALLET
The Theatre Royal Covent Garden, know affectionately as the "Garden", is the home of the Royal Opera and Royal Ballet. The Coliseum presents opera in the English language. Prices for performances vary enormously, but good tickets will be expensive.

ENGLISH NATIONAL OPERA
London Coliseum, St. Martin's Lane, WC2N 4ES. Leicester Square; Charing Cross. *0871 911 0200. www.eno.org.* Box office open 24hr.
This large Edwardian theatre was built in 1904 by Oswald Stoll to rival Drury Lane. The building is spectacular: marble pillars and lavish interior. Since 1968 it's been home to the English National Opera.

ROYAL OPERA HOUSE
Bow St, Covent Garden, WC2E 9DD.
Covent Garden. *020 7304 4000.*
www.roh.org.uk. Box office: Open Mon–Sat 10am–8pm.
In 1999 after extensive renovation, the opera house re-opened to reveal new splendour. This is one of the world's most prestigious opera houses. Tickets are quite expensive and difficult to obtain. However, there are special schemes running, with different sponsors so you can get tickets on certain days for £10.

SADLER'S WELLS THEATRE

Rosebery Ave, Islington, EC1R 4TN.
⊖Angel. ☎0844 412 4300. www.
sadlers-wells.com. Box office: Open
Mon–Sat 9am–8.30pm. 🎟️*£10–£35.*
The only London theatre to present
classical ballet and contemporary
dance.

CLASSICAL MUSIC

London offers a great range of
classical music performed by world-
class artists and orchestras. Prices
vary but if you don't mind restricted
sight, you can hear some of the best
music in the world for a few pounds.
Westminster Abbey, Westminster
Cathedral and St Paul's Cathedral all
boast superb choirs that you can hear
for free. City churches that organise
lunchtime concerts include St Bride's,
St Anne and St Agnes, St Lawrence
Jewry, St Margaret Lothbury, St Martin
-within-Ludgate, St Mary le Bow and
St Michael's Cornhill.

BARBICAN HALL

Silk St, City, EC2Y 8DS. ⊖*Barbican.*
☎020 7638 8891. www.barbican.org.
uk. Box office Mon–Sat 9am–8pm, Sun
11am–9pm.
Home to the London Symphony
Orchestra, it is also used by touring
orchestras.

ROYAL FESTIVAL HALL

Belvedere Rd, South Bank, SE1 8XX.
⊖*Waterloo. ☎0871 663 2500 (box*
office). www.southbankcentre.co.uk.
Open daily 9am–8pm.
The Royal Festival Hall, built in 1951
as part of the Festival of Britain
celebrations, is the home of the
London Philharmonic Orchestra.
Programmes range from large-scale
classical orchestral concerts, ballet,
films and staged performances of
opera, to the London Jazz Festival.
The two smaller venues, Queen
Elizabeth Hall and Purcell Room, host
contemporary dance, music theatre,
chamber music, solo recitals, world
music, poetry events and live art.

ST JAMES'S CHURCH CONCERTS

197 Piccadilly, St James's, W1J 9LL.
⊖*Piccadilly Circus. ☎020 7734*
4511. www.st-james-piccadilly.org/
eveningconcerts.html.
Lunchtime recitals (🎟️*no charge,*
suggested donation £3) and evening
concerts of classical music.

ST JOHN'S, SMITH SQUARE

Smith Sq, Westminster, SW1P 3HA.
⊖*Westminster. ☎020 7222 1061.*
www.sjss.org.uk. Ticket office: Open
Mon–Fri 10am–5pm, also evenings for
concerts.
This church, a Grade I listed building,
is the setting for the annual Lufthansa
Festival of baroque music. Lunchtime
concerts (Mon 1pm) and evening
chamber and vocal music events.

ST MARTIN-IN-THE-FIELDS

Trafalgar Sq, WC2N 4JJ. ⊖*Trafalgar*
Square. ☎020 7766 1100. www2.
stmartin-in-the-fields.org. Evening
concerts Thu–Sat at 7.30pm, tickets
available by telephone or from the Crypt
box office (open Mon–Sat 10am–5pm,
Thu–Sat 8.30pm).

ROYAL ALBERT HALL

Kensington Gore, South Kensington,
SW7 2AP. ⊖*South Kensington.*
☎020 7589 8212 (box office).
www.royalalberthall.com. Box office:
Open daily 9am–9pm; hall 45min and
restaurants 2hr before performance.
👥*Guided tours daily.*
Home to the Promenade Concerts,
held from mid-July to mid-September,
and to the Royal Philharmonic
Orchestra, the Royal Albert Hall also
hosts a wide range of other events.

WIGMORE HALL

36 Wigmore St, Marylebone, W1U 2BP.
⊖*Bond Street; Oxford Circus. ☎020*
7935 2141. www.wigmore-hall.org.uk.
Box office open daily 10am–8.30pm.
A lovely intimate hall, ideal for solo
recitals and chamber orchestras.
Sunday morning coffee-concerts are
an institution.

ROCK, ROOTS AND JAZZ
CENTRAL LONDON

Cecil Sharp House
2 Regent's Park Rd, Camden, NW1 7AY.
↬*Camden Town.* ☏*020 7485 2206.*
www.efdss.org. 🖃*From £3.*
Folk music, singing and dancing.

**Dover Street Restaurant
and Bar**
8–10 Dover St, W1S 4LQ. ↬*Green Park.*
☏*020 7491 7509. www.doverst.co.uk.*
Jazz bar-restaurant with live music
and dancing nightly from 10.30pm.
Dress smartly. 🖃*Cover charge £6–£12.*

Jazz Café
3–5 Parkway, Camden, NW1 7PG.
↬*Camden Town.* ☏*0870 060 3777.*
*www.jazzcafe.co.uk. Open daily
7pm–2am.* 🖃*£15–£25.*
Jazz, soul, Latin American and African
rap music every evening in this
intimate, two-storey club. Some of the
greatest jazzmen have played here.

Pizza Express Jazz Club
10 Dean St, Soho, W1D 3RW.
↬*Tottenham Court Road.* ☏*020 7439
8722. www.pizzaexpresslive.com. Open
daily noon–midnight.* 🖃*£17.50–£25.*
Excellent modern jazz in the basement.

Pizza on the Park
*11–13 Knightsbridge, Knightsbridge,
SW1X 7LY.* ↬*Hyde Park Corner.* ☏*0845
602 7017. Box office open 9am–5pm,
performances Wed–Sun 8.30am–11pm,*

*Sat–Sun 9.30am–midnight. Advance
booking advised.* 🖃*£10–£20.*
Nightly jazz sessions.

Ronnie Scott's★
47 Frith St, Soho, W1D 4HT.
↬*Leicester Square.* ☏*020 7439 0747.*
*www.ronniescotts.co.uk. Open Mon–Sat
6pm–3am, Sun 6pm–midnight, music
from 7.30pm.* 🖃*£26.*
Legendary Soho jazz club,
outstanding music and atmosphere.
Best to book in advance.

Shepherd's Bush Empire
Shepherd's Bush Green, W12 8TT.
↬*Shepherd's Bush.* ☏*0870 771 2000,
020 8354 3300. www.shepherds-bush-
empire.co.uk. Box office only open on
days of shows. £10–£30.*
Designed by Frank Matcham in the
early 20C, "The Empire" was bought
by the BBC in 1953 and has played a
major role in the history of television.
Today it's a concert hall with excellent
acoustics.

100 Club
100 Oxford St, W1D 1LL.
↬*Oxford Circus.* ☏*020 7636 0933.*
*www.the100club.co.uk. Open Mon–Thu
and Sun 7.30/8pm–11pm/midnight
(3am Fri, 1am Sat).* 🖃*£10–£15.*
This basement venue, where the
Sex Pistols made their debut, now
highlights jazz, modern jazz, blues
and swing.

606 Club
90 Lots Rd, Chelsea, SW10 0QD.
↬*Earl's Court.* ☏*020 7352 5953.*
*www.606club.co.uk. Open Mon
7.30pm–1am, Tue–Wed 7pm–1am,
Fri 8pm–1.30am, Sat 8pm–2am, Sun
7pm–midnight.* 🖃*Music cover charge
£10–£13.*
Book for dinner to hear top British jazz
musicians play at this atmospheric
basement venue.

Ronnie Scott's

Ronnie Scott's

SUBURBS

O2 Academy Brixton

*211 Stockwell Rd, Brixton, SW9 9SL.
⊖Brixton. ℘020 7771 3000.
www.o2academybrixton.co.uk. Open
for performances 7–11pm (later on club
nights).*◉ *£15–£40.*
Immense hall with Art Deco interior,
considered by many to be London's
best concert hall. Many greats started
out here, including the Rolling Stones,
David Bowie, Jamiroquai and UB40.
Capacity of 4 700.

The O2 Arena

*Peninsula Square. SE10 0DX.
⊖North Greenwich. ℘020 7771 3000.
www.theo2.co.uk. Open 9am till late
(last admission 1am). Thames Clippers
also runs a regular boat service from
Waterloo Pier to the O2 (www.thames
clippers.com).*
Huge concert and sports arena in the
former Millennium Dome used for
big events and big stars. Also with an
Entertainment Avenue of bars and
restaurants and a gallery space.

The Forum

*9-17 Highgate Rd, Kentish Town,
NW5 1JY. ⊖Kentish Town. ℘0844
847 2405. www.kentishtownforum.
com. Open daily 7–11pm (2am Fri–Sat).*
◉*£7–£15.*
Originally opened in 1934 as a movie
house, this art deco building on the
edge of Kentish Town has a capacity
of 2000; big bands love its intimate
charm. Performers here have included
Oasis, Iggy Pop and Macy Gray.

UNION CHAPEL

*Compton Terrace, Islington, N1 2XD.
⊖Highbury. ℘020 7226 1686. www.
unionchapel.org.uk. ◉£10–£35.*
Using the church as a concert hall was
the only way to save Union Chapel
from demolition! Music peformed
here includes rock, folk, jazz, blues
and organ concerts.

GOING OUT FOR A DRINK

PUBS

Pubs' opening hours are usually
Mon–Sat 11am–11pm and Sun,
noon–10.30pm. Many larger pubs
have later licences running up until
midnight or even 1am.

Gastropubs are ubiquitous across the
UK and offer a reasonable standard
and variety of dishes from fish &
chips to ham & eggs to burgers and
even Indian cuisine; some vegetarian
options are also available. In more
traditional pubs, you can still find
more traditional classic British dishes
(🕭*see below*).

TRADITIONAL PUB GRUB

In older, traditional pubs, you can
find staples such as **Steak & Ale
Pie** (pastry pie filled with steak in a
thick gravy), **Lasagne**, **Fish & Chips**,
baked potatoes with a choice of
fillings, pasta, burgers, sandwiches
and puddings. Most dishes come
with chips (French fries). Pubs with
atmosphere or historic associations
are listed within the Addresses
sections in the *Discovering the City*
section of the guide.

Traditional pubs are shown in red,
accompanied by a red dot on the
maps in the *Discovering the City*
section. The traditional drink is beer,
sold in pints and half pints, bottled or
draught. A freehouse sells whatever
beers it chooses. If the house is tied,
it will sell the product of its brewery
owner. Many pubs offer guest beers
and ales. Of course wines, spirits and
soft drinks are always available, too.

WINE BARS & DJ BARS

These often serve as much beer
and spirits as they do wine. Wine is
sold by the glass or the bottle. The
atmosphere is slightly more formal
than in pubs and people tend to dress
up a bit more.

Shopping

Shopping is a favourite activity most people are happy to indulge in. London shops offer the widest range of goods to satisfy the most demanding shopper. ♿*For business hours and Conversion Tables for sizes, see Basic Information in Planning Your Trip.* The main shopping centres, together with large stores like IKEA, Toys "R" Us, etc., are located on the outskirts of London in easy reach of the North Circular (Brent Cross) and South Circular Roads (Croydon), Lakeside (Thurrock), Bluewater (Dartford). The main shops are featured in the Sell Out column in Time Out.

WHAT TO BUY LOCALLY

The winter sales at Christmas and New Year and the summer sales in July and August are popular times for shopping in London, as prices are reduced on a great range of goods.

London is a good place to buy clothes, and if you know where to go, you can avoid the high-end prices likely along places like Oxford and Regent Streets. **Classic clothing styles** are sold by well-known names such as Jaeger, Burberry, Marks and Spencer, John Lewis, Debenhams and House of Fraser. **Made-to-measure** clothing for men is available in London in Savile Row (tailors) and Jermyn Street (shirt-makers).

Foodhall, Harrods
©Harrods

Shops specialising in reasonably priced **ready-to-wear clothing** appeal to a young clientele. For **trendy shops** offering styles from established and offbeat designers visit the King's Road in Chelsea, Carnaby Street in Soho, and Covent Garden. The craft studios at Oxo Tower on the South Bank and in Camden Lock Market are places to explore for a special gift.

Porcelain – The best makes: Wedgewood, Royal Worcester and Royal Doulton are available in London; seconds can be bought at the factory.

Food – Smoked salmon, Stilton cheese, pickles, marmalade) and drink (tea, gin and whisky) are also favourite items.

DEPARTMENT STORES AND SHOPS
THE CLASSICS
Harrods

87–135 Brompton Rd, Knightsbridge, SW1X 7XL. ⊖*Knightsbridge.* ☏*020 7730 1234. www.harrods. com. Open Mon–Sat 10am–8pm, Sun 11.30am–6pm.*

Harrods boasts that it can supply anything, even a pedigree dog. The food halls are particularly impressive (do not miss the displays of fish and cheese). The butcher will even sell you alligator or ostrich steaks. There is also a hairdresser's, a beauty parlour, a travel agency, and a shipping service. A world of elegance and comfort, to be visited as you would a museum.

Harvey Nichols

109–125 Knightsbridge, SW1X 7RJ. ⊖*Knightsbridge.* ☏*020 7235 5000. www.harveynichols.com. Open Mon– Sat 10am– 8pm, Sun 11.30am–6pm.*

This store regularly arouses curiosity with its unusual and daring window displays. There is a good range of fashion clothing, especially in smaller sizes, an excellent choice of hats (for Ascot!) and some fine jewellery.

John Lewis

278–306 Oxford St, W1A 1EX.
⊖*Oxford Circus.* 📞*020 7629 7711.*
www.johnlewis.co.uk. Open Mon–Fri
9.30am– 8pm (Thu 9pm), Sun noon–
6pm.
Suppliers of school uniforms and other
functional clothing, household fittings, linen and stationery. This store
has everything you need for everyday,
practical purposes and special occasions. Since its refurbishment, the
beauty department on the ground
floor is particularly good.

Liberty★★

210–220 Regent St, W1R 6AH.
⊖*Oxford Circus.* 📞*020 7734 1234.*
www.liberty.co.uk. Open Mon–Sat
9am–8pm, Sun 11.30am–6pm.
This intimate department store has a
character all its own, owing to its roots
in the East End of London: Liberty-
brand and Indian silks, Chinese
ceramics, contemporary glassware
and designer clothes. The beautiful
half-timbered Mock Tudor façade was
built in 1924.

Selfridges

400 Oxford St, W1A 1AB.
⊖*Bond Street.* 📞*0870 837 7377.*
www.selfridges.co.uk. Open Mon–
Wed and Fri–Sat 9.30am–8pm, Thu
9.30am–9pm, Sun 11.30am–6pm.
This well-known department store
sells everything from lingerie to
household articles, beauty products
and stationery.

The Westfield Centre

Westfield London, W12 7SL.
⊖*Shepherds Bush; White City;*
Wood Lane. 📞*020 3371 2300.*
www.uk.westfield.com. Open Mon–Fri
10am–9pm (Thu–Fri 10pm), Sat 9am–
9pm, Sun noon–6pm.
Europe's largest in-town shopping
centre opened at this west London
site in October 2008, with 265 shops
(including a special premium luxury
brands area, The Village) over 50
restaurants and bars and a cinema.
Take a day and take a map.

HIGH STREET CHAINS

French Connection

396 Oxford St, W1C 7JX. ⊖*Bond St.*
📞*020 7629 7766. www.frenchcon-*
nection.com. Open Mon–Wed, Fri
10am–8pm, Thu 10am–9pm, Sat
9.30am–7pm, Sun noon-6pm.
Upscale high street fashion with good
tailoring.

H & M

261–271 Regent St, W1B 2ES.
⊖*Oxford Circus.* 📞*020 7493 4004.*
www.hm.com. Open Mon–Sat
9am–9pm, Sun noon–6pm.
Flagship UK store of this trendy Swed-
ish chain of stores selling moderately
priced men's and women's fashion and
accessories. Go early on a Saturday to
avoid a scrum.

Karen Millen

247 Regent St, W1B 2EW.
⊖*Oxford Circus.* 📞*020 7629 1901.*
www.karenmillen.com. Open Mon–Fri
10am–9pm, Sat 9am–9pm, Sun noon
–6pm.
This British chain offering very
feminine and sophisticated fashion
and accessories, with an emphasis on
structured and gently tailored lines.
More expensive than high street.

Topshop

216 Oxford Street, WC1D 1LA.
⊖*Oxford Circus.* 📞*020 7636 7700.*
www.topshop.com. Open Mon–Sat
9am–9pm.
Cheap, cheerful and cutting edge,
Topshop is an institution among
fashionistas. The stock, much of it
channelling the catwalks, changes
pretty much every week – and key
pieces featured in magazines sell
out almost instantly, so if you see
something you like don't 'come back
for it'. Three floors of this flagship store
include shoes, vintage, a hairdressers
and nail bar and accessories.
Always packed, it is slightly less so
during the week.

ART AND ANTIQUES

London has always had a buoyant trade in art and antiques. Fairs are held regularly in London hotels that attract dealers from the provinces: details available from the **Antiques Trade Gazette** which comes out on Tuesdays. *For details of larger, international fairs, contact the British Antique Dealers Association, 20 Rutland Gate, SW7 1BD. ℘020 7589 4128. www.bada.org.*

BONHAMS

Montpelier St, SW7 1HH
⊖*Knightsbridge. ℘020 7447 7447. www.bonhams.com.*
Founded in 1793, Bonhams merged with Brooks in September 2000 and is now the top vintage car valuers in Britain. It is the fourth-biggest valuers in the world with expertise in 25 fields, ranging from wine to teddy bears.

CHRISTIE'S

85 Old Brompton Rd, South Kensington, SW7 3LD & 8 King St, SW1Y 6QT.
⊖*South Kensington. ℘020 7839 9060. www.christies.com. Open Mon–Fri 9am–6pm (viewing and auctions at other times).*
This internationally renowned institution, founded by James Christie in London in 1766, built up its reputation by promoting young artists such as Gainsborough but also by organising the major auctions of the 18 and 19C. The most spectacular auction remains the sale of 198 paintings by Sir Robert Walpole to Catherine the Great, now in the Hermitage museum. Christies now has offices in 15 countries and operates in almost 80 fields.

SOTHEBY'S

34–35 New Bond St, Mayfair, W1A 2AA.
⊖*Bond Street. ℘020 7293 5000. www.sothebys.com. Open Mon–Fri 9am–5pm.*
Sotheby's started out in 1744 as a book valuers. When it moved to its prestigious premises in New Bond Street, the establishment diversified into selling drawings and paintings. The sale of the Goldschmidt collection in 1958 marked a turning point, as did the concurrent opening of the New York office. Particularly memorable was the sale of the Duchess of Windsor's jewellery. Sotheby's, forward thinking, launched Internet auctioning in 1999.

MARKETS

Market stall browsing holds an enthralling fascination for antiques lovers hoping to find that desirable object. The stall holders are often amateurs, but a real find is rare. The earlier you arrive, the greater the choice. Flower stalls are a common sight in the streets of central London: in front of the Danish Embassy in Sloane St., **Gilding the Lily** at South Kensington Underground Station and **Wild at Heart** at 222 Westbourne Grove have wonderful displays. Camden Town markets specialise in clothing.

ANTIQUES AND BRIC-A-BRAC

Alfie's Antiques Market
13–25 Church St, NW8 8DT.
⊖*Edgware Road. ℘020 7723 6066. www.alfiesantiques.com. Open Tue–Sat 10am–6pm.*
Don't be put off by its slightly scruffy appearance; this market sells everything, but it is good to know what you are looking for.

Antiquarius
131–141 King's Rd, Chelsea, SW3 5EB.
⊖*Sloane Square. ℘020 7823 3900. www.antiquarius.co.uk. Open Mon–Sat 10am–6pm.*
There are 120 stalls selling art deco items, buttons, textiles, silver, glassware, jewellery, and trade versions of fashion accessories.

Bermondsey (New Caledonian) Market
Bermondsey St, Southwark, SE1 4QB.
⊖*Bermondsey; London Bridge. ℘020*

7525 5000. www.southwark.gov.uk.
Open Fri 6am–noon.
The market was revived on this site in
1950. Trade in copper and silverware,
Victorian jewellery, furniture and
other objets d'art begins by torchlight
in the early hours.

Camden Passage Antiques Market
Camden Passage, Islington, N1 5ED.
⊖Angel. ☎020 7359 0190. www.
camdenpassageislington.co.uk. Open:
General market Wed & Sat, but many
shops open on weekdays or by
arrangement.
The general Camden Passage area,
stretching over several streets, is full
of antique shops, selling just about
everything. The markets fill the rest
of the area, while the Wed and Sat
antiques market offers Oriental art,
art nouveau, art deco, silverware and
more from around 250 dealers.

Covent Garden Market
41 The Market, Covent Garden, WC2E
8RF. ⊖Covent Garden. www.covent
gardenmarket.co.uk. Open Mon–Sat
10am–7pm, Sun 11am–6pm.
In the 17C Inigo Jones created the
Piazza to create a trading space for
the original market, established by
monks before the Reformation, which
transferred to Nine Elms in 1974. The
current market buildings, designed
by Charles Fowler, were added in
1832. The flower market, haunted by
the memory of Eliza Doolittle, is now
occupied by shops, cafés, restaurants
and wine bars. The antiques market
features coins, glasses, old tools and
silverware.

Gray's Antiques Market &
Grays in the Mews
58 Davies St, W1K 5LP & 1–7 Davies
Mews, W1K 5AB. ⊖Bond Street. ☎020
7629 7034. www.graysantiques.com.
Open Mon–Fri 10am–6pm.
The market occupies a split site
incorporating 1–7 Davies Mews.
The main hall has 170 stands and
London's biggest collection of antique
jewellery.

Greenwich Antiques Market
Greenwich High Rd, SE10. ⊖Cutty Sark.
Open Wed 11am–7pm, Thu–Fri 10am–
5pm for **antiques & collectables and
arts & crafts**; open Sat–Sun, bank
holidays 10am–5.30pm **for arts &
crafts and food court**.
In this flea market expect to find
international crafts rather than real
antiques, but the atmosphere here is
pleasant, more family-orientated and
less crowded than Camden Market.

Petticoat Lane Market
Middlesex St, Wentworth St, EC1.
⊖Liverpool Street. Open Sun 9am–
2pm (Wentworth Street also open
Mon–Fri 10am–2.30pm).
A daily flea market just down the road
from its original 17C location; best
visited on Sundays.

Portobello Road
Portobello Rd, Notting Hill, W11 1AN.
⊖Notting Hill Gate; Ladbroke Grove.
☎020 7229 8354. www.portobello
road.co.uk. Open Sat 8am–5pm.
Browse for antiquities, Victoriana, later
silver, chinaware, stamps, small items.

Spitalfields Market
Brushfield St, Commercial St, E1.
⊖Liverpool Street. www.visit
spitalfields.com.
General market Mon–Fri 10am–
4pm, Sun 9am–5pm. Antiques Fair
Thu 8am–3.30pm; **Fashion market**
Fri 10am–4pm.
This large historic hall is home to
a craft market. On weekdays, the
second-hand stalls expose their wares,
but on Sunda the organic market takes
over. The atmosphere is pleasant,
with many cafés and restaurants.

CLOTHING
BRICK LANE MARKET
Brick Lane, E1. ⊖Aldgate East.
Open Sun 8am–2pm.
A vast hotchpotch of bric-a-brac and
fabrics. Leather and new clothing is
sold in the shops at the north end of
Brick Lane.

CAMDEN LOCK MARKET

Chalk Farm Rd, NW1 8AF.
⊖*Camden Town.* ℘*020 7284 2084.*
www.camdenlockmarket.com.
Open daily 10am–6pm.
Arts and crafts, designer and vintage clothes, jewellery and a wide range of goods are on sale.

CAMDEN MARKET★

Camden High St, Corner of Camden High St and Buck St, NW1. ⊖*Camden Town. www.camdenlock.net. Open daily 9.30am–6pm.*
A treasure trove for bargain leather goods and clothing, with more than 200 stands.

CAMDEN STABLES MARKET

Chalk Farm Rd, Camden, NW1 8AH.
⊖*Camden Town.* ℘*020 7485 8355.*
www.stablesmarket.com. Open daily 10am–6pm.
The centre of the alternative fashion scene with 350 shops, selling everything from leather trousers to tie-dye coats.

LEATHER LANE MARKET

Leather Lane, Chancery Lane, EC1.
⊖*Chancery Lane. www.leatherlane market.co.uk. Open Mon–Fri 10.30am–2pm.*
The market, dotted with cafés, is always full of bargains. Fashionable clothes for men and women (including sportswear), a tailor and, of course, all sorts of leatherwear: shirts, skirts, shoes and bags. ⓒ*See COVENT GARDEN.*

FOOD AND FLOWERS
BERWICK STREET

Berwick St, Soho, W1. ⊖*Tottenham Court Road; Oxford Circus. Open Mon–Sat 9am–6pm.*
Berwick Street is frequented by many nearby restaurateurs. First just a fruit and veg market, it now has fish counters, flower stalls and an excellent baker. Atmosphere of bygone times.

BOROUGH MARKET

Stoney St, Borough High St, Southwark, SE1 1TL. ⊖*London Bridge.* ℘*020 7407 1002. www.boroughmarket.org.uk. Open Thu 11am–5pm, Fri noon–6pm, Sat 8am–5pm.*
This is probably the oldest food market in London with archives dating back to 1014. It is known as "the London larder" and reputed for its organic products and its many food stalls.

BRIXTON MARKET

Atlantic Rd, SW9 8JX. ⊖*Brixton. Open Mon–Sat 8am–5.30pm (Wed from 1pm).*
One of South London's best markets for fresh food. Many exotic products.

COLUMBIA ROAD MARKET

Columbia Rd, Bethnal Green, E2. Buses 26, 48, 55. http://columbiaroad. info. Open Sun 8am–3pm.
The Columbia Road flower market east of the City is a victim of its success, but as well as the flowers, there are second-hand stores and a good bakery. The street has a country atmosphere which gives it a charm all of its own. Come to the market when the flowers are cut-price and the gardeners are at lunch. The pubs around the market serve good Sunday roasts to tuck into after you've bought your blooms.

LEADENHALL MARKET

Whittington Ave, EC3 . ⊖*Bank.* ℘*0871 789 6001. www.leadenhall market.co.uk. Open Mon–Fri 7am–4pm.*
Especially impressive is the huge Hall of Glass designed by Victorian architect Sir Horace Jones (Smithfields Market, Billingsgate Market). Apart from the poultry and fish market, there is just a small group of shops, but a good selection.

Sports Grounds

London boasts a number of Premier League and First Division **football** teams. **Cricket** was originally a British gentlemen's sport that was exported to the Colonies to encourage team spirit, discipline and sportsmanship. Wimbledon **Tennis** Championships are summer highlights. **Rugby** matches, especially the Six Nations Cup, are special events.

ALL-ENGLAND LAWN TENNIS CLUB

Church Rd, Wimbledon, SW19 5AE. ⊖*Wimbledon.* ℘*020 8944 1066.* *www.wimbledon.org.*
The All-England Championships, first held in 1877, run for 2 weeks from end June. ♿*see SUBURBS – WIMBLEDON.*

ARSENAL FC - EMIRATES STADIUM

Avenell Rd, Islington, N5 1BU. ⊖*Arsenal. www.arsenal.com. Tickets* ⊕*£25–40.* The Arsenal players are known as the "Gunners" because of the club's association with the former royal armaments factory.

THE BRIT OVAL

Kennington Oval, Kennington, SE11 5SS. ⊖*Oval.* ℘*08712 461100 (10p/min).* *www.surreycricket.com.*
London's second cricket ground, home to the Surrey County Cricket Club.

CHELSEA FC – STAMFORD BRIDGE

Fulham Rd, Fulham–Chelsea, SW6 1HS. ⊖*Fulham Broadway. www.chelseafc. co.uk.* ⊕*Tickets from £25.*
Book well in advance to support one of London's most famous football clubs, located in Fulham. Stadium tours available.

GUARDS POLO CLUB

Smith's Lawn, Windsor Great Park, Englefield Green, TW20 0HP. ⊖*Egham.* ℘*01784 434 212. www. guardspoloclub.com.*
Matches played every Saturday and Sunday at 3pm. The Cartier International tournament is held here in July. The Ladies' National Polo Championship is held at Ascot Park (Sunningdale) in early July.

HARLEQUINS STOOP MEMORIAL GROUND

Langhorn Drive, Twickenham/ Richmond, TW2 7SX. Twickenham rail (overground). ℘*0871 527 1315.* *www.quins.co.uk.*
Ground of one of London's premier rugby clubs, The Harlequins.

LORD'S CRICKET GROUND

St John's Wood Rd, NW8 8QN. ⊖*St John's Wood.* ℘*020 7432 1000.* *www.lords.org.*
London's main cricket ground. Headquarters of several autonomous bodies: the International Cricket Council that supervises the game at international level; the Marylebone Cricket Club (MCC), founded in 1787, which set up the Test and County Cricket Board to administer international matches and the county game in the United Kingdom; and the Middlesex County Cricket Club, founded in 1877.

TWICKENHAM

Rugby Rd, TW1 1DZ. ⊖*Twickenham rail.* ℘*0870 405 2000. www.rfu. com* Britain's finest rugby ground and the headquarters of the Rugby Football Union is at Twickenham, in West London. Major international matches are played on its hallowed turf, including home games in the Six Nations Tournament. The Museum of Rugby features the "Twickenham Experience": a guided tour of 14 exhibition rooms and the 50-year-old baths.

WIMBLEDON STADIUM

Plough Lane, SW17 0BL. ⊖*Tooting Broadway; Wimbledon.* ℘*0870 840 8905. www.lovethedogs.co.uk.* ⊕*£7.50.*
Famous greyhound racetrack.

INDEX

INDEX

INDEX

INDEX

INDEX

🏠 STAY

🍷 EAT

MAPS AND PLANS

Great Britain Maps: Based upon Ordnance
Survey of Great Britain with the Permission
of the Controller of Her Majesty's Stationery
Office © Crown Copyright 100000247.

REGIONAL MAPS

Michelin map 504 – South East
England, The Midlands, East Anglia
(Scale 1 : 400 000 – 1cm = 4km – 1in :
6.30 miles) covers the main regions of
the country, the network of motorways
and major roads. It provides information
on shipping routes, distances in miles
and kilometres, plan of London, services,
sporting and tourist attractions and an
index of places.

COUNTRY MAPS

The **Atlas Britain 2008** (Scale 1:
200 000) covers the whole of Great
Britain. It provides information on
route planning, distances in miles
and kilometres, town plans, services,
sporting and tourist attractions and
an index of places.

INTERNET

Users can access personalised route
plans, Michelin mapping on line, addresses of hotels and restaurants featured in
The Red Guides and practical and tourist
information through the internet:
www.ViaMichelin.com

MAP LEGEND

Highly recommended ★★★
Recommended ★★
Interesting ★

Selected monuments and sights

	Tour - Departure point
	Catholic church
	Protestant church, other temple
	Synagogue - Mosque
	Building
	Statue, small building
	Calvary, wayside cross
	Fountain
	Rampart - Tower - Gate
	Château, castle, historic house
	Ruins
	Dam
	Factory, power plant
	Fort
	Cave
	Troglodyte dwelling
	Prehistoric site
	Viewing table
	Viewpoint
	Other place of interest

Special symbols

M3	Motorway
A2	Primary route
	London wall
	City boundary
	Pub
	Underground station

Additional symbols

	Tourist information
	Motorway or other primary route
	Junction: complete, limited
	Pedestrian street
	Unsuitable for traffic, street subject to restrictions
	Steps – Footpath
	Train station – Auto-train station
	Coach (bus) station
	Tram
	Metro, underground
	Park-and-Ride
	Access for the disabled

Sports and recreation

	Racecourse
	Skating rink
	Outdoor, indoor swimming pool
	Multiplex Cinema
	Marina, sailing centre
	Trail refuge hut
	Cable cars, gondolas
	Funicular, rack railway
	Tourist train
	Recreation area, park
	Theme, amusement park
	Wildlife park, zoo
	Gardens, park, arboretum
	Bird sanctuary, aviary
	Walking tour, footpath
	Of special interest to children

Abbreviations

C	County council offices
H	Town hall
M	Museum
POL.	Police
T	Theatre
U	University

	Post office
	Telephone
	Covered market
	Barracks
	Drawbridge
	Quarry
	Mine
	Car ferry (river or lake)
	Ferry service: cars and passengers
	Foot passengers only
	Access route number common to Michelin maps and town plans
AZ B	Map co-ordinates

Michelin Apa Publications Ltd

A joint venture between Michelin and Langenscheidt

58 Borough High Street, London SE1 1XF, United Kingdom

No part of this publication may be reproduced in any form
without the prior permission of the publisher.

© 2010 Michelin Apa Publications Ltd
ISBN 978-1-906261-85-6
Printed: November 2009
Printed and bound in Germany

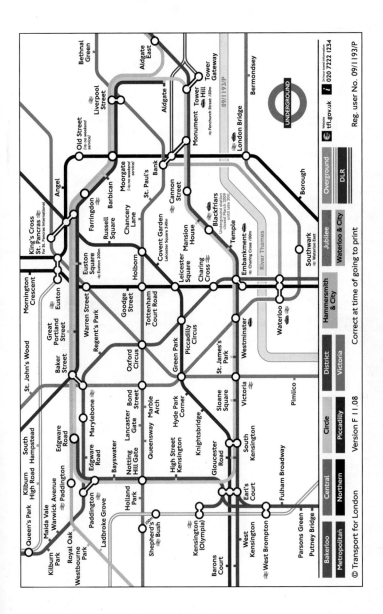

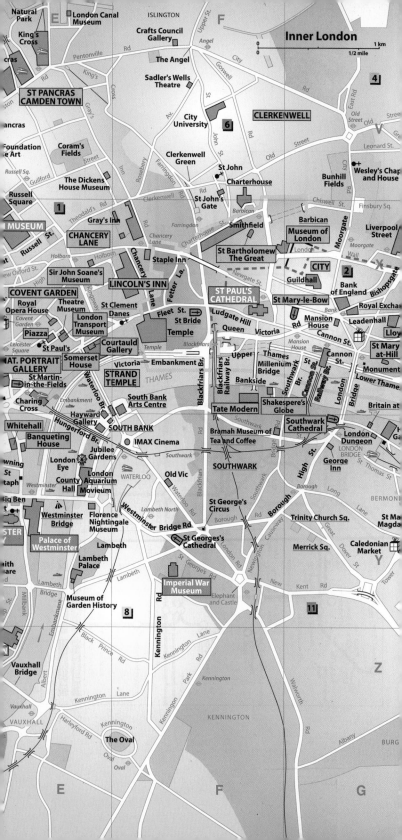